Henry James
1960-1974

a reference guide

A
Reference
Publication
in
Literature

Jack Salzman
Editor

Henry James
1960-1974

a reference guide

DOROTHY McINNIS SCURA

G.K.HALL &CO.

70 LINCOLN STREET, BOSTON, MASS.

Copyright © 1979 by Dorothy McInnis Scura

Library of Congress Cataloging in Publication Data

Scura, Dorothy McInnis.
  Henry James, 1960-1974.

  (Reference publications in literature)
  Includes indexes.
  1. James, Henry, 1843-1916—Bibliography.
I. Title. II. Series: A Reference publication in
literature.
Z8447.S38   [PS2123]   813'.4   78-27143
ISBN 0-8161-7850-X

This publication is printed on permanent/durable acid-free paper
MANUFACTURED IN THE UNITED STATES OF AMERICA

Contents

Preface

When Henry James whimsically predicted to William Dean Howells in 1888 that "someday all my buried prose will kick off its various tombstones," he could not have imagined the explosion of critical writings published in the fifteen years from 1960 to 1974. This Reference Guide of annotated criticism consists of over 2,000 books, shorter writings, and dissertations.

To identify critical trends in face of such a quantity of writing over such a short period of time is rather like standing in the midst of the whirlwind and trying to plot the direction of the storm. The single most obvious conclusion is that James's position as a major American writer is secure. The secureness of this position is supported not only by the phenomenal quantity of critical writing which shows no indication of slackening, but also by the quality of the work of many first-rate scholars who continue to publish on James. In fact, James's position seems secure if, for example, only the approximately three-hundred doctoral candidates listed in this Reference Guide whose dissertations were written wholly or partly on James continue to teach and some to publish on the subject.

In addition to the conclusion that James's continued high status in academe seems guaranteed, it is possible to identify several features and accomplishments in the mass of critical publications that extends over the fifteen years of this Guide. Several excellent bibliographical and biographical resources have been produced during the period. For information on primary bibliography, the student of Henry James should consult the definitive A Bibliography of Henry James, edited by Leon Edel and Dan H. Laurence (revised edition, 1961.A2). The summary annotations of this Reference Guide are complemented by Robert Gale's splendid essay in Eight American Authors (1971.B41), which offers evaluations and an overview of James studies and criticism. In addition, the annual essays (since 1963) published in American Literary Scholarship focus not only on the content of criticism but also evaluate that criticism. The herculean task of surveying annual James criticism for ALS has been undertaken by Bruce McElderry, Jr. (1965.B71, 1966.B62, 1967.B63, 1968.B67), Robert Gale (1972.B38), and William T. Stafford (1969.B127, 1970.B106, 1971.B114, 1973.B85, 1974.B71). Another interpretive overview of James criticism can be found in an essay by Adeline Tintner (1974.B79), which also suggests "Further Directions" that James study might profitably take.

The major biographical accomplishment in this period is the completion of Leon Edel's five-volume work, four volumes of which were published in these fifteen years (1962.A1-2, 1969.A1, 1972.A3). A recent announcement in the New York *Times* (2 July 1978, p. 32) that Avon is publishing the five volumes in paperback and that it will be a Book-of-the-Month offering indicates not only that scholars will have this work available at a modest price, but also that what the *Times* calls "the greatest literary biography written by or about an American author" will be distributed to general readers, giving some promise that the James "boom" which has thus far been confined to an academic audience may in the future reach a wider readership.

A number of treatments that introduce the writer and give an overview of his works have also been published during this fifteen year period. A student can go to four different authors with works entitled <u>Henry James</u>: Leon Edel (1960.A1), D. W. Jefferson (1960.A3), F. W. Dupee (1965.A5), and Bruce McElderry, Jr. (1965.A12). In addition, three other scholars have published introductory volumes on James: Darrel Abel (1964.A1), S. Gorley Putt (1966.A6), and Lyall H. Powers (1969.A7, 1970.A5). Oscar Cargill's <u>The Novels of Henry James</u> (1961.A1) remains the best general introduction to the long works.

A number of works that examine a particular literary, theological, philosophical, or cultural influence upon James have been published during the fifteen years of this Guide. Studies that explore various connections between James and another writer, for example, include Bruce Lowery's on Proust and James (in French, 1964.A5), George Monteiro's on John Hay and James (1965.A13), Jan W. Dietrichson's on Zola and James (1966.B20), Viris Cromer's on Ibsen and James (1973.B18), Tony Tanner's on Henry Adams and James (1968.B94), and Jeremiah J. Sullivan's on Hippolyte Taine and James (1973.B92). Studies on cultural influences include Jackson W. Heimer's "The Lesson of New England: Henry James and His Native Region" (1967.A3), Jörg Hasler's <u>Switzerland in the Life and Work of Henry James</u> (1966.A3), Christina Giorcelli's <u>Henry James e l'Italia</u> (in Italian, 1968.A5), Carl Maves's <u>Sensuous Pessimism: Italy in the Works of Henry James</u> (1973.A3), Alberta Fabris's <u>Henry James e la Francia</u> (in Italian, 1969.A2), and Jeanne Delbaere-Garant's <u>Henry James: The Vision of France</u> (1970.A2).

The influence of a number of writers on James has been explored. For example, Turgenev's influence on <u>The Princess Casamassima</u> is analyzed by Eunice C. Hamilton (1962.B40), Jeanne Delbaere-Garant (1971.B29), and Anthony D. Briggs (1972.B13). Lyall Powers points out the influence of the French naturalists (1960.B74, 1971.A5), and Balzac's influence is analyzed by J. W. Gargano (1960.B39) and Percy G. Adams (1961.B1). Several critics have discussed Hawthorne's influence: Richard Poirier (1966.B75), John Tytell (1969.B138), Robert

L. Gale (1962.B31), Tony Tanner (1967.B104), and Robert E. Long
(1973.B53). Many other writers are identified as having influenced
James--George Eliot, Mark Twain, Shakespeare, Browning, Ibsen, to
name only a few.

Beyond these influences, many studies have delineated sources and
parallel content in James's works and another author's. There is
much variety in these studies. For example, Leon Edel identifies
James's source for Gilbert Osmond as Francis Boott (1960.B27), George
Monteiro suggests Princess Casamassima's may be Princess Maria Bel-
giojoso (1962.B72), and Adeline Tintner explains that Mr. Crichton's
is Sidney Colvin and his wife's Fanny Sitwell (1974.B83). W. H.
Tilley points out that James found background material about revolu-
tionists for The Princess Casamassima in the London Times (1961.A5),
and Oscar Cargill notes that Alice James's hysteria was a source of
information for The Turn of the Screw (1963.B16). J. Kamerbeek, Jr.
traces the golden nails in The Ambassadors to Sainte-Beuve (1962.B49);
Scott Byrd finds the fractured crystal in The Golden Bowl in Middlemarch (1972.B15); and Adeline Tintner locates the Watteau fan in A
New England Primer in Balzac and Goncourt (1974.B78).

Another topic that has interested critics is the matter of
James's revisions of his fiction. Dominic J. Bazzanella analyzes
revisions of The Portrait of a Lady (1969.B13), Sacvan Bercovitch of
Roderick Hudson (1969.B16), Maqbool Aziz of "The Pension Beaurepas"
(1973.B4), Larry Reynolds of The American (1973.B70), and Sister
Stephanie Vincec of The Wings of the Dove (1972.B108). W. M. Gibson
and G. R. Petty utilize a computer to collate two versions of Daisy
Miller (1970.B42), and Professor Aziz suggests in an article on "Four
Meetings" (1968.B9) that all of the versions of a work of fiction
should be considered in analyzing the text.

Character studies are the subject of many articles. Robert L.
Gale's Plots and Characters in the Fiction of Henry James (1965.A6)
includes a dictionary of the characters. Some critics such as James
B. Colvert in his study of the Southern character (1965.B12) have
looked for a particular type of character in James, while other critics such as Linda Welshimer Wagner have explored ideas such as the
dominance of heredity in James's characterizations (1965.B117). Individual characters have received varied treatment: for example,
Isabel Archer is the subject of articles by Susan Offen, who has analyzed her fate (1964.B74); J. M. Newton, who discusses her ambition
(1967.B77); and Victor Strandberg, who explains her identity crisis
(1968.B93).

Two principal features of the critical output of this period are
the number of book-length specialized studies and the number of critical pieces on a particular portion of the James canon. A few major
studies of James which focus on specialized subjects are Viola Hopkins Winner's study of the visual arts (1970.A9), Dorothea Krook's on
consciousness (1962.A3), Sister Corona Sharp's on the confidante

(1963.A3), Ora Segal's on observers (1969.A8), Muriel Shine's on children (1969.A9), Charles P. Samuels's on ambiguity (1971.A6), Martha Banta's on the occult (1972.A1), Seymour Chatman's on style (1972.A2), and Donald Mull's on money (1973.A4). At this point, the particularized ways of looking at James's fiction seem to be inexhaustible.

The incontestable leader in James's fiction in terms of numbers of critical pieces during the period is The Turn of the Screw. Not only have an overwhelming number of articles been written on this tale; but five collections of criticism also have been published, beginning with Gerald R. Willen's A Casebook on the Turn of the Screw (1960.A6; revised edition, 1969.A11), and continuing with Robert Kimbrough's Henry James: "The Turn of the Screw": An Authoritative Text, Backgrounds and Sources, Essays in Criticism (1966.A5), Shuichi Motoda's Studies of "The Turn of the Screw" (in Japanese, 1970.A3), Jane P. Tompkins's Twentieth Century Interpretations of "The Turn of the Screw" and Other Tales (1970.A7), and E. A. Shepherd's Henry James and "The Turn of the Screw" (1974.A6). In addition, Thomas M. Cranfill and Robert L. Clark, Jr. published An Anatomy of "The Turn of the Screw" (1965.A4) which is wholly on this tale.

Other works receiving much treatment include The Portrait of a Lady (three collections of criticism: 1967.A5, 1968.A1, 1970.A4), The Ambassadors (two collections of criticism: 1964.A6, 1969.A10), The American, The Golden Bowl, The Wings of the Dove, and Daisy Miller. Such a heavy concentration on particular works has led Adeline Tintner (in 1974.B79) to call for investigation of "novels and short fiction other than the old chestnuts. Enough on The Turn of the Screw, The Ambassadors, and The Portrait of a Lady! 'Daisy Miller,' 'The Jolly Corner,' 'The Beast in the Jungle,' and such early stories as 'Madame de Mauves' . . . and 'The Real Thing' have received more than their share of attention." Tintner is not calling for a moratorium on James criticism; rather she suggests that scholars examine those of the 112 stories which have not yet been scrutinized critically.

The fifteen years encompassed in this Reference Guide are marked by several features: they have produced a major biography, several valuable bibliographical resources, studies that are both general and specialized, studies of diverse influences, comparative studies, character studies, and textual studies. Furthermore, although they have not been specifically mentioned above, there is no shortage of treatments of James's imagery, style, technique, and influence on other writers. Also prevalent are studies which compare James to another writer, and his characters to other fictional characters. And his language has been scrutinized--even his use of names and particular words. James seems to be truly a writer for all kinds of critics--even those who do not like his work. The most vituperative anti-Jamesian attack published during this period is Maxwell Geismar's Henry James and the Jacobites (1963.A2, published in England as

Henry James and His Cult), a Freudian-Marxian interpretation of James that has itself elicited many responses.

In the midst of this extensive critical attention, however, there are areas that remain to be explored. In 1974, Tintner names a number of critical areas which need further exploration. Also in 1974, a new book by Richard A. Hocks, Henry James and Pragmatistic Thought: A Study in the Relationship between the Philosophy of William James and the Literary Art of Henry James (1974.A2), provides, according to Henry L. Terrie in Sewanee Review (83 [Fall 1975], p. 99), "genuinely fresh ways of experiencing the fiction of Henry James." These two pieces of evidence suggest that there are still unexplored areas for the novice as well as the veteran James scholar, and that exciting new ways of viewing James will continue to be published.

So then, James's prophecy that his "buried prose will kick off its various tombstones" has apparently not yet been fully realized. And the James critical boom which Robert Gale has termed "one of the most astounding literary phenomena of our time" continues.

* * * *

Major bibliographic sources for this listing are: Modern Humanities Research Association Annual Bibliography of English Language and Literature; MLA Annual Bibliography; Lewis Leary's Articles on American Literature, 1950-67 (1970.B72); Robert L. Gale's essay on James in Eight American Authors: A Review of Research and Criticism (1971.B41); Maurice Beebe and William T. Stafford's 1966 listing in Modern Fiction Studies, "Criticism of Henry James: A Selected Checklist" (1966.B7); Donna Gerstenberger and George Hendrick's The American Novel: 1789-1959; A Checklist of Twentieth Century Criticism on Novels Written Since 1789. Vol. 2. Criticism Written 1960-68 (1970.B41); James Woodress's Dissertations in American Literature, 1891-1966 (1968.B114); Beatrice Ricks's Henry James: A Bibliography of Secondary Works (Scarecrow Author Bibliographies, Number 24. Metuchen, N.J.: Scarecrow Press, 1975). Also helpful have been the checklists in American Literature, David Pownall's Articles on Twentieth Century Literature: An Annotated Bibliography, 1954-1970 (1974.B55), the annual surveys (since 1963) in American Literary Scholarship, the annual surveys in The Year's Work in English Studies, and Warren S. Walker's Twentieth Century Short Story Explication (1963.B115, 1965.B118, 1967.B111).

With gratitude to all these toilers in the James bibliographical vineyards, I have attempted to collect all critical writing on James and present a comprehensive listing of criticism for the years 1960 through 1974. Material is listed in the year in which it appeared as "A--Books" (including all separately published material such as pamphlets, study guides, and collections of criticism), "B--Shorter Writings" (including articles, parts of books not primarily about James, parts of dissertations not primarily about James, and critical material included in editions of James's works), "C--Dissertations" (including dissertations primarily about James). Arrangement within each year is alphabetical by the author's last name.

Every article and book has been read and a summary annotation made. Dissertations are generally cited to <u>Dissertation Abstracts</u> or <u>Dissertation Abstracts International</u> and have been annotated from the entries in <u>DA</u> and <u>DAI</u>. Dissertations which were examined and annotated are cited to the dissertation itself. Cross reference numbers connect a dissertation with a later published book, but information is not supplied on the differences which may exist in the two items.

Any work which could not be obtained is marked by an asterisk (*) and the source of the citation noted; whenever possible, an annotation is supplied and the source of that annotation noted.

Collections of criticism are listed under the editor's name in the "Books" section. Articles are listed separately, and the original place of publication is noted, as are reprints. Cross reference numbers are given in the Reference Guide not only for reprints, but also for articles which are responses to other pieces of criticism.

Reviews of critical books on James which were listed in standard bibliographical sources have been annotated. After the annotation of a critical book on James, reviews found in the Reference Guide are listed. In addition, a selected list of citations of reviews is included whenever possible. The year is not given for reviews which appeared the same year as the book.

Foreign criticism listed in standard bibliographies in English has been included. An exception is found in the Japanese criticism, which includes many new annotated entries supplied by Ms. Michiko Naka of Keio University, Tokyo.

Reprints of material originally published before 1960 have not been included unless revisions were made or new critical material added. Reprints of material during the 1960-1974 period are noted in the original entry.

Editions of James's works are included only if there is a new critical introduction or other critical material added. Those introductions are listed in "B--Shorter Writings" under the name of the editor or author of the introduction.

Articles on film and stage adaptations of James's works are included when they appeared in standard bibliographical sources and they made specific mention of James's work. No attempt was made to include all articles on adaptations.

The index includes the names of authors, titles, characters, people, and a number of subjects (such as Biography, Comparative Studies, Expatriation, James's Influence, Textual Studies, etc.). Please see "A Note on the Index" for a full list of subjects, characters, and people indexed.

Preface

    This Reference Guide is designed to aid the student who needs a convenient and comprehensive guide to the large number of critical writings on Henry James. It is not a substitute for reading the books and articles in their entirety; indeed, each critical piece has been subjected to violence in reducing often complex arguments to one or two sentences. I hope that the brief summaries given in these annotations will serve to lead the reader to the criticism itself.

Dorothy McInnis Scura

Acknowledgments

I owe a debt of gratitude to a number of people for help with this project: to Maurice Dean for diligent and dedicated assistance; to three scholars for reading and supplying notes for foreign language criticism--Michiko Naka in Japanese, Barbara Eger in German, and Maria Borroni in Italian, French, Spanish, Portuguese, and Roumanian; to Mrs. Erwin Davis of the Interlibrary Loan Department of Boatwright Library of the University of Richmond and to Marjorie Stern of Boatwright Library, as well as Mary M. White of the Interlibrary Loan Department of Virginia Commonwealth University; to Martha Cook, Barbara Vann, and Anne Woodlief for help in proofreading; to Judith Bryant Wittenberg, Lewis Leary, Tom Inge, Grace Dean, Clay Morgan, Kristin McColgan, and George Scura for varied but concrete and measurable aid; and to Dean Gresham Riley and the Faculty Research Committee of the University of Richmond for two grants. To all of these people--thank you.

Principal Works by Henry James*

A Passionate Pilgrim, 1875 ("A Passionate Pilgrim," "The Last of
    the Valerii," "Eugene Pickering," "The Madonna of the Future,"
    "The Romance of Certain Old Clothes," "Madame de Mauves")

Transatlantic Sketches, 1875

Roderick Hudson, 1875

The American, 1877

French Poets and Novelists, 1878

Watch and Ward, 1878

The Europeans, 1878

Daisy Miller, 1878

An International Episode, 1879

The Madonna of the Future, 1879 ("The Madonna of the Future,"
    "Longstaff's Marriage," "Madame de Mauves," "Eugene Pickering,"
    "The Diary of A Man of Fifty," "Benvolio")

Confidence, 1879

Hawthorne, 1879

The Diary of A Man of Fifty, 1880 ("The Diary of A Man of Fifty,"
    "A Bundle of Letters")

Washington Square, 1880

The Portrait of A Lady, 1881

Daisy Miller: A Comedy, 1883

The Siege of London, 1883 ("The Siege of London," "The Pension
    Beaurepas," "The Point of View")

Portraits of Places, 1883

---

*For this list of James's major published works (1875-1920) and
the date of first authorized edition, I am indebted to Edel and
Laurence (revised edition, 1961.A2).

A Little Tour in France, 1884

Tales of Three Cities, 1884 ("The Impressions of a Cousin," "Lady Barberina," "A New England Winter")

The Author of Beltraffio, 1885 ("The Author of Beltraffio," "Pandora," "Georgina's Reasons," "The Path of Duty," "Four Meetings")

Stories Revived, 1885 ("The Author of 'Beltraffio,'" "Pandora," "The Path of Duty," "A Light Man," "A Day of Days," "Georgina's Reasons," "A Passionate Pilgrim," "A Landscape-Painter," "Rose-Agathe," "Poor Richard," "The Last of the Valerii," "Master Eustace," "The Romance of Certain Old Clothes," "A Most Extraordinary Case")

The Bostonians, 1886

The Princess Casamassima, 1886

Partial Portraits, 1888

The Reverberator, 1888

The Aspern Papers, 1888 ("The Aspern Papers," "Louisa Pallant," "The Modern Warning")

A London Life, 1889 ("A London Life," "The Patagonia," "The Liar," "Mrs. Temperly")

The Tragic Muse, 1890

The Lesson of the Master, 1892 ("The Lesson of the Master," "The Marriages," "The Pupil," "Brooksmith," "The Solution," "Sir Edmund Orme")

The Real Thing, 1893 ("The Real Thing," "Sir Dominick Ferrand," "Nona Vincent," "The Chaperone," "Greville Fane")

Picture and Text, 1893

The Private Life, 1893 ("The Private Life," "The Wheel of Time," "Lord Beaupre," "The Visits," "Collaboration," "Owen Wingrave")

Essays in London and Elsewhere, 1893

The Wheel of Time, 1893 ("The Wheel of Time," "Collaboration," "Owen Wingrave")

Theatricals, 1894

Theatricals, Second Series, 1894

Terminations, 1895 ("The Death of the Lion," "The Coxon Fund," "The Middle Years," "The Altar of the Dead")

Embarrassments, 1896 ("The Figure in the Carpet," "Glasses," "The Next Time," "The Way It Came")

The Other House, 1896

The Spoils of Poynton, 1897

What Maisie Knew, 1897

In the Cage, 1898

The Two Magics, 1898 ("The Turn of the Screw," "Covering End")

The Awkward Age, 1899

The Soft Side, 1900 ("The Great Good Place," "'Europe,'" "Paste,"
    "The Real Right Thing," "The Great Condition," "The Tree of
    Knowledge," "The Abasement of the Northmores," "The Given Case,"
    "John Delavoy," "The Third Person," "Maud-Evelyn," "Miss Gunton
    of Poughkeepsie")

The Sacred Fount, 1901

The Wings of the Dove, 1902

The Better Sort, 1903 ("Broken Wings," "The Beldonald Holbein," "The
    Two Faces," "The Tone of Time," "The Special Type," "Mrs. Medwin,"
    "Flickerbridge," "The Story in It," "The Beast in the Jungle,"
    "The Birthplace," "The Papers")

The Ambassadors, 1903

William Wetmore Story and His Friends, 1903

The Golden Bowl, 1904

The Question of Our Speech, The Lesson of Balzac, 1905

English Hours, 1905

The American Scene, 1907

The Novels and Tales of Henry James, "New York Edition," 1907-1909

Views and Reviews, 1908

Julia Bride, 1909

Italian Hours, 1909

The Finer Grain, 1910 ("The Velvet Glove," "Mora Montravers," "A
    Round of Visits," "Crapy Cornelia," "The Bench of Desolation")

The Outcry, 1911

A Small Boy and Others, 1913

Notes of a Son and Brother, 1914

Notes on Novelists, 1914

The Question of the Mind, 1915

The Ivory Tower, 1917

The Sense of the Past, 1917

The Middle Years, 1917

Within the Rim, 1919

Master Eustace, 1920 ("Master Eustace," "Longstaff's Marriage,"
    "Théodolinde," "A Light Man," "Benvolio")

Travelling Companions, 1919 ("Travelling Companions," "The Sweetheart of M. Briseux," "Professor Fargo," "At Isella," "Guest's Confession," "Adina," "De Grey: A Romance")

A Landscape Painter, 1920 ("A Landscape Painter," "Poor Richard," "A Day of Days," "A Most Extraordinary Case")

Writings About Henry James, 1960-1974

1   EDEL, LEON. Henry James. Pamphlets on American Writers, Num-
    ber 4. Minneapolis: Univ. of Minnesota Press, 47 pp.
        An overview of James's life and career establishes him
    as "the 'largest' literary figure to come out of America
    during the nineteenth and early twentieth centuries." Re-
    printed in 1968.B27. Reviewed: Earle F. Walbridge, Li-
    brary Journal (15 June), p. 2432; H. K. Russell, South
    Atlantic Quarterly, 60 (Winter 1961), 115-16; Modern Lan-
    guage Review (July 1961), p. 418; C. B. Green, Georgia Re-
    view (Fall 1961), p. 364; Virginia Quarterly Review, 37
    (Summer 1961), lxxxviii.

2   HORNE, HELEN. Basic Ideas of James' Aesthetics as Expressed
    in the Short Stories Concerning Artists and Writers. Mar-
    burg: Erich Mauersberger, 175 pp.
        An analysis of twenty-five of James's short stories
    dealing with art and artists in terms of the "occurrence
    and function of ideas in them." Divided into three parts:
    (1) the relevant criticism on the stories is surveyed;
    (2) the stories are interpreted; (3) the ideas in the sto-
    ries are systematically surveyed. In conclusion, "the
    agreement within the stories indicates a flexible but none
    the less existing set of basic ideas."

3   JEFFERSON, D. W. Henry James. Edinburgh: Oliver and Boyd,
    120 pp.
        This introduction to James includes biographical back-
    ground as well as a discussion of his American themes,
    English themes, developments in his method, and his late
    phase. A final chapter provides an overview of James crit-
    icism. A selected bibliography is appended. Reprinted by
    Barnes and Noble, 1961, 1965; by Capricorn Books, Writers
    and Critics Series, 1971. Reviewed: Times Literary Sup-
    plement (28 October), p. 696.

1

1960

4 MARKS, ROBERT. <u>James's Later Novels: An Interpretation</u>. New
   York: William-Frederick Press, 178 pp.
      Covers the late novels from <u>The Awkward Age</u> to <u>The Ivory
   Tower</u>. Attempts to reveal "what the novels ultimately
   mean: the sense that we shall find in him in the last
   analysis." Reviewed: <u>Nineteenth-Century Fiction</u>, 15:93;
   <u>Modern Fiction Studies</u>, 6 (1961), 374; B. R. McElderry,
   Jr., <u>South Atlantic Quarterly</u>, 60 (1961), 243-44.

5 POIRIER, RICHARD. <u>The Comic Sense of Henry James: A Study of
   the Early Novels</u>. New York: Oxford Univ. Press; London:
   Chatto and Windus, 260 pp.
      Consideration of "comic expression in James's early nov-
   els can...lead us through the language to his most vitally
   personal meanings." Since James's comedy is "usually on
   the very surface of the action and language," it is often
   ignored, but his comic sense was employed to solve the dilemma of how to grant a character dramatic freedom and not
   force him into some "system of meaning." Partially reprinted: pp. 237-46 reprinted in 1968.A1; pp. 165-82 reprinted in 1970.A8. Reviewed: 1960.B76; <u>Modern Fiction
   Studies</u>, 6:374; B. R. McElderry, Jr., <u>South Atlantic Quar-
   terly</u>, 60 (1961), 243-44; Leon Edel, <u>American Literature</u>,
   33 (1961), 87-88; Robert P. Falk, <u>Nineteenth-Century Fic-
   tion</u>, 15 (1961), 364-67.

6 WILLEN, GERALD, ed. <u>A Casebook on Henry James's "The Turn of
   the Screw."</u> New York: Crowell, 393 pp.
      Contents: This volume contains the text of the tale as
   well as an excerpt from James's Preface to <u>The Aspern Pa-
   pers</u>, fifteen critical essays, a bibliography, and a list
   of exercises for students. A brief Preface by Gerald Willen discusses the suitability of the work for a controlled
   research project for students.
      "Henry James to the Ruminant Reader: <u>The Turn of the
   Screw</u>" by Edna Kenton (pp. 102-14). Reprinted from <u>The
   Arts</u>, 6 (November 1924), 245-55." Also printed in 1966.A5.
      "The Ambiguity of Henry James" by Edmund Wilson
   (pp. 115-53). Reprinted from <u>The Triple Thinkers</u>. Revised
   and enlarged edition. New York: Oxford Univ. Press, 1948,
   pp. 83-132. A postscript dated 1959 is added to the essay.
      "Another Reading of <u>The Turn of the Screw</u>" by Nathan
   Bryllion Fagin (pp. 154-59). Reprinted from <u>Modern Language Notes</u>, 56 (March 1941), 196-202.
      "James: 'The Turn of the Screw.'" <u>A Radio Symposium</u>:
   Katherine Anne Porter, Allen Tate, Mark Van Doren
   (pp. 160-70). Reprinted from <u>The New Invitation to Learn-

ing. Edited by Mark Van Doren. New York: Random House,
1942, pp. 223-35.
"Mr. Edmund Wilson and The Turn of the Screw" by J. A.
Waldock (pp. 171-73). Reprinted from Modern Language
Notes, 62 (May 1947), 331-34.
"The Turn of the Screw as Poem" by Robert Heilman
(pp. 174-88). Reprinted from Univ. of Kansas City Review,
14 (Summer 1948), 277-89. Also reprinted in 1966.A5.
"Another Turn on James's 'The Turn of the Screw'" by
Glenn A. Reed (pp. 189-99). Reprinted from American Liter-
ature, 20 (January 1949), 413-23.
"James's Air of Evil: The Turn of the Screw" by Oliver
Evans (pp. 200-11). Reprinted from Partisan Review, 16
(February 1949), 175-87.
"Innocence and Evil in James's The Turn of the Screw" by
Charles G. Hoffman (pp. 212-22). Reprinted from Univ. of
Kansas City Review, 20 (Winter 1953), 97-105.
"Henry James as Freudian Pioneer" by Oscar Cargill
(pp. 223-38). Reprinted from Chicago Review, 10 (Summer
1956), 13-29.
"A Note on the Freudian Reading of 'The Turn of the
Screw'" by John Silver (pp. 239-43). Reprinted from Modern
Language Notes, 62 (November 1947), 433-45.
"A Pre-Freudian Reading of The Turn of the Screw" by
Harold C. Goddard (pp. 244-72). Reprinted from Nineteenth-
Century Fiction, 12 (June 1957), 1-36. Also reprinted in
1966.A5, 1970.A7.
"The Governess Turns the Screws" by John Lydenberg
(pp. 273-90). Reprinted from Nineteenth-Century Fiction,
12 (June 1957), 37-58.
"Inadequacy in Eden: Knowledge and The Turn of the
Screw" by Joseph J. Firebaugh (pp. 291-97). Reprinted from
Modern Fiction Studies, 3 (Spring 1957), 57-63.
"Point of View in The Turn of the Screw" by Alexander E.
Jones (pp. 298-318). Reprinted from Publications of the
Modern Language Association of America, 74 (March 1959),
112-22.
Contents of second edition in 1969.A11.

1960 B SHORTER WRITINGS

1   AUCHINCLOSS, LOUIS. "A Strategy for James Readers." Nation,
        190 (23 April), 364-67.
            Beginning readers of James should follow a selective
        list of his fiction that is basically chronological ending
        with his most complicated works.

1960

2   BARNET, SYLVAN, MORTON BERMAN, and WILLIAM BURTO, eds.
"Scope of the Novelist," in their The Study of Literature:
A Handbook of Critical Essays and Terms. Boston: Little,
Brown, p. 93.
    Prefatory headnote to James's "The Art of Fiction."

3   BAYLEY, JOHN. "Love and Knowledge: The Golden Bowl," in his
The Characters of Love: A Study in the Literature of Personality. New York: Basic Books, pp. 203-62.
    "Through the most artificial of forms James succeeds in
presenting to us, not only the extraordinary complications
of human motive and appearance, but their fundamental un-
knowability, a mystery in which reside both the principle
of art and the principle of love." Partially reprinted in
1962.A4.

4   BEATTIE, MUNRO. "Henry James, Novelist." Dalhousie Review,
39 (Winter), 455-63.
    Beattie rejects psychological, allegorical, and prose-
poem readings of James's works. He calls for critics "to
look straight at the conditions of the genre in which James
worked and at the means by which he made that genre yield
its utmost in interest and artistry."

5   BELL, VEREEN M. "Character and Point of View in Representative Victorian Novels." DA, 20, 3740-41 (Duke).
    Analysis of a representative novel by each of six novel-
ists (Dickens, Thackeray, Emily Bronte, George Eliot, Meredith, and Henry James) reveals "changing concepts of character [in fiction] as well as the corresponding adjustments
of fictional method." Dickens and James occupy the two
poles of presentation: Dickens "conceives his characters
as distinct and social entities," while James's characters
"are identified less vividly by complex and amorphous intellectual processes."

6   BERSANI, LEO. "The Narrator as Center in The Wings of the
Dove." Modern Fiction Studies, 6 (Summer), 131-44.
    In The Wings of the Dove the "center of consciousness"
is merged with the narrator and is assimilated into his
point of view. Boundaries between the centers' expressions
of their own thoughts and the narrator's presentation of
them cannot be clearly discerned. Merging of points of
view in the "narrative perspective" of the novel "reflects
James's failure to conceive of a meaningful contact with
the community."

7　BLACKMUR, R. P. "Henry James," in <u>Literary History of the
　　United States</u>. Edited by Robert E. Spiller et al. Revised
　　edition in one volume. New York: Macmillan, pp. 1039-64.
　　An essay which considers James's life and work.

8　BLACKMUR, R. P. "Introduction," in his edition of <u>The Ameri-
　　can</u>. The Laurel Henry James. New York: Dell, pp. 5-13.
　　　　"James was...pretty nearly right about <u>The American</u> [in
　　the Preface] when he furnished the principle or idea for
　　meditation on it that this was a Romance."

9　BOWDEN, EDWIN T. "In Defense of a Henry James Collection."
　　<u>Library Chronicle of the Univ. of Texas</u>, 6:7-12.
　　　　Given the foundation collection already built at the
　　University of Texas, the University should make an effort
　　to build a complete collection that would include James's
　　complete books, contributions to parts-of-books and period-
　　icals, and anonymous and posthumous publications.

10　BRODERICK, J. "Henry James and Gestation: A Reply." <u>College
　　English</u>, 21 (May), 497-99.
　　　　Flinn and Key have misread the text. The baby was born
　　in April following the June wedding of Isabel and Osmond.
　　Response to H. G. Flinn and Howard C. Key, "Henry James and
　　Gestation," <u>College English</u>, 21 (December 1959), 173-75.
　　<u>See</u> 1960.B52 and 1960.B90.

11　BUCKLER, WILLIAM, and ARNOLD B. SKLARE. <u>Stories from Six Au-
　　thors</u>. New York: McGraw-Hill, pp. 272-73, 415-18.
　　　　Included in this text are a biographical sketch, ques-
　　tions for discussion on "The Figure in the Carpet" and "The
　　Lesson of the Master," and an interpretation of "The Madon-
　　na of the Future."

12　BUITENHUIS, PETER, ed. <u>Henry James: French Writers and
　　American Women: Essays</u>. Branford, Conn.: Compass.
　　　　The "Introduction" (pp. i-viii) states that the six es-
　　says included, written by Henry James between 1897 and
　　1907, are on two contrasting subjects. Three are on French
　　literature and three are on the behavior of American women.
　　"A Note on the Development of James's Style" (pp. ix-x)
　　suggests that James's writing style changes during the
　　decade in which these essays were written: the first is in
　　his mature second style, while the last is in his third
　　manner.

1960

13 CAMBON, GLAUCO. "L'ombra di Henry James." <u>Fiera Letteraria</u>,
      15 (15 May), 5. [Italian]
         As in James's <u>The Portrait of a Lady</u> and "Daisy Miller,"
      the personae in Marcia Davenport's <u>The Constant Image</u> are
      individuals torn between two worlds. The descriptions,
      atmosphere, and gossip clearly follow James's style, but
      the love dialogues are more direct, spontaneous, alive.
      One could say they are almost in Hemingway's style.

14 CAMBON, GLAUCO. "What Maisie and Huck Knew." <u>Studi Ameri-
      cani</u>, no. 6, pp. 203-20.
         Despite obvious differences, Huck (as he appears in
      <u>Huckleberry Finn</u>) and Maisie share a "set of problems, cen-
      tering on the dramatized genesis, conditions and authentic-
      ity of consciousness <u>within</u> and <u>without</u> an unsustaining
      society."

15 CARGILL, OSCAR. "<u>The Ambassadors</u>: A New View." <u>Publications
      of the Modern Language Association of America</u>, 75 (Septem-
      ber), 439-52.
         The belated growth of the idealist Lewis Lambert Strether
      from innocence to maturity is achieved through his "Edenic"
      experiences with the three principal females of the novel--
      Marie de Vionnet, Maria Gostrey, and Mrs. Abel Newsome.

16 COOK, ALBERT. "The Portentous Intelligent Stillness: James,"
      in his <u>The Meaning of Fiction</u>. Detroit: Wayne State Univ.
      Press, pp. 134-66, passim.
         James refined the "tightness of structure" he received
      from Flaubert through his unique handling of the novel's
      perspective.

17 COONEY, SÉAMUS. "Awkward Ages in <u>The Awkward Age</u>." <u>Modern
      Language Notes</u>, 75 (March), 208-11.
         Two inconsistencies in ages of major characters in <u>The
      Awkward Age</u> reveal "uncertainty in one of its main concep-
      tions" and are cause to consider the book flawed by
      sentimentality.

18 COSTELLO, DONALD P. "The Structure of <u>The Turn of the Screw</u>."
      <u>Modern Language Notes</u>, 75 (April), 312-21.
         James "planted in the very structure of the story" cer-
      tain elements intended to puzzle and horrify the reader.

19   DANIELS, HOWELL. "Henry James and 'An International Epi-
       sode.'" British Association for American Studies Bulletin,
       ns 1 (September), 3-35.
         Beyond its heritage in the international tradition of
       James, "An International Episode" is a specific response to
       Laurence Oliphant's insensitive rendering of American so-
       ciety in his Tender Recollections.

20   DOVE, JOHN R. "Tragic Consciousness in Isabel Archer," in
       Studies in American Literature. Edited by Waldo McNeir and
       Leo B. Levy. Louisiana State Univ. Studies, Humanities Se-
       ries, No. 8. Baton Rouge: Louisiana State Univ. Press,
       pp. 78-94.
         Isabel's "tragic consciousness springs from her realiza-
       tion that her earlier ideals of life are irrelevant to the
       world as it is."

21   DOVE, JOHN ROLAND. "The Tragic Sense in Henry James." Texas
       Studies in Literature and Language, 2 (Autumn), 303-14.
         Concerned with personal relationships rather than socio-
       logical or metaphysical truth, James conceived of tragedy
       as the failure of personal relationships in a world in
       which the highest value was vested in those relationships.
       His protagonists (Isabel Archer, Milly Theale, Hyacinth
       Robinson) are always betrayed by a person whom they trust-
       ed; this disappointment constitutes the tragic.

22   EDEL, LEON, ed. Guy Domville: A Play in Three Acts. Key-
       stone Book. Philadelphia: Lippincott; London: Hart-
       Davis.
         Contents: Included in this book are a biographical es-
       say; the text of the play; critical responses by Shaw,
       Wells, and Bennett; and a note on the text.
         In "Henry James: The Dramatic Years" by Leon Edel
       (pp. 13-121), six biographical chapters trace James's life
       as a dramatist, beginning with his childhood experiences
       and concluding with the statement that James won a final
       victory in his playwrighting, since he found "in the scenic
       method" that which enabled him to become "one of the great
       architects of the modern novel."

23   EDEL, LEON. "Introduction," in his edition of The Ambassadors.
       Riverside Edition. Boston: Houghton Mifflin, pp. v-xvi.
         This novel's "scenes were minor, domestic, conversation-
       al, subdued; the material was refined, as civilization re-
       fines. Yet in its own quiet, unviolent way, it dealt with
       fundamental values, of the deepest and richest kind." (The
       New York Edition is the text used here with the order of

1960

chapters I and II of Book Eleventh reversed in order to
correct an error made in all American editions prior to
1957.) Reprinted in 1964.A6.

24   EDEL, LEON. "Introduction," in his edition of The Tragic
      Muse. Harper Torchbook. New York: Harper, pp. vii-xvii.
         While this novel "is outwardly a story of politics and
      painting and the stage it is in effect James's continuing
      story of the artist-dilemma in his society." In addition,
      it is one of James's "longest and most leisurely novels, a
      great cheerful mural of English life and art and talk."

25   EDEL, LEON. "Introduction," in his edition of Watch and Ward.
      Evergreen Book. New York: Grove Press, pp. 5-18.
         Henry James's first novel, "repudiated by its author,
      disregarded by criticism, is a glimpse, however shadowy,
      into the creative process of a novelist; and a harbinger of
      his greatness."

26   EDEL, LEON. "The Text of The Ambassadors." Harvard Library
      Bulletin, 14 (Autumn), 453-60.
         Six current editions of The Ambassadors can be traced to
      four earlier editions: the Anchor Edition follows the Har-
      per Edition of 1903; the Signet Edition follows the Methuen
      Edition of 1903; the Fawcett Edition follows the corrected
      Harper Edition of 1957; and the Riverside Edition and the
      Rinehart Edition follow the New York Edition with chap-
      ters XXVIII and XXIX corrected. Reprinted in 1969.A10.

27   EDEL, LEON. "Who Was Gilbert Osmond?" Modern Fiction Studies,
      6 (Summer), 164.
         The model for Gilbert Osmond could not have been H. B.
      Brewster. Osmond and Pansy are modeled on Francis Boott
      and his daughter. Response to R. W. Stallman, "Who Was
      Gilbert Osmond?" Modern Fiction Studies, 4 (1958), 127-35.
      See also 1962.B38.

28   EMERSON, DONALD. "Henry James and the American Language."
      Transactions of the Wisconsin Academy of Sciences, Arts,
      and Letters, 49 (December), 237-47.
         James had a "non-technical concern" for language and was
      well aware that the U.S. would "produce a distinguishable
      American language out of transplanted English."

29   EMERSON, DONALD. "Henry James and the Limitations of Real-
      ism." College English, 22 (December), 161-66.
         James's writings reflect three distinct, chronologically
      evolving concepts of realism.

*30   EVANS, BERGEN, ed. The Ambassadors. Greenwich, Conn.:
        Premier World Classics.
            Cited in 1966.B7, p. 136.

31   FABRIS, ALBERTA. "Note su The American Scene." Studi Ameri-
        cani, no. 6, pp. 255-73. [Italian]
            The American Scene, a bitter criticism of American mores,
        portrays many traits already present in The Ambassadors.
        In both works an abundant use of metaphors gives meaning to
        people and scenes.

32   FEINSTEIN, HERBERT. "Two Pairs of Gloves: Mark Twain and
        Henry James." American Imago, 17 (Winter), 349-87.
            Gloves in James's The Turn of the Screw and Twain's The
        Innocents Abroad provide the case material for a study in
        the use of symbols in literary interpretation.

33   FIEDLER, LESLIE. Love and Death in the American Novel. New
        York: Criterion Books, pp. 288-95, 298-300, 338-39.
            James used Hawthorne patterns of dark and light: "[I]n
        the four novels now generally considered his best, the
        archetype of the Dark Lady and Fair has arisen to possess
        him; to give his work not only technical authority and nov-
        elistic insight, but a mythic dimension as well"
        (pp. 288-95). Daisy Miller, "the Good Bad Birl," is
        "finally and unequivocally innocent" (pp. 298-300; reprint-
        ed in 1963.B99). Strether is "the trapped spectator" in-
        stead of the "'Peeping Tom,'" but James invented "the tech-
        nique of the 'center of consciousness,' i.e., a device for
        making the peeper the focus of a work of art" (pp. 338-39).
        Revised edition: 1966.B27.

34   FIEDLER, LESLIE. No! In Thunder. Boston: Beacon Press,
        p. 280, passim.
            James first set the pattern in What Maisie Knew of hav-
        ing an innocent child observe the evil of the adults, "the
        child as Peeping Tom."

35   FINKELSTEIN, SIDNEY. "Six Ways of Looking at Reality." Main-
        stream, 13 (December), 31-42.
            Six passages which describe scenes with close attention
        to outer reality demonstrate that "a faithful approach to
        the reality of the outer world" is necessary for the artist
        to gain freedom of expression. Excerpts from the following
        novels are included: Cooper's The Pioneers, Melville's
        Pierre, or The Ambiguities, James's The American, Dreiser's
        An American Tragedy, Hemingway's The Sun Also Rises, and
        Faulkner's The Old Man.

1960

36   FRANTZ, JEAN H. "Henry James and Saintine." <u>Notes and</u>
        <u>Queries</u>, ns 7 (July), 266-68.
            Saintine's romance <u>Picciola</u> influenced James's "In the
        Cage."

37   GALE, ROBERT L., ed. "Four Letters to Francis Marion Craw-
        ford: From Theodore Roosevelt, Clyde Fitch, Julia Ward
        Howe, Henry James." <u>Literary Review</u> (Fairleigh Dickinson),
        3 (Spring), 438-43.
            Four recently discovered letters received by Crawford
        are significant in that they "suggest something of the na-
        ture of their recipient."

38   GALE, RoBERT L. "James's <u>The Golden Bowl</u>, II, 307." <u>Expli-</u>
        <u>cator</u>, 19 (October), Item 5.
            Maggie's comparison of Charlotte to Io (II, 307) "re-
        enforces the strange image of Charlotte as a pet on a silk-
        en halter (II, 287, 331, 358)." Charlotte's banishment to
        America is forecast by reference to Ariadne's fate. The
        attractive interpretation aligning Maggie with Ariadne,
        Adam with Minos, and the Prince with Theseus must be re-
        jected as contrary to James's intentions.

39   GARGANO, JAMES W. "<u>The Ambassadors</u> and <u>Louis Lambert</u>." <u>Mod-</u>
        <u>ern Language Notes</u>, 75 (March), 211-13.
            James's use of the name "Lewis Lambert Strether," bor-
        rowed from Balzac's Louis Lambert, serves as "an ironic
        commentary on the overly-spiritualized philosophy pro-
        pounded by Balzac's Swedenborgian protagonist."

40   GARGANO, JAMES W. "<u>Daisy Miller</u>: An Abortive Quest for In-
        nocence." <u>South Atlantic Quarterly</u>, 59 (Winter), 114-20.
            Winterbourne, not Daisy, is the central protagonist in a
        story that is "essentially the study of a young man's quest
        for innocence, a virtue from which his society has alienat-
        ed itself." Reprinted in 1963.B99; 1968.B115.

41   GARGANO, JAMES W. "Henry James on Baudelaire." <u>Modern Lan-</u>
        <u>guage Notes</u>, 75 (November), 559-61.
            Henry James, entering into a controversy in <u>The Nation</u>
        concerning the merits of Baudelaire, denounced the "'lurid
        landscape and unclean furniture'" of Baudelaire's poems and
        denounced advocates of "art for art."

42   GRENANDER, M. E. "Henry James's <u>Capricciosa</u>: Christina Light
        in <u>Roderick Hudson</u> and <u>The Princess Casamassima</u>." <u>Publica-</u>
        <u>tions of the Modern Language Association of America</u>, 75
        (June), 309-19.

10

Christina's character is consistently developed in the
two works. The inevitable deterioration that follows the
type of life she pursues in the first work is exhibited in
her petulance and disillusionment.

43   GRENANDER, M. E., BEVERLY J. RAHN, and FRANCINE VALVO. "The
      Time-Scheme in The Portrait of a Lady." American Litera-
      ture, 32 (May), 127-35.
         James avoided the problem with the time structure of
      Roderick Hudson in The Portrait of a Lady by presenting
      Isabel over a six year period. The strictly chronological
      effect is avoided by using flashbacks and "monologue
      intérieur."

44   GROSSO, LUIGI. "Attualità di Henry James." Fiera Letteraria,
      15 (13 March), 5. [Italian]
         James's maturity can be traced in the newly developed,
      yet unmistakable, style of his Watch and Ward.

45   HINCHCLIFFE, ARNOLD P. "The Good American." Twentieth Cen-
      tury, 168 (December), 529-39.
         Three recent novels, The Nice American, The Quiet Ameri-
      can, and The Ugly American, focus on innocence, guilt, and
      morality, as does James's The American, and are "a kind of
      footnote to James's early definition of the good American."

46   HINCHCLIFFE, ARNOLD P. "Henry James's The Sacred Fount."
      Texas Studies in Literature and Language, 2 (Summer),
      88-94.
         This novel contains James's "first significant use of
      symbols" and prepares the way for The Golden Bowl; in addi-
      tion, James anticipates certain characteristics of twentieth
      century literature such as "intensity," "violence," "dislo-
      cation," and "inability of communication."

47   HOLDER, ALEX. "On the Structure of Henry James's Metaphors."
      English Studies, 41 (October), 289-97.
         An examination of James's use of three categories of
      metaphors--metaphors utilizing one metaphorical element,
      metaphors utilizing two or three elements, and metaphors
      utilizing more than three elements--reveals his virtuosity
      in combining metaphoric elements to create gradations and
      nuances in meaning and tone.

48   HOLLOWAY, JOHN. "Tess of the D'Urbervilles and The Awkward
      Age," in his The Charted Mirror: Literary and Critical
      Essays. London: Routledge and Kegan Paul, pp. 108-17.

1960

Tess and The Awkward Age share similar themes: "the
Pure Woman" in Hardy's novel and "Innocence" in James's.
Together the two novels "document a whole period of English
life," the "city plutocracy" in one and "the impoverished
countryside hidden behind it" in the other.

49 HUTCHENS, JOHN K. "One Very Dark Night in the Life of Mr.
Henry James." New York Herald Tribune Books, 37 (11 Decem-
ber), 32.
James's childhood infatuation with the theatre continued
with him until it culminated in horror at the premiere of
"Guy Domville."

50 IWASE, SHITSUU. "Isabel's Experience in The Portrait of a
Lady." Queries (Osaka Municipal Univ.), 1 (May), 38-48.
[Japanese]
Isabel's recognition changes from direct visual observation to moral insight. The ending of the novel implies a
qualitative change from experience by sight to that by
action.

51 KANZER, MARK. "The Figure in the Carpet." American Imago, 17
(Winter), 339-48.
"The Figure in the Carpet" is a psychological extension
of James's state of mind at a transitional point in his
career. The figure is presented in riddle form, with
sphinxlike and oedipal overtones, and is an illustration of
James's "idea that art . . . is more real than life itself."

52 KEY, HOWARD C. "Author's Comment." College English, 21
(May), 499-500.
Although it contains an oversight regarding the month of
Isabel's marriage, "Henry James and Gestation" (College
English, 21 [December 1959], 173-75) is basically accurate;
the article was not meant as a "malicious attack upon
James's literary artistry." See 1960.B10 and 1960.B90.

53 LID, R. W. "Tietjens in Disguise." Kenyon Review, 22
(Spring), 265-76.
Henry James, not Conrad, played the largest role in the
development of Ford Madox Ford's art.

54 LOOMIS, E. W. "Three Notes on Plot." Spectrum, 4 (Spring-
Summer), 94-99.
Plot for James comes out of the subject and "presents
itself as an idea which expresses the subject." The idea
is then developed in a manner "which suggests formal deduc-
tion but is actually nearer to that search for hypothesis
which characterizes experimental science."

55   LOWE, ALMA LOUISE. "Introduction," in her edition of English
      Hours. Second edition. Illustrations by Anthony Gross.
      New York: Orion Press; London: Heinemann, pp. xiii-xliv.
          James was "the 'sentimental tourist' and the 'analytical
      observer,' and nowhere is James the American more intimate-
      ly revealed than in his travel writings."

56   LUTWACK, LEONARD. "Mixed and Uniform Prose Styles in the
      Novel." Journal of Aesthetics and Art Criticism, 18
      (March), 350-57.
          The Ambassadors is an example of a novel which employs a
      single, uniform prose style throughout. Reprinted in
      1967.B101.

57   MacDONALD, DWIGHT. "Max Beerbohm's 'The Guerdon,'" in his
      Parodies: An Anthology from Chaucer to Beerbohm--and After.
      New York: The Modern Library, p. 147.
          "The Guerdon" was chosen for this anthology because it
      "hits off the late Jamesian style better than does The Mote
      [in the Middle Distance]."

58   MARIANI, UMBERTO. "L'esperienza italiana di Henry James."
      Studi Americani, no. 6, pp. 221-53. [Italian]
          Because of the romantic character of his first journey
      there, James introduced an unrealistic picture of Italy in
      his early works; he changed this view considerably in his
      later writings. The Italy he had once considered as a
      dream for Americans looking for an experience in the Old
      World, he transformed later into a symbol of moral values
      against which a revelation of religious and mythical Ameri-
      can values stands in all its superiority.

*59   MARKOVIĆ, VIDA. "Henry Džems." Savremenik (December),
      pp. 528-41.
          Cited in Annual Bibliography of English Language and
      Literature: 1960, Vol. 35. Edited by Marjorie Rigby and
      Charles Nilon. Cambridge, England: The Univ. Press for
      the Modern Humanities Research Assn., 1963, Item 4335.

60   MASUNAGA, KEIICHI. "Henry James and Journalism: The Rever-
      berator." Gaikoku Bungaku Kenkyu (Ritsumeikan Univ.), 3
      (December), 39-52. [Japanese]
          James intended to contrast the impudence of modern jour-
      nalism in the new world with the old world and to make use
      of that impudence to disclose the hypocrisy of the old
      world. The work contains James's usual character drama
      featuring a heroine, but the work is one of James's experi-
      ments, for he deals directly with the mechanism of modern
      journalism.

13

1960

61 MAURIAC, FRANÇOIS. Mémoires Intérieurs. Translated by Gerard
    Hopkins. New York: Farrar, Straus and Cudahy, pp. 227-30.
        Mauriac's autobiographical ruminations include a passage
    on James in which the repressed sexual elements in The Bos-
    tonians are judged to cause a weakness in the novel.

62 MAUROIS, ANDRÉ. "Un puritain hérésiarque." Nouvelles Litté-
    raires, no. 1703 (21 April), pp. 1, 4. [French]
        Maurois summarizes the impressions George Moore, Charles
    Du Bois, and H. G. Wells had of James. Maurois appreciates
    the delicate way James--the writer--treated immoral argu-
    ments, together with his ability to combine the real with
    the fantastic, but especially his primary interest: art
    and its relation to society and life.

63 MELCHIORI, GIORGIO. "The English Tradition and the American
    Tradition (1955)." Sewanee Review, 68 (Summer), 502-15.
        Contemporary English writers, such as L. P. Hartley, are
    drawing on styles and themes of nineteenth century American
    writers. Hawthorne's influence on Hartley's The Go-Between
    can be seen in method, atmosphere, and moral concern. Hen-
    ry James, touched by both Hawthorne and the English aes-
    thetic movement, achieved a "delicate balance" between the
    two novel traditions.

64 MICHAEL, MARY KYLE. "Henry James's Use of the Word Wonderful
    in The Ambassadors." Modern Language Notes, 75 (February),
    114-17.
        The word "wonderful" is an aesthetic device James em-
    ploys to tie together "resolution and art" in The
    Ambassadors.

65 MIX, KATHERINE LYON. A Study in Yellow: The "Yellow Book"
    and Its Contributors. Lawrence: Univ. of Kansas Press,
    pp. 166-72, passim.
        James's contributions to the Yellow Book (published from
    1894 to 1897) and his relationship with the editors are
    discussed.

66 MONTGOMERY, MARION. "The Flaw in the Portrait: Henry James
    vs. Isabel Archer." Univ. of Kansas City Review, 26
    (March), 215-20.
        An analysis of the protagonist's character in The Por-
    trait of a Lady reveals that the work is aesthetically
    flawed as a result of James's failure to allow the struc-
    ture of the novel to evolve as his work progressed. Re-
    printed in 1968.A1.

67   MOSS, LEONARD JEROME. "Transitional Devices in Henry James."
     CEA Critic, 22 (February), 1, 6, 12.
         The opening paragraph of Chapter 19 of The Portrait of a
     Lady illustrates James's use of all five of the most impor-
     tant transitional devices.

68   MURAKAMI, FUJIO. "The Question of the Aesthete: 'The Author
     of Beltraffio.'" Jimbun Kenkyu, 11 (June), 101-14. [Japa-
     nese]
         The story reflects the contemporary situation of the
     nineteenth century aesthetic movement in England, typified
     by the traditional Christian moral reaction to Pater's
     ideas. James apparently sides with Pater; form and content
     are one in nature, and art is to be given primacy. Yet,
     James with the knowledge of the importance of life remains
     ambivalent to aestheticism as he seems to foresee the emer-
     gence of decadence.

69   NYREN, DOROTHY, ed. "Henry James," in A Library of Literary
     Criticism: Modern American Literature. New York: Ungar,
     pp. 248-54.
         Excerpts of criticism published between 1918 and 1950
     are collected here.

70   PATERSON, JOHN. "The Language of 'Adventure' in Henry James."
     American Literature, 32 (November), 291-301.
         In his exploration of "a moral and social geography"
     James utilized the imagery of adventure novels, demonstrat-
     ing the extraordinariness latent in ordinary subjects. Re-
     printed in revised form in 1964.A6.

71   PATTERSON, REBECCA. "Two Portraits of a Lady." Midwest
     Quarterly, 1 (Summer), 343-61.
         Madame de Mauves may represent an initial draft of The
     Portrait of a Lady, and a proper appreciation of each work
     comes through the light they offer for each other.

72   PERLONGO, ROBERT A. "The Sacred Fount: Labyrinth or Parable?"
     Kenyon Review, 22 (Autumn), 635-47.
         Autobiographical in subject and parabolic in form, The
     Sacred Fount reveals James's self-doubt about the life of
     the artist.

73   PERRIN, NOEL. "The Henry James Papers." New Yorker, 36
     (12 November), 191-98.
         Noel Perrin recalls his humorous experience with a senior
     tutor at Cambridge who possessed a collection of unpub-
     lished James letters.

1960

74   POWERS, LYALL H.   "Henry James and Zola's Roman expérimental."
      Univ. of Toronto Quarterly, 30 (October), 16-30.
          The influence of the French Naturalists is most clearly
      discernible in the 1880s. In particular, The Bostonians,
      The Princess Casamassima, and The Tragic Muse, while ex-
      periments with consciousness, are "'experimental,' in
      Zola's sense, as they seem to adhere closely to his prin-
      ciples regarding the role of heredity and environment and
      the force of determinism."

75   PRIESTLEY, J. B.   Literature and Western Man. New York:
      Harper & Bros., pp. 357-62, passim.
          In this study, which places greater emphasis on the sec-
      ond half of its title than the first, some half dozen ref-
      erences to Henry James appear. They include a paragraph-
      length biographical sketch and an evaluation of James's
      accomplishment that concludes James is overrated by present
      day critics.

76   PRITCHETT, V. S.   "Babcockism." New Statesman, 59 (11 June),
      863-64.
          Despite its colorless style, Richard Poirier's The Comic
      Sense of Henry James is sensible and instinctively accu-
      rate. Review of 1960.A5.

77   RANALD, RALPH A.   "The Sacred Fount: James's Portrait of the
      Artist Manqué." Nineteenth-Century Fiction, 15 (December),
      239-48.
          Best comprehended in light of the James canon, not as an
      independent art object, The Sacred Fount is a presentation
      through inverse example of James's theories of art, morali-
      ty, and love.

78   REES, RICHARD.   "Miss Jessel and Lady Chatterley," in his For
      Love or Money: Studies in Personality and Essence. Car-
      bondale: Southern Illinois Univ. Press, pp. 115-24.
          The Turn of the Screw has a disguised theme which re-
      sembles a theme in Lady Chatterley's Lover. Peter Quint
      can be compared to Mellors; both men are "clever and deep,"
      use "bad language," possess "secret disorders and vices,"
      and have red hair. Both Miss Jessel and Connie Chatterley
      fall in love with men beneath them socially.

79   ROPER, ALAN H.   "The Moral and Metaphorical Meanings of The
      Spoils of Poynton." American Literature, 32 (May), 182-96.
          James's martial imagery provides the key to a moral in-
      terpretation that recognizes the egoism of Mrs. Gereth, the

Brigstocks, and Owen as antithetical to the selfless altru-
ism of Fleda Vetch.

80   SMITH, HENRY NASH, and WILLIAM M. GIBSON, eds., with assis-
     tance of FREDERICK ANDERSON. Mark Twain-Howells Letters.
     2 vols. Cambridge, Mass.: Belknap Press of Harvard Univ.
     Press, passim.
         A number of references to James appear in the letters
     and in the footnotes of these two volumes.

81   SNOW, LOTUS. "Some Stray Fragrance of an Ideal: Henry
     James's Imagery for Youth's Discovery of Evil." Harvard
     Library Bulletin, 14 (Winter), 107-25.
         James's three works that focus on "Youth's discovery of
     evil through the conduct of parents," The Awkward Age, "The
     Pupil" and What Maisie Knew, reveal James's evolving matu-
     rity in handling imagery and dramatic techniques.

82   STALLMAN, R. W. "Afterword," in his edition of The Ambassa-
     dors. A Signet Classic. New York: New American Library,
     pp. 377-82.
         Part I, "A Note on The Ambassadors (pp. 377-81), notes
     that the novel begins with a question by Strether "and that
     first question starts off the sequence of questions and
     answers, or theories, that comprise the nimble-minded sub-
     stance of the narrative." Part I is drawn from Modern Fic-
     tion Studies, 3 (Spring 1957), 41-56. Part II, "A Note on
     the Text of The Ambassadors" (pp. 381-82), notes that the
     1903 Methuen text is used for this edition. Reprinted in
     an expanded version in 1961.B82.

83   STALLMAN, R. W., and LILLIAN GILKES, eds. Stephen Crane Let-
     ters. New York: New York Univ. Press, pp. 243-44, passim.
         Over twenty passing references to James.

84   STEVENSON, LIONEL. The English Novel: A Panorama. Boston:
     Houghton Mifflin, pp. 394-96, 417-18, 511-12, passim.
         James's contributions to the technique of the novel are
     briefly discussed in one of two dozen references to Henry
     James in this history of the novel.

85   TADA, TOSHIO. "Henry James's The Princess Casamassima: Its
     Manners." Bungaku Ronshu (Kansai Univ.), 10 (July), 44-59.
     [Japanese]
         James's subjectivity is dividedly presented in Hyacinth
     and the Princess, revealing James's inner conflict of
     values. James's sympathy, however, goes to the youth who
     dies in homage to manners.

1960

86   TARTELLA, VINCENT. "James's 'Four Meetings': Two Texts Com-
     pared." <u>Nineteenth-Century Fiction</u>, 15 (June), 17-28.
        The revision of "Four Meetings" reflects a more fully
     delineated narrator with greater rhetorical intensity and
     precision and force.

87   THURSTON, JARVIS, O. B. EMERSON, et al., eds. <u>Short Fiction</u>
     <u>Criticism: A Checklist of Interpretation Since 1925 of</u>
     <u>Stories and Novelettes (American, British, Continental),</u>
     <u>1800-1958</u>. Denver: Alan Swallow, pp. 94-115.
        A listing of criticism published since 1925 on one hun-
     dred and five of James's works of short fiction.

88   TOCHIHARA, TOMOO. "How to Read <u>The American</u>." <u>Ronko</u> (Kwan-
     seigakuin Univ.), 7 (October), 109-23. [Japanese]
        The novel deals with the contrast between American
     idealism and French realism. Aside from the literary tech-
     nical influence of the French realists, James's primary
     concern was moralistic, ethical, and even puritanical.

89   WALKER, DON D. "Wister, Roosevelt, and James: A Note on the
     Western." <u>American Quarterly</u>, 12 (Fall), 358-66.
        Wister's failure to become a good writer is attributable
     to the absence of the help of friends, critics, and dis-
     criminating readers typified in the responses of James and
     T. Roosevelt.

90   WALLACE, JACK E. "Isabel and the Ironies." <u>College English</u>,
     21 (May), 497.
        A close look at the text of <u>The Portrait of a Lady</u> indi-
     cates that Flinn and Key in "Henry James and Gestation" are
     inaccurate in their chronology. According to the text,
     Isabel and Osmond were married in June, 1873; the baby boy
     was born in April, 1874, and died in November, 1874; Rosier
     visited Madame Merle in Autumn, 1876. Response to H. G.
     Flinn and Howard C. Key, "Henry James and Gestation," <u>Col-</u>
     <u>lege English</u>, 21 (December 1959), 173-75. (Flinn and Key
     point out that Madame Merle told Edward Rosier that Isa-
     bel's baby boy "died two years ago, six months after his
     birth" [New York Edition, II, p. 96], causing a problem in
     chronology, because the author intimates later [pp. 101,
     107] that Isabel and Osmond have only been married three
     years. This discrepancy may exist because (1) the baby was
     premature; (2) the baby was conceived out of wedlock; (3)
     Madame Merle was not exactly accurate in her time refer-
     ence; (4) James made an error [since he was a bachelor and
     perhaps "vague on gestational processes."]) <u>See</u> 1960.B10
     and 1960.B52.

91 WARD, J. A. "Evil in The Golden Bowl." Western Humanities
      Review, 14 (Winter), 47-59.
        The burden of moral evil is shared by both Europeans and
      Americans in The Golden Bowl. Since the golden bowl is
      symbolic of Maggie's marriage, the flaw in the bowl stands
      for the evil inherent in the marriage; the Ververs as well
      as the Prince and Charlotte contribute to the creation of
      the flaw.

92 WARD, J. A. "Henry James and the Nature of Evil." Twentieth-
      Century Literature, 6 (July), 65-69.
        In James's fiction, obscure and indefinite evil is an
      "ever present reality that cripples and destroys"; it is
      related to Original Sin, and every person "possesses a
      latent capacity for evil." Reprinted in 1965.B8.

93 WARD, J. A. "Henry James's America: Versions of Oppression."
      Mississippi Quarterly, 13 (Winter), 30-44.
        James explored a variety of settings to demonstrate the
      oppressive presence of evil in American society.

94 WARD, J. A. "The Ineffectual Heroes of James's Middle Peri-
      od." Texas Studies in Literature and Language, 2 (Autumn),
      315-27.
        The protagonists of the Middle Period differ from
      James's early protagonists in their diminished power, con-
      fidence, and vitality; and they typically exist in a nebu-
      lous moral world where seeming good is evil and seeming
      evil is good.

95 WARD, J. A. "Social Disintegration in The Wings of the Dove."
      Criticism, 2 (Spring), 190-203.
        In The Wings of the Dove reconciliation of the values of
      traditional society and personal ideals is impossible. The
      old order has collapsed, and the novel deals with the quest
      for identity following the collapse of civilization.

96 WASIOLEK, EDWARD. "Maisie: Pure or Corrupt?" College Eng-
      lish, 22 (December), 167-72.
        Maisie is both "pure" and "corrupt," and "at every point
      in the novel she is subtly distinct in moral coloration."

97 WASIOLEK, EDWARD. "Tolstoy's The Death of Ivan Ilyich and
      Jamesian Fictional Imperatives." Modern Fiction Studies,
      6 (Winter), 314-24.
        For James, unlike Tolstoy, successful fiction neither
      interprets experience nor prescribes what it should be.
      Experience, for James, is too complex to control by direct
      intrusion and generalization.

1960

98   WATT, IAN. "The First Paragraph of The Ambassadors: An Ex-
      plication." Essays in Criticism, 10 (July), 250-74.
         An analysis of James's stylistic techniques suggests an
      abstractness that reflects a multiplicity of visions devel-
      oped through a "progressive and yet artfully delayed clari-
      fication." Reprinted in 1964.A6; 1968.A11; 1968.B115;
      1969.A10. Response in 1961.B65. See also 1961.B95.

99   WILSON, HARRIS, ed. Arnold Bennett and H. G. Wells: A Record
      of a Personal and Literary Friendship. Urbana: Univ. of
      Illinois Press, passim.
         Henry James is mentioned a dozen times in the introduc-
      tion, notes, and letters of this record of the Bennett-
      Wells friendship.

100   WOODWARD, C. VANN. "A Southern Critique for the Gilded Age:
      Melville, Adams, and James," in his The Burden of Southern
      History. Baton Rouge: Louisiana State Univ. Press,
      pp. 109-40.
         A curious phenomenon of the Gilded Age is that "it re-
      mained for Northern writers, three of the most discerning
      critics of the age, to acknowledge the relevance of the
      Southern tradition and bring to bear that point of view in
      their critique of American society." This point of view
      was employed by Melville in Clarel, Adams in Democracy, and
      James in The Bostonians.

101   ZABEL, MORTON DAUWEN. "Memoir," in his The Art of Ruth Draper:
      Her Dramas and Characters. Garden City, N.Y.: Doubleday &
      Co., pp. 38-51.
         One of Draper's "choicest memories" was Henry James's
      encouragement of her acting career. He became her friend
      in London during 1913 and wrote her personal letters as well
      as a monologue for performance.

1960 C DISSERTATIONS

*1   DANKLEFF, RICHARD. "The Composition, Revisions, Reception,
      and Critical Reputation of Henry James's 'The Spoils of
      Poynton.'" Unpublished Doctoral Dissertation, Univ. of
      Chicago.
         Cited in Annual Bibliography of English Language and Lit-
      erature: 1961, Vol. 36. Edited by Marjory Rigby and
      Charles Nilon. Cambridge, England: University Press for
      the Modern Humanities Research Association, Item 4751.

2   HICKS, PRISCILLA GIBSON. "'The Story in It': The Design of
    Henry James's 'New York Edition.'" <u>DA</u>, 21, 895-96 (Bos-
    ton Univ.).
         Internal evidence establishes that with the arrangement
    of the New York Edition James "builds an architecture . . .
    so that each unit makes a certain 'germ' progressively
    clearer, or better enforces the same (often intricate)
    idea."

3   HOFER, ERNEST HARRISON. "The Realization of Conscience in the
    Later Henry James." <u>DA</u>, 21, 197 (Cornell).
         The novels of Henry James written after 1897 reveal that
    James "wanted the action of his story to be morally signif-
    icant." James attempted "to demonstrate that complete con-
    sciousness could be achieved." Consequently, "a practice
    of perception essentially spiritual" was implied by this
    ideal state.

4   MASBACK, FREDERIC JOSEPH. "The Child Character in Hawthorne
    and James." <u>DA</u>, 21, 338 (Syracuse).
         Although "Hawthorne and James both saw the child charac-
    ter as an innocent exposed to an evil world, and they used
    this confrontation as a device for examining and evaluating
    varying and often opposed values, conduct, and perceptions,"
    they treated their child characters in very different ways.
    In Hawthorne's fictional world, "the child's values triumph
    by prevailing, while James creates a world in which renun-
    ciation of worldly values is the only triumph."

5   NETTELS, ELSA. "The Drama of Consciousness: The Role of the
    Central Intelligence in Selected Novels of Henry James."
    <u>DA</u>, 21, 615-16 (Wisconsin).
         The "central intelligence" in seven of James's novels
    undergoes a chronological evolution that culminates in the
    last four novels with a protagonist who is simultaneously
    an objective observer and a subjective participant.

6   PURDY, STROTHER BEESON. "The Language of Henry James with
    Emphasis on His Diction and Vocabulary." <u>DA</u>, 21, 626
    (Wisconsin).
         An examination of James's language drawn principally
    from <u>The Portrait of a Lady</u>, <u>The Golden Bowl</u>, <u>The American</u>,
    <u>The Turn of the Screw</u>, "Crapy Cornelia," and "A Round of
    Visits" reveals his careful attention to individual words
    <u>qua</u> words and his recognition of their importance in the
    novel.

1960

*7   RAMADAN, A. M. "The Reception of Henry James's Fiction in the
     English Periodical Between 1875 and 1890." Dissertation,
     London.
        Cited in Beatrice Ricks, comp. Henry James: A Bibli-
     ography of Secondary Works. Scarecrow Author Bibliogra-
     phies, No. 24. Metuchen, N.J.: Scarecrow, 1975, Item 3215.

1961 A BOOKS

1   CARGILL, OSCAR. The Novels of Henry James. New York: Mac-
    millan, 505 pp.
       A reading of the novels which utilizes a wide variety of
    approaches and synthesizes the best criticism and scholar-
    ship produced on James since 1871. Partially reprinted:
    pp. 78-119 reprinted in 1967.A5. Reviewed: 1961.B45;
    1965.B6; Modern Fiction Studies, 7 (Winter 1961-1962), 380;
    J. A. Ward, Nineteenth-Century Fiction, 17 (1962), 80-84;
    Times Literary Supplement (30 November 1962), p. 938;
    W. H. Gass, South Atlantic Quarterly, 61 (1962), 285-86;
    Christof Wegelin, American Literature, 34 (1962), 382-84.

2   EDEL, LEON, and DAN H. LAURENCE, eds. A Bibliography of Henry
    James. Second edition. Soho Bibliographies, No. 8. Lon-
    don: Rupert Hart-Davis, 427 pp.
       A revised edition of the 1957 bibliography, this study
    lists original works, contributions to books, published
    letters, contributions to periodicals, translations, and
    miscellanea.

3   MORDELL, ALBERT, comp. and ed. Discovery of a Genius: Wil-
    liam Dean Howells and Henry James. Introduction by Sylvia
    E. Bowman. New York: Twayne, 201 pp.
       This collection of seventeen pieces of criticism written
    by William Dean Howells on Henry James includes fourteen
    pieces which have not been reprinted since their initial
    publication. Howells's articles and reviews show that he
    was an early, warm, true, and consistent admirer of James
    who "rendered James great service by encouraging him, by
    publishing his fiction, by calling attention to it, and by
    interpreting or defending it." Reviewed: Modern Fiction
    Studies, 7 (Winter 1961-1962), 380; John R. Willingham,
    Library Journal (1 October), p. 3284; New Yorker (30 Sep-
    tember), pp. 170-71.

4   STONE, ALBERT E. Henry James and Childhood: "The Turn of the
    Screw." Stetson University Bulletin, No. 61, 18 pp.
        James has mated the mystery story with "A classic study
    of childish innocence and its involvement with corruption."
    In plot and characters The Turn of the Screw shares the
    same tradition as Hawthorne's Pearl and Twain's Huckleberry
    Finn. Reprinted in 1964.B95.

5   TILLEY, W. H. The Background of "The Princess Casamassima."
    Univ. of Florida Monographs, Humanities, No. 5. Gaines-
    ville: Univ. of Florida Press, 61 pp.
        James used material from the London Times, published be-
    tween 1882 and 1885, to make his account of revolutionaries
    more credible, but he made his own version consistently
    more interesting than his sources. Reviewed: Modern Fic-
    tion Studies, 7 (Winter 1961-1962), 379-80.

6   WARD, JOSEPH A. The Imagination of Disaster: Evil in the
    Fiction of Henry James. Lincoln: Univ. of Nebraska
    Press, 185 pp.
        For James "evil is stasis, or restriction of develop-
    ment." This study of the "forms and implications" of evil
    in James's work reveals "the changes and patterns in
    James's characterizations of the evildoer." Reviewed:
    Robert C. LeClair, American Literature, 33:386-87; Lyall H.
    Powers, Nineteenth-Century Fiction, 16:85-87; Cornelia P.
    Kelley, Journal of English and Germanic Philology, 61
    (1962), 446; Edwin T. Bowden, South Atlantic Quarterly, 61
    (1962), 119-20.

1961 B SHORTER WRITINGS

1   ADAMS, PERCY G. "Young Henry James and the Lesson of his
    Master Balzac." Revue de Littérature Comparée, 35 (July-
    September), 458-67.
        James is indebted to Balzac for plots and characters in
    at least seven stories written early in his career: "A
    Tragedy of Error," "De Grey," "Gabrielle de Bergerac," "The
    Madonna of the Future," "The Sweetheart of M. Briseux," and
    Washington Square.

2   ALLOTT, MIRIAM. "Mrs. Gaskell's 'The Old Nurse's Story': A
    Link Between Wuthering Heights and The Turn of the Screw."
    Notes and Queries, ns 8 (March), 101-102.
        The Turn of the Screw has "important elements" in common
    with "The Old Nurse's Story," and Mrs. Gaskell's story
    bears similarity to Wuthering Heights. Reprinted in
    1966.A5.

1961

3   AUCHINCLOSS, LOUIS. "James and Bourget: The Artist and the
     Crank"; "James and the Russian Novelists"; "A Reader's
     Guide to Henry James," in his <u>Reflections of a Jacobite</u>.
     Boston: Houghton Mifflin, pp. 126-37, 157-71, 209-20.
         Conversational essays by a devoted Jamesian include dis-
     cussions of writers, each of whom had some connection with
     Henry James: Wharton, Bourget, Thackeray, George Eliot,
     Saint-Simon, Meredith, Proust, Trollope, and others. Three
     chapters specifically relate to Henry James: (1) James's
     damning appraisal of Bourget is examined; (2) his criticism
     of Tolstoy's "formlessness" and Dostoyevsky's "lost" point
     of view are examined; and (3) in the final chapter al-
     ternative reading lists are suggested for the novice ap-
     proaching James. Partially reprinted: pp. 157-71 reprint-
     ed in 1962.B10.

*4   BERKLEY, JAMES, ed. [<u>Washington Square</u>] <u>Romance and Realism</u>:
     <u>An Introduction to the Study of the Novel</u>. New York:
     Odyssey Press.
         Cited in Beatrice Ricks, comp. <u>Henry James: A Bibliog-</u>
     <u>raphy of Secondary Works</u>. Scarecrow Author Bibliographies,
     No. 24. Metuchen, N.J.: Scarecrow Press, 1975, Item 1443.

5   BLACKMUR, R. P. "Introduction," in his edition of <u>The Por-</u>
     <u>trait of a Lady</u>. The Laurel Henry James. New York: Dell,
     pp. 5-12.
         This "whole novel shows how people tamper with one an-
     other because of motives that pass like money between
     them." Reprinted in 1967.A5.

6   BLACKMUR, R. P. "Introduction," in his edition of <u>The Tragic</u>
     <u>Muse</u>. The Laurel Henry James. New York: Dell, pp. 5-15.
         In this novel "the theatre and the studio are set
     against the British Foreign Service and the House of Com-
     mons. The two sets of institutions have in common only
     that each is consciously histrionic, with the frightening
     chance that in each, if success is nearly complete, one's
     private life, one's created self, may totally disappear in-
     to one's public role, or . . . into one's work."

7   BLEHL, VINCENT F. "Freedom and Commitment in James's <u>Portrait</u>
     <u>of a Lady</u>." <u>The Personalist</u>, 42 (July), 368-81.
         In <u>The Portrait of a Lady</u> the meaning of "freedom" goes
     beyond the concept of autonomy and encompasses the capacity
     "for assent and dissent, the power to recognize or repudi-
     ate values and nonvalues, by taking an inward position in
     regard to them, and engaging the personality in defense of
     that position."

24

8   BOOTH, WAYNE C. The Rhetoric of Fiction. Chicago: Univ. of
    Chicago Press, passim.
        "Intensity of Realistic Illusion" (pp. 40-50) sug-
    gests that "From the beginning James's passion for the
    reader's sense of traveling in a real, though intensified,
    world dictates a general rhetoric in the service of real-
    ism, rather than a particular rhetoric for the most intense
    experience of distinctive effects."
        The pathos of Daisy Miller's destruction is reduced by
    James's employing a "misguided observer," Winterbourne.
    Her drama is "the drama of being misunderstood" (pp. 282-84;
    reprinted in 1963.B99).
        "'The Turn of the Screw' as Puzzle" (pp. 311-16) states
    that although James's intentions were clear in that he
    wanted the governess to be "one of his lucid--but of course
    not-too-lucid--reflectors," readers have had problems with
    the story because of the "unintentional ambiguity of ef-
    fect."
        "The Price of Impersonal Narration, II: Henry James
    and the Unreliable Narrator" (pp. 339-74) notes that James
    "fails to provide any theory relevant to one large segment
    of his own work--those stories narrated, whether in the
    first or third person, by a profoundly confused, basically
    self-deceived, or even wrong-headed or vicious reflector."
    (Includes analyses of "The Liar" and "The Aspern Papers.")

9   BORKLUND, ELMER. "Howard Sturgis, Henry James, and Belcham-
    ber." Modern Philology, 58 (May), 255-69.
        An examination of the letters exchanged by Sturgis and
    Henry James and of Sturgis's autobiographical allegory,
    "The China Pot," discredits the theory initiated by Edith
    Wharton that Sturgis's decision to abandon writing was
    prompted by James's criticism of Belchamber.

10 BURNS, LANDON C., JR. "Henry James's Mysterious Fount."
    Texas Studies in Literature and Language, 2 (Winter),
    520-28.
        The narrator's theory is substantiated in The Sacred
    Fount by the novel's theme and structure--there is a sepa-
    rate reality for a work of art although the initial stimu-
    lus is conceived in the human experience.

11 CAMBON, GLAUCO. "The Negative Gesture in Henry James."
    Nineteenth-Century Fiction, 15 (March), 335-43.
        James's heroines, Catherine Sloper and May Bartram, rise
    to moral realism and choose renunciation (negative affirma-
    tion of value); this denial is also found in Hawthorne and
    Melville. Reprinted in 1970.A8.

1961

12   COLEMAN, JOHN.   "Amusette."   New Statesman, 62 (1 December),
      854.
          Jack Clayton's The Innocents, a film adaptation of The
      Turn of the Screw, takes many liberties with James's con-
      tent, but "as a spooky piece of visual guile, as a chain of
      elegant contrivances, The Innocents is unusually subtle."

13   COURSEN, HERBERT R., JR.   "The Mirror of Allusion: The Ambas-
      sadors." New England Quarterly, 34 (September), 382-84.
          James's allusion to Shakespeare's Cleopatra in The Am-
      bassadors "coincides remarkably on many levels with his
      novel." In addition to delineating the character of Mme.
      de Vionnet, the allusion also serves to "extend the novel
      into a wider area of generalization than it enjoys
      intrinsically."

14   CROWTHER, BOSLEY.   "Screen: 'The Innocents.'" New York Times
      (26 December), p. 15.
          Jack Clayton's film adaptation of The Turn of the Screw
      is "bland": "If we're supposed to accept the creeping ter-
      ror and disintegration of the governess as inspired by
      purely mystical factors, it isn't fearful enough. And if
      we're supposed to accept them as mental disorder, it is not
      sufficiently explained."

15   DAHLBERG, EDWARD, and HERBERT READ. Truth Is More Sacred:
      A Critical Exchange on Modern Literature. New York:
      Horizon Press, pp. 121-48.
          Dahlberg objects to James's language, claiming the nov-
      elist was "the sovereign of the enervated phrase," who
      "cared more for propriety than he did for the universe."
      Read responds that James's style is "analytical and per-
      meates the whole substance of his thought." Read suggests
      that James's letters are better reading than the novels.

16   DENNEY, REUEL.   "The Discovery of the Popular Culture," in
      American Perspectives: The National Self-Image in the
      Twentieth Century. Edited for the American Studies Assn.
      by Robert E. Spiller and Eric Larrabee. Cambridge, Mass.:
      Harvard Univ. Press, 156-57.
          James's interest in the "poverty of wishes" of Americans
      became a principal theme in criticism of popular culture.

17   DICKINS, BRUCE.   "The Story of 'Washington Square.'" Times
      Literary Supplement (13 October), p. 690.
          Henry James based "Washington Square" on a story related
      to him by Fanny Kemble. A record of this in The Notebooks

of Henry James shows that the story refers to Henry Kemble
and Mary Ann Thackeray.

18 DONOVAN, A. B. "My Dear Pinker: The Correspondence of Henry
    James with His Literary Agent." Yale Univ. Library Ga-
    zette, 36 (October), 78-88.
        The Pinker correspondence (consisting of four hundred
    and eighty letters from James to Pinker) shows a strong
    friendship and dependence, James's financial concerns, and
    his detailed interest in the physical appearance of his
    books, as well as many brief insights into James's methods,
    critical opinions, and attitude toward his public reception.

19 DOVE, JOHN ROLAND. "The Alienated Hero in Le Rouge et le Noir
    and The Princess Casamassima," in Studies in Comparative
    Literature. Edited by Waldo F. McNeir. Louisiana State
    Univ. Studies, Humanities Series, No. 11. Baton Rouge:
    Louisiana State Univ. Press, pp. 130-54.
        Unlike most nineteenth-century writers, Stendahl and
    Henry James did not mitigate the problem of alienation in
    their works. Accordingly, Julien Sorel and Hyacinth Robin-
    son are prototypical of the twentieth-century alienated
    hero.

20 DURKIN, SISTER MARY BRIAN. "Henry James's Revisions of the
    Style of The Reverberator." American Literature, 33
    (November), 330-49.
        The definitive revision of 1908, although it contains no
    changes in characters, themes, scenes, or plot, is signifi-
    cantly changed through the addition of concrete nouns,
    "image-creating metaphors," and specific adjectives making
    the revision more clear, emphatic, specific, and forceful.

21 EDEL, LEON. "The Enduring Fame of Henry James." New York
    Times Book Review (3 September), pp. 1, 16-17.
        Henry James's enduring fame can be attributed to the
    "variety and contemporaneity of his subjects," his "memora-
    ble" prose, his "innovations as a craftsman," and his an-
    ticipation of modern psychology. James was the inventor
    and perfector of the international novel. Reprinted in
    1964.B18.

22 EDEL, LEON. "Introduction," in his edition of Roderick Hud-
    son. Harper Torchbook. New York: Harper; London: Hart-
    Davis, pp. vii-xvii.
        This novel "has in it the intensity James himself felt
    as he searched for his artist's footing. The book is the
    first large creation of a future master of the novel."

1961

23   EDEL, LEON, and ILSE DUSOIR LIND. "Introduction," in their
      edition of Henry James: Parisian Sketches, Letters to the
      New York "Tribune," 1875-1876. New York: Collier Books,
      pp. 9-27.
          These newspaper pieces "may be read not so much for the
      ephemeral things they chronicled as for the picture they
      offer us of a sensitive and discriminating American . . .
      sauntering through the very French scenes to which thou-
      sands of his countrymen continue to flock."

24   EJIMA, YUJI. "Henry James." Eibei-Bungakushi Kiza IX:
      19 Seiki (3) [Lectures on British and American Literature
      IX: The 19th Century]. Tokyo: Kenkyusha, pp. 274-90.
      [Japanese]
          A biographical and critical introduction to James.

*25   FIGUERA, ANGELA. Tres escritores norteamericanos: Mark
      Twain, Henry James, Thomas Wolfe. Madrid: Gredos.
          Cited in 1962 MLA International Bibliography, vol. 1,
      p. 184.

26   FOLSOM, JAMES K. "Archimago's Well: An Interpretation of The
      Sacred Fount." Modern Fiction Studies, 7 (Summer), 136-44.
          The vampire in The Sacred Fount is the narrator, "a man
      who uses his mind to feed off someone else." He is like
      Archimago in that he "gives falsehood under the guise of
      truth."

27   GALE, ROBERT L. "Henry James's Imagistic Portrait of Henry
      James." Forum (Houston), 3 (Summer), 31-34.
          An examination of the art images James used to describe
      his craft reveals that he principally perceived himself as
      a pictorial dramatist and occasionally as an embroiderer,
      an architect or a musician, but never as a dancer.

28   GALE, ROBERT L. "Roderick Hudson and Thomas Crawford." Amer-
      ican Quarterly, 13 (Winter), 495-504.
          Elements of the life and brief career of Thomas Crawford
      are evident in the characterization of Roderick Hudson.

29   GARGANO, JAMES W. "The Spoils of Poynton: Action and Respon-
      sibility." Sewanee Review, 69 (Autumn), 650-60.
          In The Spoils of Poynton James intended to show "the
      complex considerations that mass behind a single brave
      act." Fleda's renunciation of her lover must be kept in
      the context of the social situation, and Fleda must be seen
      as "the only character who possesses the comprehensive vi-
      sion in which 'ideal' solutions originate."

30 GARGANO, JAMES W. "The Turn of the Screw." Western Humani-
    ties Review, 15 (Spring), 173-79.
        James establishes the reliability of the governess by
    having the unimaginative Mrs. Grose confirm the governess's
    perceptions and by having Miles confess directly his pri-
    vate knowledge of Miss Jessel and Peter Quint.

31 GARGANO, JAMES W. "What Maisie Knew: The Evolution of a
    'Moral Sense.'" Nineteenth-Century Fiction, 16 (June),
    33-46.
        An examination of the book's "internal logic of episode
    and authorial commentary" reveals stages of revelations in
    Maisie's growth to knowledge and maturity. Reprinted in
    1968.A11 and 1973.A6.

32 GARIS, ROBERT E. "The Two Lambert Strethers: A New Reading
    of The Ambassadors." Modern Fiction Studies, 7 (Winter
    1961-1962), 305-16.
        Although James apparently did not realize it, he
    "changed his mind about Strether at the crucial point when
    he supposedly rounds out his 'education.'" The last seven
    chapters of the novel "turn against and annihilate the
    earlier ones."

33 GEISMAR, MAXWELL. "The Ambassadors: A New View." Studi
    Americani, no. 7, pp. 105-32.
        Despite the claims that have been made for its "ration-
    al" production, its structural and architectural achieve-
    ments, and its characterization triumphs, The Ambassadors
    is nothing more than a re-making of "old-fashioned popular
    travel romances," with limited human content, praiseworthy
    style, and credibility.

34 GERSTENBERGER, DONNA, and GEORGE HENDRICK. The American Nov-
    el: Volume 1: 1789-1959: A Checklist of Twentieth-
    Century Criticism. Chicago: Swallow Press, pp. 141-64.
        Criticism published on James's novels through 1959 is
    listed in three categories: under titles of individual
    novels, under general studies, and under bibliographies.

35 GIFFORD, HENRY. "Henry James: The Drama of Discrimination,"
    in The Pelican Guide to English Literature: The Modern
    Age. Vol. 7. Edited by Boris Ford. Baltimore: Penguin,
    pp. 104-18.
        This overview of James's career includes discussion of
    The Europeans, The Portrait of a Lady, The Bostonians, The
    Princess Casamassima, and his three major explorations of

1961

moral responsibility (The Ambassadors, The Wings of the
Dove, and The Golden Bowl). See 1964.B36 for revised
edition.

36 GILMAN, RICHARD. "Americans Abroad." American Heritage, 12
(October), 9-27, 89-93.
European acceptance of American art was facilitated by
the seriousness and excellence of three expatriates--John
Singer Sargent, James McNeill Whistler, and Henry James.

*37 GREENWOOD, DI CLARISSA. "Introduction," in her Città e Pae-
saggi di Toscana Visti da Henry James. Florence:
G. Barbera.
Cited in Beatrice Ricks, comp. Henry James: A Bibliog-
raphy of Secondary Works. Scarecrow Author Bibliographies,
No. 24. Metuchen, N.J.: Scarecrow, Item 1765.

38 GULLASON, THOMAS ARTHUR. "The Jamesian Motif in Stephen
Crane's Last Novels." The Personalist, 42 (Winter),
77-84.
Crane's last three works, The Third Violet, Active Ser-
vice, and The O'Ruddy, are thematically centered around the
problem of "class stratification"--a theme encouraged by
conversations with William Dean Howells and Jacob Riis, and
encouraged by Henry James (both personally and through his
writings).

39 HARDWICK, ELIZABETH. "Introduction," in her edition of The
Selected Letters of William James. New York: Farrar,
Straus and Cudahy, pp. ix-xii.
This brief sketch of the James family includes refer-
ences to Henry James. In addition, there are many mentions
of Henry James in the letters (as well as letters to Henry
James).

40 HARDY, BARBARA. "The Change of Heart in Dickens' Novels."
Victorian Studies, 5 (September), 49-67.
A gradual moral conversion characterizes the progress of
the heroes common to Dickens' novels, The Ambassadors, and
George Eliot's Middlemarch.

41 HARVEY, W. J. The Art of George Eliot. London: Chatto and
Windus, pp. 13-22, passim.
In addition to incidental references to a dozen of
James's works, the initial chapter, "George Eliot and the
Criticism of Fiction," utilizes five critical articles by
James to establish the critical perspective upon which the
subsequent chapters are built.

42 HASSAN, IHAB. <u>Radical Innocence: Studies in the Contemporary</u>
    <u>American Novel</u>. Princeton, N.J.: Princeton Univ. Press,
    pp. 43-45, passim.
        Daisy Miller consciously chooses to immolate herself to
    her own innocence.

43 HEILMAN, ROBERT B. "The Lure of the Demonic: James and Dür-
    renmatt." <u>Comparative Literature</u>, 13 (Fall), 346-57.
        Dürrenmatt's <u>The Pledge</u> corroborates James's vision of
    the experiences of Miles and Flora as objective facts of an
    illusive but observable reality.

44 HEPPENSTALL, RAYNER. <u>The Fourfold Tradition: Notes on the</u>
    <u>French and English Literatures with Some Ethnological and</u>
    <u>Historical Asides</u>. London: Barrie and Rockliff, passim.
        Passing references to James.

45 HICKS, GRANVILLE. "The Unbiased Jamesian." <u>Saturday Review</u>,
    44 (5 August), 10.
        Oscar Cargill's <u>The Novels of Henry James</u> is a useful
    contribution to the student of James as well as "to the
    understanding of the nature and function of criticism."
    Review of 1961.A1.

46 HILL, HAMLIN L., JR. "'The Revolt of the Daughters': A Sug-
    gested Source for 'The Awkward Age.'" <u>Notes and Queries</u>,
    ns 8 (September), 347-49.
        A series of magazine articles appearing in prominent
    English periodicals in 1894, entitled "The Revolt of the
    Daughters," was very probably used by James as background
    material for his novel.

47 HOFFMAN, FREDERICK J. "Freedom and Conscious Form: Henry
    James and the American Self." <u>Virginia Quarterly Review</u>,
    37 (Spring), 269-85.
        "Henry James is concerned primarily to estimate the pos-
    sibility of achieving the perfect creative consciousness,
    in terms of the forms available in society or possible to
    it."

48 HOFTUN, SIGMUND. "The Point of View in Henry James: <u>The Amer-</u>
    <u>ican</u>." <u>Edda</u>, 61 (Fall), 169-76.
        The technical immaturity of <u>The American</u> is a reflection
    of James's intellectual immaturity. James had not yet so-
    lidified his views on human nature and volition; according-
    ly, he vacillates in his handling of the novel's perspec-
    tive. Reprinted in 1972.B112.

1961

49 HOLROYD, STUART. "Henry James." John O'London's, 5
    (10 August), 171-73.
        Henry James was deeply disturbed by the outbreak of the
    War in 1914, but his last novels "had prefigured the
    catastrophe."

50 HOPKINS, VIOLA. "Visual Art Devices and Parallels in the Fic-
    tion of Henry James." Publications of the Modern Language
    Association of America, 76 (December), 561-74.
        James's visual art interest in general along with his
    propensity for Mannerism and propinquity to Impressionism
    are influences he subtly integrated into his writings. Re-
    printed in 1968.All.

51 ITAGAKI, KONOMU. "The Bostonians." The English Literature in
    Hokkaido, 7 (May), 94-104. [Japanese]
        This novel records American social history of the 1870s:
    characters representing New England high-mindedness and
    Southern gentility each struggle to win the heroine.
    James's novel is prophetic in that the America of those
    days faced reality, leaving the genteel tradition behind,
    just as the heroine was restored to her real womanhood.

52 ITO, SENICHI. "Henry James: The Turn of the Screw." The
    English Literature in Hokkaido, 7 (May), 105-13. [Japa-
    nese]
        James's modern consciousness is revealed in his inner
    uncertainty and in his strong moral concern as to what is
    evil.

53 KAPLAN, CHARLES. "James's Madame de Mauves." Explicator, 19
    (February), Item 32.
        The standard interpretation which attributes Baron de
    Mauves' suicide to the coldness of his wife is subject to
    question because of the unreliability of its source, the
    letter from "the silly Mrs. Draper." The cause of the
    Baron's suicide is less important than the fact that after-
    ward Longmore decides not to return to Madame de Mauves.

54 KAPLAN, LOUIS, comp., in association with JAMES TYLER COOK,
    CLINTON E. COLBY, JR., and DANIEL C. HASKELL. A Bibliog-
    raphy of American Autobiographies. Madison: Wisconsin
    Univ. Press, p. 152.
        James's autobiographical books are listed in four
    entries.

55   KNIGHT, ARTHUR. "Innocents Abroad." <u>Saturday Review</u>, 44
     (23 December), 38-39.
         Jack Clayton's film adaptation of William Archibald's
     "The Innocents," a dramatization of James's <u>The Turn of the
     Screw</u>, reveals a "sure, deft, cinematic hand."

*56 KOLJEVIĆ, SVETOZAR. "Pustolovina svesti u romanu Henrija
     Džejmza." <u>Putevi</u>, Banja Kuka. Nos. 2, 3, pp. 174-88,
     258-86.
         Cited in Beatrice Ricks, <u>Henry James: A Bibliography of
     Secondary Works</u>. Scarecrow Author Bibliographies, No. 24.
     Metuchen, N.J.: Scarecrow, Item 2716.1.

57   LAINOFF, SEYMOUR. "Henry James's 'The Figure in the Carpet':
     What Is Critical Responsiveness?" <u>Boston Univ. Studies in
     English</u>, 5 (Summer), 122-28.
         The central thrust of the story is not that an excep-
     tional degree of critical acumen must be applied to a work
     but that the critic must bring an "enthusiasm, affection,
     knowledge, . . . [and a] 'sense of life.'" Reprinted in
     1970.A7.

58   LEVIN, GERALD. "Why Does Vanderbank Not Propose?" <u>Univ. of
     Kansas City Review</u>, 27 (Summer), 314-18.
         Indecisiveness is not the cause of Vanderbank's failure
     to propose to Nanda. The cause is Nanda's mother and the
     exclusive quality of that mother-daughter relationship.

59   LID, R. W. "Ford Madox Ford and His Community of Letters."
     <u>Prairie Schooner</u>, 35 (Summer), 132-36.
         Ford believed that the production of literature was "es-
     sentially a communal process," and he was a contributor to
     the life of a literary community as well as a partaker of
     the community. Conrad and James were principal influences
     on Ford.

60   LOMBARDO, AGOSTINO. <u>La Ricerca del Vero: Saggi sulla Tradi-
     zione Letteraria Americana</u>. Biblioteca di Studi Americani,
     No. 6. Rome: Edizioni di storia e letteratura, pp. 213-40,
     283-98. [Italian]
         "La Critica Letteraria di Henry James" (pp. 213-40)
     notes that in addition to his numerous literary works,
     Henry James has left us a collection of literary critiques,
     magnificent in its size as well as quality, which can be
     traced to his deep artistic and spiritual consciousness.
     Nevertheless, his literary comments are at times biased,
     because of his consciousness of literary style, his aware-
     ness of impressionism, and his puritan background. "Lettre

33

1961

di James" (pp. 283-98) suggests that, though the selection is incomplete, James's Selected Letters (edited by Leon Edel) is to be considered an integral part of James's art, not only because the letters have been conceived by the author as works of art, but because they bear an awareness of formality, seriousness, and purity of style as well. Furthermore, they reveal a very affectionate, though controlled person, whose feelings appear in the numerous human characters he created in his novels.

61 LONG, E. HUDSON. "Introduction," in his edition of Short Novels of Henry James. New York: Dodd, Mead, & Co., pp. v-x.
    Brief introductory comments on "Daisy Miller," Washington Square, The Aspern Papers, "The Pupil," and The Turn of the Screw.

62 LORD, CATHERINE. "Aesthetic Unity." Journal of Philosophy, 58 (June), 321-27.
    An analysis of the congruence of a work of art and the aesthetic experience "reveals both the nature of the import of art and the character of the aesthetic experience."

63 LYDENBERG, JOHN. "American Novelists in Search for a Lost World." Revue des Langues Vivantes (Brussels), 27:306-21.
    An overview of American literature produced by Wolfe, Dos Passos, Twain, Cooper, Hemingway, Faulkner, James, and Fitzgerald reveals a dominant tone "of loss, of betrayal, [and] of fruitless search."

64 MAGALANER, MARVIN, and EDMUND L. VOLPE, eds. "Henry James," in Twelve Short Stories. New York: Macmillan, pp. 205-209.
    In the short story "Europe," James "expressed his feelings about wasted lives."

65 MAXWELL, J. C. "The Text of The Ambassadors." Essays in Criticism, 11 (January), 176.
    Ian Watt is in error to suggest that the Everyman edition and the Anchor edition both derived their variances from the Methuen edition. Response to 1960.B98. See also 1961.B95.

66 MOODY, A. D. "James's Portrait of an Ideal." Melbourne Critical Review, no. 4, pp. 77-92.
    The Portrait of a Lady suggests "that ultimately James's experience of life did not satisfy his imagination, and that he felt impelled to affirm, in his rendering of Isabel Archer's fate, a moral sense which was not dependent on any substantiating experience his imagination knew or could render."

34

67 MOONEY, STEPHEN L. "James, Keats, and the Religion of Con-
    sciousness." Modern Language Quarterly, 22 (December),
    399-401.
        When The Golden Bowl is viewed in the light of "On First
    Looking into Chapman's Homer," the novel reveals a "geogra-
    phy" which suggests "American history and fiction, English
    poetry, and European art as a force for American culture."

68 MORRISON, SISTER KRISTIN. "James's and Lubbock's Differing
    Points of View." Nineteenth-Century Fiction, 16 (Decem-
    ber), 245-55.
        The confusion in contemporary criticism over point of
    view in James is due to the fact that for James it referred
    to the "knowing center" of the narrative whether within or
    outside the novel; to Percy Lubbock and contemporary lit-
    erature and the term implies a dual meaning--the speaker of
    the narrative and the knower apprehending the narrative.

69 MURAKAMI, FUJIO. "The Aesthete in The Tragic Muse." Jimbun
    Kenkyu, 12 (June), 96-108. [Japanese]
        Gabriel Nash represents the aesthete of the 1880s, since
    he believes in the primacy of beauty, the importance of
    feelings, dandyism, and hedonism. In addition, Nash holds
    a respect for individuality, and he is a perceptive specta-
    tor, not a doer. The role of the aesthete lies in being an
    impetus-giver to others. Aestheticism, however, is flimsy
    when contrasted with the importance James attaches to art
    as an "act of life." Reprinted in 1974.B48.

70 OKITA, HAJIME. "From Henry James to Willa Cather." Albion, 8
    (November), 132-45. [Japanese]
        James's influence on the novel has been both thematic
    and technical.

71 PHILLIPS, NORMA. "The Sacred Fount: The Narrator and the
    Vampires." Publications of the Modern Language Association
    of America, 76 (September), 407-12.
        The novel's vampire theme is dramatized in the concur-
    rent depletion of the narrator's awareness and the fruition
    of Mrs. Brissenden's perceptiveness.

72 POWERS, LYALL H. "Henry James and the Ethics of the Artist:
    'The Real Thing' and 'The Liar.'" Texas Studies in Litera-
    ture and Language, 3 (Autumn), 360-68.
        Although James like Hawthorne condemns the use of other
    human beings ("The Liar" makes this point), he takes a dif-
    ferent ethical position regarding the artist; and in "The
    Real Thing," he affirms the right of the artist qua artist
    to use others for art's sake.

1961

73   POWERS, LYALL H.   "A Reperusal of James's 'The Figure in the
     Carpet.'"   American Literature, 33 (May), 224-28.
          James did not intend that the reader should be obsessed
     with discovering the illusive figure, but that he should
     give attentive perusal to the whole art work.

74   ROBERTS, J. L.   "An Approach to Evil in Henry James."   Arizona
     Quarterly, 17 (Spring), 5-16.
          Evil in James is found in "a violation of ethical stand-
     ards of human conduct" in which a character acts out of
     self-interest and may thwart "the imaginative development
     of another personality."

75   ROSENBERRY, EDWARD H.   "James's Use of Hawthorne in 'The
     Liar.'"   Modern Language Notes, 76 (March), 234-38.
          "The Liar" exhibits a "conscious or unconscious literary
     borrowing" from Hawthorne's "The Prophetic Pictures," in-
     corporating "the point of view and the interior drama of
     Hawthorne's painter."

76   RUBIN, LOUIS D., JR., and JOHN REES MOORE, eds.   The Idea of
     an American Novel.   New York: Thomas Y. Crowell,
     pp. 242-57.
          The editors have supplied headnotes for seven pieces of
     previously published criticism on Henry James by Ezra
     Pound, T. S. Eliot, H. G. Wells, Van Wyck Brooks, Sherwood
     Anderson, Wright Morris, and Marius Bewley.

77   RUHM, HERBERT, ed.   "Lady Barberina" and Other Tales: "Ben-
     volio," "Glasses," and Three Essays.   The Universal Li-
     brary.   New York: Vanguard.
          Contents: This text of James selections includes notes,
     textual variants from the manuscripts, and a selected bib-
     liography.   The "Introduction" (pp. 1-3) suggests that in
     reading James, one is "privileged to overhear, but he must
     also guess"; thus, the demands are great on the reader.
     The Note on "Lady Barberina" (pp. 11-12) states that James
     revised the text of this story thoroughly for the New York
     Edition.   That on "Benvolio" (pp. 123-24) notes that this
     tale is "evidently a symbolic expression in a smoothly mas-
     tered form of James's reflections about the artist's dual
     need for society and for solitude."   The Note on "Glasses"
     (pp. 173-74) points out that it was written in the "year
     after James turned away from his failure in the theatre de-
     termined to 'write masterpieces.'"   The Note on Three Es-
     says (p. 229) states that these three early essays (1865-
     1866) "show James even then capable of discernment and
     definition; if with less manner than he was later to

acquire, and of the analysis of character in which, in his fiction, he was only after to excel."

78   RYAN, MARJORIE. "Forster, James, and Flaubert: A Parallel." Notes and Queries, ns 8 (March), 102-103.
     Opera scenes in Forster's Where Angels Fear to Tread, Flaubert's Madame Bovary, and James's The Ambassadors all deal with the theme of the "romantic" attitude towards life. In each scene the main character, while under the influence of "spurious sentiment," makes a faulty judgment having momentous consequences.

79   SANFORD, CHARLES L. "Henry James and the American Rush of Experience," in his The Quest for Paradise: Europe and the American Moral Imagination. Urbana: Univ. of Illinois Press, pp. 203-27.
     In Europe James's characters learn "the meaning of the fall from paradise as the condition of a greater humanity, and James effects a symbolic marriage of morals and manners, of American and European civilization, not solely on American terms. At the same time, his work is a continuation of the traditional American quest for experience."

80   SELIG, ROBERT L. "The Red Haired Lady Orator: Parallel Passages in The Bostonians and Adam Bede." Nineteenth-Century Fiction, 16 (September), 164-69.
     Eliot's Dinah Morris, not Daudet's Jeanne Autheman or Eline Ebsen, is the primary influence on James's Verena Tarrant.

81   SHAHANE, V. A. "Formative Influences on E. M. Forster: Henry James--A Study in Ambivalence." Osmanic Journal of English Studies, no. 1, pp. 39-53.
     "Points of agreement as well as disagreement between Forster and the Master strengthen the evidence in support of the imperceptible manner in which" James influenced Forster.

82   STALLMAN, R. W. The Houses that James Built and Other Literary Studies. East Lansing: Michigan State Univ. Press, pp. vii-ix, 1-53.
     "Foreword" (pp. vii-ix) notes that "What my punning title--The Houses that James Built--intends is that James, both by his canon of art and by his example in fiction, influenced subsequent architects of modern fiction and built thus many more houses than his own."
     "The Houses that James Built--The Portrait of a Lady" (pp. 1-33) is a revised and expanded version of "The Houses

1961

that James Built," <u>Texas Quarterly</u>, 1 (Winter 1958-1959),
176-96. The architectural structures present in the novel
are symbolically employed to elucidate the progress of the
heroine.
"'The Sacred Rage': The Time-Theme in <u>The Ambassadors</u>"
(pp. 34-51) is a revised version of "'The Sacred Rage':
The Time-Theme in <u>The Ambassadors</u>," <u>Modern Fiction Studies</u>,
3 (Spring 1957), 41-56. "Time is the mainspring theme of
<u>The Ambassadors</u>--How to Live It."
"A Note on the Text of <u>The Ambassadors</u>" (pp. 51-53) is
an expanded version of 1960.B82. From the first publication by Harper and Brothers, the novel has been plagued by
errors in the chapter ordering, and several efforts to correct the error have resulted in additional errors. The New
American Library text (based on the 1903 Methuen edition)
renders the chapters in proper order as well as indicating
where significant variations are present in the text.

83   STALLMAN, R. W. "Time and Mrs. Newsome's 'Blue Message': A
     Reply to Leon Edel." <u>Modern Language Notes</u>, 76 (January),
     20-23.
        Stallman responds to Edel's article ("Time and the Am-
     bassadors," <u>Modern Language Notes</u>, 73 [March 1958], 177-79),
     which disagreed with Stallman's position that the timepiece
     is the "unnamed object" of Strether's riddle in <u>The Ambas-
     sadors</u>. Time is not solely mechanical in the novel and is
     "rendered symbolically."

84   STAUB, AUGUST W. "The Well-Made Failures of Henry James."
     <u>Southern Speech Journal</u>, 27 (Winter), 91-101.
        James's failure as a playwright is attributable to his
     choice of models--Scribe, Sardou, and Sarcey--to his ambiv-
     alence toward the theatre, to his "inability to gauge cor-
     rectly the intellectual potential of his audience," and to
     his "lack of critical insight."

85   STONE, EDWARD, ed. <u>Henry James: Seven Stories and Studies</u>.
     New York: Appleton-Century-Crofts.
        Seven of James's "maturest, most challenging stories"
     are reprinted along with approximately fifty commentaries
     on the stories. Included in the collection are "The Mar-
     riages," "Europe," "The Liar," "The Real Thing," "The
     Pupil," "The Beast in the Jungle," and "The Jolly Corner."

86   TANNER, TONY. "The Golden Bowl and the Reassessment of Inno-
     cence." London Magazine, ns 1 (November), 38-49.
          James perceived in his last novel that innocence con-
     tains "its own kind of sinister threat." The innocent Adam
     and Maggie redeem the experienced Prince and Charlotte aes-
     thetically, but this redemption is gained at the expense of
     dehumanizing them and turning them into "museum pieces."

87   TANNER, TONY. "The Literary Children of James and Clemens."
     Nineteenth-Century Fiction, 16 (December), 205-18.
          Clemens and James similarly used the innocent child to
     achieve a "dramatic involvement of the characters and the
     ironic disengagement of the author"; but they differed in
     their conclusions. Clemens resorts to myth and has his pro-
     tagonist eternally maintaining innocence against the world
     of experience, whereas James's children are either destroyed
     or gain maturity through the experience.

88   TERRIE, HENRY L., JR. "Henry James and the 'Explosive Prin-
     ciple.'" Nineteenth-Century Fiction, 15 (March), 283-99.
          James employs five techniques to achieve economy: "The
     functional handling of antecedent action, the double scene,
     the moment of recognition, the extended image, the closely
     observed action."

89   TILTON, ELEANOR. "Foreword," in her edition of Henry James:
     "The Marriages" and Other Stories. A Signet Classic. New
     York: New American Library, pp. vii-xiii.
          "All in all, these tales show us an intelligent ironist
     who is also a charming, kindly man of the world, a not very
     beautiful world, in which it is possible--given the illim-
     itable power of consciousness--to live and to work not ac-
     cording to complacent generalizations but according to
     one's individual algebra." (Includes "The Pension Beaure-
     pas," "The Point of View," "The Marriages," "The Real
     Thing," "Miss Gunton of Poughkeepsie," "The Two Faces,"
     "The Papers," "Fordham Castle," and "Julia Bride.")

90   TOCHIHARA, TOMOO. "Henry James and Mary (Minny) Temple:
     Henry James's Life and Artistic Manner." Eibeibungaku
     (Kansai Daigaku Univ.), 6 (November), 1-14. [Japanese]
          An examination of James's letters to his mother and to
     his brother in which he laments the death of Minny Temple
     and remembers her reveals James's attachment to her as well
     as her relation to his work, especially The Portrait of a
     Lady.

1961

*91   TOCHIHARA, TOMOO. "The Question of Henry James's Internation-
        al Theme." Ronko, 8:128-38.
            Cited in 1970.B72, p. 321.

92   TRACHTENBERG, ALAN. "The Craft of Vision." Critique, 4
        (Winter), 41-55.
            Wright Morris's craft of vision is a photographic tech-
        nique of realism which he traces to Henry James. Morris
        considers James in the community of writers searching for a
        justification of the loss of innocence and illusion as a
        gain of truth and selfhood.

93   WALKER, WARREN S., comp. Twentieth-Century Short Story Expli-
        cation: Interpretations, 1900-1960 Inclusive, of Short
        Fiction Since 1800. Hamden, Conn.: Shoe String Press,
        pp. 166-205.
            Articles published on James's short stories are arranged
        under the titles of individual stories. For revised edi-
        tion see 1967.B111.

94   WALTERS, DOROTHY JEANNE. "The Theme of Destructive Innocence
        in the Modern Novel: Greene, James, Cary, Porter." DA,
        21, 2300-01 (Oklahoma).
            Greene's The Quiet American, James's The Golden Bowl,
        Cary's The Horse's Mouth, and Porter's Noon Wine contain
        typical representations of the "active" and "passive"
        agents of "destructive innocence" and reveal its thematic
        significance in modern literature.

95   WATT, IAN. "The Text of The Ambassadors." Essays in Criti-
        cism, 11 (January), 116-19.
            The word "followed" was not intended to suggest that the
        Everyman edition was derived from the Methuen edition, but
        was intended only to note that in the particular sentence
        under consideration they both have the same words. Re-
        sponse to 1961.B65. See also 1960.B98.

96   WRIGHT, AUSTIN McGIFFERT. The American Short Story in the
        Twenties. Chicago: Univ. of Chicago Press, passim.
            During the course of a "critical-historical examination"
        of the short stories of S. Anderson, Fitzgerald, Hemingway,
        Faulkner, and K. A. Porter, multiple references are made to
        the form, content, and subject matter of James, who is
        identified with the "early period" from which the writers
        of the twenties are perceived to have developed.

97   ZABEL, MORTON D.   "Introduction," in his edition of <u>Henry
     James: Fifteen Short Stories</u>. New York: Bantam Books,
     pp. vii-xxx.
          Provides a general critical overview of Henry James's
     work and of these fifteen stories, written between 1865 and
     1908.

1961 C DISSERTATIONS

1   ARLOS, ALMA ROSENFIELD.   "'Our Doubt is Our Passion': Ambi-
     guity in Three of the Later Novels of Henry James." Dis-
     sertation, Radcliffe, 261 pp.
          James's preference for ambiguity was both "conscious"
     and "explicit" and constituted an important part of his
     general conception of life and art. His "preoccupation
     with the indefinite in form and content" is pervasive in
     <u>The Sacred Fount</u>, <u>The Golden Bowl</u>, and <u>The Wings of the
     Dove</u> and serves as a "means toward understanding the mys-
     teries and the infinite variety of life."

2   BLACKALL, JEAN FRANTZ.   "Recurrent Symbolic Elements in the
     Novels of Henry James (1896-1901)." Dissertation, Rad-
     cliffe, 361 pp.
          In the fiction published between 1896 and 1901, James
     uses meaningful patterns of symbolic elements in three
     categories--objects or places, figures of speech, and de-
     scriptive particulars--to convey subtly but persuasively
     the "effect of an evolving situation, of attitudes and
     relationships in flux" moving "toward a certain end."

3   COLES, MERIVAN ROBINSON.   "Form and Meaning in <u>The Golden
     Bowl</u>." <u>DA</u>, 21, 2712 (Bryn Mawr).
          Both the literal and symbolic meanings of the novel are
     dependent on an accurate comprehension of the formal struc-
     ture of the work.

*4   DEAKIN, MOTLEY FREEMONT.   "The Picturesque in the Life and
     Works of Henry James." Unpublished Doctoral Dissertation,
     Univ. of California, Berkeley.
          Cited in <u>Annual Bibliography of English Language and
     Literature: 1962</u>, Vol. 37. Edited by Marjory Rigby and
     Charles Nilon. Cambridge, England: The University Press
     for the Modern Humanities Research Assn., 1964, Item 5102.

1961

5 GRAGG, PERRY EARL. "The Revelation of Consciousness: The Psychology of William James and Five Novels of Henry James." DA, 21, 3097-98 (Texas).
   Four psychological principles espoused by William James are of critical importance to the novels of Henry James. The principles are (1) "the visceral origin of emotions," (2) "the stream of consciousness," (3) "the revelations of self" and (4) "volition."

6 GRIGG, WOMBLE QUAY, JR. "The Molds of Form: Comedy and Conscience in the Novels of Henry James, 1895-1901." DA, 22, 1156-57 (Pennsylvania).
   Four elements--a renewed interest in short fiction, continuing progress in his experimentation with point of view, plots with an inherent "moral drama," and a "comic vision" --characterize a distinct creative phase that produced The Spoils of Poynton, What Maisie Knew, The Awkward Age and The Sacred Fount. The four elements continue to exert a dominant influence in the "major phase"--an influence that unifies the two phases.

7 HOPKINS, VIOLA. "The Art of Seeing: Art Themes and Techniques in the Work of Henry James." DA, 21, 2275-76 (New York).
   The visual arts significantly influenced James's conception of the novel. His point of view, his imagery, and a large portion of his thematic interests are directly rooted in his affinity for visual art.

8 HOROWITZ, FLOYD ROSS. "The Ambassadors: A Modern Allegory." DA, 21, 1949 (Iowa).
   A structural analysis of the novel reveals a "three levelled allegory" that exists beyond the obvious plot design.

9 HYNES, JOSEPH ANTHONY, JR. "Henry James's William Wetmore Story and His Friends: A Critical Commentary." DA, 21, 3458 (Michigan).
   Henry James's biographical efforts were hampered by the personal interest elicited by Story's life. The ambivalence and lack of control yield a biography that is "often beautifully evocative, and reminiscent, but ultimately shapeless."

10   MLIKOTIN, ANTHONY MATTHEW. "The International Theme in the
     Novels of Turgenev and Henry James." DA, 22, 873-74
     (Indiana).
          Although both authors were influenced by their own
     "international lives," the international theme is inci-
     dentally present in Turgenev's work but of primary impor-
     tance in James's craft. For book publication see 1971.A4.

*11   REID, STEPHEN ALLEN. "The Role of Technique in Henry James's
     Later Novels." Unpublished Doctoral Dissertation, Univ. of
     California, Berkeley.
          Cited in Annual Bibliography of English Language and
     Literature: 1962, Vol. 37. Cambridge, England: The Univ.
     Press for the Modern Humanities Research Assn., 1964,
     Item 5152.

12   ROSENBAUM, STANFORD PATRICK. "Studies for a Definitive Edi-
     tion of Henry James's The Spoils of Poynton. (Volumes One
     and Two)." DA, 21, 3792 (Cornell).
          A definitive edition of The Spoils of Poynton is pre-
     pared utilizing an examination of sources, an evaluation of
     notebook entries, a collation of texts and discussion of
     revisions, and an analysis of the New York Edition's
     preface.

13   STAFFORD, WILLIAM TALMADGE. "The American Critics of Henry
     James: 1864-1943." DA, 21, 2722 (Kentucky).
          Three successive periods of critical response to Henry
     James--by his contemporaries, by the critics from 1916
     through 1929, and by the critics from 1930 through 1943--
     reveal a gradual refinement in critical techniques that is
     both a credit to the reputation of Henry James and to the
     quality of American criticism.

14   VAID, KRISHNA BALDEV. "The Tales of Henry James: A Critical
     Study." Unpublished Doctoral Dissertation, Harvard, 348 pp.
          This critique of the "neglected half of James's fiction,"
     undertaken to prove that the tales are of "equal impor-
     tance" with the novels and to examine recurrent "technical,
     thematic, and artistic preoccupations" as manifested there-
     in, emphasizes James's "method" or "craft." For book pub-
     lication see 1964.A8.

1962

1962 A BOOKS

1   EDEL, LEON. <u>Henry James: The Conquest of London, 1870-1881</u>.
    Philadelphia: Lippincott, 465 pp.
       This second volume of the biography tells of James's
    life from his return to America in 1870 to the completion
    of <u>The Portrait of a Lady</u>. These years reveal the mature
    man: "In his thirties the novelist was much more ardent
    and much less circumspect than the later James: he met
    life eagerly and often with exuberance. He was in the
    fullest sense an 'addicted artist,' but one who was guided
    at every turn by his intellect. And he was a man of action
    and a man of the world as well. No novelist of his time
    addressed himself more assiduously to wooing fame and for-
    tune." Partially reprinted: pp. 397-400 reprinted in
    1970.A8. Reviewed: 1962.B7; 1962.B9; 1962.B41; 1962.B44;
    1962.B77; 1962.B90; 1963.B11; 1963.B46; 1963.B119;
    1964.B72; 1965.B6; 1973.B8; 1973.B30; Howard Mumford
    Jones, <u>New Republic</u>, 147 (17 November), 30; Simon Nowell-
    Smith, <u>Victorian Studies</u>, 7 (1963), 103-105; Lyon N. Rich-
    ardson, <u>American Literature</u>, 35 (1963), 377-79; Kenneth S.
    Lynn, <u>New England Quarterly</u>, 36 (1963), 260-63.

2   EDEL, LEON. <u>Henry James: The Middle Years, 1882-1895</u>.
    Philadelphia: Lippincott, 408 pp.
       Volume 3 of the James biography chronicles James during
    his forties and tells "of his social entanglements and his
    attachments, as well as of his evolution from chronicler of
    the 'American girl' and 'international' comedy, into an ob-
    server and recorder of English and Continental <u>moeurs</u>. And
    at the end of this period occurs his strange attempt to
    turn himself into a man of the theatre." Reviewed:
    1962.B9; 1962.B41; 1962.B44; 1962.B77; 1963.B11; 1963.B12;
    1963.B46; 1963.B119; 1964.B72; 1965.B6; 1973.B8; 1973.B30;
    Howard Mumford Jones, <u>New Republic</u>, 147 (17 November), 30;
    <u>Modern Fiction Studies</u>, 8 (Winter 1962-1963), 419-21; Simon
    Nowell-Smith, <u>Victorian Studies</u>, 7 (1963), 103-105; Lyon N.
    Richardson, <u>American Literature</u>, 44 (1963), 330-32; Kenneth
    S. Lynn, <u>New England Quarterly</u>, 36 (1963), 260-63.

3   KROOK, DOROTHEA. <u>The Ordeal of Consciousness in Henry James</u>.
    New York: Cambridge Univ. Press, 422 pp.
       Designed for the nonspecialist reader, this is a "col-
    lection of purely elucidatory studies of a selected number
    of James's works, connected by the theme of 'being and
    seeing'--the exploration and definition of consciousness in
    James's particular meaning of the term." Connections be-
    tween works establish the "continuity of James's principal

preoccupations through various periods of his life." (Included in the text are discussions of The Portrait of a Lady, The Tragic Muse, The Turn of the Screw, The Awkward Age, The Sacred Fount, The Wings of the Dove, The Golden Bowl.) Partially reprinted: pp. 357-69 reprinted in 1968.A1; pp. 232-324 reprinted in 1973.A6. Reviewed: 1965.B6; Tony Tanner, Encounter, 19:84-86; Times Literary Supplement (30 November), p. 938; Modern Fiction Studies, 9 (1963), 182; Munro Beattie, South Atlantic Quarterly, 61 (1963), 445-46; Oscar Cargill, American Literature, 35 (1963), 97-98; J. A. Ward, Nineteenth-Century Fiction, 17 (1963), 392-95.

4 LEBOWITZ, NAOMI, ed. Discussions of Henry James. Boston: D. C. Heath, 105 pp.
      Contents: A collection of thirteen previously published pieces on James. The "Introduction" by Naomi Lebowitz (pp. vii-ix) states that in these essays James's moral vision, which is communicated by technique and atmosphere, is explored by his best critics.
      "Review of James's Hawthorne" by W. D. Howells (pp. 1-3). Reprinted from Atlantic, 45 (February 1880), 280.
      "Letter to W. D. Howells" by Henry James (p. 4). Reprinted from The Letters of Henry James. Vol. 6. Edited by Percy Lubbock. New York: Scribner's, 1920, pp. 71-73.
      "Correspondence between Henry James and H. G. Wells" (pp. 5-7). The two James letters are reprinted from The Letters of Henry James. Vol. 2. Edited by Percy Lubbock. New York: Scribner's, 1920, pp. 485-87, 488-90. The Wells letter is reprinted from Henry James and H. G. Wells. Edited by Leon Edel and Gordon Ray. Urbana: Univ. of Illinois Press, 1958.
      "The Ethics of Henry James" by Joseph Warren Beach (pp. 8-14). Reprinted from The Method of Henry James. New Haven: Yale Univ. Press, 1918.
      "The Craft of Henry James" by Percy Lubbock (pp. 15-20). Reprinted from The Craft of Fiction. London: Jonathan Cape, 1921.
      "James and the Plastic Arts" by F. O. Matthiessen (pp. 21-30). Reprinted from Kenyon Review, 5 (Autumn 1943), 533-50.
      "The Princess Casamassima" by Lionel Trilling (pp. 31-48). Reprinted from "Introduction," in The Princess Casamassima. New York: Macmillan, 1948.
      "The Portrait of a Lady" by Dorothy Van Ghent (pp. 49-59). Reprinted from The English Novel: Form and Function. New York: Holt, Rinehart, Winston, 1953.

1962

"The Portrait of a Lady" by Richard Chase (pp. 60-70).
Reprinted from The American Novel and Its Tradition. New
York: Doubleday & Co., 1957, pp. 117-35.
"The Lesson of Spiritual Beauty: The Wings of the Dove"
by Christof Wegelin (pp. 71-79). Reprinted from The Image
of Europe in Henry James. Dallas: Southern Methodist
Univ. Press, 1958.
"Love and Knowledge: The Golden Bowl" by John Bayley
(pp. 80-88). Reprinted from 1960.B3.
"The High Brutality of Good Intentions" by William H.
Gass (pp. 89-95). Reprinted from Accent, 13 (Winter 1958),
62-71. Also reprinted in 1967.A5.
"Symbolic Imagery in the Later Novels" by Austin Warren
(pp. 96-105). Reprinted from Rage for Order. Chicago:
Univ. of Chicago Press, 1948, pp. 142-61.

5   WRIGHT, WALTER F. The Madness of Art: A Study of Henry
James. Lincoln: Univ. of Nebraska Press, 269 pp.
This study of the "nature and range of Henry James's
literary work" begins by considering James's "concept of
the relation of life and art," continues "with his major
themes," and concludes "with the art of telling." Partially reprinted: pp. 193-200 reprinted in 1965.B8. Reviewed:
Harry H. Clark, American Literature, 35:379-81; Modern Fiction Studies, 9 (1963), 182-83; James K. Folsom, South Atlantic Quarterly, 62 (1963), 446-47; Lyall H. Powers,
Nineteenth-Century Fiction, 18 (1963), 295-99.

1962 B SHORTER WRITINGS

1   ABEL, DARREL, ed. Henry Blake Fuller's "Howells or James?"
in Howells: A Century of Criticism. Edited by Kenneth E.
Eble. Dallas: Southern Methodist Univ. Press, pp. 34-40.
This reprint of Fuller's 1885 paper shows that Fuller
thought "Howells' realism was more realistic than James's,
and his Americanism more American; and thought Howells himself ought to be acknowledged as the shaper and director of
American fiction." Reprinted from Modern Fiction Studies,
3 (Summer 1957), 159-64.

2   ALBÉRÈS, R. M. "L'Impressionnisme Anglais: Aux Sources du
'Nouveau Roman.'" Revue de Paris, 69 (May), 74-86.
[French]
The new novel of Nathalie Sarraute, Michel Butor, and
Alain Robbe-Grillet owes much to the impressionistic writ-
ing of Henry James and Joseph Conrad, who were more than
tellers of tales. James and Conrad captured a world in

their writings that was unknowable, heterogeneous, lyric,
and secret--in short, the world of poetry.

3 ALLOTT, MIRIAM. "Form Versus Substance in Henry James." <u>Re-
   view of English Literature</u> (Leeds), 3 (January), 53-66.
       James's critics frequently misjudge "the tone and
   'weight' of his fiction--not only those stories . . .
   justifiably labelled obscure . . . but even lightly ironical social sketches." James often adopts "techniques which
   interfere disastrously with the feeling for life which they
   are supposed to convey."

4 ANDERSON, CHARLES R. "Introduction," in his edition of <u>The
   Portrait of a Lady</u>. New York: Collier, pp. 5-11.
       Since <u>The Portrait of a Lady</u> is James's first great
   book, it has a "freshness" and "spontaneity that is possible only when an author lets himself go for the first time,
   unaware of the extent of his powers."

5 ANDREACH, ROBERT J. "Henry James's <u>The Sacred Fount</u>: The
   Existential Predicament." <u>Nineteenth-Century Fiction</u>, 17
   (December), 197-216.
       The success of the novel is in James's insight into the
   existential predicament of the narrator who is unable to
   get outside of himself and confuses his apprehension of the
   world with his real experience in it.

6 ANON. "The Accents of the Master." <u>Times Literary Supplement</u>
   (20 April), p. 264.
       In these first two volumes of James's tales or <u>nouvelles</u>,
   part of a proposed twelve-volume chronological series edited by Leon Edel, each tale is based on the "'first book
   edition' . . . thus allowing the author the benefit of a
   single . . . contemporary revision" but leaving out changes
   made by James in his later years. Review of 1962.B25.

7 ANON. "The Acceptance World." <u>Times Literary Supplement</u>
   (16 November), p. 867.
       In the second volume of James's biography, Edel "has re-
   inforced biographical facts with psychological interpreta-
   tions--subtle, brilliant, never far-fetched--of those novels and stories in which James undeliberately expressed his
   inner stress." Volumes 3 and 4 of the <u>Complete Tales of
   Henry James</u> present the tales "in the freshness with which
   they first assailed the London Public, not sophisticated by
   the Old Pretender." <u>The Three Jameses</u> is "highly recom-
   ㄱended" as an introduction to the "life and thought of

1962

three remarkable intellectuals in one American family."
Review of 1962.A1; 1962.B25; 1962.B20.

8   ANON. "The Lesson of the Master." <u>Times Literary Supplement</u>
     (19 January), p. 44.
         Jack Clayton's film <u>The Innocents</u>, which is a version of
     <u>The Turn of the Screw</u> adapted from William Archibald's play,
     <u>The Innocents</u>, fails because it attempts "to capture the
     book entire." The only way to control the book's ambiguity
     is through use of the first person narrative.

9   ARVIN, NEWTON. "The World of Henry James." <u>Nation</u>, 195
     (10 November), 310-11.
         Edel's biography is rich in fact, it is imaginatively
     written, and it is important for the "personal, familial,
     social, [and] historical" insight it gives into the milieu
     out of which James created his imaginative world. Review
     of 1962.A1 and 1962.A2.

10   AUCHINCLOSS, LOUIS. "Henry James and the Russian Novelists,"
     in <u>Novelists on Novelists</u>. Edited by Louis Kronenberger.
     Garden City, N.Y.: Doubleday, pp. 215-24.
         James did not care much for Tolstoy nor Dostoyevsky, but
     he "loved and admired" Turgenev. Reprinted from 1961.B3.

11   AUSTIN, DEBORAH. "Innocents at Home: A Study of <u>The Euro-</u>
     <u>peans</u> of Henry James." <u>Journal of General Education</u>, 14
     (14 July), 103-29.
         In order to provide a happy ending for the novel, James
     did violence to his great themes of "the struggle of the
     individual to achieve an integrity of vision" and "the
     plight of the artist."

12   BALDWIN, JAMES. "As Much of the Truth as One Can Bear." <u>New</u>
     <u>York Times Book Review</u> (14 January), p. 1.
         Strether's moral dilemma resides in his realization that
     he has "failed his manhood." Reprinted in 1964.B18.

13   BEAVER, HAROLD. "A Figure in the Carpet: Irony and the Amer-
     ican Novel." <u>Essays and Studies</u>. Compiled by Beatrice
     White. London: John Murray, pp. 101-14.
         A discussion of the coming of age of American literature
     concludes with the observation that there is a "line of de-
     scent" in America of writers who have used the tradition of
     irony (Twain, James, Nabokov), but that American writers
     have not yet "seen life coldly nor seen it whole."

14   BERLAND, ALWYN. "Henry James and the Aesthetic Tradition."
      Journal of the History of Ideas, 23 (July-September),
      407-19.
          James's fiction explores the American movement toward
      moral awareness and ideal culture (in Arnold's sense), com-
      bining the "American-Hebraic and European-Hellenic," but
      avoiding the excesses of transcendentalism and aestheticism.

15   BERNARD, KENNETH. "The Real Thing in James's 'The Real
      Thing.'" Brigham Young University Studies, 5 (Autumn),
      31-32.
          Although "the point of the story is that the artist must
      transform reality into art," the protagonist fails to
      achieve this transformation. His experiences simply teach
      him that he is a second-rate artist incapable of such
      transformation.

16   BERTHOFF, WARNER. The Example of Melville. Princeton:
      Princeton Univ. Press, passim.
          James is mentioned several times in this study of
      Melville.

17   BLACKALL, JEAN FRANTZ. "James's 'In the Cage': An Approach
      Through the Figurative Language." Univ. of Toronto Quar-
      terly, 31 (January), 164-79.
          The primary symbol of "In the Cage" is the telgraphist's
      cage, and the animal images combined with the ironic treat-
      ment James accorded the heroine "suggest that he was pre-
      occupied in particular with the implications of a point of
      view so uninformed let loose on a world so unfamiliar."

*18   BRKIĆ, SVETOZAR. "Tema 'medjunarodne situacije' i sukoba u
      delima Henri Džemza i Iva Andrića." Ivo Andrić, Institut
      za teoriju Književnosti i umetnosti, Belgrade, I, pp. 317-29.
          Cited in Annual Bibliography of English Language and
      Literature: Volume 36: 1962. Edited by Marjory Rigsby
      and Charles Nilon. Great Britain: Modern Humanities Re-
      search Association in Association with the Univ. of Colorado
      Press, 1965, p. 275.

19   BUITENHUIS, PETER. "Comic Pastoral: Henry James's The Euro-
      peans." Univ. of Toronto Quarterly, 31 (January), 152-63.
          James's The Europeans is in several areas an experi-
      mental work of considerable success: (1) James is experi-
      menting with a new form--the nouvelle; (2) he is experi-
      menting with the comic mode; and (3) he is experimenting
      with the pastoral tradition.

1962

20   CARGILL, OSCAR. "A Retrospective Introduction" and "Addendum, 1962 [to Bibliographical Notes]," in this new edition of The Three Jameses: A Family of Minds. By C. Hartley Grattan. New York: New York Univ. Press, pp. vii-x, 373-78.
      Grattan's book was originally published by Longmans, Green in 1932, before the "James revival"; but it is still "indispensable" for the study of Henry, Sr., William, and Henry, Jr. Brief essays on each of the three men bring the bibliography up to date. Reviewed: 1962.B7.

21   CASTIGLIONE, LUIGI. "Profilo di James." La Fiera Letteraria, 17 (23 September), 5. [Italian]
      Michael Swan, in his Henry James, says that James built a new and imaginary world based upon Hawthorne's moral universe. Such a line of thought, which we can find in "The Lesson of the Master," "The Four Meetings," and "The Madonna of the Future," is James's obsession and leitmotif: life is a frustrating experience, an accumulation of delusions based upon losses of meanings.

22   CORNWELL, ETHEL F. "The Jamesian Moment of Experience," in her The "Still Point": Theme and Variations in the Writings of T. S. Eliot, Coleridge, Yeats, Henry James, Virginia Woolf, and D. H. Lawrence. New Brunswick, N.J.: Rutgers Univ. Press, pp. 126-58.
      A panoramic view of James's fictive protagonists reveals that James believed self-fulfillment is achieved through a refined personal consciousness that culminates in "the moment of vision, the moment of full consciousness."

23   CREETH, EDMUND. "Moonshine and Bloodshed: A Note on The American." Notes and Queries, ns 9 (March), 105-106.
      The connection formed in The American between the Madonna and Claire de Cintré reveals the "interpenetration of the arts of painting and fiction." Reprinted in 1972.B112.

24   EBLE, KENNETH E., ed. Howells: A Century of Criticism. Dallas: Southern Methodist Univ. Press, pp. 41, 88.
      Reprints of James's 1886 essay on Howells and his 1912 "A Letter to Mr. Howells" are preceded by brief head notes. The 1886 essay is "one of the most discerning articles on Howells in the nineteenth century."

25   EDEL, LEON, ed. The Complete Tales of Henry James. Vols. 1-4. Philadelphia: Lippincott.
      Edel's "General Introduction" (Vol. 1, pp. 7-16) states that James wrote a hundred and twelve tales, all of which are included in this collected edition. Three periods can

be discerned: (1) the apprentice pieces, which are "rather melancholy and romantic"; (2) the middle tales, which "mark his emergence as a brilliant and witty observer of life on both sides of the Atlantic"; and (3) the late tales, which are often "a study of states of feeling and of dilemmas of existence." Reprinted in 1963.A1.

The "Introduction: 1864-1868" (Vol. 1, pp. 17-22) notes that these early tales "form a casual and unplanned overture to an extraordinary career in story-telling; and as in overtures small phrases offer hints of greater themes." "Introduction: 1868-1872" (Vol. 2, pp. 7-11) suggests that in these tales "the young writer embarks on his study of human types and human behavior." "Introduction: 1873-1875" (Vol. 3, pp. 7-10) states that these tales "announce certain characteristic, and indeed major, themes while reflecting the writer's personal need to understand his rôle as artist in the two worlds [America and Europe] in which he moved." "Introduction: 1876-1882" (Vol. 4, pp. 7-11) notes that some of these tales are "'potboilers,'" but that also included in the collection is "Daisy Miller," a masterpiece which caused James to be "acknowledged master of the 'international' in Anglo-American fiction." James has "discovered his characteristic theme," and in these tales "there emerges a social satire that is perceptive and humane." Reviewed: 1962.B6; 1962.B7; 1963.B89; 1965.B6.

26 EMERSON, DONALD. "Henry James on the Role of Imagination in Criticism." <u>Transactions of the Wisconsin Academy of Sciences, Arts, and Letters</u>, 51:287-94.
    In his criticism, James's developing views of the role of imagination show his "turning from judgment to 'justness of characterization' and at last to 'deep appreciation.'"

27 "Evil Emanations." <u>Time</u>, 79 (5 January), 59.
    <u>The Innocents</u> [movie adaptation of <u>The Turn of the Screw</u>] is "the most sophisticated scare show since <u>Diabolique</u>." It is flawed by its hard pressing psychological interpretation of the ghosts.

28 FINKELSTEIN, SIDNEY. "The 'Mystery' of Henry James's <u>The Sacred Fount</u>." <u>Massachusetts Review</u>, 3 (Summer), 753-76.
    <u>The Sacred Fount</u> is thematically related to James's "major phase" by its "seriousness of thought, its sharp social criticism, and the moral problem" it raises.

1962

29 FREEDMAN, WILLIAM A. "Universality in 'The Jolly Corner.'"
   Texas Studies in Literature and Language, 4 (Spring),
   12-15.
       "The Jolly Corner" achieves a universal perspective
   through its "language of totality" and its allusive connec-
   tion with "three of the greatest sources of symbolic and
   allegorical reference in all literature"--the Bible, the
   Divina Commedia and the Republic.

30 GALE, ROBERT L. "James's 'The Next Time.'" Explicator, 21
   (December), Item 35.
       The two writers referred to as undesirable alternatives
   to Shakespeare and Scott (XV, 212-13, New York Edition of
   The Novels and Tales of Henry James) are Thomas Ansteg
   Guthrie and Francis Marion Crawford, whose commercial suc-
   cess, in contrast to James's own lack of popularity, caused
   James anguish.

31 GALE, ROBERT L. "The Marble Faun and The Sacred Fount: A
   Resemblance." Studi Americani, no. 8, pp. 21-33.
       Another influence of The Marble Faun should be added to
   the already lengthy list of influences. James uses the
   pastel portrait in his fourth chapter just as Hawthorne
   uses the Guido painting in his fifteenth chapter--both "use
   challenging pictures, hung in deceptive light, to elucidate
   character and implement plot, while the postures within the
   frames are thematically symbolic."

32 GEISMAR, MAXWELL. "Henry James and the Jacobites." American
   Scholar, 31 (Summer), 373-81.
       Although a unique and notable entertainer, James is not
   a major writer because of the narrowness of his work and
   vision, and his limited self-knowledge.

33 GOSSMAN, ANN. "Operative Irony in 'The Figure in the Carpet.'"
   Descant, 6 (Spring), 20-25.
       Not the essence of the figure, but the effect it has on
   the characters is the important aspect of the story. The
   figure elicits the loyalty of Gwendolen, the humanity of
   Corvick, and the myopia of the narrator.

34 GREGOR, IAN. "The Novel of Moral Consciousness: The Awkward
   Age," in The Moral and the Story. Edited by Ian Gregor
   and Brian Nicholas. London: Faber and Faber, pp. 151-84.
       James's The Awkward Age is examined comparatively with
   the work of Hardy and the French realists (particularly
   Zola), yielding a conclusion that it "records the fine
   point of balance between 'behaviour' and 'consciousness,'

between Victorian 'innocence' and modern 'integrity.'" The
book at large, in its study of the the theme of the innocent or
guilty woman of society as she appears in literary creations of the past century, also utilizes critical evaluations made by Henry James with reference to George Eliot,
Flaubert, Hardy, and Zola.

35 GRIFFIN, R. J. "Notes toward an Exegesis: 'Four Meetings.'"
Univ. of Kansas City Review, 29 (October), 45-49.
The theme of "Four Meetings" is illustrated in the story
by the narrator's use of four devices: (1) individual
words--leitmotifs, (2) perceptual images, (3) allusions and
metaphors, and (4) symbolic parallels.

36 HAGGIN, B. H. "Music Chronicle" [on The Turn of the Screw:
Operatic Version by B. Britten]. Hudson Review, 15 (Summer), 260-61.
The New York City Opera's performance of The Turn of the
Screw revealed that Benjamin Britten exhibited "dazzling
expertise" in the music, but Myfanwy Piper's dramatic adaptation "was a simplification which entailed a loss."

37 HAGOPIAN, JOHN V. "Henry James"; "Daisy Miller," in Insight I:
Analyses of American Literature. Edited by John V. Hagopian and Martin Dolch. Frankfurt am Main: Hirschgraben-
verlag, pp. 132-39.
This biographical sketch of James, explication of the
text of Daisy Miller, and study questions on the story are
part of a book on American literature designed for use in
German schools.

38 HALPERN, MARTIN. "Henry B. Brewster (1850-1908): An Intro-
duction." American Quarterly, 14 (Fall), 464-82.
Since James did not meet Brewster until nine years after
The Portrait of a Lady was published, R. W. Stallman's at-
tempt to connect Gilbert Osmond and Brewster is refuted.
See 1960.B27.

39 HAMBLEN, ABIGAIL A. "Henry James and the Transcendentalists."
Cresset, 26 (December), 16-17.
The setting of The Bostonians is Boston in the 1870s,
the city where Transcendentalism had flourished but where
it was "devitalized, seized upon by all sorts of vulgar influences, twisted monstrously."

1962

40   HAMILTON, EUNICE C. "Henry James's The Princess Casamassima
      and Ivan Turgenev's Virgin Soil." South Atlantic Quarter-
      ly, 61 (Summer), 354-64.
          A comparison of The Princess Casamassima and Virgin Soil
      shows that Turgenev's novel was one of James's sources.

41   HICKS, GRANVILLE. "The Vision Behind the Vision." Saturday
      Review, 45 (3 November), 23.
          The publication of the second and third volumes of
      Edel's biography of James confirms the expectations raised
      by the first volume--Edel is producing a "masterly biogra-
      phy." Review of 1962.A1 and 1962.A2.

42   HIGUCHI, HIDEO. "Henry James's View of the Novel: Imagina-
      tion and Form." Shuryu (Doshisha Univ., Kyoto), 24
      (December), 24-38. [Japanese]
          In the history of English literature, James is the first
      conscious novelist who stressed the importance of form. He
      held the credo that a novel is what is deliberately con-
      ceived of life through the writer's imagination, not merely
      a faithful description of life. Characterization is a vi-
      tal element in the light of the "dramatic quality" of a
      novel, as the author should be behind the stage.

*43   HINCHCLIFFE, A. P. "Symbolism in the American Novel, 1850-
      1950: An Examination of the Findings of Recent Literary
      Critics in Respect to the Novels of Hawthorne, Melville,
      James, Hemingway, and Faulkner." Dissertation, Manchester,
      1962-1963.
          Cited in James Woodress, Dissertations in American Lit-
      erature: 1891-1966. Revised and enlarged with the assis-
      tance of Marian Koritz. Durham: Duke Univ. Press, 1968,
      Item 3482.

44   HYNES, SAMUEL. "A Small Literary Monument." Commonweal, 77
      (November), 172-74.
          The monument of James's literary reputation is enhanced
      by Leon Edel's biographical contribution but not signifi-
      cantly affected by Scribner's niggardly new edition of
      James's complete works. Review of 1962.A1 and 1962.A2.

45   IWASE, SHITSUU. "Henry James: Revision of 'Four Meetings'--
      Point of View." Queries, 3 (June), 9-22. [Japanese]
          The two texts of "Four Meetings" are compared with ref-
      erence to stylistic differences. The revised text of the
      New York Edition is superior, mainly because of the place-
      ment of the point-of-view character who is endowed with
      deepened experience.

46 JELLEMA, R. H. "Victorian Critics and the Orientation of
     American Literature, with Special Reference to the Recep-
     tion of Walt Whitman and Henry James." Dissertation, Edin-
     burgh.
          Cited in James Woodress, Dissertations in American Lit-
     erature: 1891-1966. Revised and enlarged with the assis-
     tance of Marian Koritz. Durham: Duke Univ. Press, 1968,
     Item 2681.

47 JONES, LEONIDAS M. "James's 'Four Meetings.'" Explicator, 20
     (March), Item 55.
          "Four Meetings" is a piece of "modern hagiography."
     Caroline Spencer is compared to a medieval saint, a devotee
     of the new religion of culture which has replaced the "old
     dogmatic religion." James shows how little modern dogma
     differs from the medieval by utilizing "an undercurrent of
     ironic meaning almost to the point of allegory."

48 KAEL, PAULINE. "The Innocents and What Passes for Experience."
     Film Quarterly, 15:21-36.
          Current trends in movie themes and characterization and
     critical response to The Innocents, A View from the Bridge,
     West Side Story, and The Day the Earth Caught Fire demon-
     strate that film critics are frequently "casual, indiffer-
     ent, [and] irresponsible."

49 KAMERBEEK, J., JR. "Two Golden Nails: Henry James--Sainte-
     Beuve." Revue de Littérature Comparée, 36 (July-September),
     447-51.
          The source of James's golden nail in The Ambassadors
     could be Sainte-Beuve, who employed the image both in his
     Les Cahiers and Le Clou d'Or.

50 KARIEL, HENRY S. "Notes: Rebellion and Compulsion: The
     Dramatic Pattern of American Thought." American Quarterly,
     14 (Winter), 608-11.
          In an analysis of the trends of American thought and
     language, Henry James is briefly mentioned as using "an in-
     creasingly involuted, ironic vocabulary."

51 KATAN, M., M.D. "A Causerie on Henry James's The Turn of the
     Screw." The Psychoanalytic Study of the Child. Vol. 17.
     New York: International Universities Press, pp. 473-93.
          A Freudian interpretation of the story, this analysis
     considers that it is a nightmare which reveals James's
     problems of sexual identification. Reprinted in 1969.All.

1962

52   KOMOTA, JUNZO. "Henry James--On His Early Works." Ehime
      Daigaku Kiyo, 7 (January), 203-17. [Japanese]
          James's works do not measure up to his own view of what
      a novel should be; his works are not "interesting" nor are
      they faithful "representations of life." Three factors
      contribute to James's failure: his narrow and static con-
      ception of "impression" or "experience"; his rather too-
      fastidious style, which features oxymoron, alliteration,
      and double and triple negatives; and his placing of too
      much emphasis on technique.

53   KORG, JACOB. "What Aspern Papers? A Hypothesis." College
      English, 23 (February), 378-81.
          Since there is no clear evidence that the papers exist,
      it seems probable that they are imaginary, which casts the
      actions of the narrator in a unique and ironic light. See
      1962.B87.

54   LABOR, EARLE. "James's 'The Real Thing': Three Levels of
      Meanings." College English, 23 (February), 376-78.
          James simultaneously developed the theme on three lev-
      els: social, esthetic, and moral. Reprinted in 1965.B8
      and 1970.A7.

55   LAINOFF, SEYMOUR. "James and Eliot: The Two Gwendolens."
      Victorian Newsletter, No. 21 (Spring), 23-24.
          The characterization of Gwendolen Erme in "The Figure in
      the Carpet" recalls Eliot's portrait of Gwendolen Harleth
      in Daniel Deronda.

56   LANG, P. H. "The Wings of the Dove" [the Operatic Version by
      Douglas Moore]. Music Quarterly, 48 (January), 101-102.
          This opera, sponsored by the Ford Foundation and per-
      formed at City Center, will add to Mr. Moore's popularity,
      for it "represents the high point" in his career. Libret-
      tist Ethan Ayer's "text has both force and insight."

57   LEBOWITZ, NAOMI. "The Sacred Fount: An Author in Search of
      His Characters." Criticism, 4 (Spring), 148-59.
          In The Sacred Fount James emphasizes the idea that rela-
      tionships between author and character, and character and
      character must be continually probed and reshaped. James
      explores "the possibilities of aesthetic metamorphosis dur-
      ing the very act of composition."

58 LEE, B. C. "A Felicity Forever Gone: Henry James's Last
    Visit to America." British Association for American Stud-
    ies Bulletin, no. 5 (December), pp. 31-42.
        As early as the mid-Eighteen-Seventies James realized
    that a revolution was transforming America--substituting
    for the "vital, beautiful and noble" principles of European
    civilization things that were "crude and ugly."

59 LEE, BRIAN. "Henry James's 'Divine Consensus': The Ambassa-
    dors, The Wings of the Dove, The Golden Bowl." Renaissance
    and Modern Studies (Nottingham), 6:5-24.
        These late novels are not dependent on James's father's
    Swedenborgian theology as Quentin Anderson argues; rather
    the novels show James "as a descendant of Emerson, Haw-
    thorne, Thoreau and the whole Concord school."

60 LEVY, LEO B. "A Reading of 'The Figure in the Carpet.'"
    American Literature, 33 (January), 457-65.
        Only the narrator is clearly incapable of comprehending
    Vereker's secret and epitomizes the cold intellectual crit-
    ic who focuses on form and ignores the fact that "the work
    of art is not independent of the reader's experience but
    draws upon his capacity to bring to it an appropriate moral
    and psychological readiness."

61 LEVY, LEO B. "What Does The Sacred Fount Mean?" College Eng-
    lish, 23 (February), 381-84.
        "James's novel describes the extravagant case of the
    artist attempting to find in the world precise models of
    the works of art that it is his mission to invent."

62 LINNEMAN, WILLIAM R. "Satires of American Realism, 1880-1900."
    American Literature, 34 (March), 80-93.
        Humor magazines of the late nineteenth century satirized
    both sensational, sentimental romanticism and excessively
    detailed, analytical realism, revealing a taste for liter-
    ature "that was realistic in manner but romantic in
    material."

*63 LYDENBERG, JOHN. "Romanciers Américains . . . A la Recherche
    d'un Monde Perdu." Travaux du Centre d'Etudes Anglaises et
    Américaines, 1:29-46.
        Cited in Beatrice Ricks, comp. Henry James: A Bibliog-
    raphy of Secondary Works. Scarecrow Author Bibliographies,
    No. 24. Metuchen, N.J.: Scarecrow, Item 809.

1962

64   LYNSKEY, WINIFRED, ed. "Partial Analysis of 'The Bench of
      Desolation,'" in her <u>Reading Modern Fiction: 31 Stories
      with Critical Aids</u>. Third edition. New York: Scribner's,
      pp. 306-10.
           Analysis of the story includes comments on James's in-
      tent, Dodd's life, Kate's life, theme and style.

65   MacDONALD, DWIGHT. "<u>The Innocents</u>." <u>Esquire</u>, 57 (April), 24.
           Even though Jack Clayton directed, Truman Capote wrote
      the screen play, and good actors were cast, <u>The Turn of the
      Screw</u> movie adaptation is not a good one.

66   MacKENZIE, MANFRED. "Henry James: Serialist Early and Late."
      <u>Philological Quarterly</u>, 41 (April), 492-99.
           Despite James's dislike of serialization, it provided
      him with techniques that essentially enhanced, not detract-
      ed from his art.

67   MacKENZIE, MANFRED. "<u>The Turn of the Screw</u>: Jamesian
      Gothic." <u>Essays in Criticism</u>, 12 (January), 34-38.
           "<u>The Turn of the Screw</u> is James's superfine <u>Castle of
      Otranto</u>, 'perfectly independent and irresponsible,' in
      which atmosphere is being created in a way rather like
      self-spoofing."

68   McMURRAY, WILLIAM. "Pragmatic Realism in <u>The Bostonians</u>."
      <u>Nineteenth-Century Fiction</u>, 16 (March), 339-44.
           James proposes a pragmatism in the dynamic and changing
      reality that would keep options open and allow for the
      freedom of potentiality. Reprinted in 1968.All.

69   MALIN, IRVING. <u>New American Gothic</u>. Carbondale: Southern
      Illinois Univ. Press, pp. 8-9, 79.
           "The Pupil" and "The Jolly Corner" are mentioned as ex-
      amples of American gothic.

70   MARTIN, TERENCE. "Adam Blair and Arthur Dimmesdale: A Lesson
      from the Master." <u>American Literature</u>, 34 (May), 274-79.
           James's linking of the two novels, <u>The Scarlet Letter</u>
      and <u>Adam Blair</u>, is made possible by perceiving of Arthur
      Dimmesdale as the central figure in the novel, a perception
      that ignores much of the "fictional world" Hawthorne has
      created through the symbolic letter.

71 MASUDA, YOSHIRO. "Henry James," in A Handbook of British and American Literature: 20th Century. Edited by Tsutomu Ueda. Tokyo: Nanundo, pp. 24-40. [Japanese]
      This guide to Henry James includes discussion of his biography, his works, and criticism of his works.

72 MASUNAGA, KEIICHI. "James's Literature and Doubt: The Golden Bowl." Gaikoku Bungaku Kenkyu (Ritsumeikan Univ.), 5 (December), 73-102. [Japanese]
      A discussion of Maggie Verver, who finally seems to overcome her state of American innocence.

73 MONTEIRO, GEORGE. "Another Princess." Philological Quarterly, 41 (April), 517-18.
      James need not have relied totally on his memory of Princess Christina Belgiojoso in creating Princess Casamassima, since her daughter, Princess Maria Belgiojoso, provided the same prototypical "flamboyant character and social irreverence" in the 1880s.

74 MONTEIRO, GEORGE. "Hawthorne, James, and the Destructive Self." Texas Studies in Literature and Language, 4 (Spring), 58-71.
      John Marcher's antecedent can be found in Wakefield, a character who anticipates the figure in modern literature who, like Prufrock, is so possessed with "a secret conception of self" that he destroys the possibilities of "meaningful actions" or "moral growth."

75 MONTEIRO, GEORGE. "William Dean Howells: Two Mistaken Attributions." Papers of the Bibliographical Society of America, 54 (2 October), 254-57.
      Two essays defending Daisy Miller which appeared in the February and March issues of the Atlantic Monthly (1879) were written by Constance F. Woolson and John Hay, not William Dean Howells as stated by Albert Mordell in Discovery of a Genius.

76 MUDRICK, MARVIN. "Colette and Strether." Hudson Review, 15 (Spring), 110-13.
      Colette's "Regarde" and Strether's "live" are "imperatives to describe a necessary attitude toward life, an attitude which demands that one be alert and receptive to the incidents and impressions of one's experiences"; but whereas Strether ignores his own advice, Colette heeds it and writes out of her experience.

1962

77   MUTARELLI, GEORGIO. "Una biografia di James." Le Fiera Let-
      teraria, 17 (25 November), 4. [Italian]
          Volumes 2 and 3 of Edel's biography present James's
      brilliant career, his envy of his brother William, his
      cosmopolitan experience, his love for Sarah Butler Wister,
      and his passion for Constance Fenimore Woolson. Review of
      1962.A1 and 1962.A2.

78   NAKAZATO, HARUHIKO. "Henry James's 'A Passionate Pilgrim.'"
      Rikkyo Daigaku Kenkyu Hokoku, 12 (August), 1-22. [Japa-
      nese]
          James's romantic sensitivity towards England is embodied
      in four figures in the work: James the passionate pilgrim
      in Clement Searle; the James with his eye on his native
      land in Rawson; the spectator James straddling both sides
      of the Atlantic in the narrator; and James's adored woman
      figure in Miss Searle.

79   NAKAZATO, HARUHIKO. "Henry James: Washington Square."
      Kamereon (Rikkyo Univ.), 4 (June), 75-87. [Japanese]
          James's naming the work "a tale purely American" is
      pertinent because he has succeeded in a description of his
      "native land." Without the "paraphernalia" of the old
      world, the work could concentrate on the human drama.

*80   NAMEKATA, AKIO. "The Ordeal of Isabel in James's The Portrait
      of a Lady." Essays, 15 (December), 44-59.
          Cited in Beatrice Ricks, comp. Henry James: A Bibliog-
      raphy of Secondary Works. Scarecrow Author Bibliographies,
      No. 24. Metuchen, N.J.: Scarecrow, 1975, Item 826.

81   NONAKA, RYO. "James's Consciousness." English Literature
      (Waseda), 20 (January), 5-19. [Japanese]
          In James's early works, consciousness was only vaguely
      realized; but in mid-career, his aestheticism was balanced
      with moral awareness. Finally, in his late period, what
      Freud termed "unconscious" is evident.

82   OKITA, HAJIME. "Henry James's Contribution to American Lit-
      erature (I)." Jimbun (Kyoto Prefectural Univ.), 14
      (October), 51-73. [Japanese]
          A discussion of James's relationship with William Dean
      Howells and Edith Wharton is followed by an analysis of
      James's influence on their works. See 1963.B79 and
      1964.B76 for Parts II and III.

83 OKOSO, YOSHIKO. "The Spoils of Poynton: Between Reality and
    Art." English Literature (Waseda), 21 (March), 34-41.
    [Japanese]
       The Spoils of Poynton illustrates thematically and tech-
    nically James's artistic credo that an artist must recog-
    nize and select what is essential out of the chaotic real-
    ity of life. The heroine, who symbolizes intellect, aes-
    theticism, and morality, makes it clear that art is impos-
    sible without actual life, but that art is very different
    from life.

84 OTAKE, MASARU. "Henry James (I)." Jimbun-Shizenkagaku Ronshu
    (Tokyo College of Economics), 2 (Winter), 17-69. [Japa-
    nese]
       A biographical and critical introduction of James up to
    The Turn of the Screw (1898).

*85 OTSU, EIICHIRO. "Ghost Novels of Henry James." Critica,
    no. 5 (March), pp. 34-52.
       Cited in 1970.B72, p. 315.

86 PEARCE, ROY HARVEY, and MATTHEW J. BRUCCOLI, eds. The Ameri-
    can. Riverside Edition. Boston: Houghton Mifflin,
    pp. v-xxv.
       In the "Introduction" (pp. v-xxi), Roy Harvey Pearce
    states that the 1877 version of The American is superior to
    the 1907 version: "The American is a young man's novel,
    exuberant rather than profound in its wisdom." In the New
    York Edition, James tried "to convert exuberance into pro-
    fundity." Reprinted in 1969.B106.
       In "A Note on the Text" (pp. xxiii-xxv), Matthew J.
    Bruccoli describes various editions of the novel. The
    text printed here is the first authorized English edition
    of 1879 with thirty emendations, which are listed in Ta-
    ble B.

87 PHILLIPS, ROBERT S. "A Note on 'What Aspern Papers? A
    Hypothesis.'" College English, 24 (November), 154-55.
       The biographical facts of Jane (Claire) Clairmont's life
    make untenable the hypothesis that views her as the proto-
    type of Miss Tina. See 1962.B53.

*88 PLANTE, PATRICIA R. "Edith Wharton: A Prophet Without Due
    Honor." MWQ, 16-22.
       Cited in Beatrice Ricks, comp. Henry James: A Bibliog-
    raphy of Secondary Works. Scarecrow Author Bibliographies,
    No. 24. Metuchen, N.J.: Scarecrow, 1975, Item 3142.

1962

89   POWERS, LYALL H.   "Henry James's Antinomies."   Univ. of Toron-
     to Quarterly, 31 (January), 125-35.
          Both in James's handling of international conflict and
     in the conflict of the artist with the audience, the cen-
     tral "Jamesian antinomy" is that of "being" and "doing."

90   PRITCHETT, V. S.   "Birth of a Hermaphrodite."   New Statesman,
     64 (30 November), 779-80.
          Leon Edel's interesting biography, Henry James: The
     Conquest of London, skillfully shows that the people of
     James's novels were part of his life. Because of the
     change from concentrating on heroes to heroines in the
     world, the hermaphrodite is born with Washington Square
     and The Portrait of a Lady. Review of 1962.A1.

91   PUTT, S. GORLEY.   "James the First."   English, 14 (Autumn),
     93-96.
          Several elements of the work of James's middle and late
     years are clearly present in his earliest works, where they
     are handled with confidence demonstrating the "precocious
     competence of James the First."

92   PUTT, S. GORLEY.   Scholars of the Heart: Essays in Criticism.
     London: Faber and Faber, pp. 141-235.
          The essay "'Cher Maître' and 'Mon Bon': Henry James,
     Man and Legend" (pp. 141-51) suggests that "Those who adopt
     the 'cher maître' attitude to James, watchful with esoteric
     glee for the pathetic mannered slang or the obfuscating
     parentheses, are applauding the frail means and ignoring
     the end. 'Cher maître' he certainly became, but only as a
     result of failure to break through the limitations of 'mon
     bon.'"
          "'Benvolio': 'Everyone was a little someone else'"
     (pp. 152-73) considers a theme James used in his work, ear-
     ly and late: the close relationship of two or more charac-
     ters, "figures who seem, in their fascinated complementary
     unlikeness, to be different expressions of the same larger
     character." This theme is present in "Benvolio," "The
     Great Good Place," Roderick Hudson, Watch and Ward, Washing-
     ton Square, and many other works.
          "The Private Life and the Public Life: The Princess
     Casamassima and The Bostonians" (pp. 174-203) notes that
     these two novels, both published in book form in 1886, re-
     semble each other in "certain matters of tone and in the
     evocation of that strained human anguish between the con-
     ception of a 'political' ideal and its execution in the
     face of contrary 'private' impulses."

"The Wings of the Dove: A Study in Construction"
(pp. 204-35) suggests that in this novel "a contrived and
potentially melodramatic theme is made credible because
Henry James concentrates on personality--near-perfect
though the careful elaboration of plot may be."

93 REANEY, JAMES. "The Condition of Light: Henry James's The
    Sacred Fount." Univ. of Toronto Quarterly, 31 (January),
    136-51.
        James's refusal to give the reader material clues leaves
    the reader in the same position as the narrator--dependent
    on "psychologic evidence," he must come to a knowledge of
    the truth.

94 REED, JOHN Q. "The Ambassadors: Henry James's Method." Mid-
    west Quarterly, 4 (Autumn), 55-67.
        The four stages in the evolution of The Ambassadors--
    the germinal concept, the synoptic precursor, the novel
    itself, and reflective preface of the New York Edition--
    typify the Jamesian method of creating a novel around a
    central idea.

95 REIMAN, DONALD H. "The Inevitable Imitation: The Narrator in
    'The Author of Beltraffio.'" Texas Studies in Literature
    and Language, 3 (Winter), 503-509.
        The story is a study of the implications of one person's
    trying to manipulate the will of another, and the unnamed
    American narrator is "the prime mover in the tragedy." See
    1963.B92 for response.

96 ROY, CLAUDE. "Anton Tchékhov et Henry James." Nouvelle Revue
    Française, 20 (November), 876-87. [French]
        James and Tchékhov often tell the story of a story which
    never happened. Both writers are interested in characters
    who are failures, such as Strether and Uncle Vanya, human
    beings to whom nothing ever happened, nothing of what they
    dreamed and desired.

97 RUHM, HERBERT. "Introduction," in his edition of Confidence.
    The Universal Library. New York: Grosset and Dunlap,
    pp. ix-xi.
        The text of the first American edition of Henry James's
    fifth novel is reprinted here along with an editor's note,
    changes in the text, contemporary reviews, and a selected
    bibliography.

1962

98   SANNA, VITTORIA. "I primi racconti di Henry James: 1864–
      1872." Annali Istituto Universitario Orientale, Napoli,
      Sezione Germanica, 5:213–48. [Italian]
          James's early novels reflect the same traditional Ameri-
      can spirit already expressed by Hawthorne.

*99   SAYRE, ROBERT F. "The Examined Self: Henry Adams and Henry
      James and American Autobiography." Dissertation, Yale.
          Cited in James Woodress. Dissertations in American Lit-
      erature: 1891–1966. Revised and enlarged with the assis-
      tance of Marian Koritz. Durham: Duke Univ. Press, 1968,
      Item 4167a. See 1964.B86 for book publication.

100   SHUMSKY, ALLISON. "James Again: The New New York Edition."
      Sewanee Review, 70 (Summer), 522–25.
          The first two volumes of Scribner's projected reissue of
      the New York Edition are "handsome and ceremonial," but not
      really necessary. The American is a "delight," and Roder-
      ick Hudson "remains one of James's liveliest and most read-
      able books."

101   SILVERSTEIN, HENRY. "The Utopia of Henry James." New England
      Quarterly, 35 (December), 458–68.
          George Dane encounters "a world of enchantment," a re-
      prieve from a demanding public, in "The Great Good Place."
      Dane is a "spiritual descendant of the New England trans-
      cendental movement," and his utopia is monastic, totally
      excluding women. The connection between the story and
      James's own life is noted.

102   SIMON, IRÈNE. "Jane Austen and The Art of the Novel." Eng-
      lish Studies, 43 (June), 225–39.
          Both Austen and James have as their purpose to make the
      audience see, but Austen unlike James, who felt isolated
      from his audience and accordingly maintains a single point
      of view without authorial intrusion, did not feel alienated
      from her reading public and therefore enters the story as a
      hospitable hostess counting "on a community of response be-
      tween narrator and reader."

*103 TAKUWA, SHINJI. "Hawthorne, James and Soseki: The Sense of
      Sin." Studies in English Literature and Language (Kyushu
      Univ., Fukuoka, Japan), 12 (January), 13–28.
          Cited in 1970.B72, p. 321.

104   THOMAS, A. A. "Henry James à Paris." <u>Informations et docu-</u>
       <u>ments</u>, no. 161 (15 May), pp. 25-29. [French]
            Only thirty-two, James was but a young American the
       first time he went to Europe, and he was fascinated with
       the ancient and corrupt history he found there. Sensible
       and nervous, his marvel never decreased, as if he were a
       provincial (James himself realized such an approach of his
       to Paris only five years later). It was there that he
       learned his most refined cosmopolitan style.

105   THORP, WILLARD. "Foreword," in his edition of <u>Henry James:</u>
       <u>"The Madonna of the Future" and Other Early Stories</u>. New
       York: New American Library.
            Cited in <u>1962 MLA International Bibliography</u>, vol. 1,
       p. 186.

106   THORP, WILLARD. "Foreword," in his edition of <u>"The Turn of</u>
       <u>the Screw" and Other Short Novels</u>. A Signet Classic. New
       York: New American Library, pp. vii-xv.
            "The values--human, natural, fundamental--which are at
       the center of these six nouvelles are values which were
       precious to James and to which he returned many times in
       his novels and nouvelles."

107   TOCHIHARA, TOMOO. "Henry James: <u>Watch and Ward</u>--The Charac-
       ter of the Work and the Question of Sexuality." <u>Ronko</u>
       (Kwanseiga Kuin Univ.), 9 (November), 109-84. [Japanese]
            This essay defends the novel for its precise and simple
       style. Thematically, the center of the work is naïveté in
       sexuality.

108   TODASCO, RUTH TAYLOR. "Theme and Imagery in <u>The Golden Bowl</u>."
       <u>Texas Studies in Literature and Language</u>, 4 (Summer),
       228-40.
            The novel's theme, "the quest for the full life," is
       portrayed through the imagery, which "serves primarily as
       the visible representation of subjective states of being."
       Maggie is revealed as possessing "'sound humanity,'" while
       Adam and Charlotte are bound by social forms.

109   TOMLINSON, M. "The Drama's Laws." <u>Twentieth Century</u> (Mel-
       bourne), 16:293-300.
            James's <u>Guy Domville</u> is a "bad, weak play" that fails
       because James compromised in order to seek public accep-
       tance; as a result the play is tentative and lacks the in-
       tegrity of vision of which James was capable.

1962

110 TRILLING, LIONEL. "The Princess Casamassima," in The Modern
     Critical Spectrum. Edited by Gerald Jay Goldberg and Nancy
     Marmer Goldberg. Englewood Cliffs, N.J.: Prentice-Hall,
     pp. 134-55.
         It is James's "imagination of disaster," his perception
     of social disintegration that caused the novel to fail in
     terms of contemporary public response. The same elements
     represent the source of the novel's appeal in modern
     America.

111 UEDA, TSUTOMU. "Henry James." Essays on Modern British
     Writers. Tokyo: Kenkyu-sha, pp. 40-46. [Japanese]
         Contents: Two previously published notes on James.
     (1) In An International Episode James consciously employed
     a technique designed to conceal the author from the fore-
     front of the comedy. (Originally published in a 1956
     translation of An International Episode.) (2) James's
     stylistic difficulties in his late period were due to his
     attempt to reveal fully man's psychology. (Originally
     published in the volume on James in the Series of World
     Literature, Kawade Publishers, 1959.)

112 WARREN, AUSTIN. "The New England Conscience, Henry James, and
     Ambassador Strether." Minnesota Review, 2 (Winter),
     149-61.
         James used the term "New England conscience" in an 1895
     Notebook entry which described the theme of The Ambassa-
     dors, "his most serious as well as final dealing with the
     New England conscience." In the novel Strether emancipates
     his public conscience (by allowing others to do what he
     would not do), but retains his private New England con-
     science. Reprinted in 1969.B73 and 1973.A6.

113 WATANABE, HISAYOSHI. "Past Perfect Retrospection in the Style
     of Henry James." American Literature, 34 (May), 165-81.
         The increased usage of the past perfect verb tense in
     James's late works minimizes physical action while height-
     ening the subjective experiences of the character's con-
     sciousness--"remembrance, reflection, impression, and
     interpretation."

114 WEALES, GERALD. American Drama Since World War II. New York:
     Harcourt, Brace & World, pp. 166-68.
         A brief look at the dramatic adaptations of James's The
     Turn of the Screw and Washington Square appears in this
     study.

1962

115   WEGELIN, CHRISTOF. "The Rise of the International Novel."
      Publications of the Modern Language Association of America,
      77 (June), 305-10.
           The international novel, which achieves generic distinc-
      tion with the writings of Howells, James, and Wharton,
      evolved through the writings of Cooper, Hawthorne, Long-
      fellow, Melville, and others. The expansion of tourism due
      to advancing technology contributed to the development of
      this genre.

116   WEIMANN, ROBERT. "Erzählerstandpunkt und point of view: Zu
      Geschichte und Äesthetik der Perspektive in englischen Ro-
      man." Zeitschrift für Anglistik und Amerikanistik (East
      Berlin), 10:369-416. [German]
           The two concepts of "narrator's standpoint" and "point
      of view" are defined and delineated in terms of their de-
      velopment and transformation from the epic to the modern
      novel. (James is mentioned on pp. 369, 378, 414, 416.)

117   WHITE, MORTON, and LUCIA WHITE. "The Visiting Mind: Henry
      James," in their The Intellectual Versus the City: From
      Thomas Jefferson to Frank Lloyd Wright. Cambridge, Mass.:
      Harvard Univ. Press and The M.I.T. Press, a publication of
      The Joint Center for Urban Studies, pp. 75-94.
           A study of the city as it appears in James's fiction and
      his correspondence suggests that "Henry James remained all
      his life the detached, sensitive, ironic, visiting observer
      of the American city, and within the range of his interests
      described some manifestations of urban growth with stunning
      accuracy and intense dismay at its social effects."

118   WILDE, OSCAR. The Letters of Oscar Wilde. Edited by Rupert
      Hart-Davis. New York: Harcourt, Brace & World, passim.
           A dozen references to Henry James appear in Oscar
      Wilde's correspondence.

119   WILLIAMSON, MARILYN L. "'Almost Wholly in French': The Cri-
      sis in The Ambassadors." Notes and Queries, ns 9 (March),
      106-107.
           James uses Mme. de Vionnet's French as "a device to give
      his reader a sense of the distance Strether has travelled
      as ambassador."

120   WILSON, EDMUND. Patriotic Gore: Studies in the Literature of
      the American Civil War. New York: Oxford Univ. Press,
      pp. 585-87, 654-70, 699-700, passim.
           Henry James's experience of the Civil War is discussed,
      along with three of his early stories that are concerned

1962

with the war: "The Story of a Year," "Poor Richard" and "A Most Extraordinary Case." In addition, there are many other references to James in this book.

1962 C DISSERTATIONS

1 BASS, EBEN EDWARD. "Ethical Form in the Fiction of Henry James." DA, 23, 1015 (Pittsburgh).
The use of a central consciousness was James's primary technique for joining the ethical concern of the English school with the formalistic concern of the French school to create a new kind of novel--one with an "ethical form."

2 CROTTY, SISTER M. MADELEINE, C.S.J. "The Mother in the Fiction of Henry James." DA, 23, 1698-99 (Fordham).
An overview of the mother figures pervasively present in James's fiction compared with a composite image of James's fictional presentation of Europe reveals that James infused the mother figure with symbolic value in a manner very similar to his employment of the "American girl."

3 ISLE, WALTER WHITFIELD. "Experiments in the Novel: Henry James's Fiction, 1896-1901." DA, 22, 3645-46 (Stanford).
From 1896 through 1901 were experimental years that yielded both technical and structural discoveries and advances in James's craft--discoveries and advances that became the foundation for later works. For book publication see 1968.A6.

4 MARSHALL, JAMES MORSE. "Patterns of Freedom in Henry James's Later Novels." DA, 23, 634 (Syracuse).
This reading of the late novels emphasizes their "ironical, realistic" aspect. In the context of the late novels, "The Sacred Fount stands as a germinal work" because "James here offers a symbolic suggestion of the kind of freedom his later characters seek but do not find."

5 PETESCH, NATALIE MAINES. "The Ceremony of Innocence: A Study of Narrative Techniques in Henry James." DA, 23, 1687-88 (Texas).
The theme of innocence is the common denominator in Rousseau's Confessions, Dickens's David Copperfield and Great Expectations, and in several of James's works including What Maisie Knew, The Ambassadors, The Wings of the Dove, The Golden Bowl, The Ivory Tower and Roderick Hudson. The thematic commonality produces three narrative techniques that are very similar in form.

6 RANALD, RALPH ARTHUR. "Henry James and the Social Question:
   'Freedom' and 'Life' in the Social Novels of the 1880s."
   DA, 23, 2531-32 (Princeton).
       Although James's social novels, The Princess Casamassi-
   ma, The Bostonians, and The Tragic Muse, were generally
   considered inferior by his contemporaries, they do reflect
   James's social perspicacity and contain important technical
   and thematic elements that culminated in his works at the
   turn of the century.

7 SCHOLES, JAMES BERT. "American and British Criticism of Henry
   James: 1916-1953." DA, 22, 2798-99 (Univ. of North Carolina, Chapel Hill).
       From 1916 until 1934 Henry James's critical reputation
   vacillated as different critical methods emerged and sub-
   sequently diminished in popularity. From 1934 until 1953,
   however, James's reputation has been steadily strengthened
   by the analagous strengthening of analytical criticism--a
   method that has its genesis in James's own principles.

8 SHARP, SISTER M. CORONA, O.S.U. "The Role of the Confidante
   in Henry James." DA, 23, 2139-40 (Notre Dame).
       An overview of the confidante in James's fiction reveals
   an evolving sophistication in his handling of the figure.
   An overview also suggests the role of the confidante is
   complementary to James's limited point of view technique
   and is employed as a dramatic device. For book publication
   see 1963.A3.

9 WIESENFARTH, BROTHER JOSEPH, F.S.C. "Henry James and the
   Dramatic Analogy: A Study of the Major Novels of the Middle Period." DA, 23, 241 (Catholic Univ.).
       A study of four novels--The Spoils of Poynton, What
   Maisie Knew, The Awkward Age, and The Sacred Fount--sug-
   gests that James through his handling of language, picture,
   scene, action and centre "achieved the qualities of 'intensity,' 'objectivity,' and 'economy' and thus effected a
   dramatic novel." For book publication see 1963.A4.

1963 A BOOKS

1 EDEL, LEON, ed. Henry James: A Collection of Critical Essays. Twentieth Century Views. Englewood Cliffs, N.J.:
   Prentice-Hall, 186 pp.
       Contents: Includes 18 previously published essays, a
   chronology of important dates in James's life, and a selected bibliography. In the "Introduction" (pp. 1-10),

1963

Leon Edel states that to see James among his critics is "to
encounter some large and crudely built sphinx, over whom
has been flung a prodigious coat of motley." These cri-
tiques have been included because they "are general and
broad, illustrative and 'basic.'"

"An Appreciation" by Joseph Conrad (pp. 11-17). Reprinted from Notes on Life and Letters. London: J. M.
Dent and Sons, 1905, pp. 13-23.

"Jacobean and Shavian" by Max Beerbohm (pp. 18-26). Reprinted from Around Theatres. New York: Simon and Schus-
ter, 1930, pp. 260-65, 323-26.

"A Brief Note" by Ezra Pound (pp. 27-30). Reprinted
from The Little Review (August 1918), pp. 6-9.

"The Man of Letters" by Edith Wharton (pp. 31-36). Re-
printed from two sources: Henry James in His Letters.
Edited by Percy Lubbock. New York: Macmillan, 1920;
Quarterly Review (July 1920), pp. 197-202.

"The Point of View: The Ambassadors" by Percy Lubbock
(pp. 37-46). Reprinted from The Craft of Fiction. New
York: Viking, 1921, pp. 161-71.

"The Ghost Stories" by Virginia Woolf (pp. 47-54). Reprinted from "Henry James's Ghost Stories," in Granite and
Rainbow. New York: Harcourt, Brace & World, 1921.

"A Prediction" by T. S. Eliot (pp. 55-56). Reprinted
from "A Prediction in Regard to Three English Authors,"
Vanity Fair (February 1924).

"The Pilgrimage" by Van Wyck Brooks (pp. 57-62). Reprinted from Days of the Phoenix. New York: E. P. Dutton,
1957, pp. 175-82.

"The Pilgrimage" by Edmund Wilson (pp. 63-71). Reprinted from "The Pilgrimage of Henry James," in The Shores of
Light. New York: Farrar, Straus & Young, 1952, pp. 217-28.

"The Ambassadors" by E. M. Forster (pp. 72-78). Reprinted from Aspects of the Novel. New York: Harcourt,
Brace & World, 1927, pp. 218-34.

"The New Generation" by William Troy (pp. 79-91). Reprinted from "Henry James and the Young Writers," The Book-
man (June 1931), pp. 351-58.

"The Essential Novelist?" by Pelham Edgar (pp. 92-101).
Reprinted from The Art of the Novel. New York: Macmillan,
1933, pp. 172-83.

"The Contemporary Subject" by Stephen Spender
(pp. 102-10). Reprinted from The Destructive Element.
London: Jonathan Cape, 1935, pp. 189-200.

"The Private Universe" by Stephen Spender (pp. 111-22).
Reprinted from The English Novelists. Edited by Derek
Verschoyle. London: Chatto & Windus, 1936.

"Symbolic Imagery" by Austin Warren (pp. 123-38). Re-printed from Rage for Order. Univ. of Michigan Press, 1959, pp. 142-61.
"The Museum World" by Adeline Tintner (pp. 139-55). Re-printed from "The Spoils of Henry James," Publications of the Modern Language Association, 61 (March 1946), 239-51.
"The Political Vocation" by Irving Howe (pp. 156-71). Reprinted from Politics and the Novel. New York: Horizon Press, 1957, pp. 139-56.
"The Tales" by Leon Edel (pp. 172-79). Reprinted from "General Introduction," in The Complete Tales of Henry James. See 1962.B25.

2   GEISMAR, MAXWELL. Henry James and the Jacobites. Boston: Houghton Mifflin, 463 pp. Published in England as Henry James and his Cult. London: Chatto and Windus, 1964, 463 pp.
        James has been vastly overpraised by academic critics, the James cult, who have not really understood the nature of James's work. James is not a major writer; he is "a ma-jor entertainer (something quite different) of a rare and exotic sort," an "esoteric orchid" in the garden of life and literature. His range of work was narrow; his late style "verbose and oratund"; his dramatic method resulted in the removal of "all possibilities of freedom in the nov-el itself." A reading of James's work supports the thesis that James is overrated and misunderstood. Partially re-printed: pp. 40-47 reprinted in 1968.A1; pp. 279-90 re-printed in 1969.A10. Reviewed: 1964.B17; 1965.B6; 1965.B86; 1966.B37; Philip Rahv, New York Herald Tribune Books (6 October), pp. 1, 8; Tony Tanner, Spectator (17 January 1964), p. 82; Louis Auchincloss, Virginia Quarterly Review, 40 (1964), 147-50; Modern Fiction Stud-ies, 10 (1964), 185; Oscar Cargill, South Atlantic Quar-terly, 63 (1964), 585-86; Oscar Cargill, American Litera-ture, 36 (1964), 93-94; John Lydenberg, New England Quar-terly, 37 (1964), 397-99; Kenneth Graham, Review of English Studies, 16 (1965), 218-20.

3   SHARP, SISTER M. CORONA, O.S.U. The "Confidante" in Henry James: Evolution and Moral Value of a Fictive Character. Notre Dame, Ind.: Univ. of Notre Dame Press, 305 pp.
        The use of the confidante is a dramatic device developed by James to supplement the limited point of view, thereby obtaining "greater lucidity." The confidante serves two purposes: (1) to provide the protagonist with information; and (2) to elicit information from the protagonist for the reader. Normally a subordinate character, the confidante

1963

is usually a woman; after The Portrait of a Lady James's
method and management of the confidante are unerring. Partially reprinted: pp. 67-96 reprinted in 1967.A5. For
dissertation see 1962.C8. Reviewed: 1966.B55; Modern Fiction Studies, 10 (1964), 186; Oscar Cargill, American Literature, 36 (1964), 372-73; Nineteenth-Century Fiction, 19
(1964), 311.

4   WIESENFARTH, JOSEPH. Henry James and the Dramatic Analogy:
     A Study of the Major Novels of the Middle Period. New
     York: Fordham Univ. Press, 139 pp.
        James developed a "theory of the dramatic novel" and in-
     cluded in his "dramatized narrative" five elements: "lan-
     guage, action, scene, picture, and centre." Analysis and
     evaluation of the four novels of the middle period (The
     Spoils of Poynton, What Maisie Knew, The Awkward Age, and
     The Sacred Fount) reveal the ways in which James applied
     his theory to his work. For dissertation see 1962.C9. Re-
     viewed: 1966.B55; Modern Fiction Studies, 9:183; Miriam
     Allott, Review of English Studies, 15 (1964), 442-43.

1963 B SHORTER WRITINGS

1   ABEL, DARREL. "Henry James," in his American Literature:
     Masterworks of American Realism: Twain, Howells, James.
     Vol. 3. Woodbury, N.Y.: Barron's Educational Series,
     pp. 215-363.
        A biographical and critical overview of James's life and
     work, this extended essay treats important James works in-
     dividually with plot summary and critical analysis.

2   ALTICK, RICHARD D. "Textual Study," in his The Art of Liter-
     ary Research. New York: W. W. Norton & Co., p. 49.
        In the first American edition of The Ambassadors Chap-
     ter 29 was printed before Chapter 28, an error not correct-
     ed until the 1957 Harpers edition.

3   ANDERSON, QUENTIN. "Introduction," in his edition of The Por-
     trait of a Lady. New York: Washington Square Press,
     pp. v-xiii.
        This novel "has a clear, sharp, morning freshness." It
     is a more ambitious work than its predecessors "because it
     dramatizes the connection between morality and aesthetic
     judgment."

4   AOKI, TSUGIO. "Strether's Imagination: On Henry James's <u>The</u>
    <u>Ambassadors</u>." <u>Studies in English Literature</u> (English Lit-
    erary Society of Japan, Univ. of Tokyo), 39 (March),
    33-49. [Japanese]
        The Jamesian historic sense consists of the contrast be-
    tween middle age and youth; parallels to these periods can
    be seen in the now-lost romantic period of France and the
    thriving industrial age of the United States. Strether's
    romantic imagination appears in effect more fitting for the
    past, when James's own creative imagination is much
    grander.

5   ARMS, GEORGE. "James's 'The Birthplace': Over a Pulpit-
    Edge." <u>Tennessee Studies in Literature</u>, 8:61-69.
        James's images and diction suggest that Gedge may be "a
    type of Christian minister."

6   BEAMS, DAVID W. "Consciousness in James's <u>The Sense of the</u>
    <u>Past</u>." <u>Criticism</u>, 5 (Spring), 148-72.
        The modes of consciousness employed by James in the four
    books of <u>The Sense of the Past</u> help give it "perhaps the
    most brilliant structure of any of his novels."

7   BERNARD, KENNETH. "Henry James's Unspoken Discourse in 'Mrs.
    Medwin.'" <u>Discourse</u>, 6 (Autumn), 310-14.
        Part of the success of the ironic "Mrs. Medwin" is
    achieved by characters who deal with essentially vulgar
    matters in subtly indirect verbal transactions.

8   BLACKALL, JEAN FRANTZ. "<u>The Sacred Fount</u> as a Comedy of the
    Limited Observer." <u>Publications of the Modern Language As-</u>
    <u>sociation of America</u>, 78 (September), 384-93.
        The limited observer-narrator "with his head perpetually
    in a theoretic, psychologic cloud" has an ironic relation-
    ship with the other characters that generates sustained
    high comedy.

9   BLACKMUR, R. P. "Henry James," in <u>Literary History of the</u>
    <u>United States</u>. Edited by Robert E. Spiller et al. Third
    Edition, Revised. New York: Macmillan, pp. 1039-64.
        Reprint of an essay which considers James's life and
    work.

10 BLANKE, GUSTAV H. "Aristokratie und Gentleman im Englischen
    und Amerikanischen Roman des 19. und 20. Jahrhunderts."
    <u>Germanisch-Romantische Monatsschrift, Neue Folge</u>, ns 13,
    (July), 281-306. [German]

The differing criteria of the "gentleman" in the English and American novel are discussed, as well as the relationship of the aristocracy to the other classes and various writers' portrayals of the ideal gentleman. James's ideal gentleman unites American moral integrity with European manners and aesthetic sensibility.

11 BLIVEN, NAOMI. "Lessons in the Master." New Yorker, 39 (7 September), 151-57.
    Leon Edel in the first three volumes of his biography of Henry James captures the "passion" James channeled into his art as well as "an accounting of what that channelling cost him." Review of 1962.A1 and 1962.A2.

12 BRYDEN, RONALD. "The Wounds of Judgment." Spectator, 210 (10 May), 605.
    Although Leon Edel "is not a particularly profound literary critic," his third volume of the James biography is significant for its elucidation of James's relationship with Constance Fenimore Woolson. Review of 1962.A2.

13 BURGESS, C. F. "The Seeds of Art: Henry James's Donnée." Literature and Psychology, 13 (Summer), 67-73.
    An examination of the metaphors used by James to describe the donnée in his preface to the New York Edition reveals two distinct categories that correspond to a conscious and nonconscious stage in the creative process. The predominant metaphors of the conscious stage are sensory and the predominant metaphor of the nonconscious stage is the "seed-pearl image."

14 CARGILL, OSCAR. "Afterword," in his edition of The Portrait of a Lady. A Signet Classic. New York: New American Library, pp. 547-56.
    This international novel is also a nineteenth century novel, and the portrait of Isabel Archer (along with portraits of other James heroines) belongs not "to the gallery of native art but to some cosmopolitan Louvre."

15 CARGILL, OSCAR. "Introduction," in his edition of The Ambassadors. New York: Washington Square Press, pp. v-xviii.
    "Interesting as The Ambassadors is as an expression of Henry James' philosophy, its true immortality derives from its consequence as a pioneer work of art."

16   CARGILL, OSCAR. "The Turn of the Screw and Alice James."
      Publications of the Modern Language Association of America,
      78 (June), 238-49.
          In addition to his knowledge of Freud's "The Case of
      Miss Lucy R.," James had a sister with hysteria, which
      lends credence to the belief that he purposefully wrote a
      ghost-tale with a psychological overlay. Reprinted with an
      "Afterword" in 1965.B11; also reprinted in 1966.A5.

*17   CASTELLANOS, ROSARIO. "El fin de la inocencia." Revista de
      la Universidad de Mexico, 7 (July), 4-7.
          Cited in Beatrice Ricks, comp. Henry James: A Bibliog-
      raphy of Secondary Works. Scarecrow Author Bibliographies,
      No. 24. Metuchen, N.J.: Scarecrow, Item 1212.

18   CLARK, H. H. "Henry James and Science: The Wings of the
      Dove." Transactions of the Wisconsin Academy of Sciences,
      Arts, and Letters, 52:1-15.
          The ethical and moral problems of Milly Theale's "strug-
      gle for existence" are aesthetically portrayed in terms of
      language and ideas commonly associated with scientific con-
      cepts contemporaneous with the novel (Social Darwinism be-
      ing the central concept).

19   COLOGNESI, SILVANA. "Apparenza e realtá in The Awkward Age."
      Studi Americani, no. 9, pp. 227-48. [Italian]
          The Awkward Age, though not one of the best of James's
      works, gives an intelligent insight into what can be called
      his "transition period." Nanda and Aggie come out of their
      awkward age and become women in the midst of a London so-
      ciety, itself going through an epoch of transition. In the
      novel are the strain, hurt and complications of generations
      clashing for survival, and the parallel phenomenon of a
      changing of moral values. James towers in this work in the
      portrayal of detached irony, dismounting situations, peo-
      ple, impressions.

20   COX, C. B. "Henry James and the Art of Personal Relation-
      ships," in his The Free Spirit: A Study of Liberal Human-
      ism in the Novels of George Eliot, Henry James, E. M. For-
      ster, Virginia Woolf, and Angus Wilson. London: Oxford
      Univ. Press, pp. 38-73.
          James's novels can be seen as a quest for a "vital,
      creative way of life for the free spirit" that ends with
      Maggie in The Golden Bowl.

21   CRANFILL, THOMAS M., and ROBERT L. CLARK, JR. "Caste in
     James's The Turn of the Screw." Texas Studies in Litera-
     ture and Language, 5 (Summer), 189-98.
         The caste structure of The Turn of the Screw is an im-
     portant key to understanding the relationship of the gov-
     erness and Mrs. Grose and the antipathy Mrs. Grose consis-
     tently expresses for Peter Quint.

22   DREW, ELIZABETH. "The Game of Art: Henry James: The Por-
     trait of a Lady," in her The Novel: A Modern Guide to Fif-
     teen English Masterpieces. A Laurel Edition. New York:
     Dell, pp. 224-44.
         Focuses on the human relationships in the novel.

23   EDEL, LEON. "Afterword," in his edition of The American.
     Signet Classics. New York: New American Library of World
     Literature, pp. 326-33.
         This book is "a masterpiece of American romanticism in
     which James shows us his profound grasp of what he was ul-
     timately to call 'the Americano-European legend.'"

24   EDEL, LEON. The Complete Tales of Henry James. Vols. 5-8.
     Philadelphia: Lippincott.
         Edel states in the "Introduction: 1883-1884" (vol. 5,
     pp. 7-11) that in these tales James is "writing at the top
     of his form and quite in the comic tradition of Moliere";
     he is "concerned above all with the anomalies and hypocri-
     sies of society in London and New York." In "Introduction:
     1884-1888" (vol. 6, pp. 7-12), he suggests that James
     paints "moral pictures" in the tales of these years and
     "shows the mischief created by those who meddle in other
     people's lives." The finest of the seven tales included is
     "The Aspern Papers." In "Introduction: 1888-1891" (vol. 7,
     pp. 7-13) Edel observes that with the last tale included in
     this volume, "The Pupil," James began his "most brilliant
     decade of short-story writing." In "Introduction: 1891-
     1892" (vol. 8, pp. 7-12) he notes that these thirteen tales
     were written while James was writing plays. James returns
     "constantly to the principal preoccupation of his fiction,
     the study of personal relations and, in particular, famil-
     ial relations." Reviewed: Herbert Ruhm, Sewanee Review,
     71:675-80.

25   EDEL, LEON. "Introduction," in his edition of The Portrait of
     a Lady. Riverside Editions. Boston: Houghton Mifflin,
     pp. v-xx.
         When Henry James created Isabel Archer, he placed the
     "first modern American woman" in the gallery of the world's

great fiction. Isabel was concerned with what her role in life should be . . . [and] she was egotistical enough to feel that she deserved the best the world could offer."

26   EMERSON, DONALD. "Henry James." <u>Arts in Society</u>, 2 (Spring-Summer), 126–33.
James's novels are accounts "not of what happens, but of what someone thinks about what happens."

27   EMERSON, DONALD. "Henry James: A Sentimental Tourist and Restless Analyst." <u>Transactions of the Wisconsin Academy of Sciences, Arts, and Letters</u>, 52:17–25.
James's travel accounts confirm that he was "a man of imagination" and complement other self-revelations.

28   FABRIS, ALBERTA. "La Francia di Henry James." <u>Studi Americani</u>, no. 9, pp. 173–226. [Italian]
James's love for Europe, especially for France and England, influenced his personality, both as a writer and as a man.

29   FADIMAN, CLIFTON. "Prefatory Note," in his edition of <u>Henry James: "The Beast in the Jungle</u>." Engravings by Blair Hughes Stanton. Kentfield, Calif.: Allen Press, 5 pp. (n.p.).
This tale "is the best of James's shorter fictions, combining the utmost concentration of effect with the utmost inclusiveness of meaning." Reprinted from <u>The Short Stories of Henry James</u>. New York: Random House, 1945.

30   GALE, ROBERT L. "The Abasement of Mrs. Warren Hope." <u>Publications of the Modern Language Association of America</u>, 78 (March), 98–102.
The Hopes are not the victims of the Northmores, but Mrs. Warren Hope is a paranoid who distorts reality.

31   GALE, ROBERT L. "James's 'The Middle Years,' II." <u>Explicator</u>, 22 (November), Item 22.
James leads the reader of the revised edition of "The Middle Years" to believe that the short story will have a second part. But just as Dencombe, the dying novelist of the story, is "deprived of an expected second part of his life," so, too, the reader is deprived of a second section.

1963

32   GALE, ROBERT L.   "A Note on Henry James's 'The Real Thing.'"
      Studies in Short Fiction, 1 (Fall), 65-66.
          The story's reference to black-and-white illustrations
      is a double entendre that pokes fun at the periodical,
      Black and White, in which the story first appeared.

33   GARD, A. R.   "Critics of The Golden Bowl."   Melbourne Critical
      Review, 6:102-109.
          A synthesis of the critical interpretations of The Gold-
      en Bowl postulated by J. J. Firebaugh and F. R. Leavis
      yields a new approach: James consciously develops the
      sinister aspects of the characters of the Ververs and con-
      sciously intends and achieves "total ambiguity."

34   GEISMAR, MAXWELL.   "Henry James: 'The Beast in the Jungle.'"
      Nineteenth-Century Fiction, 18 (June), 35-42.
          "The Beast in the Jungle," as the most famous of James's
      "wasted life" stories and containing many revealing auto-
      biographical elements, shows the "beast" representing not
      only Marcher's destiny (i.e. lack of destiny), but also the
      animal passions in man which Marcher had avoided, and the
      human motives which James consciously rose "above," if un-
      consciously repressed, in his works.

35   GEISMAR, MAXWELL.   "Henry James: The Psychology of the Key-
      hole."   Ramparts, 1 (March), 57-64.
          An analysis of The Sacred Fount, the "most perplexing,
      enigmatic story that Henry James ever wrote," reveals that
      "the whole later Jamesian method of psychological observa-
      tion" produced a "key-hole psychology . . . in which the
      prurient observer is not only covered with guilt and shame
      at what he has finally 'seen' (what he has always imagined
      about sexual love), but also becomes the victim of the
      sexual speculations which he has planted in the minds of
      all his assistant snoops."

36   GEISMAR, MAXWELL.   "The Wings of the Dove: or, False Gold."
      Atlantic Monthly, 212 (August), 93-98.
          In this novel James worked in "a peculiar sphere of
      values" and used "contrived methods of fiction," but this
      work holds the reader's interest and stimulates his
      imagination.

37   GENET.   "Letter from Paris."   New Yorker, 38 (12 January),
      104.
          Theatre news from Paris includes a review of a dramati-
      zation of "The Beast in the Jungle," adapted for the stage

by James Lord and Marguerite Duras: this "distinguished theatre contribution" is a "delicately suave dramatization."

38 GERBER, RICHARD. "Die Magie der Namen bei Henry James." Anglia, 81:175-97. [German]
    Henry James carefully selected names, mindful of the significance of names for the characters themselves and for their roles in his novels.

39 GHISELIN, BREWSTER. "Automatism, Intention, and Autonomy in the Novelist's Production." Daedalus, 92 (Spring), 297-311.
    Artists' use of the "subconscious" or "unconscious" mind in artistic creation is discussed and frequent reference is made to Henry James.

40 GINSBERG, ROBERT. "Criticism, Jamesian Criticism, and James's Criticism of James: 'The Turn of the Screw,'" in Criticism and Theory in the Arts. Edited by Robert Ginsberg. Paris: Parnassus Publications, pp. 20-37.
    A survey of the critical controversy caused by varied interpretations of The Turn of the Screw reveals that this story has elicited more responses than anything else James wrote. Reprinted in 1966.A5.

41 GREEN, MARTIN. "Henry James and the Great Tradition." London Magazine, ns 2 (January), 32-45.
    James seduces readers into accepting that aesthetic sensibility is a reliable guide "through every moral and intellectual tangle," but the vision of life embodied in his novels does not justify the reader's agreeing with him. Reprinted in 1965.B35.

42 HARTMAN, GEOFFREY H. "The Heroics of Realism." Yale Review, 53 (Autumn), 26-35.
    For the contemporary novel to maintain its realism the novelist must remain depersonalized from his subject matter and suspend the reader's judgment of the hero, as Henry James has done in his fiction.

43 HARVEY, W. J. "Work in Progress: I: Character and the context of things." Essays in Criticism, 13 (January), 50-66.
    For many novelists "aesthetic value becomes a metaphor for moral value." An examination of The Portrait of a Lady shows how "rich and subtly [James] exploited this interplay between aesthetics and ethics." Printed with additions as Chapter 2 in 1965.B48.

1963

44   HERX, MARY ELLEN. "The Monomyth in 'The Great Good Place.'"
       College English, 24 (March), 439-43.
         Although James's tale antedates Joseph Campbell's theory
      of the patterns of myths paralleling dreams and Jung's
      archetype of the unconscious, it presents the monomyth in
      George Dane's dream of the archetypal adventure.

45   HIRSCH, DAVID H. "William Dean Howells and Daisy Miller."
       English Language Notes, 1 (December), 123-28.
         Howells's emphasis on Daisy's merits and exclusion of
      her liabilities reflects his "gentle" approach to negative
      truths about women.

46   HOFFMAN, FREDERICK J. "The Expense and Power of Greatness:
       An Essay on Leon Edel's James." Virginia Quarterly Review,
       39 (Summer), 518-28.
         Leon Edel's biography both captures and helps explain
      the development of James, who represents "the nineteenth-
      century American imagination at its finest." Review of
      1962.A1 and 1962.A2.

47   HOLDER, ALAN. "The Lesson of the Master: Ezra Pound and
       Henry James." American Literature, 35 (March), 71-79.
         Following Pound's extensive exposure to James's work
      while preparing an article for the Little Review, James
      "became firmly established in his [Pound's] mind as a model
      of excellence, a touchstone to be employed when discussing
      other prose writers."

48   HOPKINS, VIOLA. "Gloriani and the Tides of Taste." Nine-
       teenth-Century Fiction, 18 (June) 65-71.
         Though Gloriani has talent and will in Roderick Hudson
      (1875), his art is considered less than the best because he
      lacks faith. That he then is so tremendously admired and
      successful in The Ambassadors (1909) reflects James's sen-
      sitivity to the changes in taste that had occurred in the
      intervening years.

*49   HOSHIOKA, MOTOKO. "On The Turn of the Screw." Journal of the
       Society of English and American Literature (Kwansei Gakiun
       Univ.), 7 (March), 87-96.
         Cited in Beatrice Ricks, comp. Henry James: A Bibliog-
      raphy of Secondary Works. Scarecrow Author Bibliographies,
      No. 24. Metuchen, N.J.: Scarecrow, 1975, Item 1298.

50   IVES, C. B.   "James's Ghosts in The Turn of the Screw."
     Nineteenth-Century Fiction, 18 (September), 183-89.
          A look at the appearances of the ghosts suggests they
     are the "new type," the "psychical" ghosts James claimed
     he would not but did in fact render.

51   KAYE, JULIAN B.   "The Awkward Age, The Sacred Fount, and The
     Ambassadors: Another Figure in the Carpet." Nineteenth-
     Century Fiction, 17 (March), 339-51.
          The Awkward Age and The Sacred Fount "may be read as
     preliminary sketches for The Ambassadors." Looking at The
     Ambassadors in relation to the two novels preceding it
     helps "explain not only James's ease of composition but
     also the achievement . . . of great lucidity and harmony of
     form with great complexity and richness of content."

52   KIRK, CLARA M.   "'The Brighter Side' of Fiction--According to
     Howells and James." College English, 24 (March), 463-64.
          Howells and James shared similar dislikes for the gloomy
     morbidity of Russian writers and an affinity for the joy-
     ful, happier aspects of life.

53   KNOX, GEORGE.   "Incubi and Succubi in The Turn of the Screw."
     Western Folklore, 22 (April), 122-23.
          The alignment of Miss Jessel with the role of succubi
     and Peter Quint with that of incubi could provide a key for
     interpreting the various relationships in the story.

54   LAUBER, JOHN.   "The Contrast: A Study in the Concept of Inno-
     cence." English Language Notes, 1 (September), 33-37.
          The contrasts in Royall Tyler's drama "strikingly an-
     ticipate, almost a hundred years in advance, the interna-
     tional theme of Henry James."

55   LEAVIS, F. R.   "James as Critic," in Henry James: Selected
     Literary Criticism.   Edited by Morris Shapira.   London:
     Heinemann; New York: Horizon, pp. xiii-xxiii.
          James's criticism should be read with discrimination,
     because "its interest doesn't invariably, or often wholly,
     lie in its convincing rightness and inevitableness."

56   LEVINE, GEORGE.   "Isabel, Gwendolen, and Dorothea." Journal
     of English Literary History, 30 (September), 244-57.
          James's The Portrait of a Lady incorporates the "Doro-
     thea sections of Middlemarch and the Gwendolen sections of
     Daniel Deronda in a novel of his own creation" without the
     defects of either.

1963

57 LEVINE, GEORGE. "Madame Bovary and the Disappearing Author."
    Modern Fiction Studies, 9 (Summer), 103-19.
        The author cannot disappear from his works, because the
    "characters are never autonomous, never independent of the
    mind which created them."

58 LUECKE, SISTER JANE MARIE. "The Princess Casamassima: Hya-
    cinth's Fallible Consciousness." Modern Philology, 60
    (May), 274-80.
        Hyacinth Robinson, with his "dangerous affinity" for se-
    lective perception, typifies the Jamesian protagonist and
    should not be considered heroic. Reprinted in 1968.A11.

59 LYTLE, ANDREW. "Impressionism, The Ego, and The First Per-
    son." Daedalus, 92 (Spring), 281-96.
        The success of impressionistic literature is dependent
    on a controlled first person narrative and the presence of
    an unobtrusive author.

60 MARCELL, DAVID W. "High Ideals and Catchpenny Realities in
    Henry James's The Portrait of a Lady," in Essays in Modern
    American Literature. Edited by Richard E. Langford. Stet-
    son Studies in Humanities, No. 1. Deland, Fla.: Stetson
    Univ. Press, pp. 26-34.
        Reprint of 1963.B61.

61 MARCELL, DAVID W. "High Ideals and Catchpenny Realities in
    Henry James's The Portrait of a Lady." Stetson Studies in
    the Humanities, 1:26-34.
        In the first half of the novel James traces the growth
    and refinement of Isabel's ideal; and in the second half,
    he dramatizes the "crushing impingement" of reality on the
    ideal and Isabel's "heroic response." Reprinted in
    1963.B60.

62 MASUNAGA, KEIICHI. "A Consideration of James's Technique:
    The Wings of the Dove." Gaikoku Bungaku Kenkyu, 7
    (December), 99-129. [Japanese]
        Maggie Verver is examined in relation to her change from
    a regal figure to an angelic one and in her contrast to
    Kate. In addition, James's technical experimentation with
    indirect method and the novel's central theme of life and
    death are discussed.

63   MATHEWS, J. CHESLEY. "Bibliographical Supplement: A Selec-
     tive Check List, 1955-1962," in Eight American Authors: A
     Review of Research and Criticism. Edited by Floyd Stovall.
     New York: W. W. Norton, pp. 458-66.
         An update of bibliography to supplement the essay by
     Robert E. Spiller, which had surveyed James bibliography
     through 1954. See 1963.B96.

64   MONTEIRO, GEORGE. "'Girlhood on the American Plan'--A Con-
     temporary Defense of Daisy Miller." Books at Brown, 19
     (May), 89-93.
         "Girlhood on the American Plan," published in the March
     1879 issue of the Atlantic, was in all probability the work
     of John Hay. Reprinted in full in this article, it is a
     "defense of James's 'authenticity' and of what may be
     termed his moral and patriotic responsibility."

65   MONTEIRO, GEORGE. "Henry James and John Hay." Books at
     Brown, 19 (May), 69-88.
         A complete account of the relationship of Henry James
     and John Hay, this article includes an annotated Calendar
     of Letters, which lists thirty-eight James letters, thirty-
     six to Hay and two to Mrs. Hay.

66   MONTEIRO, GEORGE. "Henry James and The American Academy of
     Arts and Letters." New England Quarterly, 36 (March),
     82-84.
         Henry James was elected unanimously as a member at the
     second meeting of the Academy. John Hay was influential in
     James's election.

67   MONTEIRO, GEORGE. "John Hay's Review of The Portrait of a
     Lady." Books at Brown, 19 (May), 95-104.
         John Hay's unsigned review of the novel, which appeared
     in the Tribune on December 25, 1881, is reprinted. Hay
     praised the book and predicted it would "remain one of the
     notable books of the time." Reprinted in 1965.A13.

68   MONTEIRO, GEORGE, ed. "Letters of Henry James to John Hay."
     Texas Studies in Literature and Language, 4 (Supplement),
     pp. 639-95.
         Thirty-six letters from James to John Hay (plus two to
     Mrs. Hay) not previously published partially document the
     thirty year friendship of Hay and James.

1963

69   MONTEIRO, GEORGE. "Letters to a 'Countryman': John Hay to
     Henry James." Books at Brown, 19 (May), 105-12.
         Seven letters from John Hay to Henry James and one let-
     ter from Mrs. Hay to Henry James are reprinted here along
     with an introduction and full notes on the content.

70   MONTEIRO, GEORGE. "The Manuscript of The Tragic Muse."
     American Notes and Queries, 1 (January), 68.
         An exchange of letters in June of 1890 between James and
     John Hay suggests the possibility that The Tragic Muse
     manuscript, although presently unlocated, may be extant.

71   MONTEIRO, GEORGE. "The New York Tribune on Henry James, 1881-
     1882." Bulletin of the New York Public Library, 67
     (February), 71-81.
         During the twelve-month period from 1881 until 1882, the
     New York Tribune shifted from enthusiastic support of James
     to harsh criticism as a result of James's "The Point of
     View" and Howells's infamous "biographical sketch" of
     James.

72   MONTEIRO, GEORGE. "An Unpublished Henry James Letter." Notes
     and Queries, ns 10 (April), 143-44.
         James responds to Henry Adams, who has requested copies
     of correspondence between James and John Hay to be included
     in the official edition of Hay's correspondence.

73   MUKHERJI, NIRMAL. "The Problem of Evil in The Turn of the
     Screw--A Study in Ambiguity." Calcutta Review, 168 (July),
     63-70.
         The nature of evil is not defined in The Turn of the
     Screw, because James intentionally portrayed evil as an
     ambiguity, which is more gruesome because it is undefinable.

74   MURRAY, DONALD M. "Henry James in Advanced Composition
     Course." College English, 25 (October), 26-30.
         James serves both as a model and an instructor for fic-
     tion writing in college composition.

75   NAIK, M. K. "The Draught from the 'Golden Bowl.'" Journal of
     the Karnatak Univ., 7:199-217.
         The impact of Europe on the American character is por-
     trayed in various ways by Henry James in his novels which
     show Americans in a European setting.

76   NIEMI, PEARL C. "The Art of <u>Crime and Punishment</u>." <u>Modern</u>
      <u>Fiction Studies</u>, 9 (Winter 1963-1964), 291-313.
           An analysis of <u>Crime and Punishment</u> using Jamesian crit-
      ical terms leads to the conclusion that in this novel
      "Dostoevsky 'out Jameses James.'"

77   O'FAOLAIN, SEAN. "O'Faolain on James," in his <u>Storytellers</u>
      <u>and Their Art</u>. Edited by Georgianne Trask and Charles
      Burkhart. Anchor Book. Garden City, N.Y.: Doubleday,
      pp. 343-52.
           James's main weakness in the short story is that "he did
      not recognize enough that in short-story writing there can
      be no development of characters."

78   OHARA, CHIYOKO. "James's Consciousness and the International
      Theme." <u>The Albion</u> (Kyoto Univ.), 9 (November), 104-23.
           James's desertion of his native land was due to the cul-
      tural void in America as well as to Americans' romantic
      view of the world. His realization of man as a social
      creature called for the international theme in which an
      innocent American confronted experience. <u>The Portrait of</u>
      <u>a Lady</u> is the culminating work utilizing this theme.

79   OKITA, HAJIME. "Henry James's Contribution to American Liter-
      ature (II)." <u>Jimbun</u> (Kyoto Prefectural Univ.), 15 (Novem-
      ber), 1-21. [Japanese]
           James's influence upon the following writers is dis-
      cussed: Henry Blake Fuller, Anne Douglas Sedgwick, Willa
      Cather, and Scott Fitzgerald. <u>See</u> 1962.B82 and 1964.B76
      for Parts I and III.

80   OLIVER, EDITH. Review of <u>The Summer of Daisy Miller</u>. <u>New</u>
      <u>Yorker</u>, 39 (8 June), 126-27.
           This dramatic adaption by Bertram Greene of <u>Daisy Miller</u>
      is "done all wrong and misses completely."

81   ONISHI, AKIO. "Henry James: Trilogy of International Theme."
      <u>Bungaku Ronshu</u> (Kansai Univ.), 12 (January), 1-45. [Japa-
      nese]
           "The Pension Beaurepas," "A Bundle of Letters," and "The
      Point of View" share the key elements of "picturesqueness,"
      "right and wrong," and "vulgarity," which are utilized to
      show the differences in European and American civilization.
      James's use of point of view reflects his understanding
      that one cannot have the absolute view.

1963

82   OWEN, ELIZABETH. "'The Given Appearance' of Charlotte Verver."
      Essays in Criticism, 13 (October), 364-74.
          A proper appreciation of Maggie in The Golden Bowl can
      only come when Charlotte is seen for what she is--"clever,
      dangerous, and brilliantly evil."

83   OZICK, CYNTHIA. "The Jamesian Parable: The Sacred Fount."
      Bucknell Review, 11 (May), 55-70.
          Read in the light of the principles of parable, The
      Sacred Fount is a key for approaching other Jamesian works.

*84   RAHV, PHILIP. "Introduction," in his edition of Eight Great
      American Short Novels. New York: Berkley Publishing Co.,
      p. 11.
          Cited in Beatrice Ricks, comp. Henry James: A Bibliog-
      raphy of Secondary Works. Scarecrow Author Bibliographies,
      No. 24. Metuchen, N.J.: Scarecrow, Item 3207.

85   REID, STEPHEN. "The Beast in the Jungle and A Painful Case:
      Two Different Sufferings." American Imago, 20 (Fall),
      221-39.
          Both James Duffy and John Marcher experience a sense of
      isolation and frustration as a result of their neurotic
      personalities--Duffy is compulsive and Marcher is phobic.
      The two authors bring their themes into a universal per-
      spective utilizing two differing methods: "James empha-
      sizes the pain and the loneliness by incorporating the un-
      pleasantness and dread within Marcher's hallucination,
      Joyce by articulating the distance Duffy stands from all
      he knows of life: Dublin."

86   ROGERS, FRANKLIN R. "The Road to Reality: Burlesque Travel
      Literature and Mark Twain's Roughing It." Bulletin of the
      New York Public Library, 67 (March), 155-68.
          Twain developed a theme in Roughing It and Innocents
      Abroad which anticipates the theme of the international nov-
      els of Henry James.

87   ROSENFIELD, CLAIRE. "The Shadow Within: The Conscious and
      Unconscious Use of the Double." Daedalus, 92 (Spring),
      326-44.
          This discussion of the use of the Double in literature
      includes a brief analysis of "The Jolly Corner," in which
      Spencer Brydon denies the existence of his double.

88 RUBIN, LOUIS D., JR. "One More Turn of the Screw." Modern
    Fiction Studies, 9 (Winter 1963-1964), 314-28.
        Douglas, introduced in the Prologue to The Turn of the
    Screw, is the same person as Miles, and the story he tells
    is about himself. This leads the reader to suspect the
    reliability of the governess as narrator and suggests that
    the story is an allegory. The governess cannot be taken as
    the heroine. The point about the puzzle of The Turn of the
    Screw is its "ultimate insolubility." Reprinted in
    1967.B86 and 1968.A11.

89 RUHM, HERBERT. "The Complete Tales of Henry James." Sewanee
    Review, 71 (Autumn), 675-80.
        These first four volumes (of a projected 12 volumes) of
    James tales, edited by Leon Edel, have the "advantage of
    comprehensiveness, textual uniformity, and developmental
    interest," but more textual scholarship leading to a vari-
    orum edition of the tales will be needed to present the
    complete picture of James's artistic development. Review
    of 1962.B25.

90 SANNA, VITTORIA. "Considerazioni intorno a The Turn of the
    Screw." Annali Istituto Universitario Orientale, Napoli,
    Sezione Germanica, 6:105-37. [Italian]
        Henry James's description of the governess in The Turn
    of the Screw was influenced by Bronte's Jane Eyre, on which
    James wrote an analysis for Harper's Weekly. The similari-
    ty exists in the identical situations (for example, when
    the two governesses are introduced into their new environ-
    ments) and in the first descriptions of their pupils.

91 SCANLON, LAWRENCE E. "Henry James's 'Compositional Resource
    and Value Intrinsic.'" Forum (Houston), 4 (Spring-Summer),
    13-19.
        An examination of James's methodological approach to the
    novel and of his conception of character and scene suggests
    that he employed mechanical and organic functionalism in
    his work.

92 SCOGGINS, JAMES. "'The Author of Beltraffio': A Reapportion-
    ment of Guilt." Texas Studies in Literature and Language,
    5 (Summer), 265-70.
        Reiman assigns the narrator too large a portion of moral
    responsibility and guilt while giving Mark Ambient too
    small a portion. Response to 1962.B95.

1963

93   SLABEY, ROBERT M.   "'The Holy Innocents' and 'The Turn of the
     Screw.'"   Die Neueren Sprachen, 12 (April), 170-73.
        The temporal structure of The Turn of the Screw is me-
     ticulously developed to make it clear that the tale is told
     on December 28, the day of the Feast of Holy Innocents, a
     fact that underscores the story's theme.

94   SNOW, LOTUS.   "'A Story of Cabinets and Chairs and Tables':
     Images of Morality in The Spoils of Poynton and The Golden
     Bowl."   Journal of English Literary History, 30 (December),
     413-35.
        In The Spoils of Poynton and The Golden Bowl James's
     primary vehicle for demonstrating "the absolute union of
     art and morality" is imagery.

95   SPILKA, MARK.   "Turning the Freudian Screw: How Not To Do
     It."   Literature and Psychology, 13 (Fall), 105-11.
        Past Freudian interpretations of The Turn of the Screw
     have not been sufficiently Freudian; they have failed to
     carry the erotic imagery of the tale to its fullest appli-
     cation--an application to the society James was criticiz-
     ing. Reprinted in 1966.A5. Response in 1964.B58. See
     also 1964.B94 and 1964.B30.

96   SPILLER, ROBERT E.   "Henry James," in Eight American Authors:
     A Review of Research and Criticism.   Edited by Floyd Sto-
     vall. New York: Norton, pp. 364-418.
        This bibliographical essay is divided into three sec-
     tions: Bibliography, Text, Manuscripts; Biography; and
     Criticism. Originally published in 1956, this essay sur-
     veys James bibliography through 1954. See 1963.B63 for
     supplement.

97   SPILLER, ROBERT E., et al., eds.   "Henry James," in Literary
     History of the United States: Bibliography.   Third Edi-
     tion, Revised. New York: Macmillan, pp. 1472-73.
        Two bibliographies published earlier (1948, 1959) are
     combined in this third edition.

98   STAFFORD, WILLIAM T.   "The Ending of James's The American: A
     Defense of the Early Version."   Nineteenth-Century Fiction,
     18 (June), 86-89.
        Given the "pattern of reversals" in the novel, the un-
     revised ending is most consonant with the thematic, struc-
     tural, and tonal elements of the work. Reprinted in
     1971.A7.

99 STAFFORD, WILLIAM T. <u>James's "Daisy Miller": The Story, The</u>
    <u>Play, The Critics</u>. Scribner Research Anthologies. New
    York: Charles Scribner's Sons.
       Contents: A collection of materials designed for use
    with students doing a "controlled-research" paper. It in-
    cludes the texts of both the tale and the comedy based on
    the tale, as well as eleven articles giving contemporary
    reactions to both story and play, seven pieces showing the
    "Social and Cultural Reaction"; and eight articles on "Lit-
    erary Considerations." Topics for research and sources for
    library research are included. (Of the twenty-four sepa-
    rate critical pieces in this anthology only the four pub-
    lished since 1960 will be listed below.)
       The "Introduction" (pp. 1-4) by William T. Stafford
    notes that no other work of James's created so much "noto-
    riety" and "fame" as <u>Daisy Miller</u>. Since James wrote both
    the story and the play, we have an example of a writer's
    work in two mediums using the same materials. This collec-
    tion provides the critical response to both story and play
    from the very beginning in newspaper reviews as well as
    James's view of the works and later critical evaluations.
       "Daisy: The Good Bad Girl" by Leslie A. Fiedler
    (pp. 140-41). Reprinted from 1960.B33.
       "<u>Daisy Miller</u>: An Abortive Quest for Innocence" by
    James W. Gargano (pp. 150-53). Reprinted from 1960.B40.
       "The Tragedy and the Comedy and the Irony" by Wayne C.
    Booth (pp. 157-58). Reprinted from 1961.B8.

100 STAFFORD, WILLIAM T. "Literary Allusions in James's Pref-
    aces." <u>American Literature</u>, 35 (March), 60-70.
       James's extensive knowledge of European and classical
    literature is evident and provides a key to those authors
    and works he emulated and to those whose shortcomings he
    sought to avoid.

101 STEEN, JAMES T. "The Vision of Henry James," in <u>Lectures on</u>
    <u>Modern Novelists</u>. Edited by Arthur T. Broes and others.
    Carnegie Series in English, Number 7. Pittsburgh: Car-
    negie Institute of Technology, pp. 55-65.
       James "was working ever farther toward the outer edge of
    consciousness, the full realization of which he had always
    held to be the highest purpose of a human being." At the
    limits of consciousness, he believed there existed "a 'pos-
    sibility' which transcended or enveloped the evil which
    poisoned it."

1963

102 STEWART, J. I. M. "Henry James," in his Eight Modern Writers.
Oxford History of English Literature. Vol. 12. New York
and Oxford: Oxford Univ. Press, pp. 71-121.
A biographical and critical overview of James's life and
work.

103 SUTTON, WALTER. Modern American Criticism. Englewood Cliffs,
N.J.: Prentice-Hall, passim.
In this historical and critical examination of five modern American critical approaches, passing references are
made to James.

104 SWAN, MICHAEL. "Introduction," in his edition of Henry James:
Selected Short Stories. Baltimore: Penguin Books,
pp. 7-11.
"From the whimsical to the profound, from the horrific
to the romantic, from the brilliant to the light-hearted,"
these stories have been chosen for the James devotee and
also for the beginning James reader. (Included are "The
Last of the Valerii," "The Real Thing," "The Lesson of the
Master," and "Daisy Miller.")

105 TADA, TOSHIO. "James's Marks of Polish: 'The Point of View.'"
Bungaku Ronshu (Kansai Univ.), 12 (January), 47-58. [Japa-
nese]
A comparison of the texts of the original edition and
the New York edition reveals that James's later style rein-
forced effective indirectness of characterization to the
degree of apparent vagueness.

106 TADOKORO, NOBUSHIGE. "The Castle of Chillon and the Colosse-
um." Bunri Ronso (Fukuoka Univ.), 7 (March), 273-92.
[Japanese]
The two sites are not only valuable as places to represent Jamesian picturesqueness and Byronic desire for freedom, but also as the effective setting in each work for the
thematic question of American innocence and European
experience.

*107 TAKAHASHI, MICHI. "The Design and 'Point of View' of Henry
James's Roderick Hudson." Essays and Studies in British
and American Literature (Tokyo Women's Christian College),
11 (Summer), 1-29.
Cited in 1970.B72, p. 321.

108 TAKANO, FUMI. "The Nature of Tragi-Comedy in Henry James."
     The Tsuda Review, 8 (November), 35-47. [Japanese]
         James's comic element is not only on the surface but is
     deep-rooted, because of "his vision of the somewhat ridicu-
     lous, certainly ineffectual heroism of his heroes, their
     beautiful quixotism which, as Faulkner has said, is a lit-
     tle sad also." Strether is carefully examined in terms of
     this comic element.

109 TANNER, TONY. "Henry James's Subjective Adventurer: The
     Sacred Fount." Essays and Studies, 16:37-55.
         James's In the Cage and The Sacred Fount deal with the
     fundamental predicament of the artist who is "excluded from
     the frame of society" but at the same time is its con-
     science and seeks to discover its meaning. Reprinted in
     1965.B107 and 1973.A6.

110 THOMSON, FRED C. "James's 'The Jolly Corner.'" Explicator,
     22 (December), Item 28.
         The "eerily luminous submarine metaphor" used by James
     "as Spencer Brydon descends the staircase to confront his
     'monstrous' alter ego" is especially appropriate, because
     it "expresses with remarkable nuance the main thematic and
     psychological substance of 'The Jolly Corner.'"

111 TOCHIHARA, TOMOO. "Henry James and Religion--Religious Con-
     sciousness and Evil in his Literary Works." Ronko (Kwan-
     seigakuin Univ.), 10 (September), 97-109. [Japanese]
         A study of James and religion which includes the in-
     fluence of his father as well as James's own attitude to
     religion and the religious aspects in his works (such as
     the external approach to Catholicism in Guy Domville and
     the supernatural evil in The Turn of the Screw) shows that
     though James was not a sectarian believer, he was an artist
     who held a Christian moral view of men.

112 TYLER, PARKER. "The Sacred Fount: 'The Actuality Pretentious
     and Vain' vs. 'The Case Rich and Edifying.'" Modern Fic-
     Studies, 9 (Summer), 127-38.
         James's personal tone is clearly present through the
     fictional "I" of the narrator in The Sacred Fount. James's
     idea is that when two people fall in love, they wage a bat-
     tle such as the one in The Sacred Fount, in which the nar-
     rator grows weary and witless, while Mrs. Briss becomes
     strong and youthful, acquiring new charm and wit.

1963

113   VAN DER BEETS, RICHARD. "A Note on Henry James's 'Western
       Barbarian.'" Western Humanities Review, 17 (Spring),
       175-78.
          The "similarities of both incident and phrase" between
       Christopher Newman and the persona of Mark Twain as re-
       vealed in The Innocents Abroad suggest a Twain influence on
       James's writing.

114   WALKER, DON D. "The Gun and Lasso of Henry James." Western
       Humanities Review, 17 (Spring), 178-80.
          The impact of the popular western novels by Bret Harte
       and Owen Wister on James is reflected in the revisions of
       several works (notably in his usage of the term "six-
       shooter" and in his employment of the lasso image).

115   WALKER, WARREN S., comp. Twentieth-Century Short Story Expli-
       cation: Supplement: Interpretations, Since 1960, of Short
       Fiction Since 1800. Hamden, Conn.: Shoe String Press,
       pp. 52-65.
          Citations for articles and parts of books which expli-
       cate James's short stories are listed under the titles of
       individual stories.

116   WANOBU, SEIJI. "Morality in Henry James's Novels." Fukuoka
       Gakugei Daigaku Kiyo, 12 (February), 81-90. [Japanese]
          The moral ambiguities in many of James's works are due to
       James's determination not to succumb to authorial prejudice
       but to give a thorough and analytical examination of the
       psychology of his characters. However, in James's major
       works moral values are put forth in a positive manner.

117   WARD, J. A. "The Double Structure of Watch and Ward." Texas
       Studies in Literature and Language, 4 (Winter), 613-24.
          In James's first novel there are indications that he was
       attracted toward an "open, or organic structure" which
       characterizes his later writings; but in this first novel,
       he binds himself to a "closed, or mechanical structure" (in
       particular the happy ending) which weakens the novel.

*118   WATANABE, TOSHIRO. "Henry James: A Study of the Heroine of
       The Portrait of a Lady." Eibunga Kukai-Kaiho, 13:34-62.
          Cited in 1970.B72, p. 323.

119   WEGELIN, CHRISTOF. "Jamesian Biography." Nineteenth-Century
       Fiction, 18 (December), 283-87.
          The first three of a projected four-volume biography of
       Henry James by Leon Edel charts a middle course between
       subjectivism and objectivism; it is artistic, imaginative,
       critical, and factual. Review of 1962.A1 and 1962.A2.

120 WELLS, ANNA MARY. Dear Preceptor: The Life and Times of
Thomas Wentworth Higginson. Boston: Houghton Mifflin, The
Riverside Press, Cambridge, pp. 259-60, passim.
This biography of Higginson includes five references to
James.

121 WHITE, BEATRICE, and T. S. DORSCH, eds. The Year's Work in
English Studies: Vol. 41: 1960. London: Published for
the English Association by the Oxford Univ. Press,
pp. 290-92.
Survey of criticism for 1960.

122 WHITE, BEATRICE, and T. S. DORSCH, eds. The Year's Work in
English Studies: Vol. 42: 1961. London: Published for
the English Association by the Oxford Univ. Press,
pp. 290-91.
Survey of criticism for 1961.

123 WILSON, EDMUND. "Meeting with Max Beerbohm." Encounter, 21
(December), 16-22.
In an account of two visits in 1954 with Beerbohm in
Rapallo, Wilson records Beerbohm's comments on George Ber-
nard Shaw, Virginia Woolf, Henry James, and others. Beer-
bohm "personally disliked Shaw" but "loved Henry James."

*124 WILSON, R. B. J. "An Attempt to Define the Meaning of Henry
James's The Wings of the Dove." Australasian Universities
Language and Literature Association: Proceedings of the
Eighth Congress 15-22 August 1962. Canberra: Australian
National Univ., pp. 76-78.
Cited in 1964 MLA International Bibliography, vol. 1,
p. 122. B. R. McElderry, Jr., in 1966.B62, writes that
this article "states perceptively the changing relationship
between Kate Croy and Densher, and the skill with which
James prepares and executes the memorable climax of the
novel."

125 ZIFF, LARZER. "The Literary Consequences of Puritanism."
Journal of English Literary History, 30 (September),
293-305.
A combination of Puritan characteristics, "plainness,
passion, and allegory," crystallized in the period of 1560-
1660 and has remained "a strong feature if not a separate
tradition in our literature."

1963

1963 C DISSERTATIONS

1   KRAFT, QUENTIN GUILD. "A Study of Point of View in Selected
    Short Stories of Henry James." DA, 24, 2036 (Duke).
       The initial point of view employed by James was that of
    omniscience. The limited point of view predominated, how-
    ever, and was used "indirectly" to emphasize the data being
    observed or "directly" to focus on the observer himself.

2   LEBOWITZ, NAOMI. "Henry James and the Moral Imperative of
    Relationship." DA, 24, 300 (Washington Univ.).
       Henry James is the "master" and in some aspects the
    "creator" of the "novel of relationship"--the novel that
    affirms the moral necessity of being open to engaging in
    individual human relationships regardless of social
    dictates.

3   SALISBURY, HOWARD E. "Wish-Fulfillment as Moral Crisis in
    Fiction of Henry James." DA, 24, 304 (Univ. of Washing-
    ton).
       The problem of reality for the idealist is resolved in
    the moral crisis of experience for the protagonists in The
    Spoils of Poynton, Washington Square, The Portrait of a
    Lady, and The Ambassadors.

1964 A BOOKS

1   ABEL, DARREL. A Simplified Approach to Henry James. Great
    Neck, N.Y.: Barron's Educational Series, 149 pp.
       An Introduction provides a biographical and critical
    overview of James and of his work, while individual treat-
    ments of James's major works contain plot summary and de-
    tailed analysis.

2   GALE, ROBERT L. The Caught Image: Figurative Language in the
    Fiction of Henry James. Chapel Hill: Univ. of North Caro-
    lina Press; London: Oxford Univ. Press, 266 pp.
       The density and proliferation of images in James's work
    exceed that in the work of almost every other major Ameri-
    can writer. His 135 works of fiction yield 16,902 figures
    of speech which should reveal much "concerning his nature
    and that of his age, ought to tell much concerning his mes-
    sage, and should, in addition, elucidate the organic nature
    of his works one by one and in toto." When the figures are
    placed into categories in terms of the content of their
    vehicles, many minor groups emerge as well as six major
    groups: water, flower, animal, war, art, religion. Re-

viewed: 1964.B22; 1966.B55; Granville Hicks, Saturday Review, 47 (30 May), 27; Frederick Crews, New England Quarterly, 37:532-35; Modern Fiction Studies, 10:185-86.

3   HOLLAND, LAURENCE BEDWELL. The Expense of Vision: Essays on
    the Craft of Henry James. Princeton: Princeton Univ.
    Press; London: Oxford Univ. Press, 414 pp.
        James clearly gave his attention "both to the complexi-
    ties and to the elemental if sometimes obvious features of
    the institutions of marriage, the family, and publishing,
    money-making and the social and economic symbolism of mon-
    ey, forms of diversion or entertainment, the institution of
    manners in America, and governing standards of taste in the
    arts in the nineteenth century." Interest in "these insti-
    tutions exerted a continuous pressure on the diction,
    structure, and import of his writings" as well as on "his
    plots, his imagery and diction, his very forms." For dis-
    sertation see 1965.C6. Reviewed: 1964.B22; 1965.B6;
    1965.B34; 1966.B55; Frederick C. Crews, New England Quar-
    terly, 37:532-35; Modern Fiction Studies, 10:185.

4   JEFFERSON, D. W. Henry James and the Modern Reader. Edin-
    burgh: Oliver and Boyd; New York: St. Martin's Press,
    240 pp.
        This introduction to James emphasizes mood, tone, point
    of view, use of language; attempts to correct some "ungen-
    erous readings"; and argues for the "readability"of James's
    works. Reviewed: Times Literary Supplement (13 August),
    p. 728; Modern Fiction Studies, 10 (Winter 1964-1965),
    391-92; Ferman Bishop, New England Quarterly, 38 (1965),
    268-70; Leon Edel, American Literature, 37 (1965), 215;
    Terence Martin, South Atlantic Quarterly, 65 (1966), 155.

5   LOWERY, BRUCE. Marcel Proust et Henry James: Une Confronta-
    tion. Paris: Librairie Plon, 415 pp. [French]
        Proust and James share similarities in their lives as
    well as in their works. Both lived in an époque of social
    conventions, appearances, and riches; both writers felt
    foreign and alone in such environments. Both were from
    wealthy families, were attached to their mothers, loved
    solitude, and grew up in very favorable cultural environ-
    ments where they acquired a strong interest in literature
    and made of art their religion. Analysis of their works
    shows a similarity in character presentation that starts
    with complex interior analysis and proceeds to a revelation
    through different layers of personalities. Both reveal
    characters through dialogue. Proust and James were art
    critics, had a strong sense of aesthetics, and gave great

importance to the artist as related to his work. Both
writers made use of an impressionistic style of writing.
Both Proust and James made use of innocent as well as ma-
cabre comicality, together with irony, to criticize the
hypocrisy, snobbism, pretensions, and conventions of their
societies. Reviewed: Times Literary Supplement (15 October), p. 931; Rainer Schulte, Comparative Literature, 17
(1965), 351-52.

6   ROSENBAUM, S. P., ed. Henry James: "The Ambassadors": An
     Authoritative Text, The Author on the Novel, Criticism.
     A Norton Critical Edition. New York: W. W. Norton,
     486 pp.
         Contents: An annotated and corrected reprint of the New
     York Edition of The Ambassadors comprises the first section
     of the book; James's critical statements on the novel,
     gleaned from his Notebooks, from one critical article that
     immediately predated the novel, and from personal letters,
     constitute the second part of the book; a collection of
     critical responses make up the third part; and a bibliog-
     raphy of published editions and of selected general criti-
     cism is included.
         "Memorandum on 'Project of Novel by Henry James'" by
     H. M. Alden (p. 413). Reprinted from The Notebooks of
     Henry James. Edited by F. O. Matthiessen and Kenneth B.
     Murdock. New York: Oxford Univ. Press, 1947, p. 372.
         "Point of View in The Ambassadors" by Percy Lubbock
     (pp. 413-21). Reprinted from The Craft of Fiction. New
     York: Viking, 1921, pp. 156-71.
         "Pattern in The Ambassadors" by E. M. Forster
     (pp. 421-27). Reprinted from Aspects of the Novel. New
     York: Harcourt, Brace & World, 1927, pp. 218-34.
         "The Ambassadors" by F. O. Matthiessen (pp. 427-38).
     Reprinted from Henry James: The Major Phase. New York:
     Oxford Univ. Press, 1944, pp. 19-41.
         "The Meaning of Paris in The Ambassadors: A Disagree-
     ment" by F. R. Leavis (pp. 438-39). Reprinted from The
     Great Tradition. New York: New York Univ. Press, 1963,
     p. 161.
         "From 'Introduction: 1954'" by Joseph Warren Beach
     (pp. 439-40). Reprinted from The Method of Henry James.
     Philadelphia: Albert Saifer, 1954, pp. xlviii-li.
         From an article by Joan Bennett (p. 441). Reprinted
     from Chicago Review, 9 (Winter 1956), 26.
         "From 'Introduction'" by Leon Edel (pp. 441-42). Re-
     printed from 1960.B23.
         "The Lesson of Social Beauty" by Christof Wegelin
     (pp. 442-58). Reprinted from The Image of Europe in Henry

<u>James</u>. Dallas: Southern Methodist Univ. Press, 1958,
pp. 86-105.
"The Language of 'Adventure' in Henry James" by John
Paterson (pp. 458-65). An abridged and slightly revised
form of an essay printed in 1960.B70.
"The First Paragraph of <u>The Ambassadors</u>: An Explication" by Ian Watt (pp. 465-84). Reprinted from 1960.B98.

7   STONE, EDWARD. <u>The Battle and the Books: Some Aspects of</u>
    <u>Henry James</u>. Athens: Ohio Univ. Press, 234 pp.
       A survey of the variety of critical response to James,
    designed in part to answer Maxwell Geismar's attack
    (1963.A2), includes critical chapters on <u>Watch and Ward</u>
    and <u>The Sense of the Past</u> as well as comment on various
    subjects, such as James's suggestive use of names for his
    characters, his affinity for the use of the fairy tale, and
    his influence on James Thurber. Reviewed: 1966.A55; <u>Times</u>
    <u>Literary Supplement</u> (25 November 1965), p. 1052; <u>Modern</u>
    <u>Fiction Studies</u>, 10 (Winter 1964-1965), 391; Terence Martin,
    <u>South Atlantic Quarterly</u>, 65 (1966), 155; B. R. McElderry,
    Jr., <u>American Literature</u>, 37 (1965), 336-37; Roger B.
    Stein, <u>New England Quarterly</u>, 38 (1965), 556-58.

8   VAID, KRISHNA BALDEV. <u>Technique in the Tales of Henry James</u>.
    Foreword by Ian Watt. Cambridge, Mass.: Harvard Univ.
    Press, 285 pp.
       Close scrutiny of 21 of James's tales (written primarily
    after 1888) reveals his technique. Dividing these tales
    according to the two narrative methods James employed
    (first person, omniscient-narrator) spotlights "distinc-
    tions--in structure, style, tone, even content, and of
    course total effect." For dissertation <u>see</u> 1961.C14. Re-
    viewed: 1966.A55; <u>Modern Fiction Studies</u>, 10 (Winter 1964-
    1965), 392; Ferman Bishop, <u>New England Quarterly</u>, 38
    (1965), 268-70; Quentin G. Kraft, <u>American Literature</u>, 37
    (1965), 335-36; B. R. McElderry, Jr., <u>Nineteenth-Century</u>
    <u>Fiction</u>, 19 (1965), 413-14; Dennis H. Burden, <u>Review of</u>
    <u>English Studies</u>, 19 (1968), 231-33; John Lucas, <u>Modern</u>
    <u>Philology</u>, 65 (1968), 422-23.

9   WEST, MURIEL. <u>A Stormy Night with "The Turn of the Screw."</u>
    Phoenix, Ariz.: Frye and Smith, 75 pp.
       A first-person narrative response to <u>The Turn of the</u>
    <u>Screw</u>, written in a colloquial style, this is supposedly an
    anonymous manuscript of the tale. The interpretation of
    the tale, however, is close to readings proposed by such
    scholars as Edna Kenton, Edmund Wilson, and Leon Edel. Re-
    viewed: E. J. Gaines, <u>Library Journal</u> (15 December),

1964

p. 4915; <u>Times Literary Supplement</u> (31 December), p. 1182;
<u>Modern Fiction Studies</u>, 10 (Winter 1964-1965), 392.

1964 B SHORTER WRITINGS

1   ALLEN, WALTER. <u>George Eliot</u>. Masters of World Literature
      Series. New York: Macmillan, pp. 162-64, passim.
        James's "<u>Daniel Deronda</u>: A Conversation" is "a fine
      piece of criticism."

2   ALLEN, WALTER. <u>The Modern Novel: In Britain and the United
      States</u>. New York: E. P. Dutton, passim.
        James is mentioned a number of times in this study of
      the novel from 1920 to 1960.

3   ALLEN, WALTER. <u>Tradition and Dream: The English and American
      Novel from the Twenties to Our Time</u>. London: Phoenix
      House, pp. 192-95, passim.
        James's influence on Elizabeth Bowen is mentioned in one
      of a dozen references to James in this history of the novel.

4   AUCHINCLOSS, LOUIS. "The World of Henry James." <u>Show</u>, 4
      (July-August), 49-55.
        James is "the Great Expatriate: Fame was his spur, Lon-
      don his main setting and the international novel, with its
      collision of Americans and Europeans, his supreme achieve-
      ment."

5   BANTA, MARTHA. "Henry James and 'The Others.'" <u>New England
      Quarterly</u>, 37 (June), 171-84.
        James, in his tales of the supernatural, hoped to reveal
      truths about the human consciousness "through the interac-
      tion of superhuman influences upon the human mind." The
      success of James's ghost stories depends upon "the degree
      of response the characters have to the meaning of the
      ghosts which face them."

6   BASS, EBEN. "Dramatic Scene and <u>The Awkward Age</u>." <u>Publica-
      tions of the Modern Language Association of America</u>, 79
      (March), 148-57.
        The moral conflict between Mrs. Brook's opportunism and
      Longdon's idealism is presented through the work's formal
      structure.

1964

7   BASS, EBEN. "James's The Europeans." Explicator, 23 (September), Item 9.
    James's comic allusion to Acteon's intrusion on Diana's bath in Greek mythology heightens the effect of Robert Acton's rejection of Baroness Münster in Chapter 9 of The Europeans. The Acteon-Diana allusion has the effect of "underscoring the moral failure of falsehood in this most charming of women."

8   BASS, EBEN. "Lemon-Colored Volumes and Henry James." Studies in Short Fiction, 1 (Winter), 113-22.
    James's evolving conception of "the public's antagonism to art and the artist's devotion to art" can be traced through "The Author of Beltraffio," "The Lesson of the Master," and the Yellow Book tales.

9   BEACHCROFT, T. O. "James, Conrad, and the Place of the Narrator," in his The English Short Story (II). London: Published for the British Council and the National Book League by Longmans, Green & Co., pp. 14-18.
    James and Conrad both employed a traditional approach to the short story, and both were interested in form.

10 BEEBE, MAURICE. "Henry James: The Ideal of Detachment," in his Ivory Towers and Sacred Founts: The Artist as Hero in Fiction from Goethe to Joyce. New York: New York Univ. Press, pp. 197-231, passim.
    For James the ideal artist is committed to an "aesthetic adventure." This commitment demands indifference to the material, "nonaesthetic" elements of life, so that in a very real sense the artist must turn his back on society. In addition to the chapter on Henry James, references to James and his works pervade this study of the artist as hero—both in terms of a literary genre and in terms of what the literature reveals about "the artistic temperament, the creative process, and the relationship of the artist to society."

11 BELLMAN, SAMUEL IRVING. "Henry James's 'The Tree of Knowledge': A Biblical Parallel." Studies in Short Fiction, 1 (Spring), 226-28.
    "The Tree of Knowledge," an inversion of the Biblical story of Jesus and Peter, is autobiographical.

1964

12   BLACKMUR, R. P.   "Introduction," in his edition of The Ambas-
     sadors. New York: Dell, pp. 5-12.
          "This is the story of a man who in middle life finds
     himself in a strange country where he gets to know about
     goodness and human freedom."

13   BLUEN, HERBERT. "The Poetry of Edgar Allan Poe." Aryan Path,
     35 (July), 316-19.
          Although Poe's poetry has been poorly received by some,
     including James, who "was temperamentally out of sympathy
     with Poe's worldly muse," it represents "a unique and per-
     manent contribution to literature."

14   BRÉE, GERMAINE. "Distrusting the Gaul." Nation, 198
     (13 April), 377-79.
          Two notable features of James's French Poets and Novel-
     ists are: (1) his instinctive dislike for "the 'Gallic'
     mind"; and (2) his admirable "critical acumen" that was
     quick to perceive the best in French writing.

15   BRENNI, VITO J., comp. "Henry James," in American English: A
     Bibliography. Philadelphia: Univ. of Pennsylvania Press,
     pp. 22-23.
          One entry lists "The Question of our Speech" and "The
     Lesson of Balzac" (1905).

16   BROOKS, CLEANTH. "The American 'Innocence': In James, Fitz-
     gerald, and Faulkner." Shenandoah, 16 (Autumn), 21-37.
          Christopher Newman, Jay Gatsby, and Thomas Sutpen are
     all "innocent" Americans. While innocence is basically a
     positive ideal, it is also "a negative thing that ought to
     disappear with the acquisition of knowledge and moral dis-
     cipline." Reprinted in 1971.B12 and 1971.A7.

17   BROPHY, BRIGID. Review of Henry James and His Cult, by Max-
     well Geismar. London Magazine, 4 (April), 89-92.
          The critical response in the British press to Geismar's
     book is summarized. Brophy terms Geismar's attack an at-
     tempted "assassination" and concludes that his "indictment
     boils down to the one charge that James wrote from his
     imagination." Review of 1963.A2. Reprinted in 1967.B11.

18   BROWN, FRANCIS, ed. Opinions and Perspectives from the "New
     York Times Book Review." Boston: Houghton Mifflin.
          Contents include:
     "The Enduring Fame of Henry James" by Leon Edel
     (pp. 102-109). Reprinted from 1961.B21.
     "As Much of the Truth as One Can Bear" by James Baldwin
     (pp. 210-11, 214). Reprinted from 1962.B12.

19   BUCHAN, ALEXANDER M. "Edith Wharton and 'The Elusive Bright-
     Winged Thing.'" <u>New England Quarterly</u>, 37 (September),
     343-62.
          Wharton's ideas on fiction are compared to those of
     James.

20   BUITENHUIS, PETER. "'The Fresh Start and the Broken Link':
     Henry James's <u>The Ivory Tower</u>." <u>Univ. of Toronto Quarter-
     ly</u>, 33 (July), 355-68.
          An examination of the design, the characterization, and
     the theme of James's incomplete last novel suggests that
     "it would almost certainly have been his best."

21   BURGESS, ANTHONY. "Treasures and Fetters." <u>Spectator</u>, 7078
     (21 February), 254.
          Elizabeth Bowen is compared to Henry James: Bowen "con-
     serves a particular place at a particular time," whereas
     James "articulates a whole culture."

22   CARGILL, OSCAR. "Occlusion and Refraction in Jamesian Criti-
     cism." <u>Nineteenth-Century Fiction</u>, 19 (December), 302-304.
          Laurence Holland's <u>The Expense of Vision</u>, a New Critical
     interpretation of the James canon, occludes the intent of
     James; whereas Robert L. Gale's <u>The Caught Image</u>, a classi-
     fication and study of James's imagery, refracts "the light
     of the author." Review of 1964.A2 and 1964.A3.

23   CAWELTI, JOHN G. "Form as Cultural Criticism in the Work of
     Henry James," in <u>Literature and Society: Nineteen Essays
     by Germaine Brée and others</u>. Edited by Bernice Slote. A
     Bison Book. Lincoln: Univ. of Nebraska Press, pp. 202-12.
          Although James did not deal with the overt social is-
     sues of his day in his art (notably, industrialism and its
     visible ramifications--strikes, trusts, working conditions,
     etc.), an examination of <u>The Ambassadors</u> reveals that he
     did deal with the social problems by designing a structure
     in which the protagonist moves "through a series of con-
     flicting social and moral roles which cannot express his
     individual needs and values and which, in their narrow
     limitations and rigid imperatives, make it almost impossi-
     ble to achieve an individual sense of identity and
     autonomy."

24   CHAUHAN, P. S. "<u>The Portrait of a Lady</u>: Its Moral Design."
     <u>Literary Criterion</u>, 6 (Summer), 56-70.
          The inspiration for <u>The Portrait of a Lady</u> was not a
     young woman but rather an engaging moral theme: "moral
     values not only condition the manner in which she would

1964

affront her destiny, but also prescribe the frame of action
beyond which even her free exploits of life are not allowed
to lure her."

25 CURTI, MERLE. The Growth of American Thought. Third edition.
New York, Evanston, London: Harper & Row, pp. 508-509.
James is "the classic example of escapism" in becoming
an expatriate.

26 DORRIS, GEORGE E. "Two Allusions in the Poetry of T. S.
Eliot." English Language Notes, 2 (September), 54-57.
The opening exchange between Sweeney and Doris in "Frag-
ment of an Agon" (Sweeney Agonistes) parallels verbally the
conversation between Miss Barrace and Little Bilham at the
garden party given by Gloriani in The Ambassadors.

*27 DUPEE, F. W. "Afterword," in his edition of The Wings of the
Dove. New York: New American Library.
Cited in Beatrice Ricks, comp. Henry James: A Bibliog-
raphy of Secondary Works. Scarecrow Author Bibliographies,
No. 24. Metuchen, N.J.: Scarecrow Press, 1975, Item 1553.

28 EDEL, LEON. The Complete Tales of Henry James. Vols. 9-12.
Philadelphia: Lippincott.
In "Introduction: 1892-1898" (Vol. 9, pp. 7-12), Edel
suggests that most of these tales "belong to two groups:
one he called his 'scenes of literary life,' and the other
his 'tales of the quasi-supernatural or gruesome.'" Edel
notes in "Introduction: 1898-1899" (Vol. 10, pp. 7-13)
that the tenth volume includes James's best-known tale,
"The Turn of the Screw," and that during this period James
returns to earlier themes but retells them "with all his
late mastery." In "Introduction: 1900-1903" (Vol. 11,
pp. 7-11), Edel states that the tales of these years are
written in James's late style, are "fairly blunt and direct" and express his "disenchantment" with life. "Introduction: 1903-1910" (Vol. 12, pp. 7-11) notes that "These
are tales of individuals lost in a crowd; and of individuals without identity or self-awareness. They are also
angry tales." Reviewed: 1965.B2.

29 EDEL, LEON. "Introduction," in his edition of Henry James:
French Poets and Novelists. New York: Grosset and Dunlap,
pp. vii-xi.
James's first collection of critical essays, published
in 1878, "has endured ever since as a significant study of
the French literary mind."

*30   EFRON, ARTHUR. "Spilka on The Turn of the Screw." Paunch,
      no. 17 (10 January), pp. 13-15.
           Cited in 1966.B7. This article is a response to
      1963.B95, 1964.B58, and 1964.B94.

31   EPIFANIO, SAN JUAN, JR. "James's The Ambassadors: The Tra-
      jectory of the Climax." Midwest Quarterly, 5 (Summer),
      295-310.
           The protagonist of The Ambassadors is the comprehending
      and accumulative central intelligence for "the whole emo-
      tional and mental nexus of the situations rendered in the
      novel." As such he is very close to James's "definition of
      'experience' as the largest possible freedom of individual
      action . . . geared toward a realization of possible roles
      and identities which either culture or individual imagina-
      tion can suggest."

32   FLEET, SIMON. "In Search of Henry James at Rye." Modern Age,
      9 (Winter), 69-76.
           The personal recollections of the townsfolk in and
      around Rye in Sussex, England, reflect some of James's
      idiosyncrasies and reflect the admiration and respect James
      has there.

33   FOFF, ARTHUR, and DANIEL KNAPP, eds. "Analysis of 'The Real
      Thing,'" in their Story: An Introduction to Prose Fiction.
      Belmont, Calif.: Wadsworth, pp. 366-68.
           "The Real Thing" is one of James's studies "of the fre-
      quently ambiguous and inside-out relations between fact and
      idea, between appearance and reality, between art and life."

34   GALE, ROBERT L. "Imagery in James's Prefaces." Revue des
      Langues Vivantes, 30 (September-October), 431-45.
           The six major categories of images present in James's
      prefaces (water, flower, animal, war, art, and religion)
      provide diversified "tenors" concerning "James's inspira-
      tions and his processes of recollecting them, James as art-
      ist, stages of his creativity, his characters and themes
      and techniques, locales used as background, his completed
      novels and stories, and his notions about readers and also
      his fellow artists and their efforts."

35   GALE, ROBERT L. "'Pandora' and Her President." Studies in
      Short Fiction, 1 (Spring), 222-24.
           The fictional president in Part I of "Pandora" is mod-
      eled after Rutherford B. Hayes; the president in Part II is
      James Abram Garfield.

1964

36   GIFFORD, HENRY. "Henry James: The Drama of Discrimination,"
       in The Modern Age. Pelican Guide to English Literature.
       Volume 7. Reprinted with revisions. Edited by Boris Ford.
       Baltimore: Penguin Books, pp. 103-18.
          An overview of James's work concludes that "very little
       in the vast body of his work can be disregarded." See
       1961.B35 for earlier edition.

37   GILBERT, ELLIOT L. "Kipling and James: A Note on Travel."
       Kipling Journal, 31, no. 152, 7-9.
          Thematically Kipling's "An Error in the Fourth Dimen-
       sion" is a superficial duplication of James's The Ambassa-
       dors.

38   GOLDSMITH, ARNOLD L. "The Maltese Cross as Sign in The Spoils
       of Poynton." Renascence, 16 (Winter), 73-77.
          The cross, which has three symbolic functions, is a key
       to the novel's structure, characterizations, imagery, and
       theme.

39   GUNN, PETER. Vernon Lee: Violet Paget, 1856-1935. London:
       Oxford Univ. Press, pp. 103-107, 136-39, 217-19.
          There are many references to James in this biographical
       critical study of Paget; three matters discussed are
       (1) Henry James's reaction to Miss Brown, which he termed
       "a deplorable mistake"; (2) Paget's parody of James in
       "Lady Tal"; (3) her analysis of James's style in The Han-
       dling of Words.

40   HALL, DONALD. "Afterword," in his edition of Washington
       Square. A Signet Classic. New York: New American Library,
       pp. 181-90.
          Washington Square is liked by everyone, but James left
       it out of the New York Edition: it "may have seemed to
       James, who wrote it during his long infatuation with the
       theater, a case of the confusion of genres, like a story-
       telling painting or a portrait-poem."

41   HAMBLEN, ABIGAIL A. "Henry James and Disease." Dalhousie Re-
       view, 44 (Spring), 57-63.
          The hopeless quality of death and disease that James ex-
       perienced at the death of his cousin, Mary Temple, has
       evolved into a cathartic experience by the time it is fic-
       tionalized in The Wings of the Dove.

42 HARDY, BARBARA. "Total Relevance: Henry James"; "The Matter
    of Treatment: Henry James," in her The Appropriate Form:
    An Essay on the Novel. London: Univ. of London, Athlone
    Press, pp. 11-29, 30-50.
        In addition to incidental references to Henry James in
    chapters on Defoe, Bronte, Hardy, Forster, Meredith, George
    Eliot, D. H. Lawrence, and Tolstoy, two chapters are devot-
    ed to James. The first deals with some of the assets and
    liabilities of Jamesian economy; the second deals with the
    price James paid in characterization for his obsession with
    aesthetic form.

43 HAYNE, BARRIE S. "The Divided Self: The Alter Ego as Theme
    and Device in Charles Brockden Brown, Hawthorne, and
    James." Dissertation, Harvard, 651 pp.
        Just as the American nineteenth-century self is divided
    "by the rival claims upon it of its homeland and its old
    home," so is the artistic self "divided between the artist
    and his representative or surrogate in the work of art" to
    whom "is transferred certain feelings of artistic insecuri-
    ty." James reveals his conflict between "the yearning for
    popular acclaim and the impulse towards artistic perfec-
    tion" through fictional pairs of artists, the artisan whose
    success has outstripped his talent and the artist "of tal-
    ent unrecognized."

44 HOFFMAN, FREDERICK J. "The Princess Casamassima: Violence
    and Decorum," in his The Mortal No: Death and the Modern
    Imagination. Princeton, N.J.: Princeton Univ. Press,
    pp. 41-50.
        In this study of death's literary images and metaphors
    in the twentieth century in the context of three basic
    terms--grace, violence, and self--James's The Princess
    Casamassima is a principal work in the opening examination
    of the "problem of manners, historical situations, and
    ideologies." (In addition, the work contains some two or
    three dozen scattered references to James.) Reprinted in
    1973.A6.

45 HOLDER, ALAN. "T. S. Eliot on Henry James." Publications of
    the Modern Language Association of America, 79 (September),
    490-97.
        Eliot's criticism of James is influenced by admiration,
    mutual interests, and ambitions and is filtered through his
    own artistic criteria.

1964

46 HOLMAN, C. HUGH. "Of Everything the Unexplained and Irre-
     sponsible Specimen: Notes on How to Read American Real-
     ism." <u>Georgia Review</u>, 18 (Fall), 316-24.
        Realism, as it was practiced in American literature be-
     tween 1870 and 1900, is defined. Also examined are "the
     characteristics which Howells and James each emphasized in
     the literary figure whom each insisted to have been his
     chief artistic model, the Russian novelist Ivan Turgenev."

47 HUDSPETH, ROBERT N. "The Definition of Innocence: James's
     <u>The Ambassadors</u>." <u>Texas Studies in Literature and Lan-
     guage</u>, 6 (Autumn), 354-60.
        Whereas Sarah Pocock represents the reprehensibleness of
     unyielding innocence, Strether represents the "American
     initiate," who has emerged from the dialectic of innocence
     and experience.

48 IWASE, SHITSUU. "Recent Studies of Henry James." <u>Queries</u>
     (Osaka Municipal Univ.), 5 (August), 25-43. [Japanese]
        A review of James studies published in the United States
     from 1955 through 1962 includes bibliographies, texts, and
     criticism.

*49 JONES, T. H. "The Essential Vulgarity of Henry James." <u>Pro-
     ceedings of the Ninth Congress of the Australasian Univer-
     sities' Languages and Literature Association</u>, 19-26 August
     1964. Edited by Marion Adams. Melbourne: Univ. of Mel-
     bourne, pp. 49-50.
        Cited in <u>1965 MLA International Bibliography</u>, vol. 1,
     p. 134.

50 KARL, FREDERICK R. <u>An Age of Fiction: The Nineteenth Century
     British Novel</u>. New York: Farrar, Straus and Giroux, The
     Noonday Press, passim.
        This study of the Victorian novel that focuses primarily
     on Austen, Scott, the Brontes, Dickens, Thackeray, Meredith,
     Eliot, and Hardy contains less than two dozen references to
     Henry James. Reprinted in 1969 as <u>A Reader's Guide to the
     Nineteenth Century British Novel</u>.

51 KAZIN, ALFRED. "The Scholar Cornered: A Procession of Chil-
     dren." <u>American Scholar</u>, 33 (Spring), 171-73, 176-83.
        Unlike the children in most American stories dealing
     with the innocence and hope of youth, Henry James's chil-
     dren are not typically American; rather they are hardened
     and precocious in the adult world.

52 KENNEY, BLAIR G. "The Two Isabels: A Study in Distortion."
    Victorian Newsletter, no. 25 (Spring), pp. 15-17.
        Although Trollope's Isabel Boncassen (The Duke's Chil-
    dren) influenced James's creation of Isabel Archer (The
    Portrait of a Lady), the works differ structurally and the
    thematic implications of Trollope's novel are reversed in
    that of James.

53 LANG, HANS-JOACHIM. "The Turns in The Turn of the Screw."
    Jahrbuch für Amerikastudien, 9:110-28.
        The "'disjunctive ambiguity'" and narrative technique of
    The Turn of the Screw follow the tradition established by
    Hawthorne (i.e., capable of simultaneous allegorical and
    individual interpretation). It is a story in which "turn-
    ing" is the controlling metaphor, and the governess is the
    one who turns and does the turning.

54 LEBOWITZ, NAOMI. "The Counterfeiters and the Epic Pretense."
    Univ. of Toronto Quarterly, 33 (April), 291-310.
        Gide's The Counterfeiters is not capable of withstanding
    comparison with the ethical and dramatic dimensions of
    James's works, because it is a work of a substantially dif-
    ferent quality--it is an experiment in "aesthetic manipula-
    tion" that utilizes the epic motif for its basic structure.

55 LONG, ROBERT E. "The Society and the Masks: The Blithedale
    Romance and The Bostonians." Nineteenth-Century Fiction,
    19 (September), 105-22.
        The similarities in these novels go much deeper than
    subject and characterization: "In these two particular
    novels, Hawthorne and James addressed themselves to truth
    and hypocrisy in American life, and attempted to say what
    seemed to them to be the essential truth of the societies
    they described."

56 LONG, ROBERT E. "A Source for Dr. Mary Prance in The Bosto-
    nians." Nineteenth-Century Fiction, 19 (June), 87-88.
        Dr. Mary Walker, a physician with the Union Army during
    the Civil War and a suffragette, may be the source of Dr.
    Mary Prance.

57 LOWERY, BRUCE. "Henry James et Marcel Proust." Revue de Pa-
    ris, 71 (April), 74-82. [French]
        Both Proust and James are idealistic writers searching
    for truth through argumentative reasonings, walls of pru-
    dence, infinite labyrinths, and masks of elegance. Under-
    neath their masks there is a deep sense of evil, cruelty,

and sadism, though this brutality never appears clearly in
their work. An excerpt from 1964.A5.

58   LYDENBERG, JOHN. "Comment on Mr. Spilka's Paper." Literature
     and Psychology, 14 (Winter), 6-8.
         Although Spilka's article "Turning the Freudian Screw"
     makes two significant contributions (it maintains a good
     interpretative balance between the religious elements of
     the story and an equally good balance between the govern-
     ess's role and that of the children), it does not represent
     the final "turn" and his certitude is unwarranted. Response
     to 1963.B95. See also 1964.B94 and 1964.B30.

59   McLEAN, ROBERT C. "The Subjective Adventure of Fleda Vetch."
     American Literature, 36 (March), 12-30.
         Since The Spoils of Poynton is interpreted through the
     unreliable subjectivity of Fleda Vetch, the reader must
     extricate the truth from the objective material available
     in four encounters between Owen and Fleda. These reveal
     Fleda as a "free spirit" to be pitied and Owen as the
     "strongest" and "most humane figure" in the work. Reprint-
     ed in 1968.A11.

60   MacSHANE, FRANK. "Introduction," in his edition of Critical
     Writings of Ford Madox Ford. Lincoln: Univ. of Nebraska
     Press, pp. ix-xiv, 107.
         Henry James is mentioned in the editor's Introduction to
     Ford's criticism, one selection of which is on Henry James:
     "The Master," reprinted from Portraits from Life. Boston:
     Houghton Mifflin, 1937.

61   MARIANI, UMBERTO. "The Italian Experience of Henry James."
     Nineteenth-Century Fiction, 19 (December), 237-54.
         To James "Italy seemed to be the mother of beauty, the
     place where nature was lovely as nowhere else in the world,
     where art and grace had adorned, and the past enriched, both
     life and nature." He moved from an initially superficial
     treatment of Italy to a deeply symbolic one.

62   MARX, LEO. The Machine in the Garden: Technology and the
     Pastoral Ideal in America. New York: Oxford Univ. Press,
     pp. 239-40, 350-53.
         Suggests that for Christopher Newman the "new world" is
     Europe (pp. 239-40); and that James sees the American land-
     scape as symbolically pastoral, because "the scenery of
     America is peculiarly hospitable to pastoral illusions"
     (pp. 350-53).

63   MAXWELL, J. C. "Henry James's 'Poor Wantons': An Unnoticed
     Version." Nineteenth-Century Fiction, 19 (December),
     301-302.
           A different account of the anecdote concerning the two
     women James deemed "the poor wantons" is found in Ada
     Leverson's The Limit (1911).

64   MAXWELL, J. C. "The Revision of Roderick Hudson." English
     Studies, 45 (June), 239.
           The New York Edition text of Roderick Hudson differs
     very little from the text of 1879.

65   MELCHIORI, GIORGIO. "Il Déjeuner Sur l'herbe di Henry James."
     Studi Americani, no. 10, pp. 201-28. [Italian]
           In most of James's works, his predilection and under-
     standing of art as an exploration of man's soul stems from
     the admiration he had and cultivated for painting. Partic-
     ularly, James's short story "A Landscape Painter" mirrors
     not only his love for art, but especially his admiration
     for John La Farge, whom he considered to be the ideal art-
     ist. Reprinted in 1974.A3.

66   MENDELSOHN, MICHAEL J. "'Drop a Tear . . . ': Henry James
     Dramatizes Daisy Miller." Modern Drama, 7 (May), 60-64.
           The failure of the dramatic version of the novel is at-
     tributable to five changes James made in preparing his nov-
     el for the stage: (1) the addition of characters; (2) his
     "use of stilted and clumsy devices"; (3) his use of "con-
     ventions and clichés"; (4) his omission of the night Colos-
     seum scene; and (5) the alterations he made in the conclu-
     sion.

67   MILLGATE, MICHAEL. "Henry James and the Business Hero," in
     his American Social Fiction: James to Cozzens. Edinburgh
     and London: Oliver and Boyd; New York: Barnes and Noble,
     pp. 1-17.
           James chose to portray only the private life of the
     businessman (as opposed to the working life) in his works;
     he was fairly successful in his treatment of minor charac-
     ters (Mr. Dosson, Mr. Ruck, Jim Pocock), but his major
     business characters are "ultimately unacceptable."

68   MILLS, A. R. "The Portrait of a Lady and Dr. Leavis." Essays
     in Criticism (Oxford), 14 (October), 380-87.
           The assessment of F. R. Leavis that The Portrait of a
     Lady is "one of the two 'most brilliant novels in the lan-
     guage'" is misguided, as is his praise for Isabel Archer;

1964

in fact, the novel is "blatantly moralistic and on occasion
even less implicit than the work of George Eliot." For response <u>see</u> 1965.B98.

69   MIZENER, ARTHUR. <u>The Sense of Life in the Modern Novel</u>. Boston: Houghton Mifflin, The Riverside Press, Cambridge,
pp. 2-5, passim.
James's prefaces have led critics to concentrate on the
structure of the novel to the exclusion of consideration of
character delineation and the society in which the characters live. (There are many references to James in this
study of "the relation of the represented life in the novel
to 'nature.'")

70   MONTEIRO, GEORGE. "The Campaign of Henry James's Disinherited
Princess." <u>English Studies</u>, 45 (December), 442-54.
Christina Light "transcends the limitations of her initial role" as a <u>ficelle</u> in both <u>Roderick Hudson</u> and <u>The
Princess Casamassima</u>. Unable to shape her destiny effec-
tively, she possesses "a strong internal consistency in her
character and a resilient bravery in her actions" and is
finally "the worthy recipient of Hyacinth Robinson's sacri-
fice."

71   MONTEIRO, GEORGE. "A Contemporary View of Henry James and
Oscar Wilde, 1882." <u>American Literature</u>, 35 (January),
528-30.
To Harriet Loring, James was "slow minded" and fastidi-
ous about his manners but an "excellent young man"; Oscar
Wilde was in appearance "most gruesome," but witty and
"very agreeable."

72   MOORE, RAYBURN S. "The Full Light of a Higher Criticism:
Edel's Biography and Other Recent Studies of Henry James."
<u>South Atlantic Quarterly</u>, 63 (Winter), 104-14.
A number of book-length critical studies of James have
appeared in the last few years, but Leon Edel continues to
play a major part in publication of James criticism. The
first three volumes of the biography present "an authoritative reconstruction of James's life and a historical and
critical treatment of his work in the context of that
life." Review of 1962.A1 and 1962.A2.

73   NAGANO, REIKO. "The Progress of Love: The Psychic Develop-
ment of Three Jamesian Heroines." <u>The Tsuda Review</u>
(Tokyo), 9 (November), 43-78. [Japanese]
<u>The Portrait of a Lady</u>, <u>The Wings of the Dove</u>, and <u>The
Golden Bowl</u> constitute a trilogy of the heroine in which

there is a distinct development in the female characters
from awareness of only the Artemis element to awareness of
both Artemis and Aphrodite elements. Maggie Verver, for
example, is a perfect Psyche who has obtained her true
womanhood through knowledge of both the redemptive and passionate aspects of love.

74   OFFEN, SUSAN. "Isabel Archer: An Analysis of Her Fate."
     Hunter College Studies, no. 2, pp. 41-50.
          Isabel Archer's character contains several foibles, in-
     cluding a lack of self-knowledge, a feeling of superiority
     toward life, a fear of reality, and a gradual drifting to-
     ward Osmond's "villainous" philosophy--all of which con-
     tribute to the large degree of responsibility she must ac-
     cept for her own fate.

75   OHMANN, CAROL. "Daisy Miller: A Study of Changing Inten-
     tions." American Literature, 36 (March), 1-11.
          In creating Daisy, James unconsciously shifts from the
     opening emphasis on comedy of manners to a final "presen-
     tation of a metaphysical ideal."

76   OKITA, HAJIME. "Henry James's Contribution to American Liter-
     ature (III)." Jimbun (Kyoto Prefectural Univ.), 16 (Octo-
     ber), 1-20. [Japanese]
          James's influence can be seen in the work of Faulkner
     and Hemingway. His influence on Light in August comes in-
     directly through Conrad. See 1962.B82 and 1963.B79 for
     Parts I and II.

77   OLIVER, CLINTON F. "Introduction," in his edition of The
     Princess Casamassima. Harper Colophon Books. New York:
     Harper & Row, pp. 5-22.
          "What distinguishes The Princess Casamassima and The
     Bostonians among James's novels is their comparatively full
     and open handling of social themes."

*78 PAIK, NAK-CHUNG. "Henry James' The Sacred Fount as a Work of
     Art and as the Portrait of Consciousness." English Lan-
     guage and Literature (English Literary Society of Korea),
     16 (June 1964-1965), 105-136.
          Cited in Beatrice Ricks, comp. Henry James: A Bibliog-
     raphy of Secondary Works. Scarecrow Author Bibliographies,
     No. 24. Metuchen, N.J.: Scarecrow, 1975, Item 1059.

1964

79 PEARCE, ROY HARVEY, ed. <u>Hawthorne Centenary Essays</u>. Colum-
      bus: Ohio State Univ. Press, pp. 271-95, 329-51.
        Contents include:
        "The Tactics of Sanctity: Hawthorne and James" by
      R. W. B. Lewis (pp. 271-95). "[I]n <u>The Bostonians</u>, James
      made his comment upon the American scene by casting a Haw-
      thornian eye upon a non-Hawthornian world: by reassembling
      themes and motives and devices and language from Hawthorne
      and then by twisting and reversing them." Reprinted as
      "Hawthorne and James: The Matter of the Heart," in
      1965.B66.
        "Our Hawthorne" by Lionel Trilling (pp. 329-51). Re-
      printed from 1964.B98.

80 POIRIER, RICHARD. "Afterword," in his edition of <u>The Euro-
      peans</u>. A Signet Classic. New York: New American Library,
      pp. 179-89.
        <u>The Europeans</u> reminds the reader of Hawthorne, "James's
      study of whom appeared a year after the novel. In their
      conjunction the two books are autobiographically important
      to any assessment of James's relation to his native cul-
      ture."

81 RODENBECK, JOHN. "The Bolted Door in James's <u>Portrait of a
      Lady</u>." <u>Modern Fiction Studies</u>, 10 (Winter 1964-1965),
      330-40.
        <u>The Portrait of a Lady</u> is "epitomized . . . in the re-
      current image of a bolted door." An examination of this
      image "alone may provide a satisfactory reading of the
      novel as a whole."

82 ROUNTREE, BENJAMIN C. "James's <u>Madame de Mauves</u> and Madame de
      La Fayette's <u>Princesse de Cleves</u>." <u>Studies in Short Fic-
      tion</u>, 1 (Summer), 264-71.
        Similarities in plot, characterization, and structure
      suggest an influence on <u>Madame de Mauves</u> by <u>La Princesse de
      Clèves</u>.

83 ROVIT, EARL. "James and Emerson: The Lesson of the Master."
      <u>American Scholar</u>, 33 (Summer), 434-40.
        The greatest single influence on James's spiritual
      thinking was exerted by Ralph Waldo Emerson.

84 SALOMON, ROGER B. "Realism as Disinheritance: Twain, How-
      ells, and James." <u>American Quarterly</u>, 16 (Winter), 531-44.
        Whereas Howells abandoned the past in his art and re-
      flected "the surface of contemporary American life," Twain

was unable to achieve "a workable relation between his
emotional ties to the past and an intellectual commitment
to the present." James, however, was able to reconcile
past and present by making the present "literally incorpo-
rate the past: make it, that is, one in body." Reprinted
in 1968.B115 and 1969.B120.

85 SANNA, VITTORIA. "I romanzi di Edith Wharton e la narrativa
jamesiana." Studi Americani, no. 10, pp. 229-91. [Ital-
ian]
Edith Wharton's novels, though sharing the theme of her
great master Henry James, are completely autonomous. The
greatest difference in her novels as compared to James's
is in the authenticity and humanity she gives to her
characters.

86 SAYRE, ROBERT F. The Examined Self: Benjamin Franklin, Henry
Adams, Henry James. Princeton, N.J.: Princeton Univ.
Press, pp. vii-xiii, 44-89, 137-208.
Contents include:
"Preface" (pp. vii-xiii). Franklin, Adams, and James
"are studied in relation to each other and against some of
the conditions of American experience, conditions which
they also help to expose."
"Henry Adams and Henry James" (pp. 44-89). Adams and
James were friends, who respected one another; however,
"In autobiography the two men had such different ideas of
form that there appears to be no reconciling them."
"The Lessons of the Boy and the Master" (pp. 137-82).
James's autobiographical works "may not be the mythic
'American life' that the Autobiography [of Franklin] is so
strangely taken to be, but, given the attention they de-
mand, they have equally as much to say about life in
America."
"Adams, James, and Autobiography" (pp. 183-208).
Adams's and James's autobiographies offer "a possible
foundation for the understanding and criticism of auto-
biography."
For dissertation see 1962.B99.

87 SCHLESINGER, ARTHUR M., JR., and MORTON WHITE, eds. Paths of
American Thought. London: Chatto & Windus, pp. 57-62,
247-49, 483-86.
Contents include:
"The Classic Literature: Art and Idea" by Richard Chase
(pp. 57-62). James is included in a discussion of the
American writer's "poverty of materials" argument.

1964

"The Realistic Novel" by Alfred Kazin (pp. 247-49).
"Like all true realists, he [Henry James] was in love with
his material, and it is this that gives the lasting polish
to James's descriptions."
"Transatlantic Portrait (III): James" (pp. 483-86) in
"America and Europe: Transatlantic Images" by Melvin J.
Lasky. Henry James "is that exquisite thing, the perfect
turning-point in the spiritual tension between Old and New
World."

*88   SCHOLES, J. B. Henry James's "The American": A Study Guide.
       New York: Shelley.
           Cited in Cumulative Book Index: 1963-64, Vol. 1. Edit-
       ed by Nina R. Thompson. New York: H. W. Wilson, 1965,
       p. 2577.

89   SEGNITZ, T. M. "The Actual Genesis of Henry James's 'Paste.'"
       American Literature, 36 (May), 216-19.
           Guy de Maupassant's "Les Bijoux," not his "La Parure,"
       is the source of "Paste."

90   SMITH, J. OATES. "Henry James and Virginia Woolf: The Art of
       Relationships." Twentieth-Century Literature, 10 (October)
       119-29.
           Virginia Woolf and Henry James both espouse metaphysical
       principles that suggest "man gains his identity, experiences
       his 'life,' in terms only of other people--other intelligent
       consciousnesses with whom he can communicate."

91   SMITH, THOMAS F. "Balance in Henry James's The Portrait of a
       Lady." Four Quarters (La Salle), 13 (May), 11-16.
           The concept of "balance," both from a thematic and a
       stylistic perspective, is an integral part of the novel's
       structure and provides the basis for a favorable judgment
       of Isabel's final decision.

92   SOLOMON, ERIC. "The Return of the Screw." University Review
       (Kansas City), 30 (Spring), 205-11.
           The Turn of the Screw is a detective story in which the
       governess, Miles, Miss Jessel, and Peter Quint are the vic-
       tims of the avaricious Mrs. Grose. Reprinted in 1966.A5.

93   SOLOMON, ERIC. Stephen Crane in England: A Portrait of the
       Artist. Columbus: Ohio State Univ. Press, pp. 67-89.
           The basis of the warm friendship between Crane and James
       was professional and artistic.

94 SPILKA, MARK. "Mr. Spilka's Reply." <u>Literature and Psychol-</u>
<u>ogy</u>, 14 (Winter), 8, 34.
The ambiguity of the tale is limited to the nature of
the evil present; such ambiguity does not defy a "definitive interpretation." Response to 1964.B58. <u>See also</u>
1963.B95 and 1964.B30.

95 STONE, ALBERT E., JR. "Henry James and Childhood: <u>The Turn</u>
<u>of the Screw</u>," in <u>American Character and Culture: Some</u>
<u>Twentieth Century Perspectives</u>. Edited by John Allen
Hague. DeLand, Fla.: Everett Edwards Press, pp. 85-100.
Reprint of 1961.A4.

96 SWINNERTON, FRANK. <u>Figures in the Foreground: Literary Remi-</u>
<u>niscences, 1917-1940</u>. Garden City, N.Y.: Doubleday & Co.,
passim.
Contains some fifteen passing references to James.

97 TAKEDA, CHIEKO. "<u>The Portrait of a Lady</u> and <u>The Wings of the</u>
<u>Dove</u>." <u>Kenkyu Nempo</u> (Gakushuin Univ.), 11 (February),
291-320. [Japanese]
The two works have in common a heroine drawn from the
same model as well as the presence of an anti-heroine, a
confidante, and an informant. There are differences in the
works, however, particularly in the direct observation and
portrayal in one novel and the symbolic indirect presentation in the other. In addition, James had a spectator attitude toward Isabel but revealed tenderness to the morally
symbolic figure of Milly.

98 TRILLING, LIONEL. "Our Hawthorne." <u>Partisan Review</u>, 31
(Summer), 329-51.
James's 1879 study of Hawthorne is "indispensable," even
though James treated Hawthorne with "condescension"; but
the modern critical view of Hawthorne is very different
from James's. Reprinted in 1964.B79.

99 TYLER, PARKER. "<u>The Sacred Fount</u>"; "The Figure in the Carpet";
and "Milly and Billy as Proto-Finnegans," in his <u>Every Art-</u>
<u>ist His Own Scandal: A Study of Real and Fictive Heroes</u>.
New York: Horizon Press, pp. 209-55.
In three separate chapters on James, the novelist's life
as artist is considered in terms of his fictive heroes,
such as the narrator in <u>The Sacred Fount</u>, Maisie Farange,
and Milly Theale.

1964

100   UCHIYAMA, TETSUJIRO. "Political Intention in <u>The Princess</u>
      <u>Casamassima</u>." <u>Jimbun-kagaku Kenkyu</u> (Niigata Univ.), 26
      (March), 85-116. [Japanese]
         Although the work depicts well the political state of
      the English labor class in the early 1880s by means of
      James's "penetrating imagination" and careful effort to
      obtain material, the focus of the work is on the relation-
      ship of characters rather than on politics itself.

101   WALSH, WILLIAM. "A Sense of Identity in a World of Circum-
      stance: <u>The Autobiography</u> of Henry James," in his <u>A Human</u>
      <u>Idiom: Literature and Humanity</u>. New York: Barnes &
      Noble, pp. 52-73.
         The theme of James's three autobiographical studies is
      the formation of a personal identity in a complex society.

102   WARD, J. A. '"James's <u>The Europeans</u> and the Structure of Com-
      edy." <u>Nineteenth-Century Fiction</u>, 19 (June), 1-16.
         The conflicting ideas of the novel, "life based on re-
      sponsibility with one based on opportunism," are presented
      in terms of a quasi-pastoral setting and simplified charac-
      terization. The resolution, however, refuses to follow
      the classic comic pattern. Reprinted in 1968.All.

103   WATANABE, HISAYOSHI. "Henry James's Late Style." <u>Eibungaku</u>
      <u>Hyoron</u> (Kyoto Univ.), 16 (October), 141-59. [Japanese]
         James's stylistic change was dependent on his artistic
      instinct rather than calculation. The culmination of
      his style is found in <u>The Ambassadors</u> and <u>The Golden Bowl</u>,
      where the style is the correlative, as it were, to James's
      theory that art is selection as life is a splendid waste,
      a confusion. James's prose is closer to poetry in these
      late books, in which he succeeds in presenting life, or
      the staked-out ground of life. Here, too, James's alle-
      giance to both the realistic and the romantic is apparent.

104   WATSON, GEORGE. "Henry James," in his <u>The Literary Critics:</u>
      <u>A Study of English Descriptive Criticism</u>. New York:
      Barnes and Noble; London: Chatto & Windus, pp. 148-60.
         James revolutionized criticism of the novel.

105   WEST, MURIEL. "The Death of Miles in <u>The Turn of the Screw</u>."
      <u>Publications of the Modern Language Association</u>, 79 (June),
      283-88.
         A close reading of the interrogation of Miles reveals
      that his death is not caused by an implausible heart at-
      tack but by the violence of the governess. Reprinted in
      1969.All.

106   WESTBROOK, JAMES SEYMOUR, JR. "Sensibility and Society: A Study in Themes." <u>DA</u>, 25, 3560 (Columbia).
        The sensibility of the protagonist within a social context is variously treated in five works--<u>Sir Charles Grandison</u>, <u>Mansfield Park</u>, <u>Shirley</u>, <u>The Amazing Marriage</u>, and <u>The Wings of the Dove</u>.

107   WHITE, BEATRICE, and T. S. DORSCH, eds. <u>The Year's Work in English Studies: Vol. 43: 1962</u>. New York: Published for the English Association by Humanities Press, pp. 315-17.
        Survey of criticism for 1962.

108   WILLIAMS, PAUL O. "James' <u>The Portrait of a Lady</u>." <u>Explicator</u>, 22 (March), Item 50.
        Gilbert Osmond's remark, in reference to his marriage with Isabel, that "We're as united, you know, as the candlestick and the snuffers" offers a perfect image which makes "an extraordinarily compact statement of certain relationships in the novel." This simile shows Osmond's contempt for Goodwood, his "summation of the state of his marriage," and his inability to perceive his own disabilities and abnormalities.

1964 C DISSERTATIONS

1   BURSTEIN, FRANCES BROWNELL. "The Picture of New England Puritanism Presented in the Fiction of Henry James." <u>DA</u>, 25, 2977-78 (Boston Univ.).
        James's presentation of the New England Puritan is both perceptive and historically accurate. Puritanism provided him with a complex moral frame of reference from which James analyzed the moral and spiritual struggles of man.

*2   CLAIR, JOHN ALOYSIUS. "The Ironic Dimension in the Fiction of Henry James." Unpublished Doctoral Dissertation, Western Reserve.
        Cited in <u>Annual Bibliography of English Language and Literature: 1965: Vol. 40</u>. Edited by Marjory Rigby, Charles Nilon, and James B. Misenheimer, Jr. Cambridge, England: MHRA, 1967, Item 6289. For book publication <u>see</u> 1965.A3.

1964

*3 DONOVAN, ALAN BARTON. "The Sense of Beauty in the Novels of
     Henry James." Unpublished Doctoral Dissertation, Yale.
     Cited in Annual Bibliography of English Language and
     Literature: 1965: Vol. 40. Edited by Marjory Rigby,
     Charles Nilon, and James B. Misenheimer, Jr. Cambridge,
     England: Modern Humanities Research Assn., 1967, Item 6295.

4   FISH, CHARLES KELLEWAY, JR. "Henry James and the Craft of
     Fiction: The Years of Exploration, 1864-1871." DA, 25,
     3568 (Princeton).
        An examination of the sixteen stories, letters, critical
     articles, travel articles, reviews, and the one novel writ-
     ten during the period from 1864 through 1871 reveals that
     it was a period of experimentation during which James
     sought to master his craft and during which he discovered
     many of the techniques and themes that became the founda-
     tion of his art.

5   GOLDSTEIN, SALLIE SEARS. "A Critical Study of Henry James's
     The Wings of the Dove, The Ambassadors, and The Golden
     Bowl." DA, 24, 5384-85 (Brandeis).
        The conflict in the three novels arises from the ten-
     sion between the force which seeks to "limit experience"
     and that which seeks to "exploit it." This tension is di-
     rectly rooted in James's own ambivalence toward experi-
     ence, which renders him incapable of resolving the conflict
     in the novel.

6   GREENE, PHILIP LEON. "Henry James and George Eliot." DA, 24,
     4188-89 (New York Univ.).
        The works of the two authors reveal similar interests in
     the areas of character, theme, and technique; and their
     critical writings are closely related in theory.

7   LEVY, EDWARD RICH. "Henry James and the Pragmatic Assumption:
     The Conditions of Perception." DA, 25, 1212 (Illinois).
        The philosophical principles manifested in James's fic-
     tion are a natural ramification of his philosophical inter-
     est and the influence of several notable thinkers including
     Chauncey Wright, Charles Sanders Peirce, Charles Darwin,
     and William James.

8   McGINTY, SISTER MARY CAROLYN, C.S.J. "The Jamesian Parenthe-
     sis: Elements of Suspension in the Narrative Sentences of
     Henry James's Late Style." DA, 24, 4193 (Catholic Univ.).
        James's use of parentheses in The Ambassadors has the ef-
     fect of enhancing the work's sense of immediacy and creat-
     ing a conversational tone that emphasizes sounds and mean-
     ings of individual words.

9   MINTER, ELSIE GRAY. "The Image in the Mirror: Henry James
     and the French Realists." DA, 24, 3340-41 (Univ. of North
     Carolina, Chapel Hill).
         The influence of the French Realists and Zola on James
     is extensive. Viewed in the successive phases of his ca-
     reer, however, the influence is less discernible as it is
     assimilated and adapted and becomes peculiarly his own in
     the major phase.

*10   TILLEY, W. H., JR. "The Background, the Writing and the Re-
      ception of The Princess Casamassima." Dissertation, Chi-
      cago.
         Cited in James Woodress. Dissertations in American Lit-
      erature: 1891-1966. Revised and enlarged with the assis-
      tance of Marian Koritz. Durham: Duke Univ. Press, 1968,
      Item 1578a. For book publication see 1961.A5.

11   TODASCO, RUTH TAYLOR. "The Humanism of Henry James: A Study
     of the Relation Between Theme and Imagery in the Later Nov-
     els." DA, 25, 3559 (Texas Tech.).
         James's humanistic philosophy with its faith in the "hu-
     man capacity to shape a constructive destiny" is articulat-
     ed through his choice of images: the predatory impulse of
     evil is portrayed in animalistic symbols; the practice of
     using other people is expressed through utilitarian images;
     and the sacredness of the human spirit is conveyed in such
     images as a harp, a fount, a bowl, and a dove's wings.

1965 A BOOKS

1   BELL, MILLICENT. Edith Wharton and Henry James: The Story of
     their Friendship. New York: Braziller, 384 pp.
         A biography of the affectionate and intimate Wharton-
     James friendship between 1903 and 1916. Their relationship
     "was of that rarest type between a man and a woman. It
     contained humor, ordinarily the enemy of infatuation, if
     not of love; it was the achievement of detached intellec-
     tual enjoyment and a sympathy qualified by irony. Each cast
     the keenest, and most appreciating, eye upon the other.
     Strangely, too, each had a kind of imaginative anticipation
     of the other." Reviewed: 1965.B2; 1965.B25; 1965.B78;
     1967.B10; R. W. B. Lewis, Nineteenth-Century Fiction,
     20:194-98; Blake Nevius, Virginia Quarterly Review,
     41:649-53; Modern Fiction Studies, 11:198; Joseph Feather-
     stone, New Republic, 142 (29 May), 21-24; Edward Stone,
     American Literature, 37 (1966), 494-95; Allan Wilson, South
     Atlantic Quarterly, 65 (1966), 153-54.

1965

2   BLACKALL, JEAN FRANTZ. <u>Jamesian Ambiguity and "The Sacred</u>
     <u>Fount."</u> Ithaca: Cornell Univ. Press, 194 pp.
        Although it is the "most problematic" of James's novels,
     <u>The Sacred Fount</u> "is explicable if one submits it to a
     variety of perspectives out of which cumulative impres-
     sions may accrue." In addition, an exploration of the
     textual origins of the ambiguities of the novel directs the
     reader "to some of the origins of Jamesian ambiguity" and
     illuminates "both analytic techniques and general implica-
     tions about James's point of view and method which are per-
     tinent to other texts of the late period, and especially
     those of the nineties." Reviewed: J. A. Ward, <u>American</u>
     <u>Literature</u>, 38 (1966), 402-403; Robert L. Gale, <u>New England</u>
     <u>Quarterly</u>, 39 (1966), 407-408; Ralph A. Ranald, <u>Nineteenth-</u>
     <u>Century Fiction</u>, 21 (1966), 199-201; <u>Modern Fiction Stud-</u>
     <u>ies</u>, 12 (Winter 1966-1967), 490; Oscar Cargill, <u>South At-</u>
     <u>lantic Quarterly</u>, 66 (1967), 124-25; Norma Phillips, <u>Novel</u>,
     1 (Fall 1967), 77-78.

3   CLAIR, JOHN A. <u>The Ironic Dimension in the Fiction of Henry</u>
     <u>James</u>. Pittsburgh: Duquesne Univ. Press, 140 pp.
        In his works James uses "two different but related ap-
     plications of irony: the formal or functional ironic ef-
     fects within the work, and the thematic irony--sometimes
     called 'irony of fate'--indicated in the concluding action
     of many of his works." He employed several devices "(1) to
     establish his dramatic ironic relationship between charac-
     ters and (2) to develop the ironic complexity of the action
     throughout." The "existence of and <u>the operation of</u>" this
     ironic principle can be demonstrated in representative
     works: "Four Meetings," "The Jolly Corner," <u>The Turn of</u>
     <u>the Screw</u>, <u>The Spoils of Poynton</u>, and <u>The Golden Bowl</u>. For
     dissertation <u>see</u> 1964.C2. Reviewed: <u>Modern Fiction Stud-</u>
     <u>ies</u>, 11 (Winter 1965-1966), 438; Oscar Cargill, <u>Nineteenth-</u>
     <u>Century Fiction</u>, 21 (1966), 101-103; <u>American Literature</u>,
     37 (1966), 520.

4   CRANFILL, THOMAS M., and ROBERT L. CLARK, JR. <u>An Anatomy of</u>
     <u>"The Turn of the Screw."</u> Austin: Univ. of Texas Press,
     195 pp.
        A survey of the criticism of <u>The Turn of the Screw</u> in
     the Introduction divides readings into "apparitionist" and
     "nonapparitionist." The book itself is a close textual
     reading of the tale which concludes that "the children suf-
     fer prolonged, helpless, lethally dangerous exposure to the
     mad governess." Flora and Miles were "victims of her end-
     less harassment and of mortal terror." A lengthy bibliog-
     raphy is annotated with symbols which indicate the contents

of each article and book. Reprinted by Gordian Press,
1971. Reviewed: W. R. Patrick, Studies in Short Fiction,
3 (1966), 458-60; Francis X. Roellinger, American Literature, 37 (1966), 492-94; Modern Fiction Studies, 12 (Winter 1966-1967), 490-91.

5   DUPEE, FREDERICK W. Henry James. Revised and expanded. A
Delta Book. American Men of Letters Series. New York:
Dell, 265 pp.
     A biographical and critical survey of James's life and
writings.

6   GALE, ROBERT L. Plots and Characters in the Fiction of Henry
James. Hamden, Conn.: Archon Books, 207 pp.
     A chronology of James's life and a chronological list of
James's fiction are followed by concise plot summaries of
the fiction as well as a dictionary of characters appearing
in the fiction. Reviewed: Times Literary Supplement
(25 November), p. 1052; Modern Fiction Studies, 11:199;
Nineteenth-Century Fiction, 20:203.

7   KELLEY, CORNELIA P. The Early Development of Henry James.
Introduction by Lyon N. Richardson. Revised edition.
Urbana: Univ. of Illinois Press., 319 pp.
     This slightly revised version of a text originally pub-
lished in 1930 follows chronologically James's essays, reviews, critical articles and fiction from 1864 to 1881.
Reviewed: Times Literary Supplement (30 December),
p. 1216.

8   KINOIAN, VARTKIS. Henry James's "Daisy Miller" and "The Turn
of the Screw." New York: Monarch, 94 pp.
     A study guide which includes biographical comments and
a selected bibliography as well as summary, critical commentary, and character analyses for each story.

9   KINOIAN, VARTKIS. Henry James's "The Ambassadors." New York:
Monarch, 101 pp.
     A study guide which includes plot summary, critical com-
mentary, character sketches and a selected bibliography.

10 KINOIAN, VARTKIS. Henry James's "The Portrait of a Lady."
New York: Monarch, 88 pp.
     A study guide which includes biographical notes, summary
of the text of the novel, criticism, analyses of characters, critical commentary, and a selected bibliography.

1965

11   LEBOWITZ, NAOMI. The Imagination of Loving: Henry James's
     Legacy to the Novel. Detroit: Wayne State Univ. Press,
     183 pp.
        James's realism was committed to human relationships,
     and his kind of novel might be called "the novel of per-
     sonal relationship." The love relationship between major
     characters (such as between Isabel Archer and Ralph Tou-
     chett and between Isabel and Gilbert Osmond in The Por-
     trait of a Lady) is the "natural and primary" relationship
     which was used as the "technical and moral center" of his
     novels. The relationship between individuals is used not
     only as a "measure of morality," but also as a "strategy
     of structure." Reviewed: Oscar Cargill, Nineteenth-
     Century Fiction, 21 (1966), 101-103; Modern Fiction Stud-
     ies, 12 (Winter 1966-1967), 491; Oscar Cargill, South
     Atlantic Quarterly, 66 (1967), 124-25; Robert C. LeClair,
     American Literature, 38 (1966), 401-402.

12   McELDERRY, BRUCE R., JR. Henry James. New York: Twayne,
     192 pp.
        A comprehensive but brief description of James's fifty-
     year career reveals that "James's achievement was enormous
     in quantity, and, at its best, superlative in quality."
     Individual treatments of each of the novels, stories, and
     plays describe James's work but do not follow a special-
     ized method of interpretation. A list of James's hundred
     and thirty-five fictional works indicates the date each
     was first published. Reviewed: Nineteenth-Century Fic-
     tion, 20:304-305; Choice, 2 (October), 484; Oscar Cargill,
     American Literature, 37 (January 1966), 516.

13   MONTEIRO, GEORGE. Henry James and John Hay: The Record of a
     Friendship. Providence, R.I.: Brown Univ. Press, 205 pp.
        A detailed analysis of the friendship of Henry James
     and John Hay is supplemented by reprints of Hay's reviews
     of Daisy Miller and The Portrait of a Lady, fifty-three
     letters (forty-five of James and eight of Hay), as well as
     a "Calendar of unlocated letters." Partially reprinted:
     pp. 65-76 reprinted in 1963.B67. For dissertation see
     1967.C10. Reviewed: Times Literary Supplement (25 Novem-
     ber), p. 1052; Modern Fiction Studies, 11 (Winter 1965-
     1966), 438; Edwin T. Bowden, New England Quarterly, 39
     (1966), 240-43; Oscar Cargill, Nineteenth-Century Fiction,
     21 (1966), 101-103; American Literature, 37 (1966), 520.

14 OKITA, HAJIME. <u>A Bibliography of Henry James in Japan</u>.
Kyoto: Aporon-sha, 198 pp.
James studies in Japan up to 1964 are cited. Comments
or quotations of important passages are supplied for about
half of the items.

15 ROBERTS, JAMES L. <u>"The Portrait of a Lady": A Critical Study</u>.
Lincoln, Neb.: Cliff's Notes, 71 pp.
A study guide for the student, this pamphlet includes
chapter summaries and commentaries, character sketches, and
study questions.

1965 B SHORTER WRITINGS

1 ANDERSON, QUENTIN. "The Critic and Imperial Consciousness."
<u>New Republic</u>, 152 (17 April), 15-17.
Van Wyck Brooks is termed "a lapsed Henry James" in this
review of Brooks's <u>An Autobiography</u>. Review of 1965.B7.

2 ANDREWS, WAYNE. "Henry James, Edith Wharton, and the Age of
Leisure." <u>Harper</u>, 230 (May), 137-40.
Leon Edel's <u>Complete Tales of Henry James</u> contains some
less noteworthy tales that could have been omitted. In
<u>Edith Wharton and Henry James: The Story of their Friend-
ship</u>, Millicent Bell is able to perceive "that rarest kind"
of friendship between the two writers. Review of 1964.B28
and 1965.A1.

*3 BELLMAN, S. I. "Henry James's 'The Madonna of the Future' and
Two Modern Parallels." <u>California English Journal</u>, 1:47-53.
Cited in 1967.B63, p. 80, by Bruce McElderry, Jr., who
explains that Bellman "finds parallels between James's story and works by Bernard Malamud and Robert Towers; as de-
scribed, the parallels seem less notable than the differences."

4 BERTHOFF, WARNER. <u>The Ferment of Realism: American Literature, 1884-1919</u>. New York: The Free Press, pp. 103-26,
passim.
James's "most worldly novels" are the two city novels,
<u>The Princess Casamassima</u> and <u>The Bostonians</u>, both of which
were failures. A survey of James's work marks him as the
"<u>grand écrivain</u>" of all the American writers of the period.

5   BIRCH, BRIAN. "Henry James: Some Bibliographical and Textual
     Matters." <u>Library</u>, 20 (June), 108-23.
         An examination of five extant texts of <u>The Ambassadors</u>
     suggests that the New York Edition, not the Methuen edition
     suggested by Edel, is "the definitive text in all respects."
     Responses in 1966.B82 and 1966.B12.

6   BORKLUND, ELMER. "Recent Approaches to Henry James." <u>Journal
     of General Education</u>, 16 (January), 327-40.
         The quintessential James has eluded in varying degrees
     both his friends and his enemies in seven studies: (1)
     Edel's <u>The Complete Tales of Henry James</u>; (2) Edel's <u>Henry
     James: The Untried Years</u>, <u>The Conquest of London</u>, and <u>The
     Middle Years</u>; (3) Booth's <u>The Rhetoric of Fiction</u>; (4)
     Geismar's <u>Henry James and the Jacobites</u>; (5) Cargill's <u>The
     Novels of Henry James</u>; (6) Krook's <u>The Ordeal of Conscious-
     ness in Henry James</u>; and (7) Holland's <u>The Expense of Vi-
     sion: Essays on the Craft of Henry James</u>. Review of
     1962.B25; 1962.A1; 1962.A2; 1963.A2; 1961.A1; 1962.A3;
     1964.A3.

7   BROOKS, VAN WYCK. <u>An Autobiography</u>. New York: E. P. Dutton,
     pp. 428-30, passim.
         A dozen passing references to James appear in Brooks's
     self-portrait. The lengthiest appearance is a defense of
     his criticism of James's late works as it appears in his
     <u>The Pilgrimage of Henry James</u>. Reviewed 1965.B1.

8   BROWNE, RAY B., and MARTIN LIGHT. "Henry James," in their
     <u>Critical Approaches to American Literature: Vol. 2: Walt
     Whitman to William Faulkner</u>. New York: Crowell,
     pp. 119-65.
         Contents include:
         "Henry James and the Nature of Evil" by Joseph A. Ward
     (pp. 119-25). Reprint of 1960.B92.
         "The American as a Young Lady" by Christof Wegelin
     (pp. 125-44). Reprinted from <u>The Image of Europe in Henry
     James</u>. Dallas: Southern Methodist Univ. Press, 1958,
     pp. 56-59, 61-80. Also reprinted in 1968.A1.
         "Point of View" by Joseph Warren Beach (pp. 145-55).
     Reprinted from <u>The Method of Henry James</u>. New Haven:
     Yale Univ. Press, 1918, pp. 56-71.
         "James's 'The Real Thing': Three Levels of Meaning" by
     Earle G. Labor (pp. 156-59). Reprint of 1962.B54.
         "The Quest for Reality [in 'The Beast in the Jungle']"
     by Walter F. Wright (pp. 159-65). Reprint of pp. 193-200
     of 1962.A5. "Though it would not be proper to call Marcher

Everyman, yet his predicament is only an accentuation of
that in which any sensitive person may be trapped."

9   BRUCCOLI, MATTHEW J. "Fitzgerald, Brooks, Hemingway, and
James: A New Fitzgerald Letter." Fitzgerald Newsletter,
no. 29 (Spring), pp. 177-78.
Scott Fitzgerald wrote Van Wyck Brooks (June 1925) in
response to The Pilgrimage of Henry James and asked Brooks
why he did not touch more on "James's impotence (physical)
and its influence?"

10 CAMPOS, CHRISTOPHE. "The Great Foreign Place (Henry James),"
in his The View of France: From Arnold to Bloomsbury.
London: Oxford Univ. Press, pp. 106-38.
James's "first expatriate, Roderick Hudson, sets off to
Europe as a pilgrim to the home of Art; his last traveller,
Strether, returns to America in order to escape European
artifice. Both Art and artifice seem to appear most clear-
ly in France."

11 CARGILL, OSCAR. Toward a Pluralistic Criticism. Carbondale:
Southern Illinois Press, pp. 69-117.
Contents include:
"William Dean Howells as Henry James's 'Moral Police-
man'" (pp. 69-94). An "Afterword" is added to this article
originally published in American Literature, 29 (January
1958), 371-98. The relationship between Howells and James
was the "longest important association in American letters."
"The Turn of the Screw and Alice James" (pp. 95-117).
An "Afterword" is added to this article originally published in 1963.B16. Henry James used the elaborately dis-
guised mental illness of his sister Alice as a source of
The Turn of the Screw, which "is at once the most horrific
and tender tale of the nineteenth century."

12 COLVERT, JAMES B. "Views of Southern Character in Some Northern Novels." Mississippi Quarterly, 18 (Spring), 59-68.
For the Northern novelist--Hawthorne, Melville, James,
and Howells--the Southerner is "wild, socially undisci-
plined, enveloped in a dark Afric primitivism, governed by
impulse, exotic and mysterious" and as such he is explored,
somewhat enviously, for the "possibilities of an abundant
experience."

1965

13   CRANFILL, THOMAS, and ROBERT CLARK, JR. "James's Revisions of
        The Turn of the Screw." Nineteenth-Century Fiction, 19
        (March), 394-98.
           In his revision of the 1908 text of The Turn of the
        Screw for the New York Edition, James made many alterations
        which improved the original text "stylistically and seman-
        tically."

14   DAVIS, J. "Intention and Achievement in Narrative Technique:
        Henry James's The Ambassadors." Kwartalnik Neofilologiczny
        (Warsaw), 12 (3 Q):245-53.
           Critics have been accurate in identifying Strether as
        the center of consciousness, but inaccurate in their in-
        sistence that the point of view is consistently rendered.
        Examples of authorial intrusion reminiscent of the tech-
        niques of writers such as Defoe, Fielding, Thackeray,
        Eliot, and Meredith include "adjectival tag[s]," editorial-
        ization, moderation, and interpretation.

15   DOMANIECKI, HILDEGARD. "Complementary Terms in The Turn of
        the Screw: The Straight Turning." Jahrbuch für Amerika-
        studien, 10:206-14.
           A consistent reading of The Turn of the Screw in terms
        of the "turning" images and their opposites, "straight"
        images, shows that the situation at Bly undergoes a com-
        plete reversal in which the originally "'straight' and
        jerky" governess becomes straightforward and the originally
        straightforward Miles becomes "feverish" and "spasmodic."

16   EASTMAN, RICHARD M. "The Psychological Novel," in his A Guide
        to the Novel. San Francisco: Chandler Publishing Co.,
        pp. 126-30.
           The birth, growth, and transformation of the modern
        psychological novel can be traced through the works of
        Eliot, James, Dostoevski, Kafka, Lawrence, Forster, Woolf,
        Proust, Joyce, Sartre, Camus, Beckett and Gide.

17   EDEL, LEON. "Foreword" and "Headnotes," in his edition of The
        Henry James Reader. New York: Scribner's, pp. vii-xiii.
           James could be cited for the many omissions in his
        works, but it is more notable to recognize his "capacity
        for transfiguring the ordinary" and for bringing life and
        literature together in his imagination.

18   EDEL, LEON. "Henry James and The Nation." Nation, 201
     (20 September), 237-40.
         James's affiliation with the fledgling Nation consti-
     tutes "a chapter not only in his own life, but that of
     American journalism and of literature."

19   EDEL, LEON. "Henry James Letters." Times Literary Supplement
     (17 June), p. 523.
         Edel reports that his search for rumored caches of James
     letters, "discovered" after the publication of the first
     three volumes of his James biography, has turned up no new
     documents. (The article also contains the correct render-
     ing of a James letter to Edmund Gosse concerning James
     Symonds and Symonds's booklet about homsexuality, The Prob-
     lem. The letter was misread by Phyllis Grosskurth in her
     biography of Symonds.) Response in 1965.B38.

20   EDEL, LEON. "Introduction," in his edition of The Diary of
     Alice James. London: Rupert Hart-Davis, pp. v-x.
         Only four copies of this diary, kept by Henry James's
     invalid sister during the last months of her life, were
     privately printed in 1894. This edition is based on the
     original manuscript.

21   EGUCHI, YUKO. "The Ordeal of Isabel Archer." Essays and
     Studies in British and American Literature (Tokyo Women's
     Christian College), 13 (September), 77-97. [Japanese]
         Isabel's nature is noble, strong, and developing.
     Through suffering she learns the meaning of renunciation.

22   ELLMANN, RICHARD, and CHARLES FEIDELSON, JR., eds. The Modern
     Tradition: Backgrounds of Modern Literature. New York:
     Oxford Univ. Press, pp. 711-14.
         In exploring the essence of the modern tradition, the
     editors include an excerpt from the preface to The Princess
     Casamassima among other works and authors representing sig-
     nificant points in the development of modernity.

23   FALK, ROBERT. The Victorian Mode in American Fiction, 1865-
     1885. East Lansing: Michigan State Univ. Press, pp. 54-91,
     138-56.
         In this study of the cultural and literary phenomenon of
     "Victorian realism," James's movement is traced from his
     early critical theories; to his first practical application
     in his prose of the early seventies, which is shaded with
     romance; to the late seventies where comedy and irony
     emerge; to the eighties--the "middle years"--which are
     characterized by satiric social criticism.

1965

*24   FARRER, ALISON. "Watch, Ward, the Jamesian Themes." Balcony:
       The Sydney Review, no. 1, pp. 23-27.
              Cited in 1970.B72, p. 303.

 25   FEATHERSTONE, JOSEPH L. "Mrs. Wharton and Mr. James." New
       Republic, 152 (29 May), 21-24.
              A review of Edith Wharton and Henry James: The Story of
       Their Friendship approves of Millicent Bell's judgement of
       the two writers but notes that the multifaceted character
       of James is projected above Wharton. Review of 1965.A1.

 26   FISH, CHARLES K. "Description in Henry James's 'A Light
       Man.'" English Language Notes, 2 (March), 211-15.
              The description of Mr. Sloane's library is calculated by
       James to reveal significant qualities about the character
       of Sloane and of Max.

 27   FISH, CHARLES K. "Indirection, Irony, and the Two Endings of
       James's 'The Story of a Masterpiece.'" Modern Philology,
       62 (February), 241-43.
              The editorially induced revision of "The Story of a
       Masterpiece" magnifies "two characteristic Jamesian
       traits": his emphasis on indirect presentation and his
       propensity for ironic detachment.

*28   FISHER, NEIL H. "Introduction," in his edition of The Ambas-
       sadors. New York: Airmont.
              Cited in Beatrice Ricks, comp. Henry James: A Bibliog-
       raphy of Secondary Works. Scarecrow Author Bibliographies,
       No. 24. Metuchen, N.J.: Scarecrow Press, 1975, Item 91.

*29   FISHER, NEIL H. "Introduction," in his edition of The Por-
       trait of a Lady. New York: Airmont.
              Cited in Beatrice Ricks, comp. Henry James: A Bibliog-
       raphy of Secondary Works. Scarecrow Author Bibliographies,
       No. 24. Metuchen, N.J.: Scarecrow Press, 1975, Item 769.

 30   FRIEND, J. H. "The Structure of The Portrait of a Lady."
       Nineteenth-Century Fiction, 20 (June), 85-95.
              A study of the structure of The Portrait of a Lady
       traces Isabel's development on her classic ironic quest.

 31   GALE, ROBERT L. "A Possible Source for Elements in The Por-
       trait of a Lady." Studi Americani, no. 11, pp. 137-41.
              The scene in which Caspar Goodwood accompanies the dying
       Ralph Touchett may have been inspired by a real life inci-
       dent in which Luther Terry, an American painter and friend

of the Crawfords, accompanied his sculptor-friend, Thomas Crawford, from Rome to Paris.

32 GINGER, RAY. An Age of Excess: The United States from 1877-1914. New York: Macmillan, passim.
Five references to James are included in this history of the U.S. for the years during which James was writing.

33 GRAHAM, KENNETH. English Criticism of the Novel: 1865-1900. Oxford: At the Clarendon Press, pp. 102-13, passim.
During the "plot-character controversy" of the 1880s, Henry James was criticized in English journals for too extensive detailing of personality and motive in his works and also for lack of plot.

34 GRAHAM, KENNETH. Review of The Expense of Vision: Essays on the Craft of Henry James, by Laurence Bedwell Holland. Review of English Studies, 16:443-45.
Holland's style "is like a parody of academic criticism" and this book is "only dimly connected with the way we actually experience the fiction it analyzes."

35 GREEN, MARTIN. "Henry James and the Great Tradition," in his Re-Appraisals: Some Commonsense Readings in American Literature. New York: W. W. Norton, pp. 145-66.
Reprint of 1963.B41.

36 GREENE, GEORGE. "Elizabeth Bowen: Imagination as Therapy." Perspective, 14 (Spring), 42-52.
Bowen's "chief mentor" is Henry James.

37 GROSS, BARRY. "Newman to Gatsby: This Side of Innocence." Papers of the Michigan Academy of Science, Arts, and Letters, 53:279-89.
Professor Kermit Vanderbilt incorrectly perceives of Jay Gatsby and Christopher Newman as parallel protagonists. In fact, they are substantively different: they have different self-conceptions, they have different moral values, and consequently they have different conclusions. Response to 1965.B116.

38 GROSSKURTH, PHYLLIS. "Henry James Letters." Times Literary Supplement (19 August), p. 722.
Grosskurth accepts Edel's correction of a quotation from a James letter used by Grosskurth in her biography of Symonds. Response to 1965.B19.

1965

39 GULLÓN, RICARDO. "Imágenes de El Otro." Revista Hispanica
   Moderna, 31:210-21. [Spanish]
       The Private Life is more than a mere love story, because
   of the transparent symbolism James inserted in the plot,
   together with the idea--universal, though inspired by
   Browning--of the individual's double; a double that can
   represent the individual in society, leaving the real self
   a pure spirit devoted to artistic creation. In The Jolly
   Corner Brydon has a confrontation with his other--and real
   --self. If The Jolly Corner is compared to El Otro, similarities are revealed in plot and character, but there is
   one major difference between Brydon and Emilio: love.
   Brydon's love will enable him to be active in front of his
   mysterious adversary, while Emilio remains passive and
   fearful.

40 HAGOPIAN, JOHN V. "In Defense of the Affective Fallacy."
   Southern Review: An Australian Journal of Literary Studies, 1:72-77.
       The text of "The Pupil" supports Hagopian's view that
   Pemberton brought about Morgan's death by taking the young
   boy on a long walk and then breaking his heart by rejecting
   him. What Spilka failed to take into account "is that all
   the events of the story are presented from the point of
   view of Pemberton." Response to 1965.B99. See 1965.B100.

41 HAIGHT, GORDON S. "Introduction," in his A Century of George
   Eliot Criticism. Boston: Houghton Mifflin Co., pp. x-xii.
       Seven of Henry James's articles on Eliot are reprinted
   in this collection, and in the Introduction the editor
   terms James an "exacting critic" of Eliot.

*42 HALL, JAMES B. Teacher's Manual for "The Realm of Fiction:
   61 Short Stories." New York: McGraw-Hill, pp. 36-37.
       Cited in Beatrice Ricks, comp. Henry James: A Bibliog-
   raphy of Secondary Works. Scarecrow Author Bibliographies,
   No. 24. Metuchen, N.J.: Scarecrow Press, 1975, Item 480.1.

43 HALL, SUSAN CORWIN, comp. Hawthorne to Hemingway: An Annotated Bibliography of Books from 1945 to 1963 about Nine
   American Authors. Edited by Robert H. Woodward. New York:
   Garrett Publishing Co., pp. 36-44, passim.
       Over fifty books on James (including criticism, biogra-
   phy, and editions of his work) are listed and annotated.
   The annotations are abstracts of reviews appearing in American Literature.

44 HALLIBURTON, D. G. "Self and Secularization in The Princess
    Casamassima." Modern Fiction Studies, 11 (Summer),
    116-28.
        The problem of society and self is focused on the char-
    acter of Hyacinth Robinson. He relates to his society and
    to "the entirety of his intellectual and moral landscape"
    by the "process of secularization."

45 HAMBLEN, ABIGAIL ANN. "The Jamesian Note in Edith Wharton's
    The Children." University Review (Kansas City), 31
    (Spring), 209-11.
        Wharton's The Children, published twelve years after
    James's death, recalls two recurrent themes from his novels
    --"that of Americans corrupted by Europe (and by wealth)
    and that of the plight of the innocent young in a corrupt
    adult world."

46 HANEY, CHARLES WILLIAM. "The Garden and the Child: A Study
    of Pastoral Transformation." DA, 26, 2212 (Yale).
        Through the course of literary history the child has
    gradually supplanted the garden as a basic pastoral motif;
    and the essential symbolism has been transformed from the
    idealized Wordsworthian child to the potentially sinister
    child in The Turn of the Screw.

47 HARTSOCK, MILDRED E. "The Dizzying Crest: Strether as Moral
    Man." Modern Language Quarterly, 26 (September), 414-25.
        Strether "bears the image of the existentialist exposed
    man, made naked by his own perceptions, pushed by them to
    the extremity of ethical rebellion, yet always committed
    to his human responsibility to act in the context of what
    it is possible for him to know." He maintains a precarious
    balance upon the "'dizzying crest'" of integrity.

48 HARVEY, W. J. Character and the Novel. Ithaca, N.Y.: Cor-
    nell Univ. Press, pp. 30-61, 81-89.
        In "The Human Context" (pp. 30-61), a discussion of
    character in fiction and in life, fictional characters are
    divided into four categories: protagonist, background,
    card, and ficelle. But it is the human context, the web of
    relationships in which characters are enmeshed, which al-
    lows the reader to define a fictional character. Original-
    ly printed in a different form in 1963.B43. Reprinted in
    1967.B101.
        The Princess Casamassima fails in "internal coherence"
    and it is a "mimetic failure": "James fails in his heroic
    attempt to extend his imaginative insight into a world of
    which he has inadequate knowledge" (pp. 81-89).

1965

49   HEILBRUN, CAROLYN. "The Woman as Hero." Texas Quarterly, 8
     (Winter), 132-41.
        The woman-hero emerged in the late 1870s, enjoyed a
     brief career under Ibsen, James, Lawrence and Forster, and
     disappeared in the early 1920s.

50   HIGUCHI, HIDEO. "Introduction to Henry James (II): Morality
     in the Novel." Gaikoku Bungaku Kenkyu (Ritsumeikan Univ.,
     Kyoto), 10 (March), 78-95. [Japanese]
        If James is considered as a critic, especially in con-
     nection with M. Arnold, Hawthorne, Zola, and H. G. Wells,
     it can be seen that James spoke basically the same truth as
     Arnold did--that poetry is a criticism of life.

51   HOLDER, ALAN. "Three Voyagers in Search of Europe: A Study
     of Henry James, Ezra Pound, and T. S. Eliot." DA, 26,
     1646-47 (Columbia).
        For substantially different reasons, the three authors
     left America. All three, however, sought a cosmopolitan-
     ism and a connection with the past; but they ultimately had
     to reconcile their idealized vision of Europe with reality.
     See 1966.B41 for book publication.

52   HOUGH, GRAHAM. "The Novelist as Innovator: Henry James."
     Listener, 73 (25 March), 447-49.
        In James's critical writing and in his novels, it is al-
     ways clear "that the most elaborate indirections are em-
     ployed only with the purpose of presenting, as fully and
     powerfully as possible, all the implications of a given
     social situation . . . . The art is not executing its ara-
     besques in a void; it is used to elucidate life."

53   HOWE, HELEN. The Gentle Americans, 1864-1960: Biography of a
     Breed. New York: Harper and Row, pp. 91-92, passim.
        A biographical portrait of M. A. DeWolfe Howe by his
     daughter is achieved through a look at the writer in his
     circle of social and literary acquaintances. The biography
     contains some dozen references to Henry James.

54   HYNES, JOSEPH A. "The Middle Way of Miss Farange: A Study of
     James's Maisie." Journal of English Literary History, 32
     (December), 528-53.
        "Game" imagery is used to focus on "the process, the
     shape and the value of renunciation" in which Maisie
     emerges a pragmatist halfway between Mrs. Wix and Sir
     Claude.

55   ISLE, WALTER. "The Romantic and the Real: Henry James's The
     Sacred Fount." Rice Univ. Studies, 51 (Winter), 29-47.
         In the last novel before the achievements of the major
     phase, James "demonstrates his mastery of form and the
     value of experiment in the novel." Reprinted in 1968.A11.

56   ITAGAKI, KONOMU. "'Merciful indirection' in The Wings of the
     Dove." Studies in English Literature (English Literary So-
     ciety of Japan, Univ. of Tokyo), 41 (March), 165-81.
     [Japanese]
         A moral interpretation of the work, this article takes
     Milly as "being," or the embodiment of perfect virtue, in
     contrast to those people of "seeing," who either admire her
     or see her without fully understanding her true quality.
     The theme, "transcendence of 'seeing' by 'being,'" is tech-
     nically assured, for the heroine is viewed by other charac-
     ters as reflecting her inner virtue, or she is being prop-
     erly treated by James's "merciful indirection."

57   IZSAK, EMILY K. "The Composition of The Spoils of Poynton."
     Texas Studies in Literature and Language, 6 (Winter),
     460-71.
         An examination of the published versions of The Spoils
     of Poynton (including serialization), James's notebook ref-
     erences to the work, and his correspondence with the editor
     of The Atlantic Monthly reveals the evolutionary and exper-
     imental nature of the novel and helps clarify its ambiguity,
     while demanding a reassessment of James's preface to the
     New York Edition.

58   KARITA, MOTOJI. "The Early American Short Stories: Henry
     James." Eigo Seinen [The Rising Generation] (Tokyo), 111
     (October), 4-5. [Japanese]
         An introduction to James's tales, a discussion of the
     various names assigned to the genre of the tale, and an
     analysis of the thematic characteristics of the three pe-
     riods of his tales.

59   KIRK, CLARA M. W. D. Howells and Art in His Time. New Bruns-
     wick, N.J.: Rutgers Univ. Press, passim.
         This study of Howells's relationship to the movements of
     art during his life contains many references to Henry

1965

60　KNOEPFLMACHER, U. C.　"'O Rare for Strether!': Antony and
　　Cleopatra and The Ambassadors."　Nineteenth-Century Fic-
　　tion, 19 (March), 333-44.
　　　　The final confrontation between Strether and Mme. de
　　Vionnet in Chapter 33 "is the culmination of a carefully
　　constructed sequence, begun early in the novel, which de-
　　picts Strether's progressive abstraction of Chad's mis-
　　tress into Shakespeare's Cleopatra, an abstraction made
　　even more ironic by his resulting, unconsciously wishful,
　　self-portrayal as the Antony of his imagined queen."　Re-
　　printed in 1969.A10.

61　KNOX, GEORGE.　"Romance and Fable in James's The American."
　　Anglia, 83:308-23.
　　　　James intended to write a "cultural parable, i.e., a
　　Romance" in this novel.　If critics would reach into "its
　　psychic depths for the fable," they would discover "a cul-
　　tural fable of success and failure, superimposed on various
　　fairy-tale motifs, allusions to marriage immurement themes
　　in Renaissance paintings, and the employment of eighteenth
　　century Gothic conventions."　Reprinted in 1972.B112 and
　　1971.A7.

62　KRAFT, QUENTIN G.　"Life Against Death in Venice."　Criticism,
　　7 (Summer), 217-23.
　　　　James practiced "the art of suggestive omission" in
　　choosing to omit the climax of Densher's portion of The
　　Wings of the Dove.　The unrepresented last meeting of Den-
　　sher and Milly must be understood in order to understand
　　the novel.　James successfully evoked this scene without
　　literally presenting it.

63　KRAFT, QUENTIN G.　"The Question of Freedom in James's Fic-
　　tion."　College English, 26 (February), 372-376, 381.
　　　　Strether's famous statement on freedom is not represen-
　　tative of James's ideal, where "in rare moments of insight
　　a freedom that is more than an illusion" is achieved.

64　LEARY, LEWIS, ed.　The Teacher and American Literature: Pa-
　　pers Presented at the 1964 Convention of the National Coun-
　　cil of Teachers of English.　Champaign, Ill.: National
　　Council of Teachers of English, pp. 134-48.
　　　　Contents include:
　　　　"Recent Scholarship on Mark Twain and Henry James" by
　　Howard Webb, Jr. (pp. 134-43).　A survey of scholarship on
　　the two authors reveals much work has been done in many
　　areas:　bibliography, textual material, collections of cor-
　　respondence, biographical material, and critical works.

"Mark Twain and Henry James: Implications for School Programs" by Frank H. Townsend (pp. 144-48). Greater emphasis should be placed on Twain and James in secondary school courses.

65 LEBOWITZ, NAOMI. "Magic and Metamorphosis in The Golden Bowl." Sewanee Review, 73 (Winter), 58-73.
Henry James "measured his most essential realism by the world of magic." In The Golden Bowl Maggie earns a life of Cinderella-like romance after her mind and heart "have gone beyond the powers of magic." Reprinted in 1968.A11.

66 LEWIS, R. W. B. Trials of the Word: Essays in American Literature and the Humanistic Tradition. New Haven, Conn.: Yale Univ. Press, pp. 77-96, 112-28.
Contents include:
"Hawthorne and James: The Matter of the Heart" (pp. 77-96). Originally published as "The Tactics of Sanctity: Hawthorne and James," in 1964.B79.
"Henry James: The Theater of Consciousness." Part I (pp. 113-20): "The Sense of Fair Play." For James "the question of beauty was located somewhere amid that lively anecdotal dialectic of the moral and the histrionic." Part II (pp. 120-28): "The Wings of the Dove." Reprinted from Modern Fiction Studies, 3 (Spring 1957), 33-40.

67 LOWERY, BRUCE. "Marcel Proust et Henry James." Informations et documents, no. 216 (15 May), pp. 20-23. [French]
Proust and James offer to their readers various similarities, perhaps dictated by the same socio-historical background. Though James makes use of a more experimental technique than Proust, both are concerned with the same themes, the primary importance of characters, the difficulty of communication among characters, and the deep analysis of real emotions. In both writers is an ambiguity of style with long, slow, precise sentences.

68 LUCAS, JOHN. "Manliest of Cities: The Image of Rome in Henry James." Studi Americani, no. 11, pp. 117-36.
An essayist, biographer, novelist, and teller of tales, James used the image of Rome in many ways. This "city incomparably endowed with the trophies of its history" was for James's American girls, "the manliest of cities."

1965

69 MACAULEY, ROBIE. "'Let Me Tell You About the Rich. . . .'" <u>Kenyon Review</u>, 27 (Autumn), 645-71.
<u>The Europeans</u> "is meant to be about money, should be about money, but . . . is not." The real issue concerns "the amenities" of wealth. In <u>Washington Square</u> money is "a purely negative fact" and wealth must have "an accompanying set of values."

70 McCLOSKEY, JOHN C. "What Maisie Knows: A Study of Childhood and Adolescence." <u>American Literature</u>, 36 (January), 485-513.
Maisie's education is not one of moral awareness, ethical development, or precocious intellectuality, but is an education in an insular environment in which Maisie's evolving egoism "culminates in the ascendancy of her ego, untrained, unrestrained, ill-formed, and ethically illiterate."

71 McELDERRY, BRUCE R. "Henry James," in <u>American Literary Scholarship: An Annual, 1963</u>. Edited by James Woodress. Durham, N.C.: Duke Univ. Press, pp. 64-71.
Survey of criticism published during 1963.

72 McLEAN, R. C. "The 'Disappointed Observer' of <u>Madame de Mauves</u>." <u>Research Studies</u> (Washington State Univ.), 33 (December), 181-96.
Longmore, not Madame de Mauves, is the central character in a study of consciousness. Longmore, a vacillating and ambivalent character, is romantically inclined and lacks critical information about Madame de Mauves, which leads to his final disappointment.

73 MASUNAGA, KEIICHI. "American Naturalism and James: Centering on Renunciation." <u>Gaikoku Bungaku Kenkyu</u>, 11 (December), 1-28. [Japanese]
When James's work is examined in relation to naturalism, it is evident that James was ten or fifteen years ahead of his time, since he was searching for inner harmony during the last years of the nineteenth century rather than focusing on the outer world. This point is aptly illustrated by comparing a Jamesian heroine's suffering in the course of awareness with that of a social climber in a naturalistic novel by H. G. Wells. In conclusion, Jamesian inner harmony is the renunciation of an outsider, a peculiarly individualistic act in the American democratic and puritanical context.

*74   MELCHIORI, GIORGIO. "Aspetti del Simbolismo di Henry James,"
       in Il Simbolismo nella Letteratura Nord-Americana: Atti
       del Symposium tenuto a Firenze 27-29 Novembre 1964.
       Florence: La Nuova Italia, pp. 169-90.
            In 1968.B67, p. 75, Bruce R. McElderry, Jr. explains
       that this article is an Italian version of 1965.B75.

 75   MELCHIORI, GIORGIO. "Cups of Gold for the Sacred Fount: As-
       pects of James's Symbolism." Critical Quarterly, 7 (Win-
       ter), 301-16.
            An examination of the use of symbolism in the later nov-
       els shows that James "goes far beyond the traditional sym-
       bolism of American fiction" and "approaches the visionary
       and mysteric symbolism of William Blake." Reprinted in
       1974.A3; printed in Italian in 1965.B74.

 76   MELCHIORI, GIORGIO. "Henry James e Tennyson," in Arte e Sto-
       ria: Studi in Onore di Leonello Vincenti. Turin: Giappi-
       chelli, pp. 341-59. [Italian]
            James's painful and intense search for his roots, his
       tradition, is revealed through his allusions and uses of
       sources among English authors such as Shakespeare and Ten-
       nyson. Reprinted in Italian in 1974.A3.

 77   MELCHIORI, GIORGIO. "Locksley Hall Revisited: Tennyson and
       Henry James." Review of English Literature, 6 (October),
       9-25.
            James's A Passionate Pilgrim "is the transposition into
       new and bitter terms of what was at the time the most fa-
       mous of Tennyson's poems"--"Locksley Hall." Reprinted in
       Italian in 1974.A3.

 78   MELLOW, JAMES R. "Edith Wharton and Henry James." Common-
       weal, 82 (18 June), 417-18.
            Wharton's and James's friendship was "more than liter-
       ary"; it was a "psychological necessity." Millicent Bell's
       Edith Wharton and Henry James: The Story of their Friend-
       ship gives us "a touching sense of the real friendship that
       existed between them." Review of 1965.A1.

 79   MURRAY, DONALD M. "The Balcony, the Pond, and the Literary
       Traveler." Antioch Review, 25 (Summer), 333-36.
            The London house at No. 34 DeVere Gardens, where Henry
       James lived and wrote from 1886 to 1897, is "a portal into
       the Jamesian world," while other literary landmarks, such
       as the Dickens house on Doughty Street in London, seem to
       lead the traveler "away from the remembered works" toward
       artifacts.

1965

80   NORMAND, JEAN. "L'Ambassadeur: Henry James, romancier des
       deux mondes." <u>Informations et documents</u>, no. 216 (5 May),
       pp. 14-19. [French]
          James is the ambassador of American literature in Europe
       and is also the ambassador of the European literary tradi-
       tion in America.

81   O'GRADY, WALTER. "On Plot in Modern Fiction: Hardy, James
       and Conrad." <u>Modern Fiction Studies</u>, 11 (Summer), 107-15.
          The "internal event" is central in <u>The Ambassadors</u>, with
       "the external situation, the internal situation, the inci-
       dents" all directed toward it.

82   ONISHI, AKIO. "Henry James: 'The Figure in the Carpet.'"
       <u>Eigo Eibungaku Ronshu</u> (Kansai Univ.), 9 (February), 53-70.
       [Japanese]
          An attempt to solve the mystery of the figure by sus-
       pecting each of the characters results in the conclusion
       that James has succeeded in portraying a sense of ambiguity
       which is reflected in a cracked mirror that gives no defi-
       nite image.

83   PARKER, HERSHEL. "An Error in the Text of James's <u>The Ameri-
       can</u>." <u>American Literature</u>, 37 (November), 316-18.
          The New York Edition, the punctuation, and the sense of
       the novel make it clear that the statement "For the girl
       herself, you may be at rest . . .", which appears late in
       Chapter XI, should be attributed to Valentin not Newman.

84   PAUL, SHERMAN. <u>Edmund Wilson: A Study of Literary Vocation
       in Our Time</u>. Urbana: Univ. of Illinois Press, pp. 17-18,
       36-38, 216-17, passim.
          In this critical-biographical study of Edmund Wilson,
       more than a dozen passing references to Henry James occur.

85   POIRIER, RICHARD. "Henry James: <u>The Portrait of a Lady</u>," in
       <u>The American Novel from James Fenimore Cooper to William
       Faulkner</u>. Edited by Wallace Stegner. New York: Basic
       Books, pp. 47-60.
          The novel contains considerable autobiographical mate-
       rial; there is a parallel between Isabel's aspiration for
       "freedom" and James's "heritage of Emersonian 'self-
       reliance.'"

86   RAHV, PHILIP. "Pulling Down the Shrine," in his <u>The Myth and</u>
     <u>the Powerhouse</u>. New York: Farrar, Straus and Giroux,
     pp. 202-208.
         Maxwell Geismar in <u>Henry James and the Jacobites</u> heaps
     upon James the most "ruthless abuse" ever directed at an
     American writer of stature. Geismar's attack is "politi-
     cally motivated." Review of 1963.B2.

87   RANDALL, JOHN H., III. "The Genteel Reader and <u>Daisy Miller</u>."
     <u>American Quarterly</u>, 17 (Fall), 568-81.
         Anticipating a genteel audience, James makes Daisy the
     victim of the genteel tradition, a tradition he criticizes
     through the implicit criticism of Winterbourne.

88   RAO, N. KRISHNA. "The Idea of Refinement in Henry James's
     The Awkward Age." <u>Literary Criterion</u>, 6:56-60.
         The maturation and refinement of Nanda Brookenham is
     achieved through her perceptive knowledge of good and evil
     in the context of her social world.

89   RASKIN, JONAH. "Henry James and the French Revolution."
     <u>American Quarterly</u>, 17 (Winter), 724-33.
         Of the images and metaphors James drew from social and
     historical contexts, those from the French Revolution are
     predominant, revealing its profound effect on his thinking
     and writing.

90   RIDDEL, JOSEPH N. "F. Scott Fitzgerald, the Jamesian Inheri-
     tance, and the Morality of Fiction." <u>Modern Fiction Stud-</u>
     <u>ies</u>, 11 (Winter 1965-1966), 331-50.
         "Fitzgerald owes a number of obvious debts to James,"
     though they are writers of "unequal abilities." The af-
     finities that James and Fitzgerald share do not consist of
     "influences or borrowings so much as inheritance."

91   ROSS, MAUDE CARDWELL. "Moral Values of the American Woman as
     Presented in Three Major American Authors." <u>DA</u>, 25,
     5262-63 (Texas).
         Five isolatable moral principles of significance to
     American women are discernible through an examination of
     Hawthorne's <u>The Scarlet Letter</u>, James's <u>The Golden Bowl</u>,
     and Faulkner's <u>The Hamlet</u>, <u>The Town</u> and <u>The Mansion</u>.

92   ROVIT, EARL. "The Ghosts in James's 'The Jolly Corner.'"
     <u>Tennessee Studies in Literature</u>, 10:65-72.
         <u>The Jolly Corner</u> is an allegory, but the referents are
     "privately idiosyncratic" and difficult for most readers to

1965

understand. Alice Staverton's dreams are significant keys
to the allegory.

93 SAMUEL, IRENE. "Henry James on Imagination and the Will to
    Power." Bulletin of the New York Public Library, 69
    (February), 117-30.
        The three principal characters in The Princess Casamas-
    sima, Hyacinth Robinson, Paul Muniment, and Christina,
    dramatize "the polarity of imagination and the will to
    power."

94 SCHNEIDER, MARCEL. "Henry James et Benjamin Britten." Nou-
    velle Revue Française, 13 (April), 713-16. [French]
        In the opera version of The Turn of the Screw, first
    presented at Venice in 1955, Benjamin Britten imitates
    Henry James by playing constantly on ambiguity and achiev-
    ing the rare feat of entering deeply into the moral and
    aesthetic intentions of James.

95 SEGAL, ORA. "'The Liar': A Lesson in Devotion." Review of
    English Studies, ns 16 (August), 272-81.
        In "The Liar' Lyon is "neither an impeccable hero nor
    a contemptible villain." At the crucial moment he fails
    to perceive the whole truth.

96 SEGAL, ORA. "The Weak Wings of Pride: An Interpretation of
    James's 'The Bench of Desolation.'" Nineteenth-Century
    Fiction, 20 (September), 145-54.
        Kate Cookman belongs in the tradition of the Jamesian
    devoted woman; and her confession--in consideration of its
    circumstance, the response of Herbert Dodd, and the value
    James places on Dodd's interpretation of the confession--
    must be taken as truth.

97 SLABEY, ROBERT M. "The Turn of the Screw: Grammar and Op-
    tics." College Language Association Journal, 9 (Septem-
    ber), 68-72.
        Three occurrences of "antecedentless" pronouns and the
    "unusually acute vision" of the governess suggest one of
    James's thematic concerns in the story is the "nature of
    imaginative truth--the 'truth' of fiction."

98 SPARSHOTT, F. E. "An Aspect of Literary Portraiture." Essays
    in Criticism, 15 (July), 359-60.
        The consistent judging of Isabel Archer by other charac-
    ters in The Portrait of a Lady and the evaluations of the
    author are not obtrusive or moralistic, as A. R. Mills sug-
    gests, but are the elements that render the novel distinc-
    tive. Response to 1964.B68.

99   SPILKA, MARK. "The Affective Fallacy Revisited." <u>Southern</u>
      <u>Review: An Australian Journal of Literary Studies</u>,
      1:57-70.
           While "the Affective Fallacy defines old sources of sub-
      jective error . . . it also eliminates feeling from the
      critical process and invites its covert re-emergence." One
      of several tonal misreadings of texts presented here is
      Hagopian's interpretation of "The Pupil." His interpreta-
      tion that Pemberton caused Morgan's death is not supported
      by the "<u>sense</u>" of the text: "the <u>tone</u> belies the critic's
      [Hagopian's] ingenuity." Response to 1965.B40. <u>See</u>
      1965.B100.

100   SPILKA, MARK. "Hagopian Revisited." <u>Southern Review: An</u>
      <u>Australian Journal of Literary Studies</u>, 1:77-79.
           Spilka responds to Hagopian's reading of "The Pupil" in
      this continuing critical debate in which Spilka explains,
      "Fundamentally we differ on the relations between litera-
      ture and life, and beyond that, on the functions of litera-
      ture which such relations imply." In interpreting "The
      Pupil" Spilka claims he stresses "aesthetic sensibility, a
      familiar aspect of James's world," while "Hagopian stresses
      homosexual aggression, something common in reality but not
      in James's fiction." Response to 1965.B40. <u>See</u> 1965.B99.

101   SPILLER, ROBERT E. <u>The Third Dimension: Studies in Literary</u>
      <u>History</u>. New York: Macmillan; London: Collier-Macmillan,
      pp. 114-15.
           Stephen Crane's use of symbol begins "where James
      pauses, at the threshold of the unconscious."

102   STANDLEY, FRED L. "Henry James to Stopford Brooke: An Unpub-
      lished Letter." <u>Victorian Newsletter</u>, no. 27 (Spring),
      p. 29.
           James's letter to Brooke reflects James's "prevalent at-
      titude" toward Italy and England, his ability to recall
      things with vividness, and his cordiality toward Brooke.

103   STEVENS, HARRIET S. "Lo que James sabía." <u>Torre</u>, 13:171-93.
      [Spanish]
           An analysis of characterization, style, structure, and
      theme in <u>What Maisie Knew</u> demonstrates that the novel is
      reflective of all the best qualities of James's work.

104   STRATMAN, CARL J., comp. <u>Bibliography of the American Theatre,</u>
      <u>Excluding New York City</u>. Chicago: Loyola Univ. Press,
      p. 137.

1965

One entry by James is listed—his review of <u>School for Scandal</u> at the Boston Museum, which was published in <u>Atlantic Monthly</u>, 33 (December 1874), 754.

105 TADOKORO, NOBUSHIGE. "The Problem of Hallucinations in <u>The Turn of the Screw</u>." <u>Kyushu American Literature</u> (Fukuoka, Japan), no. 8, pp. 25-35.
      James uses the hallucinatory phenomenon in <u>The Turn of the Screw</u> to render a complex unity in his story that surpasses the experiments of J. S. LeFanu with the same phenomenon.

106 TANNER, TONY. "The Fearful Self: Henry James's <u>The Portrait of a Lady</u>." <u>Critical Quarterly</u>, 7 (Autumn), 205-19.
      At the heart of the novel is the psychic journey Isabel Archer makes in which her "uncommitted, undefined self" seeks "the right house to live in and the right partner to live with." She chooses the wrong house and the wrong partner, but she gains the vision which will enable her to "come to a true realization of what her real self is." Reprinted in 1968.A1, 1968.A11, and 1970.A5.

107 TANNER, TONY. "Henry James," in his <u>The Reign of Wonder: Naivety and Reality in American Literature</u>. Cambridge, England: University Press, pp. 259-335.
      "The Candid Outsider" (pp. 261-77) states: "Henry James was the first, and still by far the greatest, writer to inquire into the fate of wonder when it is introduced into the clotted complexities of society and the turbulence of time." In <u>A London Life</u> James used "the candid outside eye as a strategy," subjecting it "to a dynamic, unprogrammed education."
      In "The Range of Wonderment" (pp. 278-308), an examination of <u>What Maisie Knew</u> reveals the subtlety and richness of James's analysis of the naive eye, as well as "the lessons he made it yield." "The Subjective Adventure" (pp. 309-35) is a slightly different version of 1963.B109.

108 TERRIE, HENRY L., JR. "The Image of Chester in <u>The Ambassadors</u>." <u>English Studies</u>, 46 (February), 46-50.
      James is able to make the reader know the town of Chester well, though he describes the town in only two passages. James was drawing on the "felt experience" of Chester reflected in an early essay on the town written for the <u>Nation</u> in 1872.

109 THARP, LOUISE HALL. <u>Mrs. Jack</u>. Boston: Little, Brown, passim.
      Approximately 30 passing references to Henry James appear in this biography of Isabella Stewart Gardner.

142

110 THOMSON, A. W. "The Turn of the Screw: Some Points on the Hallucination Theory." Review of English Literature, 6 (October), 26-36.

Dorothea Krook's reliance on the preface as one of four objections to Edmund Wilson's hallucination theory is undermined, since there appears to be a discrepancy between the prefatory intent and the text as it was finalized--a discrepancy that probably resulted from a change in purpose during the course of writing.

111 TILLOTSON, GEOFFREY, and KATHLEEN TILLOTSON. Mid-Victorian Studies. London: Athlone Press, passim.

James is mentioned in passing in this study which includes chapters on Trollope, George Eliot, Tennyson, Browning, Newman, and others.

112 TOCHIHARA, TOMOO. "Henry James: 'The Jolly Corner'--Borderland between the Conscious and Superconscious." Shakai-Gakubu Kiyo (Kwansei Gakuin Univ.), 11 (August), 37-45. [Japanese]

"The Jolly Corner" reflects James's "sense of loss," as does The American Scene.

113 TRACHTENBERG, STANLEY. "The Return of the Screw." Modern Fiction Studies, 11 (Summer), 180-82.

The Turn of the Screw is "a story of guilt and innocence." Douglas revealed the story in order to shed his guilt, and his character embodies the aspects of sin and redemption.

114 TRUSS, TOM J., JR. "Anti-Christian Myth in James's 'The Tree of Knowledge.'" Univ. of Mississippi Studies in English, 6:1-4.

Allegorically perceived, the story is a "gloomy myth, which connotatively is anti-authoritarian and hence anti-institutional, and perhaps even anti-Christian."

115 ULANOV, BARRY. The Two Worlds of American Art: The Private and the Popular. New York: Macmillan, pp. 210-18, passim.

At times James felt that he made his private view too public, but then his detachment would deliver him.

116 VANDERBILT, KERMIT. "James, Fitzgerald, and the American Self-Image." Massachusetts Review, 6 (Winter-Spring), 289-304.

James's The American and Fitzgerald's The Great Gatsby are "broadly parallel moral allegories of the American experience" that intersect "moral history" and become "an

important part of the current 'reconstruction' of the American character." Response in 1968.B37. Reprinted in
1972.B112.

117 WAGNER, LINDA WELSHIMER. "The Dominance of Heredity in the
Characterizations of Henry James." South Dakota Review, 2
(Spring), 69–77.
A study of the texts of Roderick Hudson, The Portrait of
a Lady, and The Ambassadors indicates that James considers
heredity, not environment, as "the incontrovertible basis
for character."

118 WALKER, WARREN S., comp. Twentieth-Century Short Story Expli-
cation: Supplement II. Interpretations, April 1, 1963-
December 31, 1964 of Short Fiction Since 1800. Hamden,
Conn.: Shoe String Press, pp. 72–86.
Published articles explicating James's stories are list-
ed under the titles of individual stories.

119 WARD, J. A. "James's Idea of Structure." Publications of the
Modern Language Association of America, 80 (September),
419–26.
Jamesian structure consists of the reconciliation of two
opposites: (1) "The Organic Principle," and (2) "The Me-
chanical Principle."

120 WARD, J. A. "Picture and Action: The Problem of Narration in
James's Fiction." Rice Univ. Studies, 51 (Winter), 109–23.
James subordinates action to picture, because temporal
events are used only to exhibit human relationships.

121 WARD, J. A. "Structural Irony in Madame de Mauves." Studies
in Short Fiction, 2 (Winter), 170–82.
Through a complex symmetrical arrangement of the characters, James utilizes a structural irony that leads the
reader to make early judgments about characters that must
later be revised.

122 WEGELIN, CHRISTOF. "Hemingway and the Decline of International Fiction." Sewanee Review, 73 (Winter), 285–98.
James is the norm for international fiction which showed
the contrast of conventional manners and institutions; Hemingway brings this kind of fiction to a close by submerging
the national differences to emphasize their irrelevance.

123 WELLEK, RENÉ. "Henry James," in his <u>A History of Modern Crit-</u>
<u>icism: 1750-1950</u>. Vol. 4. New Haven, Conn.: Yale Univ.
Press, pp. 213-37.
James is the best American critic of the nineteenth century; he "is brimful of ideas and critical concepts and has
a well-defined theory and a point of view which allow him
to characterize sensitively and evaluate persuasively a
wide range of writers."

124 WELSH, ALEXANDER. "The Allegory of Truth in English Fiction."
<u>Victorian Studies</u>, 9 (September), 7-28.
The Spenserian convention wherein truth is personified
in the pure female figure and falsehood in the seductive
female persists throughout English fiction until the end
of the nineteenth century when James transforms the tradition in <u>The Golden Bowl</u> with a newer, more plausible ideal
of the truth in Maggie Verver.

125 WHITE, BEATRICE, and T. S. DORSCH. <u>The Year's Work in English</u>
<u>Studies: Vol. 44: 1963</u>. New York: Published for the
English Association by Humanities Press, pp. 373-74.
Survey of criticism for 1963.

*126 WILDING, MICHAEL. "<u>Portrait of a Lady</u> and the World and
Choice." <u>Balcony: The Sydney Review</u>, no. 1, pp. 28-35.
Annotated by David Pownall in 1974.B55: "The quotation
from the conclusion of <u>Paradise Lost</u> in <u>The Portrait of a</u>
<u>Lady</u>, repeated twice, has its implications if we consider
that in the novel 'the wicked have all left America, have
been ejected from the garden, and come to Europe, the world
before them.'"

127 WITT, NAPIER, and JOHN LUCAS. "Introduction," in their edition of <u>Americans and Europe: Selected Tales of Henry</u>
<u>James</u>. Riverside Editions. Boston: Houghton Mifflin,
pp. viii-xx.
This anthology of eight James tales is "designed system-
atically to demonstrate his main motif, Americans confront-
ing the fact or facts of Europe." The texts, which represent the short story, the short novel, and the novel, are
all definitive versions. (Includes "Travelling Companions,"
"Madame de Mauves," <u>Daisy Miller</u>, "The Siege of London,"
<u>The Reverberator</u>, "The Pupil," "Mrs. Medwin," and "The
Jolly Corner.")

1965

128 WRIGHT, EDGAR. <u>Mrs. Gaskell: The Basis for Reassessment</u>.
     London and New York: Oxford Univ. Press, pp. 173-75,
     263-64, passim.
        In this critical reassessment of the Victorian novelist
     Mrs. Gaskell, a half-dozen passing references to Henry
     James appear.

129 WRIGHT, NATHALIA. "The Moral Field: James," in her <u>American
     Novelists in Italy: The Discoverers--Allston to James</u>.
     Philadelphia: Univ. of Pennsylvania Press, pp. 198-248.
        For James Italy was always "the sacred, the life-stored
     land." This essay includes an outline of James's Italian
     travels, a discussion of his written reactions to Italy, a
     survey of the use of Italian material in his published
     works, and an analysis of the treatment of Italy in his
     fiction.

1965 C DISSERTATIONS

 1 ASWELL, EDWARD DUNCAN. "The Art of Aggression: The Short Fic-
    tion of Henry James, 1888-1898." <u>DA</u>, 25, 4141 (Univ. of
    California, Berkeley).
       During the course of the decade from 1888 through 1898
    James examined the danger of the aggressive artist's in-
    fringing upon the rights of other and concludes "that only
    the artist can safely devote himself to a life of observa-
    tion and imagination because the person who lacks a tradi-
    tional medium for controlling what he sees and fancies will
    necessarily shape reality into fantastic patterns that will
    explain and justify the moral behavior of the aggressive
    self."

 2 BANTA, MARTHA. "The Two Worlds of Henry James: A Study in
    the Fiction of the Supernatural." <u>DA</u>, 26, 1035-36 (In-
    diana).
       James's concept of consciousness--in its essence, its
    capability, and its power--is expressed through his use of
    the supernatural.

 3 CHADDERDON, ARNOLD H. "Comic Method in Henry James's Fic-
    tion." <u>DA</u>, 26, 2205 (Yale).
       James's comic method--the method whereby he sought to
    harness the intractable elements of life--is related to
    the comedy of manners prominent in the work of Molière and
    the English Restoration and is integrally related to many
    of the stylistic features of his works.

4   HESTON, LILLA A. "A Study of Point of View in Three Novels by
    Henry James: The Spoils of Poynton, The Wings of the Dove,
    and The Golden Bowl." DA, 26, 3533 (Northwestern).
        The point of view in the three novels is that of a
    third-person author-narrator that utilizes the three female
    protagonists as reflectors.

5   HOAG, GERALD BRYAN. "Henry James and Formalist Criticism of
    the Novel in English in the Twentieth Century." DA, 26,
    2753 (Tulane).
        The critical principles scattered throughout James's
    Prefaces in the New York Edition share a basic affinity
    with Coleridge's concepts. James's concept of organic
    form has provided the foundation for the twentieth century
    progress in novelistic theory.

6   HOLLAND, LAURENCE B. "The Expense of Vision: Essays on the
    Craft of Henry James." Dissertation, Harvard, 414 pp.
        James's works are "symbolic constructs" of an "ambitious
    order whose motive lies deeper than the strictly literary
    aims which implement it." They reveal his concern "with
    the very nature of authority, particularly with the sanc-
    tioned power of important institutions in the culture and
    society he knew," and "with the authority he himself exer-
    cised as an author of fiction . . . establishing conven-
    tions of his own." For book publication see 1964.A3.

7   SCHULTE, RAINER ORTWIN. "Henry James and Marcel Proust: A
    Study in Sensibility." DA, 26, 3352 (Michigan).
        A comparison of the metaphoric and syntactic styles of
    Proust's A la recherche du temps perdu and James's The
    Wings of the Dove and The Golden Bowl reveals a basic simi-
    larity in their "wetanshauungen."

8   SOLOMON, JAN KADETSKY. "The Puritan, the Gentleman, and the
    Artist: A Study of the Conflict Between Ethics and Aesthet-
    ics in the Novels of Henry James." DA, 25, 7278-79 (Michi-
    gan).
        The dichotomy between the aesthetic and the ethical
    present in James's early works becomes less apparent as
    James seeks to emphasize the necessity of extending the
    aesthetic vision beyond the realm of the artist to the
    common man who must cope with an evil and ugly world.

1966

1966 A BOOKS

1   BUSCH, FRIEDER. Erzähler-, Figuren-, und Leserperspektive in
     Henry James' Roman, "The Ambassadors." Munich: Max Hue-
     ber, 205 pp. [German]
         This examination of perspective is divided into five
     sections: The Perspective of the Narrator, The Perspective
     of the Perceiving Figure, The Time Dimension of Perspec-
     tive, The Perspective of the Reader, and The Relationship
     of Individual Conclusions to the Work as a Whole. Re-
     viewed: Henry A. Pochman, American Literature, 40 (March
     1968), 90-91.

2   FRANKLIN, ROSEMARY F. An Index to Henry James's Prefaces to
     the New York Edition. Charlottesville: Bibliographical
     Society of the Univ. of Virginia, 29 pp.
         This analytical index of James's Prefaces includes en-
     tries for works, names of characters, literary figures,
     friends of James, as well as key words in his critical
     vocabulary.

3   HASLER, JÖRG. Switzerland in the Life and Work of Henry
     James: The Clare Benedict Collection of Letters from Henry
     James. The Cooper Monographs, No. 10. Bern: Francke,
     164 pp.
         Switzerland was relatively unimportant for James, but
     "his Swiss writings, just because of their unusually criti-
     cal tone, are invaluable to the student of his character
     and achievement." James's writings about Switzerland as
     well as his "methods of putting Swiss memories to artistic
     use" are explored. In addition, the letters James wrote to
     Mrs. Clara Benedict and her daughter, Miss Clare Benedict,
     between 1894 and 1912 are reprinted in full. Since Mrs.
     Benedict was the sister of Constance Fenimore Woolson, the
     letters contain frequent references to Miss Woolson. For
     dissertation see 1966.C3. Reviewed: Christof Wegelin,
     American Literature, 38 (1967), 568-70; Oscar Cargill,
     Modern Philology, 65 (1967), 179-80.

4   HYDE, H. MONTGOMERY. The Story of Lamb House, Rye: The Home
     of Henry James. Rye, Sussex: Adams of Rye, 83 pp.
         The history of Henry James's Sussex home, in which he
     spent most of the last eighteen years of his life, begins
     with a chapter on James Lamb, who built the house about
     1723, and concludes with genealogical tables of the James
     and Lamb families. The volume is amply illustrated. Re-
     viewed: Times Literary Supplement (4 August), p. 714.

5   KIMBROUGH, ROBERT, ed. <u>Henry James: "The Turn of the Screw"</u>:
     <u>An Authoritative Text, Backgrounds and Sources, Essays in</u>
     <u>Criticism</u>. A Norton Critical Edition. New York: W. W.
     Norton, 276 pp.
     Contents: This book is divided into three sections:
     (1) The Text of <u>The Turn of the Screw</u>, which includes an
     essay on "Textual History" as well as "Textual Notes";
     (2) Background and Sources, which includes sections enti-
     tled "James on the Ghost-Story," "James on <u>The Turn of the</u>
     <u>Screw</u>," and "Other Suggested Sources"; (3) <u>Essays in Criti-</u>
     cism, which includes "Early Reactions: 1898-1923," "Major
     Criticism: 1924-57," and "Recent Criticism." (Listed be-
     low are essays from "Other Suggested Sources," "Major Crit-
     icism" and "Recent Criticism." All are reprinted from
     earlier sources except the three written by John J. Enck,
     S. P. Rosenbaum, and Martina Slaughter.)
     Preface by Robert Kimbrough (pp. ix-x). The text of
     The Turn of the Screw follows the New York Edition.
     "The Genesis of 'The Turn of the Screw'" by Robert Lee
     Wolff (pp. 125-32). Reprinted from <u>American Literature</u>,
     13 (March 1941), 1-8.
     "Psychical Research and 'The Turn of the Screw'" by
     Francis X. Roellinger (pp. 132-42). Reprinted from <u>Ameri-</u>
     <u>can Literature</u>, 20 (January 1949), 401-12.
     "Mrs. Gaskell's 'The Old Nurse's Story': A Link Between
     'Wuthering Heights' and 'The Turn of the Screw'" by Miriam
     Allott (pp. 142-45). Reprinted from 1961.B2.
     "<u>The Turn of the Screw</u> and Alice James" by Oscar Cargill
     (pp. 145-65). Reprinted from 1963.B16.
     "A Pre-Freudian Reading of <u>The Turn of the Screw</u>" by
     Harold C. Goddard (pp. 181-209). Reprinted from <u>Ninteenth-</u>
     <u>Century Fiction</u>, 12 (June 1957), 1-36. Also reprinted in
     1960.A6, 1970.A7.
     "Henry James to the Ruminant Reader: <u>The Turn of the</u>
     <u>Screw</u>" by Edna Kenton (pp. 209-11). Reprinted from <u>The</u>
     <u>Arts</u>, 6 (November 1924), 245-55. Also printed in 1960.A6.
     "Edmund Wilson and <u>The Turn of the Screw</u>" by Martina
     Slaughter (pp. 211-14). A review of the controversy which
     followed Edmund Wilson's Freudian reading of the story in
     1934 concludes with the point that Jamesian critics divide
     into two camps: those who interpret the tale as a ghost
     story and those who see it as a psychological study. Re-
     printed in 1970.A7.
     "'The Turn of the Screw' as Poem" by Robert Heilman
     (pp. 214-28). Reprinted from <u>Univ. of Kansas City Review</u>,
     14 (Summer 1948), 277-89. Also printed in 1960.A6.

"The Point of View" by Leon Edel (pp. 228-34). Reprint-
ed from The Psychological Novel: 1900-1950. New York:
Lippincott, 1955, pp. 56-68.
"'Erlkönig' and The Turn of the Screw" by Ignace Feuer-
licht (pp. 235-37). Reprinted from Journal of English and
Germanic Philology, 58 (January 1959), 68-74.
"The Return of the Screw" by Eric Solomon (pp. 237-45).
Reprinted from 1964.B92.
"Turning the Freudian Screw: How Not to Do It" by Mark
Spilka (pp. 245-53). Reprinted from 1963.B95.
"A Note on John La Farge's Illustration for Henry
James's The Turn of the Screw" by S. P. Rosenbaum
(pp. 254-59). The distinguished artist, John La Farge, a
friend of Henry James, illustrated the first printing of
the story in Collier's Weekly, An Illustrated Journal.
That illustration "preserves something of the ambiguity of
the ghosts" and shows "how a subtle and cultivated contemporary and friend of the author interpreted his now so famous and controversial story for its magazine public."
"The Turn of the Screw & the Turn of the Century" by
John J. Enck (pp. 259-73). The story is interpreted here
in terms of the "international revolt in aesthetics" that
occurred at the turn of the century.
"James's Criticism of James" by Robert Ginsberg
(pp. 269-73). Reprinted from 1963.B40.
Reviewed: Choice, 4 (May 1967), 288-89.

6   PUTT, S. GORLEY. Henry James: A Reader's Guide. Introduction by Arthur Mizener. Ithaca, N.Y.: Cornell Univ.
Press, 432 pp. Published in England as A Reader's Guide to
Henry James. London: Thames and Hudson.
This comprehensive survey of the twenty-two novels and
one hundred and twelve tales of Henry James is arranged
thematically and designed for the beginning reader of
James. Reviewed: Oscar Cargill, American Literature, 39
(1967), 117-18; Frederick J. Hoffman, Novel, 1 (1967),
75-77; Modern Fiction Studies, 13 (Winter 1967-1968), 526;
Leon Edel, Nineteenth-Century Fiction, 22 (1968), 410-12.

7   RANALD, RALPH A. Henry James's "Washington Square." New York:
Monarch Press, 92 pp.
A study guide which includes information on James, summary and comment on each section of the work, and character
sketches.

8   TAKAHASHI, MASAO, ed. <u>Studies of Henry James</u>. Tokyo: Hoku-
      seido, 312 pp. [Japanese]
        Contents: Part I is a general introductory essay;
      Part II, "Henry James and his Literature," consists of
      three essays; Part III, "Criticisms of Works and James's
      Literary Criticism," includes six essays; and a final es-
      say surveys James criticism.
        Part I: "Henry James and Today" by Masao Takahashi.
      James's personal history obliged him to write works that
      embodied an artificiality which is relevant to the present
      day as defined by the French New Novelists: characters do
      not have a clear image, and works are open to countless
      interpretations.
        Part II;
      "Early Years: 1843-1880" by Yoshikawa Michio. James's
      later works have their germ in his early ones. This thesis
      is illustrated by a biographical reading of works produced
      in the period from "A Tragedy of Error" through <u>The Por-
      trait of a Lady</u>.
      "Middle Years: 1881-1895" by Kanichi Aihara. James's
      maturity was brought about through his knowledge of treach-
      ery gained in his experience with the drama. His middle
      period can be divided into five acts: I, "Selection in
      Life" and "Being Great"; II, <u>The Bostonians</u>; III, <u>The Prin-
      cess Casamassima</u>; IV, Italy and the Muse; and V, Drama and
      Theater.
      "Late Years: 1896-1916" by Eiichiro Otsu. This period
      began with James's devotion to art, which resulted in his
      technical experimentation with point of view and scenic
      art. James's modern meaning is in his realization of human
      situations rather than of individuals.
        Part III:
      "<u>The Portrait of a Lady</u>" by Einosuke Tamura. Isabel re-
      turns to Osmond as a result of the romantic sentiment that
      penetrates reality.
      "<u>The Princess Casamassima</u>" by Koji Kiritani. The hero's
      sensitivity is James's own, but Hyacinth's ambivalence
      seems unnatural, for he reacts only on the psychological
      level without sufficient insight into social thought. How-
      ever, the manner of existence of a sensitive artist of life
      may well reflect the internal contradiction of European so-
      ciety towards the end of the nineteenth century.
      "<u>The Turn of the Screw</u> and the Ghost" by Eiichiro Otsu.
      An examination of the characteristics of other ghost tales
      by James, as well as of critics' views, both Freudian and
      non-Freudian, suggests that James employed a psychological
      technique in the tale aimed at portraying a make-believe of
      the ghost's existence.

1966

"The Ambassadors" by Masao Nakauchi. Four elements
serve to show Strether's inner development: (1) his sense
of time; (2) his sense of fear; (3) a general indefinite
air; (4) indirectness in the characters' behavioral patterns. In addition, several stylistic devices serve the
theme of the intangibility of life.

"The Golden Bowl" by Tateo Takeichi. Two important
themes in the novel are portrayed in the bowl image and
in the moral conflict between Maggie and the Prince. This
novel is James's best, and the style is his most finished.

"James's Literary Criticism" by Kanichi Aihara. James
was born as a critic when his spirit, which had an insight
into the real, or the higher dignity and deeper psychology,
started to pursue its objective correlative, or the society. French Poets and Novelists, Hawthorne, and The Art of
Fiction illustrate James's talent as a critic.

Epilogue: "Estimation of Henry James" by Kanichi Aihara.
This brief survey of criticism groups critics into those in
favor of James and those who are not. Present-day criticism attempts to grasp James in his totality. (Van Wyck
Brooks and T. S. Eliot are examined in detail.)

9 WEXFORD, JANE. Henry James's "The Aspern Papers." New York:
Monarch, 76 pp.
A study guide which includes information on the book,
the author, the characters, and critical commentary as well
as a selected bibliography.

1966 B SHORTER WRITINGS

1 ADAMS, ROBERT M. Nil: Episodes in the Literary Conquest of
Void During the Nineteenth-Century. New York: Oxford
Univ. Press, pp. 99-102.
In "The Beast in the Jungle," Marcher takes an inward
journey in time to encounter a void, but he perceives the
truth too late to do anything about it.

2 ANDERSON, QUENTIN. "Introduction," in his edition of Hawthorne. New York: Collier Books; London: Collier-
Macmillan, pp. 7-12.
James's primary intention in Hawthorne was to show the
English reader the conditions of Hawthorne's time, place,
and cultural scene. James fulfilled his intention "admirably, producing a work exquisitely sustained in tone
which was full of excellent cultural judgments."

3   ARAUJO, VICTOR DE. "The Short Story of Fantasy: Henry James,
    H. G. Wells, and E. M. Forster." DA, 27, 200A (Univ. of
    Washington).
        Although there are significant differences in their
    techniques, all three authors used fantasy "to dramatize
    problems of personal communication and to explore man's
    psyche, his society, and his universe."

4   ASWELL, E. DUNCAN. "James's In the Cage: The Telegraphist as
    Artist." Texas Studies in Literature and Language, 8
    (Fall), 375-84.
        Although the young girl "presents herself to the reader
    as a sophisticated, compassionate, and supremely intelli-
    gent person," she is actually "naive, spiteful, and con-
    tinually engaged in self-deception."

5   ASWELL, E. DUNCAN. "James's Treatment of Artistic Collabora-
    tion." Criticism, 8 (Spring), 180-95.
        The short stories published in 1891 and 1892 about cre-
    ative people collaborating on artistic projects demonstrate
    that James saw "the impracticality of collaboration."

6   BAY, ANDRÉ. "Le cinquantenaire de Henry James: Une morale
    rayonnante." Nouvelles Littéraires, 44 (21 July), 8.
    [French]
        It has taken fifty years after Henry James's death for
    Europeans to realize that he is a supreme master of Ameri-
    can literature and his work is a precursor of the modern
    psychological novel. Characterizing James's work is his
    moral conscience as well as his extraordinary objective
    intelligence.

7   BEEBE, MAURICE, and WILLIAM T. STAFFORD. "Criticism of Henry
    James: A Selected Checklist." Modern Fiction Studies, 12
    (Spring), 117-77.
        This checklist is divided into two parts: first, gener-
    al criticism is listed; second, studies of individual works
    are listed under the title of each work. Includes most of
    the items in the checklist published in Modern Fiction
    Studies (Spring 1957).

8   BELL, MILLICENT. "The Eagle and the Worm." London Magazine,
    6 (July), 5-46.
        James referred to Wharton in witty terms as a "golden
    eagle" and a "firebird," but under the jests and mockery
    can be discerned his serious judgement of her. After
    1907, Wharton's life was "hectic and desperate," and her
    visits upset James.

9   BELLRINGER, A. W. "The Spoils of Poynton: James's Unintended
Involvement." Essays in Criticism, 16 (April), 185-200.
The consistent point of view narration of the later
style is introduced in The Spoils of Poynton, but in re-
moving the omniscient author from the text, James may have
substituted himself (in the narrator, Fleda) as "one of his
own puppets." Responses in 1966.B60; 1967.B9; 1968.B66;
1968.B13.

10   BERLAND, ALWYN. "Americans and Ambassadors: On Henry James."
Wascana Review, 1:53-82.
The characterization of Lanbert Strether is a major
achievement, James's "great tribute to the idea of
civilization."

11   BERNARD, F. V. "James's Florabella and the 'Land of the Pink
Sky.'" Notes and Queries, ns 13 (February), 70.
The tale Madame de Cintré tells her niece is parallel to
the Christopher Newman-Claire de Cintré story; therefore,
the "Land of the Pink Sky" is America.

12   BIRCH, BRIAN. "Reply [to S. P. Rosenbaum]." Library, 21
(September), 250-52.
The article "Henry James: Some Bibliographical and
Textual Matters" is accurate since it deals with "texts,"
not "editions" as Rosenbaum argues. Response to 1966.B82.
See 1965.B5.

13   BRIDGMAN, RICHARD. "Henry James and Mark Twain," in his The
Colloquial Style in America. New York: Oxford Univ.
Press, pp. 78-130.
Despite obvious differences between Henry James and Mark
Twain, when they attempted to reflect colloquial conversation in their prose they developed remarkably similar methods including the use of "repetition, interrupted phrasing,
isolation of the word, accentuated peculiarities, and patterns of sound."

14   CANADY, NICHOLAS, JR. "Portrait of Daisy: Studies by James
and Fitzgerald." Forum (Houston), 4 (Summer), 17-20.
A comparison of the portraits of Daisy Miller and Daisy
Buchanan "reveals an interesting change in the innocence-
experience theme in American literature, together with a
similarity in methods of characterization."

15   COLEMAN, ARTHUR, and GARY R. TYLER, comps. "Henry James," in
      their <u>Drama Criticism: A Checklist of Interpretation Since
      1940 of English and American Plays</u>. 2 vols. Denver: Alan
      Swallow, vol. 1, p. 98.
           Criticism of James's plays is listed.

16   COOK, GEORGE A. "Names in <u>The American</u>." <u>CEA Critic</u>, 28
      (April), 5, 14.
           An interpretation of the obviously significant names of
      characters in the novel.

17   COY, JAVIER. "Henry James en la crítica de los ultimos
      treinta años." <u>Filologia Moderna</u> (Madrid), 6:75-99.
      [Spanish]
           A survey of James criticism beginning in 1934 (and com-
      menting especially on Edmund Wilson, F. R. Leavis, John
      Crowe Ransom, F. O. Matthiessen, Quentin Anderson, Lionel
      Trilling, Marius Bewley, Leon Edel, and Maxwell Geismar)
      reveals that James criticism has progressed in no radical
      new directions.

18   DEAKIN, MOTLEY F. "The Real and Fictive Quest of Henry
      James." <u>Bucknell Review</u>, 14 (May), 82-97.
           The fictive quest motifs of James are vitalized by his
      own personal "quest for climactic moments" achieved by con-
      templation of two basic types of objects: "(1) the pros-
      pect or vista of the expansive landscape and (2) the arti-
      ficially enclosed and framed figure in the shrine."

19   DEBELLIS, JACK. "Andrew Lytle's <u>A Name for Evil</u>: A Trans-
      formation of <u>The Turn of the Screw</u>." <u>Critique</u>, 8 (Spring-
      Summer), 26-40.
           Lytle's story contains many parallels to James's, in-
      cluding characters, plot, and theme, but he notably differs
      in his complex handling of the psychological state of his
      protagonist and in his pervasive use of myth and symbol to
      explore the human predicament.

20   DIETRICHSON, JAN W. "Henry James and Emile Zola," in <u>American
      Norvegica: Norwegian Contributions to American Studies</u>.
      Edited by Sigmund Skard and Henry H. Wasser. Vol. 2.
      Oslo: Byldendal Norsk Forlag; Philadelphia: Univ. of
      Pennsylvania Press, pp. 118-34.
           James knew Zola personally and had read his works, but
      Zola's influence on James "was <u>not</u> very important." The
      two writers had "significant differences in view of life,
      range of material, and stylistic quality," but James may

be indebted to Zola for his method of note-taking for The
Princess Casamassima.

21 DORSCH, T. S., and C. G. HARLOW, eds. The Year's Work in
English Studies: Vol. 45: 1964. New York: Published
for the English Association by Humanities Press, pp. 396-98.
Survey of criticism for 1964.

22 DUBERMAN, MARTIN. James Russell Lowell. Boston: Houghton
Mifflin, The Riverside Press, pp. 261-62, 335-36, passim.
Some two dozen references to James appear in this
biography.

23 DUBLER, WALTER. "The Princess Casamassima: Its Place in the
James Canon." Modern Fiction Studies, 12 (Spring), 44-60.
The Princess Casamassima stands at a mid-point between
the early James and the James of the major phase and ex-
hibits "the essential characteristics of both periods."

24 EARNEST, ERNEST. "The American Ariel." South Atlantic Quarterly, 65 (Spring), 192-200.
The pervasiveness as well as the peculiarities of the
Ariel archetype during the second national literary renaissance represent "an important quality of the psyche of
the period."

25 EDEL, LEON. "To the Poet of Prose." Modern Fiction Studies,
12 (Spring), 3-6.
Reprinted from 1966.B26.

26 EDEL, LEON. "To the Poet of Prose." New York Herald Tribune
Books (27 February), p. 6.
Fifty years after James's death he is accepted as a
classic; "he belongs now to the permanence of American literature." Reprinted in 1966.B25.

27 FIEDLER, LESLIE. Love and Death in the American Novel. Revised edition. New York: Dell, pp. 302-308, 310-12,
343-44.
See 1960.B33.

28 FLOWER, DEAN. "Introduction," in his edition of Great Short
Works of Henry James. New York: Harper & Row, pp. vii-xi.
"Just as profound and suggestive as his long novels,
James's nouvelles regularly present his definitive state-
ments on such prevailing subjects as innocence, experience,
evil, and isolation." (This book reprints Daisy Miller,
Washington Square, The Aspern Papers, "The Pupil," The Turn

of the Screw, The Beast in the Jungle; a biographical
sketch and a bibliography are included.)

29 FRASER, JOHN. "The Turn of the Screw Again." Midwest Quar-
    terly, 7 (Summer), 327-36.
        An examination of the encounter, at the end of Chap-
    ter XV, of the governess and Miss Jessel corroborates the
    theory that The Turn of the Screw has as one of its prin-
    cipal themes the conflict and resolution experienced by a
    religiously restricted consciousness endeavoring to come to
    grips with the realities of evil.

30 FRIEDMAN, ALAN. The Turn of the Novel. New York: Oxford
    Univ. Press, pp. 26-27, 176-77.
        The American has a "closed ending," but The Portrait of
    a Lady and The Ambassadors end with the implication that
    Isabel's and Strether's moral experiences are continuing.
    The later passage suggests that the reader "can use-
    fully understand the art and the achievement" of James,
    Joyce, and Lawrence by recognizing that all three write "a
    stream of conscience."

31 FÜGER, WILHELM. "In the Cage: Versuche zur Deutung einer
    umstrittenen Henry James Novelle." Die Neueren Sprachen,
    15:506-13. [German]
        The central problems of this novella are: "What can one
    individual know of another?"; "How far removed is reality
    from the consciousness of the individual?" Several aspects
    of the work are revealing: the concept of fate, which has
    an antique, pre-Christian character; the frequent use of
    Christian terminology to describe the fantasy world of ful-
    fillment; and the symbolism of the changing seasons.

32 GALE, ROBERT L. "Names in James." Names, 14:83-108.
        Sources of names for James's approximately sixteen hun-
    dred characters include the London Times, literature, the
    theatre, friends, and family. Names are used for their
    oral appeal, symbolic suggestiveness, and to elucidate
    character, plot, tone, and theme.

33 GLIDDON, GERALD M. "James Incomplete." Times Literary Sup-
    plement (24 February), p. 148.
        Much of James is inaccessible because no effort has been
    made to produce an updated complete edition since the Com-
    plete Edition of his works went out of print. For response
    see 1966.B40.

1966

34   GOLDSMITH, ARNOLD L.   "The Poetry of Names in The Spoils of
     Poynton." Names, 14:134-42.
          The etymological and symbolic dimensions of names in The
     Spoils of Poynton give the work "an almost poetic extension
     of meaning and a subtle reinforcement of tone and theme."

35   GOODE, JOHN.   "'Character' and Henry James." New Left Review,
     40 (November-December), 55-75.
          W. J. Harvey's Character and the Novel provides the
     starting point for a discussion of Henry James's The Ambas-
     sadors, "The Turn of the Screw," and The Golden Bowl.

36   GULLÓN, RICARDO.   "Imágenes de El Otro," in Spanish Thought
     and Letters in the Twentieth Century: An International
     Symposium Held at Vanderbilt University to Commemorate the
     Centenary of the Birth of Miguel de Unamuno, 1864-1964.
     Edited by German Bleiberg and E. Inman Fox.   Nashville:
     Vanderbilt Univ. Press, pp. 257-69. [Spanish]
          Reprint of 1965.B39.

37   HALL, ROBERT A., JR.   "Some Recent Books on Henry James."
     Annali Istituto Universitario Orientale, Napoli, Sezione
     Germanica, 9:49-64.
          Of the large number of critical books published on James
     since 1960, only Maxwell Geismar's Henry James and the
     Jacobites has sounded a discordant note among the otherwise
     generally laudatory treatments.   Review of 1963.A2.

38   HALL, WILLIAM F.   "Gabriel Nash: 'Famous Centre' of The Trag-
     ic Muse." Nineteenth-Century Fiction, 21 (September),
     167-84.
          James's claim in the Preface of The Tragic Muse is a
     disguise for his ambivalent vision, so that Gabriel Nash
     becomes a "blurred centre," playing dual roles in a novel
     combining allegory with realism, and the novel is a precur-
     sor of future works that resolve the moral and aesthetic
     conflict.

39   HAMBLEN, ABIGAIL ANN.   "Henry James and the Freedom Fighters
     of the Seventies." Georgia Review, 20 (Spring), 35-44.
          In The Bostonians James captured two distinctive and un-
     changing American types, the reformer and the reactionary.

40   HART-DAVIS, RUPERT.   "James Incomplete." Times Literary Sup-
     plement (3 March), p. 167.
          In response to G. M. Gliddon, Hart-Davis lists the dif-
     ficulties involved in republishing James's works in Great
     Britain and denies the statement that his company is not
     adding to its James publications.   Response to 1966.B33.

41   HOLDER, ALAN. Three Voyagers in Search of Europe: A Study of
      Henry James, Ezra Pound, and T. S. Eliot. Philadelphia:
      Univ. of Pennsylvania Press; London: Oxford Univ. Press,
      396 pp.
          James, Pound, and Eliot "form a kind of natural triad in
      our literary history." The fact of expatriation, which
      they shared, operated "as a large and constant presence" in
      their careers. It is revealing to establish "the contents
      of each man's expatriation and the way those contents com-
      pare with their corresponding elements in the lives and
      writings of the other two men." See 1965.B51 for Disserta-
      tion. Reviewed: Modern Fiction Studies, 12 (Winter 1966-
      1967), 491; Christof Wegelin, American Literature, 38
      (1967), 568-70; Robert Lee White, Southern Review, ns 5
      (1969), 289-91.

42   HOLLERAN, JAMES V. "An Analysis of 'The Birthplace.'" Papers
      on Language and Literature, 2 (Winter), 76-80.
          "Forced into a corner by the economic and social reali-
      ties of life, Gedge sacrifices his conscience (his 'criti-
      cal sense') not to become what is greater--an artist--but
      to become what is less--a fraud."

43   HOLMAN, CLARENCE HUGH, comp. "Henry James," in his The Ameri-
      can Novel Through Henry James. Goldentree Bibliographies.
      New York: Appleton-Century-Crofts, pp. 44-53, passim.
          Bibliographical items are listed under four different
      categories: Texts, Bibliography, Biographical and Critical
      Books, and Critical Essays.

44   HOROWITZ, FLOYD R. "The Christian Time Sequence in Henry
      James's The American." College Language Association Jour-
      nal, 9 (March), 234-45.
          The progression of time in the first thirteen chapters
      of The American follows conventional literary practices;
      beginning in Chapter XIV, however, and continuing to the
      conclusion, James utilizes "an exact sequence which sym-
      bolically supports the major religious metaphor in the
      novel."

45   HOUGHTON, WALTER E. "Henry James," in his The Wellesley Index
      to Victorian Periodicals, 1824-1900. Vol. 1. London:
      Routledge & Kegan Paul, p. 953.
          A listing of eleven James works which appeared in Vic-
      torian periodicals.

1966

46   HUNT, THOMAS G.   "Moral Awareness in The Spoils of Poynton."
     Discourse, 9 (Spring), 255-62.
          Although The Spoils of Poynton is flawed by the absence
     of a "real dramatic presence," it is eminently successful
     in structuring a moral conflict between characters that is
     "real and formidable."

47   IWASE, SHITSUU.   "Henry James as a Romance-novelist."   Jimbun
     Kenkyu (Osaka Municipal Univ.), 17 (January), 100-15.
     [Japanese]
          James as an American was drawn to the romantic; and in
     trying to reconcile the realistic (manners) with the roman-
     tic, James formed the quest-romance.   Also discussed in
     this article are M. Bewley's "American problem" of the in-
     ternational situation, James's "great American disease" of
     romanticism, and James's use of the cup or bowl image as
     the reflector of reality.   James's late indirect method is
     appropriate to the romance-novelist world, since life and
     fable necessarily have to be two different things.

*48 JAMES, E. ANTHONY.   "Henry James's Mrs. Walker: Proper Matron
     or Possessive Mistress?"   Pennsylvania Council of Teachers
     of English Bulletin, no. 13 (May), pp. 15-22.
          Cited in 1968.B67, p. 77.   B. R. McElderry, Jr. explains
     that E. Anthony James "identifies Mrs. Walker as Winter-
     bourne's 'possessive mistress.'   The interpretation is pos-
     sible and ingenious, but this is not to say that genera-
     tions of readers of 'Daisy Miller' have been 'wrong' in not
     making it."

49   JEFFERSON, DOUGLAS.   "Introduction," in his edition of What
     Maisie Knew.   Classic American Texts.   London: Oxford
     Univ. Press, ix-xxvii.
          A discussion which considers biographical background as
     well as characterization and critical response to the novel
     concludes with the suggestion that the best readings of the
     novel are the ones "most akin to James's great preface."
     This book includes a "Note on the Text" (The New York Edi-
     tion text), a very brief reading list, and a selected list
     of variant readings.

50   JOST, EDWARD F.   "Love and Two Kinds of Existentialism."
     English Record (New York State English Council), 16 (Feb-
     ruary), 14-18.
          In the light of modern philosophical thinking, "The
     Beast in the Jungle" is a pre-Existentialist story wherein
     May Bartram ceases to be a person and becomes "a means, a
     victim of utensilite, something to be used and set aside."

51   KOCH, STEPHEN. "Transcendence in The Wings of the Dove."
      Modern Fiction Studies, 12 (Spring), 93-102.
           The Wings of the Dove involves a "search for a truth
      that will give the character a personal freedom beyond the
      blind isolation of personality." A change in technique by
      James in this novel gives it a "context of perception that
      must be called transcendent." The world is seen by "a
      circle of people revolving around a single figure," rather
      than through the eyes of a single person.

52   KRAMER, DALE, and CHERIS KRAMER. "James's 'The Marriages':
      Designs of Structure." University Review (Kansas City),
      33 (Autumn), 75-80.
           James utilizes a variety of structural techniques to
      force the reader into the awareness "that the informing
      center of the story is the personality of the narrator,
      Adele."

53   KUBAL, DAVID L. "Henry James and the Supreme Value." Arizona
      Quarterly, 22 (Summer), 101-14.
           In the novels of the major phase, James dealt with the
      international theme and the problem of freedom. The "su-
      preme value" in James's fiction is the "practical intel-
      lect," which allows some characters (such as Lambert
      Strether and Milly Theale) to understand the limits of
      freedom, but still "remain functional in society."

54   LEVIN, HARRY. Refractions: Essays in Comparative Literature.
      New York: Oxford Univ. Press, pp. 153-55, 194-96, 210-11,
      216-18, passim.
           Although references to Henry James appear in some two
      dozen passages, he receives no extensive treatment in this
      collection of eighteen previously published essays.

55   LEVY, LEO B. "Criticism Chronicle: Hawthorne, Melville, and
      James." Southern Review, ns 2 (April), 427-42.
           Laurence Holland's The Expense of Vision: Essays on the
      Craft of Henry James is "marked by a number of successes,"
      whereas Robert L. Gale's The Caught Image: Figurative Lan-
      guage in the Fiction of Henry James is "a monument of mis-
      directed industry." Other works on James which are criti-
      cized include: (1) Edward Stone's The Battle of the Books:
      Some Aspects of Henry James; (2) Krishna Baldev Vaid's
      Technique in the Tales of Henry James; (3) Sister M. Coro-
      na Sharp's The Confidante in Henry James: Evolution and
      Moral Value of A Fictive Character; (4) Joseph Wiesen-
      farth's Henry James and the Dramatic Analogy: A Study of

1966

the Major Novels of the Middle Period. Review of 1964.A3;
1964.A2; 1964.A7; 1964.A8; 1963.A3; 1963.A4.

56   LOCKRIDGE, ERNEST H. "A Vision of Art: Henry James's The
      Tragic Muse." Modern Fiction Studies, 12 (Spring), 83-92.
           James's vision of art in The Tragic Muse is simultane-
      ously "a vision of life in the universe." Art is "all that
      is left" in the story; it is "eternal and at the same time
      benevolent."

57   LODGE, DAVID. "Strether by the River," in his Language of
      Fiction: Essays in Criticism and Verbal Analysis of the
      English Novel. London: Routledge and Kegan Paul; New
      York: Columbia Univ. Press, pp. 189-213.
           A close analysis of the opening two paragraphs of
      Book XI, Chapter IV, of The Ambassadors, reveals that
      these paragraphs "are knitted into the fabric of the novel
      by a number of linguistic threads, but that these connec-
      tions are ironical, and serve to point up the function of
      the scene as a peripeteia."

58   LOMBARDO, AGOSTINO. "Henry James: The American e il mito di
      Otello," in Friendship's Garland: Essays Presented to
      Mario Praz on His Seventieth Birthday. Edited by Vittorio
      Gabrieli. Vol. 2. Raccolta di studi e testi, 107. Rome:
      Edizioni de storia e letteratura, pp. 107-42. [Italian]
           Shakespeare's influence on James appears clearly not
      only through James's citations and allusions to the works
      of the great dramatist, but also through his use of imag-
      ery, development of characters, and hero-concept, which are
      clearly Shakespearean. In The American the plot as well as
      the characters seem to be based on Othello. The relation-
      ship between Gabrielle and Coquelin mirrors that of Desde-
      mona and Othello.

59   LOREIS, HECTOR-JAN. "De Wortels van de Nieuwe Roman" [The
      Roots of the New Novel]. Nieu Vlaams Tijdschrift, 19
      (April), 379-408. [Dutch]
           The impressionistic works of James and Conrad are men-
      tioned as sources of the originality of the new novel.

60   LUCAS, JOHN. "The Spoils of Poynton: James's Intended Unin-
      volvement." Essays in Criticism, 16 (October), 482-89.
           Alan W. Bellringer's criticism of The Spoils of Poynton
      is in error because he fails to recognize that Owen Gereth
      is not in love with Fleda Vetch. Response to 1966.B9. See
      also 1967.B9; 1968.B66; 1968.B13.

61   McCLARY, BEN HARRIS.   "'In Abject Terror of Rising':   An Un-
      published Henry James Letter."   English Language Notes, 3
      (March), 208-11.
         James's letter to Clement King Shorter on August 18,
      1909, along with other correspondence, reveals James's
      horror of public dinners with their impromptu speeches and
      reveals Shorter's insensitivity.

62   McELDERRY, BRUCE R.   "Henry James," in American Literary
      Scholarship: An Annual, 1964.   Edited by James Woodress.
      Durham, N.C.:   Duke Univ. Press, pp. 62-72.
         Survey of criticism published during 1964.

63   MacKENZIE, MANFRED.   "Ironic Melodrama in The Portrait of a
      Lady."   Modern Fiction Studies, 12 (Spring), 7-23.
         The Portrait of a Lady is "constructed from the mate-
      rials of melodrama."   James's use of irony with these ma-
      terials is responsible for the novel's "intensities."   Re-
      printed in 1968.A1.

64   MAJOR, JOHN C.   "Henry James, Daudet, and Oxford."   Notes and
      Queries, ns 13 (February), 69-70.
         Seven James letters to Mrs. Margaret L. Woods, wife of
      the President of Trinity College, describe James's efforts
      to arrange a tour of Oxford for Alphonse Daudet.

65   MELCHIORI, GIORGIO.   "Browning e Henry James," in Friendship's
      Garland: Essays Presented to Mario Praz on His Seventieth
      Birthday.   Edited by Vittorio Gabrieli.   Vol. 2.   Storia e
      Letteratura: Raccolta di studi e testi, 107.   Rome: Edi-
      zioni de storia e letteratura, pp. 143-80.   [Italian]
         Browning was a strong influence on James.   Browning
      used prose as a medium for writing poetry, while James
      used the language and technique of poetry in his prose.
      Both writers portrayed their characters' deep psychology--
      Browning in the dramatic monolog and James through the
      stream of consciousness technique; and both writers empha-
      sized the beauty of the relationship between man and woman.
      Reprinted in 1974.A3.

66   MILLER, J. HILLIS.   "Some Implications of Form in Victorian
      Fiction."   Comparative Literature Studies, 3:109-18.
         Standing midway between the Victorian tradition and mod-
      ern literature, Conrad's subjectivism is both a culmination
      of the earlier thematic interests of Dickens, Eliot, Trol-
      lope, Meredith, Hardy and James and an early exploration of
      the nihilism to follow in Dostoevsky, Mann, Gide, Proust,
      and Camus.

1966

67 <u>Modern Fiction Studies</u>. "Henry James Number." 12 (Spring),
    177 pp.
         Includes the following articles: 1966.B25; 1966.B63;
    1966.B79; 1966.B23; 1966.B90; 1966.B56; 1966.B51; 1966.B81;
    1966.B7.

68 NEIFER, LEO J. "Durrell's Method and Purpose of Art." <u>Wis-</u>
    <u>consin Studies in Literature</u>, 3:99-103.
         Whereas James believed that Self is knowable through
    introspection, Durrell believes that man needs external
    assistance in knowing self. Whereas James believed the
    form of the novel must follow life's form, Durrell believes
    the form of life is unknowable. These basic precepts about
    the self and form provide the foundation for Durrell's
    unique writings.

69 NEWMAN, CHARLES. "The Lesson of the Master: Henry James and
    James Baldwin." <u>Yale Review</u>, 56 (Autumn), 45-59.
         A comparison of James Baldwin with his mentor, Henry
    James, and a comparison of their mutual "experience with
    the dialectic . . . reflects the cultural history of a
    half-century . . . [and] implies a good deal about the fu-
    ture of the novel."

70 NOWELL-SMITH, SIMON. "First Editions, English and American."
    <u>Library</u>, 21 (March), 68.
         An overview of James's published works on two continents
    demonstrates the necessity of distinguishing editions as
    either "First English Edition" or "First American Edition"
    and does not constitute contradictory or irrelevant desig-
    nations.

71 OKITA, HAJIME. "British and American Writers and Soseki;
    Henry James." <u>Eigo Seinen</u> [The Rising Generation] (Tokyo),
    112 (July), 45. [Japanese]
         Soseki Natsume saw James's individuality and his stylis-
    tic peculiarities as early as 1904; in addition, this Japa-
    nese writer was well acquainted with William James's work.
    There are similarities in logic and in psychological de-
    tachment in the works of all three writers, William James,
    Henry James, and Soseki.

72 O'LEARY, SISTER JEANINE, R.S.H.M. "The Function of City as
    Setting in Dickens' <u>Our Mutual Friend</u>, Trollope's <u>The Way</u>
    <u>We Live Now</u>, James' <u>The Princess Casamassima</u> and Conrad's
    <u>The Secret Agent</u>." <u>DA</u>, 26, 6048-49 (Notre Dame).
         The London of the late nineteenth and early twentieth cen-
    turies is the setting for all four works; but in each work

London is seen in a different focus, because each author makes the setting subservient to characters, themes, and the work's overall symbolic tone.

73   PEROSA, SERGIO. "Tema e technica in The Sense of the Past." Studi Americani, no. 12, pp. 169-99. [Italian]
       In The Sense of the Past James analyzes himself to realize the past is gone and unreachable. He then denies and rejects the past to find that he possesses a deep interest in the present and in the future. As a consequence, James embraces a new allegiance with the present situation in view of tomorrow's hopes.

74   PIZER, DONALD. Realism and Naturalism in Nineteenth-Century American Literature. Carbondale and Edwardsville: Southern Illinois Univ. Press, pp. 3-10, passim.
       In this examination of two literary modes, James's What Maisie Knew, Howells's The Rise of Silas Lapham, and Twain's Adventures of Huckleberry Finn provide a framework for defining realism in the late nineteenth century.

75   POIRIER, RICHARD. "Visionary to Voyeur: Hawthorne and James," in his A World Elsewhere: The Place of Style in American Literature. New York: Oxford Univ. Press, pp. 93-143, passim.
       The Blithedale Romance, Hawthorne's greatest achievement, is the novel "that clarifies the degree to which James was unable to see either the genius of Hawthorne [in his 1879 monograph Hawthorne] or the extent to which Hawthorne's concern for the self and its environment resembled what were to be his own later preoccupations." Coverdale anticipates Strether in The Ambassadors.

76   POULET, GEORGES. "Henry James," in his The Metamorphoses of the Circle. Translated by Carley Dawson and Elliott Coleman. Baltimore: Johns Hopkins Press, pp. 307-20.
       The circle with James "is pure representation of an appearance. An arbitrary cutting-out accomplished by the artist in the great fluid mass of experience, it creates a cloister in whose shelter reality can be isolated, contemplated, and represented, without running the risk of melting into the universal multiplicity of phenomena."

77   PRICE, LAWRENCE MARSDEN. The Reception of United States Literature in Germany. Univ. of North Carolina Studies in Comparative Literature, No. 39. Chapel Hill: Univ. of North Carolina Press, pp. 157-58, passim.

Several James works were translated into German between 1876 and 1880, but real interest in James did not develop until the decade following 1946.

78   PUTT, S. GORLEY. "Henry James: An Unfinished Masterpiece." _English_, 16 (Summer), 45-48.
The Ivory Tower, "a teasingly truncated masterpiece," would have forced a radical reassessment of James's literary reputation had the author lived to complete it.

79   REID, STEPHEN. "Moral Passion in The Portrait of a Lady and The Spoils of Poynton." _Modern Fiction Studies_, 12 (Spring), 24-43.
The heroine's concern with the value of a sense of obligation is a "conscious moral issue" in The Portrait of a Lady and in The Spoils of Poynton, but both novels also exhibit a "constant interplay between the . . . fact of the moral life . . . and the emotional needs that occasion our moral outlook and conflict with it." Reprinted in 1968.A1.

80   RICHARDSON, LYON N. Henry James: Representative Selections. Urbana: Univ. of Illinois Press, pp. 5-6, cxii-cxvi.
Originally published in 1941, this book has been updated with a slightly revised preface and with the addition to the Bibliography of sixty-four books published between 1941 and 1965.

81   ROSE, ALAN. "The Spatial Form of The Golden Bowl." _Modern Fiction Studies_, 12 (Spring), 103-16.
The Golden Bowl is "constructed on spatial principles." James's theme is mainly concerned with "a spatial complex of relationships among characters, moralities, backgrounds, environments, and attitudes." The theme is enhanced by "relating scenes, symbols and images in space."

82   ROSENBAUM, S. P. "The Editions of The Ambassadors." _Library_, 21 (September), 248-50.
The bibliographic information in the Norton Critical Edition of The Ambassadors is accurate. Response to 1965.B5. See 1966.B12.

83   ROSENBAUM, S. P. "Henry James and Creativity: 'The Logic of the Particular Case.'" _Criticism_, 8 (Winter), 44-52.
James's account of the germination of The Spoils of Poynton in his preface, which was written years after its first publication, does not fully agree with the account as it appears in his notebooks.

84   ROSENBAUM, S. P. "The Spoils of Poynton: Revisions and Edi-
      tions." Studies in Bibliography, 19:161-74.
         A study of the four editions of The Spoils of Poynton
      published during James's lifetime suggests the New York
      Edition is the best.

85   ROSS, MORTON L. "James's The Birthplace: A Double Turn of
      the Narrative Screw." Studies in Short Fiction, 3
      (Spring), 321-28.
         Beyond the story of Gedge's hypocrisy, The Birthplace
      is a "double-edged commentary on both the mechanics and
      the morality of literary idolatry."

86   SACHS, VIOLA. "Uwagi o Amerykańskim 'Romansie.'" Przeglad
      Humanistyczny, 10:87-93. [Polish]
         Henry James is a powerful novelist, conventional yet in-
      novative, clearly set in Hawthorne's tradition.

87   SCHNEIDER, SISTER LUCY. "Osculation and Integration: Isabel
      Archer in The One-Kiss Novel." College Language Associa-
      tion Journal, 10 (December), 149-61.
         To view Isabel in terms of the approximately twenty
      kisses she experiences in the novel is to see her growing
      in wisdom. When she returns to Rome after Caspar's pas-
      sionate kiss, she is demonstrating the freedom to act as
      "the strong woman of integrity" that she has become.

88   SHARP, SISTER M. CORONA, O.S.U. "Fatherhood in Henry James."
      University of Toronto Quarterly, 35 (April), 279-92.
         James's fictive fathers provide an index to his feelings
      toward males in general. In the early and middle years,
      James creates three types of fathers--the tyrannical, the
      adventurous, and the vanquished--but in his late work
      (notably The Golden Bowl), he reflects a mellowing atti-
      tude and creates a "good" father.

89   SIMON, JOHN KENNETH. "A Study of Classical Gesture: Henry
      James and Madame de Lafayette." Comparative Literature
      Studies, 3:273-83.
         A comparison of the works of James and Madame de
      Lafayette, in terms of setting, recurring scene, and the
      emotional genre "that is the aim of both the characters
      and author," with attention focused on La Princesse de
      Clèves and "Madame de Mauves," reveals analogies in both
      theme and method.

1966

90 SNOW, LOTUS. "'The Prose and the Modesty of the Matter':
James's Imagery for the Artist in Roderick Hudson and The
Tragic Muse." Modern Fiction Studies, 12 (Spring), 61-82.
  James "explores the disintegration of genius through the
force of passion" in both Roderick Hudson and The Tragic
Muse. The development of the imagery to more original figures in the later novel gives evidence that James changed
his position concerning the artist from "passionate and
negative" in Roderick Hudson to "intellectual and positive"
in The Tragic Muse.

91 SPENCER, BENJAMIN T. "Pound: The American Strain." Publications of the Modern Language Association of America, 81
(December), 457-66.
  A defense of Pound's true Americanism brings in his admiration of James. Both Pound and James felt a concern for
American literature, and both writers had a need for expatriation.

92 STONE, EDWARD. Voices of Despair: Four Motifs in American
Literature. Athens: Ohio Univ. Press, pp. 106-107,
passim.
  Eleven references to James.

*93 STRUBLE, GEORGE G. "Henry James and the Rise of the Cosmo-
politan Spirit in American Literature," in Proceedings of
the IVth Congress of the International Comparative Literature Association: Freiburg, 1964. 2 vols. Edited by
François Jost. The Hague: Mouton, vol. 1, pp. 80-85.
  Cited in 1967 MLA International Bibliography, vol. 1,
p. 177.

94 TAKANO, FUMI. "Liberty in the Novels of Henry James." The
Tsuda Review, 11 (November), 33-71. [Japanese]
  With James, liberty is purely subjective. His view of
individual freedom seems to diminish as one follows the
protagonists of The American, The Portrait of a Lady, and
The Wings of the Dove, who come to know of fate until its
final value appears to lie in the character's ability to
remain on the spot and to have an illusion of freedom.
James manages to reconcile his inner need of idealism with
the unheroic reality of the nineteenth century, which results in a tragi-comedy of a high order.

95 TANNER, TONY. "The Watcher from the Balcony: Henry James's
    The Ambassadors." Critical Quarterly, 8 (Spring), 35-52.
        The ambivalence James felt about life (awe at its wonder
    and fear of its terror) is made the subject of The Ambassa-
    dors, wherein Strether renounces participation in life for
    the priceless vision of the artist.

96 TEMPLE, RUTH Z., and MARTIN TUCKER, comps. and eds. "Henry
    James," in A Library of Literary Criticism: Modern British
    Literature. Vol. 2. New York: Ungar, pp. 85-95.
        Excerpts of sixteen pieces of criticism published on
    James between 1908 and 1963.

97 TUTTLETON, JAMES W. "Henry James and Edith Wharton: Fiction
    as the House of Fame." Midcontinent American Studies Jour-
    nal, 7 (Spring), 25-36.
        A study of the "New York novels" of James and Wharton
    demonstrates that like Balzac they believed "that houses,
    clothes, furniture and the externals of social existence
    . . . serve to define 'human nature.'"

98 VAN CROMPHOUT, GUSTAAF. "The Wings of the Dove: Intention
    and Achievement." Minnesota Review, 6:149-54.
        The international situation in the novel is only the
    background for a drama of universal human truth; thus the
    characters are not important as "Europeans" or "Americans,"
    but as human beings.

99 VIDAN, IVO. "James's Novel of 'Looming Possibilities,'" in
    Renaissance and Modern Essays Presented to Vivian de Sola
    Pinto. Edited by G. R. Hibbard, with the assistance of
    George A. Panichas and Allen Rodway. London: Routledge
    and Kegan Paul; New York: Barnes and Noble, pp. 137-45.
        The Princess Casamassima "contains not only the disturb-
    ing and fascinating external analogies to the modern world,
    but is full of looming potentialities which the art of the
    novel . . . has more fully discovered only in the twentieth
    century."

100 VIDAN, IVO. "The Princess Casamassima: Between Balzac and
    Conrad." Studia Romanica et Anglica Zagrabiensia, nos. 21-
    22, pp. 259-76.
        In James's The Princess Casamassima can be found paral-
    lels with Balzac's Les Illusions Perdues, as well as analo-
    gies with Conrad's The Secret Agent.

1966

101 WADE, DAVID. "Shadows of Henry James." <u>Listener</u>, 75
(10 March), 365.
Radio adaptations of "The Lesson of the Master" and <u>The
Turn of the Screw</u> provide evidence that "radio deals indif-
ferently with Henry James."

102 WALCUTT, CHARLES CHILD. "The Illusion of Action in Henry
James," in his <u>Man's Changing Mask: Modes and Methods of
Characterization in Fiction</u>. Minneapolis: Univ. of Minne-
sota Press, pp. 175-211.
An examination of two stories--"The Real Thing" and "The
Beast in the Jungle"--and four novels--<u>The Bostonians</u>, <u>The
Portrait of a Lady</u>, <u>The Golden Bowl</u>, and <u>The Ambassadors</u>--
reveals that "the rich heady flow of James's own sensibili-
ty" obscures his characterizations. They "fail to achieve
a solid form" because the action of the novel is illusive.

103 WARREN, AUSTIN. "Henry James," in his <u>The New England Con-
science</u>. Ann Arbor: Michigan Univ. Press, pp. 143-56.
James's close observation and attentive analysis of the
New England conscience is exemplified in <u>The Europeans</u>, <u>The
Bostonians</u>, and <u>The Ambassadors</u>.

104 WEIMER, DAVID R. "Babylons Visited: Henry James," in his <u>The
City as Metaphor: Studies in Language and Literature</u>. New
York: Random House, pp. 34-51.
For James, "expressive cities" in his fiction "are al-
ways European, never American." James's use of "city-
place" in <u>Roderick Hudson</u>, <u>The Portrait of a Lady</u>, and <u>The
American</u> is discussed.

105 WIESENFARTH, BROTHER JOSEPH. "Henry James: Action and the
Art of Life." <u>Four Quarters</u> (La Salle), 15 (January),
18-26.
"In <u>Pride and Prejudice</u> the meaning of life is stable
and real, and Elizabeth has only to share in it. In <u>The
Portrait of a Lady</u>, Isabel must create a vision of life and
strive to make it actual for herself." The imaginative
faculty is a danger in Austen's novel and a means for ful-
fillment in reality in James's.

106 WILLEY, FREDERICK. "The Free Spirit and the Clever Agent in
Henry James." <u>Southern Review</u>, ns 2 (Spring), 315-28.
In <u>The Spoils of Poynton</u> and <u>The Portrait of a Lady</u>,
through the key word "clever" James conveys his "vision of
human character" and explores "the ethical and psychological implications of seeing and feeling."

107 WILSON, RICHARD. "Henry James and 'The Note Absolute.'" Eng-
     lish Studies, 47 (February), 31-35.
          James was intolerant of criticism of his work and of his
     own imperfect works. Accordingly, he either isolated him-
     self from critics or ignored their writings and rejected or
     revised many of his early writings that did not measure up
     to his later ideals.

108 WOLF, H. R. "What Maisie Knew: The Rankian Hero." American
     Imago, 23 (Fall), 227-34.
          The characteristics of the hero delineated in Otto
     Rank's The Myth of the Birth of the Hero are obvious in the
     character of Maisie, and the mythic mechanism is a vehicle
     for exploring the forbidden sexual content in acceptable
     moral terms.

109 ZIETLOW, EDWARD R. "A Flaw in The American." College Lan-
     guage Association Journal, 9 (March), 246-54.
          The resolution of this early work, which consists of
     Newman's vindication according to James's stated intention,
     is "forced," since James does not deal with the implica-
     tions of Newman's personal disposition of criminal evi-
     dence. Reprinted in 1972.B112.

110 ZIFF, LARZER. "Literary Absenteeism: Henry James and Mark
     Twain," in his The American 1890's: Life and Times of a
     Lost Generation. New York: Viking, pp. 50-66, passim.
          During the decade of the 1890s James's themes "modulat-
     ed from freedom to the nature of art to the need for pas-
     sion, each successive theme retaining the motifs of the
     earlier ones and building upon them. By the flames of the
     nineties he was refined as few American artists have ever
     been refined."

*111 ZOLLA, ELEMIRE. "Henry James e i morti." Elsinore, 3:49-71.
          Cited in 1970.B72, p. 324.

1966 C DISSERTATIONS

  1 EAKIN, PAUL J. "Henry James and the New England Conscious-
     ness." Dissertation, Harvard, 280 pp.
          Henry James's exploration of "the moral and aesthetic
     confusion of the age of Emerson, Hawthorne, and Margaret
     Fuller" is revealed in his "dramas of consciousness," pub-
     lished between 1876 and 1886, which center around "New Eng-
     land Heroines" who evince "a gift of a sensibility dis-
     tinctly Transcendentalist in cast."

1966

2   FLOWER, DEAN SCOTT. "The Art of the Nouvelle: Henry James."
    DA, 27, 179A (Stanford).
        Under the influence of Mérimée, Hawthorne, Maupassant,
    Turgenev, and Balzac, Henry James formulated his own con-
    cept of the nouvelle which included special techniques,
    themes, and characters.

*3 HASLER, JÖRG. "Switzerland in the Life and Work of Henry
    James: The Clare Benedict Collection of Letters from Henry
    James." Dissertation, Basel.
        Cited in James Woodress, Dissertations in American Lit-
    erature: 1891-1966. Revised and enlarged with the assis-
    tance of Marian Koritz. Durham: Duke Univ. Press, 1968,
    Item 1490.
        For book publication see 1966.A3.

4   LEONARD, VIVIEN ROSE. "An Introductory Study of Imagery in
    the Prefaces to the New York Edition of the Novels and
    Tales of Henry James." DA, 27, 1826A-27A (Columbia).
        Since most of James's ideas are presented in his imag-
    ery, a study of the "nature" and the "patterning" of those
    images provides meaningful insight into both his craft and
    his individual works.

5   MAIXNER, PAUL ROGER. "Henry James and the Question of Formal
    Unity." DA, 27, 1828A-29A (Columbia).
        For James formal unity was only a portion of his larger
    concern with cultural unity. The unity James sought to
    achieve was between the "moral" and the "aesthetic" as
    represented in American and European cultures. James be-
    lieved "the value and unity of a work are proportional to
    the degree of integration of the 'moral' and the 'aesthet-
    ic' values."

6   MAYS, MILTON ANDREW. "Uptown and Downtown in Henry James's
    America: Sexuality and the Business-Society." DA, 26,
    6046 (Minnesota).
        The traditional sex roles in America were perceived by
    James to have been obliterated as a result of the males'
    preoccupation with capitalistic responsibilities.

7   MOSSMAN, ROBERT E. "An Analytical Index of the Literary and
    Art Criticism by Henry James." DA, 27, 1790A (Pittsburgh).
        Utilizing reviews, essays, notebooks, letters, prefaces,
    and other materials, an attempt has been made to index
    every known discussion by James to "persons, places, and
    theoretical concepts."

8   WHITE, SIDNEY HOWARD. "Henry James's The American Scene."
      DA, 26, 6055 (Southern California).
         The American Scene is an important entity in the Jamesi-
      an canon because of its historical accuracy and the insight
      it provides into the author's creative process.

1967 A BOOKS

1   GALE, ROBERT L. Key-Indexed Study Guide to Henry James' "The
      Ambassadors." Philadelphia: Educational Research Associ-
      ates in association with Bantam Books, 114 pp.
         A thorough and comprehensive guide for the undergraduate
      student, this study includes biographical background on
      James along with critical information and a bibliography.

2   GALLOWAY, DAVID. Henry James: "The Portrait of a Lady."
      Studies in English Literature, No. 32. London: Edward
      Arnold, 64 pp.
         This critical overview of the novel includes discussion
      of biographical background, plot, theme, point of view, and
      the use of symbols. Isabel's return to Osmond is analyzed
      with the conclusion that she lost her "soaring and improb-
      able freedom which intoxicated Ralph," but she gained "wis-
      dom and dignity to compensate for that loss." Reprinted
      1973.

3   HEIMER, JACKSON W. The Lesson of New England: Henry James
      and His Native Region. Ball State Monograph, Number 9.
      Publications in English, Number 5. Muncie, Ind.: Ball
      State Univ., 26 pp.
         James had roots in New England and retained connections
      with the region throughout his life. His relationship with
      New England was not consistent, and three different periods
      may be isolated in terms of his feelings of acceptance
      (1843-1875), condemnation (1876-1903), and reconciliation
      (1904-1916).

4   KEYNES, GEOFFREY. Henry James in Cambridge. Cambridge:
      Heffer, 23 pp.
         Geoffrey Keynes, a Pembroke undergraduate, and two li-
      brarians at Cambridge initiated a correspondence with Henry
      James on New Year's Eve, 1907, which resulted in James's
      reluctantly visiting Cambridge in May, 1909. (James's
      letters to the trio are reprinted here.)

1967

5   STAFFORD, WILLIAM T. <u>Perspectives on James's "The Portrait of a Lady": A Collection of Critical Essays</u>. New York: New York Univ. Press; London: Univ. of London Press, 303 pp.
Contents:
"Introduction" by William T. Stafford (pp. x-xix). The twenty selections in this book constitute a sampling of the literary history of the novel. Various perspectives are employed--"in time, in approach, in distance." A bibliography is included.
Excerpts from James's <u>Notebooks</u> and his Preface to the novel are reprinted (pp. 1-20).
"A Survey of Early Reviews--American" by Richard N. Foley (pp. 25-28). Reprinted from <u>Criticism in American Periodicals of the Works of Henry James from 1866 to 1916</u>. Washington, D.C.: Catholic Univ. of America Press, 1944, pp. 26-30.
"An American Review--James's <u>The Portrait of a Lady</u>" by William C. Brownell (pp. 29-34). Reprinted from <u>Nation</u>, 34 (2 February 1882), 102-103.
"A Survey of Early Reviews--English" by Donald M. Murray (pp. 35-38). Reprinted from "The Critical Reception of Henry James in English Periodicals, 1875-1916." Unpublished Dissertation, New York Univ., 1951, pp. 45-49.
"An English Review--<u>The Portrait of a Lady</u>" by Anonymous (pp. 39-41). Reprinted from <u>The Athenaeum</u> (26 November 1881), p. 699.
"From <u>The Method of Henry James</u>" by Joseph Warren Beach (pp. 45-50). Reprinted from <u>The Method of Henry James</u>. New Haven: Yale Univ. Press, 1918, pp. 205-11.
"From <u>The Early Development of Henry James</u>" by Cornelia Pulsifer Kelley (pp. 51-62). Reprinted from <u>The Early Development of Henry James</u>. Urbana: Univ. of Illinois Press, 1965.
"The Painter's Sponge and Varnish Bottle" by F. O. Matthiessen (pp. 63-88). Reprinted from <u>Henry James: The Major Phase</u>. New York: Oxford Univ. Press, 1944, pp. 152-86.
"From <u>An Introduction to the English Novel</u>" by Arnold Kettle (pp. 91-112). Reprinted from <u>An Introduction to the English Novel</u>. Vol. 2. London: Hutchinson, 1953, pp. 13-34.
"From <u>The English Novel: Form and Function</u>" by Dorothy Van Ghent (pp. 113-31). Reprinted from <u>The English Novel: Form and Function</u>. New York: Holt, Rinehart and Winston, 1953, pp. 211-28.
"From <u>The English Novel: A Short Critical History</u>" by Walter Allen (pp. 132-35). Reprinted from <u>The English Novel: A Short Critical History</u>. New York: Dutton, 1954, pp. 314-18.

"From 'The Heiress of All the Ages'" by Philip Rahv
(pp. 139-47). Reprinted from Image and Idea. Norwalk,
Conn.: New Directions, 1957, pp. 51-52, 62-70.
"The Lesson of the Master" by Richard Chase (pp. 148-65).
Reprinted from The American Novel and Its Tradition. New
York: Doubleday, 1957, pp. 117-37.
"The Portrait of a Lady: Vis Inertiae" by William
Bysshe Stein (pp. 166-83). Reprinted from Western Humani-
ties Review, 13 (Spring 1959), 177-90.
"The Wings of the Dove and The Portrait of a Lady: A
Study of Henry James's Later Phase" by Ernest Sandeen
(pp. 187-205). Reprinted from Publications of the Modern
Language Association of America, 69 (December 1954),
1060-75.
"The High Brutality of Good Intentions" by William H.
Gass (pp. 206-16). Reprinted from Accent, 18 (Winter
1958), 62-71. Also reprinted in 1962.A4.
"From The Confidante in Henry James" by Sister M. Corona
Sharp, O.S.U. (pp. 217-44). Reprinted from 1963.A3.
"The Portrait of a Lady" by R. P. Blackmur (pp. 247-55).
Reprinted from 1961.B5.
"The Portrait of a Lady" by Oscar Cargill (pp. 256-96).
Reprinted from 1961.A1.
Reviewed: Richard Lehan, Nineteenth-Century Fiction, 23
(1968), 122-23; Times Literary Supplement (28 March 1968),
p. 311; Modern Fiction Studies, 13 (Winter 1967-1968), 527.

6 TANIGUCHI, RIKUO, ed. Guide to 20th Century English and American Literature I: Henry James. Tokyo: Kenkyusha,
   302 pp. [Japanese]
   Contents: This convenient guide to James consists of
three main parts along with a brief chronology of James's
life and a bibliography.
   I: "Henry James: The Man and Life" by Rikuo Taniguchi.
A biographical survey, this essay includes discussion of
James's family background, his youth, his artistic intentions, his crisis as an artist, and the major phase of his
career.
   II: Works. Each work is summarized; critical questions
are discussed; and an informative note is included telling
of the circumstances at the time of the work's creation.
The works covered are: Roderick Hudson (Yuji Ejima), The
American (Yuji Ejima), The Portrait of a Lady (Shigetoshi
Katsurada), The Bostonians (Akio Onishi), The Princess Ca-
samassima (Akio Onishi), What Maisie Knew (Shitsuu Iwase),
The Wings of the Dove (Konomu Itagaki), The Ambassadors
(Tsugio Aoki), The Golden Bowl (Akio Namekata); Other Nov-
els, including Watch and Ward, The Europeans, The Tragic

1967

Muse, The Sacred Fount, and others (Akio Onishi and Akio
Namekata); Tales and Short Stories (Shigetoshi Katsurada
and Shitsuu Iwase); and Critical Works (Fujio Murakami).
    III: "Estimation" by Rikuo Taniguchi. Includes a sur-
vey of James criticism and an introduction of the major
critical works on James.

7 WARD, JOSEPH A. The Search for Form: Studies in the Struc-
    ture of James's Fiction. Chapel Hill: Univ. of North
    Carolina Press, 228 pp.
        A study of the structure in James's works reveals that
    he built his works both "in accordance with some prede-
    termined ideal of what the shape should be" and "in accor-
    dance with the organic development of the 'germ.'" In all
    of his writing he continued the "search for form." Chap-
    ters are devoted to analyzing the following works: Watch
    and Ward, "Madame de Mauves," The Europeans, The Princess
    Casamassima, The Wings of the Dove, and The Golden Bowl.
    Reviewed: Modern Fiction Studies, 13 (Winter 1967-1968),
    526; Oscar Cargill, American Literature, 40 (1968), 92-93;
    B. R. McElderry, Jr., Nineteenth-Century Fiction, 23
    (1968), 111-13; William T. Stafford, Novel, 1 (1968),
    284-85; Times Literary Supplement (3 March 1969), p. 233;
    Dale Kramer, Studies in Short Fiction, 8 (1971), 495-97.

1967 B SHORTER WRITINGS

1 ALDRICH, C. KNIGHT, M.D. "Another Twist to The Turn of the
    Screw." Modern Fiction Studies, 13 (Summer), 167-78.
        The Turn of the Screw is "a tragedy about an evil older
    woman" (Mrs. Grose) who drove the governess out of her mind
    and who indirectly caused Miles's death. Reprinted in
    1969.A11.

2 ALLEN, GAY WILSON. William James: A Biography. New York:
    Viking, passim.
        Henry James played a large part in his brother's life
    and there are many references to him in this biography.

3 ALLINGHAM, WILLIAM. William Allingham's Diary. Carbondale:
    Southern Illinois Univ. Press, p. 378.
        James is mentioned once in Allingham's Diary; at a tea-
    party James describes himself as an "'unmitigated cockney.'"

4   ANDERSON, CHARLES R.   "Person, Place, and Thing in James's The
    Portrait of a Lady," in Essays on American Literature in
    Honor of Jay B. Hubbell. Edited by Clarence Gohdes. Dur-
    ham, N.C.: Duke Univ. Press, pp. 164-82.
        With the publication of The Portrait of a Lady James
    shifted "from the argument of a thesis to the creation of
    characters" with the result that his theme is indirectly
    conveyed to the reader through a process whereby "persons"
    develop relationships with one another through the symbolic
    facilitation of "places" and "things."

5   ANDREACH, ROBERT J.   "Literary Allusion as a Clue to Meaning:
    James's 'The Ghostly Rental' and Pascal's Pensées." Com-
    parative Literature Studies, 4:299-306.
        Allusions to the Pensées in "The Ghostly Rental" are
    functional and "supply the clue to the tale's meaning."

6   BANTA, MARTHA.   "The House of the Seven Ushers and How They
    Grew: A Look at Jamesian Gothicism." Yale Review, 57
    (October), 56-65.
        To the Gothic tradition James added "a New Gothicism
    which . . . revealed the self as a victim of its own
    villainy."

7   BARNHART, CLARENCE, with the assistance of WILLIAM D. HALSEY.
    "Henry James," in their The New Century Handbook of English
    Literature. Revised edition. New York: Appleton-Century-
    Crofts, pp. 620-21.
        Briefly surveys James's life and lists his major works.

8   BEATTIE, MUNRO.   "The Many Marriages of Henry James," in Pat-
    terns of Commitment in American Literature. Edited by
    Marston La France. Toronto: Univ. of Toronto Press,
    pp. 93-112.
        An overview of James's fiction reveals the centrality
    of the marriage relationship to his art; it is central to
    much of his theme, and is "an instrument of composition,
    controlling and defining the pattern of a tale or a novel."
    Originally presented as a public lecture at Carleton Univ.,
    Autumn 1965.

9   BELLRINGER, ALAN W.   "The Spoils of Poynton: James's Inten-
    tions." Essays in Criticism, 17 (April), 238-43.
        A look at James's prefaces and Notebooks contradicts
    John Lucas's interpretation of Fleda; furthermore, his
    interpretation accentuates the peril of "authorial dis-
    tance." Response to 1966.B60. See also 1966.B9; 1968.B66;
    1968.B13.

1967

10   BIDDLE, FRANCIS. "The Eagle and the Worm." Sewanee Review,
      75 (Summer), 533-39.
          This review of Millicent Bell's Edith Wharton and Henry
      James (an "engaging book") includes comment on James's
      relationships with other women writers: George Eliot,
      Vernon Lee, and Constance Fenimore Woolson. Review of
      1965.A1.

11   BROPHY, BRIGID. "Henry James," in her Don't Never Forget:
      Collected Reviews and Re-Reviewers. New York: Holt, Rine-
      hart and Winston, pp. 203-18.
          Reprinted from 1964.B17.

12   CALISHER, HORTENSE. "A Short Note on a Long Subject: Henry
      James." Texas Quarterly, 10 (Summer), 57-59.
          James's work is an "extraordinary affirmation of human
      consciousness." Reprinted in 1971.B20.

13   CECIL, L. MOFFITT. "'Virtuous Attachment' in James's The Am-
      bassadors." American Quarterly, 19 (Winter), 719-24.
          The novel is a dialectical examination of a "sensitive
      individual consciousness" struggling "to transcend group
      or code morality."

14   CLAES, ASTRID, trans. "Henry James: Europa und Amerika: Aus
      dem Tagebuch" [Henry James: Europe and America: From the
      Diary]. Text und Kritik, 15-16:9-11. [German]
          This is the translation of a diary entry dated 25 Novem-
      ber 1881, in which James, who has recently returned to
      America, reflects on the previous six years spent in
      Europe.

15   COTTON, GERALD B., and HILDA MARY McGILL. "Henry James," in
      Fiction Guide: British and American. Hamden, Conn.:
      Archon Books and Clive Bingley, p. 15.
          For "The Literary Aspect" of the Novel, the reader is
      directed to James's critical writings on the novel.

16   COX, C. B. "Henry James's Unravished Brides." Spectator, 218
      (17 March), 308-309.
          James's heroines reflect his undefined sexual fears—
      fears James makes "subservient to a great artistic vision
      of innocence threatened and menaced by life."

17 DELBAERE-GARANT, J. "The Redeeming Form: Henry James's 'The Jolly Corner.'" Revue des Langues Vivantes, 33:588-96.
The tale is examined "in the light of James's conception of art and of the creative act." Brydon gives form to his obsession of Self, discovers his life has been wasted, "recognizes the vanity of his former pride and finds salvation in human love."

18 DOMANIECKI, HILDEGARD. "Die Daumenschrauben der Erziehung: Eine Interpretation der short story 'The Turn of the Screw.'" Text und Kritik, 15-16:45-61. [German]
Ambiguities are inherent in this artistically unified short story, which is explored by considering the function of the half-frame, point of view, the reader's perception of the governess, the structure of the narrative, and problems involved in translating the work.

19 DORSCH, T. S., and C. G. HARLOW, eds. The Year's Work in English Studies: Vol. 46: 1965. New York: Published for the English Association by Humanities Press, pp. 460-63.
Survey of criticism for 1965.

20 DUFFY, JOHN J. "Ernest Dowson and the Failure of Decadence." University Review (Kansas City), 34 (Autumn), 45-49.
Ernest Dowson's "The Diary of a Successful Man," the donnée for which is lifted from Henry James's The American, illustrates the limitations of the literary aesthetics of the "decadent nineties."

21 EDEL, LEON. "Henry James: The Americano-European Legend." Univ. of Toronto Quarterly, 36 (July), 321-34.
The writings of James as well as his relationship with Europe reflect an admirably sympathetic cosmopolitanism and catholicity of spirit not commonly shared by his contemporary fellow-Americans.

22 EDEL, LEON. "Henry James Looked Ahead." New York Times Book Review, 12 (November), 2, 70-72.
In The American Scene Henry James prophetically observed many of the problems which haunt Americans today. He observed the alienation and isolation of people as well as the blighting of cities, the lack of tradition, the despoiling of the land. Reprinted in 1968.B33.

1967

23 EDEL, LEON. "Introductions," in his The Bodley Head Henry
   James. Vols. 1-4. London: Bodley Head.
   In the "Introduction" to The Europeans and Washington
   Square, Edel states: "Washington Square stands today as a
   recognized classic and an admirable study in psychological
   realism. The Europeans remains a fresh and lucid illustration of James's comic spirit." He introduces The Awkward
   Age as "a fine dramatic comedy" placed "within the novel-
   form." This story of two adolescent girls "would qualify
   as an outmoded Victorian novel were it not for James's
   grasp of the essence of his subject--and the formidable
   technique he uses to give it a frame." Edel's "Introduction" to The Bostonians notes that this novel is an American tale which treats social reformers satirically and is
   both "a fascinating work of fictional art" and "a fascinating social document." And in his "Introduction" to The
   Spoils of Poynton, he observes that this novel was written
   just after James's theatre failure in 1895 and is "the
   first to possess the characteristics of his most advanced
   work." The novel is characterized "by its concision, its
   swift scenic deployment of its four characters, its shrewd
   personal relations, its measured moral atmosphere."

24 FELSTINER, JOHN. "Max Beerbohm and the Wings of Henry James."
   Kenyon Review, 29 (September), 449-71.
   Beerbohm reveals much about the nature of fiction in his
   parodies and caricatures, and his "criticism of certain
   aims and inadequacies in James was indirect self-evaluation,
   a kind of literary transference."

25 FISH, CHARLES. "Form and Revision: The Example of Watch and
   Ward." Nineteenth-Century Fiction, 22 (September), 173-90.
   James's revisions in Watch and Ward of the alternating
   "centers of interest" achieve a refined form, although the
   attempts at perfection do not equal any of his later novels.

26 FRIESE, FRÄNZE. "Auf der Suche dem Muster im Teppich: Eine
   Einfuhrung in den Roman The Ambassadors." Text und Kritik,
   15-16:22-43. [German]
   Central to The Ambassadors is the development of Strether's consciousness, which is the key to understanding the
   novel.

27 GARGANO, JAMES W. "The Theme of 'Salvation' in The Awkward
   Age." Texas Studies in Literature and Language, 9 (Summer),
   273-87.
   The novel's action and its moral and psychological elements are based on the theme of salvation dramatized as a

"collision between competing saviors, one representing innocence [Mr. Longdon] and the other 'intrigue' and experience [Mrs. Brook]."

28 GARRETT, PETER K. "Scene and Symbol: Changing Mode in the
    English Novel from George Eliot to Joyce." DA, 27, 4251A
    (Yale).
        "This study examines changes in fictional mode between
    George Eliot's Middlemarch and Joyce's Ulysses under the
    aspect of increasing symbolism and in terms of scenic
    method."

29 GERBER, RICHARD. "Henry James." Neue Rundschau, 78:307-17.
    [German]
        James, with his interest in art for its own sake, de-
    parted from the dominant "life-oriented," "non-literary"
    tradition of the Anglo-American novel. Particularly sig-
    nificant in James's novels is the richness of nuance.

30 GILLESPIE, GERALD. "Novella, Nouvelle, Novella, Short Novel?
    --A Review of Terms." Neophilologus (Groningen), 51
    (April), 117-27; continued in Neophilologus (Groningen),
    51 (July), 225-30.
        An historical investigation of the terms used for short
    prose fiction in English, French, Spanish, German, and
    Italian includes mention of James's "The Bench of Desola-
    tion" and "The Beast in the Jungle" and closes with a call
    for "the establishment of a qualitative definition" of the
    nouvelle.

31 GOETSCH, PAUL. "Henry James," in his Die Romankonzeption in
    England: 1880-1910. Heidelberg: Carl Winter, pp. 371-87.
    [German]
        The following topics are discussed: the unique position
    of Henry James; James as a critic, 1864-1880; James's early
    works, 1864-1880; and The Portrait of a Lady.

32 GOODE, JOHN. "The Art of Fiction: Walter Besant and Henry
    James," in Tradition and Tolerance in Nineteenth-Century
    Fiction: Critical Essays on Some English and American
    Novels. Edited by David Howard, John Lucas, and John
    Goode. New York: Barnes and Noble; London: Routledge
    and Kegan Paul, pp. 243-81.
        The theoretical principles delineated by James in re-
    sponse to Besant's lecture with its techniques for "suc-
    cess" are clearly present in The Bostonians, but are ulti-
    mately renounced in The Princess Casamassima. James's es-
    say constitutes an important marker in the development of
    letters from Victorianism to modernism.

1967

33   GOTTSCHALK, JANE. "The Continuity of American Letters in The Scarlet Letter and 'The Beast in the Jungle.'" Wisconsin Studies in Literature, 4:39-45.

Analysis of these two works by Hawthorne and James reveals a continuing tradition in American literature: "Both works depend on a perception of values that are not material, both subordinate action and dialogue to an analysis of conduct, and both works have universal application despite their differences in approach and execution."

34   GREEN, DAVID BONNELL. "Witch and Bewitchment in The Bostonians." Papers on Language and Literature, 3 (Summer), 267-69.

The novel's themes are conveyed through pervasive witch imagery that includes the "white witch," Verena Tarrant.

35   GREENE, PHILIP L. "Point of View in The Spoils of Poynton." Nineteenth-Century Fiction, 21 (March), 359-68.

James "produces in Fleda Vetch a reliable reflector of his values"; her reliability is shown by James's constant violation of her point of view (thus closing distance between him and Fleda).

36   GREENE, SARAH EPSTEIN. "Love and Duty: The Character of the Princesse de Clèves as Reflected in Certain Later English and American Novels (Studies in Richardson's Clarissa Harlowe, Jane Austen's Sense and Sensibility and Persuasion, Charlotte Bronte's Jane Eyre, George Eliot's Middlemarch, and Henry James's The Wings of the Dove and The Portrait of a Lady)." DA, 28, 230A-31A (New Mexico).

Princesse de Clèves is an early prototype of a recurring fictional character in Romantic, Victorian, and American literature.

37   GROSSKURTH, PHYLLIS. "The Smile on the Face of the Tiger: A Profile of Leon Edel." Canadian Literature, 34 (Autumn), 24-31.

Edel's aims and methods have been different from Boswell's and Froude's, who wrote of the impact that Dr. Johnson and Carlyle had on them; Edel has created literary biography, "a study of the mind inside the man who held the pipe or the pen."

38   HAGAN, JOHN. "A Note on a Symbolic Pattern in The Wings of the Dove." College Language Association Journal, 10 (March), 256-62.

Milly's development is marked by three phases: "she charts a painful course from initial acceptance of London

182

society, through disillusionment, to the renunciation she
first disdains." Each of the three stages is defined "by
an image of her on a height contemplating the world before
her."

39   HAMBLEN, ABIGAIL ANN.   "Two Almost-Forgotten Innocents."
      Cresset, 30 (October), 16-17.
          Booth Tarkington's Claire Ambler and Henry James's Daisy
      Miller are notably similar in their innocence; and they
      have their parallels in modern America where "young women,
      . . . in jeans and mini-skirts and flowing hair, go to re-
      mote corners of the earth to 'help' the natives, or to
      'study conditions' in totalitarian governments."

40   HARNACK, CURTIS.   "Week of the Angry Artist. . . ."   Nation,
      204 (20 February), 245-48.
          Some political activist writers, who are protesting
      against the Viet Nam War, see Henry James as an example of
      the writer who ignored the great political problems of his
      time.

41   HARRISON, STANLEY R.   "Through a Nineteenth Century Looking
      Glass: The Letters of Edgar Fawcett." Tulane Studies in
      English, 15:107-57.
          Fawcett, a minor writer, was acquainted with Henry
      James, whom he worshipped. Excerpts from Fawcett's letters
      on James (pp. 129-31) include the comment: "James (take my
      word for it) is a very big man. He includes a good many
      Howellses."

42   HARTSOCK, MILDRED E.   "The Exposed Mind: A View of The Awk-
      ward Age." Critical Quarterly, 9 (Spring), 49-59.
          Although Nanda Brookenham is involved in a favorite
      Jamesian theme, the exploration of consciousness, she is
      not so myopic as to be insensitive to social realities and
      ethical responsibilities.

43   HARTSOCK, MILDRED E.   "Unweeded Garden: A View of The Aspern
      Papers." Studies in Short Fiction, 5 (Fall), 60-68.
          With its ability to evoke affectual responses in the
      reader, this story serves as an example to argue against
      critics who perceive of James's art as a purely intellec-
      tual experience.

44 HARVEY, PAUL, comp. and ed. "Henry James," in The Oxford Com-
    panion to English Literature. Fourth edition, revised by
    Dorothy Eagle. Oxford: Clarendon Press, 424-25.
        A brief entry surveys James's life and mentions his
    best-known works.

45 HARVEY, W. J. "The Human Context," in The Theory of the Nov-
    el. Edited by Philip Stevick. New York: The Free Press,
    pp. 231-47.
        Reprinted from 1965.B48.

46 HAYASHI, TETSUMARO. "Henry James: A Semantic View of His
    Short Stories." The Indian P.E.N., 33 (February), 35-38.
        In his short stories, James forces the reader to "feel"
    the meaning of his story and his characters by carefully
    choosing words that must be interpreted in light of how the
    reader experiences the character--not merely on the basis
    of what is said.

47 HÖNNIGHAUSEN, LOTHAR. "The Velvet Glove--zur Erzähltechnik in
    Henry James' Spätwerk." Germanisch-romanische Monats-
    schrift, Neue Folge, 48 (July), 307-22. [German]
        Certain aspects of the narrative technique in Henry
    James's later works, such as the varying degrees of inten-
    sity in erlebte Rede, the central intelligence technique,
    and problems of time and tense, are illuminated in examin-
    ing this previously neglected work.

48 HOWE, IRVING. "Henry James's Return to America." New Repub-
    lic, 157 (30 September), 23-26.
        James's writings reflect two visions, one American and
    another European, that converge in The American Scene.

49 HOWE, IRVING. "Introduction," in his edition of The American
    Scene. New York: Horizon, pp. v-xvi.
        James has deftly and subtly woven his ideas into his
    travel record--ideas that explore the impact of social
    change and industrial expansion on "the beauty of spirit
    of Emersonian America." (Includes photographs from the
    period of James's 1904-1905 visit.) Reprinted in 1970.B59.

50 HYDE, H. MONTGOMERY. "The Lamb House Library of Henry James."
    Book Collector, 16 (Winter), 477-80.
        When James died in 1916, he left a library of 2000 vol-
    umes in his Sussex home, Lamb House, Rye. Most of these
    books were eventually sold by a bookseller to individual
    customers, but one hundred and forty volumes are preserved
    in the Henry James Room at Lamb House. Lists of the large-

ly utilitarian library, which was richest in modern first
editions, do survive.

51   HYMAN, STANLEY E., ed. <u>William Troy: Selected Essays</u>. New
     Brunswick, N.J.: Rutgers Univ. Press, pp. 45-64.
         Contents include:
         "The Lesson of the Master" by William Troy (pp. 45-57).
     Originally published as "Henry James and Young Writers."
     <u>Bookman</u> (June 1931). Hyman explains in the "Introduction"
     that Troy, in this 1931 essay, was doing "a sort of
     criticism-by-generation along the lines of T. S. Eliot's
     in 'Baudelaire in Our Time.'"
         "The Altar of Henry James" by William Troy (pp. 58-64).
     Reprinted from <u>New Republic</u>, 108 (15 February 1943),
     228-30. Hyman points out that Troy suggested in this 1943
     essay that James was influenced by his father's Sweden-
     borgian mysticism.

52   IRLE, GERHARD. "Auswirkung des Wahns auf eine Gemeinschaft:
     Eine Untersuchung anhand von Henry James 'The Turn of the
     Screw.'" <u>Studium Generale</u>, 20:700-708. [German]
         Literary models offer interesting and relevant domains
     for psychiatric observation since certain psychopatholog-
     ical occurrences become more comprehensible when expressed
     in literary form. The changing relationships of the char-
     acters in the story can be interpreted from a psychiatric
     point of view.

53   JOHNSON, COURTNEY. "Henry James's 'The Jolly Corner': A
     Study in Integration." <u>American Imago</u>, 24 (Winter),
     344-59.
         The threat perceived by Spencer Brydon is that of cas-
     tration--both masculine and feminine anxiety are present.
     With the assistance of Alice Staverton, however, Brydon is
     able to overcome his anxiety by acknowledging and accepting
     both the strength (the masculine aspect of his personality)
     and the weakness (the feminine aspect) of his vision.

54   KANE, PATRICIA. "Mutual Perspective: James and Howells as
     Critics of Each Other's Fiction." <u>Minnesota Review</u>,
     7:331-41.
         Howells assumed the role of "justifier and friend" in
     most of his criticism of James, while James in his writings
     on Howells admired what Howells did superbly, recognizing
     still that the novel could do other things.

1967

55 KEHLER, HAROLD. "James's 'The Real Thing.'" Explicator, 25
    (May), Item 79.
        "The Real Thing" contains an example of James's "fond-
    ness for attributive names" in the word-play suggested by
    "Churm," the artist's model. "Churm" is a witty distortion
    of "charm."

56 KETTLE, ARNOLD. "Henry James: The Portrait of a Lady," in
    his An Introduction to the English Novel. Vol. 2. New
    edition. London: Hutchinson, pp. 14-32.
        In The Portrait of a Lady "James's manner, his obsession
    with style, his intricate and passionate concern with pre-
    sentation, do not spring from a narrow 'aesthetic' attitude
    to his art."

57 KIMMEY, J. L. "The Princess Casamassima and the Quality of
    Bewilderment." Nineteenth-Century Fiction, 22 (June),
    47-62.
        James shows Hyacinth's vacillating nature as a series of
    paradoxes resulting from and reflected in his background,
    his career, his appearance and his attitudes, as well as
    the attitudes and desires of his friends. These friends,
    more important to him than their ideas or cause, are divid-
    ed into two social classes, each trying to gain entry into
    the class of which he (or she) is not naturally a member.

58 KING, KIMBALL. "Theory and Practice in the Plays of Henry
    James." Modern Drama, 10 (May), 24-33.
        James's failure as a playwright is a result of his fail-
    ure to apply the three basic principles of art delineated
    in "The Art of Fiction" to his plays.

59 KRAFT, JAMES. "An Unpublished Review by Henry James." Stud-
    ies in Bibliography, 20:267-73.
        James's second earliest extant manuscript appears to be
    a review written for the North American Review in which the
    youthful James is "harshly critical" of Elizabeth Stoddard's
    Two Men.

60 LANE, MARGARET. "The Disappearing Ghost-Story: Some Reflec-
    tions on Ghost-Stories, in Particular on Henry James's The
    Turn of the Screw." Cornhill Magazine, no. 1052 (Summer),
    pp. 136-46.
        There has been a decline in the ghost story because
    readers no longer believe in the supernatural. For the
    same reason, critics have proposed the Freudian reading of
    James's The Turn of the Screw, since that interpretation
    calls the ghosts hallucinations.

61 LIDDELL, ROBERT. "Percy Lubbock." Kenyon Review, 29 (Septem-
    ber), 493-511.
        This memoir of Lubbock's life and work includes personal
    anecdotes about Henry James, as well as a survey of Lub-
    bock's scholarly work on James.

62 McDONALD, JAMES L. "The Novels of John Knowles." Arizona
    Quarterly, 23 (Winter), 335-42.
        An examination of Knowles's Indian Summer and Morning in
    Antibes reveals a promising artist who shares the literary
    affinities and "aesthetic preoccupations" of Henry James
    and F. Scott Fitzgerald.

63 McELDERRY, BRUCE R. "Henry James," in American Literary
    Scholarship: An Annual, 1965. Edited by James Woodress.
    Durham, N.C.: Duke Univ. Press, pp. 69-81.
        Survey of criticism published during 1965.

64 McLEAN, ROBERT C. "The Completed Vision: A Study of 'Madame
    de Mauves' and The Ambassadors." Modern Language Quarter-
    ly, 28 (December), 446-61.
        The Ambassadors is "an elaborate and deliberate rework-
    ing" of a theme James had explored earlier in "Madame de
    Mauves."

65 McLEAN, ROBERT C. "'Poetic Justice' in James's Aspern Pa-
    pers." Papers on Language and Literature, 3 (Summer),
    260-66.
        Miss Bordereau's confrontation with the narrator over
    the financial arrangements for the papers is an important
    element in the story that suggests the study is comic--a
    "study of poetic justice in which rewards and punishments
    are appropriately distributed."

66 MAGUIRE, C. E. "James and Dumas, fils." Modern Drama, 10
    (May), 34-42.
        L'Etrangère was produced while James was working on The
    American. James's bitter criticism of the play may have
    been caused by the remarkable similarities between Mr.
    Clarkson, whom Dumas satirizes, and Christopher Newman,
    whom James wanted taken seriously.

67 MARTIN, JAY. "Henry James: The Wings of the Artist," in his
    Harvests of Change: American Literature, 1865-1914.
    Englewood Cliffs, N.J.: Prentice-Hall, pp. 310-64,
    passim.
        The literary career of Henry James, a career enclosed on
    either end by war, at times reflects and at other times an-
    ticipates the concerns of the American psyche.

1967

68   MARTINEAU, STEPHEN FRANCIS. "Opposition and Balance: A Characteristic of Structure in Hawthorne, Melville, and James."
DA, 28, 1441 A (Columbia).
    Present in The Scarlet Letter, The Confidence-Man, The
Sacred Fount and The Golden Bowl is a recurring structural
device based on "radical disunities" that enables the authors of the works to produce a "very conscious, controlled
form with an unusual textural combination of clarity and
complexity."

69   MELCHIORI, GIORGIO. "Shakespeare and Henry James." Shake-
speare Newsletter, 17 (December), 56.
    The influence of Othello can be seen in A Passionate
Pilgrim and The American, but the most Shakespearean of
James's works are the late novels.

70   MERCER, CAROLINE G. "Adam Verver, Yankee Businessman." Nineteenth-Century Fiction, 22 (December), 251-69.
    James has created a shrewd Yankee figure in Adam Verver
by drawing from, but refining, the tradition of American
humor.

71   MILLER, JAMES EDWIN. Quests Surd and Absurd: Essays in American Literature. Chicago and London: Univ. of Chicago
Press, pp. 55-56, passim.
    A brief comparison of James and Faulkner reveals that
both writers "use a convolute, entangled and entangling
style to probe deep into the complexities of reality."

72   MILLER, PERRY. Nature's Nation. Cambridge, Mass.: The
Belknap Press of Harvard Univ. Press, pp. 262-78.
    A discussion of the novel and the romance focuses on the
four major writers of the post-Civil-War period--Henry
James, Howells, Twain, Adams--all of whom were noncombat-
ants during the war.

73   MIZENER, ARTHUR. "The Ambassadors," in Twelve Great American
Novels. New York: New American Library, pp. 49-67.
    James wrote "novels of manners, comedies in the old,
full sense of the word. But his 'poor gentlemen' come as
close as any figures of American fiction to being the tragic heroes of modern Western culture."

74   MOTODA, SHUICHI. "Interpretations of The Turn of the Screw
(I)." Bungaku Kenkyu (Kyushu Univ.), 64 (March), 35-61.
[Japanese]
    A close examination of the theories (Freudian and non-
Freudian) concerning the governess's psychosis is followed

by a reading based on Fromm which delineates the governess's character as being both sadistic and masochistic.

75 MUNFORD, HOWARD M. "Der geteilte Strom: Zur Kunstauffassung
    von Henry James." Translated by Amei Ortmann. Text und
    Kritik, 15-16:12-21. [German]
        The modern novel has taken two directions: one is real-
    ism and is represented by H. G. Wells; the other is the
    conception of the novel which comes from James, who viewed
    the expanding of human consciousness as the domain of the
    novel.

76 NAKANO, K. "G. K. Chesterton's View of James." English Lit-
    erature and Language (Sophia Univ.), 4 (December), 63-82.
    [Japanese]
        Chesterton's understanding of James can be divided into
    four phases: (1) in the beginning he sometimes referred to
    James in a derogatory fashion; (2) after knowing James per-
    sonally, he raised his previous estimation of James's work
    to compare it with Meredith's; (3) at James's death, he
    held James as the novelist, just as Shakespeare was the
    dramatist; (4) after James's death, Chesterton was proud of
    having known him and remembered the novelist humorously.

77 NEWTON, J. M. "Isabel Archer's Disease and Henry James's."
    Cambridge Quarterly, 2 (Winter), 3-22.
        The ambition and imagination of Isabel are not to be
    praised but are to be recognized as indicators of her
    "spiritual disease," a disease which James, lacking courage
    and honesty, fails to bring to its natural conclusion.

78 NODA, HISASHI. "A Note on Mrs. Tristram and the Education of
    Christopher Newman." Kyushu American Literature (Fukuoka,
    Japan), 10:50-60.
        Mrs. Tristram, the only realistically conceived charac-
    ter in the novel, offers another objective viewpoint to
    complement the viewpoints of Christopher Newman, the nar-
    rator, and the intervening author.

79 ORTMANN, AMEI. "Henry James: Ein Leben für die Literatur."
    Text und Kritik, 15-16:1-8. [German]
        James's experiences--his life, travels, and places of
    residence--are related to his literary production.

1967

80 OWEN, ELIZABETH. "The Awkward Age and the Contemporary Eng-
    lish Scene." Victorian Studies, 11 (September), 63-82.
        It can be demonstrated that The Awkward Age is a product
    of its cultural age, a demonstration that clarifies the
    aim of the novel and provides a basis "for a judgment of
    its successes and limitations in both content and form."

81 PISAPIA, BIANCAMARIA. "George Eliot e Henry James." Studi
    Americani, no. 13, pp. 235-80. [Italian]
        George Eliot plays a very prominent role in Henry James's
    life, and special attention is given to her by the author in
    his Autobiography.

82 PURDY, STROTHER B. "Henry James's Use of 'Vulgar.'" American
    Speech, 42 (February), 45-50.
        The word "vulgar" is employed with precision in four dif-
    fering connotative contexts.

83 PURDY, STROTHER B. "Language as Art: The Ways of Knowing in
    Henry James's 'Crapy Cornelia.'" Style, 1 (Spring),
    139-49.
        The thematic center of "Crapy Cornelia" hinges upon the
    word "know" in a single scene, where Cornelia and White-
    Mason are "courting in word-play."

84 REARDON, JOHN. "Hemingway's Esthetic and Ethical Sportsmen."
    University Review (Kansas City), 34 (Autumn), 22-23.
        Although they tell very different stories, Hemingway and
    James share a "fusion of the physical-esthetic-ethical in
    one action by one unified vision."

85 REILLY, ROBERT J. "Henry James and the Morality of Fiction."
    American Literature, 39 (March), 1-30.
        James shared his brother's skepticism of religious dogma
    and preferred an "infinite variety of religious affections
    in their inchoate state." He also believed that imitative
    art, like life, provided "the context in which we perform
    our moral acts." Reprinted in 1971.B67.

86 RUBIN, LOUIS, JR. "One More Turn of the Screw," in his The
    Curious Death of the Novel. Baton Rouge: Louisiana State
    Univ. Press, pp. 67-87.
        Reprint of 1963.B88.

87   RUBIN, LOUIS, JR. "The Presence of the Master," in his The
      Teller in the Tale. Seattle and London: Univ. of Washing-
      ton Press, pp. 83-102.
            "To attempt, therefore, to understand The Ambassadors
      without taking into account how much of the story's wonder-
      ful charm and suspense depend upon our consciousness of the
      authorial personality revealing it to us is to leave out
      much of the book's attraction for us."

88   RULAND, RICHARD. The Rediscovery of American Literature:
      Premises of Critical Taste, 1900-1940. Cambridge, Mass.:
      Harvard Univ. Press, pp. 78-81, 255-65, passim.
            In this study of the influence of moral values and
      philosophical propensities on the critical production of
      a four-decade period in America, a dozen passing references
      to Henry James appear.

89   SANDERS, THOMAS E. The Discovery of Fiction. Glenview, Ill.:
      Scott, Foresman & Co., pp. 289-303, 331-33.
            The style of the opening paragraph of "The Real Thing"
      is examined; then the story itself is explicated.

90   SCHNEIDER, DANIEL J. "The Ironic Imagery and Symbolism of
      James's The Ambassadors." Criticism, 9 (Spring), 174-96.
            A study of imagery and symbolism in The Ambassadors re-
      veals a "pervasive irony" which undercuts the extravagant
      praise of Paris and Mme. de Vionnet. James's repudiation
      of Paris is "at least as violent as his rejection of
      Woolett."

91   SCHOLES, ROBERT. The Fabulators. New York: Oxford Univ.
      Press, p. 162.
            Scholes accepts James's view that the critic's responsi-
      bility is to interpret the "central figure" in a writer's
      "carpet."

92   SLACK, ROBERT C., ed. "Henry James," in Bibliographies of
      Studies in Victorian Literature. Urbana: Univ. of Illi-
      nois Press, passim.
            In this reprinting of the annual Victorian bibliogra-
      phies for the years 1955-1964, which were published in
      Modern Philology (1956-1957) and Victorian Studies (1958-
      1965), there are seventeen references to Henry James.

1967

93   SOLOMON, ERIC. "Joseph Conrad, William Faulkner, and the
        Nobel Prize Speech." Notes and Queries, 14 (July), 247-48.
           Faulkner's Nobel Prize Speech reflects ideas similar to
        those expressed in Conrad's "Henry James: An Apprecia-
        tion," particularly the dual nature of the human heart.

94   SPACKMAN, W. M. "James, James," in his On the Decay of Human-
        ism. New Brunswick, N.J.: Rutgers Univ. Press, pp. 33-81.
           Henry James "lacked the professional self-discipline
        which is the very heart of the role that academic criticism
        assigns him. He wrote too much, and reflected on what he
        wrote far too little."

95   STALLMAN, R. W. "Introduction," in his edition of The Por-
        trait of a Lady. Illustrations by Colleen Browning. Bal-
        timore: Printed for the Members of the Limited Editions
        Club by the Garamond Press, pp. v-xii.
           "Isabel Archer belongs to life--as well as to art--
        because her plight is that of any young girl confronting
        her unknown destiny." Although a fictive creature, Isabel
        comes alive for readers.

96   STANFORD, DEREK. "A Larger Latitude: Three Themes in the
        'Nineties Short Story." Contemporary Review, 210 (Febru-
        ary), 96-104.
           The three most commonly encountered themes are "the life
        of sex, the life of art, [and] bohemian and declassé exis-
        tence."

97   STEIN, ROGER B. John Ruskin and Aesthetic Thought in America,
        1840-1900. Cambridge: Harvard Univ. Press, pp. 209-17,
        passim.
           An account of James's objections to "the narrow dogma-
        tism" of Ruskin's "point of view which left out of account
        the complexities of art" is included in the study along with
        a number of other references to Henry James.

98   STEPHENS, ROBERT O., and JAMES ELLIS. "Hemingway, Fitzgerald,
        and the Riddle of 'Henry's Bicycle.'" English Language
        Notes, 5 (September), 46-49.
           The allusion to the mystery of "Henry's bicycle" in The
        Sun Also Rises has generally been interpreted as a refer-
        ence to the "obscure hurt" that rendered Henry James impo-
        tent. Fitzgerald wrote in a 1926 letter to Maxwell Perkins
        that he did not find the reference "objectionable but then
        he [Henry James] seems to me to have been dead for fifty
        years."

99   STEVENSON, LIONEL. <u>The History of the English Novel: Volume XI--Yesterday and After</u>. New York: Barnes and Noble,
passim.
    This volume, which should be read "conjointly" with Er-
nest Baker's tenth volume in order to get a complete picture of the Edwardian and Georgian eras, contains thirty-
six references to Henry James.

100   STEVICK, PHILIP. "The Theory of Fictional Chapters." <u>Western
Humanities Review</u>, 20 (Summer), 231-41.
    A theoretical discussion of chapters includes brief
mention of <u>The Aspern Papers</u>: chapter division "makes the
narration possible." Reprinted in 1967.B101. Radically
revised in 1970.B107.

101   STEVICK, PHILIP, ed. <u>The Theory of the Novel</u>. New York:
Free Press.
    Contents include:
    "The Theory of Fictional Chapters" by Philip Stevick
(pp. 171-84). Reprinted from 1967.B100.
    "Mixed and Uniform Prose Styles in the Novel" by Leonard
Lutwack (pp. 208-19). Reprinted from 1960.B56.
    "The Human Context" by W. J. Harvey (pp. 231-51). Re-
printed from 1965.B48.

102   STROUT, CUSHING. "Henry James and the International Theme
Today." <u>Studi Americani</u>, no. 13, pp. 281-97.
    Although the two countries which provided the dialectic
structure for James's international studies have been dra-
matically altered in the twentieth century, James's method,
which is superior to that of any of his predecessors, could
be employed by today's authors to dramatize "how both the
parity and the disparity of our lives influence the individual meaning of freedom and limitation, of the pursuit of
happiness and the acceptance of sorrow."

103   SWARTZ, D. L. "Bernard Shaw and Henry James." <u>Shaw Review</u>,
10 (May), 50-59.
    James and Shaw moved in the same circles, and their paths
crossed particularly during James's playwriting experiences,
but the full story of their relationship awaits publication
of their letters.

104   TANNER, TONY. "Introduction" and "Notes," in his edition of
<u>Henry James's "Hawthorne."</u> London: Macmillan; New York:
St. Martin's Press, pp. 1-21.
    James's debt to Hawthorne is surveyed: "in matters of
subject, theme, and even technique (particularly with re-

1967

gard to the symbolism in James's late work) the influence
of Hawthorne is pervasive." Indeed, James thought of Hawthorne during his whole life, for Hawthorne's life and
works demonstrated to James that "'an American could be an
artist.'" Reviewed: 1968.B45.

105   THORBERG, RAYMOND. "Terror Made Relevant: James's Ghost Stories." Dalhousie Review, 47 (Summer), 185-91.
James's late ghost stories--The Turn of the Screw, The
Beast in the Jungle and The Jolly Corner--have a strong
autobiographical influence that renders them especially
relevant and vivid.

106   TOOR, DAVID. "Narrative Irony in Henry James's 'The Real
Thing.'" University Review (Kansas City), 34 (Winter),
95-99.
An examination of the narrator's credibility reveals
that he is unreliable: accordingly, the reader cannot take
seriously the esthetic theory he articulates. Reprinted in
1970.B7.

107   TRACHTENBERG, ALAN. "The American Scene: Versions of the
City." Massachusetts Review, 8 (Spring), 281-95.
"The presentational forms through which our writers
(particularly James in The American Scene) have projected
the city's disordered mind are . . . of incalculable value
as history and as art."

108   TRIESCHMANN, MARGARET. "The Golden Bowl: An Analysis of the
Sources of Evil in Human Relationships." Iowa English
Yearbook, 12 (Fall), 61-67.
The conflict between American and European values does
not define the moral dilemma of the novel, which "is a
study of the sources of evil as it arises in human relations, a complex demonstration that even the innocent and
well-intentioned may bear responsibility for it."

109   TRILLING, LIONEL. "Commentary" on Henry James's "The Pupil,"
in his The Experience of Literature. New York: Holt,
Rinehart & Winston, pp. 591-93.
Pemberton fails as a "moral agent," and he is account-
able for Morgan's death.

110   VAN KAAM, ADRIAN, and KATHLEEN HEALY. "Marcher in James' 'The
Beast in the Jungle,'" in their The Demon and the Dove:
Personality Growth Through Literature. Duquesne: Duquesne
Univ. Press, pp. 197-224.

"'The Beast in the Jungle' is perhaps his [James's] most penetrating presentation--through the power of negation, to be sure--of man's existential situation."

111   WALKER, WARREN S., comp. Twentieth-Century Short Story Explication: Interpretations, 1900-1966, of Short Fiction Since 1880. Second edition, revised. Hamden, Conn.: Shoe String Press, pp. 296-354.
      Articles published on James's short stories are arranged under the titles of individual stories. For earlier edition see 1961.B93.

112   WILLETT, MAURITA. "Henry James's Indebtedness to Balzac." Revue de Littérature Comparée, 41 (April-June), 204-27.
      Parallels in settings, themes, plots, characters, and imagery between The American and Le Père Goriot reveal that James's debt to Balzac is greater than critics have realized. James's statements of indebtedness to Balzac are verified.

113   WILSON, ANGUS. "Evil in the English Novel." Kenyon Review, 29 (March), 167-94.
      In this survey of the treatment of evil in the English novel, Henry James is considered to have transcended right and wrong in his works so as to have created "a real feeling of evil," principally in the actions of Kate Croy and Densher in The Wings of the Dove.

114   WINNER, VIOLA HOPKINS. "Pictorialism in Henry James's Theory of the Novel." Criticism, 9 (Winter), 1-21.
      James's fiction and his critical theory were fundamentally influenced by his "conception and experience of the visual arts and his ability to put his perceptions into words."

1967 C DISSERTATIONS

1   ALEXANDER, CHARLOTTE ANNE. "The Emancipation of Lambert Strether: A Study of the Relationship Between the Ideas of William and Henry James." DA, 28, 661A-62A (Indiana).
    William James's belief that moral character is developed through "experience and pragmatic reflection" is a belief held in common by his brother--a fact that is reflected in the experiences of the protagonist in The Ambassadors.

1967

2   BONTLY, THOMAS JOHN. "The Aesthetics of Discretion: Sexual-
      ity in the Fiction of Henry James." DA, 27, 3446A-47A
      (Stanford).
         Sexuality is a prominent aspect in James's novel. The
      oblique manner in which James presented it, however, is
      not indicative of perversion or pathology but of a sensi-
      tive appreciation of the importance of sexuality to man and
      a conscious decision to handle the subject discreetly in
      his fiction.

3   COLEMAN, ELIZABETH. "Henry James's Criticism: A Reëvalua-
      tion." DA, 28, 1428A-29A (Columbia).
         James's principal contribution to critical theory is not
      found in his technical innovations and evaluations, but in
      his moral insight and application of that morality to his
      art.

4   DUNCAN, KIRBY LUTHER. "The Structure of the Novels of Henry
      James." DA, 28, 2242A-43A (South Carolina).
         A study of thirteen of James's novels reveals a basic
      structural similarity present in all, with four variations
      on the common three-element structure. The three elements
      present in all thirteen novels are "one or more central
      characters, and the two opposing poles which he or they
      must choose between, attempt to synthesize, or reject."

5   FLORY, SISTER ANCILLA MARIE, S.B.S. "Rhythmic Figuration in
      the Late Style of Henry James." DA, 27, 3044A-45A (Catho-
      lic Univ.).
         An analysis of the rhythmic pattern of James's late
      style supports the contention that "the prosodic structure
      of James's prose is appropriate to the other elements of
      the late style and to the subject matter."

6   HABEGGER, ALFRED CARL. "Secrecy in the Fiction of Henry
      James." DA, 28, 1077A-78A (Stanford).
         The ignorant protagonist is present in James's fiction
      in four forms: "the deluded hero, the suspicious fiance,
      the obsessed quester, and the innocent American."

7   JOHNSON, COURTNEY, JR. "The Problem of Sex in the Writings of
      Henry James." DA, 28, 679A-80A (Michigan).
         An overview of James's treatment of sex reveals a con-
      cept in evolution. Through the evolving process, however,
      James is consistent in his handling of sexual passion--
      passion is treated as both a physical and a spiritual enti-
      ty; and he is consistent in his attitude toward sex:
      (1) the effects of love transcend the physical elements,

(2) sexual activity disassociated from "the whole continuum
of life is anathema," and (3) the solutions to sexual problems have moral, spiritual and aesthetic implications.

8   LABRIE, ERNEST ROSS. "The Role of Consciousness in the Fic-
    tion of Henry James, 1881-1899." DA, 28, 1438A (Toronto).
        In order to understand James's fiction accurately, it is
    imperative that the reader recognize that "the phenomenon
    of consciousness permeates life in the Jamesian world. The
    pursuit of greater consciousness is the characteristic form
    of activity in that world; consciousness is the decisive
    force in James's conflict situations; and it provides the
    underpinning for the moral system in that world."

9   MENIKOFF, BARRY HAROLD. "Style and Point of View in the Tales
    of Henry James." DA, 28, 686A-87A (Wisconsin).
        A study of specific narrative and stylistic techniques
    employed by James in his early, middle, and late tales re-
    veals a consistent movement toward devices that require the
    reader to participate in the story.

10 MONTEIRO, GEORGE. "Henry James and John Hay: A Literary and
    Social Relationship." DA, 28, 1824A (Brown).
        Biographical research, identification of articles pub-
    lished anonymously by John Hay, and examination of personal
    letters exchanged by Hay and James establish that the two
    men made literary and social exchanges during a three-
    decade span (1875-1905). For book publication see
    1965.A13.

11 MULL, DONALD LOCKE. "Sublime Economy: Money as Symbolic
    Center in Henry James." DA, 27, 2537A (Yale).
        An examination of James's Autobiography and several of
    his works that span his career, including The Portrait of
    a Lady, The Golden Bowl, The American Scene, and The Ivory
    Tower, reveals that he conceived of money both as "a sym-
    bolic equivalent for the potentialities of the imagination
    and a commercial limit upon that imagination." For book
    publication see 1973.A4.

12 STEER, HELEN VANE. "Henry James on Stage: A Study of Henry
    James's Plays, and of Dramatizations by other Writers Based
    on Works by James." DA, 28, 826A (Louisiana State Univ.).
        A study of James's fifteen plays shows his plays were
    "highly conventional; mostly comedies; with upper class
    characters . . .; [and] his settings were always playable."
    A study of the varying success of subsequent playwrights
    who utilized James's material offers "proof that James's

works can be successfully dramatized, when the right playwright chooses the right Jamesian material."

13   TEICHGRAEBER, STEPHEN EMILE.   "The Treatment of Marriage in
the Early Novels of Henry James."   DA, 28, 1830A (Rice).
A study of marriage as handled by James in seven novels
of his early period reveals an evolving complexity both in
the treatment of marriage and in the stylistic elements
consistently associated with the subject.

1968 A BOOKS

1   BUITENHUIS, PETER, ed.   Twentieth Century Interpretations of
"The Portrait of a Lady":   A Collection of Critical Essays.
Englewood Cliffs, N.J.:   Prentice-Hall, 122 pp.
Contents: Includes nineteen essays on the novel re-
printed from other sources, a chronology of important
dates, and a selected bibliography.
"Introduction" by Peter Buitenhuis (pp. 1-13).   Includes
biographical background on Henry James as well as a criti-
cal overview of the novel.
"The Lesson of the Master" by Richard Chase (pp. 15-28).
Reprinted from The American Novel and Its Tradition.   New
York: Doubleday, 1957, pp. 117-35.
"Drama in The Portrait of a Lady" by Richard Poirier
(pp. 20-36).   Reprinted from 1960.A5.
"Some Rooms From 'The Houses that James Built'" by R. W.
Stallman (pp. 37-44).   Reprinted from Texas Quarterly, 1
(Winter 1958), 181-84, 189-92.
"Nostalgic Poison" by Maxwell Geismar (pp. 45-50).   Re-
printed from 1963.A2.
"News of Life" by Quentin Anderson (pp. 51-54).   Re-
printed from The American Henry James.   New Brunswick,
N.J.:   Rutgers Univ. Press, 1957, pp. 187-92.
"The American as a Young Lady" by Christof Wegelin
(pp. 55-59).   Reprinted from The Image of Europe in Henry
James.   Dallas: Southern Methodist Univ. Press, 1958,
pp. 72-78.
"The Flaw in the Portrait" by Marion Montgomery
(pp. 60-66).   Reprinted from 1960.B66.
"The Fearful Self" by Tony Tanner (pp. 67-82).   Reprint-
ed from 1965.B106.
"Ironic Melodrama in The Portrait of a Lady" by Manfred
Mackenzie (pp. 83-96).   Reprinted from 1966.B63.
"Two Problems in The Portrait of a Lady" by Dorothea
Krook (pp. 97-106).   Reprinted from 1962.A3.

Brief excerpts of previously printed criticism are in-
cluded in the section titled "View Points" (pp. 107-15).
The following critics have work included here: F. O. Mat-
thiessen, Arnold Kettle, Sister Corona Sharp (from 1963.A3),
Walter F. Wright (from 1962.A5), Leon Edel (from 1968.B32),
Pelham Edgar, Edmond L. Volpe, F. W. Dupee, and Stephen
Reid (from 1966.B79).
    Reviewed: G. Matheson, <u>Dalhousie Review</u> (Winter 1968-
1969), p. 577; J. D. O'Hara, <u>Modern Language Journal</u>, 53
(March 1969), 207; S. Dick, <u>Queen's Quarterly</u> (Summer
1969), p. 364.

*2 FITZPATRICK, KATHLEEN. <u>Henry James and the Influence of
    Italy</u>. Sydney: Sydney Univ. Press.
        Robert L. Gale in 1972.A38, p. 100, states that this
    "tiny 'book' on an enormous subject. . . . presents ele-
    mentary biographical evidence that James loved Italy, and
    supports the truism by alluding to some of his fictional
    and nonfictional prose dealing with Italy and Italians."

3   FOX, HUGH. <u>Henry James, A Critical Introduction</u>. Conesville,
    Iowa: Westburg, 109 pp.
        This critical survey of James's work from 1869 to 1917
    concludes with the observation that in his last work, <u>With-
    in the Rim</u>, he was able to leave the past and "live with
    valor in the present." Reviewed: Edwin T. Bowden, <u>Ameri-
    can Literature</u>, 42:582-84; <u>Choice</u>, 6 (September 1969), 816.

4   GARD, ROGER, ed. <u>Henry James: The Critical Heritage</u>. The
    Critical Heritage Series. General editor B. C. Southam.
    London: Routledge and Kegan Paul; New York: Barnes and
    Noble, 566 pp.
        Reprints of contemporary responses to James's work from
    British and American sources between 1866 and 1920 are ar-
    ranged in chronological order and present a record of
    James's reception. Most of the comments taken from reviews
    and articles in books and periodicals, letters (to, from,
    and about James), memoirs, and allusions to James in fic-
    tion and parody concern the novels and stories. Five nov-
    els receive full treatment: <u>The Europeans</u>, <u>The Portrait of
    a Lady</u>, <u>The Tragic Muse</u>, <u>The Awkward Age</u>, and <u>The Golden
    Bowl</u>. Included in the book are an introduction, index,
    appendix of "important" bibliographic omissions, and an ap-
    pendix of book sales. Reviewed: Ashley Brown, <u>Spectator</u>,
    (11 October), p. 517; <u>Times Literary Supplement</u> (26 Septem-
    ber), p. 1070; B. R. McElderry, Jr., <u>Modern Fiction Studies</u>,
    15 (Winter 1969-1970), 554.

1968

5   GIORCELLI, CHRISTINA. Henry James e l'Italia. Rome: Edi-
     zioni di Storia e Letteratura, 159 pp. [Italian]
         Italy, and mostly Rome, was for James more than a symbol
     of nature, ancient civilization, and art. It represented a
     memory of youth, an inspiration for new projects and
     dreams. It was especially a place to rest and a source of
     new ideas. Reviewed: Times Literary Supplement (6 March
     1969), p. 233; Leon Edel, Comparative Literature, 23 (Sum-
     mer 1971), 284-85.

6   ISLE, WALTER. Experiments in Form: Henry James's Novels:
     1896-1901. Cambridge, Mass.: Harvard Univ. Press; London:
     Oxford Univ. Press, 251 pp.
         An examination of the five novels James published be-
     tween 1896 and 1901 points to "James's continually changing
     and developing fictional techniques, his constant experi-
     mentation with style, subject matter and form." James was
     "at the height of his creative powers" during this period
     of experimentation, when he moved toward "what is typically
     recognizable" as the twentieth century novel. For disser-
     tation see 1962.C3. Reviewed: Times Literary Supplement
     (26 September), p. 1070; Laurence B. Holland, Nineteenth
     Century Fiction, 23:361-65; Modern Fiction Studies, 13
     (Winter 1967-1968), 526-27; Leon Edel, American Literature,
     40 (1969), 562-64.

7   LEYBURN, ELLEN DOUGLASS. Strange Alloy: The Relation of
     Comedy to Tragedy in the Fiction of Henry James. Foreword
     by William T. Stafford. Chapel Hill: Univ. of North Caro-
     lina Press, 180 pp.
         James was interested in "the mixture and interaction of
     what he regularly calls comic with the painful in human ex-
     perience," and he portrayed comedy and tragedy as insepa-
     rable. Reviewed: Times Literary Supplement (6 March 1969),
     p. 233; Modern Fiction Studies, 14 (Summer), 235-36; Lau-
     rence B. Holland, Nineteenth-Century Fiction, 23:361-65.

8   SEARS, SALLIE. The Negative Imagination: Form and Perspec-
     tive in the Novels of Henry James. Ithaca, N.Y.: Cornell
     Univ. Press, 231 pp.
         A close examination of James's last three novels reveals
     that the conflict in the novels arises out of tensions
     formed by a character's limited choice and his desire to
     "reject limitations." If the character attempts "to create
     a new reality," sometimes with the aid of another charac-
     ter, then a new universe is created, which is worse than
     "the one left behind." A "process of annihilation" follows,
     thereby establishing a tension in James's works "between

the 'certainty' of the patterning of events and the uncer-
tainty of the significance of both terms and events." In
the late novels James's negative imagination (negative "because James could not assert positive values with any degree of success or conviction") took the form of an "unre-
solved debate about the promise and meaning of life, a
debate between a voice of yearning and a voice of restric-
tion." Reviewed: J. A. Ward, Modern Fiction Studies, 15
(1969), 283-86; Walter Isle, American Literature, 41
(1969), 439-40; Walter F. Wright, Modern Philology, 67
(1970), 389-90; Leon Edel, Nineteenth-Century Fiction, 25
(1970), 116-18.

9   SIEGEL, ELI. James and the Children: A Consideration of
    Henry James's "The Turn of the Screw." Edited by Martha
    Baird. New York: Definition Press, 162 pp.
       These edited lectures, originally delivered in 1953,
    present discussions of The Turn of the Screw in terms of
    Siegel's "Aesthetic Realism." In this reading Miles and
    Flora represent evil. Reviewed: 1968.A58; J. A. Ward,
    Modern Fiction Studies, 15 (1969), 283-86.

10 SPIEGEL, MARSHALL. "The Turn of the Screw"--"Daisy Miller."
    New York: Barnes and Noble, 96 pp.
       A study guide which includes a brief overview of James's
    work as well as summaries, critical analyses, critical
    opinions, and study questions for each novel.

11 TANNER, TONY, ed. Henry James: Modern Judgements. London:
    Macmillan.
       Contents: Twenty essays on James published since 1943
    were selected to represent "the different kinds of intelli-
    gence, patient research, imaginative interpretation and
    sensitive study which have been exercised in the field of
    James studies in the last twenty-five years or so." In-
    cluded are a chronology of James's life and a selected
    bibliography.
       "Introduction" by Tony Tanner (pp. 11-41). Criticism of
    James published before 1943 is analyzed.
       "The Altar of Henry James" by William Troy (pp. 46-51).
    Reprinted from New Republic, 108 (15 February 1943),
    228-30.
       "Henry James: The Poetics of Empiricism" by J. H.
    Raleigh (pp. 52-70). Reprinted from Publications of the
    Modern Language Association of America, 66 (March 1951),
    107-23.

"The Turned Back of Henry James" by Maurice Beebe (pp. 71-88). Reprinted from South Atlantic Quarterly, 53 (October 1954), 521-39.

"Visual Art Devices and Parallels in the Fiction of Henry James" by Viola Hopkins (pp. 98-115). Reprinted from 1961.B50.

"Points of Departure from The American" by William Maseychik (pp. 116-27). Physical environment is very important to James's characters, for they "are under the sway of the places from which they come, and whatever worlds they enter."

"The Europeans and the Structure of Comedy" by J. A. Ward (pp. 128-42). Reprinted from 1964.B102.

"The Fearful Self: Henry James's The Portrait of a Lady" by Tony Tanner (pp. 143-59). Reprinted from 1965.B106.

"Pragmatic Realism in The Bostonians" by William McMurray (pp. 160-65). Reprinted from 1962.B68.

"Henry James at the Grecian Urn" by Daniel Lerner and Oscar Cargill (pp. 166-83). Reprinted from Publications of the Modern Language Association of America, 66 (June 1951), 316-31.

"The Princess Casamassima: Hyacinth's Fallible Consciousness" by J. M. Luecke (pp. 184-93). Reprinted from 1963.B58.

"James's The Tragic Muse--Ave Atque Vale" by Lyall H. Powers (pp. 194-203). Reprinted from Publications of the Modern Language Association of America, 73 (June 1958), 270-74.

"The Subjective Adventure of Fleda Vetch" by Robert C. McLean (pp. 204-21). Reprinted from 1964.B59.

"What Maisie Knew: The Evolution of a 'Moral Sense'" by James W. Gargano (pp. 222-35). Reprinted from 1961.B31.

"'Wonder' and 'Beauty' in The Awkward Age" by H. K. Girling (pp. 236-44). Reprinted from Essays in Criticism, 8 (October 1958), 370-80.

"The Romantic and the Real: Henry James's The Sacred Fount" by Walter Isle (pp. 245-65). Reprinted from 1965.B55.

"The Abyss and The Wings of the Dove: The Image as a Revelation" by Jean Kimball (pp. 266-82). Reprinted from Nineteenth-Century Fiction, 10 (March 1956), 281-300.

"The First Paragraph of The Ambassadors: an explication" by Ian Watt (pp. 283-303). Reprinted from 1960.B98.

"Metaphor in the Plot of The Ambassadors" by William Gibson (pp. 304-15). Reprinted from New England Quarterly, 24 (September 1951), 291-305.

"Maggie Verver: Neither Saint nor Witch" by Walter
Wright (pp. 316-26). Reprinted from Nineteenth-Century
Fiction, 12 (June 1957), 59-71.
"Magic and Metamorphosis in The Golden Bowl" by Naomi
Lebowitz (pp. 327-39). Reprinted from 1965.B65.
Reviewed: Times Literary Supplement (26 September),
p. 1070; D. Grant, Critical Quarterly (Winter 1969),
p. 380.

1968 B SHORTER WRITINGS

1   ABEL, ROBERT H. "Gide and Henry James: Suffering, Death, and
Responsibility." Midwest Quarterly, 9 (Summer), 403-16.
For Gide suffering is a means of individual exaltation
that culminates in perfection, but for James suffering is
a means of individual suppression that leaves society
culpable.

*2   ALEXANDRESCU, SORIN. "Introduction" to "Henry James sau
poezia enigmei" [Henry James, or the Poetry of the Puz-
zle], in Henry James' "Daisy Miller," The Great Short
Novels. Bucureşti: Editura pentru literatură,
pp. v-xxxiii.
Cited in Annual Bibliography of English Language and
Literature: Volume 43: 1968. Edited by John Horden and
James B. Misenheimer, Jr. Great Britain: MHRA, 1970,
p. 403.

3   ANON. "Recent Acquisitions--Manuscripts." Princeton Univ.
Library Chronicle, 30 (Autumn), 55-63.
Among new acquisitions of the Princeton Library are nine
Henry James letters: six to Lady Trevelyan and one each to
E. Gosse, W. D. Howells, A. S. Van Westrum.

4   ANTUSH, JOHN VINCENT. "Money in the Novels of James, Wharton,
and Dreiser." DA, 29, 558A (Stanford).
In his characteristic style each author presents "in
realistic social situations the spirit's yearning for
transcendence through money."

*5   ANZILOTTI, ROLANDO. "Un racconto italiano di Henry James:
Daisy Miller," in Studi e ricerche di letteratura ameri-
cana. Florence: La Nuova Italia, pp. 173-81.
Robert L. Gale in 1972.B38, p. 110, explains that
Anzilotti "curiously regards Winterbourne as less a character than a 'punto di vista.' Anzilotti takes up the characteristic 'ambiguita' in the story and asks the usual

1968

> unanswerable questions raised by it. Interestingly, he
> suggests that just as the full-length <u>Portrait of a Lady</u>
> follows 'Daisy Miller,' which was only a study, so Ralph
> Touchett is a 'personaggio derivato da Winterbourne.'"

6   APLASH, MADHU. "Methods of Characterization in <u>The Portrait</u>
    <u>of a Lady</u>," in <u>Variations in American Literature</u>. Edited
    by Darshan Singh Maini. New Delhi: U.S. Educ. Foundation
    in India, pp. 58-63.
       James's dynamic characters, who are enigmatic to each
    other and to the reader, are developed by the use of vari-
    ous methods: pictorial and dramatic presentations, the au-
    thor's observations, foreshadowing devices, parallelism and
    contrast, flashback technique, multiple points of view,
    sense of place, imagery and metaphor.

7   ASSELINEAU, ROGER. "The French Stream in American Litera-
    ture." <u>Yearbook of Comparative and General Literature</u>,
    17:29-39.
       A "transatlantic migration" of influences between France
    and America has been in effect since the seventeenth cen-
    tury and is recognizable in the writings of some of Ameri-
    ca's major writers.

8   ASWELL, E. DUNCAN. "Reflections of a Governess: Image and
    Distortion in <u>The Turn of the Screw</u>." <u>Nineteenth-Century</u>
    <u>Fiction</u>, 23 (June), 49-63.
       The simplistic morality of the governess, which makes
    confession a prerequisite to salvation, leads her to become
    the unwitting tempter of the children (a role at which she
    succeeds), while consciously endeavoring to save them (a
    role at which she fails).

9   AZIZ, MAQBOOL. "'Four Meetings': A Caveat for James Critics."
    <u>Essays in Criticism</u>, 18 (July), 258-74.
       Criticism of "Four Meetings" demonstrates that few crit-
    ics take into account the various versions of James's works.
    Aziz proposes that James's "multiple-version texts" should
    be considered "as various stages in the growth" of a par-
    ticular work.

10 BALLOU, ELLEN B. "Scudder's <u>Atlantic</u>." <u>Harvard Library Bulle-</u>
    <u>tin</u>, 16 (October), 326-53.
       James's relationship with the editor of the <u>Atlantic</u>
    <u>Monthly</u> during the 1890s is discussed in this account of
    Scudder's editorship.

11   BAXTER, ANNETTE K. "Archetypes of American Innocence: Lydia
      Blood and Daisy Miller," in The American Experience: Ap-
      proaches to the Study of the United States. Edited by
      Hennig Cohen. New York: Houghton Mifflin, pp. 148-56.
          A brief bibliographical note is added to this article
      which compares James's Daisy Miller and Howells's Lady of
      the Aroostook. Reprinted from American Quarterly, 5
      (Spring 1953).

12   BEACHCROFT, T. O. The Modest Art: A Survey of the Short
      Story in English. London: Oxford Univ. Press, passim.
          A number of references to James's works are found in
      this study of the short story.

13   BELLRINGER, ALAN W. "The Spoils of Poynton: The 'Facts.'"
      Essays in Criticism, 18 (July), 357-59.
          Since Owen is presented obliquely, the reader does not
      know the nature of his feelings for Mona and Fleda. Nei-
      ther can the reader be sure that Fleda's attitude to Mrs.
      Brigstock is treated ironically by James. Response to
      1966.B60. See also 1966.B9; 1967.B9; 1968.B66.

*14 BERNER, R. L. "Douglas in The Turn of the Screw." EN, 3
      (Winter 1968-1969), 3-6.
          William T. Stafford explains in 1971.B114, p. 104, that
      this "is simply another defense of the 'non-apparitionist'
      reading, emphasizing here the importance of the introduc-
      tory comments by Douglas to support that well-known view."

16   BIER, JESSE. The Rise and Fall of American Humor. New York:
      Holt, Rinehart & Winston, pp. 390-93, passim.
          James employs self-satire, comic anticlimax, and para-
      dox in his work. Targets of his satire are American chil-
      dren and vacuous females.

*16 BONINCONTRO, MARILIA. "Le ascendenze austeniane del Portrait
      of a Lady di Henry James." Pensiero e Scuola, 4:31-39.
          Cited in 1970 MLA International Bibliography, vol. 1,
      p. 115.

17   BROME, VINCENT. "James and Anderson." Times Literary Sup-
      plement (13 June), p. 621.
          For the British Museum to deny access to the Henry
      James-Hendrik Christian Andersen correspondence, claiming
      that such access would breach copyright laws, represents a
      "total travesty of its meaning."

1968

18   BRUNEAU, JEAN. "Une lettre inédite de Henry James à Gustave
      Flaubert: Autour de Monckton Milnes, Lord Houghton." Re-
      vue de Littérature Comparée, 42 (October-December), 520-33.
      [French]
          An 1878 letter from James to Flaubert is the only sur-
      viving record of the friendly relationship between the two
      novelists. It is a letter of introduction for Lord Hough-
      ton, a statesman and a writer.

19   CAMERON, KENNETH WALTER. Hawthorne Among His Contemporaries.
      Hartford: Transcendental Books, passim.
          This chronologically ordered collection of comments on
      Hawthorne printed in Victorian periodicals includes a num-
      ber of James's critical pieces on Hawthorne.

20   CORE, GEORGE. "Introduction," in his Regionalism and Beyond:
      Essays of Randall Stewart. Foreword by Norman Holmes Pear-
      son. Nashville: Vanderbilt Univ. Press, pp. xxiv-xxv.
          Stewart's "The Moral Aspect of Henry James's 'Interna-
      tional Situation,'" originally published in University Re-
      view, 9 (Winter 1943), 109-13, is reprinted in this collec-
      tion. According to Core, Stewart's essay "illuminates the
      fusion of the moral element in James's international novels
      with the enveloping action which flows out of the tension
      between the societies of the old world and the new."

21   D'AVANZO, MARIO L. "James's 'Maud-Evelyn': Source, Allusion,
      and Meaning." Iowa English Yearbook, 13 (Fall), 24-33.
          Browning's "Evelyn Hope," the literary source of James's
      "Maud-Evelyn," is central to an appreciation of the "mean-
      ing, design, character, motivation and ironies" of James's
      story.

22   DONOGHUE, DENIS. "Plot, Fact, and Value," in his The Ordinary
      Universe: Soundings in Modern Literature. New York: Mac-
      millan, pp. 69-77.
          "James's sense of the person is the animating value of
      his fiction: it accounts for the scope, the radiance of
      The Portrait of a Lady."

23   DOOLEY, D. J. "The Hourglass Pattern in The Ambassadors."
      New England Quarterly, 41 (June), 237-81.
          The "hourglass pattern" in The Ambassadors, which E. M.
      Forster discusses in Aspects of the Novel, "will never be
      complete." The reader can never be sure about what Streth-
      er does and does not know. Part of "James's subtlety lies
      in his insinuation of the hourglass pattern into the read-

er's mind leaving unanswered the question of whether the
pattern fits."

24 DORSCH, T. S., and C. G. HARLOW, eds. The Year's Work in Eng-
    lish Studies: Vol. 47: 1966. New York: Published for
    the English Association by Humanities Press, pp. 351-52.
    Survey of criticism for 1966.

25 DRYDEN, EDGAR A. Melville's Thematics of Form: The Great Art
    of Telling the Truth. Baltimore: Johns Hopkins Univ.
    Press, pp. 12-18.
    The importance James places on "the special nature of
    the writer's consciousness" is discussed.

26 EDEL, LEON. "The Deathbed Notes of Henry James." Atlantic
    Monthly, 221 (June), 103-105.
    The last days of Henry James, from December 1, 1915
    through February 28, 1916, are succinctly chronicled.

27 EDEL, LEON. "Henry James," in Six American Novelists of the
    Nineteenth Century. Minneapolis: Univ. of Minnesota
    Press, pp. 191-225.
    This collection of reprints of University of Minnesota
    Pamphlets on American Writers includes Number 4, Edel's
    Henry James, 1960.A1.

28 EDEL, LEON. "Henry James and Sir Sydney Waterlow: The Unpub-
    lished Diary of a British Diplomat." Times Literary Sup-
    plement (8 August), pp. 844-45.
    Sydney Waterlow penned "one of the most fascinating"
    diaries of James's life at Lamb House. In it "we hear
    . . . the authentic tone, the nuanced inflection, the
    ironic vision of life, of art--and the ineradicable sense
    of human values."

29 EDEL, LEON. "Henry James's 'Last Dictation.'" Times Literary
    Supplement (2 May), pp. 459-60.
    Edel here makes public the "last dictation" of Henry
    James, which James gave to his secretary, Theodora Bosan-
    quet, during his final illness in December 1915. The Na-
    poleonic legend is the subject of the dictation. For re-
    sponses see 1968.B53; 1968.B30; 1968.B54; 1968.B31;
    1968.B55.

1968

30   EDEL, LEON. "Henry James's 'Last Dictation.'" <u>Times Liter-</u>
      <u>ary Supplement</u> (23 May), p. 529.
           Edel claims that he had not suggested that anything il-
      legal was involved in H. Montgomery Hyde's use of the
      Bosanquet papers, and that Hyde's stated intention had been
      to use the manuscripts for a pamphlet for the National
      Trust on Lamb House. Response to 1968.B53. <u>See also</u>
      1968.B29; 1968.B54; 1968.B31; 1968.B55.

31   EDEL, LEON. "Henry James's 'Last Dictation.'" <u>Times Liter-</u>
      <u>ary Supplement</u> (6 June), p. 597.
           Edel denies H. Montgomery Hyde's statement that it was
      by Edel's instigation that Hyde was asked to sign a state-
      ment promising not to use the Bosanquet letters at Harvard
      Library. <u>See</u> 1968.B29; 1968.B53; 1968.B30; 1968.B54;
      1968.B55.

32   EDEL, LEON. "Introduction," in his edition of <u>The Portrait of</u>
      <u>a Lady</u>. <u>The Bodley Head Henry James</u>. Vol. V. London:
      Bodley Head, pp. 5-12.
           With this novel James "placed a large and beautiful can-
      vas of an American woman in the great gallery of the world's
      fiction." Reprinted in 1968.A1.

33   EDEL, LEON. "Introduction" and "Notes," in his edition of <u>The</u>
      <u>American Scene</u>. Bloomington: Indiana Univ. Press,
      vii-xxiv.
           Over fifty years after the first publication of this
      book "we can see that in fundamental matters there has been
      little change in America, only an accentuation of the con-
      fusion, distortion, and fragmentation James discerned."
      (Includes a description of the text, list of periodical
      publications of parts published previously, notes, and a
      chronology of James's 1904-1905 visit.) Reprint of
      1967.B22 included in "Introduction."

34   EDELSTEIN, TILDEN G. <u>Strange Enthusiasm: A Life of Thomas</u>
      <u>Wentworth Higginson</u>. New Haven and London: Yale Univ.
      Press, pp. 361-62, passim.
           Higginson's criticisms of James "for abandoning Ameri-
      ca" are recounted.

35   ENGELBERG, EDWARD. "James and Arnold: Conscience and Con-
      sciousness in a Victorian 'Künstlerroman.'" <u>Criticism</u>, 10
      (Spring), 93-114.
           <u>Roderick Hudson</u> encompasses the entire debate over the
      artist and his function and shows that Imagination, when
      stressed at the expense of life, is confining and deadly.

James's novel is "an exemplum of late Victorian ambiguity about Romanticism." Reprinted in 1973.A6.

36 FEIDELSON, CHARLES. "The Moment of The Portrait of a Lady." Ventures, 8:47–55.
    In The Portrait of a Lady James removed many of the so-cial reference points and placed the "subject" of his novel in the context of the consciousness with the result that Isabel Archer expands from "a mere slim shade" to a heroine of tragic proportions.

37 FINCH, G. A. "A Retreading of James' Carpet." Twentieth Century Literature, 14 (July), 98–101.
    James's "The Figure in the Carpet," which contrasts "the great public void, the general mind closed to reading" and the few who are "benighted" and believe "the search for clues has importance," continues to be relevant in the second half of the twentieth century.

38 GARD, ROGER. "Introduction," in his Henry James: The Critical Heritage. New York: Barnes and Noble, pp. 1–18.
    Critical comment is excerpted and arranged in chrono-logical order in this book with the purpose of recapturing the contemporary response to James's novels. (An histori-cal overview of James's critical reception is set forth.)

39 GARG, NEERA. "The Return of Isabel Archer," in Variations on American Literature. Edited by Darshan Singh Maini. New Delhi: U.S. Educ. Foundation in India, pp. 64–69.
    Isabel's return to Rome is evidence of the strength of her human spirit. She was determined to bear the conse-quences of her error in marrying Osmond without ever pub-licly admitting that error.

40 GARLAND, HAMLIN. Hamlin Garland's Diaries. Edited by Donald Pizer. San Marino, Calif.: Huntington Library, passim.
    Contains four references to James.

41 GIRLING, H. K. "The Strange Case of Dr. James & Mr. Steven-son." Wascana Review, 3:65–76.
    Could Robert Louis Stevenson's The Strange Case of Dr. Jekyll and Mr. Hyde and James's The Turn of the Screw rep-resent a portion of their ongoing critical repartee ini-tiated by Stevenson's "Remonstrance" of James's "Art of Fiction"?

1968

42 GOLDFARB, CLARE R. "Names in The Bostonians." Iowa English
    Yearbook, 13 (Fall), 18-23.
        Verena Tarrant's first name suggests "spring," while
    Olive Chancellor's name connotes "rank" and "importance,"
    as well as "battle" and "defeat" (Chancellorsville). Basil
    Ransom's first name brings to mind "royalty," while his
    last name predicts that he will "ransom" Verena.

43 GROVER, PHILIP. "Henry James and Several French Critics:
    Sources and Comparisons." Philologica Pragensia, 11:45-52.
        James owes much of his critical theory to French influ-
    ence: (1) he relied heavily on Taine; (2) he relied heav-
    ily on Sainte-Beuve; and (3) although he apparently did not
    borrow from Mérimée, they shared a common appreciation for
    certain elements of art. (James's reviews of Continental
    writers are compared to those of French critics written on
    the same works.)

44 GROVER, P. R. "Mérimée's Influence on Henry James." Modern
    Language Review, 63 (October), 810-17.
        The most important lessons James learned from Mérimée
    were "the construction of a well-conducted action, the con-
    veying of emotion through significant detail, the presence
    of strong passions." More important, however, may be the
    possibility that Mérimée's work introduced James to
    Turgenev.

45 GROVER, P. R. "A Tanner in the Works." Cambridge Review, 89A
    (3 May), 430-31.
        Tony Tanner's introduction to the reissue (Macmillan,
    1967) of Henry James's Hawthorne covers the "essential and
    lasting connections between Hawthorne and James." Review
    of 1967.B104.

46 HAGEMANN, E. R. "Life Buffets (and Comforts) Henry James,
    1883-1916: An Introduction and An Annotated Checklist."
    Papers of the Bibliographical Society of America, 62 (2Q),
    207-25.
        The "Introduction" establishes the critical credentials
    of Life's editors and writers; the Checklist contains a
    chronologically ordered entry for every discovered refer-
    ence to Henry James during the thirty-three year period.

47 HALL, WILLIAM F. "James's Conception of Society in The Awk-
    ward Age." Nineteenth-Century Fiction, 23 (June), 28-48.
        The novel presents an accurate image of the "awkward
    age" of upper-class English society in the 1880s and 1890s,

and presents an idea pursued in later novels--"the deep human need of the group for the institution itself."

48   HAMBLEN, ABIGAIL ANN. "Henry James and the Power of Eros:
      What Maisie Knew." Midwest Quarterly, 9 (Summer), 391-99.
           Maisie Farange's loss of innocence and growth of moral
      perception are presented in explicitly sexual terms. It is
      the story of innocence being educated by "a force that can
      both dignify and degrade, that can create life and destroy
      it."

49   HARRIS, WENDELL V. "English Short Fiction in the Nineteenth
      Century." Studies in Short Fiction, 6 (Fall), 45-58.
           James's significance is noted, along with Stevenson and
      Kipling, as an important transitional figure in the develop-
      ment of the short story in late nineteenth century England.

50   HARTSOCK, MILDRED E. "Henry James and the Cities of the
      Plain." Modern Language Quarterly, 29 (September),
      297-311.
           The theme of sexual inversion recurs throughout James's
      works, especially in The Bostonians, The Tragic Muse, and
      "The Pupil."

51   HASLAM, GERALD. "Olive Chancellor's Painful Victory in The
      Bostonians." Research Studies (Washington State Univ.),
      36 (September), 232-37.
           Not Olive's homosexuality, but her "desperate need to
      commit herself totally" is the key to her characterization.
      She triumphs at the close of the novel, because she over-
      comes her fear and is willing to face the unfriendly
      audience.

52   HILL, J. S. "Henry James: Fitzgerald's Literary Ancestor."
      Fitzgerald Newsletter, no. 40 (Winter), pp. 305-309.
           James's influence on Scott Fitzgerald is generally con-
      sidered to be indirect (through Joseph Conrad), but The
      Ambassadors and The Great Gatsby share a common attitude
      of "disillusionment about the American dream."

53   HYDE, H. MONTGOMERY. "Henry James's 'Last Dictation.'" Times
      Literary Supplement (9 May), p. 481.
           Hyde made no direct quotations from the Bosanquet manu-
      script material in the Harvard Library, and Leon Edel's
      accusation that he used the papers of Miss Bosanquet
      (James's secretary) in his book is unfounded. Response to
      1968.B29. See also 1968.B30; 1968.B54; 1968.B31; 1968.B55.

1968

54   HYDE, H. MONTGOMERY. "Henry James's 'Last Dictation.'" Times
      Literary Supplement (30 May), p. 553.
          The Hyde-Edel controversy over access to the Bosanquet
      papers (containing James's "Last Dictation") continues.
      See 1968.B29; 1968.B53; 1968.B30; 1968.B31; 1968.B55.

55   HYDE, H. MONTGOMERY. "Henry James's 'Last Dictation.'" Times
      Literary Supplement (18 June), p. 621.
          Hyde claims that he had agreed not to use the Bosanquet
      papers as a result of a letter from Leon Edel to the Har-
      vard librarian. Response to 1968.B31. See also 1968.B29;
      1968.B53; 1968.B30; 1968.B54.

56   IWAYAMA, TAJIRO. "Novelistic 'Morality' in Henry James's
      'The Art of Fiction': Its Place in Other Essays on the
      Novel in the Latter Half of the 19th Century." American
      Studies (Japan), 2 (March), 46-70. [Japanese]
          Beginning with the controversy between James and Walter
      Besant, this article explains James's conception of the
      novel in which sincerity in trying to give an illusion of
      life promises morality. A comparison between English and
      American writers of the late 19th century concerning the
      question of morality and the novel includes discussion of
      Besant, Leslie Stephen, Hardy, Howells, Garland, Norris,
      and others.

*57   KARITA, MOTOSHI. "Shosetsu to Denki no Shud ai-sentaku to
      Imi." Sophia: Studies in Western Civilization and the
      Cultural Interaction of East and West (Tokyo), 17:29-45.
          Cited in 1970 MLA International Bibliography, vol. 1,
      pp. 106-107, which describes the contents of the article
      as containing a discussion of "matter and meaning in fic-
      tion and biog. in Hawthorne and H. James."

58   KENNER, HUGH. "Critic of the Month: III--Ghosts and Bene-
      dictions." Poetry, 113 (November), 109-25.
          Excerpts from The Pound Era, a book-in-progress, and a
      review of Eli Siegel's James and the Children (1968.A9) are
      connected by Henry James: "The perfusing presence is that
      of Henry James: he broods over our century."

59   KIMMEY, JOHN L. "The Bostonians and The Princess Casamassi-
      ma." Texas Studies in Literature and Language, 9 (Winter),
      537-46.
          An examination of The Princess Casamassima and The Bos-
      tonians, James's notebook references to the two novels, and
      his correspondence with his brother William suggest that
      the problems James experienced with the earlier novel were

the catalyst for the aesthetically successful The Princess
Casamassima.

*60   KOHLI, RAJ K. "Huck Finn and Isabel Archer: Two responses to
       the Fruit of Knowledge." Banasthali Patrika, 11 (July),
       73-82. (Special No. on American Literature. Edited by
       Rameshwar Gupta. Proceedings of the Seminar on American
       Literature, 2-3 March 1968 at Banasthali Vidyapath.)
             Cited in 1968 MLA Bibliography, vol. 1, pp. 198, 23.
       See 1969.B101 for annotation of content of article.

61   KONO, YOTARO. "The Victorian Realists in the United States:
       Henry James and William Dean Howells." In Maekawa Shunichi
       Kyoju Kanreki Kinen Ronbunshu [Essays and Studies in Com-
       memoration of Professor Sunichi Maekawa's Sixty-First Birth-
       day]. Tokyo: Eihosha, pp. 177-90. [Japanese]
             A comparison of James and Howells reveals that both were
       faithful in the observation and presentation of reality;
       both saw the novel as having an enlightening quality; and
       both understood that the question of opposing values (such
       as romance and reality, imagination and fact) was to be
       solved dialectically.

62   KRAFT, JAMES. "'Madame de Mauves' and Roderick Hudson: The
       Development of James's International Style." Texas Quar-
       terly, 11 (Autumn), 143-60.
             In "Madame de Mauves" and Roderick Hudson, James began
       to handle the international theme with assurance and "found
       greater stylistic control and symbolic power."

63   KUDO, YOSHIMI. "Strether and Prufrock." Eigo Seinen [The
       Rising Generation] (Tokyo), 114 (December), 2-3. [Japa-
       nese]
             Both Strether and Prufrock live in the wasteland of the
       modern age, knowing self-abandonment. However, while Eliot
       reaches to see the object to which one can surrender one's
       self, the absolute existence, James has none. James, in
       this respect, is a martyr to art.

64   LABRIE, ERNEST ROSS. "Henry James's Idea of Consciousness."
       American Literature, 39 (January), 517-29.
             The metaphors James used suggest he viewed the human
       consciousness as the center of life with organic, quantita-
       tive, qualitative, discriminative, and sacred features.

1968

65 LEVY, LEO B. "The Comedy of Watch and Ward." Arlington
    Quarterly, 1 (Summer), 86-98.
        James's first novel is "largely a comedy," but in the
    last three chapters "lightness and wit give way to a
    sombre sketch of a humble heart surviving its ordeal."

66 LUCAS, JOHN. "James's Intentions: The Spoils of Poynton."
    Essays in Criticism, 18 (January), 107-11.
        A. W. Bellringer's argument, which refers to a James
    entry in the Notebooks, is not valid since James may have
    rewritten the chapter after the Notebook entry. Fleda
    Vetch is an "unreliable narrator," and the story "explores
    and betrays as illusion the idea of the free spirit." Re-
    sponse to 1967.B9. See also 1966.B9; 1966.B60; 1968.B13.

67 McELDERRY, BRUCE R. "Henry James," in American Literary
    Scholarship: An Annual, 1966. Edited by James Woodress.
    Durham, N.C.: Duke Univ. Press, pp. 65-78.
        Survey of criticism published during 1966.

68 MacKENZIE, MANFRED. "Obscure Hurt in Henry James." Southern
    Review: An Australian Journal of Literary Studies,
    3:107-31.
        Not guilt, but shame is the "central psychological ex-
    perience" informing James's work. Shame is associated with
    feelings of inadequacy and inferiority arising "from the
    failure to reach goals or ideals."

69 MAINI, DARSHAN SINGH. "The Style of Henry James." Indian
    Journal of English Studies, 9:18-29.
        The evolving Jamesian style, viewed in terms of the com-
    monly identified three phases, "is truly organic and poet-
    ical, having a cognitive function," and it is an evocative
    outgrowth of James's psyche.

70 MATHESON, GWEN. "Portraits of the Artist and the Lady in the
    Shorter Fiction of Henry James." Dalhousie Review 48
    (Summer), 222-30.
        An examination of James's Stories of Artists and Writers
    reveals a close correlation between the artist's character
    and femininity. At other times James used women--the pro-
    creating force of life--to oppose artists--the creative
    force of art.

71 MAYS, MILTON A. "Henry James in Seattle." <u>Pacific Northwest</u>
    <u>Quarterly</u>, 59 (October), 186–89.
       James's praise for Seattle, where he visited his nephew,
    Edward H. James, and Oliver H. P. LaFarge, contrasts with
    his criticism of the East and South and indicates that he
    probably would not have succeeded in writing of Western
    America because it was too far removed from his experience.

72 MAYS, MILTON A. "Henry James, or, the Beast in the Palace of
    Art." <u>American Literature</u>, 39 (January), 467–87.
       A simultaneous "terror" of and attraction to life is at
    the center of James's thematic concern and is "the dynamic
    of James's very creative process."

73 MELLARD, JAMES M. "Modal Counterpoint in James's <u>The Aspern</u>
    <u>Papers</u>." <u>Papers on Language and Literature</u>, 4 (Summer),
    299–307.
       In <u>The Aspern Papers</u> James utilized the "contrapuntal
    elements" of romance and realism to expand his treatment of
    the theme and to expand the reader's awareness.

74 MITGANG, HERBERT. "Introduction," in his edition of <u>Italian</u>
    <u>Hours</u>. Illustrations by Joseph Pennell. New York: Hori-
    zon Press, pp. v-xi.
       <u>Italian Hours</u> represents "fine travel writing in the
    classical tradition." James's travels in Italy provided
    him with countless themes, characters, settings, and situa-
    tions for his other works. Edited version in 1968.B75.

75 MITGANG, HERBERT. "Springtime for Henry." Edited by Horace
    Sutton. <u>Saturday Review</u>, 51 (6 April), 46–47.
       James's travels in Italy were to revitalize in his mind
    the artistic life that once existed there and, at the same
    time, enhance his own creative potential by "accumulating
    impressions for his own fiction." Horace Sutton edited
    this adaptation of 1968.B74.

76 MOTODA, SHUICHI. "Interpretations of <u>The Turn of the Screw</u>
    (II)." <u>Bungaku Kenkyu</u> (Kyushu Univ.), 65 (March), 189–98.
    [Japanese]
       The work is basically a Gothic romance with much influ-
    ence from psychism. It succeeds as both an allegorical
    ghost story and a psycho-realistic novel, thereby linking
    itself to Poe and Hawthorne.

1968

77   MUELLER, LAVONNE.   "Henry James: The Phenomenal Self as the
      'Real Thing.'"   Forum (Houston), 6 (Spring), 46-50.
         The behavior and the thoughts of Major and Mrs. Monarch
      are determined by their concepts of themselves; thus "it
      is the phenomenological frame of reference that is under-
      scored" in "The Real Thing."

78   MUKERJI, N.   "Sense of Place in The Portrait of a Lady."   Lit-
      erary Criterion (Mysore) (Winter), pp. 12-25.
         James's sense of place in The Portrait of a Lady is em-
      ployed in "physical setting" as well as in "a complex meta-
      phorical framework."   Places "become the symbol of the
      drama of confrontation and involvement" and "a part of
      James's moral vision."

79   NEWLIN, PAUL ARTHUR.   "The Uncanny in the Supernatural Short
      Fiction of Poe, Hawthorne and James."   DA, 28, 5064A-65A
      (U.C.L.A.).
         Poe, Hawthorne, and James employed "uncanny" literary
      motifs to enhance the effect of their supernatural stories.
      These literary motifs are the precursors to twentieth-
      century interior-monologue and stream-of-consciousness
      writings.

80   NOBLE, DAVID W.   "The Realists: Mark Twain, William Dean
      Howells, Henry James," in his The Eternal Adam and the New
      World Garden: The Central Myth in the American Novel Since
      1830.   New York: George Braziller, pp. 79-98.
         "James, like his midwestern contemporaries [Twain and
      Howells], turned to the novel as the means of exploring
      the cause of this gap between the ideal of a harmonious
      New World Eden and the reality of the disorderly and dis-
      harmonious society which covered the land with its crude
      imperfections."

81   POWERS, LYALL H. P.   "Addenda, 1968," in The Portable Henry
      James.   Edited with an Introduction by Morton Dauwen Zabel.
      Revised by L. H. P. Powers.   New York: Viking, pp. 37-38.
         A supplementary bibliography is included in this volume,
      originally published in 1951, and The Turn of the Screw has
      been added to the collection, while two tales and a nou-
      velle have been removed.

*82   PRITCHETT, V. S.   "Great Horse-faced Bluestocking."   Tri-
      Quarterly, 11 (11 October), 463-64.
         Cited in Beatrice Ricks, comp. Henry James: A Bibliog-
      raphy of Secondary Works.   Scarecrow Author Bibliographies,
      No. 24.   Metuchen, N.J.:   Scarecrow, 1975, Item 3188.

83   RALEIGH, JOHN HENRY. "Henry James: The Poetics of Empiri-
      cism," in his Time, Place, and Idea: Essays in the Novel.
      Carbondale: Southern Illinois Univ. Press, pp. 3-24.
          James wrote on many themes in his works, but "he always
      asked his 'questions' and thus gave his 'answers' in a cer-
      tain manner--roughly in terms of the assumptions of empiri-
      cism concerning personality and experience and their inter-
      action--and this was his 'technique.'" Reprint of article
      in Publications of the Modern Language Association of Amer-
      ica, 66 (March 1951), 107-23.

84   RALEIGH, JOHN HENRY. "The Novel and the City: England and
      America in the Nineteenth Century." Victorian Studies, 11
      (March), 291-328.
          Although most nineteenth century novelists focused on
      non-urban subjects (James being a notable exception), the
      city exerted a profound influence on life and accordingly
      on the novel; for Melville the city was a "Metaphysical
      Entity," for Dickens it was a visual background, and for
      James it was an "Anthropomorphic 'Being.'" The Princess
      Casamassima provides one of the "most convincing pictures
      of a large city in English or American fiction."

85   SAMUELS, CHARLES THOMAS. "At the Bottom of the Fount." Novel:
      A Forum on Fiction, 2 (Fall), 46-54.
          The Sacred Fount is ambivalent, and the book can be read
      as existing to expose the narrator or as existing to con-
      firm his speculations. At the bottom of the Fount is
      James's evasion of portraying clearly either vice or virtue.

86   SAMUELS, CHARLES THOMAS. "Giovanni and the Governess." Amer-
      ican Scholar, 37 (Autumn), 655-78.
          The Turn of the Screw, an amusette that ambivalently
      presents the governess's "moral heroism and moral arro-
      gance," was significantly influenced by Hawthorne's
      "Rappaccini's Daughter."

87   SHIBUYA, YUZABURO. "A Short Study of James's The Wings of
      the Dove: On Milly Theale." Kyoyo Ronshu (Meiji Univ.),
      40 (March), 80-98. [Japanese]
          The characterization of Milly fails because of James's
      indirect presentation. This is particularly apparent in
      James's avoidance of the critical scene where she and
      Densher must face each other. Milly appears to be a piti-
      able girl rather than one with great eagerness to live.
      This failure in characterization resides also in James's
      excessive explanations and in the inconsistency among
      "reflectors."

1968

88   SHULMAN, ROBERT.   "Henry James and the Modern Comedy of Knowl-
     edge." Criticism, 10 (Winter), 41-53.
          The stylistic characteristics of the mature James serve
     as the basis for comedy which is "inseparable from the gen-
     eral difficulty of knowing in the modern world." "The Next
     Time" and "Flickerbridge" are early examples of a comedy
     form James realized fully in What Maisie Knew and The Awk-
     ward Age.

89   SIEGEL, PAUL N.   "'Miss Jessel': Mirror Image of the Govern-
     ess." Literature and Psychology, 18, no. 1, 30-38.
          An examination of the four encounters between Miss Jes-
     sel and the governess makes it clear that the apparition is
     a projection, a "shadowy portion" the governess will not
     accept.

90   STANFORD, DEREK.   "The 'Nineties Short-Story: Birth of a New
     Genre." Contemporary Review, 212 (February), 97-104.
          The short story in the 1890s, with its "artistic strin-
     gency, and a moral permissiveness," was an outgrowth of its
     culture.

91   STEIN, WILLIAM BYSSHE.   "The Method at the Heart of Madness:
     The Spoils of Poynton." Modern Fiction Studies, 14 (Sum-
     mer), 187-202.
          In The Spoils of Poynton Fleda "brings a temporary, lim-
     ited perfection" into a disordered world, making human con-
     duct "conform to the . . . absolute ideals of a spiritual
     community." She fails because "her paradise is an infantile
     fantasy."

92   STONE, DONALD DAVID.   "The English Novel, in the 1880's:
     George Meredith, Henry James, and the Development of Modern
     Fiction." Dissertation, Harvard.
          This study examines a crucial period of transition and
     two contrasting exemplars: George Meredith, who failed "to
     perpetuate Victorian idealism into the modern world"; and
     Henry James, who successfully escaped from Victorian con-
     straints to affirm the "modern sensibility." James per-
     sonifies "the move from the Victorian novel, which harmo-
     nized and reconciled extremes, to the modern novel, which
     has tended to emphasize the individual over his world and
     the individual author over anything referential."

93   STRANDBERG, VICTOR H.   "Isabel Archer's Identity Crisis: The
     Two Portraits of a Lady."   University Review (Kansas City),
     34 (Summer), 283-90.
          The structure of The Portrait of a Lady builds around
     the tension and resolution of the conflict between Isabel
     Archer's persona and her inner self.

94   TANNER, TONY.   "Henry James and Henry Adams."   Tri-Quarterly,
     11 (Winter), 91-108.
          James's Autobiographies and Henry Adams's Education sug-
     gest that "whereas Adams set out to unravel the secrets of
     nature, James set out to explore the mystery of his own
     consciousness" which "helped him to negotiate that 'void of
     nothingness' out of which Adams, for all his theories,
     found no guide."

95   TANNER, TONY.   "Introduction," in his edition of Three Novels:
     "The Europeans," "The Spoils of Poynton," "The Sacred
     Fount."   A Perennial Classic.   New York: Harper & Row,
     pp. vii-xxviii.
          "The three novels collected here all concern themselves
     with forms of 'art':   The Europeans dwells on the symbolic
     implications of clothes and personal adornments, The Spoils
     of Poynton centres on a beautiful house full of rare ob-
     jects and rich furnishings, while The Sacred Fount explores
     the ambiguous nature of the artistic instinct to create
     imaginary pictures and patterns out of the given actuali-
     ties of existence."

96   TAYLOR, MARION A.   "Henry James' American and American Mil-
     lionaires."   Litera, 9:78-85.
          James's 1875 portrayal of the millionaire Christopher
     Newman is judged as realistic when Newman's qualities are
     measured against the characteristics of the American mil-
     lionaire of the 1960s.

97   TEMPLE, RUTH Z., comp. and ed.   "Henry James," in Twentieth
     Century British Literature: A Reference Guide and Bibliog-
     raphy.   New York: Frederick Ungar Publishing Co.,
     pp. 183-84.
          A listing of first publication of James's works includ-
     ing letters, notebooks, and plays.

98   THORBERG, RAYMOND.   "Henry James and the Real Thing: 'The
     Beldonald Holbein.'"   Southern Humanities Review, 3 (Win-
     ter), 78-85.
          "'The Beldonald Holbein' is about art, and about life,
     and about the relation of art to life, with life rather
     than art providing the final measure . . . ."

1968

99　TILLOTSON, GEOFFREY, and DONALD HAWES, eds.　Thackeray: The
　　Critical Heritage.　The Critical Heritage Series.　London:
　　Routledge and Kegan Paul; New York:　Barnes and Noble Inc.,
　　passim.
　　　　Less than a dozen references to Henry James appear in
　　this collection of reviews and essays.

100　TRIBBLE, JOSEPH L.　"Cherbuliez's Le Roman d'une Honnête
　　Femme:　Another Source of James's The Portrait of a Lady."
　　American Literature, 40 (November), 279-93.
　　　　James's knowledge of Cherbuliez's work and similarities
　　in characterization, theme, and events suggest it is the
　　primary source for The Portrait of a Lady.

101　VAN CROMPHOUT, G.　"Artist and Society in Henry James."　Eng-
　　lish Studies, 49 (April), 132-40.
　　　　James's realization that the artist is necessarily
　　alienated from society and must develop spiritual inde-
　　pendence in order to retain his artistic integrity is
　　clearly reflected in "The Lesson of the Master," "The Mid-
　　dle Years," "The Death of the Lion," "The Next Time," and
　　"The Figure in the Carpet."

102　VANDERBILT, KERMIT.　The Achievement of William Dean Howells:
　　A Reinterpretation.　Princeton, N.J.:　Princeton Univ.
　　Press, pp. 127-32, passim.
　　　　In this critical reassessment of Howells some two dozen
　　references to Henry James appear.　The lengthiest passage
　　focuses on Howells's defense of Daisy Miller.

103　VANDERSEE, CHARLES.　"James's 'Pandora':　The Mixed Conse-
　　quences of Revision."　Studies in Bibliography, 21:93-108.
　　　　In revising "Pandora," James shifted the tone and made
　　six types of "verbal changes," yet the revision contains
　　"neither striking improvement nor fatal tampering."

104　VAN NOSTRAND, A. D.　"The Dense Totality of Henry James," in
　　his Everyman His Own Poet:　Romantic Gospels in American
　　Literature.　New York:　McGraw-Hill, pp. 149-74.
　　　　The concept of "subjective reality" is at the center of
　　all of James's work.　This "subjective reality" evolved
　　from the influence of idealism and is evident in the par-
　　ticular techniques James developed to dramatize his world
　　view.

105 WAGER, WILLIS. "Mainly the Novel, Amateur to Professional:
Twain to James," in his American Literature: A World View.
New York: New York Univ. Press, pp. 145-56.
A discussion of Henry James's life and work is included
in this survey of prose fiction between the Civil War and
World War I. Howells, Twain and James were the outstanding
writers of the period. Published London: Univ. of London
Press, 1969.

106 WALCUTT, CHARLES CHILD, and J. EDWIN WHITESELL. The Explicator Cyclopedia. Vol. 3. Chicago: Quadrangle, pp. 92-98.
Previously published explications of five James works
are reprinted here. Works treated are: "Four Meetings,"
The Golden Bowl, "Madame de Mauves," The Turn of the Screw,
and "The Two Faces."

107 WATT, IAN. "Conrad, James, and Chance," in Imagined Worlds:
Essays on Some English Novels and Novelists in Honour of
John Butt. Edited by Maynard Mack and Ian Gregor. London:
Methuen, pp. 301-22, passim.
James and Conrad knew one another for two decades, but
the relationship was "elusive and obscure." In his only
published critique of Conrad (reprinted in Notes on Novelists), James wounded him in criticizing the narrative method of Chance.

108 WEAVER, RICHARD. "The American as a Regenerate Being." Edited by George Core and M. E. Bradford. Southern Review, 4
(Summer), 633-46.
American literature is the record of a vision of polari-
ty that sees the American man as simultaneously regenerate
and unregenerate. In James's work the character who embodies American virtues usually "emerges in a superior
light": this can be seen in the cases of Christopher Newman
and Basil Ransom.

109 WEBER, CARL J. "Hardy and James." Harvard Library Bulletin,
16 (January), 18-25.
Three unpublished Hardy letters (two about James and one
to him) help elucidate the two writers' relationship.

110 WEST, RAY B., JR. The Writer in the Room: Selected Essays.
East Lansing: Michigan State Univ. Press, pp. 60-82.
Contents include:
"Henry James: The American" (pp. 60-73). Allegory in the
novel subsists on three levels: social, artistic, and
moral.

1968

> "Henry James: The Ambassadors" (pp. 74-82). After a
> belated initiation, Strether rejects life in the complex
> form "in favor of both European manners and American
> morality."

*111 WILDING, MICHAEL. "Introduction," in Three Tales: "Louisa
      Pallant," "Sir Edmund Orme," "The Real Thing." The Gateway
      Library. Hicks.
          Cited in Cumulative Book Index: 1969. Edited by Nina
      R. Thompson. New York: H. W. Wilson, 1970, p. 1118.

112   WILDING, MICHAEL. "James Joyce's 'Eveline' and The Portrait
      of a Lady." English Studies, 49:552-56.
          The similarity of the climactic section of Dubliners in
      idea, language, and imagery to the ending of The Portrait
      of a Lady suggests a Jamesian influence.

113   WINNER, VIOLA HOPKINS. "The Artist and the Man in 'The Author
      of Beltraffio.'" Publications of the Modern Language Asso-
      ciation of America, 83 (March), 102-108.
          Artistically perceived, Mark Ambient is a positive char-
      acter in whom James's aesthetic ideas are posited; psycho-
      logically and morally, however, he is weak and culpable.

114   WOODRESS, JAMES. Dissertations in American Literature, 1891-
      1966. Revised and enlarged with the assistance of Marian
      Koritz. Durham, N.C.: Duke Univ. Press, Items 1434-1588.
          Listing of dissertations on Henry James.

115   YOUNG, THOMAS DANIEL, and RONALD EDWARD FINE. "Henry James,"
      in American Literature: A Critical Survey. Vol. 2. New
      York: American Book Co.
          Contents include:
          "Realism as Disinheritance: Twain, Howells, and James"
      by Roger B. Salomon (pp. 198-212). Reprinted from
      1964.B84.
          "'Daisy Miller': An Abortive Quest for Innocence" by
      James W. Gargano (pp. 275-80). Reprinted from 1960.B40.
          "The First Paragraph of The Ambassadors: An Explica-
      tion" by Ian Watt (pp. 282-300). Slightly revised and re-
      printed from 1960.B98.

1968 C DISSERTATIONS

1   BALDWIN, RICHARD EUGENE. "The Influence of Emerson on the
      Fiction of Henry James." DA, 28, 4162A (Univ. of Califor-
      nia, Berkeley).

James's chief philosophical indebtedness to Emerson is
for his "conception of the individual as the center of
relations."

2   BRYLOWSKI, ANNA SALNE. "The House of Irony: A Study of Irony
    in Henry James." DA, 28, 5044A-45A (Michigan State).
        A chronological study of irony in James's fiction shows
    different techniques and emphases at work at different
    times; but it demonstrates that "irony is an integral part
    of the art of Henry James; it lies behind his craft, marks
    his selection of material and his own attitude toward
    life."

3   FELDMAN, STEPHEN MICHAEL. "The Dynamics of Innocence in Henry
    James: A Guide to the Jamesian Vision." DA, 28, 4626A-27A
    (Yale).
        A study of innocence as it appears in James's fiction
    provides the basis for the postulate that James, like Haw-
    thorne and Melville, was a realist who dramatized the fall
    from innocence as a fatality for the protagonist.

4   FERGUSON, LOUIS ALOYSIUS. "Henry James and Honoré de Balzac:
    A Comparative Study in Literary Techniques." DA, 29, 1537A
    (Fordham).
        Balzac and James used similar technical and thematic
    devices to resolve the problem "of how best to 'render' a
    subject so that it is made to stand out from its background
    in a life-like way."

5   FISCHER, WILLIAM COVERLY, JR. "The Representation of Mental
    Processes in the Early Fiction of William Dean Howells and
    Henry James." DA, 28, 4597A-98A (Univ. of California,
    Berkeley).
        An overview of the works of the two authors reveals that
    each author used three "compositional devices" unique to
    their purposes to convey how their characters think and
    feel.

6   HOCKS, RICHARD ALLEN. "Henry James and Pragmatic Thought."
    DA, 28, 3639A-40A (North Carolina).
        In the writings of Henry James and particularly in his
    "style, point of view, the comic discipline, the dramatic
    method, the portrayal of consciousness, [and] the ethical
    sensibility" the philosophical concepts of William James
    are "uniquely actualize[d]." For book publication see
    1974.A2.

1968

7   HOFFA, WILLIAM WALTER. "A Study of Theme and Technique in the
    Autobiography of Henry James." DA, 28, 3186A (Wisconsin).
        "By not simply arguing for the creative power of the
    imagination, but also demonstrating it through the writing
    of his Autobiography in the waning years of his life, James
    provides an example worthy of consideration, emulation, and
    respect."

8   KRAFT, JAMES LOUIS ANTHONY. "The Early Tales of Henry James:
    1864-1880." DA, 28, 4179A-80A (Fordham).
        In the thirty-seven stories that preceded the serializa-
    tion of The Portrait of a Lady, James discovered and pol-
    ished the characters and themes that later provided the
    foundation of his craft. For book publication see 1969.A5.

9   MAYER, CHARLES WRIGHT. "Percy Lubbock: Disciple of Henry
    James." DA, 29, 904A (Michigan).
        The theories, practices, successes, and failures of
    Percy Lubbock are directly traceable to the influence of
    Henry James.

*10 MILTON, DOROTHY. "The Unquiet Hearthside: A Study of the
    Parent-Child Relationship in the Fiction of Henry James."
    Dissertation, Chicago.
        Cited in Beatrice Ricks, comp. Henry James: A Bibliog-
    raphy of Secondary Works. Scarecrow Author Bibliographies,
    No. 24. Metuchen, N.J.: Scarecrow, 1975, Item 2993.1.

11 SCHULTZ, ELIZABETH AVERY. "Henry James and the Impossible and
    Irresistible Romance." DA, 28, 5069A-70A (Michigan).
        Despite a professed dislike for the romance, James con-
    tinually utilizes romance motifs in his works. His "major
    characters reflect the traditional, socially oriented ro-
    mance hero, the isolated and anguished nineteenth-century
    romantic hero, and persistently the anti-romance hero."

12 SHINE, MURIEL GRUBER. "Children, Childhood, and Adolescence
    in the Novels and Tales of Henry James." DA, 29, 273A-74A
    (New York Univ.).
        The fictional children of James serve a variety of tech-
    nical and thematic roles in their diverse appearances. In
    general, however, the child was "a 'convenient image'
    through which to express dissatisfaction with the values
    of the age . . . ." For book publication see 1969.A9.

13   THOMAS, WILLIAM B. "The Novelist's Point of View: A Study
     in the Technique of Henry James." <u>DA</u>, 29, 1236A (Bowling
     Green).
          It is in <u>The Ambassadors</u>, not his later works, that
     James comes closest to the point of view common in the
     twentieth-century.

14   WEINMAN, GEOFFREY STEPHEN. "Life Into Art: A Literary Anal-
     ysis of Henry James's <u>Autobiography</u>." <u>DA</u>, 29, 1882A-83A
     (Johns Hopkins).
          James's <u>Autobiography</u> is a "unified, carefully construct-
     ed, imagistically consistent literary work."

15   WEINSTEIN, PHILIP M. "Open Windows and Closed Doors: Imagi-
     nation and Experience in the Fiction of Henry James."
     Dissertation, Harvard, 243 pp.
          This study of five James novels is an effort to inter-
     pret "one of the chief paradoxes in James's fiction," the
     "tension between the impulse to plunge into 'experience'
     and the impulse to renounce it," as exemplified by the dis-
     crepancy between Lambert Strether's advice to "Live all you
     can!" and his failure to do so. For book publication <u>see</u>
     1971.B8.

16   WOLF, HOWARD ROBERT. "Forms of Abandonment in Henry James."
     <u>DA</u>, 28, 5031A-32A (Michigan).
          An examination of the extensive occurrences of abandoned
     children in James's fiction reveals both his perceptiveness
     of psychological complexities and his talent for exploiting
     such complexities in his craft.

1969 A BOOKS

 1   EDEL, LEON. <u>Henry James: The Treacherous Years, 1895-1901</u>.
     Philadelphia: Lippincott, 381 pp.
          Volume 4 of the biography of James focuses on the years
     when James suffered "spiritual illness," but "rid himself
     of his private demons by writing about them." The novels
     and tales written during these years "deal with children
     and ghosts--with the phantasmagoric--and the ways in which
     the imagination endows reality with realities of its own."
     James experimented technically in these works and pointed
     the way "to the innovations of Joyce and Virginia Woolf and
     the 'interior journey' of Proust." Reviewed: 1969.B3;
     1969.B80; 1969.B128; 1970.B39; 1970.B56; 1970.B116;
     1973.B8; 1973.B30; Robert L. Gale, <u>Modern Fiction Studies</u>,
     16 (1970), 212-14; Blake Nevius, <u>Nineteenth-Century Fiction</u>,

25 (1970), 118-21; Oscar Cargill, American Literature, 44 (1972), 330-32.

2 FABRIS, ALBERTA. Henry James e la Francia. Biblioteca di Studi Americani, No. 18. Roma: Edizioni di Storia e Letteratura, 363 pp. [Italian]
    A study of James's travels and impressions of France, together with his interest in French literature (particularly the Romantic period and the theatre) reveals the deep mark these interests made on James, whose work shows the influence of French civilization and arts, namely painting and architecture. Reviewed: James Woodress, American Literature, 42 (1970), 415-17; David A. Leeming, Comparative Literature, 24 (1972), 374-77.

3 HYDE, H. MONTGOMERY. Henry James at Home. New York: Farrar, Straus & Giroux, 322 pp.
    The story of James's home life in England from 1876 to his death in 1916 includes accounts of his friendships of the time (Edmund Gosse, Edith Wharton, Ford Madox Hueffer, and others), as well as discussion of many matters which concerned James, such as the management of Lamb House, problems with his publisher, worries over finances. Reviewed: Lyon N. Richardson, American Literature, 42 (1970), 355-56; George Monteiro, Modern Fiction Studies, 19 (1973-1974), 590-95.

4 KOSSMANN, RUDOLF R. Henry James: Dramatist. Groningen, Netherlands: Wolters-Noordhoff N.V., 136 pp.
    James's life-long interest in the drama--as a spectator, critic, and playwright--is explored, including his early experience of the theatre (1843-1868), his first attempts at writing plays (1869-1883), his full scale "siege of the theatre" (1890-1895), his later playwrighting (1907-1910), and his work as a drama critic. For dissertation see 1969.C7. Reviewed: Quentin Anderson, American Literature, 43 (May 1971), 294-96; G. Rowell, The Yearbook of English Studies, 1 (1971), 316.

5 KRAFT, JAMES. The Early Tales of Henry James. Carbondale: Southern Illinois Univ. Press; London: Feffer and Sons, 143 pp.
    A survey of thirty-seven early stories and short novels by James, published between 1864 and 1879, reveals connections to James's other fiction (written at the same period and later). These early works make possible "a clearer understanding of the foundations of James's fiction" as well as "the evolution of his art." For dissertation see

1968.C8. Reviewed: William T. Stafford, <u>Nineteenth-Century Fiction</u>, 25 (1970), 237-42; Quentin Anderson, <u>American Literature</u>, 43 (1971), 294-96; Walton R. Patrick <u>Studies in Short Fiction</u>, 8 (1971), 338-39; George Monteiro, <u>Modern Fiction Studies</u>, 19 (Winter 1973-1974), 590-95.

6   MARKOW-TOTEVY, GEORGES. <u>Henry James</u>. Translated by John Cumming. Preface by Andre Maurois. London: Merlin; New York: Funk and Wagnalls, 151 pp.
     This study begins with a brief biographical sketch and then surveys James's work, concluding with an evaluation of the novelist's place in fiction. An unpublished letter (1888) to Minnie and Paul Bourget is appended, along with a selected bibliography and a chronology of James's life. Reviewed: Edwin T. Bowden, <u>American Literature</u>, 42 (1971), 582-84; George Monteiro, <u>Modern Fiction Studies</u>, 19 (Winter 1973-1974), 590-95.

7   POWERS, LYALL H. <u>Guide to Henry James</u>. Merrill Guides. Columbus, Ohio: Charles E. Merrill, 39 pp.
     A concise overview of James's life, work, and his contribution to letters.

8   SEGAL, ORA. <u>The Lucid Reflector: The Observer in Henry James' Fiction</u>. New Haven and London: Yale Univ. Press, 265 pp.
     A close examination of the role of the observer in selected novels and <u>nouvelles</u> establishes that the Jamesian observer "fulfills most of the authorial functions of the traditional omniscient author" and "is a flexible and complex functional character." In the fiction the observer develops from holding a subsidiary role (as "choric commentator, <u>raissoneur</u>, or confidant") to a "central intelligence with a personal perspective that fully controls the story." In addition, James's treatment of the observer is increasingly refined. Reviewed: William T. Stafford, <u>Nineteenth-Century Fiction</u>, 25 (1970), 237-42; Joseph J. Firebaugh, <u>American Literature</u>, 42 (1971), 581-82; George Monteiro, <u>Modern Fiction Studies</u>, 19 (Winter 1973-1974), 590-95.

9   SHINE, MURIEL G. <u>The Fictional Children of Henry James</u>. Chapel Hill: Univ. of North Carolina Press, 192 pp.
     A careful study of James's portrayal of children and adolescents reveals certain "thematic patterns which fused in the 1890's to produce the uniquely Jamesian child." All of James's children are "deeply sentient miniature adults," while his young people are "a shade too watchful and pre-

cious." James played "an active role in the movement to
sweep away outmoded convention and prejudice and to establish the child in literature as a worthy object of complete
and honest investigation." For dissertation <u>see</u> 1968.C12.
Reviewed: William T. Stafford, <u>Nineteenth-Century Fiction</u>,
25 (1970), 237-42; Quentin Anderson, <u>American Literature</u>,
43 (1971), 294-96; George Monteiro, <u>Modern Fiction Studies</u>,
19 (Winter 1973-1974), 590-95.

10   STONE, ALBERT E., JR., ed.   <u>Twentieth Century Interpretations</u>
     <u>of "The Ambassadors": A Collection of Critical Essays</u>.
     Englewood Cliffs, N.J.: Prentice-Hall, 121 pp.
        Contents: Consists of eleven selections in Part One--
     View Points, and nine essays in Part Two--Interpretations.
     A chronology of important dates and a selected bibliography
     are included.
        "Introduction" by Albert E. Stone, Jr. (pp. 1-20). Dis-
     cusses the background of the novel and provides an overview
     of the criticism collected in this book.
        Eleven selections are reprinted from various sources
     (pp. 21-36) and include an 1895 excerpt from James's <u>Note-</u>
     <u>books</u>; a 1903 letter from James to the Duchess of Suther-
     land; a 1904 review of the novel by Annie R. Logan, which
     appeared in <u>The Nation</u>; a 1912 letter from James to Hugh
     Walpole; and brief critical comments from Arnold Bennett,
     Yvor Winters, Elizabeth Stevenson, E. K. Brown, F. W. Dupee,
     F. R. Leavis, and Wayne Booth.
        "Full Prime" by Joseph Warren Beach (pp. 37-42). Re-
     printed from <u>The Method of Henry James</u>. New Haven: Yale
     Univ. Press, 1918, pp. 255-56, 258-59, 260-62, 266-70.
        "The Ambassadors" by F. O. Matthiessen (pp. 43-48). Re-
     printed from <u>Henry James: The Major Phase</u>. New York: Ox-
     ford Univ. Press, 1944, pp. 18-23, 38-41.
        "The Loose and Baggy Monsters of Henry James" by Richard
     Blackmur (pp. 49-56). Reprinted from <u>The Lion and the</u>
     <u>Honeycomb: Essays in Solicitude and Critique</u>. New York:
     Harcourt, Brace & World, 1951, pp. 276-77, 279-83, 284-88.
        "The Art of Henry James: The Ambassadors" by Joan Ben-
     nett (pp. 57-65). Reprinted from <u>Chicago Review</u>, 9 (Win-
     ter 1956), 12-26.
        "James The Old Intruder" by John E. Tilford, Jr.
     (pp. 66-74). Reprinted from <u>Modern Fiction Studies</u>, 4
     (Summer 1958), 157-64.
        "The First Paragraph of The Ambassadors: An Explica-
     tion" by Ian Watt (pp. 75-87). Reprinted from 1960.B98.
        "The Text of The Ambassadors" by Leon Edel (pp. 88-95).
     Reprinted from 1960.B26.

"The Achieved Life à la Henry James" by Maxwell Geismar
(pp. 96-105). Reprinted from 1963.A2.
"'O Rare for Strether!': Antony and Cleopatra and The
Ambassadors" by U. C. Knoepflmacher (pp. 106-16). Reprinted from 1965.B60.
Reviewed: Choice, 6 (October 1969), 1020; Booklist, 66
(15 February 1970), 710.

11 WILLEN, GERALD, ed. A Casebook on Henry James's "The Turn of
the Screw." Second Edition. New York: Crowell, 393 pp.
Contents: Added to this edition are four critical es-
says, an Appendix which includes four James letters and a
Notebook Entry, an expanded bibliography, and new Exercises
for students. A new Preface by Gerald Willen includes a
discussion of the large number of responses to the tale.
"A Causerie on Henry James's 'The Turn of the Screw'" by
M. Katan, M.D. (pp. 319-37). Reprinted from 1962.B51.
"The Death of Miles in The Turn of the Screw" by Muriel
West (pp. 338-49). Reprinted from 1964.B105.
"One More Turn of the Screw" by Louis D. Rubin, Jr.
(pp. 350-66). Reprinted from 1963.B88.
"Another Twist to The Turn of the Screw" by C. Knight
Aldrich, M.D. (pp. 367-78). Reprinted from 1967.B1.
See 1960.A6 for the first edition.

1969 B SHORTER WRITINGS

1 ALLEN, WALTER. The Urgent West: The American Dream and Modern Man. New York: E. P. Dutton, pp. 103-104, passim.
James's equating Americans with "idealistic innocence"
and Europeans with "cynical corruption" is termed a "common
American attitude in the nineteenth century."

2 ANON. "Commentary," Times Literary Supplement (11 September),
p. 1000.
Basil Ashmore, in directing Robert Myers's adaptation of
The Spoils of Poynton, reverted to Jamesian dialogue in the
play without informing Myers of his intentions. For responses see 1969.B37; 1969.B7; 1969.B103.

3 ANON. "Gloom and Some Friendships." Times Literary Supplement (30 October), pp. 1245-46.
Volume 4 of Edel's biography is "the most penetrative
and persuasive of the series." Review of 1969.A1.

1969

4   ANTUSH, JOHN V.   "Money as Myth and Reality in the World of
     Henry James."   Arizona Quarterly, 25 (Summer), 125-33.
        Money moves plots and motivates characters; it also
     makes possible the development of an individual's powers,
     as well as sometimes representing "an oppressive weight of
     corruption."

5   AOKI, TSUGIO.   "Lies in 'The Liar.'"   Eigo Seinen [The Rising
     Generation] (Tokyo), 115 (April), 26-27.   [Japanese]
        The painter character is the worst liar because the
     couple's lies have a saving grace.

6   ARSENESCU, ADINA.   "Henry James."   Orizont, no. 12 (December),
     pp. 55-59.   [Roumanian]
        James's literary works are interpreted in terms of his
     social life.

7   ASHMORE, BASIL.   "Henry James on Stage."   Times Literary Sup-
     plement (9 October), p. 1158.
        Ashmore defends his alteration of Robert Myers's script
     of The Spoils of Poynton, maintaining that the true author
     of the play he was directing was Henry James, and that "the
     interests of dead authors . . . should be protected when-
     ever possible."   Response to 1969.B2.   See 1969.B37;
     1969.B103.

8   BALLORAIN, ROLANDE.   "The Turn of the Screw: L'adulte et
     l'enfant, Ou les deux regards."   Etudes Anglaises, 22
     (July-September), 250-58.   [French]
        It is a mistake to analyze the governess as a character
     separated from the context of the works written in the same
     period, with the result of reducing her to a sex-obsessed
     figure.   If all of these works are group-analyzed, a re-
     curring obsessive theme or conflict prevails: youth vs.
     adulthood, thus leading to the question: are there any
     more adults, or how can one become an adult?

9   BANTA, MARTHA.   "The Quality of Experience in What Maisie
     Knew."   New England Quarterly, 42 (December), 483-510.
        A study of the quality of Maisie's experience by examin-
     ing the language of the novel ("the quality of its imagery
     and the violence of its hyperbole") reveals that What
     Maisie Knew is in the tradition of comedy mixed with tragic
     violence found in Jacobean drama.

10   BANTA, MARTHA. "Rebirth or Revenge: The Endings of Huckleberry Finn and The American." Modern Fiction Studies, 15
(Summer), 191-207.
Both Huckleberry Finn and The American "recognize the
complexity of the experience they portray and the two-fold
nature of their characters' responses, and thus side-step
simplifying moral evaluations that would be at odds with
the very special kind of morality which drives through
their pages, first to last."

11   BAREISS, DIETER. "The Golden Bowl," in his Die Vierpersonen-
konstellation im Roman: Strukturuntersuchungen zur Per-
sonenführung. Vol. 1. Europäische Hochschulschriften,
Reihe, 14. Bern: Herbert Lang, pp. 73-92. [German]
The past and present bilateral relationships of the four
central characters in The Golden Bowl are examined along
with the central symbol of the novel.

12   BAYM, NINA. "Fleda Vetch and the Plot of The Spoils of Poynton." Publications of the Modern Language Association of
America, 84 (January), 102-11.
The characterization of Fleda Vetch is not one whole
creation formed from James's notebooks, the preface, and
the novel; instead she is three separate characters, recast
in each stage of James's writing.

13   BAZZANELLA, DOMINIC J. "The Conclusion to The Portrait of a
Lady Re-examined." American Literature, 41 (March), 55-63.
In response to contemporary criticism that pointed to an
unintentional ambiguity, James revised the New York Edition
with two results: (1) a clarification of Isabel's character, and (2) an achievement of "aesthetic distance for his
narrator."

14   BEKER, MIROSLAV. "T. S. Eliot's Theory of Impersonality and
Henry James: A Note." Studia Romanica et Anglica Za-
grabiensia, 27-28 (July-December), 163-67.
Eliot's theory of depersonalization of the artist can be
compared with James's thoughts on this subject as reflected
in his prefaces.

15   BELL, MILLICENT. "The Dream of Being Possessed and Possessing:
Henry James's The Wings of the Dove." Massachusetts Review,
10 (Winter), 97-114.
James considers the effects of money, comparing a traditional religious feeling by which the soul is not for sale
(represented by Milly) with the psychology of the market-
place (represented by Kate and Densher).

1969

16 BERCOVITCH, SACVAN. "The Revision of Rowland Mallet."
    Nineteenth-Century Fiction, 24 (September), 210-21.
        In his revisions of Roderick Hudson, James intended to
    draw attention to Rowland Mallet's perversity that under-
    lies his rational, patient, altruistic sensibility and
    highlights his limitations by stressing the darker quali-
    ties of his mind.

17 BERSANI, LEO. "The Jamesian Lie." Partisan Review, 36 (Win-
    ter), 53-79.
        The tension between the emphasis in James's prefaces on
    structural composition and the emphasis on psychological
    development in the novels themselves creates a drama that
    is "often violent" and "occasionally lurid . . . involving
    the mutation of lies into redemptive fiction."

18 BLANCK, JACOB, comp. "Henry James," in Bibliography of Ameri-
    can Literature. 5 vols. New Haven, Conn.: Yale Univ.
    Press, vol. 5, pp. 117-81.
        A descriptive listing of first editions of James's work,
    reprints of James's own books, reprinted James material
    (with James's name on the title page), and a brief list of
    secondary materials on James.

19 BOCHNER, JAY. "Life in a Picture Gallery: Things in The Por-
    trait of a Lady and The Marble Faun." Texas Studies in
    Literature and Language, 11 (Spring), 761-77.
        James's concern with the actuality of things, especially
    houses, allows us to see what reality means to Isabel and
    unifies The Portrait of a Lady, whereas The Marble Faun is
    a failure because Hawthorne, overwhelmed by Italian cul-
    ture, includes too many things and symbols, causing a lack
    of unity.

20 BONTLY, THOMAS J. "Henry James's 'General Vision of Evil' in
    The Turn of the Screw." Studies in English Literature,
    1500-1900, 9 (Autumn), 721-35.
        The symbolic meaning of the ghosts can be found in the
    governess's reaction to them, for the ghosts "symbolize the
    origins of human fear in the adult's sense of sexual guilt."

21 BONTLY, THOMAS J. "The Moral Perspective of The Ambassadors."
    Wisconsin Studies in Literature, 6:106-17.
        In James's work "technique is itself the expression of
    moral value"; thus The Ambassadors may be seen as "an
    anatomy of the moral act, an investigation of the condi-
    tions of true morality."

22 BROWN, DANIEL RUSSELL. "The Cosmopolitan Novel: James and
Lewis." Sinclair Lewis Newsletter, 1 (Spring), 6-9.
In The Ambassadors and Dodsworth James and Lewis have
transcended the traditional conventions of the novel deal-
ing with foreign travel and have rendered "artful depic-
tions of a higher informational value--of the moralities,
the psychologies, and the truths of human relationships."

23 BRYLOWSKI, ANNA SALNE. "In Defense of the First Person Narrator in The Aspern Papers." Centennial Review, 13
(Spring), 215-40.
Examined in the context of the principles of the dramatic monologue delineated in Robert Langbaum's The Poetry of
Experience, The Aspern Papers, with its alleged oscillating
narrator, emerges as an artistic poetic success.

24 BUFKIN, E. C. "A Pattern of Parallel and Double: The Function of Myrtle in The Great Gatsby." Modern Fiction Studies, 15 (Winter 1969-1970), 517-24.
James is the source of much of Fitzgerald's knowledge of
the craft of fiction. Myrtle "functions as a source of
Jamesian operative irony."

25 BUITENHUIS, PETER. "The Return of the Novelist: Henry
James's The American Scene." Canadian Association for
American Studies, 4 (Spring-Summer), 54-103.
Reflected in The American Scene, a work to which James
"brought to bear all the psychological penetration, the in-
tense analytical consciousness and the sophistication of
form that he had perfected in writing the three great novels of the major phase," is James's dislike of twentieth-
century America and his fear of "the naked power that this
giant of a country was . . . displaying in so many areas."

26 BURNS, GRAHAM. "The Bostonians." The Critical Review,
12:45-60.
Beyond the personal and psychological level of the novel, a level that is notably successful, the Feminist movement provides James with two additional levels of vision:
(1) "as being in itself symptomatic of the state of society"; and (2) "as a convenient image . . . to suggest the
quality and intensity of life . . . in post-Civil War
America."

1969

27   CARTINAU, VIRGINIA. "Aspecte ale romanului modern şi contem-
poran englez." Via̧ta Românească, 22:93-103. [Roumanian]
The greatest figures in Modern English novels are Henry
James, James Joyce, Joseph Conrad, Virginia Woolf, Aldous
Huxley, D. H. Lawrence, John Cowper Powys, and Graham
Greene. James is universal, having knowledge of both
European and American cultures, as well as the ability to
discover and describe the internal conflict and tumult ex-
isting in each individual.

*28   CAZAN, ILEANA. "Postscript: Henry James," in Portretul unei
doamne [The Portrait of a Lady]. Bucharest: Editura pen-
tru literatură universală, pp. 564-76.
Cited in Annual Bibliography of English Language and
Literature: Volume 44: 1969. Edited by John Horden and
J. B. Misenheimer. Great Britain: MHRA, 1971, p. 417.

29   CHANDA, A. K. "Art and Artists in The Portrait of a Lady."
Indian Journal of English Studies, 10:109-21.
In The Portrait of a Lady James uses the artist and
artistic terms to demonstrate the incompatability and
antagonism that result from an attempt to mold life--or
to apply art to life.

30   CLUNY, CLAUDE MICHEL. "Retour à Henry James." Lettres Fran-
çaises, 1275 (19 March), 11-12. [French]
The recent revival of interest in James is due to new
French editions of the Notebooks and of works such as The
Ambassadors, What Maisie Knew, The Aspern Papers, The Turn
of the Screw, and The Spoils of Poynton.

31   COY, JUAN JOSÉ. "Washington Square: o el folletin bien
hecho." Papeles de son Armadans (Mallorca), 55:26-47.
[Spanish]
An explication of structure, symbolism, characterization, and meaning of James's Washington Square establishes
that the novel is "very well made."

32   DAVIS, O. B. Introduction to the Novel. Rochelle Park, N.J.:
Hayden Book Co., pp. 83, 134-41, 166-74.
A brief biographical-critical introduction to Henry
James precedes the text of "Daisy Miller," following which
there are forty questions designed to elicit responses from
students. In "Daisy Miller: An Afterword," Davis states:
"He [Winterbourne] is by no means the admirable person
Daisy is and he fails to make the right decisions, but the
external story of Daisy is the internal story of Winter-
bourne, and he . . . is the main character of the novel."

In "Benito Cereno and Daisy Miller: Comments and Questions," comments which compare and contrast the two works
are followed by questions and passages from the works.

33 DEAKIN, M. F. "Daisy Miller, Tradition, and the European
    Heroine." Comparative Literature Studies, 6 (March),
    45-59.
        Daisy Miller's creation was influenced by European lit-
    erary heroines as much as by real American girls. Placing
    Daisy in this European tradition shifts interpretation of
    her character "from the conventional emphasis on her inno-
    cence to her equally significant rebellious independence"
    and makes her death "a social and symbolic necessity."

34 DIETRICHSON, JAN W. "The Image of Money in the Works of Henry
    James," in his The Image of Money in the American Novel of
    the Gilded Age. Oslo: Universitetsforlaget; New York:
    Humanities Press, pp. 24-164.
        For James the love of money and material goods repre-
    sented a false standard that "conflicted with a spiritual
    and moral concept of human existence." The only way to
    reach "the lofty moral stature" propounded by James was to
    be "free of money."

35 DOW, EDDY. "James' 'Brooksmith.'" Explicator, 27 (January),
    Item 35.
        In the third paragraph of "Brooksmith" the sentence
    "'The explanation is usually that our women have not the
    skill to cultivate it--the art to direct through a smiling
    land, between suggestive shores, a sinuous stream of
    talk,'" gives the reader a premonition of the identity of
    the real artist of Offord's salon.

36 DRAPER, R. P. "Death of a Hero? Winterbourne and Daisy Mil-
    ler." Studies in Short Fiction, 6 (Fall), 601-608.
        Winterbourne, not Daisy, is the central protagonist in
    this story that focuses on his "slow, lingering, and almost
    comically un-dramatic death . . . and his ironically dis-
    tanced, but unavailing struggle for life."

37 DRUCKER, LEON. "Henry James on Stage." Times Literary Sup-
    plement (18 September), p. 1027.
        Kate O'Mara, as Fleda Vetch, brought "life and a touch
    of real distinction" to a mediocre production of The Spoils
    of Poynton. See 1969.B2; 1969.B7; 1969.B103.

1969

38   DUMITRIU, GEORGETA. "Aspecte ale metodie narative în romanul
      lui Henry James." Revista de Istorie și Theorie Literara,
      18:235-47. [Roumanian]
          James's contribution to modern romance ranges from his
      style, narrative method, and structure (which gives to his
      prose the characteristics of drama) to his psychological
      analysis of his characters.

*39   DUMITRIU, GHEORGHIȚA. "Middlemarch și geneza Isabelei Archer"
      [Middlemarch as the Genesis of Isabel Archer]. Analele
      Universitătii Bucuręst. Literatură universală și com-
      parată, 18:77-84.
          Cited in Annual Bibliography of English Language and
      Literature for 1970: Volume 45. Edited by John Horden
      and J. B. Misenheimer. Great Britain: MHRA, 1972, p. 426.

40   DUNCAN-JONES, E. E. "Some Sources of Chance." Review of Eng-
      lish Studies, 20 (November), 468-71.
          James's The Turn of the Screw is a possible source for
      Joseph Conrad's Chance.

41   EBINE, SHIZUE. "Milly's Consciousness: The Wings of the
      Dove." Kobe Daigaku Kyoyobu Jimbungakkai Ronshu (Kobe
      Univ. Liberal Arts-Humanities Essays), 6 (March), 1-19.
      [Japanese]
          The question of how to reconcile Milly's mildness with
      her strong desire to live can be answered by the fact that
      her consciousness, which is full of insight into others,
      has a positive quality that accepts and actively engages
      others in a favorable way, however passive she may appear.

42   EDEL, LEON. "Henry James: The Ambassadors," in Landmarks of
      American Writing. Edited by Hennig Cohen. New York:
      Basic Books, pp. 182-93.
          The Ambassadors is a carefully structured philosophical
      novel with unified scenes and symbols that examines the
      existential struggle of Lambert Strether.

43   EDEL, LEON. "Introductions," in his The Bodley Head Henry
      James. Vols. VI-VII. London: Bodley Head.
          In his "Introduction" to What Maisie Knew (vol. vi,
      pp. 5-10), Edel notes that Maisie is the "first in a series
      of fictions dealing with the emotional life of little girls,
      from early childhood to late adolescence." In his "Intro-
      duction" to The Wings of the Dove (vol. vii, pp. 5-12),
      he states: "The centre of emotion in this novel is fixed
      in Densher, but it is Kate and Milly who are the tragic
      figures. Kate fights both nobly and sordidly to escape

from the material indignities of her life as Milly strug-
gles to escape its physical indignities."

44 EMERSON, DONALD. "The Relation of Henry James's Art Criticism
    to His Literary Standards." Transactions of the Wisconsin
    Academy of Sciences, Arts and Letters, 57:9-19.
        Although James spoke less authoritatively in his criti-
    cism of visual arts than he did of literary art, his criti-
    cal emphasis on the imagination is apparent in both areas.

45 FALK, ROBERT. "The Tragic Muse: Henry James's Loosest, Bag-
    giest Monster?" in Themes and Directions in American Liter-
    ature, Essays in Honor of Leon Howard. Edited by Ray B.
    Browne and Donald Pizer. Lafayette, Ind.: Purdue Univ.
    Studies, pp. 148-62.
        When this novel is "analyzed through the perspective of
    James's own ideal of its possible thematic consistency and
    structural form, one may surely modify the uninterrupted
    tendency to call it one of his loosest and baggiest mon-
    sters of serialized fiction."

46 FERNANDEZ, DIANE. "Henry James et la Symétrie." Les Lettres
    Nouvelles (June-July), pp. 77-90. [French]
        James's systematic and symmetric style is the result of
    his constant effort to establish order in his confused sub-
    conscious. Hence, we find in his writings parallels of
    death, resentment, fatality, and failure, resulting in an
    overflowing artistic creation.

47 FERNANDEZ, DIANE. "Henry James Revisited." Quinzaine Litté-
    raire, 68 (15 March), 4-5. [French]
        James's fascination with ghosts and memories may have
    resulted from a form of physical castration James suffered
    (as a result of his trying to identify with his father who
    had to have a leg amputated), or from a masochism that led
    James to avoid women as well as wars.

48 FIDERER, GERALD. "Henry James's 'Discriminated Occasion.'"
    Critique: Studies in Modern Fiction, 11:56-69.
        The "keys" to James's late fiction are "spiritual dis-
    cernment and moral growth through renunciation." His late
    novels "may stand as the monument--a last tribute to the
    enduring worth of discriminated, fine, honorable human
    conduct."

1969

49 FINK, GUIDO. "I bambini terribili di Henry James." Paragone,
    no. 236, pp. 4-28. [Italian]
        All of James's "children"--Maisie, Miles and Flora, Mor-
    gan Moreen, and Dolcino--are somehow as disturbing as lit-
    tle Pearl in Hawthorne's The Scarlet Letter. These chil-
    dren are all extremely precocious, strangely wise, very
    sensitive, and especially beautiful. They all receive a
    very unusual education and share a knowledge of the fasci-
    nating and disturbing secrets of their families. Unlike
    little Pearl, though, it is their knowledge and wisdom that
    will lead them to a violent death. Only in the later
    "Maud-Evelyn" does a child follow a completely different
    destiny; and in The Ambassadors Lambert Strether will sac-
    rifice himself for Chad, perhaps to expiate the sins of
    James's "fathers," and of the novelist as well.

50 FREDERICK, JOHN T. "Henry James," in his The Darkened Sky:
    Nineteenth-Century American Novelists and Religion. Notre
    Dame, Ind.: Univ. of Notre Dame Press, pp. 229-253.
        Although James is probably "more religious" than
    Cooper, Hawthorne, Melville, Twain, or Howells, religion
    is not an important subject in his fiction since his father
    had already dealt with the major religious issues of the
    nineteenth century prior to Henry James's birth.

51 FREDERICK, JOHN T. "Patterns of Imagery in Chapter XLII of
    Henry James's The Portrait of a Lady." Arizona Quarterly,
    25 (Spring), 150-56.
        The success of Chapter XLII (wherein Isabel realizes her
    situation) is due partly to the "sustained and elaborated
    patterns of imagery." Central is the prison image, which
    contrasts with space and freedom images. Other image pat-
    terns exist: darkness and light, cold and heat.

52 GARGANO, JAMES W. "Age and Innocence in What Maisie Knew."
    Research Studies (Washington State Univ.), 37 (September),
    218-26.
        A close reading of the text shows that Maisie was only
    eleven years old at the close of the novel, too young to
    make a sexual advance to her step-father, as some critics
    have suggested. In addition, Maisie retains her childlike
    innocence throughout her remarkable experiences.

53 GARRETT, PETER K. "Henry James: The Creations of Conscious-
    ness," in his Scene and Symbol from George Eliot to James
    Joyce: Studies in Changing Fictional Mode. Edited by
    Richard S. Sylvester. Yale Studies in English, 172. New
    Haven: Yale Univ. Press, pp. 76-159.

James's experimental technique with reference to consciousness in the novel is centrally located in the transi-
tion from George Eliot's realism to the increasing symbolism of the twentieth century.

54 GARST, TOM. "Beyond Realism: Short Fiction of Kipling, Con-
    rad, and James in the 1890's." <u>DAI</u>, 30, 1167A (Washington
    Univ.).
      The narrative techniques of the limited point of view
    and the compromised narrator, and the thematic emphasis on
    personal experience are seen in the late short stories of
    Kipling, Conrad, and James whereas their early works are in
    the conventional mode of realism. The shift both reflects
    the changing form of the short story in the late 1890s and
    gives impetus to subsequent changes in the twentieth cen-
    tury.

55 GILLEN, FRANCIS XAVIER. "The Relationship of Rhetorical Con-
    trol to Meaning in the Novels of Henry James, Virginia
    Woolf, and E. M. Forster." <u>DAI</u>, 30, 1525A (Fordham).
      In the dramatic novel of James, the stream of conscious-
    ness novel of Woolf, and the "traditional" novel of For-
    ster, rhetorical devices are used to control and direct the
    reader's response to the fictional characters presented in
    their various works.

56 GOULD, CECIL. "Henry James." <u>Times Literary Supplement</u>
    (22 May), p. 558.
      No written evidence of homosexual activity by Henry
    James has been found. H. Montgomery Hyde's opinions that
    homosexual activity would discredit James, and his confi-
    dence that no evidence will be found, are questionable.
    Response to 1969.B69. <u>See</u> 1969.B122.

57 HABEGGER, ALFRED. "'The Siege of London': Henry James and
    the <u>Pièce Bien Faite</u>." <u>Modern Fiction Studies</u>, 15 (Sum-
    mer), 219-30.
      "The Siege of London" contains numerous references at-
    testing to its sources. Augier's <u>L'aventurière</u> and <u>Le
    demi-monde</u> by Dumas <u>fils</u> "disclose James's exact intentions
    in his <u>nouvelle</u>" and "define James's connections with . . .
    the <u>pièce bien faite</u>."

58 HAMBLEN, ABIGAIL ANN. "<u>Confidence</u>: The Surprising Shadow of
    Genius." <u>University Review</u> (Kansas City), 36 (Winter),
    151-54.
      Despite the artistic inadequacies of the story, Gordon
    Wright's willful disregard for Victorian morality and ap-

1969

plication of "situational ethics" demonstrate James's grasp of universal human nature.

59   HAMBLEN, ABIGAIL A.   "The Inheritance of the Meek: Two Novels by Agatha Christie and Henry James."   Discourse, 12 (Summer), 409-13.
      Besides similarities of plot, setting, and characterization, Agatha Christie's Endless Night and James's The Wings of the Dove have a common theme--"they have showed us vividly the terrible power of innocence."

60   HAMPSHIRE, STUART.   "Henry James," in his Modern Writers, and Other Essays.   London: Chatto & Windus; New York: Knopf, pp. 96-101.
      James was obsessed with the defense of "the private life."   Even after three volumes of Edel's biography, it appears that "the artist's defense may indeed prove stronger than the biographer's attack."

61   HARLOW, GEOFFREY, and JAMES REDMOND, eds.   The Year's Work in English Studies: Vol. 48:   1969.   London: Published for the English Association by John Murray, p. 396.
      Survey of criticism for 1969.

62   HARTSOCK, MILDRED E.   "A Light Lamp: The Spoils of Poynton as Comedy."   English Studies (Anglo-American Supp.), 50:xxix-xxxvii.
      Comedy, not tragedy or villainy, is the best word to describe The Spoils of Poynton, a "mock-epic" that satirizes "the triviality of human nature, the idea that virtue always triumphs, the ubiquitous practice of dispossessing the widow in English society, certain types of British character, [and] over-devotion to things."

63   HARTSOCK, MILDRED E.   "The Princess Casamassima: The Politics of Power."   Studies in the Novel, 1 (Fall), 297-309.
      The Princess Casamassima is a social commentary that evokes relevance and reality through James's ability to present characters and issues that are palpably believable.

64   HOFFA, WILLIAM.   "The Final Preface: Henry James's Autobiography."   Sewanee Review, 77 (Spring), 277-93.
      James's Autobiography is not a "'Family Book,'" as originally intended, but rather a "Preface" which "uncovers certain 'formative' principles" about James's life.   It is a "plea for the values of art and civilization."

65   HOLLOWAY, JOHN. "Introduction," in his edition of <u>Henry</u>
<u>James: "Daisy Miller."</u> Illustrations by Gustave Nebel.
Cambridge, England: Printed for the Members of The Limited Editions Club at the Univ. Printing House, pp. v-xvi.
   When <u>Daisy Miller</u> was first published in <u>The Cornhill</u>
<u>Magazine</u> (1878), it "caught the spirit of that time." It
was, in a certain sense, typical. The story has a "crisp,
summery charm," revealing James's "rich response to the
landscape of Europe."

66   HOUGHTON, DONALD E. "Attitude and Illness in James' <u>Daisy</u>
<u>Miller</u>." <u>Literature and Psychology</u>, 19:51-60.
   Characters in <u>Daisy Miller</u> who go to Europe without apprehension are healthy, whereas those who go with a negative attitude suffer from a variety of maladies; and in
the case of Daisy, the final result is death.

67   HOWARD-HILL, T. H. <u>Bibliography of British Literary Bibliog-</u>
<u>raphies</u>. Oxford: At the Clarendon Press, pp. 371-72.
   Listing of James bibliographies.

68   HUX, SAMUEL. "Irony in <u>The Aspern Papers</u>: The Unreliable
Symbolist." <u>Ball State Univ. Forum</u>, 10 (Winter), 60-65.
   Symbolically, the Aspern Papers represent "a controlling
moral corruption," the symbolic significance of which the
narrator remains ironically ignorant.

69   HYDE, H. MONTGOMERY. "Henry James." <u>Times Literary Supple-</u>
<u>ment</u> (15 May), p. 525.
   James's letters to Edmund Gosse are "in no way personally 'compromising'"; and the rumor that James engaged in a
homosexual affair is untrue. Responses in 1969.B122;
1969.B56.

70   JOHNSON, COURTNEY. "Adam and Eve and Isabel Archer." <u>Re-</u>
<u>nascence</u>, 21 (Spring), 134-44, 167.
   Isabel Archer's "struggle with her own fate parallels
the <u>sexual</u> struggle of Adam . . . in essence, this struggle
is between the Tree of Life and the Tree of Knowledge."

71   JOHNSON, COURTNEY. "John Marcher and the Paradox of the 'Un-
fortunate' Fall." <u>Studies in Short Fiction</u>, 6 (Winter),
121-35.
   Although the relationship of John Marcher and May Bar-
tram holds the potential for Marcher's redemption, his pro-
jections lead him to reject May, thereby rejecting his
chance for salvation.

1969

*72   KAUL, R. K. "Henry James on the Creative Process." <u>Rajasthan</u>
        <u>Univ. Studies in English</u> (Jaipur, India), 6:33-44.
            Cited in <u>1972 MLA International Bibliography</u>, vol. 1,
        p. 147.

73   KAZIN, ALFRED, ed. <u>The Ambassadors</u>. With an Introduction,
        biographical sketch, and a selection of background materi-
        als and commentaries. Bantam Critical Editions. Toronto,
        New York, London: Bantam.
            Contents include:
            "Introduction" by Alfred Kazin (pp. vii-xv). "The power
        of James's determination as a master planner and plotter,
        working things up for us, holding the rhythm--that is what
        most holds and charms us."
            James's "Preface to <u>The Ambassadors</u>," followed by the
        text of the novel and a brief biographical sketch.
            "Critical Supplement" (pp. 461-553). This section in-
        cludes James's comments on the novel, contemporary reviews,
        and comment by seven modern critics. (Selections by Percy
        Lubbock, E. M. Forster, F. W. Dupee, F. R. Leavis, Yvor
        Winters, Austin Warren, and Richard Chase are reprinted.
        <u>See</u> 1962.B112 for the Warren selection.)

74   KLEINBERG, SEYMOUR. "Ambiguity and Ambivalence: The Psychol-
        ogy of Sexuality in Henry James' <u>The Portrait of a Lady</u>."
        <u>Markham Review</u>, [1] (May), [2-7].
            "The function of James's ambiguity in <u>The Portrait of a</u>
        <u>Lady</u> is to express obliquely the psychology of sexual
        ambivalence."

75   KOLB, HAROLD HUTCHINSON, JR. <u>The Illusion of Life: American</u>
        <u>Realism as a Literary Form</u>. Charlottesville: Univ. Press
        of Virginia, passim.
            Three writers in the mid-1880s--James, Twain, and How-
        ells--represent the point of maturity in the American real-
        ism movement. Their works, while vastly different, contain
        a commonality of style that emphasizes the importance of
        stylistic techniques in defining realism. Their works also
        provide a pivotal base from which romanticism and natural-
        ism may be examined. (This book includes a bibliography of
        published works by James, Twain, and Howells from 1884-1886,
        an alphabetically ordered index of subjects and personali-
        ties of the period, and a selective bibliography on Ameri-
        can Realism.) <u>See</u> 1969.B76 for dissertation.

76   KOLB, HAROLD HUTCHINSON, JR. "The Illusion of Life: American
      Realism as a Literary Form in the Writings of Mark Twain,
      Henry James, and W. D. Howells in the Mid-1880's." DA, 29,
      3102A (Indiana).
         A study of realism based on its appearance in the mid-
      1880s in the works of Twain, Howells, and James suggests
      that the genre is "best defined by a consideration of its
      philosophy, subject matter, morality, and style." See
      1969.B75 for book publication.

77   KOSSICK, SHIRLEY. "Henry James: The Europeans." Unisa Eng-
      lish Studies (May), pp. 29-38.
         In The Europeans Eugenia and Felix embody European cul-
      ture and moral values. In their encounters with Wentworth
      and the Actons the values "of New England emerge as supe-
      rior to those of Europe."

78   KRAFT, JAMES L. "A Perspective on 'The Beast in the Jungle.'"
      Literatur in Wissenschaft und Unterricht (Kiel), 2:20-26.
         The complexity and contradictoriness of life is por-
      trayed in the relationship of John Marcher and May Bartram,
      a relationship symbolically portrayed through the settings,
      the cyclic structure, and the names in the story. Reprint-
      ed in 1970.A7.

79   KRAFT, QUENTIN G. "The Central Problem of James's Fictional
      Thought: From The Scarlet Letter to Roderick Hudson."
      Journal of English Literary History, 36 (June), 416-39.
         James's handling of freedom and morality in his first
      novel, Roderick Hudson, "relates . . . back to the problem
      of The Scarlet Letter and forward to the problems James
      confronts in his subsequent novels."

80   KRAMER, HILTON. "Henry James in the Nineties." New Leader,
      52 (26 May), 14-16.
         Leon Edel's The Treacherous Years is a "masterly biogra-
      phy . . . [and] a deeply moving act of literary faith."
      Review of 1969.A1.

81   KRONENBERGER, LOUIS. "Washington Square," in his The Polished
      Surface: Essays in the Literature of Worldliness. New
      York: Knopf, pp. 233-45.
         Washington Square "is of worldliness all compact, is
      indeed in the artistic sense superbly compact, superbly
      organized--something which carries on from the manner of
      Jane Austen without repeating it."

1969

82   KROOK, DOROTHEA. "Critical Principles." New Statesman, 222
        (9 May), 658.
           Critics today need a flexible set of principles similar
        to those espoused in James's The Art of Fiction.

83   KROOK, DOROTHEA. Elements of Tragedy. New Haven and London:
        Yale Univ. Press, passim.
           In this generic study, which draws its principal exam-
        ples from Sophocles, Ibsen, Chekhov, Middleton and Shake-
        speare, some two dozen passing references to James and his
        works appear.

84   LABRIE, ERNEST ROSS. "Sirens of Life and Art in Henry James."
        Lakehead Univ. Review (Port Arthur, Ont.), 2:150-69.
           Four works by James--The Tragic Muse, "The Lesson of the
        Master," "The Figure in the Carpet," and "Sir Dominick Fer-
        rand"--suggest he believed the successful artist must find
        a balance between the "intensity of the pull of life" and
        the necessity for aesthetic detachment. The artist must
        constantly be aware of the dangers of being overcome by
        either extreme.

85   LEEMING, DAVID ADAMS. "Henry James and George Sand." Revue
        de Littérature Comparée, 43 (January-March), 47-55.
           Sand "served as a source of discussion for a question
        which fascinated James throughout his career--the question
        of the relationship between art and experience, between the
        artist and the life of the 'world.'"

86   LIBMAN, VALENTINA A. Russian Studies of American Literature:
        A Bibliography. Translated by Robert V. Allen. Edited by
        Clarence Gohdes. Chapel Hill, N.C.: Univ. of North Caro-
        lina Press, p. 110.
           Five "Genri Dzheims" entries, which appeared in Russian
        sources between 1881 and 1963, are listed.

87   LONG, ROBERT E. "The Ambassadors and the Genteel Tradition:
        James's Corrections of Hawthorne and Howells." New England
        Quarterly, 42 (March), 44-64.
           The Ambassadors refers back to Hawthorne and Howells and
        is "a correction of their understanding of the American
        mind." A correction of Howells's choice of duty rather
        than life, it is also "an implicit correction of Haw-
        thorne's moral dramas of renunciation of the world."

88 LYNEN, JOHN F. The Design of the Present: Essays on Time and
    Form in American Literature. New Haven and London: Yale
    Univ. Press, passim.
        Jonathan Edwards, Benjamin Franklin, Irving, Cooper,
    Poe, Whitman and Eliot are the principal authors consid-
    ered in this study which contains a dozen passing refer-
    ences to James.

89 McDONALD, WALTER R. "The Inconsistencies in Henry James's
    Aesthetics." Texas Studies in Literature and Language, 10
    (Winter), 585-97.
        Despite James's critical perceptiveness, an examination
    of his diverse criticism, both in theory and in practice,
    reveals the absence of a clear theoretical position with
    the result that he is inconsistent in several areas:
    (1) on the subject of selectivity as opposed to inclusive-
    ness; (2) on the differences between Romance and Realism;
    (3) on the differences between the story and the novel; and
    (4) on the subject of organic growth vis à vis artistic
    control.

90 McDOUGAL, EDWARD D. "Henry James." Times Literary Supplement
    (13 November), p. 1313.
        On the same night that James was "hooted off the stage"
    after a performance of Guy Domville (January 5, 1895),
    Julian Field's Too happy by half was received with thun-
    derous applause by the same audience.

91 McMASTER, JULIET. "'The Full Image of a Repetition' in The
    Turn of the Screw." Studies in Short Fiction, 6 (Summer),
    377-82.
        Through consistent "ironic reversals of locations" and
    carefully employed imagery of windows, glass, and mirrors,
    James has created a story for dual appreciation: it is
    both a ghost story and a psychological novel.

*92 MARKOVIĆ, VIDA. "Conflict and Controversy Between Henry James
    and H. G. Wells." Zbornik radova (Belgrade), pp. 197-216.
        Cited in Annual Bibliography of English Language and
    Literature: Vol. 44. Edited by John Horden and James B.
    Misenheimer, Jr. London: MHRA, 1971, Item 7202.

93 MARTIN, ROBERT K. "Henry James and Rodolphe Töpffer: A
    Note." Romance Notes, 10 (Spring), 245-46.
        The suggestion that James was significantly influenced
    by Töpffer is corroborated by the presence of two volumes
    listed in the Lamb House Library, Voyages en Zigzag and

1969

Nouveaux Voyages en Zigzag, and by a recorded borrowing of Causeries du Lundi, which contains an essay on Töpffer, from the Harvard College Library.

94   MARTIN, ROBERT K. "Henry James and the Harvard College Library." *American Literature*, 41 (March), 95-103.
       James's borrowings from the College Library provide an index to the broad spectrum of his literary and cultural interests.

95   MAYNARD, REID. "The Irony of Strether's Enlightenment." *Lock Haven Review*, 11:33-44.
       Maria Gostrey serves to intensify Strether's "romantic idealizations." Strether ironically mistakes "this sensitive heightening . . . for the beginning of a profound change in his sense of values."

96   MELCHIORI, BARBARA. "Feelings about Aspects: Henry James on Pierre Loti." *Studi Americani*, no. 15, pp. 169-99.
       Loti was an Impressionist in prose who "loosened up the form and structure of the novel." James admired him, but found his subject matter "vulgar." Reprinted in 1974.A3.

97   MELDRUM, RONALD M. "Three of Henry James' Dark Ladies." *Research Studies* (Washington State Univ.), 37 (March), 54-60.
       Olive Chancellor, the governess in *The Turn of the Screw*, and Kate Croy are three of James's archetypal "Dark Ladies," whose natural sexuality is perverted and used for egoistic purposes.

98   MEWS, SIEGFRIED. "German Reception of American Writers in the Late Nineteenth Century." *South Atlantic Bulletin*, 34 (March), 7-9.
       Henry James is noted among American writers who were read and translated in Germany in the nineteenth century, but he received poor reader reception because he failed to portray distinctive American traits--subject matter appealing to a country that wanted to know about the raw and unrefined America.

99   MONTEIRO, GEORGE. "Addendum to Edel and Laurence: Henry James's 'Future of the Novel.'" *Papers of the Bibliographical Society of America*, 63 (2Q), 130.
       With the subheading "An Analysis and a Forecast," James's essay "The Future of the Novel" first appeared in the *Saturday Review of Books and Art* on 11 August 1900, p. 541.

100   MONTEIRO, GEORGE. "Henry James and His Reviewers: Some
      Identifications." Papers of the Bibliographical Society
      of America, 63 (4Q), 300-304.
         The authors of twenty-one reviews of James's work,
      which were anonymously published, are identified to pro-
      vide information not included in Roger Gard's Henry James:
      The Critical Heritage (1968.B38).

101   MUKHERJEE, SUJIT, and D. V. K. RAGHAVACHARYULU, eds. Indian
      Essays in American Literature: Papers in Honour of Robert
      E. Spiller. Bombay: Popular Prakashan, pp. 139-178.
         Contents include:
         "The Idea of Refinement in James' Roderick Hudson" by
      N. Krishna Rao (pp. 139-47). The James canon can be read
      as a statement on human refinement, "that element in human
      nature, and in the structure of society, which implicates
      the self in the possibility and fact of human change,
      growth, and transformation." Roderick, who fails to "com-
      prehend or exercise intellectual refinement," is without
      self-control, a slave to life's passions, while Roland,
      who is intellectually refined, is lacking in spiritual re-
      finement, evidenced by his meddling in Roderick's life.
         "The Albany Cousin and Two Heroines of Henry James" by
      O. P. Sharma (pp. 149-65). The image of Minny Temple,
      freed from time and mortality in 1870, is transformed to
      live "in an eternal moment in the realm of art" and even-
      tually finds "aesthetic salvation" in Isabel Archer and
      Milly Theale. A personal symbol for James attains the
      "immanence and universality of archetypal feminine expe-
      rience" through the "process of transmutation."
         "Isabel Archer and Huck Finn: Two Responses to the
      Fruit of Knowledge" by Raj K. Kohli (pp. 167-78). Both
      The Portrait of a Lady and Huckleberry Finn are "master-
      pieces," "almost contemporaneous," "novels of education
      which exploit the picaresque mode and use the archetypal
      journey." Huck and Isabel maintain "their individual in-
      tegrity" throughout their encounters with the "fruit of
      knowledge" and offer opposing responses to the experience
      --Huck asserts freedom, while Isabel submits to fate. Re-
      print of 1968.B60.

102   MUKHERJI, N. "The Role of Pansy in The Portrait of a Lady,"
      Calcutta Review, ns 1:585-94.
         Pansy is a functional character who makes indispensable
      contributions to the novel's texture and plot in addition
      to her "important role of revealing and reflecting the main
      characters" and their relationships.

1969

103 MYERS, ROBERT MANSON. "Henry James on Stage." Times Literary
Supplement (16 October), p. 1211.
Myers supports the account given in "Commentary"
(11 September 1969), which reported that he tried to can-
cel the London opening of Basil Ashmore's production of
The Spoils of Poynton. Myers defends his right as an
artist to preserve the integrity of his own work. Response to 1969.B2. See also 1969.B37; 1969.B7.

104 NOWELL-SMITH, SIMON. "Texts of The Portrait of a Lady, 1881-
1882: The Bibliographical Evidence." Papers of the Bibliographical Society of America, 63 (4Q), 304-10.
Sufficient evidence exists to formulate a tentative
chronology for the order in which the texts of The Portrait
of a Lady "may be said to have come into being." This order does not correspond with either the printing or publication order.

105 PEARCE, BRIAN. "Introduction," in his edition of Washington
Square. Modern English Language Texts. London: Heinemann
Educational Books, 8 pp.
Catherine Sloper, "dull and unattractive," is also "honest, generous and capable of deep feeling." Her happiness
is destroyed by her realization that the man she loves is
"an insincere heiress-chaser," and by her realization that
her "adored father does not love her, either." (This book
includes a "Note on New York in 1850" and "Glossary and
Notes.")

106 PEARCE, ROY HARVEY. "Henry James and His American," in his
Historicism Once More: Problems and Occasions for the
American Scholar. Princeton, N.J.: Princeton Univ. Press,
pp. 240-60.
Reprint of 1962.B86.

107 PERLOFF, MARJORIE. "Cinderella Becomes the Wicked Step-
mother: The Portrait of a Lady as Ironic Fairy Tale."
Nineteenth-Century Fiction, 23 (March), 413-33.
Thwarted in her effort to subjugate Gilbert Osmond, Isabel finds Pansy a more submissive subject. Isabel fails to
comprehend that in trying to get Pansy to act freely, not
dutifully, she is actually acting negatively and destruc-
tively.

108 PICCINATO, STEFANIA. "The Wings of the Dove: Dal progetto
     alla forma." Studi Americani, no. 15, pp. 131-68. [Ital-
     ian]
     If James's drama Guy Domville had been a painful fail-
     ure, his novel The Wings of the Dove can be considered the
     essence of James's dramatic technique. Its characteristics
     are a dialogue implying a constant interior search, a tight
     debate, and a deep knowledge of man's subconscious.

109 PIZER, DONALD. "A Primer of Fictional Aesthetics." College
     English, 30 (April), 572-80.
     A discussion of four approaches to fictional aesthetics
     notes James's significant place in the establishment of the
     novel as an aesthetic form.

110 PORTE, JOEL. "James," in his The Romance in America: Studies
     in Cooper, Poe, Hawthorne, Melville, and James. Middle-
     town, Conn.: Wesleyan Univ. Press, pp. 193-226.
     Three works by James, The American, The Turn of the
     Screw, and The Golden Bowl, contain romantic affinities
     with the works of Cooper, Poe, Hawthorne, and Melville.
     James follows the American romance tradition that explores
     "large questions" through the use of archetypal, mythical,
     and symbolical devices.

111 PRITCHETT, V. S. "The Traveller Returns." New Statesman, 77
     (21 February), 259-60.
     James's The American Scene, written from intensely per-
     sonal experiences, contains "an essential America that is
     still recognisable today."

112 PURDY, STROTHER B. "Conversation and Awareness in Henry
     James's 'A Round of Visits.'" Studies in Short Fiction, 6
     (Summer), 421-32.
     An analysis of the conversation of Monteith and Winch
     reveals a gradual shift from verbal to "extra-lingual" com-
     munication, whereby Monteith becomes responsible for Winch's
     death.

113 PURDY, STROTHER B. "Henry James and the Mot Juste." Wiscon-
     sin Studies in Literature, 6:118-25.
     Henry James was a "marked linguistic innovator": "The
     word that ended Henry James's search was the complex word
     of William Empson, or the autonomous word of Leo Spitzer,
     rather than the invisible mot juste of Malherbe and the
     Flaubert of Madame Bovary."

1969

114 PURDY, STROTHER B. "Henry James and the Sacred Thrill."
    Philological Quarterly, 48 (April), 247-60.
        In consideration of James's employment of "sacred" in
    phrases such as "sacred rage," "sacred fount," and "sacred
    thrill," and his translation of the word from French, it is
    clear that the connotation is not Christian but rather re-
    flects a religion that reveres "art and memories of child-
    hood."

115 PUTT, S. GORLEY. "Editorial Note," in his edition of Roderick
    Hudson. Penguin Modern Classics. Baltimore: Penguin,
    pp. 5-7.
        The first revised text of 1878 is used for this edition
    of Roderick Hudson because there is a freshness in this
    version not present in the final version of the New York
    Edition.

116 PUTT, S. GORLEY. "Introduction," in his edition of The Turn of
    the Screw, and Other Stories. Penguin Modern Classics.
    Baltimore: Penguin, pp. 5-6.
        Miles (in The Turn of the Screw) and Morgan (in "The Pu-
    pil") are both "presented by James as being quite literally
    too good for the world of disillusioned adults." The third
    story in this collection, "The Third Person," is an "amus-
    ing spoof on spooking."

117 RAYMOND, JOHN. "Beyond the Usual." New Statesman, 77
    (30 May), 778-79.
        A review of Anthony Trollope: The Critical Heritage by
    Donald Smalley includes Henry James's objection to the con-
    clusion of several of the novels as well as excerpts from
    the essay written by James to amend his rebukes after
    Trollope's death.

118 ROSE, ALAN M. "Conrad and the Sirens of the Decadence."
    Texas Studies in Literature and Language, 11 (Spring),
    805-808.
        Conrad and James took similar positions during the 1890s
    in standing apart from both the "art for art's sake" writ-
    ers and the didactic writers.

119 SABISTON, ELIZABETH JEAN. "The Provincial Heroine in Prose
    Fiction: A Study in Isolation and Creativity." DAI, 30,
    1150A (Cornell).
        A study of the similarities among Austen's Emma, Flau-
    bert's Emma, Eliot's Dorothea, and James's Isabel provides

an argument for the existence of a type of heroine who is "trying against insurmountable odds . . . to realize her 'ideal conception of her own personality.'"

120 SALOMON, ROGER B. "Time and the Realists," in Intellectual History in America. Edited by Cushing Strout. New York: Harper, pp. 47-59.
Reprinted from 1964.B84. Also printed in 1968.B115.

121 SCHERTING, JOHN. "Roderick Hudson: A Re-evaluation." Arizona Quarterly, 25 (Spring), 101-19.
The examination of Rowland Mallet's "character, motives, and deeds" leads to "the central meaning of the novel."

122 SCHNEIDER, DANIEL J. "The 'Full Ironic Truth' in The Spoils of Poynton." Connecticut Review, 2 (April), 50-66.
"Analysis of the innumerable innuendos and implications of James's phrasing" and the symbolic patterns of The Spoils of Poynton "discloses not only that Fleda is sometimes dishonest and self-deluded but also that she is conceived, in almost purely naturalistic terms, . . . as the pathetic victim of her own cravings."

123 SCOTT, R. H. F. ["Henry James"]. Times Literary Supplement (22 May), p. 558.
"Mr. Montgomery Hyde is a rare bird. He can scotch a canard without producing a lame duck." Response to 1969.B69. See 1969.B56.

124 SHRIBER, MICHAEL. "Cognitive Apparatus in Daisy Miller, The Ambassadors, and Two Works by Howells: A Comparative Study of the Epistemology of Henry James." Language and Style, 2 (Summer), 207-25.
Whereas a study of Howells's early and late usage of the "cognitive apparatus" (i.e. the patterns of verbs, adverbs, and grammatical constructions utilized to denote and connote cognitions) suggests a movement toward a rationalist perspective, James's movement is toward an empirical view. A comparison of Howells's A Chance Acquaintance and The Son of Royal Langbrith with James's Daisy Miller and The Ambassadors illustrates the two authors' representation of cognition.

125 SMITH, CHARLES R. "'The Lesson of the Master': An Interpretive Note." Studies in Short Fiction, 6 (Fall), 654-58.
On the basis of internal and biographical evidence, the story is not to be interpreted ironically or humorously,

1969

but in a literal fashion that emphasizes the Master's
weakness and the demanding terms on which Overt must ob-
tain his ideal.

126   SMITH, HERBERT F., and MICHAEL PETNOVICH. "The Bostonians:
       Creation and Revision." Bulletin of the New York Public
       Library, 73 (May), 298-308.
          James's underrating of The Bostonians by excluding it
       from the New York Edition is considered. Even though its
       initial publication history and poor public reception
       caused unhappiness for the author, pride in his achievement
       is obvious because of the careful revisions from serial
       form to novel.

127   STAFFORD, WILLIAM T. American Literary Scholarship: An An-
       nual, 1967. Edited by James Woodress. Durham, N.C.:
       Duke Univ. Press, pp. 73-85.
          Survey of criticism published during 1967.

128   STAFFORD, WILLIAM T. "'Blighted Houses and Blighted Child-
       hood': James's Treacherous Years." Virginia Quarterly
       Review, 45 (Summer), 526-30.
          Leon Edel's fourth biographical volume of Henry James
       is "eminently and dramatically its own justification."
       Review of 1969.A1.

129   STONE, EDWARD. "Henry James," in A Certain Morbidness: A
       View of American Literature. London: Feffer & Simons;
       Carbondale and Edwardsville: Southern Illinois Univ.
       Press, pp. 43-52, passim.
          William Mumford Baker's Mose Evans is a probable source
       of James's "The Author of Beltraffio." In James's short
       story, he broadens the reader's understanding of morbidity.

130   SZALA, ALINA. "Henry James's The American Simplified."
       Kwartalnik Neofilologiczny (Warsaw), 16:61-64.
          The Polish version of The American (Amerykanin, 1879),
       which may have been translated from the German edition is
       a careless translation. The most obvious changes are in
       the character of Newman, who emerges as a stereotyped
       American.

131   TAHARA, SETSUKO. "Henry James: What Maisie Knew and The
       Awkward Age." Ohara Kyoko Sensei Kinen Eibeibungaku Ron-
       shu (Essays and Studies of British and American Literature
       in Commemoration of Professor Kyoko Ohara). Tokyo,
       pp. 241-59. [Japanese]

1969

These two works and "The Pupil" deal commonly with spiritual growth in childhood (or adolescence) and the acquisition of moral awareness with the help of an adult guardian
figure. James satirizes the immorality of society in contrast to the delicate sensitivity of a child.

132   TANIGUCHI, RIKUO. "Henry James," in The Writers of the Lost
      Generation. Revised edition. Tokyo: Nanundo, pp. 161-207.
      [Japanese]
      This discussion of James includes a consideration of
      America and American literature in relation to European
      civilization and literature. James's cosmopolitanism is at-
      tributed to his preference for regarding America as on the
      same plane as Europe (and not as inferior to Europe). Fur-
      thermore, James's spectator attitude in his works is perhaps
      due to his physical problem and to his feelings of inferi-
      ority with respect to his brother William. Finally, the
      relativity in James's works may be due to the novelist's
      lack of a home.

133   TANNER, TONY. "James in the terrible tank." Spectator, 222
      (21 February), 240-41.
      James's The American Scene records his "shock at all the
      brutal obliterations which seem to be an inherent part of
      the development of modern America."

134   TAYLOR, GORDON O. "The Friction of Existence: Henry James,"
      in his The Passages of Thought: Psychological Representa-
      tion in the American Novel, 1870-1900. New York: Oxford
      Univ. Press, pp. 42-84.
      Roderick Hudson, The Portrait of a Lady, and The Ambas-
      sadors provide the basis for a study of James's "movement
      toward firm control and full artistic use of a concept of
      narrative in which the processes of a character's mind are
      centrally 'interesting,' and which therefore acknowledges
      the representation of mental process as its basic 'princi-
      ple of continuity.'"

135   THORBERG, RAYMOND. "'Flavien,' 'Tenants,' and The Portrait of
      a Lady." South Atlantic Bulletin, 34 (May), 10-13.
      In addition to James's use of "affronting" in his pref-
      ace to The Portrait of a Lady, similarities of character,
      incident, and plot with Rivière's "Flavien" and "Tenants"
      suggest James perceived Isabel in a "French Context."

1969

136 THORBERG, RAYMOND. "Henry James and the 'New England Conscience.'" Notes and Queries, ns 16 (June), 222-23.
The term "The New England Conscience" does not appear
to be used pejoratively by James, and his earliest usage of
the term appears to be in approximately 1879 in the manuscript of Confidence.

137 TOURNADRE, C. "Propositions pour une psychologie sociale de
The Turn of the Screw." Etudes Anglaises, 22 (July-
September), 259-69. [French]
The Turn of the Screw might be considered as a parable
of English society in which Flora and Miles reflect a dying
aristocracy whose only nourishment can be provided by "inferior" people--Quint, Miss Jessel, and all of the servants
--at the risk of its own integrity. But if Flora betrays
her class with her departure, Miles remains faithful,
though his only salvation is in his death.

138 TYTELL, JOHN. "Henry James and the Romance." Markham Review,
[1], no. 5 (May), [1-2].
"De Grey" reflects the influence of Poe and Hawthorne
on James's conception of romance form.

139 VANDERMOERE, H. "Baroness Münster's Failure." English Studies, 50 (February), 47-57.
Eugenia fails to marry Robert Acton because both of them
possess "suspicion, fastidiousness, egoism, self-suffi-
ciency." Neither one is open or detached, because each is
locked into his respective world.

140 VITELLI, JAMES R. Van Wyck Brooks. Twayne's United States
Authors Series, No. 134. New York: Twayne, pp. 99-109,
passim.
Brooks's The Pilgrimage of Henry James was an attempt to
illuminate "James 'the man.'" Brooks held James's Puritan
inheritance responsible for James's failure.

141 WARD, J. A. "The Ambassadors as a Conversion Experience."
Southern Review, ns 5 (Spring), 350-74.
The Ambassadors, not the explicitly religious The Wings
of the Dove, typifies the "familiar Jamesian paradigm of
the American's 'Conversion' by Europe."

142 WATSON, GEORGE, ed. "Henry James," in The New Cambridge Bibliography of English Literature, 1800-1900. Cambridge,
England: Cambridge Univ. Press, vol. 3, pp. 992-1000.
A listing of bibliographies, collections of James's
work, primary bibliographical material, and criticism.

143 WEGELIN, CHRISTOF. "Edith Wharton and the Twilight of the
     International Novel." Southern Review, ns 5 (Spring),
     398-418.
         Edith Wharton began in the "shadow" of James, the pre-
     eminent international novelist, "but soon stepped out into
     the light of her own talent and of her own experience and
     observation."

144 WHITE, WILLIAM. "Unpublished Henry James on Whitman." Review
     of English Studies, ns 20 (August), 321-22.
         James's letter to Dr. John Johnston in 1898 reflects a
     different opinion of Whitman than that published in Nation
     in 1865.

145 WISE, JAMES N. "The Floating World of Lambert Strether."
     Arlington Quarterly, 2 (Summer), 80-110.
         A synopsis by James of The Ambassadors, entitled "Proj-
     ect of Novel by Henry James," reveals "a pattern of fluidi-
     ty references and height/depth relationships which epito-
     mizes Lambert Strether's psychological, as well as physical,
     journey through the novel." These references are present
     in the completed novel showing Strether as a passive charac-
     ter, who floats "through the action of the novel."

1969 C DISSERTATIONS

  1 ALEXANDER, ELIZABETH. "Henry James as a Playwright." DA, 29,
     3123A (Wisconsin).
         Inattention to the dramaturgical aspects of his plays,
     inadequate comic appeal, poor dialogue, shallow characters,
     and an insensitivity to the changing theatrical preferences
     of his culture all converged to prevent James from succeed-
     ing at a life-long ambition.

  2 CONN, PETER JAMES. "The Tyranny of the Eye: The Observer as
     Aggressor in Henry James's Fictions." DA, 30, 1556A (Yale).
         "Human aggression as Henry James represents it is typi-
     cally accompanied by recurring and definable patterns of
     perceptual activity" in which the "perceptual activity" is
     a means of aggression.

  3 COOPER, SUZANA RIGOLETH. "Art as Deception: A Study of Some
     Fictional Characters of Thomas Mann and Henry James." DA,
     30, 3002A-03A (Illinois).
         Although James conceived of "art . . . [as] the highest
     good and the artist . . . [as] the embodiment of the supe-
     rior, enlightened, profoundly moral spirit," there are

1969

times when the artist is treated ambiguously and there are
suggestions that the artist is a "guilty outsider, . . .
[a] criminal, or [a] charlatan" thus "unwittingly paving
the way for Mann's concept of the artist-illusionist."

*4   COY FERRER, JUAN J. "La Novelistica de Henry James. Inicia-
ción y Primera Madurez. 1864-1881." Unpublished Doctoral
Dissertation, Univ. of Madrid.
    Cited in Annual Bibliography of English Language and
Literature: 1969: Vol. 44. Edited by John Horden and
James B. Misenheimer, Jr. London: Modern Humanities Re-
search Association, 1971, Item 7156.

5   CUMMINS, ELIZABETH KEYSER. "Henry James: Irony and the Limited Observer." DA, 29, 2670A (Claremont).
    The limited observers of Madame de Mauves, "The Pupil,"
The Beast in the Jungle, The Ambassadors, The Aspern Papers, The Liar, and The Sacred Fount cannot be identified
with James. They are instead the objects of his ironic
treatment and serve to demonstrate that "for James there
can be no true consciousness without self-consciousness,
and there can be no self-consciousness without a recognition of the self's need to love and be loved."

6   GORDON, JULIE PEYTON. "The Idea of Decadence and the Novels
of Henry James." Dissertation, Harvard, 354 pp.
    "Decadence as a phase in the literary history of France
and England in the last half of the nineteenth century"
provides an intellectual and aesthetic context for a reading of James's novels, which exhibit both "direct" and "indirect" evidence of influence by major "decadent" writers.

*7   KOSSMANN, RUDOLF RICHARD. "Henry James: Dramatist." Gro-
ningen: Wolters-Noordhoff, Dissertation, Univ. of Leiden.
    Cited in Annual Bibliography of English Language and
Literature: 1969: Vol. 44. Edited by John Horden and
James B. Misenheimer, Jr. London: Modern Humanities Research Association, 1971, Item 7196. For book see 1969.A4.

8   O'BRIEN, ELLEN TREMPER. "Henry James and Aestheticism." Dissertation, Harvard, 265 pp.
    This study attempts "to place James in relation to aes-
theticism, particularly as formulated by Pater," and "to
reveal the special nature of [James's] own aestheticism,"
his "notion of 'taste' that makes us feel the identity [of
aesthetic and moral perception] as a reality in his fiction."

9   RECCHIA, EDWARD JOHN. "Form and the Creative Process: Lesson
      and Example in Eleven of Henry James's Artist Tales." DAI,
      30, 2495A-96A (Ohio State).
         A structural analysis of James's eleven stories about
      writers and artists "reveals his emphasis on the necessity
      of the artist's achievement of an impersonal, unrestricted
      sense of life in order that he may suggest the qualities of
      life he perceives through the formal structure of his work."

10   SAUL, FRANK JOSEPH. "Autobiographical Surrogates in Henry
      James: The Aesthetics of Detachment." DAI, 30, 2549A-50A
      (Johns Hopkins).
         The sense of alienation from the world felt by James and
      his need to achieve some integration with it, as reflected
      in his autobiographical writings, are similarly expressed
      in the fictional protagonists of The American, The Princess
      Casamassima, and The Ambassadors.

11   SCHWERTMAN, MARY POGUE. "Henry James's Portraits of Ladies."
      DA, 29, 2282A (Univ. of North Carolina).
         In two of James's early works, Madame de Mauves and
      Daisy Miller, he created the two types of heroines to which
      he would repeatedly turn in his later works: (1) the true
      heroine, who is notable for her self-awareness and absence
      of romantic illusions; and (2) the limited heroine, who is
      immersed in romantic illusions, fears emotional involvement,
      and denies her true feelings.

12   TYTELL, JOHN. "Henry James: From Omniscience to Inner Reali-
      ty: The Experimental Novels, 1895-1901." DAI, 30, 343A-44A
      (New York Univ.).
         From 1895 to 1901 James abandoned the "omniscient novel"
      and experimented with techniques that enabled him to convey
      a character's conception of reality directly to the reader
      --techniques that "involved the reader more directly in the
      pursuit of inner reality."

13   WHITMORE, PAUL EUGENE. "The Image of the City in the Art of
      Henry James." DAI, 30, 1579A (Fordham).
         An examination of fourteen novels and nineteen shorter
      works reveals an evolution in James's technique for present-
      ing his vision of the city. The technique of simple de-
      scription evolves into complex metaphoric and symbolic
      devices in the later works that reflect James's sense of
      alienation from the modern city.

1970

1970 A BOOKS

1   BUITENHUIS, PETER. The Grasping Imagination: The American
    Writings of Henry James. Toronto: Toronto Univ. Press,
    288 pp.
        A close textual analysis of James's American writings
    (fiction set in the United States as well as critical es-
    says and travel notes) set in the context of biography
    (that part of James's life spent in the U.S.) establishes
    that James used all of the viewpoints of his characters
    "to give a spectrum of opinion about America that amounts
    to one of the most comprehensive criticisms that any writer
    made of his own country." Reviewed: 1971.B37; 1972.B34;
    1972.B111; David K. Kirby, New England Quarterly, 44
    (1971), 337-39; Krishna Baldev Vaid, American Literature,
    43 (1971), 461-62; Modern Fiction Studies, 19 (1973),
    263-66.

2   DELBAERE-GARANT, JEANNE. Henry James: The Vision of France.
    Paris: Société d'Editions "Les Belles Lettres," 441 pp.
        An examination of James's attitude to France (as ex-
    pressed in letters, travel writing, and autobiography), his
    criticism of French writers, and his use of French settings
    and French characters reveals that "James indeed defined
    himself through his attitude to the French mind and through
    his criticism of French writers just as his own Anglo-Saxon
    heroes define themselves through their reaction to the
    French environment." Reviewed: Leon Edel, American Liter-
    ature, 43 (1972), 662-63; Sallie Sears, Modern Fiction
    Studies, 19 (1973), 263-66.

3   MOTODA, SHUICHI, ed. Neji no Kaiten eno Apurochi [Studies of
    "The Turn of the Screw"]. Tokyo: Bunri-Shoin, 88 pp.
    [Japanese]
        Contents: A collection of papers originally presented
    at a symposium of the Kyushu Chapter of English Literature
    Society of Japan, Miyazaki Univ., November 1969.
        "Reality of The Turn of the Screw" by Shuichi Motoda.
    The charm of the work is due to two aspects it contains:
    the symbolic meaning of James's intention in "the air of
    evil" and the psychological realism made valid through
    point of view.
        "James's Reaction to Hallucination" by Nobushige Tado-
    koro. James had full knowledge of hallucination and much
    interest in J. S. Le Fanu. A comparison of James and Le
    Fanu reveals that James appears more involved with hallu-
    cination without scientific distance in his work. Refer-

ences are made in this essay to James's own hallucinatory experience, the Society for Psychical Research, Swedenborg, and the beast image in hallucination.

"Mythic Approaches to <u>The Turn of the Screw</u>" by Okibumi Yonezu. The two qualities of an artistic work, the mythical and the individual, correspond to James's novelistic and romantic elements. <u>The Turn of the Screw</u> is a romance, in which James's vision of evil is more important than the (non-)existence of the ghost.

"Chaotic Situation in <u>The Turn of the Screw</u>" by Kazuto Ono. The disorder in the work reflects James's own inner disorder after his failure in drama, as well as the chaos in the European situation of the time.

4 POWERS, LYALL H. <u>Henry James: An Introduction and Interpretation</u>. American Authors and Critics Series. New York: Holt, Rinehart and Winston, 164 pp.

A consideration of James's biography as well as of his prose fiction and literary criticism demonstrates "the fundamental unity of James's moral attitude and the consistency of aim in his artistic endeavor." Reviewed: Edwin T. Bowden, <u>American Literature</u>, 42 (1971), 582-84; William Wallis, <u>Prairie Schooner</u>, 45 (1971), 179-80.

5 POWERS, LYALL H., comp. <u>The Merrill Studies in "The Portrait of a Lady."</u> Columbus, Ohio: Merrill, 122 pp.

Contents include:

"Preface" by L. H. Powers (pp. iii-iv). Three early responses to the novel plus seven critical pieces written since World War II were selected to illustrate a variety of approaches to the novel and to provide assistance toward understanding the novel for students.

"James's <u>The Portrait of a Lady</u>" by John Hay (pp. 1-8). Reprinted from <u>New York Tribune</u> (25 December 1881), p. 8.

"From '<u>The Portrait of a Lady</u> and <u>Dr. Breen's Practice</u>'" by Horace Scudder (pp. 9-12). Reprinted from <u>Atlantic Monthly</u>, 49 (January 1882), 126-30.

"From 'James's <u>Portrait of a Lady</u>'" by William C. Brownell (pp. 13-18). Reprinted from <u>The Nation</u>, 34 (2 February 1882), 102-103.

"From 'The Heiress of All the Ages'" by Philip Rahv (pp. 19-27). Reprinted from <u>Literature and the Sixth Sense</u>. Boston: Houghton Mifflin, 1969, pp. 104-25. Originally printed in <u>Partisan Review</u>, 10 (May-June 1943), 227-47.

"On <u>The Portrait of a Lady</u>" by Dorothy Van Ghent (pp. 28-45). Reprinted from <u>The English Novel: Form and</u>

1970

Function. New York: Holt, Rinehart and Winston, 1953, pp. 211-28.
"Henry James: The Portrait of a Lady" by Arnold Kettle (pp. 46-66). Reprinted from An Introduction to the English Novel. Vol. 2. London: Hutchinson, 1953, pp. 13-34.
"From 'News of Life'" by Quentin Anderson (pp. 67-79). Reprinted from The American Henry James. New Brunswick, N.J.: Rutgers Univ. Press, 1957, pp. 183-98.
"From 'The Disconcerting Poetry of Mary Temple: A Comparison of the Imagery of The Portrait of a Lady and The Wings of the Dove'" by Lotus Snow (pp. 80-93). Reprinted from New England Quarterly, 31 (September 1958), 312-23, 336-39.
"The Portrait of a Lady" by Leon Edel (pp. 94-105). Reprinted from 1962.A1.
"The Fearful Self: Henry James's The Portrait of a Lady" by Tony Tanner (pp. 106-22). Reprinted from 1965.B106.

*6 SEIFFERT, ALICE. Schraubendrehungen, Aus Dem Amerikanisschen Übertragen. Mit einem Nachwort von Rudolf Suhnel. Stuttgart: Reclam.
Cited in Beatrice Ricks, comp. Henry James: A Bibliography of Secondary Works. Scarecrow Author Bibliographies, No. 24. Metuchen, N.J.: Scarecrow, 1975, Item 1374.1.

7 TOMPKINS, JANE P. Twentieth Century Interpretations of "The Turn of the Screw" And Other Tales. Englewood Cliffs, N.J.: Prentice-Hall, 115 pp.
Contents: Consists of twelve critical essays: ten are reprints of previously published criticism and two are published for the first time. Also included are a chronology of important dates and a selected bibliography.
"Introduction" by Jane P. Tompkins (pp. 1-10). An overview of the seven tales discussed in these essays includes an assessment of James's achievement in writing short fiction: "James achieved scope and complexity through concentration of focus, and the virtues of his method--subtlety of analysis and an imaginative grasp of possibilities--are passed on to the attentive reader of his stories in the form of a broader awareness of life arrived at through sharper perceptions."
"James's 'The Pupil': The Art of Seeing Through" by Terence J. Martin (pp. 11-21). Reprinted from Modern Fiction Studies, 4 (Winter 1958-1959), 335-45.
"'The Pupil': The Education of a Prude" by William Bysshe Stein (pp. 22-28). Reprinted from American Quarterly, 15 (Spring 1959), 13-22.

"James's 'The Real Thing': Three Levels of Meaning" by
Earle Labor (pp. 29-32). Reprinted from 1962.B54.

"Narrative Irony in Henry James' 'The Real Thing'" by
David Toor (pp. 33-39). Reprinted from 1967.B106.

"Henry James' 'The Figure in the Carpet': What is
Critical Responsiveness?" by Seymour Lainoff (pp. 40-46).
Reprinted from 1961.B57.

"Art as Problem in 'The Figure in the Carpet' and 'The
Madonna of the Future'" by Charles Feidelson, Jr.
(pp. 47-55). "Translated into the subject-matter of fiction, James's experience of the problematical in art yielded the artist-fable; this kind of ironic legend, half-
farcical and half-tragic, was his most immediate interpretation of the circles of significance that seemed to inhere
in the dubious practice of fiction."

"Edmund Wilson and The Turn of the Screw" by
M. Slaughter (pp. 56-59). Reprinted from 1966.A5.

"A Pre-Freudian Reading of The Turn of the Screw" by
Harold C. Goddard (pp. 60-87). Reprinted from Nineteenth-
Century Fiction, 12 (June 1957), 1-36. Also reprinted
1960.A6; 1966.A5.

"Imagination and Time in 'The Beast in the Jungle'" by
Elisabeth Hansot (pp. 88-94). "When the Beast has sprung
and Marcher is forced to see the real measure of his past
'in the chill of his egotism and the light of her use' it
is too late. Unknown to himself he had lived, been measured, and found wanting--by ordinary time."

"A Perspective on 'The Beast in the Jungle'" by James
Kraft (pp. 95-98). Reprinted from 1969.B78.

"The Ghost in the Jolly Corner" by Maxwell Geismar
(pp. 99-105). Reprinted from 1963.A2.

"Universality in 'The Jolly Corner'" by William A.
Freedman (pp. 106-109). Reprinted from 1962.B29.

8 WILLEN, GERALD, ed. Henry James, "Washington Square": A
Critical Edition. New York: Crowell.
Contents: Ten previously published essays and four new
ones constitute the "Criticism and Commentary" section of
this book. Also included are the text of the novel, a
preface, note on the text, James's Notebook Entry, and a
bibliography.

"Preface" by Gerald Willen (pp. v-vii). James himself
did not like Washington Square, and the novel has suffered
critical neglect.

"Note on the Text" by Gerald Willen (pp. vii-viii).
This text follows the Macmillan edition of 1881.

"From the Introduction to The American Novels and Stories of Henry James" by F. O. Matthiessen (pp. 175-77).

1970

Reprinted from <u>The American Stories and Novels of Henry</u>
<u>James</u>. New York: Knopf, 1947, pp. xi-xii.
    "From <u>The Method of Henry James</u>" by Joseph Warren Beach
(pp. 177-81). Reprinted from <u>The Method of Henry James</u>.
New Haven: Yale Univ. Press, 1918, pp. 228-32.
    "From <u>The Early Development of Henry James</u>" by Cornelia
Pulsifer Kelley (pp. 181-87). Reprinted from <u>The Early De-</u>
<u>velopment of Henry James</u>. Urbana: Univ. of Illinois
Press, 1930, pp. 278-83.
    "From <u>Turn West, Turn East</u>" by Henry Seidel Canby
(pp. 187-88). Reprinted from <u>Turn West, Turn East</u>. Boston: Houghton Mifflin, 1951, pp. 152-53.
    "From <u>Henry James</u>" by F. W. Dupee (pp. 188-90). Re-
printed from <u>Henry James</u>. New York: William Morrow, 1951,
pp. 62-65.
    "From <u>The Themes of Henry James</u>" by Edwin T. Bowden
(pp. 190-96). Reprinted from <u>The Themes of Henry James</u>.
New Haven: Yale Univ. Press, 1956, pp. 40-44.
    "From <u>The Comic Sense of Henry James</u>" by Richard Poirier
(pp. 196-215). Reprinted from 1960.A5.
    "From <u>Henry James: The Conquest of London</u>" by Leon Edel
(pp. 215-18). Reprinted from 1962.A1.
    "The Negative Gesture in Henry James" by Glauco Cambon
(pp. 218-21). Reprinted from 1961.B11.
    "The Dehumanizing Mind in <u>Washington Square</u>" by Leo
Gurko (pp. 230-43). "A principal theme of <u>Washington</u>
<u>Square</u> is the distortion imposed on the human personality
by the domination of one particular trait." The only
"balanced and whole" characters are Mrs. Almond and Mrs.
Montgomery. The narrative itself is "a remarkable revelation of the concealed liaisons between reason and passion."
    "Reason under the Ailanthus" by Mina Pendo (pp. 243-52).
In <u>Washington Square</u> "James gave us a novel about place, as
his title suggests, but not about people <u>living</u> in that
place."
    "The Critical Sublime: A View of <u>Washington Square</u>" by
Philip Roddman (pp. 252-63). Dr. Sloper "most nearly re-
sembles the Jamesian narrator of the later fiction, especially when early in his family ordeal the Doctor describes
his mind as a geometer's medium reflecting the surfaces and
profundities of human behavior, of what is visibly, in-
tensely there."
    "<u>Washington Square</u>: A Psychological Perspective" by
David J. Gordon (pp. 263-71). <u>Washington Square</u> is a
"sophisticated comedy, containing tragic elements and fea-
turing characters with highly refined manners." It is a
psychological tale, which is not worked out mechanically
but rather by the characters seeming to work out their own
destinies.

9 WINNER, VIOLA HOPKINS. Henry James and the Visual Arts.
   Charlottesville: Univ. Press of Virginia, 201 pp.
       An analysis of James's aesthetic and art criticism, his
   use of the visual arts in technique (both in the conception
   of fiction and in the writing of fiction), and his treatment of the artist figure and the connoisseur in his novels
   shows that an intimate relation exists between James's visual responses and his creative impulse. In various ways
   "James's cultivation of the art of seeing found expression
   in his practice and conception of the art of fiction." The
   culmination of his practice of converting "visual art experience into literary form" is found in The Golden Bowl.
   Reviewed: David K. Kirby, South Atlantic Quarterly, 70
   (1971), 420-21; Robert Falk, Nineteenth-Century Fiction,
   26 (1971), 239-42; Robert Emmet Long, New England Quarterly,
   44 (1971), 170-72; Lyall H. Powers, American Literature, 44
   (1972), 159-60; Adeline R. Tintner, Modern Fiction Studies,
   20 (1974), 273-79.

1970 B SHORTER WRITINGS

1 ANDERSEN, KENNETH. "Mark Twain, W. D. Howells, and Henry
     James: Three Agnostics in Search of Salvation." Mark
     Twain Journal, 15 (Winter), 13-16.
       The moral quest for "earthly salvation" ends quite dif-
     ferently in Twain's A Connecticut Yankee in King Arthur's
     Court, Howells's A Hazard of New Fortunes, and James's The
     Ambassadors: Hank Morgan's quest is a failure that ends in
     death; Basil March's quest brings salvation "within soci-
     ety"; and Lambert Strether's quest brings salvation at a
     high price—self-ostracism from society.

2 BASS, EBEN. "Henry James and the English Country House."
     Markham Review, 2 (February), [4-10].
       The key to understanding James's fictional country
     houses, which serve many purposes including thematic, sym-
     bolic, aesthetic, moralistic, and character elucidation, is
     most frequently found in their respective names.

3 BECK, RONALD. "James' The Beast in the Jungle: Theme and
     Metaphor." Markham Review, 2 (February), [17-20].
       "The beast in the jungle . . . is an extremely complex
     controlling metaphor that serves as the major unifying ele-
     ment of the story."

1970

4   BELLRINGER, ALAN W. "The Tragic Muse: 'the objective cen-
    tre.'" Journal of American Studies, 4 (July), 73-89.
        Although Miriam Rooth is the central character, she
    lacks the discriminative ability to be an interesting cen-
    tral consciousness. Sherringham and Dormer consequently
    carry "the weight of human interest."

5   BERRY, THOMAS ELLIOTT. The Newspaper and the American Novel,
    1900-1969. Metuchen, N.J.: Scarecrow Press, pp. 40-44.
        Merton Densher is a newspaper journalist, but James does
    not deal with Densher's work. And newspaper reporters in-
    vade the privacy of characters in The Reverberator, but the
    subject matter in this novel "transcends national bounda-
    ries." Thus James touched journalism very lightly in his
    works.

6   BEWLEY, MARIUS. "Death and the James Family" and "Henry
    James's English Hours," in his Masks & Mirrors: Essays in
    Criticism. New York: Atheneum, pp. 107-18, 119-38.
        Alice James's attitude toward imminent death, which is
    shared by her siblings, has its foundations in the theology
    of the elder James.
        For three reasons James's English Hours is of interest
    to Jamesian students: (1) its stylistic contrast with The
    American Scene reveals an evolving artistic process that
    culminates in a fusion of metaphor and meaning; (2) it con-
    tains passages that exemplify the pitfalls of detachment
    and nonparticipation; and (3) it lucidly reflects James's
    Anglophilian proclivity.

7   BIER, JESSE. "The Romantic Coordinates of American Litera-
    ture." Bucknell Review, 18 (Fall), 16-33.
        American Romanticism and Realism establish "coordinates
    for our whole consciousness" and prepare "for our inter-
    mittent accesses to the truth between the extremes and to
    a future wisdom which may yet be our consummation."

8   BIXLER, J. SEELYE. "James Family Letters in Colby College Li-
    brary." Colby Library Quarterly, 9 (March), 35-47.
        The Colby Collection of James family letters includes
    fifty-two letters from William (Henry's brother), sixteen
    from William's wife (Alice Gibbens James), twelve from
    Henry James, one from Alice James, two from Robertson
    James. Most of the letters were written to Mrs. Julius H.
    Seelye (Elizabeth Tillman James) and her sister, Mrs. Wil-
    liam H. Prince (Katharine Barber James). (Letters from
    Henry James's father, Alice James, Robertson James, and
    William James are included in the text.)

9   BLEICH, DAVID. "Utopia: The Psychology of a Cultural Fanta-
     sy." <u>DAI</u>, 30, 4935A-36A (New York Univ.).
          From 1870 through 1914 represents a transition period in
     Europe and America during which the utopian fantasy reached
     its zenith in popularity and then immediately began to de-
     cline. Accordingly, it offers a unique epoch for examining
     the utopian phenomenon. (<u>The Golden Bowl</u> is discussed.)

10   BOURAOUI, H. A. "Henry James and the French Mind: The Inter-
     national Theme in 'Madame de Mauves.'" <u>Novel</u>, 4 (Fall),
     69-76.
          "Madame de Mauves," an early James work, contains an
     openness toward and a perceptive grasp of French culture
     that will later culminate in his blending of European and
     American cultures.

11   BRENNAN, JOSEPH GERARD. "Three Novels of <u>Dépaysement</u>." <u>Com-</u>
     <u>parative Literature</u>, 22 (Summer), 223-36.
          James's <u>The Ambassadors</u>, André Gide's <u>L'Immoraliste</u>, and
     Thomas Mann's <u>Der Zanberberg</u> share a thematic interest in
     <u>Dépaysement</u>, the illusion that a change in the physical mi-
     lieu will be followed by moral changes.

12   BUITENHUIS, PETER. "Henry James and American Culture," in
     <u>Challenges in American Culture</u>. Edited by Ray B. Browne,
     Larry N. Landrum, and William K. Bottorff. Bowling Green,
     Ohio: Bowling Green Univ. Popular Press, pp. 199-208.
          Although James did not write specifically about the sub-
     ject we call popular culture, he did establish "the rela-
     tionship between manners and morals, between the need for
     articulateness and clarity in speech and that for articu-
     late criticism and clarity of vision about the ugliness of
     the man-made part of the American environment."

13   BURGESS, CHARLES E. "Henry James's 'Big' Impression: St.
     Louis, 1905." <u>Missouri Historical Society Bulletin</u>, 27
     (October), 30-63.
          James did not ever write the travel book that would have
     included his impressions of the western leg of his 1905
     tour, but he does make passing reference to St. Louis in
     <u>The American Scene</u>. (Includes reprint of a pamphlet, <u>Henry</u>
     <u>James: A Colloquy</u>, which reproduces James's conversation
     with members of the University Club of St. Louis on
     March 8, 1905.)

1970

14   BYATT, A. S. "Prophet and Doubter." <u>New Statesman</u>, 79
      (2 January), 16.
          There are two Robert Brownings--a fact not unobserved by
      Henry James--"the prophet who creates meaning and energy,
      and the doubter whose skepticism about the processes of
      self-knowledge and 'life' he creates are part of the crea-
      tion."

15   CARY, RICHARD. "Henry James Juvenilia: A Poem and a Letter."
      <u>Colby Library Quarterly</u>, 9 (March), 58-63.
          In the Colby Library James collection is an untitled
      poem found among the papers of Lilla Cabot Perry (Mrs.
      Thomas Sergeant Perry) in an envelope inscribed "Youthful
      poem of Harry James." The poem is probably a product of
      James's adolescence, but a brief letter in the Colby col-
      lection seems to have been written to a cousin (Katharine
      Barber James Prince) when James was only six years old.
      He asks for "a good strong tin sword" for Christmas.

16   CARY, RICHARD. "Vernon Lee's Vignettes of Literary Acquaint-
      ances." <u>Colby Library Quarterly</u>, 9 (September), 179-99.
          In the Vernon Lee letters at Colby are found more refer-
      ences to Henry James than to any other author. She referred
      to James as "kind," "wise," and "pleasant"; he was one of
      the few people who escaped her "noxious pellets."

17   CHESHIRE, DAVID, and MALCOLM BRADBURY. "American Realism and
      the Romance of Europe: Fuller, Frederic, Harland." <u>Per-
      spectives in American History</u>, 4:285-310.
          Three important minor fiction writers (Henry Blake Ful-
      ler, Harold Frederic, Henry Harland) knew Europe well. In
      tracing their views of Europe and of romance, "an interest-
      ing stage in the development of the literary expatriate
      sensibility" is illuminated.

18   CIXOUS, HÉLÈNE. "Henry James: L'écriture comme placement ou
      de l'ambiguité de l'intérêt." <u>Poetique</u>, 1:35-50. [French]
          James enjoys his own writing and regards his writing self
      as separate from himself. The wound which prevented his
      fighting in the Civil War led him to see himself not as an
      actor, but as a writer who replaced being with vision.

19   <u>Colby Library Quarterly</u>. "Special James Number." 9 (March),
      62 pp.
          Includes: 1970.B8; 1970.B67; 1970.B16.

20 CONN, PETER J. "Seeing and Blindness in 'The Beast in the
     Jungle.'" Studies in Short Fiction, 7 (Summer), 472-75.
        The destructive force in the story, which is centered in
     Marcher's blindness, is conveyed through carefully employed
     perceptual imagery.

21 CRANFILL, THOMAS M., and ROBERT L. CLARK, JR. "The Provoca-
     tiveness of The Turn of the Screw." Texas Studies in Lit-
     erature and Language, 12 (Spring), 93-100.
        James's provocative story, in addition to generating a
     plethora of criticism, has been the catalyst for many "cre-
     ative writers, parodists, anthologizers, illustrators," and
     dramatists.

22 CUMMINS, ELIZABETH. "'The Playroom of Superstition': An
     Analysis of Henry James's The Pupil." Markham Review, 2
     (May), [13-16].
        Pemberton is a deterrent to Morgan's education to reali-
     ty; and by encouraging Morgan to remain under the illusions
     of false beliefs and superstitions, Pemberton becomes re-
     sponsible for his death.

23 CURTIN, WILLIAM, ed. The World and the Parish: Willa Cath-
     er's Articles and Reviews, 1893-1902. 2 vols. Lincoln:
     Univ. of Nebraska Press, passim.
        Henry James is mentioned several times in Cather's arti-
     cles and reviews.

24 DITSKY, JOHN. "The Watch and Chain of Henry James." Univ. of
     Windsor Review, 6 (Fall), 91-101.
        Both John Fowles in The French Lieutenant's Woman and
     Saul Bellow in Mr. Sammler's Planet employ "a genuinely
     Jamesian mode of expression, an expansiveness born of ca-
     pacity and a richness of materials."

25 DOMMERGUES, PIERRE. "L'art romanesque de Henry James." Le
     Monde, 27 (7 March), iv. [French]
        Not until the centenary of James's birth did the United
     States accept the Jamesian concept of the novel. A James
     novel is the account the narrator makes; it is not charac-
     ter that interests James, but the relationships of charac-
     ters.

26 DONOGHUE, DENIS. "James's The Awkward Age and Pound's
     'Mauberley.'" Notes and Queries, ns 17 (February), 49-50.
        Pound's "Hugh Selwyn Mauberley" contains a passage which
     echoes the opening chapters of The Awkward Age. "Mauber-
     ley" contains several references to James.

1970

27   DUMITRIU, GHEORGHITA. "Henry James teoretician al romanului"
      [Henry James: The Theorist of the Novel], in Studii de
      literatură universală şi comparată [Studies on World and
      Comparative Literature]. Bucharest: Editura Academiei
      Republicii Socialiste România, pp. 181-99. [Roumanian]
            This essay considers James's ideas regarding the well-
      written novel as they are revealed in his critical writ-
      ings, particularly the Prefaces to his novels. Especially
      noted is James's insistence on a central consciousness and
      his use of "reflectors."

28   EAGLETON, TERRY. Exiles and Emigres: Studies in Modern Lit-
      erature. New York: Schocken Books, pp. 9-19.
            Henry James is mentioned several times in the Introduc-
      tion to this study of the theme of expatriation in twen-
      tieth-century literature.

29   EDEL, LEON. "Introduction," in his edition of The Ambassadors.
      The Bodley Head Henry James. Vol. VIII. London: The Bod-
      ley Head, pp. 5-10.
            "There is a legend that this book is 'tragic,' but to
      say this is to forget its humor, its ironies, its relaxed
      tone, its incomparable baroque style." The Ambassadors is a
      "milestone" in fiction, for it "inaugurated the fiction of
      the twentieth century."

30   EDEL, LEON. "Introduction," in his edition of Partial Por-
      traits. Ann Arbor Paperbacks. Ann Arbor: Univ. of Michi-
      gan Press, pp. v-xviii.
            James's personal experience with the craft of fiction
      and his personal contact with those about whom he was writ-
      ing renders his collection an "enduring book" with a style
      that "raises it above the flood of critical writing in re-
      cent decades."

31   EDEL, LEON, ed. "Introduction" and "Headnotes," in his edi-
      tion of Stories of the Supernatural. New revised edition.
      New York: Taplinger, pp. v-xlv, passim.
            A chronologically ordered collection of eighteen super-
      natural tales includes a prefatory note to each that pro-
      vides a historical, biographical, and critical context for
      the story. James's ghost stories grew out of his own ex-
      periences and family experiences with the occult and ex-
      traordinary dreams; his fictional treatment of the superna-
      tural presents an "impenetrable and mysterious" force which
      is not susceptible to precise definition or intelligent ra-
      tionalization. Originally published as The Ghostly Tales
      of Henry James.

1970

32 EDELSTEIN, ARNOLD. "'The Tangle of Life': Levels of Meaning
    in The Spoils of Poynton." Hartford Studies in Literature,
    2:133-50.
        The "unpredictable margin of difference" evident in the
    diverse critical responses to The Spoils of Poynton is in-
    dicative of the depth and complexity of the novel, which
    elicits responses (often contradictory) on varying levels
    and emphasizes the necessity of recognizing "the range of
    responses to the work that are possible."

33 FALK, ROBERT P. "The Writers' Search for Reality," in The
    Gilded Age. Edited by H. Wayne Morgan. Revised and en-
    larged edition. Syracuse: Syracuse Univ. Press,
    pp. 223-37.
        "James, the most truly original and talented artist of
    the period, was an American Victorian despite his distrust
    of much of the American scene and his rediscovery of Europe
    as a source of value."

34 FERNANDEZ, DIANE. "Henry James ou la richesse des possibles."
    Quinzaine Littéraire (16 February), pp. 77-90. [French]
        James's vision not only embraces and is sensitive to
    symbols of nature, it is as well a mirror and a memory of
    his childhood and adolescence. The multiple personalities
    of James's literary characters, though, are not a mere re-
    flection of his relatives and friends; each of them embod-
    ies a particular characteristic of James, as if each were
    a facet of a diamond. Similarly, homosexuality, though un-
    mistakably present, is not the secret key of James's works:
    it is only one of the many truths behind the author's mask,
    the author's art.

35 FISCHER, WILLIAM C., JR. "William Dean Howells: Reverie and
    the Nonsymbolic Aesthetic." Nineteenth-Century Fiction, 25
    (June), 1-30.
        "Howells's stylistic ideal is a graphic one, as opposed
    to James's symbolic uses of language that reach behind ap-
    pearances to metaphysical meanings."

36 FORDE, SISTER VICTORIA M. "The Aspern Papers: What Price--
    Defeat." Notre Dame English Journal, 6:17-24.
        An examination of Juliana's bargaining for the apart-
    ment, the first of three bargaining episodes, suggests
    "the dramatic density of all three scenes."

1970

37　FRANK, CHARLES P. _Edmund Wilson_. Twayne's United States Au-
　　thors Series, 152. New York: Twayne, pp. 49-55, passim.
　　　　"The Ambiguity of Henry James" is careless, ambiguous,
　　and weakened by Wilson's "biographical preoccupation."

38　GARDNER, JOSEPH HOGUE. "Dickens in America: Mark Twain, How-
　　ells, James, and Norris." _DAI_, 30, 4409A-10A (Univ. of
　　California, Berkeley).
　　　　Themes, techniques, characters, plots, incidents, and
　　literary devices borrowed from Dickens are "a massive pres-
　　ence" in the creations of Twain, Howells, James, and Norris.

39　GARIS, ROBERT. "Anti-Literary Biography." _Hudson Review_, 23
　　(Spring), 143-53.
　　　　Leon Edel's _The Treacherous Years: 1895-1901_ fails "to
　　demonstrate the validity or the relevance or the plain use-
　　fulness of . . . the secret of James' life." Review of
　　1969.B1.

40　GASS, WILLIAM H. "A Spirit in Search of Itself," "In the
　　Cage," and "The High Brutality of Good Intentions," in his
　　Fiction and the Figures of Life. New York: Knopf,
　　pp. 157-90.
　　　　In the first essay on William James, a comparison of
　　William and Henry is included. "In the Cage" is about
　　Henry James's life and Edel's biography, while the third
　　essay discusses Henry James as a moralist and contains an
　　analysis of _The Portrait of a Lady_.

41　GERSTENBERGER, DONNA, and GEORGE HENDRICK. _The American Nov-
　　el: 1789-1959: A Checklist of Twentieth Century Criticism
　　on Novels Written Since 1789. Vol. 2. Criticism Written
　　1960-68_. Chicago: Allan Swallow, pp. 189-218.
　　　　This checklist of criticism is arranged alphabetically
　　under titles of individual James works. A section of "gen-
　　eral" criticism is included.

42　GIBSON, W. M., and G. R. PETTY. "Project _Occult_: The Ordered
　　Computer Collation of Unprepared Literary Text," in _Art and
　　Error: Modern Textual Editing_. Edited by Ronald Gottesman
　　and Scott Boyce Bennett. Bloomington: Indiana Univ.
　　Press, pp. 279-300.
　　　　Occult, a revolutionary computer program designed to
　　collate forms of a text swiftly and accurately, was uti-
　　lized to collate the last pages of the 1879 and 1909 texts
　　of _Daisy Miller_. Analysis of the print-out demonstrates
　　the advantages of this method of collation.

43   GIOLI, GIOVANNA M. "Racconto psicologico e Romance in 'Daisy
      Miller.'" Studi Americani, no. 16, pp. 231-54. [Italian]
          The story of a pretty American girl on a tour of Europe,
      "Daisy Miller" is seen and narrated by Winterbourne. James
      makes use of this plot to carry an international theme, to
      portray the thematic opposition of a free, innocent, strong
      America against a traditional and corrupt Europe.

44   GOLDFARB, RUSSELL M. Sexual Repression and Victorian Litera-
      ture. Lewisburg: Bucknell Univ. Press, pp. 59-61, 63.
          James's Watch and Ward had been before the public
      ninety-two years when Leon Edel first pointed out the sexu-
      al overtones in the text.

45   GRIFFITH, ALBERT J. Peter Taylor. Twayne United States Au-
      thors Series, 168. New York: Twayne, pp. 24, 149-50,
      passim.
          Henry James's influence on Taylor is mentioned in this
      study.

46   GUNN, GILES B. "Criticism as Repossession and Responsibility:
      F. O. Matthiessen and the Ideal Critic." American Quarter-
      ly, 22 (Fall), 629-48.
          Matthiessen's description of the "Ideal Critic," who
      would make of "criticism nothing less than an act of the
      fully responsive and engaged self," is as relevant today as
      it was when it was formulated. Matthiessen was indebted to
      Henry James and realized "the close relationship between
      James and [T. S.] Eliot."

47   GUNTHNER, FRANTZ. "Henry James--Le romancier comme critique."
      Le Monde, 27 (7 March), v. [French]
          James's critical thought and critical terminology as ex-
      plained in his Prefaces have become part of the Anglo-Saxon
      theory of the novel. Contrary to Proust, James never nar-
      rated a novel by using the first-person point of view. In-
      stead, he employed a reflector, and the reader never knows
      more of happenings than the impressions of that reflector.

48   GURKO, LEO. "The Missing Word in Henry James's 'Four Meet-
      ings.'" Studies in Short Fiction, 7 (Spring), 298-307.
          The missing word in the opening paragraph is probably
      "alive."

1970

49　GUTWINSKI, WALDEMAR FRANCISZEK. "Cohesion in Literary Texts: A Study of Some Grammatical and Lexical Features of English Discourse." DAI, 30, 2990A (Connecticut).
　　A study of cohesion--"the relations obtaining among the sentences and clauses of a text"--is a useful linguistic approach to literary texts. Applied to two major American writers, it shows how James relied on the "grammatical features" of his work to achieve cohesion, while Hemingway is more balanced in his use of grammatical and lexical features to achieve cohesion.

50　HABEGGER, ALFRED. "The Disunity of The Bostonians." Nineteenth-Century Fiction, 24 (September), 193-209.
　　The Bostonians lacks unity because the successful Book One, showing James's social realism and ability as a satirist, is supplanted by the less successful Book Two, in which presentation of events, tone, and point of view are changed and an intrigue plot is introduced, showing James's other side as a psychological realist.

51　HAGEMANN, E. R. "'Unexpected light in shady places': Henry James and Life, 1883-1916." Western Humanities Review, 24 (Summer), 241-50.
　　Over a thirty-year period Life consistently confronted Henry James from several perspectives: (1) he was wittily satirized; (2) his expatriation was "strongly resented"; (3) his style was criticized; (4) he was parodied; and (5) his works were seriously reviewed.

52　HALL, WILLIAM F. "Caricature in Dickens and James." Univ. of Toronto Quarterly, 39 (April), 242-57.
　　Dickens and James differ in their use of "caricature of likeness" but are related in their subtly and complexly employed "caricature of equivalence," a method "that complicates rather than simplifies character motive and interpretation."

53　HAN, PIERRE. "Organic Unity in 'Europe.'" South Atlantic Bulletin, 35 (May), 40-41.
　　The opening sentence of "Europe" starts a rhetorical pattern which is completed with the final sentence of the story, demonstrating James's principle of organic unity.

54　HARDY, BARBARA, ed. Critical Essays on George Eliot. London: Routledge and Kegan Paul, passim.
　　Seventeen passing references to James.

272

55   HARLOW, GEOFFREY, and JAMES REDMOND, eds. The Year's Work in
      English Studies: Vol. 49: 1968. London: Published for
      the English Association by John Murray, pp. 400-402.
      Survey of criticism for 1968.

56   HARTSOCK, MILDRED E. "Biography: The Treacherous Art."
      Journal of Modern Literature, 1 (First Issue), 116-19.
         Despite the biographer's ability to evoke a living sub-
      ject, Edel's fourth volume is inconsistent in part with
      preceding volumes and appears to force the psychological
      premise at times where it does not naturally fit. Review
      of 1969.A1.

57   HOGSETT, ELIZABETH A. "'The Beast in the Jungle' and 'Old Mr.
      Marblehall': A Comparison." Laurel Review, 10:70-75.
         These two short stories by James and Eudora Welty are
      ironical horror stories that make use of symbols, but the
      most striking similarity is found in the two Prufrockian
      protagonists, Marcher and Marblehall.

58   HORRELL, JOYCE TAYLOE. "A 'shade of a Special Sense': Henry
      James and the Art of Naming." American Literature, 42
      (May), [203]-20.
         James's conscious use of names, chosen from nature, his-
      tory, and myth for their connotative value, reflects his
      values and interests; they are used to parody; to heighten
      awareness of social class distinctions, vocations, and na-
      tionalities; and to suggest moral or allegoric overtones.

59   HOWE, IRVING. "Henry James and The American Scene," in his
      Decline of the New. New York: Harcourt, Brace & World,
      pp. 112-21.
         Reprint of 1967.B49.

60   HUNTLEY, H. ROBERT. The Alien Protagonist of Ford Madox Ford.
      Chapel Hill: Univ. of North Carolina Press, pp. 118-20,
      passim.
         Ford's first novel, An English Girl (1907), was influ-
      enced by James.

61   IWASE, SHITSUU. "The American Scene and James's Creative
      Method." Studies in English Literature (English Literary
      Soc. of Japan), 46 (March), 141-52. [Japanese]
         The American Scene shows James's peculiar manner of
      creation, his "execution" or "doing." James's creativity
      is one with his being a "restless analyst" who tries to fix
      "Style" in the very void of American scenes. James's meth-
      od is related to the American Transcendentalists' view of

1970

style in which more meaning is attached to how to appreciate an object than to the object itself.

62 JOHNSON, RICHARD COLLES, and G. THOMAS TANSELLE. "The
Haldeman-Julius 'Little Blue Books' as a Bibliographical
Problem." Papers of the Bibliographical Society of America, 64 (1Q), 29-78 (Henry James, pp. 64, 65, 73).
    The publication in the 1920s and 1930s of the enormously
popular "Little Blue Books" raises a bibliographical problem. An addition to the Edel-Laurence Bibliography of Henry James indicates that the original issue of Daisy Miller
in the Little Blue Books was in the Ten Cent Pocket Series.

63 KARL, FREDERICK R. "Three Conrad Letters in the Edith Wharton
Papers." Yale Univ. Library Gazette, 44 (January),
148-51.
    Three previously unpublished letters are significant for
two reasons: (1) one indicates that Conrad and James tried
to "maintain their friendship" despite James's harsh criticism of Chance; and (2) the other two shed light on Conrad's critical preferences as revealed in his comments on
Wharton's Summer.

64 KAUL, A. N. "The Portrait of a Lady: Henry James and the
Avoidance of Comedy," in his The Action of English Comedy:
Studies in the Encounter of Abstraction and Experience from
Shakespeare to Shaw. New Haven and London: Yale Univ.
Press, pp. 250-83.
    One main problem with The Portrait of a Lady is that it
is "a comic novel laboring under an imposed sense of tra-
gedy."

65 KAY, WALLACE G. "The Observer and the Voyeur: Theories of
Fiction in James and Robbe-Grillet." Southern Quarterly, 9
(October), 87-91.
    While Robbe-Grillet is voyeuristically obsessed with
"the shapes and surfaces of things" and the facade of his
characters, James's interest in "things" is confined to
their ability to elucidate the depths of his character's
mind.

66 KELLOGG, GENE. The Vital Tradition: The Catholic Novel in a
Period of Convergence. Chicago: Loyola Univ. Press,
pp. 111, 114, 115.
    James influenced Graham Greene, particularly in "the use
of personality reflectors."

67 KENNEY, BLAIR G. "Henry James's Businessmen." Colby Library
    Quarterly, 9 (March), 48-58.
        One of the only nineteenth century novelists to treat
    the businessman with sympathy, James constantly portrayed
    him as possessing both shrewdness and naivete. Generally,
    James drew three types of businessmen: the type absolute-
    ly identified with his money (Jim Pocock); the Grand Old
    Man of business, who is both "ironic and complex" (Adam
    Verver); and the man whose "force and shrewdness" brought
    him success in business but not in human relationships
    (Christopher Newman).

68 KENNEY, WILLIAM. "Doctor Sloper's Double in Washington
    Square." University Review (Kansas City), 36 (Summer),
    301-306.
        Doctor Austin Sloper and Morris Townsend are remarkably
    similar (even where they initially appear dissimilar), so
    that the Doctor's insistence that Catherine abandon Town-
    send is an ironic insistence that she abandon the negative
    influence of both men.

69 KIMMEY, JOHN L. "The Tragic Muse and Its Forerunners." Amer-
    ican Literature, 41 (January), 518-31.
        The germinal themes, characters, and structures of The
    Bostonians and The Princess Casamassima are brought to
    aesthetic fruition in The Tragic Muse.

70 KORNFELD, MILTON HERBERT. "A Darker Freedom: The Villain in
    the Novels of Hawthorne, James, and Faulkner." DAI, 31,
    2883A (Brandeis).
        Villainy in the work of the three authors, although it
    is manifested in different forms, is commonly present in a
    protagonist who is using other people for his own selfish
    purposes. Chronologically examined, the three authors suc-
    cessively diminish the villain's ability to apprehend his
    own villainous nature.

71 KUHLMANN, SUSAN. "Knave, Fool, and Genius: The Confidence
    Man as He Appears in Nineteenth-Century American Fiction."
    DAI, 32, 4006A (New York Univ.).
        "The confidence man reveals much about the nineteenth-
    century American character and about the way in which that
    character was observed and evaluated by many of its signif-
    icant writers of that period." (Chapter Four studies
    James's adaptation of the character of the confidence man
    to the international scene.)

1970

72   LEARY, LEWIS, comp. <u>Articles on American Literature, 1950-67.</u>
     Carolyn Batholet and Catharine Roth, assistants. Durham,
     N.C.: Duke Univ. Press, pp. 296-324.
        A bibliographical listing of critical articles published
     on James from 1950 to 1967.

73   LE VOT, ANDRÉ. "Henry James--Le critique comme romancier."
     <u>Le Monde</u>, 27 (7 March), iv. [French]
        James turned from the realism of Wells and Zola to em-
     brace a theory of literature akin to that of Mallarmé.
     James's method has influenced the writers of today more
     than his work; his affirmation of threatened individualism
     has inspired major writers more than his subtle analysis of
     human relationships.

74   LIEBMAN, SHELDON W. "The Light and the Dark: Character De-
     sign in <u>The Portrait of a Lady</u>." <u>Papers on Language and
     Literature</u>, 6 (Spring), 163-79.
        The secondary characters in <u>The Portrait of a Lady</u> are
     psychologically and morally one-sided figures who either
     facilitate (the light figures) or impede (the dark figures)
     the quest of the protagonist in her movement to moral and
     aesthetic superiority.

75   LIND, SIDNEY E. "'The Turn of the Screw': The Torment of
     Critics." <u>Centennial Review</u>, 14 (Spring), 225-40.
        "The Turn of the Screw" is a literary case study of an
     hysteric (the governess). Contemporary in its psychologi-
     cal origins, it is also "the culmination of a particular
     kind of narrative technique."

76   LOMBARDI, OLGA. "Il Mito dell'America." <u>Nuova Antologia</u>,
     508 (February), 274-80. [Italian]
        In an anthology, the <u>Americana</u>, edited by Vittorini, the
     opinion of Henry James is biased due to Vittorini's dislike
     of any form of intellectualism, particularly that found in
     James's works.

77   LYNN, K. S. "Howells in the Nineties." <u>Perspectives in Amer-
     ican History</u>, 4:27-82.
        Howells suffered "a personal and artistic despair" dur-
     ing the 1890s, which was just as profound as the "more
     celebrated glooms" that afflicted Henry Adams, Henry James,
     and Mark Twain. (James mentioned in passing.)

78   McDOWELL, M. B. "Edith Wharton's Ghost Stories." <u>Criticism</u>,
     12 (Spring), 133-52.
          Wharton shares an "awareness of the metaphysical and
     symbolical implications of experience" with James and
     Hawthorne.

79   MAROVITZ, SANFORD E. "<u>Roderick Hudson</u>: James's <u>Marble Faun</u>."
     <u>Texas Studies in Literature and Language</u>, 11 (Winter),
     1427-43.
          The extensive similarities between James's <u>Roderick Hud-</u>
     <u>son</u> and Hawthorne's <u>The Marble Faun</u> include themes, con-
     flicts, settings, methods of construction, and characters.

80   MENIKOFF, BARRY. "Punctuation and Point of View in the Late
     Style of Henry James," <u>Style</u>, 4 (Winter), 29-47.
          In his late style James changed his punctuation and
     sentence structure "to facilitate his method of interior
     narration."

81   MILLER, JAMES E., JR. "The 'Classic' American Writers and
     the Radicalized Curriculum." <u>College English</u>, 31 (March),
     565-70.
          The often radical visions of Poe, Hawthorne, Melville,
     Emerson, Thoreau, Whitman, Twain, James, and Dickinson give
     them contemporary relevance. "The Beast in the Jungle" and
     <u>What Maisie Knew</u> are especially suitable for today's stu-
     dents.

*82 MIROIU, MIHAI. "The Makers of the Stream of Consciousness
     Novel." <u>Analele Universității București, Limbi germanice</u>,
     19:137-49.
          Cited in <u>Annual Bibliography of English Language and</u>
     <u>Literature for 1971: Volume 46</u>. Edited by John Horden
     and J. B. Misenheimer. Great Britain: MHRA, 1973, p. 455.

83   MORGAN, ALICE. "Henry James: Money and Morality." <u>Texas</u>
     <u>Studies in Literature and Language</u>, 12 (Spring), 75-92.
          The metaphoric and symbolic use of renunciation in the
     later works of James is prepared for in the early works
     where renunciation is seen on both a financial and an emo-
     tional level and is seen as being capable of both positive
     and negative potential.

84   MORSE, SAMUEL FRENCH. <u>Wallace Stevens</u>. New York: Pegasus,
     passim.
          Several references to Henry James.

1970

85 NAMEKATA, AKIO. "Some Notes on <u>The Spoils of Poynton</u>."
    <u>Studies in English Literature</u> (English Literary Society of
    Japan), English No., pp. 19-35.
       In Fleda Vetch's four encounters with Owen Gereth she
    emerges a triumphant and successful character by virtue of
    her ability to maintain "her idealistic moral sense and
    sympathetic imagination" and to act in a fashion that is
    never inconsistent with those ideals.

86 NETTELS, ELSA. "<u>The Ambassadors</u> and the Sense of the Past."
    <u>Modern Language Quarterly</u>, 31 (June), 220-35.
       Strether's personal longing to recapture his youth is
    intricately bound up in the passing of the old values em-
    bodied in Madame de Vionnet and the emerging new age iden-
    tified with Chad Newsome.

87 NICOLOFF, PHILIP L. "At the Bottom of All Things in Henry
    James's 'Louisa Pallant.'" <u>Studies in Short Fiction</u>, 7
    (Summer), 409-20.
       The avuncular narrator is the "hidden protagonist" in a
    story that deals with motives, intuitions, and perceptions,
    not the external events of the more visible characters.

88 NILON, CHARLES H. "Henry James," in his <u>Bibliography of Bib-
    liographies in American Literature</u>. New York and London:
    R. R. Bowker & Co., pp. 105-108.
       A listing of more than fifty sources of bibliographical
    information on James.

89 PEARCE, BRIAN. "Perpetuated Misprints." <u>Times Literary Sup-
    plement</u> (4 June), p. 613.
       There are a number of "perpetuated misprints" in <u>Wash-
    ington Square</u>, caused by the mechanical repetition of
    printer's errors from one edition to the next.

90 PILKINGTON, JOHN, JR. <u>Henry Blake Fuller</u>. Twayne United
    States Authors Series, 175. New York: Twayne, passim.
       Over twenty references to James.

91 POIRIER, RICHARD. "What Is English Studies, and If You Know
    What That Is, What Is English Literature?" <u>Partisan Re-
    view</u>, 37:41-58.
       To be relevant, English studies "cannot be the body of
    English literature but it can be at one with its spirit:
    of struggling, of wrestling with words and meaning."
    (James is compared to Herbert Marcuse; both considered that
    "art and literature are essentially higher forms of life.")

92 PRICE, REYNOLDS. "Introduction: The Wings of the Dove--a
    single combat," in The Wings of the Dove. Columbus, Ohio:
    Charles E. Merrill, pp. v-xix.
        This novel is not James's "masterpiece," but it is a
    work which demonstrates intensely and movingly "the dilemma
    of the artist whose subject has seized him and will not
    relent."

93 PURDY, STROTHER B. "Henry James, Gustave Flaubert, and the
    Ideal Style." Language and Style, 3 (Summer), 163-84.
        Although Henry James and Gustave Flaubert both espoused
    the style of the mot juste, a look at James's use of the
    word "clever" demonstrates not only the impossibility of
    the ideal but that his style in fact is opposite the impli-
    cations of the phrase.

94 PURDY, STROTHER B. "Henry James's Abysses: A Semantic Note."
    English Studies, 51 (October), 424-33.
        An analysis of the metaphoric uses of the word "abyss"
    shows "that the semantic range and thematic weight James
    applied to 'abyss' were unusually great."

95 REED, KENNETH T. "Henry James, Andrew Marvell, and The Aspern
    Papers." Notre Dame English Journal, 6:25-28.
        The thematic and imagistic similarities between James's
    novella and Marvell's "The Mower's Song" and "The Garden"
    suggest the novelist is indebted to the poet.

96 ROGERS, ROBERT. A Psychoanalytic Study of the Double in Lit-
    erature. Detroit: Wayne State Univ. Press, pp. 70-72,
    99-108, 113-14, passim.
        "The Jolly Corner," The Portrait of a Lady, and The Am-
    bassadors provide illustrative material for this examina-
    tion of the literary double.

97 RUPP, RICHARD H. Celebration in Postwar American Fiction:
    1945-1967. Coral Gables, Fla.: Univ. of Miami Press,
    p. 210.
        James's "esthetic method forced him away from the com-
    munal sharing and praise of life that underlie all celebra-
    tions."

98 SCHEYER, ERNEST. The Circle of Henry Adams: Art and Artists.
    Detroit: Wayne State Univ. Press, passim.
        In this study of the relationship of Henry Adams with
    Henry Hobson Richardson, John LaFarge, and Augustus Saint-
    Gaudens, a dozen passing references are made to James.

1970

99   SCHUHMANN, KUNO. "Ethic und Äesthetic im Spätwerk von Henry
      James." Jahrbuch für Amerikastudien, 15:77-87. [German]
         In the Prefaces to the New York Edition and in the later
      novels "ethical questions are presented in aesthetic
      terms." Strether in The Ambassadors is the artist whose
      experience leads him to see and then to understand; this
      aesthetic experience prepares him to make a moral decision.

100   SEARS, DONALD A., and MARGARET BOURLAND. "Journalism Makes
      the Style." Journalism Quarterly, 47:504-509.
         A comparison of four "journalist-novelists," Stephen
      Crane, Theodore Dreiser, Ernest Hemingway, and John Hersey,
      with four "non-journalistic writers," Henry James, Edith
      Wharton, Thomas Wolfe, and Truman Capote, demonstrates that
      "the style of four with journalistic background displays a
      tendency toward the elimination of semantic noise, charac-
      terized by compressed syntax, clear and active word choice,
      and concrete, objective detail."

101   SENANU, K. E. "Anton Chekhov and Henry James." Ibadan Stud-
      ies in English, 2:182-97.
         Despite the apparent differences between James's ideal-
      ism and Chekhov's realism, and despite the fact that the
      two authors apparently were unfamiliar with one another's
      works, they both dealt with the problem of form in very
      similar fashions and achieved very similar results.

102   SMITH, HERBERT F. Richard Watson Gilder. Twayne United States
      Authors Series, 166. New York: Twayne, pp. 81-85.
         While editor of The Century, Gilder probably neglected
      Henry James because of James's voluntary expatriation and
      because of James's unpopularity with Century readers.

103   SPECK, PAUL S. "A Structural Analysis of Henry James's Rod-
      erick Hudson." Studies in the Novel, 2 (Fall), 292-304.
         Structurally perceived, the theme of the novel can be
      represented in terms of concentric circles in which Roder-
      ick's rise and fall is intimately linked to Rowland's
      concerns.

104   SPILLER, ROBERT E., ed. The Van Wyck Brooks-Lewis Mumford
      Letters: The Record of a Literary Friendship, 1921-63.
      New York: E. P. Dutton, passim.
         Eleven references to Henry James in this collection,
      some of which reveal information about Brooks's The Pil-
      grimage of Henry James (1925).

105 SQUIRES, RADCLIFFE. "Allen Tate's The Fathers." Virginia
     Quarterly Review, 46 (Autumn), 629-49.
        The Fathers is termed "a triumph of the Jamesian view-
     point."

106 STAFFORD, WILLIAM T. "Henry James," in American Literary
     Scholarship: An Annual, 1968. Edited by J. Albert Rob-
     bins. Durham, N.C.: Duke Univ. Press, pp. 84-99.
        Survey of criticism published during 1968.

107 STEVICK, PHILIP. The Chapter in Fiction: Theories of Narra-
     tive Division. Syracuse: Syracuse Univ. Press, pp. 1-33.
        Radically revised version of 1967.B100.

108 STOEHR, TAYLOR. "Words and Deeds in The Princess Casamassi-
     ma." Journal of English Literary History, 37 (March),
     95-135.
        The Jamesian ideal of the relationship between language
     and reality ("to speak 'as people speak when their speech
     has had for them a signal importance'") was his "guarantee
     of authenticity" and his "defense against 'uncreating
     word' of the propagandist of the 'universal darkness' of
     the terrorist."

109 SWEETAPPLE, R. "Accepting the Unacceptable," in Australasian
     Universities Language and Literature Association: Proceed-
     ings and Papers of the Twelfth Congress Held at the Univer-
     sity of Western Australia, 5-11 February, 1969. Edited by
     A. P. Treweek. New South Wales: AULLA, pp. 224-30.
        A persistent feature of James's writing is his "use of
     the double," which is "consistently used in every short
     story and shows itself to be a corollary of the personality
     crisis, the central situation of his writing."

110 TERRAS, VICTOR. "Turgenev's Aesthetic and Western Realism."
     Comparative Literature, 22 (Winter), 19-35.
        Turgenev's eclectic aesthetic principles are inconsis-
     tent with those of Hippolyte Taine, Alphonse Daudet, Émile
     Zola, Edmond de Goncourt, and Henry James.

111 THORBERG, RAYMOND. "Germaine, James's Notebooks, and The
     Wings of the Dove." Comparative Literature, 22 (Summer),
     254-64.
        An examination of James's Notebooks reveals a more sig-
     nificant literary debt to Edmond About's Germaine than was
     acknowledged by Matthiessen and Murdock.

1970

112 TICK, STANLEY. "Henry James's The American: Voyons." Stud-
     ies in the Novel, 2 (Fall), 276-91.
         Tom Tristram and Newman are contrasted with Mrs. Tris-
     tram and Valentin de Bellegarde; whereas the latter pair is
     perceptive, the former pair fails to develop the "refine-
     ment of observation" necessary for moral discernment.

113 TOMPKINS, JANE P. "'The Beast in the Jungle': An Analysis of
     James's Late Style." Modern Fiction Studies, 16 (Summer),
     185-91.
         Use of parenthetical statement is the most outstanding
     feature of James's late style and "furnishes a key to his
     narrative mentality." In The Beast in the Jungle "the
     hard-won syntactical resolutions, delayed by frustrating
     qualifications, share, by virtue of their intensity and the
     sense they afford of welcome relief, the orgasmic nature of
     the story's conclusion."

*114 VAN AKEN, PAUL. "Crisis en Eenzamheid in de Jeud (II)."
     Nieuw Vlaams Tijdschrift, 23 (May-June), 504-20.
         Cited in Beatrice Ricks, comp. Henry James: A Bibliog-
     raphy of Secondary Works. Scarecrow Author Bibliographies,
     No. 24. Metuchen, N.J.: Scarecrow, 1975, Item 1408.

115 WAGENKNECHT, EDWARD. "The Mark Twain Papers and Henry James:
     The Treacherous Years." Studies in the Novel, 2 (Spring),
     88-98.
         Although Edel's biography contains much useful informa-
     tion, it is speculative in its Freudian interpretation.
     (Includes review of book on Twain.) Review of 1969.A1.

116 WALT, JAMES. "Stevenson's 'Will O' the Mill' and James's 'The
     Beast in the Jungle.'" Unisa English Studies, 8 (June),
     19-25.
         The similarities of Will and Marcher and of the thematic
     implications of the two works suggest that James's story
     was "directly inspired by 'Will o' the Mill.'"

117 WEINSTEIN, PHILIP M. "The Exploitative and Protective Imagi-
     nation: Unreliable Narration in The Sacred Fount," in The
     Interpretation of Narrative: Theory and Practice. Edited
     by Morton Bloomfield. Harvard English Studies 1. Cam-
     bridge: Harvard Univ. Press, pp. 189-209.
         The narrator "embodies a profound, if skeptical, version
     of the artist himself at work"; moreover, his theory "en-
     tails a process of verification" and "posits a view of ex-
     perience that are essential elements in James's fictive
     world."

118 WILLIAMS, RAYMOND. "The Parting of the Ways," in his The English Novel: From Dickens to Lawrence. New York: Oxford Univ. Press, pp. 119-39.
A discussion of the novel between the 1890s and 1914 includes the works of James, Conrad, Forster, Wells, Bennett, and Galsworthy.

119 WOLFE, DON M. The Image of Man in America. Second edition. New York: Thomas Y. Crowell, passim.
James is mentioned several times in this intellectual history.

120 WOODRESS, JAMES. Willa Cather: Her Life and Art. Pegasus American Authors. New York: Pegasus, passim.
Contains sixteen passing references to James.

121 WOODWARD, ROBERT H. "Punch on Howells and James." American Literary Realism, 3 (Winter), 76-77.
Harold Frederic reprinted in the Utica Observer and Albany Journal (21 April 1883) a satirical poem from the London Punch (24 March 1883), which was a humorous response to William Dean Howells's essay on Henry James in Century (November 1882).

122 YOUNG, MAHONRI SHARP. "Duveneck and Henry James: A Study in Contrasts." Apollo, 92 (September), 210-17.
The contrasting personalities of Duveneck and James are salient in their differing relationships with Lizzie Boott.

123 ZIMMERMAN, EVERETT. "Literary Tradition and 'The Turn of the Screw.'" Studies in Short Fiction, 7 (Fall), 634-37.
The governess's effort to explore and explain events in terms of literary frameworks reflects James's concern for the dangers inherent in the artistic process of "ordering" and distortion.

1970 C DISSERTATIONS

1 BURDE, EDGAR J. "The Double Vision of Henry James: An Essay on the Three Late Novels." DAI, 31, 1753A (Claremont).
The Ambassadors, The Wings of the Dove, and The Golden Bowl are characterized not by ambiguity but by their "clarity of double vision." In order to appreciate the novels the reader must alternately employ a "symbolistic" and a "realistic" mode of perception as James dramatizes "two irreconcilable points of view, the transcendent and the worldly."

1970

2　CHAPMAN, SARA SIMMONS.　"Henry James's Developing Perspective
　　of America:　An Examination of the Tales." DAI, 31, 2908A
　　(Ohio Univ.).
　　　　Divided into three periods, 1864-1879, 1880-1889, and
　　1890-1910, the hundred and twelve Tales reveal a balanced
　　attitude toward America.　Although James is critical of
　　America and toward the end of his career modulated "toward
　　despair and bitterness," there is a pervasive element of
　　"sympathic concern" that appears throughout his writings.

3　GREWAL, OM PRAKASH.　"Henry James and the Ideology of Culture:
　　A Critical Study of The Bostonians, The Princess Casamas-
　　sima and The Tragic Muse." DAI, 30, 5444A-45A (Rochester).
　　　　Present in each novel is a coherent ideology that "in-
　　fluences the development of action in each novel and de-
　　termines the deployment of characters as well as the degree
　　of sympathy extended to them."　Ultimately, James's ideo-
　　logical biases are responsible for the weaknesses present
　　in the works.

4　JONES, GRANVILLE HICKS.　"The Jamesian Psychology of Expe-
　　rience:　Innocence, Responsibility, and Renunciation in
　　the Fiction of Henry James." DAI, 30, 5447A (Pittsburgh).
　　　　The James canon conforms to "a single comprehensive
　　thesis:　that James saw and represented life as a prede-
　　termined process of initiation, frustration, retreat, and
　　reflection."　In this process James presents "innocence as
　　a given condition, responsibility as the common denominator
　　of involvement, and renunciation as the morally imperative
　　consequence of experience."

5　MacNAUGHTON, WILLIAM ROBERT.　"The First-Person Fiction of
　　Henry James." DAI, 31, 1805A-06A (Wisconsin).
　　　　An examination of fifty-one occurrences of the first-
　　person narrator from 1865 through 1901 provides a basis for
　　concluding that "the narrators of 'The Turn of the Screw'
　　and The Sacred Fount are important as methods and as
　　characters."

6　MAVES, CARL EDWIN.　"Sensuous Pessimism:　Italy in the Work of
　　Henry James." DAI, 30, 5450A-51A (Stanford).
　　　　Three themes--those of romance, betrayal, and sensuous-
　　ness--can be traced through their earliest and simplest ex-
　　pression in five short stories from 1870 to 1873 to James's
　　"crowning work of the international and Italian themes to-
　　gether," The Golden Bowl, where Prince Amerigo embodies
　　James's concept of the "Italian emotion."　For book publi-
　　cation see 1973.A3.

7   TEDFORD, BARBARA WILKIE. "Henry James's Admiration of Ivan
    Turgenev, an Early Influence 'Ineradicably Established.'"
    DAI, 31, 2404A (Pittsburgh).
        The influence of Turgenev, traced from its earliest oc-
    currence in the mid-1850s, is most obvious in James's char-
    acter portrayal—the aspect of Turgenev's art for which
    James had the highest praise.

8   THOMAS, GLEN RAY. "The Freudian Approach to James's 'The Turn
    of the Screw': Psychoanalysis and Literary Criticism."
    DAI, 31, 770A (Emory).
        An overview of the psychoanalytic interpretations of
    "The Turn of the Screw" reveals two common critical mis-
    takes: (1) they emphasize the early theories of Freud to
    the exclusion of his later more complex ideas; and (2) they
    demonstrate "too little concern with the assessment of lit-
    erature as literature."

9   VEEDER, WILLIAM RICHARD. "Watch and Ward: The Mixed Begin-
    ning." DAI, 31, 772A (Univ. of California, Berkeley).
        James's first novel is an exploration of impotence which
    can be related "back to Hawthorne's emasculated protagonists
    and forward to many sexually ambivalent males of Twentieth
    Century literature." Stylistically examined, the novel has
    five distinct elements that coalesce in his later works—
    "Augustan, essay, legal, coordinate and perceptual."

10 WEITHAUS, SISTER BARBARA MARIE, O.S.F. "Represented Discourse
    in Selected Novels of Henry James." DAI, 31, 407A-08A
    (Catholic Univ.).
        "Represented Discourse" in the form of "Represented
    Speech" is prominent in The Portrait of a Lady, The Princess
    Casamassima, The Bostonians, and The Tragic Muse. An exami-
    nation of this narrative technique in the four works reveals
    that it "makes a substantial contribution to James's narra-
    tive art by reason of its mimetic qualities and by making
    available a variety of stylistic options."

11 WOODARD, JAMES EDWIN, JR. "Pragmatism and Pragmaticism in
    James and Howells." DAI, 31, 408A (New Mexico).
        Both James and Howells rejected social and moral dogma-
    tism. James, like his brother William, "subscribed to an
    introspective method of self-knowledge"; whereas Howells,
    like another leading philosopher of the period, Charles
    Sanders Peirce, subscribed to an opposite epistemology—"to
    a perspectival method of self-knowledge, arguing that images
    of reality exist outside the human mind and that only fig-
    ments exist in the mind."

1971

<u>1971 A BOOKS</u>

1   BATTILANA, MARILLA. <u>Venezia Sfondo e simbolo nella narrative</u>
    <u>di Henry James</u>. Le Esperienze fiflesse, 2. Milan: Labo-
    ratorio delle Arti, 251 pp. [Italian]
        James's "Travelling Companions" and <u>The Art of Travel</u>
    relate his first impressions of Venice along with his en-
    chantment with the city. The influence of Venice can be
    seen in the works James wrote after his Venetian experience,
    works such as <u>The Princess Casamassima</u>, "The Aspern Papers,"
    and <u>Italian Hours</u>, as well as <u>The Wings of the Dove</u>, "The
    Chaperon," and others. James saw Venice with innocent and
    puritan eyes, which reduced him to a passive observer, ac-
    companied by constant regret that he could not experience
    the Venice Veronese and Tintoretto had painted.

2   FLOWER, DEAN. <u>Henry James in Northampton: Visions and Revi-</u>
    <u>sions</u>. Northampton, Mass.: Friends of the Smith College
    Library, 26 pp.
        Henry James visited Northampton, Massachusetts, on
    May 6, 1905, just after completing his national tour. He
    gave a lecture at Smith College and was photographed by
    Katherine Elizabeth McClellan, the Smith College photogra-
    pher. In <u>The American Scene</u> James remembered Northampton
    "with 'a pleased vision,' and associated it with a time of
    self-discovery and sudden productivity." (Includes twelve
    photographs of Henry James made by Katherine McClellan on
    his visit to Smith College in 1905.)

*3 MacGREGOR, MARGARET SCOTT. <u>The Conflict of Europe and America</u>
    <u>in Henry James until 1889</u>. Toronto: Univ. of Toronto
    Press, 128 pp.
        Cited in <u>The National Union Catalog: 1968-72</u>. Vol. 59.
    Ann Arbor: J. W. Edwards, 1973, p. 245.

4   MLIKOTIN, ANTHONY M. <u>Genre of the "International Novel" in</u>
    <u>the Works of Turgenev and Henry James: A Critical Study</u>.
    Univ. of Southern California Series in Slavic Humanities,
    No. 2. Los Angeles: Univ. of Southern California Press,
    149 pp.
        Prolonged periods of living abroad influenced both the
    themes and structures of James's and Turgenev's novels. In
    this study the "International Lives" of the two novelists
    are examined; three novels by each one are explicated in
    terms of the international theme; then, the two writers are
    compared in their application of international materials to
    fiction. <u>The American</u>, <u>The Portrait of a Lady</u>, and <u>The Am-</u>
    <u>bassadors</u> are discussed. Both Turgenev and James "accepted

cosmopolitanism as a noble effort to make their positions valid in the face of both their strong native instincts and their avidity for foreign cultures." For dissertation see 1961.C10. Reviewed: R. Freeborn, Slavonic and East European Review (July 1974), pp. 459-60.

5   POWERS, LYALL H. Henry James and the Naturalist Movement. East Lansing: Michigan State Univ. Press, 200 pp.
     The change in James's fiction during the 1880s, apparent in The Bostonians, The Princess Casamassima, and The Tragic Muse, is due to the influence on his work by the group of writers he called "the grandsons of Balzac," realist and naturalist writers he met in 1875: Gustave Flaubert, Edmond de Goncourt, Ivan Turgenev, Emile Zola, Alphonse Daudet, and Guy de Maupassant. More significant than direct influences which these writers may have had on particular works is the "broader general influence of the aesthetic principles and the professional attitude to the art of fiction which the group as a whole shared among themselves." James adapted the "literary mode and manners" of these writers in order to accomplish his own artistic purposes. Reviewed: 1972.B74; 1972.B87; 1973.B17; Martha Banta, New England Quarterly, 44:681-83; David A. Leeming, Comparative Literature, 24 (1972), 374-77; David K. Kirby, South Atlantic Quarterly, 71 (1972), 274-75; Leon Edel, Nineteenth-Century Fiction, 26 (1972), 498-99; James E. Miller, Jr., Modern Fiction Studies, 19 (1973), 267-70.

6   SAMUELS, CHARLES THOMAS. The Ambiguity of Henry James. Urbana: Univ. of Illinois Press, 235 pp.
     James faced two challenges in his fiction: "How to assert the essential difference between good and evil without oversimplifying their opposition, how to establish the validity of moral judgments without ignoring personal bias." His achievement in dealing with "moral antinomies" in his fiction is various, and his work can be evaluatively divided into three categories: "confused novels" (such as The Turn of the Screw and The Sacred Fount); "ambiguous" novels (such as The Bostonians and The Portrait of a Lady); and novels of "achieved complexity" (What Maisie Knew and The Ambassadors). Reviewed: 1972.B17; 1972.B34; Maurice Beebe, South Atlantic Quarterly, 71 (1972), 447-48; Leo B. Levy, American Literature, 44 (1972), 328-29; David K. Kirby, New England Quarterly, 45 (1972), 137-39; Sallie Sears, Modern Fiction Studies, 19 (1973), 263-66.

1971

7   STAFFORD, WILLIAM T., comp. <u>Merrill Studies in "The Ameri-</u>
     <u>can."</u> Columbus, Ohio: Merrill, 126 pp.
        Contents: Part 1, "From the Author," reprints three
     James selections, from <u>The Notebooks</u>, from an 1877 letter
     to William Dean Howells, and the Preface to <u>The American</u>.
     Part 2, "From the Reviews," includes George Saintsbury's
     1877 review and two anonymous responses to the novel, both
     published in 1877, one from <u>The Nation</u> and one from <u>Atlan-</u>
     <u>tic Monthly</u>. Part 3, "From Book-Length Studies," consists
     of excerpts from Joseph Warren Beach's <u>The Method of Henry</u>
     <u>James</u>, Constance Rourke's <u>American Humor: A Study of Na-</u>
     <u>tional Character</u>, and Oscar Cargill's <u>The Novels of Henry</u>
     <u>James</u>. The articles in Parts 4, 5, and 6 are listed below:
     Part 4, "Special Approaches" (George Knox and John A.
     Clair); Part 5, "Special Achievements" (James W. Gargano,
     D. W. Jefferson, Floyd C. Watkins, and William T. Staf-
     ford); Part 6, "The Context" (Cleanth Brooks).
        "Preface" by William T. Stafford (pp. iii-viii). <u>The</u>
     <u>American</u> is an "ideal introduction" to James's fiction be-
     cause of its "early place in the James canon; its progeni-
     tive treatment of the international theme; its balanced
     blend of melodrama and comedy; its free and easy style; its
     memorable fabulistic protagonist, Christopher Newman; and
     . . . the richly varied interpretative comment it has pro-
     voked."
        "Romance and Fable in James's <u>The American</u>" by George
     Knox (pp. 65-79). Reprinted from 1965.B61.
        "<u>The American</u>: A Reinterpretation" by John A. Clair
     (pp. 80-91). Reprinted from <u>Publications of the Modern</u>
     <u>Language Association of America</u>, 74 (December 1959),
     613-18. Also reprinted in 1972.B112.
        "Foreshadowing in <u>The American</u>" by James W. Gargano
     (pp. 95-97). Reprinted from <u>Modern Language Notes</u>, 74
     (December 1959), 600-601.
        ["Mrs. Tristram and a 'Sense of Type'"] by D. W. Jeffer-
     son (pp. 98-99). Reprinted from 1964.A4, pp. 89-90. In
     his characterization of Mrs. Tristram, James "depicts the
     restless, unsatisfied American woman."
        "Christopher Newman's Final Instinct" by Floyd C. Wat-
     kins (pp. 100-103). Reprinted from <u>Nineteenth-Century Fic-</u>
     <u>tion</u>, 12 (June 1957), 85-88.
        "The Ending of James's <u>The American</u>: A Defense of the
     Early Version" by William T. Stafford (pp. 104-107). Re-
     printed from 1963.B98.
        "The American 'Innocence': In James, Fitzgerald, and
     Faulkner" by Cleanth Brooks (pp. 111-26). Reprinted from
     1964.B16.

8 WEINSTEIN, PHILIP M. <u>Henry James and the Requirements of the
Imagination</u>. Cambridge: Harvard Univ. Press, 207 pp.
One of the chief paradoxes of James's fiction exists in
the "space between" the two modes of living identified by
Strether in his advice ("Live all you can!") and his example (renunciation). An understanding of this paradox illuminates what James means in his fiction by "living."
Analysis of such works as <u>Roderick Hudson</u>, <u>Portrait of a
Lady</u>, <u>The Ambassadors</u>, and <u>The Golden Bowl</u> shows James
treating the "fundamentally irreconcilable" two modes of
living, "vision and action." For dissertation <u>see</u> 1968.C15.
Reviewed: 1972.B87; 1972.B17; 1972.A34; William T. Stafford, <u>American Literature</u>, 44 (1972), 16-61; David K. Kirby, <u>New England Quarterly</u>, 45 (1972), 137-39; Sallie Sears,
<u>Modern Fiction Studies</u>, 19 (1973), 263-66.

1971 B SHORTER WRITINGS

1 ANDERSON, QUENTIN. <u>The Imperial Self: An Essay in American
Literary and Cultural History</u>. New York: Knopf,
pp. 166-244.
Contents include:
"<u>The Golden Bowl</u> as a Cultural Artifact" (pp. 166-200).
In James "the nascent imperial self conquers the great
world of European culture and art and carries it home in
triumph. This venture was launched in the 1870's and is
achieved with the publication of <u>The Golden Bowl</u>."
"The Coming Out of Culture" (pp. 201-44). "Henry James's
late work incarnates the claims of the imperial self in
form--the esthetic shape of particular novels--and marks a
further step in the process of our disassociation from the
imaginative priority of communal life."

2 AOKI, TSUGIO. "Language of Love and Language of Things:
Henry James's <u>The Wings of the Dove</u>." <u>Studies in English
Literature</u> (English Literary Society of Japan) (English
No.), 48 (October), 55-71.
<u>The Wings of the Dove</u> has "suggestive characteristics of
a psychological fable about the predicament of the free but
'disinherited' American spirit." Milly's attempt to par-
ticipate in life "takes the form of searching after the
possibilities of human relation, particularly of love."

1971

*3 ASOCIACION ARGENTINA DE ESTUDIOS AMERICANOS. Sextas jornados
de historia y literatura norteamericana y rioplatenese.
2 vols. Buenos Aires, [not paged].
Cited in 1971 MLA International Bibliography, vol. 1,
p. 2. Contents include:
"Los fantasmas de Henry James ante la critica" by Virginia Erhart [7 pp.].
"Nathaniel Hawthorne: Entre Henry James y el psicoanál-
sis" by Rosa Pastalosky [6 pp.].
"Henry James y el arte de la novela" by Jaime Rest
[4 pp.].

4 AUCHINCLOSS, LOUIS. "Introduction," in "The Spoils of Poynton" and Other Stories. Garden City, N.Y.: Doubleday,
pp. vii–xiv.
These five pieces are what is "needed to prepare the
person not already indoctrinated to read the great novels of
the master's final style." (Included are The Spoils of
Poynton, The Turn of the Screw, The Aspern Papers, "Daisy
Miller," and Washington Square.)

5 AUCHINCLOSS, LOUIS S. "Introduction," in Washington Square.
Illustrated by Lawrence Beall Smith. Mount Vernon, N.Y.:
Printed for Members of the Limited Editions Club at the
Thistle Press, pp. v–xii.
"The chief beauty of Washington Square . . . lies in its
expression––by background, characterization, and dialogue––
of its mild heroine's mood of long-suffering patience."

6 BELL, INGLIS F., and JENNIFER GALLUP. A Reference Guide to
English, American and Canadian Literature. Vancouver:
Univ. of British Columbia Press, p. 98, passim.
This practical introduction to research, designed for
the undergraduate, contains a number of annotated entries
for reference books about Henry James.

7 BERTHOFF, WARNER. Fictions and Events: Essays in Criticism
and Literary History. New York: E. P. Dutton, passim.
James is mentioned several times in this collection of
essays.

8 BHATNAGAR, O. P. "The American: A Revaluation." Indian
Journal of American Studies, 1 (November), 51–61.
The central problem of the novel, "that of knowing what
one is to one's own self," manifests itself in two different forms: (1) the Bellegardes and Mrs. Tristram wear social facades; and (2) Newman and de Cintre masquerade as
innocents. The problem is solved in typical Jamesian fashion as Newman expands his awareness and grasps his autonomy.

9   BIANCHINI, ANGELA. "Henry James e la Remington." <u>Nuova Anto-</u>
     <u>logia</u>, 511 (Fall), 259-63. [French]
          James spent the last years of his life trying to escape
     loneliness. As a consequence he had some homosexual expe-
     riences, described in Leon Edel's biography <u>The Treacherous</u>
     <u>Years</u>.

10   BLEICH, DAVID. "Artistic Form as Defensive Adaptation: Henry
     James and <u>The Golden Bowl</u>." <u>Psychoanalytic Review</u>, 58
     (Summer-Fall), 223-44.
          <u>The Golden Bowl</u> is both a culminating defensive reaction
     and "an adaptive and creative maneuver" that "transforms
     the unpleasant and frustrating experience in the theater
     into a technique of novel writing."

11   BLUEFARB, SAM. "The 'Radicalism' of the Princess Casamassima."
     <u>Barat Review</u>, 6 (Spring-Summer), 68-73.
          The motives of Christina Light typify those frequently
     found in upper-class radicals--she is selfishly involved
     in order to inject excitement into her bored existence.

12   BROOKS, CLEANTH. "The American 'Innocence': In James, Fitz-
     gerlad, and Faulkner," in his <u>A Shaping Joy: Studies in</u>
     <u>Writer's Craft</u>. London: Methuen, pp. 181-97.
          Reprinted from 1964.B16.

13   BROWN, ASHLEY. "Landscape into Art: Henry James and John
     Crowe Ransom." <u>Sewanee Review</u>, 79 (Spring), 206-12.
          James's Charleston chapter in <u>The American Scene</u> is the
     source for Ransom's "Old Mansion." In this book, James
     transcends the "social milieu" and makes his landscapes
     speak.

14   BROWN, R. CHRISTIANI. "The Role of Densher in <u>The Wings of</u>
     <u>the Dove</u>, by Henry James." <u>Moderna Språk</u>, 65:5-11.
          Merton Densher is the central character in <u>The Wings of</u>
     <u>the Dove</u>; it is through him that James presents his theme--
     "renunciation and sacrifice are a higher form of love and
     more to be sought than the consummation of passion."

15   BURGESS, CHARLES E. "The Master and the <u>Mirror</u>." <u>Papers on</u>
     <u>Language and Literature</u>, 7 (Fall), 382-405.
          The opinions of James as a person and as a writer which
     were expressed by the influential critic William Marion
     Reedy and his contributors to the St. Louis <u>Mirror</u> have
     thus far been ignored. Although Reedy had "genuine respect"
     for James, references to the novelist in the <u>Mirror</u> empha-
     size "his obscure style and supposed snobbishness" as well
     as his expatriation.

1971

16   BYERS, JOHN R., JR. "The Turn of the Screw: A Hellish Point
      of View." Markham Review, 2 (May), 101-104.
           James's prefatory words "supposititious" and "amusette"
      are pivotal in an interpretation that perceives of the
      governess as a dissembler, a lurer, and an agent of the
      devil that destroys Miles and deceives the audience.

17   BYRD, SCOTT. "Henry James's 'Two Old Houses and Three Young
      Women': A Problem in Dating and Assemblage." Papers of
      the Bibliographical Society of America, 65 (4 Q), 383-89.
           James's dating of this essay (1899) refers to the date
      he assembled the disparate material, not to the dates of
      composition which are several.

18   BYRD, SCOTT. "The Spoils of Venice: Henry James's 'Two Old
      Houses and Three Young Women' and The Golden Bowl." Amer-
      ican Literature, 43 (November), 371-84.
           The case of Prince Amerigo recalls the "endless strange
      secrets, broken fortunes and wounded hearts" of James's
      "Two Old Houses and Three Young Women," both of which focus
      on the effects historical plunder and despoilment in Venice
      have on young Italian nobility.

19   CADY, EDWIN. "Three Sensibilities: Romancer, Realist, Natu-
      ralist," in his The Light of Common Day: Realism in Ameri-
      can Fiction. Bloomington: Indiana Univ. Press, pp. 23-52.
           James's realism in "The Beast in the Jungle" stems from
      the technique whereby the story "proceeds through ever-
      intensifying suspense to simultaneous moments of emotional
      release and revelation for John Marcher and the reader."

20   CALISHER, HORTENSE. "Henry James," in Atlantic Brief Lives:
      A Biographical Companion to the Arts. Edited by Louis
      Kronenberger. An Atlantic Monthly Press Book. Boston:
      Little, Brown, pp. 405-407.
           Reprinted from 1967.B12.

21   CAPELLÁN, ANGEL. "Estudio estructural de las obras tempranas
      de Henry James." Atlántida, 9:586-603. [Spanish]
           Roderick Hudson and Portrait of a Lady can be analyzed
      in terms of visual and verbal techniques of formalistic
      criticism which reveal dramatic structures and internal
      architectures.

22 CERVO, NATHAN A. "'Our Lady of the Gulls': A Case of Polite
    Revenge." Barat Review, 6 (Fall-Winter), 22-32.
       The subject of this story is "policy and revenge; in
    short, polite but punitive warfare." In refusing to for-
    give the Baron for his indiscretions, Madame de Mauves,
    whose name can be translated "Our Lady of the Gulls," is
    "inflexible," "hardhearted," and shows herself to be "of
    the 'race' of Puritans."

23 CHAN, LOIS MAI. "Figures in the Carpet: A Study of Leading
    Metaphors in Six Realistic Novels." DAI, 31, 5354A (Ken-
    tucky).
       An examination of the metaphorical elements of Flau-
    bert's Madame Bovary, Tolstoy's Anna Karenina, Fontane's
    Effi Briest, Thackeray's Vanity Fair, James's Portrait of a
    Lady, and Ts'ao Hsüeh-Ch'in's Dream of the Red Chamber re-
    veals a similarity in the use of the metaphor to perform
    "various functions simultaneously, through its relation to
    setting, theme, characterization, structure, and often
    tone" that is not attributable to cultural or literary
    traditions.

24 CHARTIER, RICHARD. "The River and the Whirlpool: Water
    Imagery in The Ambassadors." Ball State Univ. Forum, 12
    (Spring), 70-75.
       Pervasive water imagery illuminates structure and mean-
    ing as well as perhaps serving as "the clearest and most
    lucid unifying element in the novel."

25 CHATMAN, SEYMOUR. "Henry James et le style de l'intangibili-
    té." Translated by Henri Quéré. Poétique, 6:155-72.
    [French]
       James's style in the late novels might be termed "in-
    tangible." James believed that the things worthy of inter-
    est in the world were not objects, but abstract construc-
    tions of a personal or cultural origin; his style reflects
    this belief. Excerpt reprinted from 1972.A2.

26 CONGER, S. M. "The Admirable Villains in Henry James's The
    Wings of the Dove." Arizona Quarterly, 27 (Summer), 151-60.
       James states the "moral ambiguities of life" by portray-
    ing sympathetic villains in Kate Croy and Merton Densher in
    order "to give his reader a refined notion of what is ethi-
    cal." Kate, though clever and socially adept, is neither
    good nor virtuous. The "trustworthy and conscientious"
    Densher is not always ethical.

1971

27   CONN, PETER J. "Roderick Hudson: The Role of the Observer."
     Nineteenth-Century Fiction, 26 (June), 65-82.
          In Rowland Mallet, James presents an observer, whose
     perception of events is analogous to an aesthetic act, or
     act of providence, in re-creation.

28   CROWL, SUSAN R. "Aesthetic Allegory in The Turn of the
     Screw." Novel, 4 (Winter), 107-22.
          "The Turn of the Screw," Jamesian autobiography, reveals
     his "awareness of a turning point in both his life and his
     art."

29   DELBAERE-GARANT, JEANNE. "Henry James's Divergences from His
     Russian Model in The Princess Casamassima." Revue des
     Langues Vivantes, 37:535-44.
          While maintaining the same basic characters and situa-
     tion, James altered his version of Virgin Soil to include
     a more elaborate design, to evoke a different tone, and to
     emphasize his particular thematic preoccupations.

30   DYSON, A. E. "On Knowing What Maisie Knew, Perhaps," in On
     the Novel: A Present for Walter Allen on His 60th Birth-
     day from His Friends and Colleagues. Edited by B. S.
     Benedikz. London: Dent, pp. 128-39.
          "But perhaps what Maisie has basically come to know is
     social realism: her choice is a final perception of the
     law of her life."

31   EDEL, LEON. "Introduction," in his edition of The Golden
     Bowl. The Bodley Head Henry James. Vol. IX. London:
     The Bodley Head, pp. 7-13.
          "In its imagination and its language The Golden Bowl is
     a work of great beauty and intensity, an exemplar of the
     ways in which a novel could deal . . . with 'the great
     relation'--that is the life of the emotions and passions
     on other than the simplified terms of sexual coupling."

32   EICHELBERGER, CLAYTON L., comp., assisted by Karen L. Bickley,
     et al. A Guide to Critical Reviews of United States Fic-
     tion, 1870-1910. Metuchen, N.J.: Scarecrow Press,
     pp. 177-82.
          Critical reviews of James's work are listed under in-
     dividual works.

33 ENGSTRØM, SUSANNE. "Epistemological and Moral Validity in
Henry James's The Ambassadors." Language and Literature,
1:50-65.
The reader of The Ambassadors is faced with the problem
of Strether's reliability as a narrator, as well as his
"moral validity." For response see 1972.B36. See also
1973.B22.

34 FAHEY, PAUL. "What Maisie Knew: Learning Not to Mind." The
Critical Review, 14:96-108.
As the study of Maisie evolved, the problem of how to
deal with the intensity of her emotions became an increasingly intractable problem, one which James was unwilling to
confront, until Maisie and "the prose itself . . . breaks
down."

35 FINGLETON, DAVID. "The Knot Garden and Owen Wingrave: Operatic Development or Experiment?" Contemporary Review, 119
(November), 246-51.
Whereas Tippett's The Knot Garden, which was written for
the Opera House, appears to have potential for a television
performance, Britten's Owen Wingrave, which may have been
subconsciously written for television, is limited by the
medium in terms of its "passion," "pathos," and "positive
musical development."

36 FINN, C. M. "Commitment and Identity in The Ambassadors."
Modern Language Review, 66 (July), 522-31.
The modernity of The Ambassadors is evident in the "semi-
naturalistic account of a consciousness searching for identity." A new direction and moral commitment follow the
found identity.

37 FLYNN, T. E. "Henry James's Journey from the Interior." Dalhousie Review, 51 (Spring), 96-104.
Peter Buitenhuis's The Grasping Imagination is a "highly
readable, richly informative and often remarkably perceptive" reading of James's "American" works, but it is weakened by a misapplication of Gombrichean schemata—the
schemata governing the major phase is not literary but
philosophical and psychological. Review of 1970.A1.

38 FRANK, FREDERICK S. "The Two Taines of Henry James." Revue
des Langues Vivantes, 45:350-65.
Throughout his life James was simultaneously attracted
to Taine, "the pure artist, the sensitive prose-impression-
ist, the refined image-maker and stylist," and antagonized

1971

by Taine, "the narrowminded critic, intractable, over-
methodic, self-doxological, pontificating and harshly
formulaic in his views."

39   FREEMAN, ARTHUR. "Henry James and Dickens." Times Literary
Supplement (12 March), p. 296.
A Letter to the Editor suggests that The Princess
Casamassima is completely inaccurate as a picture of political life in London and must not be taken for a "literal
as well as literary" interpretation of the world. Response
to 1971.B101. See also 1971.B100; 1971.B68; 1971.B69;
1971.B102.

40   FUJITA, EIICHI. "Fleda's Free Spirit: Henry James: The
Spoils of Poynton." Kenkyu Ronshu (Kansai Gaikokugo
Univ.), 16 (February), 35-60. [Japanese]
Fleda is a free spirit, who is perceptive to life, especially to love and beauty, and is endowed with imagination
and a keen moral sense. Poynton symbolizes modern contra-
diction and disorder, and the spoils represent a precursor
of modern evil.

41   GALE, ROBERT L. "Henry James," in Eight American Authors: A
Review of Research and Criticism. Edited by James Woodress.
Revised edition. New York: Norton, pp. 321-75.
This essay surveying James scholarship is divided into
five major sections: Bibliography, Editions, Manuscripts,
Biography, and Criticism.

42   GETTMANN, ROYAL A. "Landscape in the Novel." Prairie Schoo-
ner, 45 (Fall), 239-44.
This article on landscape mentions "James's call for
unity and 'close texture'" in the novel as well as his
opinion that "the way to achieve the closest possible texture is to see the external world through the eyes of a
character in the novel."

43   GILLEN, FRANCIS. "The Dramatist in His Drama: Theory vs. Effect in The Awkward Age." Texas Studies in Literature and
Language, 12 (Winter), 663-74.
James's novelistic instinct necessitated his intrusion
in The Awkward Age in order to control the novel's meaning.

44   GINDIN, JAMES. "Howells and James," in his Harvest of a Quiet
Eye: The Novel of Compassion. Bloomington: Indiana Univ.
Press, pp. 102-28.
An overview of the literary productions of both Howells
and James reveals a movement toward fiction that was de-

creasingly moralistic and increasingly sympathetic bringing
their writings into confluence with "the tradition of compassion already apparent in English fiction."

45 GIOLI, GIOVANNA MOCHI. "The Turn of the Screw nelle sue oppo-
    sizioni strutturali." Studi Americani, no. 17, pp. 75-92.
    [Italian]
    The Turn of the Screw is composed of two major parallel
    plots: one dealing with the children, Miles and Flora, and
    their relations with the phantoms; the other with the
    governess-observer-narrator. Symbolically, not only light
    takes an important place with all of its shades of glow,
    glitter, gloom, glimmer, and glare, but Miles himself is a
    symbol of the coexistence of two opposite values: the Good
    and the Evil. Miles, furthermore, shares characteristics
    of isolation, exceptional beauty, intelligence, regality,
    musicality, happiness, isolation, as well as supernatural,
    angelic and devilish elements, together with images of
    sickness, old age and violent death, with Dolcino in "The
    Author of Beltraffio" and Morgan in "The Pupil."

46 GROSS, THEODORE L. "Henry James: The Illusion of Freedom,"
    in his The Heroic Ideal in American Literature. New York:
    Free Press; London: Collier-Macmillan, pp. 68-84.
    James's early fiction features Emersonian heroes who are
    convinced they are free; but with the novels of the 1880s
    and 1890s, James is searchingly questioning the ideal of
    freedom. Finally, in The Ambassadors Strether speaks of
    "the illusion of freedom."

47 GROVER, P. R. "Two Modes of Possessing--Conquest and Appreci-
    ation: The Princess Casamassima and L'éducation sentimen-
    tale." Modern Language Review, 66 (October), 760-71.
    Not the common French subjugation, but a radical, sympa-
    thetic and "receptive assimilation" characterizes James's
    response to "the agglutinative imagination of man as he
    tries to subsume the world to himself."

48 HABEGGER, ALFRED. "Reciprocity and the Market Place in The
    Wings of the Dove and What Maisie Knew." Nineteenth-
    Century Fiction, 25 (March), 455-73.
    What Maisie Knew and The Wings of the Dove show, in
    their distinction between contract and gift, that the prin-
    ciple of reciprocity is an important part of James's "moral
    sensibility"; it is connected with beauty (as symmetry),
    responsibility, and intelligence.

1971

49   HALL, WILLIAM F. "The Continuing Relevance of Henry James'
      The American Scene." Criticism, 13 (Spring), 151-65.
          In The American Scene James delineates the problems of
      American identity, American society, and American art as
      they confront the modern American.

50   HALVERSON, JOHN. "Late Manner, Major Phase." Sewanee Review,
      79 (Spring), 214-31.
          James's early style has "grace and wit and strength,"
      but the late style is mannered: "James's verbal tics are
      generally ludicrous, his vocabulary inflated, his syntax
      ponderous; his ear is pure tin." Perhaps "the loss of
      stylistic elegance was the price James had to pay for the
      vision of the major phase . . . ."

51   HARLOW, GEOFFREY, ed. The Year's Work in English Studies:
      Jubilee Volume: No. 50: 1969. London: Published for
      the English Association by John Murray, pp. 408-409.
          Survey of criticism for 1969.

52   HARTSOCK, MILDRED E. "The Conceivable Child: James and the
      Poet." Studies in Short Fiction, 8 (Fall), 569-74.
          In "The Birthplace" James is illustrating the necessity
      of tempering the facts of criticism and biography with ar-
      tistic imagination.

53   HARVEY, J. R. Victorian Novelists and Their Illustrators.
      New York: New York Univ. Press, pp. 166-67, 176.
          James objected to the illustrating of novels, which
      should themselves be "pictorial enough."

54   HATCHER, JOE B. "Shaw the Reviewer and James's Guy Domville."
      Modern Drama, 14 (December), 331-34.
          Shaw's review, which reflects his tolerance and critical
      acumen, is primarily critical of James but does praise his
      perceptiveness.

55   HAVLICE, PATRICIA P. "Henry James," in Index to American Au-
      thor Bibliographies. Metuchen, N.J.: Scarecrow Press,
      pp. 90-91.
          A listing of fourteen James bibliographies.

56   HEILMAN, ROBERT B. "Foreword" [to Eric Voegelin's "A Letter
      to Robert Heilman"]. Southern Review, 7 (January), 6-8.
          Eric Voegelin's interpretive letter on The Turn of the
      Screw is complex, anticipatory of later interpretations,
      and unique in three points: "his interpretation of employ-
      er and governess, his emphasis on the problem of communica-

tion, and his view of the incestuous relationships as symbolic rather than simply psychological." Foreword to
1971.B126. See also 1971.B115; 1971.B127.

57 HELLMAN, GEOFFREY T. "Leon Edel." New Yorker, 47 (13 March),
    43-86.
        Edel has worked on James since his 1932 doctoral disser-
    tation at the Sorbonne. In addition to the biography, he
    has made countless major contributions to James studies.
    His major work, beginning in the 1940s, played a signifi-
    cant part in the revival of critical interest in Henry
    James.

58 HUMMA, JOHN B. "The 'Engagement' of Daisy Miller." Research
    Studies, 39:154-55.
        In sending the repeated message to Winterbourne that she
    is not engaged, Daisy's purpose is to indicate to him
    through "a sort of euphemistic shorthand" that she is
    innocent.

59 KEATING, P. J. The Working Classes in Victorian Fiction.
    London: Routledge and Kegan Paul, pp. 46-52.
        In this study of the "urban and industrial working
    classes" James's The Princess Casamassima is examined in a
    demonstration of how even a major literary talent fails to
    break away from the class stereotypes dictated by literary
    and social conventions.

60 KENNEY, WILLIAM. "The Death of Morgan in James's 'The Pupil.'"
    Studies in Short Fiction, 8 (Spring), 317-22.
        Since there is no clear evidence that Pemberton rejected
    Morgan, the Moreens are morally responsible for Morgan's
    death.

61 KING, SISTER M. JUDINE. "An Explication of 'At the Grave of
    Henry James,' by W. H. Auden." Horizontes, 25:61-65.
        Like Milton's "Lycidas," Auden's elegiac tribute to
    Henry James becomes a vehicle for exploration of the poet's
    own personal concerns and emotions.

62 KIRBY, DAVID K. "Two Modern Versions of the Quest." Southern
    Humanities Review, 5 (Fall), 387-95.
        W. H. Auden's assessment of the durability of the quest
    motif is validated in James's The Turn of the Screw and
    Thomas Pynchon's The Crying of Lot 49.

1971

63 KIRKHAM, E. BRUCE. "A Study of Henry James's 'Mdme. de
    Mauves.'" <u>Ball State Univ. Forum</u>, 12 (Spring), 63-69.
        In James's study of an international conflict situation,
    the principal character, Longmore, avoids the extreme re-
    actions of Euphemia and the de Mauves family and achieves
    a degree of self-understanding.

64 KNIEGER, BERNARD. "James's 'Paste.'" <u>Studies in Short Fic-
    tion</u>, 8 (Summer), 468-69.
        Charlotte is a foil to the ignoble Arthur and Mrs. Guy,
    and her decision to return the pearls is evidence of her
    moral perspicacity, not excessive scrupulousness.

65 LABRIE, ERNEST ROSS. "The Morality of Consciousness in Henry
    James." <u>Colby Library Quarterly</u>, 9 (December), 409-24.
        A study of <u>Washington Square</u>, <u>The Portrait of a Lady</u>,
    <u>The Bostonians</u>, and <u>The Awkward Age</u> reveals a conception of
    morality, developed under James's proclivity for intellec-
    tualism, that integrates levels of consciousness with good
    and evil.

66 LAUER, KRISTIN O. "Backdoor to James: The Nature of Plot-
    ting." <u>Michigan Academician</u>, 3 (Spring), 107-11.
        The plots of the later novels are in two modes, tragic
    and romantic. The tragic plot may be labeled "internal,"
    and the romantic (or comic) plot may be labeled "external."

67 LEARY, LEWIS, ed. <u>Criticism: Some Major American Writers</u>.
    New York: Holt, Rinehart & Winston, pp. 165-92.
        Includes "Henry James" by Lewis Leary, a brief biblio-
    graphical essay on James; and "Henry James and the Morality
    of Fiction" by Robert J. Reilly, reprinted from 1967.B85.

68 LEAVIS, F. R. "Henry James and Dickens." <u>Times Literary Sup-
    plement</u> (5 March), p. 271.
        Leavis responds to S. Gorley Putt's claim that James's
    pictures of London life in <u>The Princess Casamassima</u> came
    from first-hand views by maintaining that the novel has a
    "radical dependence" on <u>Little Dorrit</u>. Further, Leavis
    denies any discordance between his 1937 and 1971 opinions
    concerning James's novel. Response to 1971.B100. <u>See also</u>
    1971.B101; 1971.B39; 1971.B69; 1971.B102.

69 LEAVIS, F. R. "Henry James and Dickens." <u>Times Literary Sup-
    plement</u> (19 March), p. 325.
        <u>The Princess Casamassima</u> is a "miserable failure." <u>See</u>
    1971.B100; 1971.B68; 1971.B101; 1971.B39; 1971.B102.

70 LIEBMAN, SHELDON W. "Point of View in The Portrait of A Lady."
    English Studies, 52 (April), 136-47.
        Isabel Archer discovers "that points of view are as nu-
    merous as the people who have them." Her sympathy and
    understanding are the result of the knowledge "that points
    of view are not one--but multi-dimensional."

71 LINCECUM, J. B. "A Victorian Precursor of the Stream-of-
    Consciousness Novels: George Meredith." South-Central
    Bulletin: Studies, 31 (Winter), 197-200.
        Meredith's experiments with the subject matter and the
    forms of the stream of consciousness novel establish his
    seminal role in the development of the genre. Henry James,
    whose experiments with point of view are regarded as "ush-
    ering in stream of consciousness," knew Meredith's work
    well.

72 LODGE, DAVID. The Novelist at the Crossroads and Other Essays
    on Fiction and Criticism. Ithaca, N.Y.: Cornell Univ.
    Press, passim.
        In this collection of previously published critical es-
    says, two dozen passing references to James appear.

73 LONG, ROBERT E. "Adaptations of Henry James's Fiction for
    Drama, Opera, and Films; with a Checklist of New York The-
    atre Critics' Reviews." American Literary Realism, 4
    (Summer), 268-78.
        A checklist of James's work adapted for film and stage
    includes thirteen stage adaptations, two opera versions,
    four film productions, as well as a listing of New York re-
    views for James plays presented in New York City between
    1929 and 1962.

74 LUCAS, WILLIAM JOHN. "Conservatism and Revolution in the
    1880s," in his Literature and Politics in the Nineteenth
    Century. London: Methuen (distributed by Barnes and
    Noble), pp. 195-217.
        A comparison of Mallock's The Old Order and Gissing's
    Demos with James's The Princess Casamassima reveals that
    "James comes much closer to their ideas and errors than it
    has been the usual practice to notice."

75 McCARTHY, HAROLD T. "Henry James and the American Aristocra-
    cy." American Literary Realism, 4 (Winter), 61-71.
        The "American elite," who were James's associates in
    both America and Europe, provided the subject matter for
    novels portraying the international theme (such as The
    American, Daisy Miller, The Ambassadors) in which James

1971

criticized these Americans for being "opposed to what was
traditionally valued as distinctive in the American spirit."
James saw the danger of the wealthy, powerful, and exclu-
sive forces "to a society that had prided itself on being
open, generous, and dedicated to an ideal of human community."

76   McELRATH, JOSEPH R. "Thoreau and James: Coincidence in
      Angles of Vision?" in Thoreau Symposium, American Trans-
      cendental Quarterly, 11 (Summer), 14-15.
           Walden's "'I' voice" and Lord Warburton have a compara-
      ble "angle of vision" suggesting a possible Thoreauvian
      influence.

77   McLEAN, ROBERT C. "The Bostonians: New England Pastoral."
      Papers on Language and Literature, 7 (Fall), 374-81.
           James's controlling motif in The Bostonians is derived
      from pastoral literature. He exploits two basic pastoral
      metaphors in order to give his novel structure, and give
      "symbolic significance to its setting, and insight into
      its major characters."

78   McMANIS, JO AGNEW. "Edith Wharton's Hymns to Respectability."
      Southern Review, 7 (Autumn), 986-93.
           The suffering from self-sacrifice and self-denial of
      Wharton's characters is a theme associated more with the
      works of Marcel Proust than with Henry James's work.

79   MAIXNER, PAUL. "James on D'Annunzio--'A High Example of Ex-
      clusive Estheticism.'" Criticism, 13 (Summer), 291-311.
           James's essay on D'Annunzio in Quarterly Review (1904)
      is an important critical announcement, suggesting that "the
      value of a work and its unity of form are proportional to
      the degree of integration of the moral and the aesthetic."
      D'Annunzio, who holds the aesthetic principle uppermost, is
      a "'masterful specimen'" of the aesthetic.

80   MALIN, IRVING. "The Authoritarian Family in American Fic-
      tion." Mosaic, 4:153-73.
           Certain archetypes such as the "rigid father," the "in-
      effectual son," and the "terrifying shrew" recur in the
      works of Cooper, Poe, Hawthorne, Melville, James, and
      Faulkner. James's portrayal of women, authoritative or
      passive, is more significant than his treatment of the
      "father-son relationship."

1971

81 MARKS, SITA PATRICIA. "The Sound and the Silence: Nonverbal
    Patterns in The Wings of the Dove." Arizona Quarterly, 27
    (Summer), 143-50.
        Silence is used as "communication and pattern in the
    novel." Milly's life is lost and Kate's and Merton's rela-
    tionship destroyed "by the power of silence."

82 MENIKOFF, BARRY. "The Subjective Pronoun in the Late Style of
    Henry James." English Studies, 52 (October), 436-41.
        James uses the third person pronoun to engage the reader
    in "the character's subjective adventure."

83 MIKKELSEN, NINA M. "A Redefinition of the International Nov-
    el: Studies in the Development of an American Genre."
    DAI, 32, 5191A (Florida State).
        Simply stated, the international novel is one in which
    "the theme, conflict and character traits arise from or
    serve to emphasize an inter-cultural relationship between
    nations." Although James wrote international novels of
    notable distinction, he is neither the originator of nor
    the norm for the form.

84 MILLER, JAMES E., JR. "Henry James: A Theory of Fiction."
    Prairie Schooner, 45 (Winter 1971-1972), 330-56.
        A systematized theory of fiction is gleaned from James's
    many writings on the subject. Reprinted in 1972.B72.

85 MONTEIRO, GEORGE. "Addendum to Edel and Lawrence: Henry
    James in Portuguese." Papers of the Bibliographical Soci-
    ety of America, 65 (3 Q), 302-304.
        Listed here are fifteen novels, novellas, short stories,
    and essays known to have been translated into Portuguese.

86 MONTGOMERY, JUDITH H. "The American Galatea." College Eng-
    lish, 32 (May), 890-99.
        The treatment of women by Hawthorne in The Blithedale
    Romance, James in The Portrait of a Lady, and Wharton in
    The House of Mirth demonstrates the influence of the Pyg-
    malion and Galatea myth on American writing.

87 MULL, DONALD L. "Freedom and Judgment: The Antinomy of Ac-
    tion in The Portrait of a Lady." Arizona Quarterly, 27
    (Summer), 124-32.
        The world of paradox manufactured by Isabel Archer is
    due to her essentially dualistic notion of freedom as ac-
    tion and freedom as thought.

1971

88 MULQUEEN, JAMES E. "Perfection of a Pattern: The Structure
of The Ambassadors, The Wings of the Dove, and The Golden
Bowl." Arizona Quarterly, 27 (Summer), 133-42.
    All three novels share a similar pattern of "deception,
discovery, and resolution." Perfection in the pattern is
achieved in The Golden Bowl.

89 MUNZAR, JIŘÍ. "Graham Greene, Essayist." Philologica Pra-
gensia, 14:30-38.
    Greene was fascinated by James's idea of religion, that
is, a belief in the eternal battle between good and evil,
where evil is always victorious. Greene was also interested in the "judas complex" particular to most of James's
protagonists. Moreover, Greene was concerned with James's
failure in writing dramas, as well as his exceptional ability in the conscious writing of prefaces.

90 MURRAY, D. M. "Candy Christian as a Pop-Art Daisy Miller."
Journal of Popular Culture, 5 (Fall), 340-48.
    Terry Southern's Candy is related to Mark Twain in genre
and to James in subject, but the technique is that of the
Pop Art school.

91 NAGEL, PAUL C. This Sacred Trust: American Nationality,
1798-1898. New York: Oxford Univ. Press, pp. 214-15,
passim.
    James expressed confidence in America's national renew-
al in 1867, but his expectations dwindled through the years.

92 NASH, DEANNA COLLINGWOOD. "The Web as an Organic Metaphor in
The Marble Faun, Middlemarch: A Study of Provincial Life,
and The Golden Bowl: The Growth of Contextualism as an
Aesthetic Theory in the Nineteenth Century." DAI, 31,
4131A (Univ. of North Carolina, Chapel Hill).
    The basic metaphor whereby Hawthorne, Eliot, and James
expressed their world views in which "all men are inter-
connected in a vast web of society, with each character an
inextricable part of the social web" was the web.

93 NEWLIN, PAUL A. "The Development of Roderick Hudson: An
Evaluation." Arizona Quarterly, 27 (Summer), 101-23.
    An examination of the literary influences and the influ-
ence of William Wetmore Story on Roderick Hudson reveals
the significance of this first novel as an indication of
James's commitment to art and his conception of the novelist.

94 NORTON, RICTOR. "The Turn of the Screw: Coincidentia Opposi-
    torum." American Imago, 28 (Winter), 373-90.
        The Turn of the Screw is an illustration of Jungian
    coincidentia oppositorum; it is developed after the model
    of a three-act mystery play; and the ambivalence is re-
    flective of James's latent homosexuality.

95 PAULY, THOMAS HARRY. "The Travel Sketch-Book and the American
    Author: A Study of the European Travelogues of Irving,
    Longfellow, Hawthorne, Howells, and James." DAI, 32, 928A
    (Univ. of California, Berkeley).
        For all five authors the "sketch" was of artistic value
    and was a "critical exercise" that provided the basis for
    subsequent "more finished" works. James adapted the
    sketch-book genre in Italian Hours.

96 PETERSON, WILLIAM. "Henry James on Jane Eyre." Times Liter-
    ary Supplement (30 July), pp. 919-20.
        Henry James's "detailed observations" on Jane Eyre are
    to be found in Mrs. Humphry Ward's 1899 Introduction to
    the Haworth Edition of Bronte's novel.

97 POIRIER, RICHARD. "The Performing Self," in Twentieth-Century
    Literature in Retrospect. Edited by Reuben A. Brower.
    Harvard English Studies 2. Cambridge: Harvard Univ.
    Press, pp. 87-109.
        Reprinted from 1971.B98.

98 POIRIER, RICHARD. The Performing Self: Compositions and De-
    compositions in the Languages of Contemporary Life. New
    York: Oxford Univ. Press, pp. 86-111.
        This discussion of the artist as "performing self" fo-
    cuses on Robert Frost, Norman Mailer, and Henry James, the
    last two of whom are termed "notorious self-advertisers
    when it comes to literary performances." Reprinted in
    1971.B97.

99 PORAT, TSFIRA. "Ha'aman Ve-ha-omenet" [The Artist and Art].
    Mo'oznayim (Tel Aviv), 33:240-46. [Hebrew]
        The Turn of the Screw is James's most popular story be-
    cause it is many-sided, contains hints of the forbidden
    life, and is about death. James deals with the education
    of the children in a romantic style, but adds his own dis-
    tinctive insights to the treatment.

1971

100   PUTT, S. GORLEY. "Henry James and Dickens." <u>Times Literary</u>
      <u>Supplement</u> (19 February), p. 213.
            James was not dependent upon memories of <u>Little Dorrit</u>
      for his pictures of London life. James's first-hand view
      of London and his visits to several prisons are more impor-
      tant as sources. Response in 1971.B68. <u>See also</u> 1971.B101;
      1971.B39; 1971.B69; 1971.B102.

101   PUTT, S. GORLEY. "Henry James and Dickens." <u>Times Literary</u>
      <u>Supplement</u> (12 March), p. 296.
            Putt maintains his position that James's first-hand
      views of London were more important sources for <u>The Prin-</u>
      <u>cess Casamassima</u> than <u>Little Dorrit</u>. (F. R. Leavis has
      argued that the Dickens novel is an important source.)
      Response to 1971.B68. <u>See also</u> 1971.B100; 1971.B39;
      1971.B69; 1971.B102.

102   PUTT, S. GORLEY. "Henry James and Dickens." <u>Times Literary</u>
      <u>Supplement</u> (26 March), p. 353.
            Putt's disagreement with F. R. Leavis is not on critical
      opinion (whether <u>The Princess Casamassima</u> is a success or
      failure), but on verifiable facts (whether James had first-
      hand knowledge of the London setting). Putt summarizes the
      sources of biographical information which prove James's
      first-hand knowledge. <u>See</u> 1971.B100; 1971.B68; 1971.B101;
      1971.B39; 1971.B69.

103   RAMSEY, ROGER. "The Available and the Unavailable 'I': Con-
      rad and James." <u>English Literature in Transition</u>,
      14:137-45.
            <u>The Turn of the Screw</u> and <u>Heart of Darkness</u> are similar
      in format and intent, but in James's psychological mystery
      the "I" disappears and in Conrad's the "I" remains present
      to the end of the story.

104   RAO, ADAPTA R. "Gleams and Glooms: A Reading of <u>The Turn of</u>
      <u>the Screw</u>." <u>Osmania Journal of English Studies</u>, 8:1-9.
            James's own statements about the tale refute both Wil-
      son's psychological reading (the governess as "sexually re-
      pressed spinster") and Heilman's reading of the story as a
      parallel to the "Loss of Paradise myth" (the governess as
      "redeemer").

105   RICHMOND, LEE J. "Henry James and the Comedy of Love: <u>The</u>
      <u>Golden Bowl</u>." <u>Erasmus Review</u>, 1 (September), 47-62.
            Adam Verver is not a philanthropist but a tyrant; Maggie
      Verver's innocence is not a strength but is an agent of
      self-deception; Amerigo is not a sympathetic character but

is a Machiavellian opportunist. These characters along with the Assinghams are stock figures James borrowed from the Commedia dell' Arte tradition to stage his satire of "the emptiness of love in this Victorian world."

106 ROSELLI, DANIEL N. "Max Beerbohm's Unpublished Parody of Henry James." Review of English Studies, ns 22 (February), 61-63.
Max Beerbohm's library at Merton College, Oxford, contains an unpublished parody of James, which is pencilled into Beerbohm's copy of James's Terminations (1895, second edition).

107 SAALBACH, R. P. "Literature and Morality." Publications of the Modern Language Association of America, 86 (October), 1031.
A Letter to the Editor proposes that James was not justified in placing the "aesthetic" first in his value hierarchy.

108 SASAKI, MIYOKO. "A Consideration of Evil in James." Oberon, 34 (December), 72-80. [Japanese]
In James's international works American moral values and European cultural decorum are contrasted. Though James seems to see vice hidden in Europe, he is more or less ambivalent in his final judgement of either America or Europe. This is especially so when one is aware of the time in historical context from Emersonian optimism through Henry Adams's premonition of the end of innocence and of the diversified age to come.

109 SCHRAMM, MINTZI SCHNAIDMAN. "The Art of the Nouvelle: Theme and Technique in the Genre." DAI, 32, 6392A-93A (Michigan).
Thematically, the nouvelle focuses on social concerns, and the genre flourishes when "divisive" elements erupt in society. Technically, the nouvelle uses dramatic techniques and economy. A "specific corpus of nouvelles" by Henry James is used to examine problems resulting from a traditionally negative critical attitude towards this genre. Both technical structure, linking the form to drama, and thematic focus are discussed and related to irony.

110 SCHRERO, ELLIOT M. "The Narrator's Palace of Thought in The Sacred Fount." Modern Philology, 68 (February), 269-88.
James's narrator counted on an audience informed by the "scientific materialism" of Münsterberg and the "pragmatic

1971

humanism" of William James, F. C. S. Schiller and others
to appreciate his intellectual quest.

111   SCHULTZ, ELIZABETH. "The Bostonians: The Contagion of Ro-
      mantic Illusion." Genre, 4 (March), 45-59.
           Basil Ransom is a hero of romance, but in order to res-
      cue Verena, he had "to utilize the obviously tainted wea-
      pons of romance, thereby deceiving himself in romantic
      terms." He sees Verena as a victim; but in rescuing her,
      he, too, victimizes her.

112   SINGH, BRIJRAJ. "A Study of the Concepts of Art, Life and
      Morality in the Criticism of Five Writers from Pater to
      Yeats." DAI, 32, 3331A-32A (Yale).
           Two strains, one decadent and the other humanistic, are
      present in the criticism of Pater. The two strains are
      variously received and modified by Lionel Johnson, Arthur
      Symons, and Henry James. William Butler Yeats "is able to
      pull all these diverse strains together into an unusual and
      transcendent unity."

*113 SKOUMAL, ALOYS. Afterword: "Na okraj Jamesovy 'Maisie,'" in
      Henry James's Co všechno věděla Maisie. Translated by Hana
      Skoumalová. Praha: Odeon.
           Cited in 1973 MLA International Bibliography, vol. 1,
      p. 147.

114   STAFFORD, WILLIAM T. "Henry James," in American Literary
      Scholarship: An Annual, 1969. Edited by J. Albert Rob-
      bins. Durham, N.C.: Duke Univ. Press, pp. 89-107.
           Survey of criticism published during 1969.

115   STANFORD, DONALD E. "A Prefatory Note" [to Eric Voegelin's
      "A Letter to Robert Heilman"]. Southern Review, 7 (Janu-
      ary), 3-5.
           Eric Voegelin's epistolary essay on The Turn of the
      Screw, beyond its critical insight, is especially meaning-
      ful since it "represents the initial impact of one of the
      most distinguished literary minds of the late Victorian
      period on one of the most distinguished philosophical and
      historical minds of the twentieth century." Preface to
      1971.B126. See also 1971.B56; 1971.B127.

116   STANZEL, FRANZ K. Narrative Situations in the Novel: "Tom
      Jones," "Moby Dick," "The Ambassadors," "Ulysses." Trans-
      lated by James P. Pusack. Bloomington: Indiana Univ.
      Press, pp. 92-120.

Of two possible narrative methods--"authorial" and "figural"--James's works show a gradual movement toward the
latter. In The Ambassadors, although remnants of authorial
narration are present, the figural method predominates and
is exploited for its dramatic effectiveness in presenting
the consciousness of the protagonist.

117 STEIN, WILLIAM BYSSHE. "The Sacred Fount and British Aestheticism: The Artist as Clown and Pornographer." Arizona
Quarterly, 27 (Summer), 161-73.
If the "method of craftsmanship" in The Sacred Fount is
related to the "design of the narrator's experience," the
novel can be read as a parody of British aestheticism and
decadence which debunks the Wilde, Beardsley, Pater circle.
James has objectified the l'art pour l'art technique by
portraying a protagonist who channels the energies of the
imagination "into the fruitless creation of pornographic
fancies of illicit wish-fulfillment."

118 SUMNER, NAN, and NATHAN SUMNER. "A Dickinson-James Parallel."
Research Studies, 39 (June), 144-47.
Although no direct influence between James's "The Jolly
Corner" and Dickinson's "I years had been from Home" and
"One need not be a Chamber-to be Haunted--" can be estab-
lished, they contain striking parallels in theme, struc-
ture, and imagery.

119 TANNER, TONY. City of Words: American Fiction, 1950-1970.
New York: Harper & Row, passim.
There are fifteen references, most of them significant,
to Henry James in this book.

120 THOMAS, WILLIAM B. "The Author's Voice in The Ambassadors."
Journal of Narrative Technique, 1 (May), 108-21.
James is consistent and skillful in using the point of
view he called the "center," a point of view which differs
from the twentieth century third-person protagonist's view-
point.

121 TINTNER, ADELINE R. "James's Mock Epic: 'The Velvet Glove,'
Edith Wharton, and Other Late Tales." Modern Fiction
Studies, 17 (Winter 1971-1972), 483-99.
"The Velvet Glove" is a mock-epic, understructured by
classical mythology, with Wharton as heroine and object of
the literary joke.

1971

122   TOMSICH, JOHN. <u>A Genteel Endeavor: American Culture and</u>
       <u>Politics in the Gilded Age</u>. Stanford: Stanford Univ.
       Press, passim.
           This book, which reconstructs and explains the Genteel
       Tradition by examining the lives and thought of eight men
       who worked within the tradition, contains passing refer-
       ences to Henry James, a realist who was devoted to fiction
       rather than poetry, as the idealists were.

123   TRAVIS, MILDRED K. "Hawthorne's 'Egotism' and 'The Jolly Cor-
       ner.'" <u>Emerson Society Quarterly</u>, 63 (Spring), 13-18.
           "Egotism; or the Bosom Serpent" and "The Jolly Corner"
       contain "solipsistic characters with gnawing secrets in
       their breasts" as well as "the concept of the alter-ego,
       where the other self is seen as a hostile beast of prey
       termed in serpent imagery." In each story the "redemptive
       power of love" brings about a happy ending.

124   TYTELL, JOHN. "The Jamesian Legacy in <u>The Good Soldier</u>."
       <u>Studies in the Novel</u>, 3 (Winter), 365-73.
           Ford's novel is indebted to James for "much of its mi-
       lieu, its idea of character, and its structure."

125   VEEDER, WILLIAM. "Strether and the Transcendence of Lan-
       guage." <u>Modern Philology</u>, 69 (November), 116-32.
           The process of transcendency whereby Strether overcomes
       two basic limitations, "a tendency to judge experience by
       Woollett's rigid, a priori, Calvinist code, and a romantic
       tendency to idealize nature into art and women into inno-
       cents," is reflected in his syntax, diction, and "mental
       processes."

126   VOEGELIN, ERIC. "A Letter to Robert B. Heilman" [on <u>The Turn</u>
       <u>of the Screw</u>]. <u>Southern Review</u>, 7 (January), 9-24.
           James's novella is an allegorical dramatization of the
       mystery of good and evil "in relation to the complex of
       consciousness--conscience--virtue." <u>See</u> 1971.B115;
       1971.B56; 1971.B127.

127   VOEGELIN, ERIC. "Postscript: On Paradise and Revolution"
       [in <u>The Turn of the Screw</u>]. <u>Southern Review</u>, 7 (January),
       25-48.
           Edenic imagery is central to the meaning of <u>The Turn of</u>
       <u>the Screw</u>; but it is a Jamesian Eden derived from the an-
       drogynic tradition and influenced by Swedenborg. <u>See</u>
       1971.B115; 1971.B56; 1971.B126.

128   VOEGELIN, ERIC. "The Turn of the Screw." Southern Review, 7
       (January), 3-48.
          Consists of four separate articles: 1971.B115;
       1971.B56; 1971.B126; 1971.B127.

129   VORPAHL, BEN M. "Henry James and Owen Wister." Pennsylvania
       Magazine of History and Biography, 95 (July), 291-338.
          The "long and complex personal relationship" between
       James and Wister is evident in the Jamesian elements of
       The Virginian.

130   WISTER, FANNY KEMBLE. "Caroline Lewis and Henry James."
       Pennsylvania Magazine of History and Biography, 95 (July),
       339-50.
          A series of sketches by Caroline Lewis constitutes a
       pictorial record of her meeting with James.

131   WOLF, H. R. "The Psychology and Aesthetics of Abandonment in
       The Ambassadors." Literature and Psychology, 21:133-47.
          The residual ambivalence of childhood relationships with
       the mother is dramatized in Strether's fear of being aban-
       doned by Mrs. Newsome while being attracted to the moral
       and sensuous autonomy Maria and Madame de Vionnet repre-
       sent.

132   WYATT, BRYANT N. "Naturalism as Expedience in the Novels of
       Frank Norris." Markham Review, 2 (February), 83-87.
          The Pit (1903) "is remarkably in the manner of Howells
       and James."

1971 C DISSERTATIONS

1   BIDDLE, ARTHUR WILLIAM. "The Emerging Consciousness: A Study
      of the Development of the Centre of Consciousness in the
      Early Novels of Henry James." DAI, 31, 6046A (Michigan
      State).
        A study of James's critical pronouncements and of three
      novels, Roderick Hudson, The American, and The Portrait of
      a Lady, reveals a "growth in subtlety and scope of the cen-
      tre of consciousness."

2   COLE, ROBERT CARLTON. "These Strange Relations: Henry James'
      'The Turn of the Screw.'" DAI, 32, 382A (Lehigh).
        Joseph Sheridan LeFanu's Uncle Silas provides the source
      of James's tale, which is not a ghost story but a psycho-
      logical exploration of the relationship of the governess,
      Mrs. Grose, Miles, and Flora. The social inequities that

1971

exist between the governess and her employer, not a repression of sexual love, are responsible for her strange behavior.

3   CROWL, SUSAN RICHARDSON.   "The Beholder's Eye: Romantic and
    Critical Perspective Through Style in James's 'Turn of the
    Screw,' The Wings of the Dove, and The Golden Bowl." DAI,
    31, 5357A (Indiana).
       The late style of James encompasses "both romantic and
    critical extremes . . . [that] demand an engagement by the
    reader in accordance with the experience the style dis-
    closes."

4   FARNHAM, MARY DAVIS.   "Henry James on Three Victorian Novel-
    ists: Concepts of the Novel." DAI, 31, 6054A (Univ. of
    North Carolina, Chapel Hill).
       James's conception of the novel owes a substantial lit-
    erary debt to his studies of Eliot, Trollope, and Steven-
    son.

5   FINNEY, MARTHA COLLINS.   "The Mingled Vision: Point of View
    in the Novels of Henry James, 1871-1900." DAI, 32,
    1468A-69A (Iowa).
       "Although the narrator's vision and voice are often de-
    tached from the character's vision and thoughts in the
    early novels, James attempts from the beginning to find a
    method of presenting characters, scenes, and action from
    the point of view of a limited number of characters."

6   GARN, DENNIS STEWART.   "Experience Disengaged: Henry James's
    Use of the Romance." DAI, 32, 429A (Michigan State).
       A study of the romance elements utilized by James yields
    three conclusions: (1) "James uses elements of the romance
    in ways that are essential to his works"; (2) romance ele-
    ments appear in all periods of James's work; and (3) James
    utilizes romance elements to enhance the realistic aspects
    of his novels.

7   GEARY, EDWARD ACORD.   "A Study of the Androgynous Figure in
    the Fiction of Henry James." DAI, 32, 1509A (Stanford).
       "Some of James's most important characters display an-
    drogynous traits, and . . . Henry James himself possessed
    an androgynous mind, combining an unusual sensitivity to
    feminine modes of consciousness with some uncertainty about
    his masculine identity."

8   GÉRACHT, MAURICE ARON. "Windows on the House of Fiction:
        James's Perspectives on Some French and English Figures."
        DAI, 31, 5401A (Wisconsin).
            A study of James's theoretical statements about criti-
        cism as they occur in his reviews, articles, and essays and
        of his criticism of six major literary figures--Balzac,
        Trollope, Sand, Eliot, Zola, and Turgenev--reveals that,
        for James, "the 'individual vision,' the 'personal' point
        of view is . . . a central and controlling idea."

9   GOODMAN, CHARLOTTE MARGOLIS. "Views of the Artist and His Art
        in the Writing of Henry James." DAI, 32, 2686A (Brandeis).
            James ambivalently approached four major issues regard-
        ing the artist in his works: (1) he treats both the posi-
        tive and negative aspects of expatriation; (2) he extols
        commitment while noting the losses; (3) he sees the artist
        as the victim and the suitor of the public; and (4) while
        denying that art should be moral or political, he laments
        the artist's failure to "ameliorate the lot of mankind."

*10   HABICHT, LOUISE ANN. "Henry James and Joseph Conrad: A Study
        in Relationship." Dissertation, Brown.
            Cited in Beatrice Ricks, comp. Henry James: A Bibliog-
        raphy of Secondary Works. Scarecrow Author Bibliography,
        No. 24. Metuchen, N.J.: Scarecrow, 1975, Item 2462.1.

11   HALLAB, MARY CLARK YOST. "Psychoanalytic Criticism of the
        Life and Works of Henry James." DAI, 32, 966A (Louisiana
        State).
            The psychoanalytic approach to James and his works has
        yielded Freudian, Jungian, and Neo-Freudian interpreta-
        tions; it has yielded a few perceptive interpretations and
        a plethora of misapplied and over-simplified ones; it has
        been used to elevate and denigrate the author; and it has
        elucidated his works and obfuscated his works.

12   HODGDON, DAVID CROCKETT. "Henry James: The Texture of Lan-
        guage in the Later Novels, 1897-1901." DAI, 32, 434A
        (State Univ. of New York, Binghamton).
            "A close reading of four novels, The Spoils of Poynton,
        The Awkward Age, What Maisie Knew, and The Sacred Fount,
        makes clear that language is the subject as well as the
        medium of Henry James's later work."

1971

13   HUFFMAN, JAMES RICHARD. "The Sense of the Past in Henry
      James." DAI, 32, 434A-35A (Michigan State).
          James's "sense of the past" is central to his philoso-
      phy, his themes, his techniques, his use of archetypes, and
      his character creations.

14   JOHNSON, ROBERT G. "A Study of the Style of Henry James's
      Late Novels." DAI, 32, 2092A (Bowling Green).
          A study of The Ambassadors, The Wings of the Dove, The
      Golden Bowl, Daisy Miller, Watch and Ward, and The Ameri-
      can "utilizing quantitative and reductionist analysis" re-
      veals James emphasizes "stress relation and modification,
      abstraction, states of being, and arrested forward move-
      ment" in his late style.

15   LANDRY, LOWELL. "Genres of Short Fiction in the Works of Hen-
      ry James." DAI, 31, 4776A-77A (Tulane).
          A structural examination of the works James identified
      as either an anecdote, a picture, or a nouvelle "proves
      that, for James, generic distinctions are based upon his
      treatment of the tension between objective and subjective
      reality."

16   LAUER, KRISTIN OLSON. "The Interior Monologue in The Ambas-
      sadors and The Golden Bowl." DAI, 31, 6015A (Michigan
      State).
          The three occurrences of interior monologue in The Am-
      bassadors and the eleven occurrences in The Golden Bowl
      provide a basis for defining the "Jamesian interior mono-
      logue."

17   LIBBY, MARION JEAN VLASTOS. "Self-Affirmation: The Challenge
      to Self-Sacrifice in the Fiction of Henry James." DAI, 32,
      1478A-79A (Stanford).
          Two themes are pervasive in James's works--self-affirma-
      tion and self-sacrifice. James's own propensity for the
      Christian concept of self-sacrifice dictates the design of
      his work. A comparative evaluation, however, of the pro-
      tagonist who sacrifices self with the protagonist who
      espouses self-preservation and self-affirmation shows the
      latter protagonist is the more attractive character.

18   MARKS, SITA PATRICIA SMITH. "Character Patterns in Henry
      James's The Wings of the Dove and The Golden Bowl." DAI,
      31, 6063A (Michigan State).
          The identification of "circular" and "spiral" patterns
      in the two novels is the key to understanding the charac-
      ters and tracing "the development of James's conception of

good and evil from the modes of innocence and experience to
patterns of moral perception and moral blindness."

19   MELTZER, SHARON BITTENSON. "The Fiction of Henry James, 1895–
     1901." DAI, 32, 445A (Yale).
        The period from James's theatrical failure (1895) to his
     major phase (1901) is a distinct period during which he is
     "poised between the abstract solutions of idealizing phi-
     losophy and the existential metaphysic emerging in the
     nineteenth century . . . [and in which he] comes gradually
     to synthesize idealizing consciousness and an existential
     metaphysic in an ethical and artistic solution to his phil-
     osophical dilemma."

20   NICHOLAS, CHARLES ANDREW. "Henry James's Personal Theory of
     Art." DAI, 32, 1522A (Michigan).
        Emphasis on the technical aspects of James's craft and
     theory has obscured his insistence that the personality of
     the writer become a part of the critical and creative
     process.

21   O'NEILL, JOHN PATRICK. "The Story in It: The Design of Ac-
     tion and Situation in Henry James's Fiction." DAI, 32,
     927A (Stanford).
        In The Portrait of a Lady, The Princess Casamassima, The
     Spoils of Poynton, The Awkward Age, and The Wings of the
     Dove, James uses "polar opposition," not to emphasize the
     moral, social, or psychological elements of the work, but
     to arouse excitement in the reader in response to "the phe-
     nomenon of radical conflict."

22   PETERSON, DALE EARL. "One Much-Embracing Echo: Henry James's
     Response to Ivan Turgenev." DAI, 32, 1524A (Yale).
        "To varying extents, all of the early Jamesian novels
     before 1881 are structurally or thematically or 'relation-
     ally' derivative of the Turgenevan novel."

23   RAMBEAU, JAMES MORRIS. "The American Scene and James's Late
     Fiction (1907-1914)." DAI, 32, 981A (Rutgers).
        James's American tour significantly affected his style
     in The Ivory Tower and five short stories of the late pe-
     riod--"Julia Bride," "The Jolly Corner," "Crapy Cornelia,"
     "A Round of Visits," and "The Bench of Desolation." The
     affected works differ from those of the major phase in vo-
     cabulary and tone as a "result of James's perceptions dur-
     ing his American tour."

1971

24   REDDICK, BRYAN DEWITT. "Tone in Dramatic Narrative." DAI, 31
      (1970), 2397A (Univ. of California, Davis).
          "Tone" is of primary importance in the dramatic narra-
      tive because it "directly controls the relationship between
      reader and story-world." Accordingly, careful attention to
      the tone of Austen's Emma, James's The Golden Bowl, Joyce's
      Portrait of the Artist, and Lawrence's Women in Love is es-
      sential for an adequate understanding of "their structure
      and their meaning."

25   RICE, LOREE McCONNELL. "Henry James's Theory of the Novel--
      Static or Dynamic?" DAI, 31, 6022A-23A (Oklahoma State).
          A comparative analysis of James's critical pronounce-
      ments as they appear in his "The Art of Fiction" and his
      Prefaces to the New York Edition reveals that his theories
      underwent substantive changes during the interim years.

26   SMITH, WILLIAM FRANCIS, JR. "Sentence Structure in Three
      Representative Tales of Henry James." DAI, 31, 3520A
      (Michigan State).
          A syntactical study of a representative short story from
      each period of James's craft ("The Madonna of the Future,"
      "The Death of the Lion," and "The Jolly Corner") yields
      four conclusions: (1) the average sentence length progres-
      sively increases; (2) sentence types differ in each period;
      (3) there is a progressive increase in the use of preposi-
      tional phrases, subordinate and relative clauses, and noun
      and verb phrases; and (4) "in general, James matches his
      content and style to a great extent."

27   TRACY, BRUCE PHILIP. "Henry James's Representation of Inner
      Consciousness in Meditation Scenes from the Late Novels."
      DAI, 32, 1533A (Michigan State).
          A comparative analysis of rhetorical and grammatical
      components present in meditative scenes in three late nov-
      els with those of three non-meditative scenes reveals how
      the style of the meditative scenes contributes "to the il-
      lusion of having stepped inside a character's mind."

28   WADDEN, ANTHONY T. "The Novel as Psychic Drama: Studies of
      Scott, Dickens, Eliot, and James." DAI, 31, 4737A (Iowa).
          A psychoanalytic examination of Philip Pirrip in Great
      Expectations, Peter Pattieson in The Heart of Midlothian,
      the narrator in The Mill on the Floss, and Lambert Strether
      in The Ambassadors suggests "that novels function as au-
      tonomous and dynamic models of psychic life, unconsciously
      grounding their imagery and structure in the archetypal
      opposition between conscious and unconscious attitudes

which conflict or unite within the psyche as the basic
sources of dramatic action."

1972 A BOOKS

1   BANTA, MARTHA. Henry James and the Occult: The Great Exten-
    sion. Bloomington: Indiana Univ. Press, 273 pp.
        Although James was a secular man, who viewed the world
    "humanistically and agnostically" and whose "full faith"
    resided in "the powers of human consciousness," he used ar-
    tistically "notions extracted from contemporary attitudes
    toward the supernatural." His "use of the supernatural as
    vocabulary, metaphor, theme, and atmosphere altered great-
    ly, however, in the degree of its quality and importance of
    symbolic essence. James's conception of the supernatural
    changed in kind as well; it changed to an instinctive sense
    that there was more often 'something there' to fascinate
    than to be lightly dismissed." Reviewed: James E. Miller,
    Jr., Modern Fiction Studies, 19 (1973), 267-70; Howard
    Kerr, Nineteenth-Century Fiction, 28 (1973), 101-103; David
    K. Kirby, New England Quarterly, 46 (1973), 331-34; John
    Lydenberg, American Literature, 45 (1974), 619-20.

2   CHATMAN, SEYMOUR. The Later Style of Henry James. New York:
    Barnes and Noble; Oxford: Blackwell's, 135 pp.
        The elements of James's later style can be described.
    The main characteristic is "abstractness," or "intangibili-
    ty," which "results from a preoccupation with mental states
    and social relations, that these--as much as, or even more
    than the characters themselves--are topics commented upon
    and hence cast as syntactically important nouns; and final-
    ly that other stylistic phenomena, like the increased meta-
    phorizing of the later novels, might be explained, in part
    at least, as a need to prevent intangibility from leading
    to dryness." Analysis of two parodies of James reveals
    that the more successful parody (by Max Beerbohm) employs
    syntactic and lexical devices used by James, such as in-
    tangible subjects, profusions of prepositions, deictic and
    expletive constructions, ellipsis, parallelism and antith-
    esis, unusual collocation, and metaphors combining the in-
    tangible with the physical. Excerpt reprinted in French in
    1971.B25. Reviewed: Sidney J. Krause, American Litera-
    ture, 44:494-96; James E. Miller, Jr., Modern Fiction Stud-
    ies, 19 (1973), 267-70; Barry Menikoff, Nineteenth-Century
    Fiction, 27 (1973), 492-94; David Lodge, Novel, 7 (Winter
    1974), 187-89.

1972

3 EDEL, LEON. Henry James: The Master, 1901-1916. Philadel-
    phia: Lippincott, 591 pp.
       The fifth volume of the biography focuses on James's
    final years when he was "the master": the writing of the
    three great novels, the American journey which resulted in
    The American Scene, the production of the New York Edition,
    the friendship with Edith Wharton, the death of William
    James, and James's final illness. Reviewed: 1972.B1;
    1972.B2; 1972.B10; 1972.B33; 1972.B60; 1972.B83; 1972.B98;
    1973.B8; 1973.B17; 1973.B30; 1974.B47; Joseph Wiesenfarth,
    Commonweal, 96:44-45; Oscar Cargill, American Literature,
    44 (May), 330-32; Times Literary Supplement (18 August),
    pp. 957-59; Mark Krupnik, Novel, 6:257-65.

4 EGAN, MICHAEL. Henry James: The Ibsen Years. Vision Criti-
    cal Studies. London: Vision Press, 154 pp.
       After his disastrous experience in the theater, James
    attempted to apply what he had learned as a playwright to
    his fiction; thus he developed his dramatic method. Sur-
    rendering the portrait metaphor of his earlier work, he
    evolved a metaphor drawn from drama and drew upon Ibsen's
    dramatic methods, ideas, and techniques. James learned
    from Ibsen that realism and symbolism are compatible. The
    shaping presence of Ibsen can be found in The Spoils of
    Poynton, The Other House, Covering End, The Turn of the
    Screw, What Maisie Knew, The Awkward Age. Reprinted by
    Harper, 1973. Reviewed: 1973.B11; Times Literary Supple-
    ment (18 August), p. 958; Motley F. Deakin, Modern Fiction
    Studies, 19 (Winter 1973-1974), 595-98.

5 FRIEDL, HERWIG. Die Funktion der Bildlichkeit in den Kriti-
    schen und Theoretischen Schriften von Henry James: Ein
    Entwurf Seiner Literaturtheorie. Heidelberg: Carl Winer,
    200 pp.
       A study of the function of imagery in James's writings
    in which literary opinions are expressed reveals that his
    practices as a theorist represent a literary manifestation
    of William James's radical empiricism. Reviewed: James E.
    Miller, Jr., Modern Fiction Studies, 19 (1973), 267-70.

6 GOODE, JOHN, ed. The Air of Reality: New Essays on Henry
    James. London: Methuen, 368 pp.
       Contents:
       "Introduction" by John Goode (pp. 1-4). Essays do not
    follow "any method or line," but the editor suggests "that
    the book as a whole should have what M. H. Abrams calls a
    'mimetic orientation'--that we might profit most by asking

318

questions about the relationship of the work to the world
it takes account of."

"The American" by R. W. Butterfield (pp. 5-35). James's
The American is pervaded with allegorical overtones in
which Christopher Newman, who variously represents the
"New American man, 'western Barbarian,' 'nature's noble-
man,' 'child of nature,' 'innocent abroad,' . . . [and] the
American as optimist," vacillates in his choice between the
aggressive "life" of America and the oppressive "death" of
Europe.

"Washington Square" by John Lucas (pp. 36-59). Washington Square is a "triumph of disinterested observations" and
exemplifies James's social perceptiveness "with all that
that implies of tone, habits of deference, poise, conscious
civility, [and] calculated decorum."

"The Bostonians" by David Howard (pp. 60-80). The controlling concept in the novel, whether it be public or private, is "union"--union that generates a conflict ending in
either victory or defeat.

"The reference of The Tragic Muse" by D. J. Gordon and
John Stokes (pp. 81-167). Characters in The Tragic Muse
are revealed through their relationships with the physical
"things" and ideas associated with the cities of Paris and
London; the subject of the novel is topical, reverberating
with echoes of contemporary critical debates; but the novel
is also personal, reflecting the concern of the author with
the meaning of success.

"What Maisie Knew: portrait of the artist as a young
girl" by Juliet Mitchell (pp. 168-89). In the novel "seeing is knowing," and there are two ways to see: (1) Maisie
sees "straight" while maintaining innocence (this does not
imply that she does not see evil); and (2) Mrs. Wix sees
"crooked" (her seeing is "pornographic").

"Keeping the place tidy for the young female mind: The
Awkward Age" by Margaret Walters (pp. 190-218). The Awkward Age shares the social and epistemological concerns of
James's other novels of the Nineties. It is the story of
an adolescent upon whom the facade of "emphasized virgini-
ty" is projected by her elders. Although Nanda is intel-
lectually aware of the falsehood, she accepts the projected
ideal on an emotional level.

"The Ambassadors and The Sacred Fount: the artist
manqué" by Bernard Richards (pp. 219-43). The characterizations of the narrator and Strether, the methodology, and
the thematic concerns of the two novels are very similar.
Although both protagonists have artistic proclivities,
neither is an artist; but each man is a "futile Mephis-

topheles" who desires to manipulate the people surrounding
him.

"The pervasive mystery of style: The Wings of the Dove"
by John Goode (pp. 244-300). Although the novel clearly
manifests a "parabolic direction," its texture and thematic content are much too complex to be evaluated on a solely
parabolic level. "The novel is concerned with the connex-
ions between ways of seeing and modes of relationship, in
the context of the social role of money in general and
large accretions of money in particular; and in its concern
it embodies highly representative visions and attitudes
which are relevant to the historical situation out of which
the novel grows."

"The novel to end all novels: The Golden Bowl" by
Gabriel Pearson (pp. 301-62). The Golden Bowl "represents
James's ultimate attempt to salvage imaginatively the
ideals of a civilization that his deepest instincts warned
him was doomed"; and "every subsequent novel can be viewed
as in some way post-novelistic--parasitic, parodic, nostalgic, ironic--or in some more or less posthumous relationship to the great classic nineteenth-century novel,
whose last paradoxical example is The Golden Bowl."

Reviewed: Motley F. Deakin, Modern Fiction Studies, 19
(Winter 1973-1974), 595-98; William T. Stafford, American
Literature, 45 (1974), 618-19.

7   HOAG, GERALD. Henry James and the Criticism of Virginia
    Woolf. Wichita State Univ. Studies, No. 92. Wichita,
    Kans.: Wichita State Univ., 11 pp.
        Woolf's critical ideas share "a kinship with James's
    criticism." However, she considers "form as an unconscious
    phenomenon beyond the reach of analysis by either writer or
    reader," and in this view "she does not stand in the tradi-
    tion of James."

8   KRISHNA RAO, N. The Quest for Refinement: A Study of the
    Novels of Henry James. Visakhapatnam: Vagdevi, 122 pp.
        The idea of refinement is viewed thematically in this
    study as the "central premise in the Jamesian ethic." The
    subject investigated is "the dramatic relationship between
    refinement and selfhood in the novels of Henry James as it
    develops through the four major movements of his artistic
    creation. The problem is viewed in terms of the growth and
    education of the Jamesian individual whose quest for a
    meaningful selfhood becomes identified with the analogous
    quest for the refinements of life. The metamorphic cycle
    of individual growth is traced in terms of its archetypal
    pattern: the quest, the ordeal, the crisis and fulfill-
    ment."

9   VANN, J. DON, ed. <u>Critics on Henry James</u>. Coral Gables,
      Fla.: Univ. of Miami Press, 99 pp.
          Includes a brief introduction, a table of important
      dates in James's life, a selected bibliography, reprints of
      six early reviews of James's work, and fifteen critical ex-
      cerpts. All of the critical pieces were originally pub-
      lished before 1960, and selections by the following writers
      are included: Elizabeth Cary, T. S. Eliot, Ezra Pound,
      Percy Lubbock, Van Wyck Brooks, Edith Wharton, Yvor Win-
      ters, F. O. Matthiessen, Lionel Trilling, Allen Tate, Leon
      Edel, Dorothy Van Ghent, R. P. Blackmur, Richard Chase, and
      Harold C. Goddard. Reviewed: 1973.B17; D. K. Kirby, <u>New
      England Quarterly</u>, 45 (December), 591-93; G. Core, <u>Michigan
      Quarterly Review</u> (Winter 1973), p. 82; <u>Choice</u>, 9 (February
      1973), 1593.

<u>1972 B SHORTER WRITINGS</u>

1   ALDRIDGE, JOHN W. "The Anatomy of Passion in the Consummate
      Henry James." <u>Saturday Review</u>, 55 (12 February), 65-68.
          The fifth volume of Edel's biography of James is "one of
      the truly distinguished works of creative scholarship of
      our time." Information about James is given its "appro-
      priate meaning" through "being placed within the context of
      James's emotional torments." Review of 1972.A3.

2   ANDERSON, QUENTIN. "Leon Edel's 'Henry James.'" <u>Virginia
      Quarterly Review</u>, 48 (Autumn), 621-30.
          Leon Edel's fifth volume of James biography provides a
      needed factual chronicle of the last years and is well
      written, but Edel "is not to be trusted with evidence about
      the psyche." Review of 1972.A3.

3   ANON. "From the James Family Libraries." <u>Bancroftiana</u>, 52
      (April), 1-2.
          Sixty-eight volumes which originally belonged to various
      members of the James family have been given to the Bancroft
      Library, University of California, Berkeley. The most no-
      table item is one of the four published copies of the <u>Diary</u>
      of Alice James.

4   ANTUSH, JOHN V. "The 'Much Finer Complexity' of History in
      <u>The American</u>." <u>Journal of American Studies</u>, 6 (April),
      85-95.
          The American Dream myth and the Horatio Alger hero in
      Christopher Newman are stripped down to reveal the truth
      of history and the human condition in America--the reality
      of losing.

1972

5   AOKI, TSUGIO. "Conservative Sense in James." Eigo Seinen
     [The Rising Generation] (Tokyo), 118 (November), 494-95.
          Defends Henry James from the contemporary attack of the
     intelligentsia, including William James, which charged that
     Henry James was a conservative lacking a sense of reality.
     When the difference between Henry's placement of a personal
     viewpoint and William's plural points of view is noted, it
     is clear that Henry James was not a narrow-sighted artist
     but a far-sighted one with a satirical view of the time.
     "Friends of Friends" is a warning to the then fashionable
     pseudo-science of psychics.

6   BACKUS, JOSEPH M. "'Poor Valentin' or 'Monsieur le Comte':
     Variation in Character Designation as Matter for Critical
     Consideration (in Henry James's The American)." Names,
     20:47-55.
          Name variations used by James to elucidate character in
     The American include full names, surnames with prefixes,
     first names, nicknames, and epithets.

7   BARZUN, JACQUES. "The Jameses." Times Literary Supplement
     (15 September), p. 1060.
          Barzun disagrees with Edel's interpretation (in
     1972.B29) of William James's character and points out
     how the letter used as "damning evidence" against William
     has been "twisted and garbled" by Edel. (William James's
     letter refusing membership in the National Institute of
     Arts and Letters is reprinted.) Responses in 1972.B30 and
     1972.B103.

8   BAŠIĆ, SONJA. "Love and Politics in The Bostonians: A Note
     on Motivation." Studia Romanica et Anglica Zagrabiensia,
     33-36:293-303. [Roumanian]
          The Bostonians, though a story of struggle for love, is
     as well a socio-political, highly satirized parable. There
     is too much vagueness in the novel, which destroys the uni-
     ty, flattens the satire, and gives it a repetitive, monoto-
     nous aspect.

9   BELLRINGER, ALAN W. "The Sacred Fount: The Scientific Meth-
     od." Essays in Criticism, 22 (July), 244-64.
          "The Sacred Fount is . . . primarily a study in the ob-
     scurity of the loss and gain of lovers; what is presented
     to us is the narrator's fight with uncertainty."

1972

10 BLIVEN, NAOMI. "Home, James." New Yorker, 48 (29 April),
    137-40.
        Edel's final volume, The Master: 1901-1916, captures
    "the distance between the secret sufferer and the Literary
    Cham." Review of 1972.A3.

11 BOCAZ, SERGIO HERNÁN. "La novelística de José Donoso y su
    cosmogonía estética a través de dos influencias principa-
    les: Marcel Proust y Henry James." DAI, 33, 1714A (Colo-
    rado).
        The influence of Proust's A la Recherche du Temps Perdu
    and James's The Turn of the Screw and The Beast in the Jun-
    gle on Donoso coalesces with his own vast thought, produc-
    ing his obsession with "God's cruelty in having created man
    as he is, an urning, a perverted creature with an abnormal
    essence."

12 BRIGGS, ANTHONY D. "Alexander Pushkin: A Possible Influence
    on Henry James." Forum for Modern Language Study, 8:52-60.
        The remarkable similarities of incident, characteriza-
    tion, imagery, theme, and structure between The Aspern Pa-
    pers and three Pushkin works (Yevgeniy Onegin, The Queen of
    Spades, and The Bronze Horseman) defy the possibility of co-
    incidence and argue for a Pushkin influence which probably
    derived through French translations.

13 BRIGGS, ANTHONY D. "Someone Else's Sledge: Further Notes on
    Turgenev's Virgin Soil and Henry James's The Princess Casa-
    massima." Oxford Slavonic Papers, ns 5:52-60.
        In his attempt to improve on Turgenev's Virgin Soil
    James found himself increasingly dependent on his source as
    a result of the initial boundaries he established for him-
    self. The close parallels are especially salient in the
    protagonists, who share similar births, physical traits,
    cultural attitudes, sociological settings, political views,
    and climactic conclusions.

14 BROOKS, PETER. "The Melodramatic Imagination." Partisan Re-
    view, 39:195-212.
        Although James's technique is "subtler" and "more re-
    fined," both James and Balzac aim at a "total articulation
    of the grandiose moral terms of the drama, an assertion
    that what is being played out within the realm of manners
    is charged with significance from the realm of the moral
    occult."

1972

15   BYRD, SCOTT. "The Fractured Crystal in Middlemarch and The
      Golden Bowl." Modern Fiction Studies, 18 (Winter 1972-
      1973), 551-54.
           James developed a minor image from Middlemarch into a
      central symbol in The Golden Bowl.

16   CARGAS, HARRY J. "Seeing, But Not Living: Two Characters
      from James and Wharton." New Laurel Review, 1:5-7.
           Lawrence Selden and Lambert Strether provide "the point
      of greatest similarity in The House of Mirth and The Ambas-
      sadors"; both men "see," but neither "lives."

17   CHERNAIK, JUDITH. "Henry James as Moralist: The Case of the
      Late Novels." Centennial Review, 16 (Spring), 105-21.
           Ambiguities in the late novels are puzzling, but James's
      characters are debating the choice between good and evil.
      The characters may have difficulty seeing the difference
      between good and evil, but this does not imply that James
      was uncertain about values.

18   COLEMAN, ALEXANDER. "Notes on Borges and American Litera-
      ture." Tri-Quarterly, 25 (Fall), 356-77.
           Borges's Introducción a la literatura norteamericana "is
      a most unsatisfactory exposition of a body of literature";
      it is flawed by "considerable gaps and summary dismissals"
      and a restrictive preoccupation with the "world of inner-
      most symbol."

19   COX, JAMES M. "Henry James: The Politics of International-
      ism." Southern Review, 8 (July), 493-506.
           Not James's political The Princess Casamassima, but his
      International novels reveal his political vision of the
      "New World renewing the Old" at its best.

20   COY, JAVIER. "El Concepto de la inocencia en Henry James."
      Filología Moderna (June), pp. 221-45. [Spanish]
           When the fiction is examined against the backdrop of the
      biographical details of James's life, the theme of inno-
      cence is revealed through his use of the figures of for-
      eigners, children, artists and ghosts.

21   CURRIE, WILLIAM. "The Light Going Out: Henry James as Social
      Critic in The Portrait of a Lady and 'The Pupil.'" English
      Literature and Language (Tokyo), 9:145-50. [Japanese]
           These two works share a parallel theme in the central
      issue of "innocence in confrontation with selfishness, de-
      ceit, and moral confusion." In "The Pupil" James was more
      distinctly aware of a society, though both works deal with

"mediocrity, selfishness, dullness and vulgarity" in ascendancy in a modern society.

22 DEANS, THOMAS R. "Henry James' The Ambassadors: The Primal
    Scene Revisited." American Imago, 29 (Fall), 233-56.
        Marie de Vionnet is the substitute lost wife and Chad is
    the surrogate son in an oedipal conflict scene in which
    Strether rejects the sexual rivalry and obtains secondary
    erotic satisfaction by "visually incorporating the forbid-
    den scene."

23 DEBO, ELIZABETH LEA. "The Narrator in Henry James, Joseph
    Conrad and Ford Madox Ford." DAI, 32, 3946A-47A (Nebras-
    ka).
        An examination of the narrative techniques reveals the
    presence of three types of narrators and two distinct per-
    sonae. The omniscient narrator is a "social critic" of a
    changing society; the limited omniscient narrator criti-
    cizes a static society as he focuses on one individual;
    and the first person narrator is used to "achieve ambigui-
    ty." The conscious persona enhances the reliability of the
    narrator; but the unconscious persona frequently undermines
    reliability.

24 DONNELLY, J. B. "Cultural Consolations During the Great
    War." Topic, 12 (Spring), 22-34.
        James is briefly mentioned in this discussion of the
    effects of World War I on artists: James retreated from
    the "unspeakable" war by working on a novel set in the
    Regency period, The Sense of the Past.

25 DUNN, ALBERT A. "The Articulation of Time in The Ambassa-
    dors." Criticism, 14 (Spring), 137-50.
        James utilizes a variety of techniques--including paral-
    lel presentation of mental and "social" time and comple-
    mentary use of temporal and spatial perspectives--to pre-
    sent the education of Strether.

26 DUPEE, F. W., ed. The Ambassadors. Rinehart Book. New York:
    Holt, Rinehart and Winston.
        Contents: This volume contains Henry James's Preface
    to the novel and the text of the New York Edition. Ex-
    cerpts from Henry James's Notebooks and two letters (one
    to William Dean Howells and one to Hugh Walpole) are found
    in Appendix I; critical comments from E. M. Forster (As-
    pects of the Novel), F. O. Matthiessen (Henry James: The
    Major Phase), and F. W. Dupee (Henry James) are in Appen-
    dix II; "A Note on the Text" and a Selected Bibliography

comprise Appendix III and IV. In "A Note on the Text"
F. W. Dupee describes textual problems with the novel and
states that a comparison of the first edition and the New
York Edition reveals that "revision was in its own way
thorough, consistent and in conformity with a definite
principle."

27   DYSON, A. E. "Murderous Innocence: James's The Turn of the
       Screw," in his Between Two Worlds: Aspects of Literary
       Form. London: Macmillan, pp. 53-80.
          The psychotic Governess is responsible for Flora's mal-
       ady and Miles's death.

28   EDEL, LEON. "Introduction," in his edition of The Princess
       Casamassima. The Bodley Head Henry James. Vol. X. Lon-
       don: Bodley Head, pp. 5-12.
          This novel's "atmosphere is conspiratorial; its theme is
       revolution, its voice is a strange mixture of anguish and
       aestheticism."

29   EDEL, LEON. "The Jameses." Times Literary Supplement
       (13 October), pp. 1226-27.
          Edel defends his account in the final volume of his
       James biography of the strained relationship between Wil-
       liam and Henry James, stating that his interpretation is
       based on over two thousand letters and other family docu-
       ments, whereas Barzun's objection is based on a single let-
       ter. Response to 1972.B7. Controversy continues in
       1972.B103 and 1972.B30.

30   EDEL, LEON. "The Jameses." Times Literary Supplement
       (3 November), p. 1342.
          Edel restates his position against Barzun and Trilling,
       maintaining that he looked at all the evidence and "not
       that of a single document." The affections and animosi-
       ties of the brothers developed over a long period of time
       and were traced by Edel in earlier volumes of his biography
       of Henry James. Response to 1972.B7 and 1972.B103. See
       also 1972.B29.

31   EGAN, MICHAEL. "Henry James and Ibsen," in his edition of
       Henrik Ibsen: The Critical Heritage. London: Routledge
       and Kegan Paul, pp. 16-18.
          In 1891 James became an Ibsen supporter, and with The
       Other House in 1893 he began to write drama modelled on
       Ibsen's plays. After 1895 his novels and tales were "quite
       consciously modelled on the drama," and it was Ibsen's
       drama which "proffered the really fruitful analogies."

James's response to Ibsen is documented in three letters to
Edmund Gosse printed for the first time in this collection
(January 1889, October 1890, April 1891).

32   ENGELBERG, EDWARD. "The Tyranny of Conscience: Arnold, James,
      and Conrad's Lord Jim," in his The Unknown Distance: From
      Consciousness to Conscience, Goethe to Camus. Cambridge,
      Mass.: Harvard Univ. Press, pp. 144-85.
          Writing under the influence of Arnold, James constructed
      a dialectic in Roderick Hudson that is not capable of syn-
      thesis, only "mutual annihilation"--a dialectic between
      Hebraism and Hellenism.

33   EPSTEIN, JOSEPH. "The Greatest Biography of the Century."
      Chicago Tribune Book World (6 February), pp. 1, 3, 9.
          Leon Edel's The Master: 1901-1916 is "a biography that,
      in its scholarship, refinement, and subtlety of understand-
      ing does not pale beside its subject's own magnificent
      achievement." Review of 1972.A3.

34   FALK, ROBERT P. "Jacobites and Anti-Jacobites: Three Recent
      Studies of Henry James." Nineteenth-Century Fiction, 27
      (September), 224-28.
          Peter Buitenhuis, a Jacobite, has written an "orthodox"
      book in The Grasping Imagination: "its strength lies in
      the knowledge of previous work in the subject and in a
      balanced critical point of view." Charles Samuels in The
      Ambiguity of Henry James and Philip Weinstein in Henry
      James and the Requirements of the Imagination "represent
      in different ways the subjective, evaluative approach with
      a 'revisionist' emphasis." Weinstein's book is "well writ-
      ten and discriminating, with close and careful insights
      into the text of the novels under consideration." Samuels,
      however, "takes up the cudgels where Wilson and Geismar
      left them and proposes to distinguish the good from the bad
      in the whole of James's work." Review of 1970.A1; 1971.A6;
      1971.A8.

35   FRASER, G. S. "The English Novel," in The Twentieth-Century
      Mind: History, Ideas, and Literature in Britain: Vol. 2:
      1918-1945. Edited by C. B. Cox and Anthony Edward Dyson.
      London: Oxford Univ. Press, p. 374.
          In this survey of the major figures in the English nov-
      el, James is mentioned briefly as an influence on Graham
      Greene and L. P. Hartley.

1972

36 FREDERIKSEN, BODIL FOLKE. "Moral or Historical Validity:
   Henry James, The Ambassadors." Language and Literature,
   1:58-66.
      The Ambassadors can best be appreciated from a histori-
   cal perspective--a perspective that recognizes it as the
   outgrowth of a "specific cultural and social epoch." In
   turn, not only does the epoch illuminate the novel, but the
   novel illuminates the epoch. Response to 1971.B33. See
   1973.B22.

37 FRIEDMAN, ALAN. "The Novel," in The Twentieth-Century Mind:
   History, Ideas, and Literature in Britain: Vol. 1: 1900-
   1918. Edited by C. B. Cox and A. E. Dyson. London: Oxford
   Univ. Press, pp. 415-22.
      Early in this century "the structure of the novel gradu-
   ally underwent a change" and "the energy of the novel
   shifted . . . to an unbalanced concentration in the self."
   (Includes readings of James's last three novels.)

38 GALE, ROBERT L. "Henry James," in American Literary Scholarship: An Annual: 1970. Edited by J. Albert Robbins.
   Durham, N.C.: Duke Univ. Press, pp. 90-115.
      Survey of criticism published during 1970.

39 GILL, RICHARD. Happy Rural Seat: The English Country House
   and the Literary Imagination. New Haven and London: Yale
   Univ. Press.
      Contents include:
      "The Great Good Place: Henry James and the Country
   House" (pp. 19-93). A comprehensive examination of James's
   use of the country house shows that the house is an actuality and also a symbol, "one of the most attractive vari-
   ants of the 'great good place.'" The importance of houses
   to James is revealed in "their number, carefully chosen
   names, and evocative power." (Special attention is given
   The Princess Casamassima, The Portrait of a Lady, and The
   Spoils of Poynton.)
      "Tradition and an Individual Talent: The Literary Back-
   ground of the Country House in James's Fiction"
   (pp. 255-59). Hawthorne was the major influence on James
   in his treatment of the country house, but other influences
   are Balzac, English novelists of the nineteenth century,
   and Gothic novelists.

40 GOODMAN, CHARLOTTE. "Henry James's Roderick Hudson and Nathaniel Parker Willis's Paul Fane." American Literature,
   43 (January), 642-45.

1972

Since the two works are similar in characterization,
genre, and theme, and since James knew Willis, Willis
should be added to the list of influences on <u>Roderick
Hudson</u>.

41 GRIFFITH, JOHN. "James's 'The Pupil' as Whodunit: The Question of Moral Responsibility." <u>Studies in Short Fiction</u>,
9 (Summer), 257-68.
This tale is "black high comedy." Morgan's death can be
considered either uncaused or self-caused. The issue of
moral responsibility is a product of excessive critical in-
genuity not James's textual ambiguity.

42 GROSSMAN, EDWARD. "Henry James & the Sexual-Military Complex." <u>Commentary</u>, 53 (April), 37-50.
<u>The Bostonians</u>, the action of which is set one hundred
years ago, contains remarkable relevance; it is uncanny in
its reflection of a changing civilization and seemingly
prophetic in its anticipation of the sexual-military complex of the twentieth century.

43 HALPERIN, JOHN WILLIAM. "The Language of Meditation: Four
Studies in Nineteenth-Century Fiction." <u>DAI</u>, 32, 6976A-77A
(Johns Hopkins).
An examination of "meditation" scenes from seven novels
by Jane Austen, George Eliot, George Meredith, and Henry
James provides a framework for discovering the similarities
and differences in the authors' conception of the human
mental process. (<u>The Portrait of a Lady</u> is analyzed.)

44 HARLOW, GEOFFREY, ed. <u>The Year's Work in English Studies:
Vol. 51: 1970</u>. New York: Humanities Press, pp. 431-33.
Survey of criticism for 1970.

45 HINZ, EVELYN J. "Henry James's Names: Tradition, Theory, and
Method." <u>Colby Library Quarterly</u>, 9 (September), 557-78.
James's onomastic techniques, which follow the Puritan
and novel of manners traditions, include: (1) the use of
names simultaneously to particularize and suggest types;
(2) the use of names to enhance his pictorial techniques,
point of view, and dramatic techniques; and (3) the use of
names to elucidate character.

46 HINZ, EVELYN J. "The Imagistic Evolution of James's Businessmen." <u>Canadian Review of American Studies</u>, 3 (Fall), 81-95.
The dominant image associated with James's business type
is "appetite." Within the range of the imagery a gradual
evolution is present as James moves from the vulgar and

voracious esthetic "mouth" of Christopher Newman to the
rapacity of Abel Gaw.

47 HOFFMAN, MICHAEL J. "Realism as Vision and Style: Daisy Mil-
ler and the Social Octopus," in his The Subversive Vision:
American Romanticism in Literature. Port Washington, N.Y.:
Kennikat Press, pp. 117-28.
Daisy Miller fails in her attempts to protect her indi-
viduality in a repressive society.

48 HOUGH, GRAHAM. "English Criticism," in The Twentieth-Century
Mind: History, Ideas and Literature in Britain: Vol. 1:
1900-1918. Edited by C. B. Cox and A. E. Dyson. London:
Oxford Univ. Press, pp. 475-84.
James's criticism "forms a majestic survey of the prob-
lems of prose fiction."

49 HOUGHTON, WALTER E. The Wellesley Index to Victorian Periodicals. Vol. 2. Toronto and Buffalo: Univ. of Toronto
Press, p. 961.
Four works by James which appeared in Victorian periodicals are listed. (Supplements 1966.B45)

50 HUBBELL, JAY. "Henry James," in his Who Are the Major Ameri-
can Writers? Durham, N.C.: Duke Univ. Press, pp. 122-35,
passim.
An overview of James's place in American fiction, of
James's literary opinions, and of the critical view of
James.

51 HYDE, H. MONTGOMERY. "Henry James & Theodora Bosanquet."
Encounter, 39 (October), 6-12.
Theodora Bosanquet's personal recollections of James
provide significant insight into his life and character.
(Unpublished excerpts of Bosanquet's diary are reprinted.)

52 IUCHI, YUSHIRO. "Formation of a Sense of Fall: The Princess
Casamassima." Jimbun Shizen Kagaku Kenkyu (Waseda), 9
(January), 29-44. [Japanese]
This novel is the tragedy of Hyacinth Robinson, an individual of extreme aesthetic delicacy, who is unable to
bear the conflicts of reality. In addition, James portrays
the fall of the civilization embodied in the cultural aristocracy and the rise of the lower class at the end of the
nineteenth century.

53   JOHNSON, RICHARD COLLES, and G. THOMAS TANSELLE. "BAL Adden-
     da: Haldeman-Julius Blue Books." Papers of the Biblio-
     graphical Society of America, 66 (1Q), 67-71.
          Addenda for the fifth volume of the BAL should include
     omissions and corrections for the following: Irving,
     James, Landon, Lanier, Locke, London, and Longfellow.

54   KAMBARA, TATSUO. "James's Gothic: Gothic in American Novels
     (5)." Bungakubu Kiyo (Tokyo Univ. of Education), 88
     (March), 49-65. [Japanese]
          For James, the supernatural was complementary to and
     helpful in understanding the real world; he tried to show
     the dark force in order to express the uncertainty of life.
     In James's Gothic tales, the grotesque perceived by con-
     sciousness is more to be stressed than that perceived by
     the senses. (Treated in detail in this article are "Sir
     Edmund Orme," The Turn of the Screw, "The Private Life,"
     "The Beast in the Jungle," and "The Jolly Corner.")

55   KEPPLER, C. F. The Literature of the Second Self. Tucson:
     Arizona Univ. Press, pp. 164-72.
          Spencer Brydon in The Jolly Corner deliberately seeks
     out his second self, which he had left in his ancestral
     home many years earlier; this second self "is simultaneous-
     ly not only both Spencer Brydon and the opposite of Spencer
     Brydon, but also a past memory and a present reality." In
     The Sense of the Past Ralph Pendrel confronts his second
     self, who lived a century earlier.

56   KERR, HOWARD. "The Young Prophetess: Memories of Spiritual-
     ism and Intimations of Occult Consciousness in Henry
     James's The Bostonians," in his Mediums, and Spirit-
     Rappers, and Roaring Radicals: Spiritualism in American
     Literature, 1850-1900. Urbana: Univ. of Illinois Press,
     pp. 190-222.
          James had a "combination of social and psychological in-
     terests" in spiritualism, and as a result "The Bostonians
     resembled both the anti-spiritualistic, anti-reform satires
     and the magnetic responses of the 1850's, while also anti-
     cipating the studies of psychical consciousness which lay
     ahead in James's supernatural fiction."

57   KIRBY, DAVID K. "Henry James: Art and Autobiography." Dal-
     housie Review, 52 (Winter), 637-44.
          In James's autobiographical writings, he "often attempts
     to make his objects real by the superimposition of art upon
     --or even the substitute of art for--memories of actual
     persons, places, and things."

1972

58   KIRBY, DAVID K. "Henry James's The Other House: From Novel
     to Play." Markham Review, 3 (May), 49-53.
         Both the novel and the play suffer from poor character-
     ization and flawed structure, but through compression the
     play succeeds where the novel failed.

59   KORNFELD, MILTON. "Villainy and Responsibility in The Wings
     of the Dove." Texas Studies in Literature and Language,
     14 (Summer), 337-46.
         James uses the amoral Kate Croy and the embryonic moral
     consciousness of Merton Densher to explore man's motivation
     in the will to good and evil and the meaning of responsi-
     bility and choice, and to force the reader into making
     moral decisions about the characters.

60   KRAMER, HILTON. "Henry James." New York Times Book Review
     (6 February), pp. 1, 32-33.
         The final volume of Edel's biography of James exhibits
     "legendary patience and consummate artistry"; it is a
     "first-class work of art." Review of 1972.A3.

61   LACASSIN, FRANCIS. "Henry James ou l'entrée des fantômes."
     Magazine Littéraire, 67-68 (August-September), 66-72.
     [French]
         The best of James's fine ghost stories is The Turn of
     the Screw, which conforms to the fantastic tradition
     through a conjunction of love and death. James could not
     have written several of the best examples of fantastic lit-
     erature had he not given "his own unconscious some vigorous
     turns of the screw."

62   LYRA, FRANCISZEK, ed. "Correspondence of Helena Modrzejewska
     (Modjeska) to Henry James." Kwartalnik Neofilologiczny
     (Warsaw), 19:89-96.
         Seven letters written by Modrzejewska to James survive;
     the last two reveal that she refused James's request to
     play Madame Vibert in his play Tenants. Correction stating
     that five of these letters were addressed to Longfellow is
     in 1972.B63.

*63 LYRA, FRANCISZEK. "A Note to 'Correspondence of Helena Mod-
     rzejewska (Modjeska) to Henry James.'" Kwartalnik Neo-
     filologiczny (Warsaw), 19:325-26.
         Cited in William T. Stafford, "Henry James," in American
     Literary Scholarship: An Annual/1974. Edited by James
     Woodress. Durham, N.C.: Duke Univ. Press, 1976, p. 89.
         Stafford explains that Lyra "corrects her previous iden-
     tification . . . of seven letters from Modjeska to James to

332

accommodate the later-discovered fact that only the sixth
and seventh of those were to the Master. The first five
had been addressed to Longfellow!" Correction of 1972.B62.

64 McDOWELL, BILL D. "The Use of 'Everything' in The Wings of
    the Dove." Xavier Univ. Studies, 11 (Spring), 13-20.
        James consistently and consciously employs a different
    meaning for the word "everything" for each major charac-
    ter. This varying usage is a structural device that en-
    hances the novel's unity.

65 MacKENZIE, MANFRED. "Communities of Knowledge: Secret Soci-
    ety in Henry James." Journal of English Literary History,
    39 (March), 147-68.
        James's international novels and stories follow a com-
    plex sociological paradigm wherein the protagonist rejects
    American society for European society only to find himself
    simultaneously included and excluded, and as a result he
    must forcibly gain entrance or else lack a social identity.

66 McLEAN, ROBERT C. "'Love by the Doctor's Direction': Disease
    and Death in The Wings of the Dove." Papers on Language
    and Literature, 8, supp.: 128-48.
        For Milly Theale the effect of familial misfortune and
    sexual repression is hysteria, manifested in egocentricty,
    jealousy, indulgent self-pity and a neurotic proclivity
    for fantasizing, that culminates in suicide.

67 MAGLIN, NAN BAUER. "Fictional Feminists in The Bostonians and
    The Odd Women," in Images of Women in Fiction: Feminist
    Perspectives. Edited by Susan K. Cornillon. Bowling
    Green, Ohio: Bowling Green Univ. Popular Press,
    pp. 216-36.
        Though James treated the women's movement with "disgust
    and mockery" and Gissing's attitude showed "support and
    concern," both novels portray the "passion and power" of
    the women's movement as well as giving valid portrayals of
    the leadership and of anti-feminists (Basil Ransom, Edmund
    Widdowson).

68 MARTINEAU, BARBARA. "Portraits Are Murdered in the Short Fic-
    tion of Henry James." Journal of Narrative Technique,
    2:16-25.
        "The Liar," "The Story of a Masterpiece," and "The Bel-
    donald Holbein" contain slashed portraits and reflect an
    evolving concept of the relationship between actuality and
    ʾrtistic representation.

1972

69 MAYNARD, REID. "The Image of Venice in Milly Theale's American Dream of Europe." Studies in the Humanities, 3 (October), 45-50.
Milly Theale's "image of Venice is the controlling symbol of the novel, for this image encompasses all that old
Europe means to her. It is the vision towards which her
aesthetic experience moves as she retreats from the world
outside Palazzo Leporelli, and it is the vision in which
her American dream of Europe is finally confirmed."

70 MAYS, MILTON A. "Down-Town with Henry James." Texas Studies
in Literature and Language, 14 (Spring), 107-22.
In "The Question of Our Speech," "The Speech of American
Women," "The Manners of American Women," and The American
Scene, James's view of an America in which man has aban-
doned his civilizing and cultural role for business is expressed, as well as his pessimism that man will ever re-
cover that role from women.

71 MAZZELLA, ANTHONY J. "James' The Portrait of a Lady." Explicator, 30 (January), Item 37.
The ending of Volume I (Volume III in the New York Edition) of The Portrait of a Lady is "significantly revised
and in a fashion that parallels the ending of Volume II."
The paired revisions of the New York Edition emphasize the
theme of Isabel's complete freedom of choice.

72 MILLER, JAMES EDWIN. Introduction: "A Theory of Fiction in
Outline: Henry James," in his Theory of Fiction: Henry
James. Lincoln: Nebraska Univ. Press, pp. 1-26.
This book presents selections and excerpts from all of
James's work (between 1865 and 1915) in a "comprehensive
and definitive" fashion so as to reveal James's theory of
fiction. James's total theory is outlined in the Introduction under five major headings: The Writer, Preliminary
Concepts, The Work in its Elements, The Work in its Unity,
and Meaning and Impact. Included are a Bibliography of
Sources, an Index to authors and works referred to, and a
list of critical terms. Introduction reprinted from
1971.B84. Reviewed: 1973.B17.

73 MILLER, THEODORE C. "The Muddled Politics of Henry James's
The Bostonians." Georgia Review, 26 (Fall), 336-46.
Basil Ransom manifests five distinct and inconsistent
roles and demonstrates James's inability to present a novelistic defense of conservatism that is unaffected by his
ambivalence.

74 MONTEIRO, GEORGE. Review of Lyall H. Powers's <u>Henry James and
    the Naturalist Movement</u>. <u>American Literature</u>, 44 (Novem-
    ber), 493-94.
        Powers's book is "lucid, closely argued and well-
    balanced." Review of 1971.A5.

75 MOYNAHAN, JULIAN. "Pastoralism as Culture and Counter-Culture
    in English Fiction, 1800-1928." <u>Novel</u>, 6 (Fall), 20-35.
        The pastoral tradition, which idealizes the female image
    in English literature, maintains its value from the begin-
    ning of the nineteenth century into the twentieth century
    despite the imposition of modern society and culture on the
    concept. James is briefly mentioned for maintaining this
    tradition of the feminine ideal when he recounts charac-
    terizing Isabel Archer in the Preface to <u>The Portrait of a
    Lady</u>.

76 NETTELS, ELSA. "Action and Point of View in 'Roderick Hud-
    son.'" <u>English Studies</u>, 53 (June), 238-47.
        The subject of the novel is the consciousness of Rowland
    Mallet, but the character who performs the action is Roder-
    ick. Later James would make the central consciousness not
    only the observer but also the main actor.

77 NETTELS, ELSA. "James and Conrad on the Art of Fiction."
    <u>Texas Studies in Literature and Language</u>, 14 (Fall),
    529-43.
        James and Conrad are similar in matters of form, method,
    the artist's freedom, and their belief that the novel re-
    flects the author's mind and character; they differ, how-
    ever, in their principal preoccupations (James with struc-
    ture and point of view, Conrad with style) and in their
    opinions of the relationship between author and character.

78 NICHOLAS, CHARLES A. "A Second Glance at Henry James's 'The
    Death of the Lion.'" <u>Studies in Short Fiction</u>, 9 (Spring),
    143-46.
        James is satirizing "the kind of journalistic biographi-
    cal criticism that turns an artist into a public figure and
    a social asset while totally ignoring his work."

79 PATRICK, MICHAEL D. "Henry James's Literary Criticism."
    <u>Illinois Quarterly</u>, 35 (December), 20-33.
        Despite the flaws in some of his critical works, James's
    principles of criticism are the bedrock of modern criticism.

1972

80   PODHORETZ, NORMAN. "A Minor Cultural Event." Commentary, 53
      (April), 7-8, 10.
           Philip Rahv's use of political criteria to judge
      James's art and his shift from the ranks of critics bol-
      stering James's resurgent popularity to the ranks of the
      denigrators qualify as a "minor cultural event." Response
      to 1972.B83. See also 1972.B99 and 1972.B82.

81   POWERS, LYALL H. "James's Debt to Alphonse Daudet." Compara-
      tive Literature, 24 (Spring), 150-62.
           Beyond his thematic and structural indebtedness in cre-
      ating The Bostonians, James was influenced in a more gen-
      eral way by Daudet's "poetic naturalism."

82   RAHV, PHILIP. "Digging James." New York Review of Books, 18
      (6 April), 37-38.
           In response to A. Tintner, there are at least three su-
      perior biographies; Tintner's defense of the late novels
      manifests her unperceptiveness; and the fact that her chil-
      dren read James is not representative of today's youth.
      Response to 1972.B98. See also 1972.B80; 1972.B83.

83   RAHV, PHILIP. "Henry James and his Cult." New York Review of
      Books, 18 (10 February), 18-22.
           Edel's voluminous biography of James (1972.A3) with its
      "excessive" and "rapturous" praise typifies the James cult
      that fails to recognize his inadequacies and the fact that
      he is not a great writer on an international scale. Review
      of 1972.A3. Responses in 1972.B80; 1972.B98; 1972.B82.

84   SAITO, HIKARU. "Henry James and the Japanese Readers."
      Gakuto (Tokyo: Maruzen), 69 (November), 8-11. [Japanese]
           James has been much discussed in Japan among students of
      American and British literature, but the general reading
      public has not paid as much attention to him as to Poe,
      Melville, Twain, Hemingway, Faulkner, and Steinbeck. The
      neglect may be due to Soseki Natsume's comment on James's
      stylistic difficulty. James is particularly relevant to
      today's Japanese readers, who have come to take an interest
      in knowing their own national character in this interna-
      tional age.

85   SALZBERG, JOEL. "The Gothic Hero in Transcendental Quest:
      Poe's 'Ligeia' and James' 'The Beast in the Jungle.'"
      Emerson Society Quarterly, ns 18 (2 Q), 108-14.
           Parallel in plot, characterization, and theme, "Ligeia"
      and "The Beast in the Jungle" both adapt the demonic lover-
      gothic maiden fable of the gothic tale. Marcher, however,

finally realizes his lack of humanity, but Poe's protagonist never does. The stories both demonstrate the failure
of the obsessed idealist to come to terms with the value of
personal love.

86 SALZBERG, JOEL. "Love, Identity, and Death: James' The Princess Casamassima Reconsidered." Bulletin of the Rocky
Mountain Modern Language Association, 26:127-35.
The Princess Casamassima is a "study of how love gal-
vanizes Hyacinth's identity into being and how lovelessness
destroys it."

87 SCHWARTZ, ARTHUR. "James in Search of Himself." CEA Critic,
35 (November), 37-39.
Lyall Powers's Henry James and the Naturalist Movement
and Philip M. Weinstein's Henry James and the Requirements
of the Imagination are complementary studies--one external
and one internal--that provide a key to the "quintessential
James." Review of 1971.A5 and 1971.A8.

88 SHANKOVSKY, MARILLA BATTILANA. "Sei personaggi in cerca di
nome." Ateneo Veneto, 10:217-30. [Italian]
James's historical references in "Two Old Houses and
Three Young Women" are like pieces on a chessboard when
only one final move is left to accomplish the game.

89 SIMMS, L. MOODY, JR. "Henry James and the Negro Question."
American Notes and Queries, 10 (April), 127-28.
James had little contact with the southern Negro, so he
deliberately chose not to "lecture" or "moralize" about the
race problem in the South.

90 SMITH, MARTHA STRIBLING. "A Study of the Realistic Treatment
of Psychic Phenomena in Selected Fiction of William Dean
Howells, Hamlin Garland, Henry James, Frank Norris, and
Theodore Dreiser." DAI, 33, 1743A-44A (Univ. of North
Carolina, Chapel Hill).
In the late nineteenth and early twentieth centuries,
characteristically realistic writers were able to include
"ghosts, telepathy, spiritualistic manifestations, and
other mysterious events within realistic settings, leaving
room for physicalistic interpretations as well as specula-
tive ones." (Analysis of The Turn of the Screw is included.)

1972

91 STEIN, WILLIAM BYSSHE. "The Sacred Fount: The Poetics of
       Nothing." Criticism, 14 (Fall), 373-89.
          The language of The Sacred Fount is "constantly charged
       with double meanings," with the literal statements dis-
       torting the character of the objective world. The protag-
       onist's account catalogues the rationalizations he himself
       uses to alleviate his anxieties.

92 STEVENSON, ELIZABETH. "On Henry James." Commentary, 54
       (August), 12.
          A Letter to the Editor states that though James's
       reputation may again suffer "eclipse," he will be redis-
       covered again.

*93 STOENESCU, STEFAN. Introduction, in Ambasadorii [The Ambas-
       sadors]. Bucuresti: University, pp. 5-23.
          Cited in Annual Bibliography of English Language and
       Literature for 1972. Edited by John Horden and J. B.
       Misenheimer. Great Britain: MHRA, 1974, p. 438.

94 STONE, DONALD D. Novelists in a Changing World: Meredith,
       James, and the Transformation of English Fiction in the
       1880's. Cambridge, Mass.: Harvard Univ. Press, pp. 1-5,
       173-337.
          Contents include:
          Introduction: "Two Novelists" (pp. 1-5). Meredith and
       James are "the two finest novelists" of the 1880s and
       "embody opposing trends of the decade."
          "Henry James and the Americanization of English Fiction"
       (pp. 173-330). In his writing of the 1880s "the tension
       between James's early ambitions [to objectivity and real-
       ism] and his emerging subjectivity is most evident." Fi-
       nally, in The Tragic Muse "James advocated the withdrawal
       from all obligations other than to the practice of art."
       The English novel followed James, "unimpressed by Mere-
       dith's warning [against subjectivity] in opposition."
          "Conclusion: Two Novelists" (pp. 332-37). During the
       1880s "Meredith went to pieces in the effort to save the
       best of the Victorian world from dissolution; James, by
       shifting his values from the world to his own inner world
       and his own artistic standards, successfully salvaged the
       writing of fiction--and the need for fiction--for the mod-
       ern world."

95 STONE, DONALD D. "Victorian Feminism and the Nineteenth-
       Century Novel." Women's Studies, 1:65-91.
          A survey of feminism in the Victorian novel reveals that
       male novelists and not their female counterparts were the

supporters of women's rights. A number of late Victorian
novelists portrayed the new woman in a favorable light:
George Meredith, George Gissing, George Moore, Grant Allen,
Thomas Hardy, and Henry James.

96   STONE, EDWARD. "More About Gatsby's Guest List." Fitzgerald-
     Hemingway Annual, pp. 315-16.
         Fitzgerald's "guest list" may have been suggested to him
     by James's "Aspern Papers," in which the narrator comments
     on the guests of Tita and Miss Bordereau.

97   TINTNER, ADELINE R. "Balzac's Two Maries and James's The Am-
     bassadors." English Language Notes, 9 (June), 284-87.
         The similar functions of James's two "Maries" and the
     two "Maries" in Une Fille d'Ève suggest not a Biblical but
     a secular source.

98   TINTNER, ADELINE. "Digging James." New York Review of Books,
     18 (6 April), 37-38.
         In defense of Edel and James, Edel's biographical accom-
     plishment may be the greatest of the century and James's
     last three novels do not "violate 'our sense of reality'";
     they do not indicate snobbery; and "they are popular with
     today's young." Review of 1972.A3. Response to 1972.B83.
     See also 1972.B80 and 1972.B82.

99   TINTNER, ADELINE R. "Hyacinth at the Play: The Play Within
     the Play as a Novelistic Device in James." Journal of Nar-
     rative Technique, 2 (September), 171-85.
         In The Princess Casamassima, as well as in The American
     and The Ambassadors, James used the play within a play
     technique, borrowed both from Hamlet and Balzac's La Comé-
     die humaine, to heighten the awareness of his protagonists.

100 TINTNER, ADELINE R. "The Influence of Balzac's L'envers de
     l'histoire contemporaine on James's 'The Great Good
     Place.'" Studies in Short Fiction, 9 (Fall), 343-51.
         James borrowed heavily from Balzac in creating the
     characterization, language, and tone of "The Great Good
     Place."

101 TINTNER, ADELINE R. "'The Old Things': Balzac's Le curé de
     Tours and James's The Spoils of Poynton." Nineteenth-
     Century Fiction, 26 (March), 436-55.
         Beyond James's admitted indebtedness to Balzac for the
     work's concept, the two stories are similar in plot, theme,
     characterization, and structure and utilize identical ma-
     terial objects, motifs, and words.

1972

102   TODOROV, TZVETAN. "The Structural Analysis of Literature:
The Tales of Henry James," in <u>Structuralism: An Introduc-</u>
<u>tion</u>. Wolfson College Lecture 1972. Edited by David
Robey. Oxford: Clarendon, pp. 73-103.
    A structuralist reading of the tales with the purpose of
discovering "the figure in Henry James's carpet, the primal
plan on which everything depends" reveals that "James's
tales are based on the quest for an absolute and absent
cause."

103   TRILLING, LIONEL. "The Jameses." <u>Times Literary Supplement</u>
(20 October), p. 1257.
    Trilling agrees with Barzun that Leon Edel misinter-
preted the letter in which William James refused election
to the National Institute of Arts and Letters. Affection
between Henry James and William "was strong and remained
unbroken." William did not maintain a "'hidden animus'"
against Henry and was not "strikingly deficient in good
faith." <u>See</u> 1972.B29; 1972.B7; 1972.B30.

104   TUTTLETON, JAMES W. "Henry James: The Superstitious Valua-
tion of Europe," in his <u>The Novel of Manners in America</u>.
Chapel Hill: Univ. of North Carolina Press, pp. 48-85.
    Henry James's "sense of character in relation to soci-
ety, his commitment to civilization, his artistic intelli-
gence, his command of language, the particular felicity of
his style, the characteristic comedy of his phrasing and
diction--it is these that make him not only America's best
novelist of manners but our best novelist."

105   TUVESON, ERNEST. "<u>The Turn of the Screw</u>: A Palimpsest."
<u>Studies in English Literature, 1500-1900</u>, 12 (Autumn),
783-800.
    <u>The Turn of the Screw</u> contains two levels of influence
and interest: on the one hand, it is an exploration of
the inner self similar to activities of the Society for
Psychical Research; on the other hand, it reflects the
spiritual emphasis of Swedenborgianism.

106   UROFF, M. D. "Perception in James's 'The Real Thing.'"
<u>Studies in Short Fiction</u>, 9 (Winter), 41-46.
    James is dramatizing the perils of deluded, myopic, and
distorted perceptions of reality.

*107   VINAROVA, B. "Postscript," in <u>Henri Džejmz: Život i tvor-</u>
<u>čestvo</u> [Henry James: Life and Work], in <u>Henri Džejmz:</u>
<u>Portret na Edna Dama</u> [The Portrait of a Lady]. Sofia:
Narodna Kultura, pp. 639-43.
    Cited in <u>Annual Bibliography of English Language and</u>
<u>Literature for 1972</u>. Edited by John Horden and J. B.
Misenheimer. Great Britain: MHRA, 1974, p. 439.

108   VINCEC, SISTER STEPHANIE. "A Significant Revision in <u>The</u>
<u>Wings of the Dove</u>." <u>Review of English Studies</u>, 23
(February), 58-61.
    In Chapter XXX James corrects a factual error that in
the first American and English edition identified St. Mark
as a column in the arcade which should have been St. Theodore, the Byzantine patron of Venice. Ruskin is possibly
the source of the correction.

109   WALLACE, RONALD. "Comic Form in <u>The Ambassadors</u>." <u>Genre</u>, 5
(March), 31-50.
    <u>The Ambassadors</u>, which resembles <u>The Tempest</u>, is a "com-
bination of international comedy of manners and archetypal
displacement myth."

110   WATANABE, HISAYOSHI. "Memory and Creation: Henry James's
Meaning to the Generations to Follow." <u>Eibungaku Hyoron</u>
(Kyoto Univ.), 28 (January), 24-39. [Japanese]
    Examines the meaning of James's statement, "It is art
that makes life." James knew well that for an artist
"reality forms only in memory," as Proust explained--that
is, that time and distance are essential to the symbolic
meaning of poetry.

111   WESTBROOK, MAX. "Fiction and Belief." <u>Canadian Review of</u>
<u>American Studies</u>, 3 (Spring), 63-67.
    Marston La France's <u>A Reading of Stephen Crane</u> and Peter
Buitenhuis's <u>The Grasping Imagination</u> focus on the authors'
themes, sources, structures and languages in order to show
"those ineluctable brush strokes by which Crane and James
affirm ethical values while seeming to deny any possible
basis for belief." Review of 1970.A1.

112   WILLEN, GERALD, ed. <u>The American</u>. The Crowell Critical Library. New York: Crowell, 468 pp.
    Contents: Includes the text of the novel, the Original
Ending of the novel, James's Preface, a bibliography, and
ten critical articles.
    "Preface" and "A Note on the Text" by Gerald Willen
(pp. v-viii). This novel's "theme of the American as a

1972

self-conceived aristocrat rejecting his society by attempt-
ing to escape from it or its limitations" was not a new
theme when James employed it, and it still has relevance
for Americans today. The text reprinted here is the New
York Edition.

"Henry James's Revision of The American" by Royal Gett-
man (pp. 365-82). Reprinted from American Literature, 6
(January 1945), 275-95.

"Criticism of The American" by Cornelia Pulsifer Kelley
(pp. 382-88). Reprinted from The Early Development of Henry James. Urbana: Univ. of Illinois Press, 1930,
pp. 238-44.

"The Point of View in Henry James: The American" by
Sigmund Hoftun (pp. 389-96). Reprinted from 1961.B48.

"Henry James and the Millionaire" by Irving Howe
(pp. 396-402). Reprinted from Tomorrow, 9 (January 1950),
53-55.

"The Limitations of Christopher Newman" by H. R. Hays
(pp. 402-13). With this novel James originated a tradition
of anxiety in American letters and thought. James attempts
two things in the characterization of Newman: "to create
a type and to raise questions of values."

"A Flaw in The American" by Edward R. Zietlow
(pp. 413-21). Reprinted from 1966.B109.

"Moonshine and Bloodshed: A Note on The American" by
Edmund Creeth (pp. 422-24). Reprinted from 1962.B23.

"The American: A Reinterpretation" by John A. Clair
(pp. 424-35). Reprinted from Publications of the Modern
Language Association of America, 74 (December 1959),
613-18.

"Romance and Fable in James's The American" by George
Knox (pp. 435-49). Reprinted from 1965.B61.

"James, Fitzgerald, and the American Self-Image" by
Kermit Vanderbilt (pp. 449-63). Reprinted from 1965.B116.

113   WOLFF, ERWIN. "James: The Portrait of a Lady," in Der ameri-
kanische Roman: Von den Anfängen bis zur Gegenwart. Hans-
Joachim Lang. Düsseldorf: August Bagel, pp. 168-93.

Includes an analysis of James's theoretical preface, an
analysis of the character of Isabel Archer, an examination
of the figure of the narrator, and an investigation of the
relationships of the minor characters to each other, the
narrator, and the novel as a whole.

114 WOOD, ANN. "Reconsideration: Daisy Miller." New Republic,
     167 (23 & 30 December), 31-33.
         Daisy Miller reflects "the fact that the American girl
     is absolutely and quintessentially public property."

115 YU, FREDERICK YEH-WEI. "Andrew Lytle's A Name for Evil as a
     Redaction of The Turn of the Screw." Michigan Quarterly
     Review, 11 (Summer), 186-90.
         A look at the changes introduced in Lytle's redaction
     suggests that his purpose was to take a critical look at
     the Agrarian movement associated with Vanderbilt in the
     1920s.

1972 C DISSERTATIONS

  1 BERTOLOTTI, DAVID SANTO, JR. "A Concordance of Foreign Words
     and Phrases for the New York Edition of Henry James." DAI,
     33, 2361A (Michigan State).
         James used foreign words and phrases from French, Ital-
     ian, German, Greek, and Latin. Each occurrence is record-
     ed, translated, and the location is identified.

 *2 BORDEN, DIANE M. "Threads for the Labyrinth: Style and Sym-
     bol in Henry James." Dissertation, Santa Cruz, Calif.
         Cited in Ricks, Beatrice, comp. Henry James: A Bibli-
     ography of Secondary Works. Scarecrow Author Bibliogra-
     phies, No. 24. Metuchen, N.J.: Scarecrow, 1975, Item
     1968.1.

  3 BOSCH, LOUIS ALAN. "Henry James's The American: The Novel
     and the Play." DAI, 32, 5774A (Indiana).
         Whereas the novel has many of the important elements
     necessary for good theatre, the play lacks these same ele-
     ments. The few changes made following the initially poor
     critical reception were insufficient to improve subsequent
     reception.

  4 CORE, GEORGE ERIC. "Everything of the Shade of the Real: The
     Fiction of Henry James 1902-1914." DAI, 32, 5223A (Univ.
     of North Carolina, Chapel Hill).
         A critical and analytical examination of the major fic-
     tion from 1902 through 1914, utilizing biographical and
     historical sources, provides the basis for two conclusions:
     (1) that James's fiction is organically related to a whole;
     and (2) that the romance elements of his fiction are sub-
     ordinate to the comic and realistic elements.

1972

5   DYSON, JOHN PETER. "The Soft Breath of Consciousness: A
    Critical Analysis of Some of the Later Tales of Henry
    James." DAI, 32, 4608A (Princeton).
        A careful reading of "The Two Faces," "The Middle Years,"
    "Fordham Castle," "The Velvet Glove," and "The Bench of
    Desolation" reveals how James uses "various manifestations
    of consciousness" to establish an analogy between the "cre-
    ative activity of the artist in relation to his fictional
    characters and to his readers, and the creative activity of
    the fictional characters in relation to each other" and to
    establish "a fictional reality for his readers" just as
    "the characters create fictional reality for themselves and
    other characters."

6   EDELSTEIN, ARNOLD STANLEY. "The Triumph of Fantasy: Ambigu-
    ity and Ambivalence in the Fiction of Henry James." DAI,
    33, 271A-72A (Univ. of California, Berkeley).
        The ambiguity in James's work can be traced to the au-
    thor's psyche. As reflected in his art, ambiguity "results
    from the tension that arises between James's conscious in-
    tentions on the surface level and the frequently contra-
    dictory direction of the fantasy level."

7   FIELD, MARY LEE. "Henry James's Criticism of French Litera-
    ture." DAI, 33, 2370A (Wayne State).
        An overview of James's critical pronouncements on French
    Literature reveals which topics he most frequently comment-
    ed on (leading topics include the problems of translations,
    the differences between the French and British traditions,
    vulgarity in literature, and the topics of form, style, and
    realism); it reveals "that James did not comment as exten-
    sively on form and technique in French literature as he did
    on morality and on the lives and imaginative processes of
    French authors"; and it reveals that significant changes
    occurred between his early and late evaluations.

8   GWIAZDA, RONALD E. "The Spiral Staircase and the Blank Wall:
    Fantasy and Anxiety in Three Early Novels by Henry James."
    Dissertation, Columbia.
        "From Roderick Hudson, The American, and The Portrait of
    a Lady, there emerges a central character through whose
    eyes, through whose emotional responses and observations,
    the fictional world is primarily presented." The three
    protagonists--Rowland Mallet, Christopher Newman, and Isa-
    bel Archer--are all American and "all share in common a
    sense of intense anxiety." Since the world appears to each
    of them to be "sinister and destructive," they are "exam-
    ples of the Jamesian threatened self." These "novels ex-

hibit a strong bent toward fantasy and dreams, toward theories and abstractions, all of which serve the <u>threatened
self</u> as a means of avoiding anxiety and conflict." In addition, these novels "convey a sense of circularity, of re-
turning again and again to the same imagery and symbolism."

9   HALL, SALLIE JEAN. "The Integrated Self: A Reading of the
    Novels of Henry James." <u>DAI</u>, 32, 5738A (Florida).
       A study of nine novels (<u>Washington Square</u>, <u>The Bosto-
    nians</u>, <u>The Aspern Papers</u>, <u>The Portrait of a Lady</u>, <u>The Prin-
    cess Casamassima</u>, <u>Roderick Hudson</u>, <u>The American</u>, <u>The Ambas-
    sadors</u>, <u>The Wings of the Dove</u>) reveals three variations of
    a basic dialectic structure present in each work--the pro-
    tagonist's attempt at self-realization is challenged by the
    "opposite force of self-serving ego gratification."

10 HODGE, JUDITH BUSH. "The Essential Constant: A Focusing De-
    vice in Selected Novels by Henry James." <u>DAI</u>, 33, 1727A
    (Pennsylvania).
       In his lengthy novels James uses recurring experiences to
    relate individual scenes to "larger concerns of the novel."
    These recurring experiences represent an "essential con-
    stant" other authors have established by means of narrative
    techniques. (Includes discussion of <u>The Portrait of a
    Lady</u>, <u>The Bostonians</u>, and <u>The Ambassadors</u>.)

11 JOHNSON, LEE ANN. "The Art of Characterization: James's De-
    piction of the 'Protector' Figure." <u>DAI</u>, 33, 1685A (Univ.
    of California, Los Angeles).
       A comparative study of the "protector" as he appears in
    <u>Watch and Ward</u>, <u>The Awkward Age</u>, <u>Roderick Hudson</u>, <u>The Prin-
    cess Casamassima</u>, <u>The Bostonians</u>, <u>The Spoils of Poynton</u>,
    <u>What Maisie Knew</u>, and <u>The Turn of the Screw</u> reveals a char-
    acter that, "through his misguided moral rigidity, serves
    more frequently to circumscribe his protégé's freedom than
    to foster it."

12 JONES, OLIVER PERRY. "Fables of the Imagination: First-
    Person Narrative in Henry James." <u>DAI</u>, 33, 1729A (State
    Univ. of New York, Buffalo).
       "'The Aspern Papers,' 'The Turn of the Screw,' and <u>The
    Sacred Fount</u> are fables of the imagination which comment
    on the 'penetrating imagination' and the desire to wrest
    some ultimate truth from existence."

1972

13   KIRBY, DAVID KIRK. "Some Implications of the Technique of
     Foreshortening in the Writings of Henry James." DAI, 32,
     6982A (Johns Hopkins).
        James's use of the term "foreshorten" has an analogy in
     the pictorial arts--proportional representation. In the
     craft of fiction the term has meaning in terms of scene,
     character, narrator, and style. (Includes discussion of
     The Wings of the Dove and The Other House.)

14   KLEINBARD, ELAINE ZABLOTNY. "Citadels of Withdrawal: Psycho-
     logical Themes in the Tales of Henry James." DAI, 33,
     2381A (Yale).
        James's portrayal of the individual incapable of pas-
     sionate commitment to another individual reveals keen
     psychological insight into a type of schizoid personality
     identified by W. R. D. Fairbairn and Harry Guntrip years
     later.

15   KRISHAN, BAL. "Henry James and the Nature of Nouvelle."
     DAI, 33, 1688A (Utah).
        Under the influence of Merimee, Maupassant, and Tur-
     genev, James formulated his own ideal of the nouvelle.
     The ideal called for a "large subject" with adequate
     "scope for development" while maintaining control in order
     to "preserve the unified impression of the tale."

16   LAVENDER, KENNETH ERNEST. "Henry James: From Drama to Meta-
     phor, 1896-1904." DAI, 33, 1733A (Univ. of California,
     Santa Barbara).
        James's "major phase" derives its unique quality from
     his concepts of the drama as they are applied to the novel
     and "combined with his structural use of metaphor and
     symbol."

17   LEEMING, DAVID ADAMS. "Henry James and the French Novelists."
     DAI, 32, 5234A (New York Univ.).
        A study of James's critical responses to the French
     novelists, with particular emphasis on Balzac, George
     Sand, Flaubert, Zola, Maupassant, and Daudet, reveals how
     the French provided a life-long touchstone for James's own
     exploration of the "creative imagination" and how he bor-
     rowed elements from each man.

18   LUXFORD, ANSEL FRANK, JR. "Henry James's Forgotten Phase:
     A Critical Analysis of the Late Fiction." DAI, 32, 4618A
     (Virginia).
        The common suggestion that The Sense of the Past, The
     Ivory Tower, and The Finer Grain are works that reflect

1972

James's despair and bitterness is untenable. They are, in fact, thematically related to James's earlier works and can be termed "tragi-comic" novels that emphasize the value of human relationships.

19 RAUNHEIM, JOHN PETER. "A Study of the Revisions of the Tales of Henry James Included in the New York Edition." DAI, 33, 7330A (New York Univ.).

An analysis of the textual differences between the New York Edition and earlier editions provides the basis for a general conclusion that although "not all the revisions were felicitous, . . . the weight of the evidence shows James's constant artistic concern for the improvement of his work."

20 ROWE, JOHN CARLOS. "Restless Analysts: Henry Adams and Henry James: A Study in the Function of Modern Symbolism." DAI, 33, 1739A-40A (State Univ. of New York, Buffalo).

Henry Adams and Henry James are representative of a struggle that was occurring at the end of the nineteenth-century--a "struggle to find an appropriate form for communication and meaning in a world where the absolute foundations for language and thought" had disappeared.

21 SKLEPOWICH, EDWARD ANTHONY. "The Play of Tone: Henry James and the Concept of Social Artifice." DAI, 32, 4633A-34A (Virginia).

"The ideal in the Jamesian social universe is a balance between moral spontaneity and social artifice, between innate, expressed goodness and the self-conscious and stylized use of manners."

22 THOMAS, JEAN LANDERS. "The Technical Synthesis of Henry James: A Study of the Method of 'The Major Phase.'" DAI, 32, 4027A (New York Univ.).

The "major phase" is differentiated from James's earlier psychological novels by his successful infusion of dramatic techniques that enhance the unity and tone of the works.

23 UNRUE, DARLENE HARBOUR. "Henry James and Gothic Romance." DAI, 32, 4028A (Ohio State).

The romance elements in James's works can be more narrowly identified as Gothic elements--elements James borrowed and modified to fit his unique aesthetic and philosophic vision.

1972

24   WALLACE, RONALD WILLIAM. "Henry James and the Comic Form: A
     Study of the Major Novels." DAI, 32, 4029A (Michigan).
        An analysis of James's major novels in terms of charac-
     ters, plots, themes, and styles reveals that the comic
     genre is characteristic of the James canon.

25   YEAZELL, RUTH BERNARD. "The Late Style of Henry James: A
     Study of Style in the Novel." DAI, 32, 7016A (Yale).
        The style, dialogue, and imagery in three products of
     the "major phase," The Ambassadors, The Wings of the Dove,
     and The Golden Bowl, reflect James's concern with "the con-
     flict between complete consciousness and the need for
     order."

1973 A BOOKS

1   GROVER, PHILIP. Henry James and the French Novel: A Study in
     Inspiration. Novelists and Their World Series. London:
     Elek Books Ltd., 221 pp.
        James's work shows important links with French nine-
     teenth-century writers, especially in the area of formal
     elements: he borrowed themes as well as subjects; he
     adapted and developed certain of their techniques; he re-
     sponded critically to a number of French authors; he as-
     similated many of their critical ideas. Three general
     areas reveal the French relationship: "the lesson of Bal-
     zac, the importance of Flaubert and the significance of the
     L'Art pour l'Art movement for James." Reviewed: Adeline
     R. Tintner, Modern Fiction Studies, 20 (1974), 273-77;
     George J. Becker, American Literature, 46 (1974), 233-34;
     J. A. Ward, Nineteenth-Century Fiction, 29 (June 1974),
     107-109.

2   MAINI, DARSHAN SINGH. Henry James: The Indirect Vision:
     Studies in Themes and Techniques. Major American Authors
     Series. Bombay and New Delhi: Tata McGraw-Hill, 228 pp.
        This study of the principal themes and techniques of
     Henry James elucidates the novels of all three of James's
     phases.

3   MAVES, CARL. Sensuous Pessimism: Italy in the Works of Henry
     James. Bloomington: Indiana Univ. Press, 169 pp.
        James visited Italy fourteen times between 1869 and
     1907, and his response to Italy can be found in his fic-
     tion. From the beginnings, James's writings about Italy
     "show a remarkable continuity" and "are dominated by three
     general motifs . . . . of romance, of treachery, and of

sensuousness." For dissertation see 1970.C6. Reviewed:
Motley F. Deakin, Modern Fiction Studies, 19 (Winter 1973-
1974), 595-98; David K. Kirby, New England Quarterly, 47
(1974), 173-75.

4   MULL, DONALD L. Henry James's 'Sublime Economy': Money as
Symbolic Center in the Fiction. Middletown, Conn.: Wes-
leyan Univ. Press, 195 pp.
A tension in James's mind existed "between his sense of
money as the source of imaginative experience and his sense
of it as the mere hard cash by which one had to live."
That tension became in his fiction a metaphor for a greater
tension, "the dilemma of the imagination in its encounter
with the world." The subject of money is examined in selected fiction: early tales and novels, The Portrait of a
Lady ("in which the fact of money is the nexus of meaning"), and The Golden Bowl ("in which the metaphorical language of money becomes the vessel of the dialectic"). For
dissertation see 1967.C11. Reviewed: Adeline R. Tintner,
Modern Fiction Studies, 20 (1974), 273-77; Viola Hopkins
Winner, American Literature, 46 (1974), 232-33; Laurence B.
Holland, Nineteenth-Century Fiction, 29 (1974), 97-100;
David K. Kirby, New England Quarterly, 47 (1974), 342-44.

5   O'NEILL, JOHN P. Workable Design: Action and Situation in
the Fiction of Henry James. National University Publications Series on Literary Criticism. Port Washington, N.Y.:
Kennikat, 152 pp.
A formal analysis of action and situation in five major
novels (The Portrait of a Lady, The Princess Casamassima,
The Spoils of Poynton, The Awkward Age, The Wings of the
Dove) reveals that answers to the problem of motivation in
James "can be found by taking a careful look at a long ne-
glected element in James's work: the extraordinarily
powerful effects of the action and situation in which his
characters appear." Reviewed: Adeline R. Tintner, Modern
Fiction Studies, 20 (1974), 273-77; Martha Banta, American
Literature, 46 (1974), 231-32.

6   POWERS, LYALL H., ed. Henry James's Major Novels: Essays in
Criticism. East Lansing: Michigan State Univ. Press,
461 pp.
Contents: This collection consists of eighteen essays,
all but one of which were published in the past twenty
years, on James's twelve major novels. A selected bibliography is included.
"Introduction" by Lyall H. Powers (pp. xiii-xxi).
James's important achievements in fiction and in critical

writing along with his considerable influence on narrative
technique in the modern novel mark him "as a dominant figure: if not the Master of American Prose Fiction, James
is nevertheless unmistakably a lion in our path."

"James and Arnold: Conscience and Consciousness in a
Victorian Kunstlerroman" by Edward Engelberg (pp. 3-27).
Reprinted from 1968.B35.

"The American" by Constance Rourke (pp. 31-50). Reprinted from American Humor. New York: Harcourt, Brace &
World, 1931, pp. 235-65.

"The Portrait of a Lady" by Arnold Kettle (pp. 53-72).
Reprinted from An Introduction to the English Novel.
Vol. 2. London: Hutchinson, 1951, pp. 13-34.

"The Portrait of a Lady: 'The Eternal Mystery of
Things'" by Lyall H. Powers (pp. 73-85). Reprinted from
Nineteenth-Century Fiction, 14 (September 1959), 143-55.

"The Bostonians" by Lionel Trilling (pp. 89-99). Reprinted from The Opposing Self. New York: Viking, 1955,
pp. 104-17.

"The Princess Casamassima" by Lionel Trilling
(pp. 103-32). Reprinted from "Introduction," in The
Princess Casamassima. New York: Macmillan, 1948.

"The Princess Casamassima: Violence and Decorum" by
Frederick J. Hoffman (pp. 133-45). Reprinted from
1964.B44.

"The Tragic Muse" by Lyall Powers (pp. 149-68). Reprinted from Publications of the Modern Language Association, 73 (June 1958), 270-74.

"What Maisie Knew: The Evolution of a 'Moral Sense'"
by James W. Gargano (pp. 171-84). Reprinted from 1961.B31.

"The Pragmatism of Henry James" by Joseph J. Firebaugh
(pp. 187-201). Reprinted from Virginia Quarterly Review,
27 (Summer 1951), 419-35.

"The Sacred Fount" by Leon Edel (pp. 205-23). Reprinted
from "Introduction," in The Sacred Fount. New York: Grove
Press, 1953.

"Henry James's Subjective Adventurer: 'The Sacred
Fount'" by Tony Tanner (pp. 224-40). Reprinted from
1963.B109.

"The Wings of the Dove" by Dorothea Krook (pp. 243-74).
Reprinted from 1962.A3. This novel is the "most heroic of
James's late works."

"The Wings of the Dove" by Laurence Holland (pp. 275-
313). Reprinted from 1964.A3.

"The Ambassadors" by Frederick C. Crews (pp. 317-45)
Reprinted from The Tragedy of Manners. New Haven: Yale
Univ. Press, 1957, pp. 30-56.

"The New England Conscience, Henry James, and Ambassador Strether" by Austin Warren (pp. 346-57). Reprinted from 1962.B112.

"The Function of Slang in the Dramatic Poetry of the 'Golden Bowl'" by H. K. Girling (pp. 361-76). Reprinted from Nineteenth-Century Fiction, 11 (September 1956), 130-47.

"The Golden Bowl" by Dorothea Krook (pp. 377-458). Reprinted from 1962.A3.

Reviewed: Robert Emmet Long, New England Quarterly, 46 (September), 489-91; G. B. Tennyson, Nineteenth-Century Fiction, 28 (September), 242-47; John R. Marvin, Library Journal, 98 (15 April), 1286.

1973 B SHORTER WRITINGS

1 APPIGNANESI, LISA. "Henry James: Femininity and the Moral Sensibility," in her Femininity and the Creative Imagination: A Study of Henry James, Robert Musil, and Marcel Proust. London: Vision, pp. 20-80.

Since femininity in James's works "is a call to inwardness and introspection, the prerequisite of all true relationship and action," it is this quality that "introduces into the Jamesian world the possibility of full consciousness."

2 ASHTON, JEAN WILLOUGHBY. "The Contact of Flint with Steel: A Study of History, Self, and Form in the Autobiographies of Howells, Adams, James, and Twain." DAI, 33, 4328A (Columbia).

In content the four autobiographies are dissimilar, but in form they are analogous. The formal similarity is the result of a "common urge to explore and define the self" in terms of the historical changes of their generation.

3 AUCHINCLOSS, LOUIS. "The Ambassadors." Horizon, 15 (Summer), 118-19.

Strether is an example of "how desperately human beings, particularly in later life, can try to fool themselves."

4 AZIZ, MAQBOOL. "Revisiting The Pension Beaurepas: The Tale and its Texts." Essays in Criticism, 23 (July), 268-82.

The satiric and comic elements of The Pension Beaurepas are intensified in the revised versions of the tale.

1973

5   AZIZ, MAQBOOL. The Tales of Henry James. Vol. 1: 1864-1869.
     Oxford: Clarendon Press.
         Contents: Contains a chronological listing of James's
     tales with place and date of initial publication, the texts
     of fourteen tales, a preface to each tale with an account
     of its publishing history, a compilation of some of the
     early and private notices about the tales, and textual var-
     iants in seven tales. The "Introduction" by Maqbool Aziz
     (pp. xvii-l) states that the serial texts of the tales
     written by James during the first five years of his career
     are reproduced here.

6   BAILEY, N. I. "Pragmatism in The Ambassadors." Dalhousie Re-
     view, 53 (Spring), 143-48.
         Parallels with pragmatic theory illuminate the meaning
     of the novel, particularly in showing the conclusion of the
     novel to be affirmative.

7   BAKER, ROBERT S. "Gabriel Nash's 'House of Strange Idols':
     Aestheticism in The Tragic Muse." Texas Studies in Litera-
     ture and Language, 15 (Spring), 149-66.
         Gabriel symbolizes the aestheticism of the eighties and
     "stands as an indictment of the aesthete," who abandons
     both life and society to devote "his mind and soul to a
     peculiarly Jamesian version of narcissism."

8   BELL, MILLICENT. "Henry James: The Man Who Lived." Massa-
     chusetts Review, 14 (Spring), 391-414.
         Edel's five volume biography of James is "reared with
     learning and art and the patience of a lifetime," but it
     is "a failure." (This careful analysis of the Edel Vol-
     umes includes much information on Jamesian biography.)
     Review of 1962.A1; 1962.A2; 1969.A1; 1972.A3.

9   BLASING, MUTLU. "Double Focus in The American." Nineteenth-
     Century Fiction, 28 (Summer), 74-84.
         Newman's character is seen only from the outside until
     the Bellegardes reject him, whereupon the focus shifts to
     Newman's consciousness as his self-awareness grows; the
     presence of double focus causes two movements, each having
     distinct plot, humor, and manner of presenting the charac-
     ters.

10   BOBBITT, JOAN. "Aggressive Innocence in The Portrait of a
     Lady." Massachusetts Studies in English, 4:31-37.
         "Ultimately Isabel Archer's 'aggressive' innocence
     proves to be her destruction."

352

1953

11 BRENNEMAN, BETSY. Review of Michael Egan's The Ibsen Years.
    Library Journal, 98 (July), 2106.
        "Egan sufficiently investigates Ibsen's unique influence
    which surfaced in James's later novels with his new manner
    of working out scenic schemes and the expansion of meta-
    phors into symbols." Review of 1972.A4.

12 CANAVAN, THOMAS L. "The Economics of Disease in James's 'The
    Pupil.'" Criticism, 15 (Summer), 253-64.
        Complementary themes of economic success or failure and
    physical health or sickness are present throughout "The
    Pupil."

13 CHAPMAN, SARA S. "The 'Obsession of Egotism' in Henry James's
    'A Round of Visits.'" Arizona Quarterly, 29 (Summer),
    130-38.
        James's last story recounts Mark Monteith's development
    from self-interest to an awareness of the necessity of
    reaching beyond self to others.

14 COOK, DAVID A. "James and Flaubert: The Evolution of Percep-
    tion." Comparative Literature, 25 (Fall), 289-307.
        James's four essays on Flaubert, written between 1874
    and 1902, contain an evolving appreciation that moves from
    a harshly oppressive moralistic assessment, to an ambiva-
    lent appreciation of his artistic talents, to a final per-
    ceptive critical position that marks the final essay as a
    classic piece of Flaubert criticism.

15 COOK, JOHN A. "The Fool Show in Roderick Hudson." Canadian
    Review of American Studies, 4 (Spring), 74-86.
        Roderick Hudson can be read as an ironic tragedy similar
    in themes to King Lear, with Roderick playing the fool, who
    acts out Rowland's unconscious fears and desires.

16 CORE, GEORGE. "Henry James and the Comedy of the New England
    Conscience," in The Comic Imagination in American Litera-
    ture. Edited by Louis D. Rubin, Jr. New Brunswick, N.J.:
    Rutgers Univ. Press, pp. 179-93.
        An examination of four novels--The American, The Golden
    Bowl, The Portrait of a Lady, The Wings of the Dove--
    reveals James's propensity for the comic mode, which he
    uses to praise and celebrate "man's folly."

1973

17   CORE, GEORGE. "Henry, Leon, and Other Jamesians." <u>Michigan
      Quarterly Review</u>, 12 (Winter), 82-88.
          Of six critical works on James, not a single one offers
      a thoroughly convincing and consistent interpretation of
      his work. The six books under consideration are: (1) <u>Hen-
      ry James: The Master</u>, by Leon Edel; (2) <u>Theory of Fiction:
      Henry James</u>, edited by James E. Miller; (3) <u>Henry James and
      the Naturalist Movement</u>, by Lyall H. Powers; (4) <u>The Ambi-
      guity of Henry James</u>, by Charles Thomas Samuels; (5) <u>Crit-
      ics on Henry James</u>, edited by J. Don Vann; and (6) <u>Henry
      James and the Requirements of the Imagination</u>, by Philip M.
      Weinstein. Review of 1972.A3; 1972.B72; 1971.A5; 1971.A6;
      1972.A9; 1971.A8.

18   CROMER, VIRIS. "James and Ibsen." <u>Comparative Literature</u>, 25
      (Spring), 114-27.
          James uses the values and criteria he employs in his own
      art to criticize Ibsen. The resulting criticism praises
      Ibsen's realism and dramatic mastery but questions the
      scope of his vision.

19   DEAN, SHARON WELCH. "Lost Ladies: The Isolated Heroine in
      the Fiction of Hawthorne, James, Fitzgerald, Hemingway, and
      Faulkner." <u>DAI</u>, 34, 2616A (New Hampshire).
          The elements common to all five writers in their treat-
      ment of the "lost lady" are "sexuality, isolation, and
      sacrifice." Each author, while making changes necessary to
      his unique purpose, uses the type "as a vehicle for explor-
      ing the conflict between isolation and society." (Includes
      discussion of <u>The Wings of the Dove</u> and <u>The Golden Bowl</u>.)

*20   DUMITRIU, GHEORGHITA. "Henry James's Use of Imagery in <u>The
      Wings of the Dove</u>." <u>Analele Universității</u>, <u>București</u>,
      <u>Limbi Germanice</u>, 22:61-74.
          Cited in <u>1974 MLA International Bibliography</u>, vol. 1,
      p. 159.

21   DUMITRIU, DANA. "Un eseu despre Henry James: O aventură
      primejdioasă." <u>Romania Literara</u>, 15 (March 15), 28-29.
      [Roumanian]
          Visible in Henry James is his internal, omnipresent con-
      flict; a conflict coming from his American background (new,
      young, imaginative, and energetic) and his love for a deca-
      dent, structuralized Old World.

22   ENGSTRØM, SUSANNE. "Historical or Moral Validity, or Two
     Kinds of Norms." Language and Literature, 1:83-86.
          In her article on The Ambassadors (1971.B33), Engstrøm
     was interested in the problem of finding the norms com-
     municated by the "implied author" of the novel. Response
     to 1972.B36.

23   FABIAN, BERNHARD. "Henry James: The Portrait of a Lady," in
     Der englische Roman im 19. Jahrhundert: Interpretationen.
     Zu Ehren von Horst Oppel. Edited by Paul Goetsch, Heinz
     Kosok, and Kurt Otten. Berlin: Erich Schmidt, pp. 232-42.
     [German]
          For James, character is more important than plot. In
     this novel a character is portrayed through a dual perspec-
     tive: (1) from the point of view of the central figure
     herself, as she perceives present events; (2) from the
     point of view of the narrator, who provides biographical
     and temporal background.

24   FEIDELSON, CHARLES. "James and the 'Man of Imagination,'" in
     Literary Theory and Structure: Essays in Honor of William
     K. Wimsatt. Edited by Frank Brady, John Palmer, and Martin
     Price. New Haven and London: Yale Univ. Press, pp. 331-52.
          When James speculates about the "man of imagination" in
     the preface to The Ambassadors and in Notes of a Son and
     Brother, he is dramatizing a "problematic interplay" be-
     tween "Romantic premises and the premises of a 'realistic'
     social novelist."

25   FRYER, JUDITH JOY. "The Faces of Eve: A Study of Women in
     American Life and Literature in the Nineteenth Century."
     DAI, 34, 2558A (Minnesota).
          Unlike Adam, who is easily traced in American litera-
     ture, Eve is many-faceted, and frequently only one aspect
     of her character is discernible at one time. Four aspects
     of Eve are: (1) "The Temptress," (2) "The American Prin-
     cess," (3) "The Great Mother," and (4) "The New Woman."

26   FULLER, ROY. "The Two Sides of the Street." Southern Review,
     9 (July), 579-94.
          Since James the novel has assimilated poetic qualities,
     but this development does not signal the demise of poetry;
     whereas prose fiction has adopted poetic elements--"the-
     matic imagery, ambiguous characterization, [and] critical
     morality"--poetry cannot adopt novelistic techniques.

1973

27   GARGANO, JAMES W.   "'The Aspern Papers': The Untold Story."
     Studies in Short Fiction, 10 (Winter), 1-10.
     The narrator's limited perception of the superficial,
     sensory experiences of the story dramatically illustrates
     the consequences of "unseen and unrealized opportunities."

28   GEISMAR, MAXWELL.   "Evading Art and Society."   Chicago Review,
     24 (Spring), 85-92.
     Henry James represents an "exotic and singular curiosi-
     ty" in American literature.   He is not a major writer, al-
     though he is a "talented literary entertainer."

29   GIRGUS, SAM B.   "The Other Maisie: Inner Death and Fatalism
     in What Maisie Knew."   Arizona Quarterly, 29 (Summer),
     115-22.
     Maisie's childhood is a "form of internal, psychological
     death from which she can never escape."

30   GONZALO, ANGEL CAPELLAN.   "Un Monumento Biográfico a Henry
     James."   Studia Neophilologica, 3:82-90.
     Leon Edel has employed a praiseworthy accuracy, method
     and critical acumen in his five-volume biography of Henry
     James.   Review of 1962.A1; 1962.A2; 1969.A1; 1972.A3.

31   GREENE, MILDRED S.   "Les liaisons dangereuses and The Golden
     Bowl: Maggie's 'Loving Reason.'"   Modern Fiction Studies,
     19 (Winter 1973-1974), 531-40.
     Similarities can be found between Maggie Verver and
     Mme. de Merteuil.

32   GROVER, P. R.   "Henry James and the Theme of the Adventuress."
     Revue de Littérature Comparée, 47 (October-December),
     586-96.
     James's "The Diary of a Man of Fifty" and "Louisa Pal-
     lant" contain echoes of situation, plot, characterization,
     and dialogue from Dumas the Younger's Le Demi-Monde and
     Augier's l'Aventurière and Le Mariage d'Olympe, but the
     theme is presented in James's "own idiom and with his own
     quite different moral complexities."

33   HALPERIN, JOHN.   "Henry James (1843-1916)," in his The Lan-
     guage of Meditation: Four Studies in Nineteenth-Century
     Fiction.   Elms Court, Ilfracombe, Devon: Arthur H. Stock-
     well Ltd., pp. 116-55.
     James's The Portrait of a Lady and The Golden Bowl re-
     veal his emphasis on concreteness in the epistemological
     process: relationships are perceived spatially; charac-
     ters tend to "pictorialize"; and architectural metaphors
     abound.

34   HAMBLEN, ABIGAIL ANN. "Literary Ramble: Architectural Imag-
     ery in The Golden Bowl." Architectural Forum, 139 (July-
     August), 98, 100.
          Architectural figures abound in The Golden Bowl.

35   HARLOW, GEOFFREY, ed. The Year's Work in English Studies:
     Vol. 52: 1971. New York: Humanities Press, pp. 453-55.
          Survey of criticism for 1971.

36   HEINEY, DONALD, and LENTHIEL H. DOWNS. "Henry James," in
     Recent American Literature to 1930. Barron's Educational
     Series. Woodbury, N.Y.: Barron, pp. 33-51.
          A critical overview of James's work precedes individual
     summaries and interpretations of his chief works.

37   HEROLD, EVE GRIFFITH. "A Study of the Bildungsroman in Ameri-
     can Literature." DAI, 34, 2562A (Ohio State).
          James is one of the authors examined in this study which
     seeks "to illuminate generally the relationship between the
     Bildungsroman and social criticism."

38   HILL, JOHN EDWARD. "Dialectical Aestheticism: Essays on the
     Criticism of Swinburne, Pater, Wilde, James, Shaw, and
     Yeats." DAI, 33, 3648A-49A (Virginia).
          Swinburne's William Blake contains the premise shared by
     Pater, Wilde, James, Shaw and Yeats--that "the critic as
     artist shares the sensibility of the artist as artist."

39   HOUSTON, N. B. "Henry James's 'Maud-Evelyn': Classic Folie
     à Deux." Research Studies, 41:28-41.
          Marmaduke and the Dedricks exhibit the seven-fold symp-
     toms characteristic of folie à deux, as defined by Alexander
     Gralnick, thereby anticipating an as yet unidentified
     psychosis.

40   JOHNSON, LEE ANN. "'A Dog in the Manger': James's Depiction
     of Roger Lawrence in Watch and Ward." Arizona Quarterly,
     29 (Summer), 169-76.
          Utilizing a variety of characterization techniques,
     James succeeds in depicting Roger Lawrence as a man of
     moral complexity and ambiguity--a depiction that is an-
     ticipatory of many of James's later protagonists.

41   KAU, JOSEPH. "Henry James and the Garden: A Symbolic Setting
     for 'The Beast in the Jungle.'" Studies in Short Fiction,
     10 (Spring), 187-98.
          The vigil of Marcher and May evokes an overtone of the
     Garden of Passion through the use of sustained Biblical

1973

imagery. The effect of the overtone is to heighten the
emphasis given decision.

42   KEHLER, JOEL R. "Salvation and Resurrection in James' 'The
       Beast in the Jungle.'" Essays in Literature (Univ. of
       Denver), 1:13-29.
          An examination of the relationship of the two central
       characters in the context of three mythic patterns employed
       by James ("John Marcher and May Bartram are portrayed vari-
       ously as the archetypal (1) spirits of seasons, (2) Christ
       and Everyman, and (3) Madonna and Child") reveals that it
       is May, not Marcher, who must suffer, whose fate is sealed,
       and who provides the means of Marcher's psychological and
       symbolic salvation.

43   KENNEDY, IAN. "Frederick Winterbourne: The Good Bad Boy in
       Daisy Miller." Arizona Quarterly, 29 (Summer), 139-50.
          The observable behaviors of Winterbourne make him a very
       attractive character; but internally he is a man "whose re-
       pressed libidinal instincts and romantic self-deceptive,
       [and] squinted vision of reality make him potentially a
       very dangerous character."

44   KENNEDY, J. GERALD. "Jeffrey Aspern and Edgar Allan Poe: A
       Speculation." Poe Studies, 6 (June), 17-18.
          James, in addition to his acknowledged prototype for
       Jeffrey Aspern, may have used Edgar Allan Poe as described
       in an essay by T. W. Higginson.

45   KIRBY, DAVID K. "A Possible Source for James's 'The Death of
       the Lion.'" Colby Library Quarterly, 10 (March), 39-40.
          The Autobiography of William Powell Frith contains an
       incident about the poet Thomas Moore which may be the
       source for James's story.

46   KRAFT, JAMES. "On Reading The American Scene." Prose, 6
       (Spring), 115-36.
          In order to maximize the reading experience of The Amer-
       ican Scene, the reader must become a "restless analyst" and
       along with James examine the potentialities of man in the
       democratic experiment.

47   KRIER, WILLIAM JOHN. "A Pattern of Limitations: The Hero-
       ine's Novel of the Mind." DAI, 34, 277A-78A (Indiana).
          This study of "the evolving use by novelists of heroines
       trapped in the powerless position" (which is termed the
       "feminine situation") includes two chapters on Henry James.
       Analysis of "Madame de Mauves," "Daisy Miller," and The

Portrait of a Lady is presented in terms of James's use of the "feminine situation."

48 KROOK, DOROTHEA. "The Madness of Art: Further Reflections on the Ambiguity of Henry James." Hebrew University Studies in Literature, 1 (Spring), 25-38.
    Dorothea Krook updates her book, The Ordeal of Consciousness in Henry James (1962.A3), "eliminating some of the errors of emphasis and proportion . . . and drawing out some further implications."

49 KUHLMANN, SUSAN. "To the Old World," in her Knave, Fool, and Genius: The Confidence Man as He Appears in Nineteenth-Century Fiction. Chapel Hill: Univ. of North Carolina Press, pp. 91-103.
    Caroline Spencer in Four Meetings is the innocent American who is duped out of her savings in Europe by her cousin, a confidence man. And Isabel Archer and Milly Theale are innocents who are victims of confidence women, Serena Merle and Kate Croy.

50 LABRIE, ROSS. "The Power of Consciousness in Henry James." Arizona Quarterly, 29 (Summer), 101-14.
    The emphasis of the consciousness in The Sacred Fount and The Golden Bowl is different from the emphasis in The Bostonians. In the later works the epistemological problems related to consciousness are not focused on; rather James seems to have "recovered his faith" in the potency of the consciousness.

51 LANGBAUM, ROBERT. "Thoughts for Our Time: Three Novels on Anarchism." American Scholar, 42 (Spring), 227-50.
    Joseph Conrad's The Secret Agent, Dostoevsky's The Possessed, and Henry James's The Princess Casamassima share a common thematic interest in anarchism and as a group point simultaneously to the limitations of politics and the dangers of revolution.

52 LARSON, JUDY. "The Drama Criticism of Henry James." Yale/ Theatre, 4:103-109.
    James's drama criticism includes appraisals of the drama audience, evaluations of the state of the art in various nations, judgments of specific actors, and criticism of playwrights (Dumas and Ibsen are praised, while Edmond Rostand is deplored).

1973

53   LONG, ROBERT E. "James's <u>Washington Square</u>: The Hawthorne
      Relation." <u>New England Quarterly</u>, 46 (December), 573-90.
           James placed himself in the tradition of novelists such
      as Eliot and Hawthorne, who "'care for the moral ques-
      tions'" and "'are haunted by a moral ideal.'" James found
      American sources from which to draw for <u>Washington Square</u>
      in Hawthorne and the convention of the gothic tale. Cath-
      erine's fate has "local" qualities which help make the nov-
      el "a tale truly American."

54   McELROY, JOHN. "The Hawthorne Style of American Fiction."
      <u>Emerson Society Quarterly</u>, 71 [ns 18] (1Q), 117-23.
           As literary descendants of Hawthorne, James and Faulkner
      are deeply aware of the importance of "native place" and
      of "native social tradition." Both writers frequently "in-
      voke the past." Hawthorne's chief legacy, however, was the
      "invention of retroaction, or the style of fiction that
      progresses by discovering what has gone before."

55   McMASTER, JULIET. "The Portrait of Isabel Archer." <u>American
      Literature</u>, 45 (March), 50-66.
           An exploration into Isabel Archer's ambivalent nature
      reveals her proclivity toward life, liberation, and happi-
      ness in conflict with a desire for suffering and self-
      imprisonment in a "paralysing aestheticism" as a work of
      art for Osmond.

56   MALIN, IRVING. "American Gothic Images." <u>Mosaic</u>, 6 (Spring),
      145-71.
           The American "nightmare" can be examined in the literary
      manifestations of three images: (1) the castle haunted by
      authoritarianism; (2) the voyage with its perils; and
      (3) the masquerade with its duplicity. (Works discussed
      include <u>The Portrait of a Lady</u>, <u>The Sense of the Past</u>,
      "The Jolly Corner," "The Beast in the Jungle," <u>The Ambas-
      sadors</u>, and <u>The Golden Bowl</u>.)

57   MARTINEZ, INEZ. "Introduction," in <u>The Speech and Manners of
      American Women</u>. Edited by E. S. Riggs. Lancaster, Pa.:
      Lancaster House Press, pp. 3-12.
           "These essays about American women are an indirect com-
      mentary on American society and a plea for social commit-
      ment to consciousness and to form." According to James,
      American women lack "manners and language," and their fail-
      ure is due to "infantilism."

58 MERRILL, ROBERT. "What Strether Sees: The Ending of The Am-
    bassadors." Bulletin of the Rocky Mountain Modern Language
    Association, 27 (June), 45-52.
       The climax of Strether's growth does not consist of a
    rejection of any person but of a rejection of his old way
    of perceiving experience.

59 MORRIS, R. A. "Classical Vision and the American City: Henry
    James's The Bostonians." New England Quarterly, 46 (Decem-
    ber), 543-57.
       Henry James attempted "to invest the American urban
    scene with an aesthetic significance." The "classical
    vision" can be traced throughout The Bostonians and shows
    that James was trying to "come to grips imaginatively with
    the difficult, anomic facts of contemporary American urban
    life."

60 NELSON, CARL. "James's Social Criticism: The Voice of the
    Ringmaster in The Awkward Age." Arizona Quarterly, 29
    (Summer), 151-68.
       The reader must grasp that the narrator is the showman
    who joins in "the spiritual and immoral charades of the
    age" and understand that the novel is "a condemnation of
    the circus atmosphere that is presented."

61 NETHERY, WALLACE. "Tragedy of Errors: A Note on The Bosto-
    nians." Coranto, 8:34-41.
       Among the social and artistic "errors" which may have
    contributed to the failure of The Bostonians are: the
    lesbian relationship between Olive and Verena; the casting
    of a Southerner as protagonist; the characterization of
    Miss Birdseye, who reminded readers of Elizabeth Peabody;
    and the portrayal of Boston, which some Bostonians regard-
    ed as an attack on their native city.

62 NORTON, RICTOR CARL. "Studies of the Union of Love and
    Death: I. Heracles and Hylas: The Homosexual Archetype.
    II. The Pursuit of Ganymede in Renaissance Pastoral Liter-
    ature. III. Folklore and Myth in Who's Afraid of Virginia
    Woolf? IV. The Turn of the Screw: Coincidentia Opposi-
    torum." DAI, 33, 5190A-91A (Florida State).
       "James's story systematically creates a Hegelian union
    of opposites or Jungian coincidentia oppositorum. The
    story is a ritual drama with three acts which correspond
    to the three stages of inquisitorial torture: the prepara-
    tory torture, the question definitif, and the question
    extraordinaire."

1973

63   PATERSON, JOHN. <u>The Novel as Faith: The Gospel According to</u>
      <u>James, Hardy, Conrad, Joyce, Lawrence and Virginia Woolf.</u>
      Boston: Gambit, pp. 3-39, 230-93, passim.
          The first six chapters of this book "define the theories
      of the individual novelists"; a final chapter "defines the
      relations (and disrelations) between them."

64   PENDLETON, JAMES D. "The James Brothers and 'The Real Thing':
      A Study in Pragmatic Reality." <u>South Atlantic Bulletin</u>, 38
      (November), 3-10.
          William and Henry shared identical philosophical prem-
      ises on the subjects of truth and reality.

65   PICKERING, SAMUEL F. "The Sources of 'The Author of Beltraf-
      fio.'" <u>Arizona Quarterly</u>, 29 (Summer), 177-90.
          Sources include not only an anecdote about John Adding-
      ton Symonds, but also more significant experiences from
      James's memory such as W. Besant's criticism, an 1869 visit
      to William Morris, and paintings by the Pre-Raphaelites and
      Joshua Reynolds.

66   PORTER, CAROLYN JANE. "Form and Process in American Litera-
      ture." <u>DAI</u>, 34, 1291A (Rice).
          A study of the tension that exists "between (1) the need
      for a formal structure·through which experience is ordered
      and given meaning, and (2) the recognition that human ex-
      perience occurs in a world always changing, in process, and
      thus resisting the formal urge" in terms of four major au-
      thors, Emerson, Whitman, James, and Faulkner, reveals that
      "beneath the decisive shift from form as given to form as
      created, there persists a fundamental tension between the
      need for pattern and the desire to transcend all patterns."
      (Includes interpretation of <u>The Golden Bowl</u>.)

*67   RADHA, K. "<u>The Turn of the Screw</u>: A Critical Examination of
      Its Meaning," in <u>Literary Studies: Homage to Dr. A. Siva-</u>
      <u>ramasubramonia Aiyer</u>. Edited by K. P. K. Menon, M. Manuel,
      and K. Ayyappa Paniker. Trivandrum: St. Joseph's Press
      for the Dr. A. Sivaramasubramonia Aiyer Memorial Committee,
      pp. 103-11.
          Cited in <u>1973 MLA International Bibliography</u>, vol. 1,
      p. 148.

68   RANDALL, JOHN H., III. "Romeo and Juliet in the New World:
      A Study in James, Wharton, and Fitzgerald: 'Fay ce que
      vouldras.'" <u>Costerus</u>, 8:109-75.
          "Daisy Miller," <u>The House of Mirth</u>, and <u>The Great Gatsby</u>
      are versions of the Romeo and Juliet legend in which the

authors have written "tales of romantic love" and
freighted "them with meanings that are, in the broad
sense, political."

69   RECCHIA, EDWARD. "James's 'The Figure in the Carpet': The
     Quality of Fictional Experience." Studies in Short Fic-
     tion, 10 (Fall), 357-65.
          The critic-narrator reveals the potential fallacy of
     searching for esoteric meanings in art works, whereas
     George Corvick represents an emulative critical approach
     that focuses on the reader's experiential response.

70   REYNOLDS, LARRY J. "Henry James's New Christopher Newman."
     Studies in the Novel, 5 (Winter), 457-68.
          In the New York Edition of The American, James substan-
     tively changed the character of Christopher Newman five
     ways, thereby making him "a more engaging and sympathetic
     hero."

71   RIMMON, SHLOMITH. "Barthes' 'Hermeneutic Code' and Henry
     James's Literary Detective: Plot-Composition in 'The Fig-
     ure in the Carpet.'" Hebrew University Studies in Litera-
     ture, 1:183-207.
          The hermeneutic code postulated by Barthes is an ideal
     tool for explicating James's "metaliterary story." The
     three structural hermeneutic units--"exposition," "body,"
     and "dévoilement"--are clearly present with the dévoile-
     ment being delayed by five reproductions of the quest
     motif.

72   ROSE, HARRIET. "The First-Person Narrator as Artist in the
     Works of Charles Brockden Brown, Nathaniel Hawthorne, and
     Henry James." DAI, 33, 6373A (Indiana).
          A study of Brown's Arthur Mervyn, Hawthorne's The
     Blithedale Romance, and James's Stories of Writers and
     Artists provides a composite portrait of a characteristic
     American type--the writer who displays "criminal overtones,"
     is "guilty of aesthetic fraudulence," and nearly always
     ends a "creative failure."

73   ROSE, SHIRLEY. "Waymarsh's 'Sombre Glow' and Der Fliegende
     Holländer." American Literature, 45 (November), 438-41.
          The import of James's recurring description of Waymarsh
     --"sombre glow"--is found in its Wagnerian source.

1973

74   ROWE, JOHN C.   "The Symbolization of Milly Theale: Henry
        James's The Wings of the Dove." Journal of English Liter-
        ary History, 40 (Spring), 131-64.
           Maud Manningham, Kate Croy, Merton Densher, Lord Mark
        and Susie Stringham view Milly archetypally, projecting
        their individual needs on her; it is Milly's ability to
        "individualize" herself that represents the triumph of her
        humanity and helps the others to recognize their humanity.

75   RUGGIERO, CLAUDIA CORRADINI.   "Henry James as a Critic: Some
        Early French Influences." Revista di Letterature Moderne
        e Comparate (Florence), 26:285-306.
           Analyzes French influences on James's early criticism
        with particular attention to a chronological and textual
        comparison of Edmond Scherer's criticism with James's.

76   SABISTON, ELIZABETH.   "The Prison of Womanhood." Comparative
        Literature, 25 (Fall), 336-51.
           Austen's Emma Woodhouse, Flaubert's Emma Bovary, Eliot's
        Dorothea Brooke, and James's Isabel Archer "exhibit re-
        markably similar aspirations and failings, in that each
        attempts to impose on life a romantic ideal, which crum-
        bles after a series of confrontations with reality."

77   SCHECHTER, HAROLD.   "The Unpardonable Sin in 'Washington
        Square.'" Studies in Short Fiction, 10 (Spring), 137-41.
           Dr. Austin Sloper is of a character like the Hawthorne
        protagonists who commit the Unpardonable Sin of suppressing
        the affectual responses while elevating the intellectual
        ones.

78   SECOR, ROBERT.   "Christopher Newman: How Innocent Is James's
        American?" Studies in American Fiction, 1 (August),
        141-53.
           In the last fifth of The Ambassadors, Newman's potential
        for evil is explored. Since he considered revenging him-
        self by using family secrets, he shows himself to be "nei-
        ther eternally innocent nor absolutely good."

79   SHINN, THELMA J.   "A Question of Survival: An Analysis of
        'The Treacherous Years' of Henry James." Literature and
        Psychology, 23:135-48.
           Following the failure of "Guy Domville," James engaged
        for the next five or six years in two tasks--his own emo-
        tional reconstruction and experimentation with form--that
        culminated in his greatest personal and literary success,
        The Golden Bowl.

80   SHUCARD, ALAN R. "Diplomacy in Henry James's The Ambassa-
      dors." Arizona Quarterly, 29 (Summer), 123-29.
          The "splendidly knotted thread of diplomacy" is an im-
      portant structural device for the novel. The novel's dic-
      tion reflects the basically diplomatic relationships in
      which Strether is an "unprofessional emissary on a diplo-
      matic mission."

81   SMITH, WILLIAM F., JR. "Sentence Structure in the Tales of
      Henry James." Style, 7 (Spring), 157-72.
          The development of James's style can be traced through
      a syntactical analysis of "The Madonna of the Future,"
      "The Death of the Lion," and "The Jolly Corner."

82   SORESCU, ROXANA. "Henry James, precursor al romanului mo-
      dern." Revista de Istorie şi Theorie Literară, 22:387-95.
      [Roumanian]
          James's theme and method usually involve a superficial
      level and a stream of consciousness level. For example,
      both The Ambassadors and "The Beast in the Jungle" develop
      in two interwoven layers: characters' relationships and
      psychological explanations of their subconscious.

83   SPILKA, MARK. "Henry James and Walter Besant: 'The Art of
      Fiction' Controversy." Novel, 6 (Winter), 101-19.
          Walter Besant's lecture "The Art of Fiction" precipi-
      tated James's essay of the same title and marked the begin-
      ning of "an adventure of immense importance to the novel's
      history."

84   SPILKA, MARK. "Ian Watt on Intrusive Authors, or the Future
      of an Illusion." Hebrew University Studies in Literature,
      1:1-24.
          James was the first modern novelist to focus on the
      problem of the intrusive author; and now the "modern author
      is in fact an immanent rather than an omniscient narrator,
      working through techniques rather than with them, to create
      that audience of uncommon readers which his problematic
      fiction demands."

85   STAFFORD, WILLIAM T. "Henry James," in American Literary
      Scholarship: An Annual: 1971. Edited by J. Albert Rob-
      bins. Durham, N.C.: Duke University Press, pp. 86-103.
          Survey of criticism published during 1971.

1973

*86   STAFFORD, WILLIAM. <u>An Index to Henry James' Criticism and</u>
      <u>Essays</u>. Washington, D. C.: NCR Microcard Editions.
           Cited in Beatrice Ricks, comp. <u>Henry James: A Bibliog-</u>
      <u>raphy of Secondary Works</u>. Scarecrow Author Bibliographies,
      No. 24. Metuchen, N.J.: Scarecrow, Item 1640.2.

*87   STANCULESCU, LIANA. "Henry James's Use of Metaphor in <u>The</u>
      <u>Golden Bowl</u>." <u>Analele Universității, București, Litera-</u>
      <u>tură Universala Comparată</u>, 22:117-31.
           Cited in <u>1974 MLA International Bibliography</u>, vol. 1,
      p. 160.

88   STERN, J. P. <u>On Realism</u>. London and Boston: Routledge and
      Kegan Paul, passim.
           Less than a dozen passing references to Henry James ap-
      pear in this critical study of realism.

89   STIMPSON, CATHARINE. "The Case of Miss Joan Didion." <u>Ms.</u>, 1
      (January), 36-41.
           Joan Didion's limitations in portraying the essential
      and complex issue of freedom of women are apparent when
      her work is compared to Henry James's <u>The Bostonians</u>, a
      peculiarly modern novel that treats richly the "possession
      of one person by another."

90   STONE, WILLIAM B. "On the Background of James's <u>In the Cage</u>."
      <u>American Literary Realism</u>, 6 (Summer), 243-47.
           James's presentation of the working girl of <u>In the Cage</u>,
      while not absolutely accurate factually, shows a familiar-
      ity with "telegraphers' general working conditions and a
      certain awareness of the details of these conditions."

91   STONE, WILLIAM B. "Towards a Definition of Literary Realism."
      <u>Centrum</u>, 1:47-60.
           Literary realism consists of a balance between objective
      reality and aesthetic order. Where the theme of a work,
      utilizing setting, plot, characterization and symbolism, is
      presented in an "unobtrusive" manner, the work tends toward
      realism, but as these devices increase in obtrusiveness,
      the work moves further from realism.

92   SULLIVAN, JEREMIAH J. "Henry James and Hippolyte Taine: The
      Historical and Scientific Method in Literature." <u>Compara-</u>
      <u>tive Literature Studies</u>, 10 (March), 25-50.
           James at times admired the analytical and objective
      method of Taine's criticism, his view of the novelist as
      historian of "race, milieu and moment," and his emphasis
      on aesthetic use of the scientific method. Taine's

366

influence can be detected in James's art criticism, his
criticism of Hawthorne, his essay on Balzac, his use of
types in The American and The Bostonians, and in other literary endeavors.

93 SWINDEN, PATRICK. "Registration: Henry James," in his Unofficial Selves: Character in the Novel from Dickens to the
Present Day. New York: Barnes and Noble, pp. 100-19,
passim.
    Discussion of James includes a consideration of James's
theory of the novel and a reading of The Golden Bowl.

94 THOMPSON, DAVID JOSEPH SIMON. "Societal Definitions of Individualism and the Critique of Egotism as a Major Theme in
American Fiction." DAI, 33, 4435A (Brown).
    The concept of individualism championed by the general
public of America "was in the eyes of Hawthorne, James,
Faulkner, and Warren an inadequate and morally reprehensi-
ble basis for society." The attention given to egotism, or
individualism, by major American writers qualifies it as a
central theme of American Literature. (Includes discussion
of The Portrait of a Lady.)

95 THORNTON, LAWRENCE. "Rosamond Lehmann, Henry James, and the
Temporal Matrix of Fiction." Virginia Woolf Quarterly, 1
(Spring), 66-75.
    Rosamond Lehmann's female protagonist is similar to
James's female protagonists. Lehmann, however, turns what
appears to be the very defects of James's women into attri-
butes in The Ballad and the Source.

96 TINTNER, ADELINE R. "Balzac's 'Madame Firmiani' and James's
The Ambassadors." Comparative Literature, 25 (Spring),
128-35.
    The Ambassadors resembles Balzac's "Madame Firmiani" in
plot, in method of presentation, in theme, and in pastoral
tone, and reveals the persisting influence of the French
author.

97 TINTNER, ADELINE R. "The Elgin Marbles and Titian's 'Bacchus
and Ariadne': A Cluster of Keatsian Associations in Henry
James." Notes and Queries, 20 (July), 250-52.
    The Elgin Marbles and the "Bacchus and Ariadne" of
Titian are joined in The Princess Casamassima as in Keats's
life and poetry, because James "saw them as the two great
heuristic experiences" of Hyacinth.

1973

98 TINTNER, ADELINE R. "The House of Atreus and Mme. de Belle-
    garde's Crime." Notes and Queries, 20 (March), 98–99.
       Early versions of The American imply that Mme. de Belle-
    garde is "an adultress as well as a murderess." Reference
    to Balzac in the 1907 revision reinforces the adultery
    theme.

99 TINTNER, ADELINE R. "Keats and James and The Princess Casa-
    massima." Nineteenth-Century Fiction, 28 (September),
    179–93.
       Keatsian poetry and biography were primary influences on
    the creation of Hyacinth.

100 TINTNER, ADELINE R. "Maggie's Pagoda: Architectural Follies
    in The Golden Bowl." Markham Review, 3 (May), 113–15.
       The pagoda of The Golden Bowl, which need not be an
    imaginary creation since James could have had any number
    of prototypes in mind including ones in Kew Gardens, Alton
    Towers, Moor Park and the Pavilion at Brighton, is more
    than a metaphor; it is a "concrete correlative" for the
    novel's basic theme.

101 TOMPKINS, JANE P. "The Redemption of Time in Notes of a Son
    and Brother." Texas Studies in Literature and Language,
    14 (Winter), 681–90.
       The purposefulness with which James sustained a "cele-
    bratory attitude" and maintained a tone of innocence by
    guarding "against the incursions of a later and grimmer
    reality" suggests that his autobiography was a religious
    experience--"a means of salvation."

102 VANDERBILT, KERMIT. "Notes Largely Musical on Henry James's
    'Four Meetings.'" Sewanee Review, 81 (Fall), 739–52.
       The "musical analogy" in James's works recurs in moments
    when he measures his character's "responsiveness to art and
    life." "Four Meetings," in its revised form, "can best be
    described by analogy to musical composition." Such an
    analogy clears up the mystery enveloping the final pages.

103 WALDRON, RANDALL H. "Prefiguration in 'The Beast in the Jun-
    gle.'" Studies in American Fiction, 1 (Spring), 101–104.
       The conversation at Weatherend between Marcher and May
    Bartram in Part I prefigures the fireplace scene in
    Part IV and forecasts both the major events and themes of
    the story.

104   WALLACE, RONALD. "Gabriel Nash: Henry James's Comic Spirit."
      Nineteenth-Century Fiction, 28 (September), 220-24.
          Nash, with his "high comic affirmation of life," pro-
      vides the touchstone for interpreting the James canon.

105   WALLACE, RONALD. "Maggie Verver: Comic Heroine." Genre, 6
      (December), 404-15.
          Maggie Verver is the comic heroine of The Golden Bowl,
      which is written in a basically comic form closely resem-
      bling A Midsummer Night's Dream. The theme of both works
      is "love madness."

106   WEGELIN, CHRISTOF. "Henry James and the Treasure of Consci-
      ousness." Die Neueren Sprachen, 22:484-91.
          James's use of the limited point of view is more than a
      compositional innovation; it is an artistic outgrowth of
      his beief that the human consciousness is the "most real
      thing we know."

1973 C DISSERTATIONS

  1   ASWAD, BETSY B. "The Crucible of Conversation: A Study of
      Jamesean Dialogue." DAI, 34, 1890A (State Univ. of New
      York, Binghamton).
          In writing The Awkward Age and The Sacred Fount James
      was experimenting with the technical and thematic possi-
      bilities of dialogue, thus preparing the way for The Wings
      of the Dove--a novel that is a "virtual anatomy of human
      language."

  2   BENNETT, BARBARA LOUISE. "The Ethics of Henry James's Nov-
      els." DAI, 34, 304A-05A (Univ. of North Carolina, Chapel
      Hill).
          "In general, the ethical beliefs expressed in James's
      novels fall within the eudaemonistic tradition."

  3   BURTNER, WILLIAM THOMAS, JR. "Ideal and Actual Society:
      Theme and Technique in Henry James's The American Scene."
      DAI, 34, 1850A-51A (Miami Univ.).
          A tension existed between James's ideal America, which
      was "traditional and aristocratic" in nature, and the Amer-
      ica James saw on tour. This tension became the "internal
      structural principle" of The American Scene.

1973

4   COMMANDAY, SUSAN NANCY. "Imagery in Henry James's Late Sto-
     ries (1898-1910)." <u>DAI</u>, 34, 1235A (New York Univ.).
        An analysis of James's last thirty-three stories in
     terms of eight categories of imagery ("archetypal imagery,
     imagery of sensation, of nature, of the supernatural and
     spiritual, of abstract thought and feeling, of the physical
     world of things, of the moral world of values, and of man's
     outer social and inner personal world") reveals certain
     images are consistently used to describe various subjects.
     For example, fire is associated with passion; height with
     success; warmth with contentment; and flight with imagina-
     tiveness.

5   DWYER, JOHN FRANCIS. "A Medium for Sexual Encounter: Henry
     James's Return to the International Theme, 1899-1904."
     <u>DAI</u>, 33, 4408A-09A (State Univ. of New York, Buffalo).
        James's handling of sexual passion in <u>The Ambassadors</u>,
     <u>The Wings of the Dove</u>, and <u>The Golden Bowl</u> differs from his
     earlier treatment. Renunciation characterized his earlier
     treatment, whereas engagement characterizes the later. Ac-
     cordingly, it appears that James returned to the interna-
     tional novel--a medium with which he felt especially com-
     fortable--in order to resolve the issue of sexual passion.

6   FRIEDLING, SHEILA. "Problems of Perception in the Modern
     Novel: The Representation of Consciousness in Works of
     Henry James, Gertrude Stein, and William Faulkner." <u>DAI</u>,
     34, 3391A (Wisconsin).
        The fiction of James, Stein, and Faulkner reveals their
     individual responses to the cultural questions being raised
     about the nature of perception by contemporary "philosophy,
     aesthetics, and the theory of fiction." (Includes discus-
     sion of <u>The Portrait of a Lady</u>, <u>The Golden Bowl</u>, and <u>The
     Sacred Fount</u>.)

7   GILLETTE, JANE BROWN. "Medusa/Muse: Women as Images of Chaos
     and Order in the Writings of Henry Adams and Henry James."
     <u>DAI</u>, 33, 6909A (Yale).
        For Henry Adams and Henry James the "Medusa/Muse" con-
     cept provided "a focal point for the investigation of the
     paradoxical interrelations of self and society."

8   GRUMMAN, JOAN MARY. "Henry James's Great 'Bad' Heroines."
     <u>DAI</u>, 33, 5177A-78A (Purdue).
        While the "great bad heroine" in James's fiction is
     selfish and manipulating, she directs the "protagonist to
     an awareness of good and evil." (Includes discussion of
     <u>The Portrait of a Lady</u>, <u>The Awkward Age</u>, <u>Roderick Hudson</u>,

The Bostonians, The Ambassadors, The Wings of the Dove, and The Golden Bowl.)

9   HELLER, SHIRLEY HILMER. "Nature as Design in the Novels of
    Henry James." DAI, 34, 317A (Tulsa).
        James used the metaphors and symbols of nature for two
    purposes: (1) to enhance plot, character, theme and form;
    and (2) to indicate different levels of awareness within
    his characters.

10 HOVANEC, EVELYN ANN. "Henry James and Germany." DAI, 34,
    2628A-29A (Pittsburgh).
        A study of fictional and non-fictional references to
    Germany and German things by James reveals a consistent
    dislike for "the German element."

11 IRLEN, HARVEY STUART. "Henry James and the Victorian Novel."
    DAI, 33, 6313A (Minnesota).
        A study of James's critical comments on the Victorian
    novel reveals that his conception of the Victorian novel
    became the basis for his own theories and principles.
    (Includes discussion of Roderick Hudson, The American, The
    Bostonians, and The Princess Casamassima.)

12 KAUFMAN, JULE SUZANNE. "Possibilities for Freedom in the Nov-
    els of Henry James." DAI, 34, 1284A (Stanford).
        The possibilities for freedom differ in the three phases
    of James's career: during the early novels the failure of
    the protagonists to achieve freedom is tempered by the wit
    and tone of the works; during the middle novels, "freedom
    in action" fails, and the novels are pessimistic in tone;
    during the late novels, freedom succeeds through "triumph
    of action."

13 KOZOL, CLARA BARBARA. "Creator and Collector: The Unpub-
    lished Letters of Henry James to Isabella Stewart Gardner."
    DAI, 34, 3407A (Columbia).
        The one hundred letters received by Mrs. Gardner from
    Henry James over a thirty-five year period reveal a rela-
    tionship that was "mutually influential."

14 MAZZELLA, ANTHONY JOHN. "The Revised Portrait of a Lady:
    Text and Commentary." DAI, 33, 4424A-25A (Columbia).
        A comparison of the extensive differences between the
    American Edition (1881) and the New York Edition (1908) of
    The Portrait of a Lady suggests that they are two different
    works. The New York Edition is superior to the earlier
    edition.

1973

15   MORRISON, PEGGY ANN R.   "The Connoisseur in the Novels of
     Henry James." <u>DAI</u>, 33, 3660A (Brandeis).
        An examination of eight novels--<u>Roderick Hudson</u>, <u>The</u>
     <u>Europeans</u>, <u>The Princess Casamassima</u>, <u>The Tragic Muse</u>, <u>The</u>
     <u>Portrait of a Lady</u>, <u>The Spoils of Poynton</u>, <u>The Ambassadors</u>,
     and <u>The Golden Bowl</u>--reveals that the connoisseur is forced
     to use his aesthetic criteria to evaluate his own conduct
     and morality.

16   SEBOUHIAN, GOERGE.   "The Emersonian Idealism of Henry James."
     <u>DAI</u>, 34, 739A (Ohio State).
        A fuller appreciation of James's canon is possible when
     the reader realizes that "Emersonian idealism" is at the
     center of his work and that "James is a part of the ideal-
     ist tradition that informs the work of Emerson, and that
     James dramatizes that tradition in his work."

17   STOWELL, H. PETER.   "The Prismatic Sensibility: Henry James
     and Anton Čexov as Impressionists." <u>DAI</u>, 34, 288A-89A
     (Univ. of Washington).
        An overview of the developing impressionism of Henry
     James and Anton Čexov reveals that although there are dif-
     ferences, they share basic similarities and a common
     aesthetic goal--"the fusion of form and meaning through
     the portrayal of the human condition compressed into a
     network of brilliantly concentrated momentary impressions."

18   TRAVIS, KAREN CORINNE PETERSON.   "Henry James: The Fiction of
     the First Ten Years Particularly as It Relates to the De-
     velopment of the Strether-Figure." <u>DAI</u>, 33, 6328A-29A
     (Michigan).
        "The character which embodies all that James learned
     [from 1864 through 1874] in terms of both technique and
     content is Lewis Lambert Strether."

19   WATERFALL, GAILLARD FITZSIMONS.   "The Manipulation Theme in
     the Works of Nathaniel Hawthorne and Henry James." <u>DAI</u>,
     34, 1874A (South Carolina).
        There are five identifiable manipulatory types in Haw-
     thorne's fiction: "the wayward theologian, the warped
     idealist, the earthy materialist, the prying artist, and
     the god-like scientist." The same basic types are identi-
     fiable in Henry James's fiction. Although James makes the
     types his own, they do reveal a strong Hawthorne influence.
     (Includes discussion of <u>Roderick Hudson</u>, <u>The American</u>, <u>The</u>
     <u>Golden Bowl</u>, and <u>The Wings of the Dove</u>.)

1974

20   YARINA, MARGARET ANNE. "The Functions of Language in the
     Early Tales of Henry James: 1864-1872." DAI, 34, 1302A
     (State Univ. of New York, Binghamton).
         A study of the language in James's first nineteen tales
     reveals that the words are more than vehicles for communi-
     cating thoughts or action. Words are used to portray the
     "distinctively limited awareness of the sayers and doers."

1974 A BOOKS

1   DOMANIECKI, HILDEGARD. Zum Problem literarischer Ökonomie:
    Henry James' Erzählungen Zwischen Markt und Kunst. Stutt-
    gart: J. B. Metzlersche, 335 pp. [German]
        This study of James's hundred and twelve tales focuses
    on the forces that "essentially determined" his creativity:
    (1) his love for the art of fiction; and (2) his financial
    dependence on the literary marketplace. The first part
    covers "the economic conditions with which James had to
    cope, the world of periodicals, editors, and publishers
    both in the United States and Great Britain." The second
    part discusses his theory of fiction, his art in creating
    the tale as well as "his practical working mode and the
    resulting tales."

2   HOCKS, RICHARD A. Henry James and Pragmatistic Thought: A
    Study in the Relationship between the Philosophy of William
    James and the Literary Art of Henry James. Chapel Hill:
    Univ. of North Carolina Press, 258 pp.
        A study of the relationship of William's philosophy and
    Henry's writing establishes "that William James's pragma-
    tistic thought is literally actualized as the literary art
    and idiom of his brother Henry James especially so in the
    later work." For dissertation see 1968.C6. Reviewed:
    J. Barzun, American Literature, 47 (May 1975), 279-80;
    H. L. Terrie, Jr., Sewanee Review, 83 (Fall 1975), 695-703;
    Christof Wegelin, Modern Fiction Studies, 21 (Summer 1975),
    284-87; Times Literary Supplement (5 September 1975),
    p. 990; Review of English Studies, ns 27 (November 1976),
    495-98.

3   MELCHIORI, BARBARA, and GIORGIO MELCHIORI. Il Gusto di Henry
    James. Turin: Guilio Einaudi editore, 277 pp. [Italian]
        Contents: A collection of previously published articles
    on Henry James. (Includes 1964.B65, 1965.B75, 1965.B76,
    1965.B77, 1966.B65, 1969.B96.)
        By examining James's ambiguity, taste, and technique,
    together with his political and social considerations

1974

(these last two based on The Princess Casamassima), the authors evaluate James's constant aspiration and research in
refining his style. The result is his original, pure, perfect, discriminatory, and "classic" vision of humanity, as
it transpires from his writings.

4   MOORE, HARRY T.   Henry James.   New York: Viking; London:
    Thames and Hudson, 128 pp.
        A biographical text is amply illustrated with photo-
    graphs, including illustrations of James, other members of
    the James family, James's friends, places James visited and
    lived, scenes from productions of his plays. Reviewed:
    Stephen Spender, New Statesman, 88 (27 September), 426-27;
    Wayne McGuire, Library Journal, 99 (1 September), 2068;
    Christian Science Monitor, 66 (7 August), 10.

5   PIRIE, GORDON.   Henry James.   Literature in Perspective Se-
    ries. London: Evans Brothers, 152 pp.
        A concise treatment of James's life, selected short sto-
    ries, and five novels (The Europeans, Washington Square,
    The Portrait of a Lady, The Bostonians, What Maisie Knew)
    verifies that he achieved "a wide range of comic and tragic
    effects," brought high "standards of craftsmanship" to fic-
    tion, and "dramatised moral problems with unique subtlety."
    Reviewed: Viola Hopkins Winner, American Literature, 47
    (November 1975), 463; David K. Kirby, Library Journal, 100
    (15 May 1975), 988-89; Choice, 12 (July 1975), 683.

6   SHEPPARD, E. A.   Henry James and "The Turn of the Screw."
    Auckland: Auckland Univ. Press; New York: Oxford Univ.
    Press, 292 pp.
        The text of the nouvelle is scrutinized closely in terms
    of its context ("the circumstances of its production, the
    literary tradition in which it was conceived, and the in-
    fluences that helped to shape it") and James's "expressed
    intentions." Reviewed: David K. Kirby, Library Journal,
    100 (15 May 1975), 989; Quentin G. Kraft, American Litera-
    ture, 48 (May 1976), 237; Kenneth Graham, Review of English
    Studies, ns 27 (November 1976), 495-98.

1974 B SHORTER WRITINGS

1   AKIYAMA, MASAYUKI.   "Henry James's The Ambassadors: Strether's
    Inner Self." Annual Report of the Researches (Mishima Col-
    lege, Nihon Univ.), 23:45-67. [Japanese]
        The inner drama of Strether's consciousness is the moral
    struggle between sophisticated Europe and puritanical
    America.

2   ATKINSON, F. G. "Henry James and 'The Sign of Sympathy.'"
    Notes and Queries, 21 (October), 363-65.
        A letter written by James to A. T. Quiller-Couch in
    October 1901 is of interest because it gives documentary
    confirmation of a connection between the two and because
    it reveals James's warm and delighted response to Quiller-
    Couch's proposed dedication.

3   BAILEY, BRUCE. "A Note on The Waste Land and James' In the
    Cage." T. S. Eliot Newsletter, 1 (Fall), 2.
        James's nouvelle bears striking parallels to Eliot's
    The Waste Land, Part II of which was originally titled "In
    the Cage."

4   BASS, EBEN. "Flannery O'Conner and Henry James: The Vision
    of Grace." Studies in the Twentieth Century, no. 14
    (Fall), pp. 43-67.
        O'Connor used James's restrictive point of view by
    adapting to her own needs James's practice and theory.

5   BEDFORD, R. C. "Henry James's 'mere mistake and a worry and
    a joke.'" Annual Reports (Doshisha Women's College,
    Kyoto), 25:136-80. [Japanese]
        The Turn of the Screw should be taken as it is and not
    read as a ghost tale nor a psychological study of a psy-
    chotic hallucination. The reader must differentiate be-
    tween the more mature narrator and the younger governess,
    whose hyperimagination was stimulated by adolescent
    peculiarities.

6   BLACKMUR, R. P. "Henry James," in Literary History of the
    United States. Edited by Robert E. Spiller et al. Fourth
    edition. Revised. New York: Macmillan, pp. 1039-64,
    1510.
        Reprint of essay and bibliography published in the third
    edition (1963).

7   BOARDMAN, ARTHUR. "Mrs. Grose's Reading of The Turn of the
    Screw." Studies in English Literature, 1500-1900, 14
    (Autumn), 169-35.
        The reader should accept Mrs. Grose's interpretation of
    the governess's story, since Mrs. Grose serves as a reli-
    able "first reader," who is honest and possesses sound
    judgment.

1974

8 BÖKER, UWE. "Henry James, Graham Greene, und das Problem der Form." Literature in Wissenschaft und Unterricht (Kiel), 7 (May), 16-33. [German]
Greene was not only a popular writer interested in theological questions, but also an author who, in the tradition of Henry James, was deeply concerned with the form and underlying structure of the novel.

9 BOURAOUI, H. A. "Henry James's The Sacred Fount: Nouveau Roman avant la lettre?" International Fiction Review, 1 (July), 96-105. [French]
The Sacred Fount, James's fullest treatment of the problem of the artist, anticipates the French "new novel," particularly Nathalie Sarraute's Portrait d'un inconnu.

10 BROWN, BERNADINE. "The Turn of the Screw: A Case of Romantic Displacement." Nassau Review (Nassau [N.Y.] Community College), 2:75-82.
At the heart of the novel is the governess's infatuation with and rejection by the uncle, which causes her "to displace her romantic fantasies on two other couples: Peter Quint and Miss Jessel, and Miles and Flora."

11 COHEN, S. B. "The Ambassadors: A Comedy of Musing and Manners." Studies in American Humor, 1 (October), 79-90.
One of James's most comic novels, The Ambassadors evokes cerebral laughter; "it is a comedy of subtle musing and obvious manners."

12 DAVIDSON, ARNOLD E. "James's Dramatic Method in The Awkward Age." Nineteenth-Century Fiction, 29 (December), 320-35.
The novel is made up of "dramatized action," and the reader must pay particular attention to the specific events that are dramatized in order to assess what a character is doing, what his motives might be, and what implications can be drawn from his actions.

13 DONOGHUE, DENIS. "The American Style of Failure." Sewanee Review, 82 (Summer), 407-32.
James deals with dismal situations in his fiction by "creating a verbal world as rich as the situation is poor." To James the difference between apparently unhappy and apparently pleasant situations is "not as great as it is to common minds, because James sees possibility where a common mind sees only defeat."

*14   EBINE, SHIZUE. "The Central Theme of Henry James." Studies
       in English Literature (Japan), English no., pp. 53-60.
       [Japanese]
           Cited by William T. Stafford in American Literary Schol-
       arship: An Annual/1974. Edited by James Woodress. Dur-
       ham, N.C.: Duke Univ. Press, p. 97. Stafford explains
       that according to an English synopsis appended to the
       article, this "is still another study of the last three
       novels and their concerns with consciousness, freedom, and
       social relationships."

15   EDEL, LEON. "Introduction," in his edition of "Daisy Miller"
       and "The Turn of the Screw." The Bodley Head Henry James.
       Vol. XI. London: Bodley Head, pp. 5-11.
           James's two most popular stories, both of which reveal
       his "fascination with the mind and manners of the young
       female adult," remain "as alive today as when they were
       written, one in 1878 and the other in 1898."

16   EDEL, LEON, ed. "Introduction and Brief Chronology," in Henry
       James Letters. 2 vols. Cambridge, Mass.: Harvard Univ.
       Press.
           The first volume of representative letters "constitutes
       one of the greatest self-portraits in all literature." In
       addition, the letters "provide vivid pictures of character
       and personality, and glimpses into art, into life, into the
       meaning of literary genius and literary power." This first
       volume reveals James the schoolboy, James the adolescent,
       and James the young professional (through the publication
       of Roderick Hudson). The letters of the second volume show
       James the professional laying "siege to Paris" and then
       establishing "the center and focus of his art in London."

17   EICHELBERGER, CLAYTON L. A Guide to Critical Reviews of United
       States Fiction, 1870-1910. Vol. 2. Metuchen, N.J.:
       Scarecrow, pp. 149-52.
           This list of critical reviews of James's work supplements
       1971.B32.

18   FIELD, MARY LEE. "Henry James's Criticism of French Litera-
       ture: A Bibliography and a Checklist." American Literary
       Realism, 7 (Autumn), 379-94.
           This bibliography is chronologically ordered and each
       entry is identified in consonance with Edel's and Lau-
       rence's Henry James: A Bibliography. The checklist of
       authors and works criticized by James is alphabetized by
       author's last name.

1974

19   FLETCHER, PAULINE. "The Sense of Society in <u>The Ambassadors</u>."
      <u>English Studies in Africa</u> (Johannesburg), 17 (September),
      79-88.
         In the late novels society is not portrayed by surface
      naturalistic detail, but James does achieve "most solidly
      his sense of society as a structure of mutual relationships
      from which the individual cannot escape."

20   GABBAY, LYDIA RIVLIN. "The Four Square Coterie: A Comparison
      of Ford Madox Ford and Henry James." <u>Studies in the Novel</u>,
      6 (Winter), 439-53.
         Ford uses <u>The Good Soldier</u> "as a vehicle whereby he
      might expose the absurdity of James's values, the amorality
      and the stupidity of his protagonists, the falsity of
      James's belief in the delicacy and restraint of the aristo-
      cratic soul, and thereby to kill his own Jamesian passion."

21   GORDON, CAROLINE. "Rebels and Revolutionaries: The New Amer-
      ican Scene." <u>Flannery O'Connor Bulletin</u>, 3 (Autumn),
      40-56.
         O'Connor's debt to James is evident in a number of af-
      finities she shared with the older novelist: both are
      "masters of illusionism"; both had a family heritage that
      included an "interest in theology"; both created protago-
      nists who were visionaries; both had a concern with struc-
      ture in their novels and short stories; and both "had a
      vision which demanded for its embodiment a revolutionary
      technique."

22   GRANT, WILLIAM E. "'Daisy Miller': A Study of a Study."
      <u>Studies in Short Fiction</u>, 11 (Winter), 17-26.
         Winterbourne studying Daisy Miller is the object of
      James's study.

23   HALPERIN, JOHN. "<u>The Portrait of a Lady</u>," in his <u>Egoism and
      Self-Discovery in the Victorian Novel</u>. New York: Burt
      Franklin, pp. 247-76.
         Virtually all of James's novels employ the theme of "the
      expansion of the individual's moral sensibility": "It is
      <u>The Portrait of a Lady</u>, however, that most clearly and ful-
      ly embodies that pattern of egoism, despair, and self-
      education--the ordeal of moral education--which is at the
      heart of so much nineteenth-century fiction."

24 HARRIS, JOSEPHINE. "The Sacred Fount: The Geometry in the
    Jungle." Michigan Quarterly Review, 13 (Winter), 57-73.
        There are three distinct tones in The Sacred Fount--
    comic, ironic, and romantic. The differing tones represent
    a tension between James's stated intentions and his natural
    proclivities.

25 HARTSOCK, MILDRED E. "Dizzying Summit: James's 'The Altar of
    the Dead.'" Studies in Short Fiction, 11 (Fall), 371-78.
        The story is an affirmative statement about "the bonds
    of life and death and the bonds of love and life."

26 HARTSOCK, MILDRED E. "Unintentional Fallacy: Critics and The
    Golden Bowl." Modern Language Quarterly, 35 (September),
    272-88.
        The Golden Bowl, which is neither "rarefied" nor "re-
    mote" but is relevant and comprehensible, has suffered from
    three "unintentional fallacies" of criticism: "the common
    use of the invalid criteria; the frequently careless or in-
    attentive reading of the text . . . ; [and] the attribution
    of a critic's own incomprehension to an excessive ambiguity
    in James."

27 HENDERSON, HARRY B., III. "James's Sense of the Past and The
    Europeans," in his Versions of the Past: The Historical
    Imagination in American Fiction. New York: Oxford Univ.
    Press, pp. 209-13.
        "Superficially a holist historical novel written out of
    a critical but sympathetic understanding of Hawthorne, The
    Europeans reveals the tendency of the holist historical
    novel in one of its metamorphoses to become pure surface,
    with no effort to represent historical forces or movements
    at all."

28 HOBERMAN, MARY ANN. "Henry James: On a Tour of the Prov-
    inces." New York Times (24 November), Sect. 10, pp. 1,
    16-17.
        Henry James's "A Little Tour in France" served as a
    travel guide for Hoberman's visit to France in October of
    1973. James's book contains architectural critiques, lit-
    erary and historical references, and evaluations of various
    inns. Hoberman compares her views with James's of October,
    1882.

1974

29 JOHANNSEN, ROBERT. "The Two Sides of Washington Square."
    South Carolina Review, 6 (April), 60-65.
        In the early part of Washington Square the Sloper home
    is associated with a chivalric, romantic motif, a motif
    that is rejected for a tragic motif of domination and sac-
    rifice--the tragic aspects of which are ultimately overcome.

30 JOHNSON, LEE ANN. "James's Mrs. Wix: The 'Dim, Crooked Re-
    flector.'" Nineteenth-Century Fiction, 29 (September),
    164-72.
        Mrs. Wix is "neither a malevolent figure nor a standard
    of serious respectability." She is "a significant comic
    character whose self-interested, misguided attempts to edu-
    cate her charge serve as a source of humor and irony within
    the novel."

31 JOHNSON, LEE ANN. "The Psychology of Characterization:
    James's Portraits of Verena Tarrant and Olive Chancellor."
    Studies in the Novel, 6 (Fall), 295-303.
        In James's first novel following "The Art of Fiction,"
    where he emphasized the necessity of "solidity of specifi-
    cation," he simultaneously failed and succeeded. The in-
    congruous inclusion of romance elements in Verena Tarrant's
    character is a failure compared to the credible Olive Chan-
    cellor, whose character is delineated through psychological
    presentation.

32 JONES, GRANVILLE H. "Henry James's 'Georgina's Reasons': The
    Underside of Washington Square." Studies in Short Fiction,
    11 (Spring), 189-94.
        On the basis of characterizations, settings, and struc-
    tures, it appears that Georgina Gressie is James's fiction-
    al antithesis for Catherine Sloper.

33 KAMAN, JOHN MICHAEL. "The Lonely Hero in Hawthorne, Melville,
    Twain and James." DAI, 34, 5974A-75A (Stanford).
        A study of Hawthorne's The Blithedale Romance, Melville's
    Pierre, Twain's Adventures of Huckleberry Finn and James's
    The Ambassadors reveals a "peculiarly American conception"
    of heroism that does not conform to the classical comic or
    tragic conceptions.

34 KING, MARY JANE. "The Touch of the Earth: A Word and a
    Theme in The Portrait of a Lady." Nineteenth-Century Fic-
    tion, 29 (December), 345-47.
        James's frequent use of the word "touch" relates a major
    theme the book; that is, "behind the harmless ring of

this word lurks the suggestion of not only the loss of
freedom but also the acquisition of responsibility."

35   KIRSCHKE, JAMES. "Henry James's Use of Impressionist Painting
     Techniques in The Sacred Fount and The Ambassadors." Stud-
     ies in the Twentieth Century, 13 (Spring), 83-116.
         In his later novels James employed a literary impres-
     sionism which utilized the techniques and philosophy of the
     Impressionist painters.

36   LEMCO, GARY. "Henry James and Richard Wagner: The American."
     Hartford Studies in Literature, 6:147-58.
         Mythically perceived, Lohengrin and Christopher Newman
     are remarkably similar.

37   LING, AMY. "The Pagoda Image in Henry James's The Golden
     Bowl." American Literature, 46 (November), 383-88.
         C. F. Gordon Cumming's "Pagodas, Aurioles, and Umbrel-
     las" provides the metaphor with which James "triumphs in
     expressing the subtle emotions of his heroine through a
     device much like a metaphysical conceit."

38   LOHMANN, CHRISTOPH K. "Jamesian Irony and the American Sense
     of Mission." Texas Studies in Literature and Language, 16
     (Summer), 329-48.
         James used three devices in The Ambassadors to criticize
     ironically the sense of mission expressed in America: "the
     conjunction of financial and moral redemption, ironic re-
     versals, and diction replete with allusions to Christian
     religion."

39   LOUVRE, ALFRED WILLIAM. "The Limits of Living in Style."
     DAI, 34, 7238A (Cornell).
         The "romantic" interpretation of major nineteenth cen-
     tury and twentieth century writers that prevails needs to
     be re-interpreted in light of the prevalent political,
     psychological, and social influences contemporaneous with
     the authors.

40   MacKENZIE, MANFRED. "A Theory of Henry James's Psychology."
     Yale Review, 63 (Spring), 347-71.
         "The Jolly Corner" exemplifies a theme that permeates
     James's works--psychological "shock," the fear of exposure
     followed by shame.

1974

41   MacNAUGHTON, W. R. "The First-Person Narrators of Henry
      James." Studies in American Fiction, 2 (August), 145-64.
          Of the fifty first-person tales James published between
      1865 and 1901, the majority remain "uncriticized and un-
      read." Analysis of "A Passionate Pilgrim," "The Author of
      Beltraffio," "The Special Type," and "The Tone of Time" re-
      veals that the more or less myopic narrator cannot be de-
      scribed as a "disinterested observer."

42   MacNAUGHTON, W. R. "Turning The Screw of Ordinary Human Vir-
      tue: The Governess and the First-Person Narrators." Cana-
      dian Review of American Studies, 5 (Spring), 18-25.
          If The Turn of the Screw is viewed in the context of
      James's first-person fiction (including forty-nine stories
      and The Sacred Fount), it can be seen that the story shares
      many characteristics with the other first-person stories,
      particularly "the importance of the narrator as a function
      of technique and character important in her own right."

43   MARKS, SITA PATRICIA. "A Silent Morality: Non-Verbal Expres-
      sion in The Ambassadors." South Atlantic Bulletin, 39
      (May), 102-106.
          James conveys his study of Strether's moral development
      to the reader in terms of his expanding verbal and nonver-
      bal sensitivity.

44   MATHEWS, J. W. "Fowles's Artistic Freedom: Another Stone
      from James's House." Notes on Contemporary Literature,
      4:2-4.
          The fiction of John Fowles reveals the similarities of
      his idea of artistic freedom and its relationship to reality
      with that of James.

45   MEYERS, JEFFREY. "Bronzino, Veronese and The Wings of the
      Dove." Artist International, 18 (October), 10, 41, 42, 55.
          Bronzino's Lucrezia Panciatichi and Veronese's Marriage
      Feast at Cana play crucial roles in The Wings of the Dove's
      structure, characterization, tone, and thematic development.

46   MONTEIRO, GEORGE. "Addendum to Edel and Laurence: Henry
      James's 'Two Old Houses and Three Young Women.'" Papers of
      the Bibliographical Society of America, 68 (3Q), 331.
          The first publication of James's essay was 7 September
      of 1899 in The Independent, not 1909 as has been previously
      believed.

47   MOORE, RAYBURN S. "Henry James, Ltd., and the Chairman of the
      Board: Leon Edel's Biography." South Atlantic Quarterly,
      73 (Spring), 261-69.
          Edel's biography is the best present source of informa-
      tion on James's life, but some of his interpretations of
      James's life and work are open to question (especially his
      treatment of James's relationship with Constance Fenimore
      Woolson). Review of 1972.A3.

48   MURAKAMI, FUJIO. Literature of Hawthorne and James. Osaka:
      Ko-Murakami Fujio Kyoju Rombunshu Kankokai (Society for
      Publishing the Studies and Essays by the Late Professor
      Fujio Murakami), 134 pp. [Japanese]
          Contents: A collection of essays which originally ap-
      peared in Jimbun-Kenkyu (Osaka Municipal Univ.). On James
      are the following: "The Real in Henry James," 9, no. 6
      (1958); "The Aesthete in The Tragic Muse," 1961.B69; "The
      Creative Process of The Princess Casamassima," 16, no. 2
      (1965); "James on the Novel: 'Vicarious Experience,'" 17,
      no. 11 (1966); and "James's The Europeans," 20, part 7
      (1968).

49   NETTELS, ELSA. "The Portrait of a Lady and the Gothic
      Romance." South Atlantic Bulletin, 39 (November), 73-82.
          The Portrait of a Lady, while utilizing Gothic conven-
      tions to explore the depths of Isabel Archer, "calls into
      question several of the ideas and assumptions underlying
      the Gothic romance."

50   NETTELS, ELSA. "The Scapegoats and Martyrs of Henry James."
      Colby Library Quarterly, 10 (September), 413-27.
          Two martyrs, Olive Chancellor and Hyacinth Robinson, and
      two scapegoats, Lambert Strether and Maggie Verver, are in-
      verted by James so that all four are the victims not of so-
      ciety but of their own psychological needs.

51   PAGE, PHILIP. "The Curious Narration of The Bostonians."
      American Literature, 46 (November), 374-83.
          The failure of the narrator to reveal the thoughts of
      Verena Tarrant, his inconsistent attitude toward charac-
      ters, his sensitive awareness of and ambivalence toward the
      reader, and his arbitrary scene selection are calculated
      techniques James employs to force total immersion in the
      reading experience.

1974

52 PAYNE, JAMES ROBERT. "Style and Meaning in American Autobiography: William Dean Howells, Henry James, Hamlin Garland." DAI, 34, 6653A-54A (Univ. of California, Davis).
   "In autobiography Howells, James, and Garland, committed as writers to individual, imaginative 'inwardness' and as 'realists' to their time and world in its complex actuality, found an accommodating, congenial genre."

53 PEARCE, HOWARD D. "Witchcraft Imagery and Allusion in James's Bostonians." Studies in the Novel, 6 (Summer), 236-47.
   The combined effect of witchcraft imagery, demonic metaphor, and supernatural allusion endows the novel with a larger than life quality where Basil and Olive are destructive spellcasters and Verena Tarrant is a redemptive figure.

54 POPESCU, CONSTANTIN C. "Fantastic Elements in Nineteenth-Century American Prose." DAI, 34, 7718A-19A (Univ. of Wisconsin, Milwaukee).
   In nineteenth-century American literature, "fantastic literature" is born in the early writings of Irving and Hawthorne, comes to fruition in the works of Poe, Bangs, Crawford, and James, and then "discarding the heavy Gothic trappings" reflects "national traits toward the end of the century."

55 POWNALL, DAVID E. Articles on Twentieth Century Literature: An Annotated Bibliography: 1954-1970. Vol. 4. New York Kraus-Thomson Organization Ltd., pp. 1705-1852.
   An annotated list of articles published on James is divided into one general section in the beginning and then separate sections for individual works by James.

56 PRONO, JUDYTH KAE. "The Spectator Figure as Counter-Culture Spokesman in American Fiction, 1850-1925." DAI, 34, 5987A-88A (Stanford).
   The role of the spectator in The Blithedale Romance, A Modern Instance, The Rise of Silas Lapham, Democracy, Daisy Miller, The Portrait of a Lady, The Ambassadors, The House of Mirth, The Age of Innocence, and The Great Gatsby implies "that the best a man of principle can do is make a separate peace with his own conscience" in the absence of a "coherent moral and social order" in America.

57   PUTT, S. GORLEY.   "Henry James Haggles over Terms for <u>Guy Dom-</u>
     <u>ville</u>." <u>Times Literary Supplement</u> (11 January), pp. 35-36.
          Four letters from Henry James to Austen Henderson and a
     letter written to James by George Alexander concern terms
     for the performance of <u>Guy Domville</u>.

58   PUTT, S. GORLEY.   "James," in <u>The English Novel: Select</u>
     <u>Bibliographical Guides</u>. Edited by A. E. Dyson. London:
     Oxford, pp. 280-99.
          A bibliographical essay is divided into five sections:
     Texts, Critical Studies and Commentary, Biographies and
     Letters, Bibliography, and Background Reading. Also in-
     cluded are a "chronological checklist of the novels and
     tales" and a bibliographical listing of sources for each
     topic covered in the essay.

59   PYRON, JOHN E., JR.   "American Romance and Italian Reality in
     the Nineteenth Century." <u>DAI</u>, 35, 1120A (Pittsburgh).
          A comparison of the fictional representations of Italy,
     as reflected in the writings of Cooper, Crawford, Fuller,
     Hawthorne, Howells, Irving, James, Stowe, and Woolson, with
     the non-fictional accounts by Cooper, Greeley, Hawthorne,
     Howells, Irving, James, Lowell, Melville, Parkman, Story,
     and Twain "points up the striking incompleteness of the
     traditional nineteenth-century American romantic picture
     of Italy."

60   REDMOND, JAMES, et al., eds.   <u>The Year's Work in English Stud-</u>
     <u>ies: Vol. 53: 1972</u>. New York: Humanities Press, 461-63.
          Survey of criticism for 1972.

61   REYNOLDS, GORDON DUNCAN.   "Psychological Rebirth in Selected
     Works by Nathaniel Hawthorne, Stephen Crane, Henry James,
     William Faulkner, and Ralph Ellison." <u>DAI</u>, 34, 7719A
     (Univ. of California, Irvine).
          An overview of individual works by five American authors
     reveals a basic pattern of psychological rebirth that "in-
     cludes the breaking down of a character's immature, inade-
     quate mental identity, aberrations in perception and other
     mental processes, the appearance of guides, entrance into
     a deathlike state, awakening to a new mode of perception of
     the familiar, [and] suggestions that the character is a new
     or newborn person."

1974

*62   RIEDEL, D. C. "Até a última espiral." <u>Minas Gerais, Supplemento Literário</u>, 23 (February), 2-3.
        Cited in <u>1974 MLA International Bibliography</u>, vol. 1, p. 160, which notes that the article discusses <u>The Turn of the Screw</u>.

63   RODGERS, PAUL C., JR. "Motive, Agency, and Act in James's <u>The Aspern Papers</u>." <u>South Atlantic Quarterly</u>, 73 (Summer), 377-87.
        In <u>The Aspern Papers</u> Juliana greatly influences the events following her death by scheming. James rearranged and added to the facts from his source so as to increase the "unity, irony, and dramatic impact" of the story.

64   SCHNEIDER, DANIEL J. "The Theme of Freedom in James's <u>The Tragic Muse</u>." <u>Connecticut Review</u>, 7 (April), 5-15.
        An examination of the symbolic and structural elements of <u>The Tragic Muse</u> reveals a thematic interest, not in the particularized issues of the artist, but in the "general problem of freedom--. . . that problem considered with special reference to the coercive or restrictive aspects of a career."

65   SHAW, SHARON. "Gertrude Stein and Henry James: The Difference Between Accidence and Coincidence." <u>Pembroke Magazine</u> (Pembroke, N.C.), 5:95-101.
        Although Stein shared several ideas with James about America, human nature, and the "necessity for expanding consciousness," Stein's writing is "accidental" (spontaneous) whereas James's is coincidental--"he writes to fill out a larger, abstract but wholly pre-conceived framework."

66   SHELDON, PAMELA JACOBS. "American Gothicism: The Evolution of a Mode." <u>DAI</u>, 35, 1634A-35A (Kent State).
        An overview of American Gothicism beginning with Charles Brockden Brown's <u>Wieland</u> and ending with James's "The Jolly Corner" (other works by James as well as works by Poe and Hawthorne are included in the overview) reveals the same "psychological undercurrents" as are present in Walpole's <u>The Castle of Otranto</u> and William Godwin's <u>Caleb Williams</u>.

67   SHELDON, PAMELA JACOBS. "Jamesian Gothicism: The Haunted Castle of the Mind." <u>Studies in the Literary Imagination</u> (Georgia State College), 7 (Spring), 121-34.
        James uses gothic techniques in "The Jolly Corner" to symbolize Brydon's spiritual and psychological condition.

68   SPENDER, STEPHEN. "Henry James as Centre of the English-
      American Language," in his <u>Love-Hate Relations: A Study of
      Anglo-American Sensibility</u>. London: Hamish Hamilton,
      pp. 53-100.
          James went to England "with the intention of writing the
      novels of the Anglo-Saxon world," but he returned in 1904
      to find that Americans did not understand what he was say-
      ing. "Having made it his life ambition to fuse Anglo-
      American Literature into a single whole in which the ob-
      server could not trace the line that marked the 'join,' he
      had, it seemed, succeeded only in separating it neatly into
      two halves": the English language he championed and the
      American language he found incomprehensible.

69   SPILLER, ROBERT E., et al, eds. "Henry James," in <u>Literary
      History of the United States: Bibliography</u>. Fourth Edi-
      tion. Revised. New York: Macmillan, pp. 584-90, 938-42,
      1232-36.
          Listings of three bibliographies published in earlier
      editions (1959, 1963, 1972).

70   STAFFORD, WILLIAM T. "An 'Easy Ride' for Henry James: or, Is
      Captain America Christopher Newman(?)--The Master and Pop
      Kultur, a Note from the Midwest." <u>Journal of Popular Cul-
      ture</u>, 8 (Fall), 320-27.
          Dennis Hopper's <u>Easy Rider</u> corroborates James's uncanny
      ability to read the "American character."

71   STAFFORD, WILLIAM T. "Henry James," in <u>American Literary
      Scholarship: An Annual, 1972</u>. Edited by J. Albert Rob-
      bins, Durham, N.C.: Duke Univ. Press, pp. 92-113.
          Survey of criticism published during 1972.

72   STAFFORD, W. T. "A Whale, an Heiress, and a Southern Demigod:
      Three Symbolic Americas." <u>College Literature</u>, 1:100-12.
          Although <u>Moby-Dick</u>, <u>The Wings of the Dove</u>, and <u>Absalom,
      Absalom!</u> have in common a "cosmic scope, prophecy, [and] a
      strange, complex, wholly American double vision about the
      ambivalent nature of whiteness and perpetuity," they repre-
      sent three distinctive conceptions of the American expe-
      rience.

73   STEIN, ALLEN F. "The Beast in 'The Jolly Corner': Spencer
      Brydon's Ironic Rebirth." <u>Studies in Short Fiction</u>, 11
      (Winter), 61-66.
          Spencer Brydon is a thoroughly corrupt protagonist; he
      is not reborn, and he does not evidence change following
      his experience at "Jolly Corner."

1974

74   STEIN, ALLEN F.   "The Hack's Progress: A Reading of James's
      'The Velvet Glove.'" Essays in Literature (Western Illi-
      nois Univ.), 1 (Fall), 219-26.
          Berridge is not a serious or honest artist, but is a
      comic figure who is a self-deluded and pompous "hack"
      representative of James's talent for subtly revealing his
      characters.

75   STERNER, D. W.   "Henry James and the Idea of Culture in 'The
      American Scene.'" Modern Age, 18 (Summer), 283-90.
          "Lacking a historical vision of America's place in time,
      too dependent on observations of manners and forms for a
      knowledge of people's hearts, torn between a desire to ad-
      mire and even to help the country of his birth on the one
      hand and an ideal of culture which it breached on the other,
      James battered his judgment against the anomaly of a nation
      both prosperous and cheap, beautiful and ugly, for which he
      cares in spite of himself."

76   THORBERG, RAYMOND.   "Henry James and the Sense of the Past."
      Modern Age, 18 (Summer), 272-82.
          For James the present owes its meaningfulness "in large
      part to the relations it can establish with the past. Out
      of these relations comes a sense of distance, of the pas-
      sage of time, as well as of immediacy from the perception
      of likeness."

77   TINTNER, ADELINE R.   "The Countess and Scholastica: Henry
      James's 'L'Allegro' and 'Il Penseroso.'" Studies in Short
      Fiction, 11 (Summer), 267-76.
          Following the classic pattern of John Milton, James's
      allegory, "Benvolio," presents the polarities of human
      temperament through the Countess and Scholastica.'

78   TINTNER, ADELINE R.   "Henry James and a Watteau Fan." Apollo,
      99 (June), 488.
          The use of the Watteau fan in James's A New England
      Primer can be traced both to Balzac's use in Le Cousin Pons
      and to an inventory in Goncourt's L'Art du Dixhuitième
      Siècle of Watteau's works owned and read by James.

79   TINTNER, ADELINE R.   "Henry James Criticism: A Current Per-
      spective." American Literary Realism, 7 (Spring), 155-68.
          A comprehensive overview of critical background and of
      current trends in James studies suggests several areas that
      need and deserve further study: (1) novels and short sto-
      ries which have been comparatively neglected; (2) short
      stories in their groupings; (3) James's use of the works of

other writers (both past and contemporary); (4) James as
Edwardian and Georgian; (5) James's attitude to and use of
newspapers; (6) James's relation to the American realists
of 1885-1915; and (7) James's relation to the visual arts.

80 TINTNER, ADELINE R. "'The Hermit and the Wild Woman': Edith
    Wharton's 'Fictioning' of Henry James." Journal of Modern
    Literature, 4 (September), 32-42.
        Wharton used elements of James's character to create her
    hermit; and James's "The Velvet Glove" and Wharton's "The
    Hermit and the Wild Woman" and "Ogrin the Hermit" may re-
    present a literary repartee between the two artists.

81 TINTNER, A. R. "James's Monologue for Ruth Draper and The
    Tragic Muse: A Parody of the 'Usurping Consciousness.'"
    Studies in English Literature (English Literary Society of
    Japan), English no., pp. 149-54.
        The monologue James wrote for Ruth Draper in 1913 has
    its source in The Tragic Muse and is an unintentional paro-
    dy of James's "experiments in perception."

82 TINTNER, A. R. "Octave Feuillet: La petite comtesse and
    Henry James." Revue de Littérature Comparée, 48:218-32.
        The Princess Casamassima demonstrates a characteristic
    James technique for imaginatively combining personal and
    literary encounters to produce his own creations.

83 TINTNER, ADELINE R. "Sir Sidney Colvin in The Golden Bowl:
    Mr. Crichton Identified." Colby Library Quarterly, 10
    (September), 428-31.
        Mr. Crichton's prototype was Sidney Colvin, Keeper of
    Prints and Drawings at the British Museum from 1884-1916,
    and Fanny Assingham is his wife Fanny Sitwell.

84 TOMLINSON, T. B. "An American Strength: James's The Ambas-
    sadors." The Critical Review (Melbourne; Sydney), no. 17,
    pp. 38-58.
        James exhibited a continuing naiveté about the superi-
    ority of Europe, but he remained "thoroughly American" in
    The Ambassadors.

85 UENO, KAZUKO. "Henry James's Point of View." Eibungaku
    (Waseda), 40 (March), 78-88. [Japanese]
        James's ambiguity and sense of treachery are due to the
    shadowy parts hidden behind the point-of-view character.
    His technical employment of a ficelle has much to do with
    the psychological description prevalent in his later works.

1974

86 VON EGMOND, PETER. "Henry James' Autobiographies: The Growth
of a Poet's Mind," in Americana-Austriaca: Beiträge Zur
Amerikakunde. Band 3. Edited by Klaus Lanzinger. Wien
and Stuttgart: Braumüller, pp. 109-20.
James's autobiographical writing provides "an account of
the growth of his imagination, as it is molded and shaped
by virtually everything he apprehends."

87 WATANABE, HISAYOSHI. "Henry James's Late Style." Eigo Seinen
[The Rising Generation] (Tokyo), 119 (February), 106-107.
[Japanese]
James's late orientation toward "intangibility" (Seymour
Chatman's term) should be dealt with in the larger context
of the American cultural void, as well as in terms of
James's skilled but limited hand as a writer.

88 WEINSTEIN, ARNOLD. "Enclosed Vision: Conrad, Ford, and
James," in his Vision and Response in Modern Fiction.
Ithaca, N.Y.: Cornell Univ. Press, pp. 50-90.
James is preoccupied with "the forms of vision and
awareness, for James, through example and especially
theory, inaugurates the literature of perception and
creates the narrative strategies to embody it." (Includes
analyses of The Ambassadors and The Turn of the Screw.)

89 WELLS, CELIA TOWNSEND. "Introduction," in her edition of The
Bostonians. New York: Crowell, pp. v-xvi.
Verena Tarrant is an "American princess," who is faced
with alternatives not available to other "princesses" of
her time, but she makes "the worst of all possible choices"
in deserting "her vocation, her feminist views, and her
deep friendship with Olive Chancellor."

90 YEAZELL, RUTH. "The New 'Arithmetic' of Henry James." Criticism, 16 (Spring), 109-19.
In The Golden Bowl, a novel in which James's "late style
is most mannered and extreme," James ironically "acknowl-
edges the potential absurdity of that style" through the
comic dialogue of the Assinghams.

91 YOUNG, THOMAS BEETHAM. "Thematic Emphasis and Psychological
Realism in Lawrence Durrell's Alexandria Quartet." DAI,
34, 5214A-15A (Ohio State).
The thematic variation of the Alexandria Quartet produces "psychological realism," a technique employed by
such notable writers as Conrad in Victory and James in
The Ambassadors.

92 ZAK, MICHELE WENDER. "Feminism and the New Novel." DAI, 34,
    5215A (Ohio State).
        A study of the "significant" works of George Eliot,
    Henry James, Virginia Woolf, and Doris Lessing reveals the
    influence of the "feminine principle" on the "new" novel.

1974 C DISSERTATIONS

1 BEPPU, KEIKO. "The Education of the Sensibility in the Fiction of Henry James and Walter Pater." DAI, 35, 439A-40A
   (Michigan).
       In the writings of Pater and James, there is a conflu-
   ence of the aesthetic and the moral. For both writers it
   is through the "perception of beauty" that "man fully
   realizes his true nature."

2 BLOUNT, JOSEPH DONALD. "Marcel Proust and Henry James in the
   Tradition of Lyric Description." DAI, 34, 5956A-57A
   (South Carolina).
       The economical lyric descriptions in James's The Ambas-
   sadors and the profuse lyric descriptions in Proust's A la
   recherche du temps perdu (both authors use lyric descriptions to indicate unconscious states in their characters)
   "indicate the poles between which other writers may be
   arranged."

3 COLLAS, JUDITH CAROL. "Henry James and His Father's Ideas:
   A Study of The American." DAI, 35, 1042A-43A (Univ. of
   California, Los Angeles).
       A close reading of The American reveals James's indebt-
   edness to his father's ideas. "James seems to have made
   extensive fictional use of the symbolic values that his
   father attached to America and Europe" and of his father's
   "theories of selfhood, conscience, and consciousness."

4 DAUGHERTY, SARAH BOWYER. "The Literary Criticism of Henry
   James, 1864-1884." DAI, 34, 5096A-97A (Pennsylvania).
       The early criticism written by James contains two dis-
   tinct elements--one is "neo-classical," and the other is
   "romantic." (Includes discussion of French Poets and
   Novelists.)

5 DONADIO, STEPHEN LOUIS. "The Dream of Art Triumphant: An Essay on Nietzsche and Henry James." DAI, 34, 7702A (Columbia).
       Nietzsche and James are related by a fundamental "belief
   in the necessity and power of art as a form-giving and

1974

value-creating activity." (Includes discussion of The Golden Bowl.)

6   GOLDENTHAL, JANICE B. "Henry James and Impressionism: A Method of Stylistic Analysis." DAI, 35, 2967A (New York Univ.).
    In The Ambassadors, The Wings of the Dove, and The Golden Bowl, verbal, syntactical, and narrative devices are employed by James to achieve impressionistic effects analogous to those achieved in impressionistic paintings.

7   GORNTO, ELEANOR FRANCES. "A Study of the Influence of the Fairy Tale on the Fiction of Henry James." DAI, 34, 7754A (Univ. of Illinois, Urbana-Champaign).
    James used fairy tales (Sleeping Beauty and Cinderella were most frequently utilized) "to heighten the moral reality which was his particular concern as a novelist and to intensify the ironic, as well as the romantic, melodramatic, and tragic dimensions of his fiction."

8   HAPPY, REUEL LYNN. "The Function of the Ending in the Later Novels of Henry James." DAI, 35, 1046A (Univ. of Missouri, Columbia).
    An analysis of four novels from James's late phase--The Spoils of Poynton, The Turn of the Screw, What Maisie Knew, and The Ambassadors--reveals that contrary to the opinion of some who feel he was unwilling to bring the issues he raised in his novels to a resolution, James consciously concluded his endings. These endings (except in the case of The Turn of the Screw where "the novel's pessimistic, disjunctive ending in itself reveals the nature and value of the negated synthesis") are "successful attempts to synthesize the antithetical principles" portrayed in the novels.

9   HELDER, JACK. "The Commedia dell'arte Tradition and Three Later Novels of Henry James." DAI, 35, 1047A (Bowling Green).
    A study of autobiographical, biographical, critical, and historical resources, and a close analysis of What Maisie Knew, The Awkward Age, and The Golden Bowl reveal that James adapted elements of the Commedia dell'arte tradition for his novelistic purposes.

10 KORMALI, SEMA GÜNISIK. "The Treatment of Marriage in Repre-
    sentative Novels of Jane Austen and Henry James." DAI, 35,
    2228A-29A (Texas Tech.).
        A study of six novels by Jane Austen (Sense and Sensi-
    bility, Pride and Prejudice, Mansfield Park, Emma, North-
    anger Abbey, and Persuasion) and six novels by James (Daisy
    Miller, The Portrait of a Lady, The Wings of the Dove, The
    Golden Bowl, The Bostonians and The Awkward Age) reveals
    that both authors used the conflicts of the protagonists to
    epitomize "the conflict between the moral and social values
    of a visionary or romantic life view and those of a real-
    istic or conventional life view."

11 LABADIE, PATRICIA BARTON. "Critical Response to the Prefaces
    of Henry James: A History of the Development of Under-
    standing and Appreciation of James's Theory of Fiction."
    DAI, 35, 3688A (Cincinnati).
        "The uneven but steady growth in appreciation of James's
    Prefaces was, in general, always preceded by improved un-
    derstanding of his fiction. This understanding was, in
    turn, generally a consequence of current critical theories
    of current developments in fiction at a given time."

12 LAUINGER, JOSEPH LEONARD, JR. "Internationalism in the Life
    and Fiction of Henry James, 1864-1881." DAI, 35, 1109A
    (Princeton).
        Three international novels written during James's early
    career--Roderick Hudson, The American, and The Portrait of
    a Lady--are parts of a "psychological puzzle" that revolves
    around his conscious decision to move to England.

13 PAGE, EUGENE PHILIP. "'The Intimate Connexion of Things':
    Narrative Form in The Portrait of a Lady, The Bostonians,
    The Princess Casamassima, and The Tragic Muse." DAI, 34,
    4277A (Johns Hopkins).
        Utilizing different techniques in the four novels,
    James employs a "narrative strategy" in each that "insists
    on the intimate connections among the characters, the au-
    thor, the narrators and the reader."

14 PATNODE, DARWIN NICHOLAS. "Love and Death in the Jamesian
    Novel." DAI, 35, 3760A-61A (Minnesota).
        A study of eighteen novels that span James's career
    suggests that he "deliberately avoids situations allowing
    for the consummation of happy, healthy, heterosexual love,
    preferring instead situations of absent love, of abnormal
    love, of frustrated love, and of love tinged with morbidity
    and death."

1974

15   PORTER, KATHLEEN ZAMLOCH. "The Epistemological Novels of
      Joseph Conrad and Henry James." DAI, 34, 6654A-55A
      (Syracuse).
           Both Conrad and James were epistemological skeptics. As
      such, both authors were in search of adequate techniques
      whereby they might "most fully portray the opacity of their
      separate novelistic worlds." (Includes discussion of The
      Ambassadors, The Golden Bowl, The Wings of the Dove, and
      The Turn of the Screw.)

16   SARMAD, NAHID. "Henry James: Elements of Drama and Theatre
      in the Major Novels of the Early Period: 1874-1881." DAI,
      34, 7721A (New York Univ.).
           A study of James's life-long interest in the theatre and
      an examination of four early novels, Roderick Hudson, The
      American, The Europeans, and Washington Square, reveal that
      James employed dramatic techniques not only in his late
      works but in his early works as well.

17   SMITH, CARL SHELDON. "Henry James, Henry Adams, and American
      Travel." DAI, 35, 3010A-11A (Yale).
           For Henry Adams and Henry James, travel was more than a
      pleasure, it was a "means of understanding the world" and
      of "making their ventures into dynamic and multi-levelled
      experiences that were of major importance in their lives
      and their work." (Includes discussion of Transatlantic
      Sketches, Italian Hours, The Sense of the Past, and "Trav-
      elling Companions.")

18   TERRILL, ROBERT E. "Artist Failures in the Fiction of Henry
      James." DAI, 35, 2302A-03A (Loyola, Chicago).
           James displays "considerable depth and insight" in his
      handling of the artist who, as a result of his "intensified
      consciousness," withdraws "from society and faces conflicts
      that can create artistic failure." Although James produced
      one major work related to this theme during each phase of
      his career (Roderick Hudson--early, The Tragic Muse--
      middle, The Sacred Fount--late), he still had "few resolu-
      tions" to offer.

19   WEINER, ROSEMARIE BODENHEIMER. "The Terrible Algebra: Images
      of the Self in Henry James." DAI, 35, 3016A (Boston Col-
      lege).
           A study of the imagery of The Portrait of a Lady, The
      Wings of the Dove, and The Golden Bowl reveals an evolving
      conception of selfhood in the author. In the end, his
      views fall "between earlier nineteenth-century novelists'

1974

subordinations of the self to society and late romantic
versions of the self . . . as a partially asocial or
'given' quality."

A Note on the Index

In addition to authors and titles (of books, articles, chapters of books, dissertations on James and James's works), this index includes names of people and characters (in James's works) and a number of subject entries. The reader should not, of course, presume that these topics are exhaustively surveyed.

People, characters, and subjects can be located in the appropriate alphabetical place in the index. However, titles of Henry James's works are found listed alphabetically under "James, Henry: Works."

Index numbers direct the reader to the year, section, and number of an entry. For example, 1965.B82 is found in the listing for the year 1965, the "B--Shorter Writings" section, entry number 82. Item numbers underlined for emphasis indicate significant treatments of the item indexed.

Subjects Indexed:

Aesthetics and Aestheticism

Ambiguity in Henry James's works

American Women

Artist (figure of the artist in Henry James's works)

Autobiography

Bibliography

Bio-Critical Surveys

Biography

Center of consciousness

Character Studies (including types of characters)

Children in the works of Henry James

Comic method (including comic sense, comic mode, comic spirit)

A Note on the Index

Comparative Studies

Correspondence

Critical Writings of Henry James

Criticism of Henry James

Double (use of the double in Henry James's works)

Drama

Expatriation

Film adaptations (of James's works)

General surveys (studies ranging over a number of James's works)

Gothic (Henry James's use of the Gothic)

Imagery Studies

International Theme

James and America

James and Art

James and France

James and French Writers

James and Italy

James and Russian Writers

James's influence

Language Studies

Money (James's treatment of money)

Morality

Name studies

Narrator

Naturalism

New York Edition

Parodies

Point of view

Pragmatism

Psychological studies

Realism

Religion

Renunciation

Revisions

Romance

Short stories, tales, and nouvelles

Sources, Influences, and Parallels

Stage adaptations (including opera)

Structure Studies

Study Aids

Style

Symbolism

Technique

Textual Studies

Theme Studies

Tragic Sense

Transcendentalism

Translations

Travel Writings

Word Studies

Characters Indexed:

Christina Light, Christopher Newman, Daisy Miller, Frederick Winterbourne, Hyacinth Robinson, Isabel Archer, Lewis Lambert Strether,
Maggie Verver, Maisie Farangue, Milly Theale

People Indexed:

Adams, Henry

Balzac, Honoré de

Beerbohm, Max

Besant, Walter

Boott, Francis

Bosanquet, Theodora

Brewster, H. B.

Browning, Robert

Cather, Willa

Clemens, Samuel

Conrad, Joseph

Crane, Stephen
Dickens, Charles
Draper, Ruth
Dumas, Alexander
Eliot, George
Eliot, T. S.
Emerson, Ralph Waldo
Faulkner, William
Fitzgerald, F. Scott
Flaubert, Gustave
Ford, Ford Madox
Forster, E. M.
Freud, Sigmund
Hardy, Thomas
Hawthorne, Nathaniel
Hay, John
Hemingway, Ernest
Howells, William Dean
Ibsen, Henrik
James, William
James, Alice
Lee, Vernon
Melville, Herman
Meredith, George
Poe, Edgar Allan
Proust, Marcel
Scudder, Horace
Shakespeare, William
Shaw, George Bernard
Stevenson, Robert Louis
Swedenborg, Emanuel
Taine, Hippolyte
Temple, Mary
Thurber, James

Index

"Analysis of 'The Birthplace,'
An," 1966.B42
"Analysis of 'The Real Thing,'"
1964.B33
"Analytical Index of the Literary
and Art Criticism by Henry
James, An," 1966.C7
"Anatomy of Passion in the Con-
summate Henry James, The,"
1972.B1
Anatomy of "The Turn of the
Screw," An, 1965.A4
Andersen, Kenneth, 1970.B1
Anderson, Charles R., 1962.B4;
1967.B4
Anderson, Frederick, 1960.B80
Anderson, Quentin, 1963.B3;
1965.B1; 1966.B2; 1968.A1;
1970.A5; 1971.B1; 1972.B2
Andreach, Robert J., 1962.B5;
1967.B5
"Andrew Lytle's A Name for Evil
as a Redaction of The Turn of
the Screw," 1972.B115
"Andrew Lytle's A Name for Evil:
A Transformation of The Turn of
the Screw," 1966.B19
Andrews, Wayne, 1965.B2
Anonymous, 1967.A5; 1968.B3;
1969.B2-3; 1972.B3
"Another Princess," 1962.B73
"Another Reading of The Turn of
the Screw," 1960.A6
"Another Turn on James's 'The
Turn of the Screw,'" 1960.A6
"Another Twist to The Turn of
the Screw," 1967.B1 (rpt.
1969.A11)
"Anti-Literary Biography,"
1970.B39
"Anton Chekhov and Henry James,"
1970.B101
"Anton Tchékhov et Henry James,"
1962.B96
Antush, John Vincent, 1968.B4;
1969.B4; 1972.B4
Anzilotti, Rolando, 1968.B5
Aoki, Tsugio, 1963.B4; 1967.A6;
1969.B5; 1971.B2; 1972.B5
Aplash, Madhu, 1968.B6

"Apparenza e realta' in The
Awkward Age," 1963.B19
Appignanesi, Lisa, 1973.B1
"Appreciation, An," 1963.A1
"Approach to Evil in Henry
James, An," 1961.B74
Appropriate Form: An Essay on
the Novel, 1964.B42
Araujo, Víctor de, 1966.B3
"Archetypes of American Innocence:
Lydia Blood and Daisy Miller,"
1968.B11
"Archimago's Well: An Interpre-
tation of The Sacred Fount,"
1961.B26
"Aristokratie und Gentleman im
Englischen und Amerikanischen
Roman des 19. und 20. Jahr-
hunderts," 1963.B10
Arlos, Alma Rosenfield, 1961.C1
Arms, George, 1963.B5
Arnold Bennett and H. G. Wells:
A Record of a Personal and
Literary Friendship, 1960.B99
Around Theatres, 1963.A1
"Art and Artists in The Portrait
of a Lady," 1969.B29
Art and Error: Modern Textual
Editing, 1970.B42
"Art as Deception: A Study of
Some Fictional Characters of
Thomas Mann and Henry James,"
1969.C3
"Art as Problem in 'The Figure in
the Carpet' and 'The Madonna of
the Future,'" 1970.A7
Articles on American Literature,
1950-67, 1970.B72
Articles on Twentieth Century
Literature: An Annotated
Bibliography: 1954-1970,
1974.B55
"Articulation of Time in The
Ambassadors, The," 1972.B25
Artist (figure of the artist in
Henry James's works), 1960.A2,
B24, B72, B77; 1961.B72, B77;
1962.B11, B15, B61, B83;
1963.B109 (rpt. 1965.B107,
1973.A6); 1964.B8, B10, B43,
B99; 1965.C1, C8; 1966.B5,

(Bibliographies and Checklists)
1971.B6, B32, <u>B41</u>, B55, B67,
B73, B85; 1972.<u>B3</u>, B49, B53;
1973.B5; 1974.B17-18, B46,
B55, B58
Bibliographies of Bibliographies, 1969.B67; 1970.B88;
1971.B55
Collections, (Univ. of Texas)
1960.B9; (Lamb House)
1967.B50; (Princeton Univ.)
1968.B3; (Colby College Lib.)
1970.B8, (Colby College Lib.)
B15; (Bancroft Lib., Univ. of
California) 1972.B3
Critical Reception and Reputation, 1960.C1; 1962.C7;
1966.B77; 1968.A4; 1969.B86,
B98
Indexes, (plots and characters)
1965.A6; (to James's Prefaces) 1966.A2, (to literary
and art criticism) C7
<u>Bibliography of American Auto-
biographies, A</u>, 1961.B54
<u>Bibliography of American Litera-
ture</u>, 1969.B18
<u>Bibliography of Bibliographies in
American Literature</u>, 1970.B88
<u>Bibliography of British Literary
Bibliographies</u>, 1969.B67
<u>Bibliography of Henry James, A</u>,
1961.A2
<u>Bibliography of Henry James in
Japan, A</u>, 1965.A14
<u>Bibliography of the American
Theatre, Excluding New York
City</u>, 1965.B104
Bickley, Karen L., 1971.B32
Biddle, Francis, 1967.B10;
1971.C1
Bier, Jesse, 1968.B15; 1970.B7
Bio-Critical surveys, 1960.A1
(rpt. 1968.B27), <u>A3</u>, <u>B7</u>;
1961.B24, B35; 1962.<u>B70</u>, B84;
1963.B1, B9, B102; 1964.A1;
<u>1965.A5</u>, <u>A12</u>; 1967.A6, B7, B44;
<u>1969.A7</u>; <u>1970.A4</u>; 1973.B36;
1974.A5, B6, B69
Biography, 1960.B22, B49, B101;
1961.B18, B39, B49, B90;

<u>1962.A1-2</u>, B20, B120; 1964.B32;
1965.A1; 1966.A4, B61;
1967.B76; 1968.B26, B28-31,
B53-55, B71; <u>1969.A1</u>, A3, B47,
B56, B60, B94; <u>1970.B6</u>, B15,
B18, B34; 1971.B130; <u>1972.A3</u>,
B1-2, B7, B10, B29-30, B33,
B51, B60, B82-83, B98, B103;
1973.B8, B30; 1974.A4, B16,
B47
"Biography: The Treacherous
Art," 1970.B56
Birch, Brian, 1965.B5; 1966.B12
"Birth of a Hermaphrodite,"
1962.B90
Bixler, J. Seelye, 1970.B8
Blackall, Jean Frantz, 1960.B36;
1961.C2; 1962.B17; 1963.B8;
1965.A2
Blackmur, R. P., 1960.B7-8;
1961.B5-6; 1963.B9; 1964.B12;
1967.A5; 1969.A10; 1972.A9;
1974.B6
Blanck, Jacob, 1969.B18
Blanke, Gustav H., 1963.B10
Blasing, Mutlu, 1973.B9
Blehl, Vincent F., 1961.B7
Bleich, David, 1970.B9; 1971.B10
"'Blighted Houses and Blighted
Childhood': James's Treacher-
ous Years," 1969.B128
Bliven, Naomi, 1963.B11; 1972.B10
Blount, Joseph Donald, 1974.C2
Bluefarb, Sam, 1971.B11
Bluen, Herbert, 1964.B13
Boardman, Arthur, 1974.B7
Bobbitt, Joan, 1973.B10
Bocaz, Sergio Hernán, 1972.B11
Bochner, Jay, 1969.B19
<u>Bodley Head Henry James, The</u>,
1967.B22; 1968.B32; 1969.B43
Böker, Uwe, 1974.B8
"Bolted Door in Henry James,
The," 1964.B81
Bonincontro, Marilia, 1968.B16
Bontly, Thomas John, 1967.C2;
1969.B20-21
Booth, Wayne C., 1961.B8;
1963.B99; 1969.A10
Boott, Francis, 1960.B27
Borden, Diane M., 1972.C2

"'Easy Ride' for Henry James: or,
Is Captain America Christopher
Newman (?)--The Master and Pop
Kultur, a Note from the Mid-
west, An," 1974.B70
Ebine, Shizue, 1969.B41; 1974.B14
Eble, Kenneth E., 1962.B24
"Economics of Disease in James's
'The Pupil,' The," 1973.B12
Edel, Leon, 1960.A1, B22-27;
1961.A2, B21-23; 1962.A1-2,
B25; 1963.A1, B23-25; 1964.A6,
B28-29; 1965.B17-20; 1966.A5,
B25-26; 1967.B21-23, B37;
1968.A1, B27-33; 1969.A1, A10,
B42-43; 1970.A5, A8, B29-31;
1971.B31, B57; 1972.A3, A9,
B28-30; 1973.A6; 1974.B15-16
Edelstein, Arnold, 1970.B32;
1972.C6
Edelstein, Tilden G., 1968.B34
Edgar, Pelham, 1963.A1; 1968.A1
"Edith Wharton and Henry James,"
1974.B78
Edith Wharton and Henry James:
  The Story of their Friendship,
1965.A1
"Edith Wharton and 'The Elusive
Bright-Winged Thing,'" 1964.B19
"Edith Wharton and the Twilight
of the International Novel,"
1969.B143
"Edith Wharton: A Prophet With-
out Due Honor," 1962.B88
"Edith Wharton's Ghost Stories,"
1970.B78
"Edith Wharton's Hymns to
Respectability," 1971.B78
"Editions of The Ambassadors,
The," 1966.B82
Edmund Wilson, 1970.B37
"Edmund Wilson and The Turn of
the Screw," 1966.A5 (rpt.
1970.A7)
Edmund Wilson: A Study of Lit-
erary Vocation in Our Time,
1965.B84
"Education of the Sensibility in
the Fiction of Henry James and
Walter Pater, The," 1974.C1
Efron, Arthur, 1964.B30

Egan, Michael, 1972.A4, B31
Egoism and Self-Discovery in the
  Victorian Novel, 1974.B23
Eguchi, Yuko, 1965.B21
Eibei-Bungakushi Kiza IX:
  19 Seiki, 1961.B24
Eichelberger, Clayton L.,
1971.B32; 1974.B17
Eight American Authors: A Review
  of Research and Criticism,
1963.B63, B96; 1971.B41
Eight Great American Short
  Novels, 1963.B84
Eight Modern Writers: Oxford
  History of English Literature,
1963.B102
Ejima, Yuji, 1961.B24; 1967.A6
"El Concepto de la inocencia en
Henry James," 1972.B20
Elements of Tragedy, 1969.B83
"El fin de la inocencia,"
1963.B17
"Elgin Marbles and Titian's
'Bacchus and Ariadne': A
Cluster of Keatsian Associa-
tions in Henry James," 1973.B97
Eliot, George, 1961.B40-41, B80;
1962.B55; 1963.B56; 1964.B1,
B68, C6; 1967.B10, B28, B35,
B81; 1970.B54; 1971.B91, C4,
C28; 1972.B15, B43; 1973.B76
Eliot, T. S., 1963.A1; 1964.B26,
B45; 1965.B51; 1968.B63;
1969.B14, B39; 1970.B46;
1972.A9; 1974.B3
"Elizabeth Bowen: Imagination
as Therapy," 1965.B36
Ellis, James, 1967.B98
Ellmann, Richard, 1965.B22
"Emancipation of Lambert
Strether: A Study of the
Relationship Between the Ideas
of William and Henry James,
The," 1967.C1
"Emerging Consciousness: A
Study of the Development of
the Centre of Consciousness in
the Early Novels of Henry
James, The," 1971.C1
Emerson, Donald, 1960.B28-29;
1962.B26; 1963.B26-27; 1969.B44

"Felicity Forever Gone: Henry
James's Last Visit to America,
A," 1962.B58
Felstiner, John, 1967.B24
Femininity and the Creative
Imagination: A Study of Henry
James, Robert Musil, and Marcel
Proust, 1973.B1
"Feminism and the New Novel,"
1974.B92
Ferguson, Louis Aloysius,
1968.C1
Ferment of Realism: American
Literature, 1884-1919, The,
1965.B4
Fernandez, Diane, 1969.B46-47;
1970.B34
Feuerlicht, Ignace, 1966.A5
Fictional Children of Henry
James, The, 1969.A9
"Fictional Feminists in The
Bostonians and The Odd
Women," 1972.B67
"Fiction and Belief," 1972.B111
Fiction and the Figures of Life,
1970.B40
Fiction Guide: British and
American, 1967.B15
"Fiction of Henry James, 1895-
1901, The," 1971.C19
Fictions and Events: Essays in
Criticism and Literary History,
1971.B7
Fiderer, Gerald, 1969.B48
Fiedler, Leslie, 1960.B33-34;
1963.B99; 1966.B27
Field, Mary Lee, 1972.C7;
1974.B18
Figuera, Angela, 1961.B25
"Figure in the Carpet, The,"
(Kanzer) 1960.B51; (Tyler)
1964.B99
"Figure in the Carpet: Irony
and the American Novel, A,"
1962.B13
"Figures in the Carpet: A Study
of Leading Metaphors in Six
Realistic Novels," 1971.B23
Figures in the Foreground: Lit-
erary Reminiscences, 1917-1940,
1964.B96

Film adaptations, 1961.B12, B14,
B55; 1962.B8, B27, B48, B65;
1971.B73
"Final Preface: Henry James's
Autobiography, The," 1969.B64
Finch, G. A., 1968.B37
Fine, Ronald Edward, 1968.B115
Fingleton, David, 1971.B35
Fink, Guido, 1969.B49
Finkelstein, Sidney, 1960.B35;
1962.B28
Finn, C. M., 1971.B36
Finney, Martha, 1971.C5
Firebaugh, Joseph J., 1960.A6;
1973.A6
"First Editions, English and
American," 1966.B70
"First Paragraph of The Ambas-
sadors: An Explication, The,"
1960.B98 (rpt. 1964.A6;
1968.A11, B115; 1969.A10)
"First-Person Fiction of Henry
James, The," 1970.C5
"First-Person Narrator as Artist
in the Works of Charles Brock-
den Brown, Nathaniel Hawthorne,
and Henry James, The," 1973.B72
"First-Person Narrators of Henry
James, The," 1974.B41
Fischer, William Coverly, Jr.,
1968.C5; 1970.B35
Fish, Charles Kelleway, Jr.,
1964.C4; 1965.B26-27; 1967.B25
Fisher, Neil H., 1965.B28-29
"Fitzgerald, Brooks, Hemingway,
and James: A New Fitzgerald
Letter," 1965.B9
Fitzgerald, F. Scott, 1961.B96;
1964.B16 (rpt. 1971.A7);
1965.B9, B37, B90, B116 (rpt.
1972.B112); 1966.B14;
1967.B62, B98; 1968.B52;
1969.B24; 1972.B96; 1973.B19,
B68
Fitzpatrick, Kathleen, 1968.A2
"Flannery O'Connor and Henry
James: The Vision of Grace,"
1974.B4
Flaubert, Gustave, 1960.B16;
1961.B78; 1963.B57; 1968.B18;
1970.B93; 1971.A5; 1973.A1,
B14, B76

Hill, John Edward, 1973.B38
Hill, J. S., 1968.B52
Hinchcliffe, Arnold P.,
 1960.B45-46; 1962.B43
Hinz, Evelyn J., 1972.B45-46
Hirsch, David H., 1963.B45
"Historical or Moral Validity, or
 Two Kinds of Norms," 1973.B22
Historicism Once More: Problems
 and Occasions for the American
 Scholar, 1969.B106
History of Modern Criticism:
 1750-1950, A, 1965.B123
History of the English Novel:
 Volume XI--Yesterday and After,
 The, 1967.B99
Hoag, Gerald Bryan, 1965.C5;
 1972.A7
Hoberman, Mary Ann, 1974.B28
Hocks, Richard Allen, 1968.C6;
 1974.A2
Hodgdon, David Crockett, 1971.C12
Hodge, Judith Bush, 1972.C10
Hofer, Ernest Harrison, 1960.C3
Hoffa, William Walter, 1968.C7;
 1969.B64
Hoffman, Charles G., 1960.A6
Hoffman, Frederick J., 1961.B47;
 1963.B46; 1964.B44; 1973.A6
Hoffman, Michael J., 1972.B47
Hoftun, Sigmund, 1961.B48;
 1972.B112
Hogsett, Elizabeth A., 1970.B57
Holder, Alan, 1963.B47; 1964.B45;
 1965.B51; 1966.B41
Holder, Alex, 1960.B47
Holland, Laurence Bedwell,
 1964.A3; 1965.C6
Holleran, James V., 1966.B42
Holloway, John, 1960.B48;
 1969.B65
Holman, C. Hugh, 1964.B46;
 1966.B43
Holroyd, Stuart, 1961.B49
"'The Holy Innocents' and 'The
 Turn of the Screw,'" 1963.B93
"Home, James," 1972.B10
Hönnighausen, Lothar, 1967.B47
Hopkins, Gerard, 1960.B60
Hopkins, Viola. See Viola
 Hopkins Winner.

Horne, Helen, 1960.A2
Horowitz, Floyd Ross, 1961.C8;
 1966.B44
Horrell, Joyce Tayloe, 1970.B58
Hoshioka, Motoko, 1963.B49
Hough, Graham, 1965.B52; 1972.B48
Houghton, Donald E., 1969.B66
Houghton, Walter E., 1966.B45;
 1972.B49
"Hourglass Pattern in The
 Ambassadors, The," 1968.B23
"House of Atreus and Mme. de
 Bellegarde's Crime, The,"
 1973.B98
"House of Irony: A Study of
 Irony in Henry James, The,"
 1968.C2
"House of the Seven Ushers and
 How They Grew: A Look at
 Jamesian Gothicism, The,"
 1967.B6
Houses that James Built and Other
 Literary Studies, The, 1961.B82
"Houses that James Built--The
 Portrait of a Lady, The,"
 1961.B82
Houston, N. B., 1973.B39
Hovanec, Evelyn Ann, 1973.C10
Howard, David, 1972.A6
Howard-Hill, T. H., 1969.B67
"Howard Sturgis, Henry James, and
 Belchamber," 1961.B9
Howe, Helen, 1965.B53
Howe, Irving, 1963.A1; 1967.B48-
 49; 1970.B59; 1972.B112
Howells, William Dean, 1961.A3;
 1962.B1, B75, B82; 1963.B45,
 B52; 1964.B46, B84 (rpt.
 1968.B115; 1969.B120);
 1965.B11-12, B59; 1966.B74;
 1967.B41, B54, B72; 1968.B11,
 B61, B80, B102, C5; 1969.B75-
 76, B87, B123; 1970.B1, B35,
 B38, B77, B121, C11; 1971.A7,
 B44, B95; 1972.B90; 1973.B2;
 1974.B52
Howells: A Century of Criticism,
 1962.B1, B24
"Howells and James," 1971.B44
"Howells in the Nineties,"
 1970.B77

Knapp, Daniel, 1964.B33
"Knave, Fool, and Genius: The
    Confidence Man as He Appears
    in Nineteenth-Century American
    Fiction," 1970.B71
Knave, Fool, and Genius: The
    Confidence Man as He Appears
    in Nineteenth-Century Fiction,
    1973.B49
Knieger, Bernard, 1971.B64
Knight, Arthur, 1961.B55
Knoepflmacher, U. C., 1965.B60;
    1969.A10
"The Knot Garden and Owen
    Wingrave: Operatic Development
    or Experiment?" 1971.B35
Knox, George, 1963.B53; 1965.B61;
    1971.A7; 1972.B112
Koch, Stephen, 1966.B51
Kohli, Raj K., 1968.B60;
    1969.B101
Kolb, Harold Hutchinson, Jr.,
    1969.B75-76
Koljević, Svetozar, 1961.B56
Komota, Junzo, 1962.B52
Kono, Yotaro, 1968.B61
Korg, Jacob, 1962.B53
Kormali, Sema Günisik, 1974.C10
Kornfeld, Milton Herbert,
    1970.B70; 1972.B59
Kossick, Shirley, 1969.B77
Kossman, Rudolf R., 1969.A4, C7
Kozol, Clara Barbara, 1973.C13
Kraft, James, 1967.B59; 1968.B62,
    C8; 1969.A5, B78; 1970.A7;
    1973.B46
Kraft, Quentin Guild, 1963.C1;
    1965.B62-63; 1969.B79
Kramer, Cheris, 1966.B52
Kramer, Dale, 1966.B52
Kramer, Hilton, 1969.B80
Krier, William John, 1973.B47
Krishan, Bal, 1972.C15
Krishna Rao, N. See Rao,
    N. Krishna.
Kronenberger, Louis, 1962.B10;
    1969.B81
Krook, Dorothea, 1962.A3;
    1968.A1; 1969.B82-83; 1973.A6,
    B48
Kubal, David L., 1966.B53

Kudo, Yoshimi, 1968.B63
Kuhlmann, Susan, 1970.B71;
    1973.B49

L

Labadie, Patricia Barton,
    1974.C11
Labor, Earle, 1962.B54; 1965.B8;
    1970.A7
Labrie, Ernest Ross, 1967.C8;
    1968.B64; 1969.B84; 1971.B65;
    1973.B50
Lacassin, Francis, 1972.B61
"La Critica Letteraria di Henry
    James," 1961.B60
"La Francia di Henry James,"
    1963.B28
Lainoff, Seymour, 1961.B57;
    1962.B55; 1970.A7
"L'Ambassadeur: Henry James,
    romancier des deux mondes,"
    1965.B80
"Lamb House Library of Henry
    James, The," 1967.B50
Landry, Lowell, 1971.C15
"Landscape in the Novel,"
    1971.B42
"Landscape into Art: Henry James
    and John Crowe Ransom,"
    1971.B13
Lane, Margaret, 1967.B60
Lang, Hans-Joachim, 1964.B53
Lang, P. H., 1962.B56
Langbaum, Robert, 1973.B51
"Language as Art: The Ways of
    Knowing in Henry James's
    'Crapy Cornelia,'" 1967.B83
"Language of 'Adventure' in
    Henry James, The," 1960.B70;
    1964.A6
Language of Fiction: Essays in
    Criticism and Verbal Analysis
    of the English Novel, 1966.B57
"Language of Henry James with
    Emphasis on His Diction and
    Vocabulary," 1960.C6
"Language of Love and Language
    of Things: Henry James's The
    Wings of the Dove," 1971.B2

"Letter from Paris," 1963.B37

"Letters of Henry James to John Hay," 1963.B68

Letters of Oscar Wilde, The, 1962.B118

"Letters to a 'Countryman': John Hay to Henry James," 1963.B69

"Letter to Robert B. Heilman [on The Turn of the Screw], A," 1971.B126

"Lettre di James," 1961.B60

Levin, Gerald, 1961.B58

Levin, Harry, 1966.B54

Levine, George, 1963.B56-57

Le Vot, André, 1970.B73

Levy, Edward Rich, 1964.C7

Levy, Leo B., 1962.B60-61; 1966.B55; 1968.B65

Lewis, R. W. B., 1965.B66

Lewis Lambert Strether, 1960.B15, B33, B39; 1961.B32; 1962.B12 (rpt. 1964.B18), B76, B112 (rpt. 1973.A6); 1963.B4, B108; 1964.B47; 1965.B10, B47, B60 (rpt. 1969.A10), B63; 1966.B10; 1967.C1; 1969.B42, B95, B145; 1971.B131; 1973.B3, B58, C18; 1974.B1. See The Ambassadors.

Leyburn, Ellen Douglass, 1968.A7

"'The Liar': A Lesson in Devotion," 1965.B95

Libby, Marion Jean Vlastos, 1971.C17

"Liberty in the Novels of Henry James," 1966.B94

Libman, Valentina A., 1969.B86

Library of Literary Criticism: Modern American Literature, A, 1960.B69

Library of Literary Criticism: Modern British Literature, A, 1966.B96

Lid, R. W., 1960.B53, 1961.B59

Liddell, Robert, 1967.B61

Liebman, Sheldon W., 1970.B74; 1971.B70

"Lies in 'The Liar,'" 1969.B5

"Life Against Death in Venice," 1965.B62

"Life Buffets (and Comforts) Henry James, 1883-1916: An Introduction and An Annotated Checklist," 1968.B46

"Life in a Picture Gallery: Things in The Portrait of a Lady and The Marble Faun," 1969.B19

"Life Into Art: A Literary Analysis of Henry James's Autobiography," 1968.C14

Light, Martin, 1965.B8

"Light and the Dark: Character Design in The Portrait of a Lady, The," 1970.B74

"Light Going Out: Henry James as Social Critic in The Portrait of a Lady and 'The Pupil,' The," 1972.B21

"Light Lamp: The Spoils of Poynton as Comedy, A," 1969.B62

Light of Common Day: Realism in American Fiction, The, 1971.B19

"Limitations of Christopher Newman, The," 1972.B112

"Limits of Living in Style, The," 1974.B39

"L'Impressionnisme Anglais: Aux Sources du 'Nouveau Roman,'" 1962.B2

Lincecum, J. B., 1971.B71

Lind, Ilse Dusoir, 1961.B23

Lind, Sidney E., 1970.B75

Ling, Amy, 1974.B37

Linneman, William R., 1962.B62

Lion and the Honeycomb: Essays in Solicitude and Critique, The, 1969.A10

"Literary Absenteeism: Henry James and Mark Twain," 1966.B110

"Literary Allusion as a Clue to Meaning: James's 'The Ghostly Rental' and Pascal's Pensées," 1967.B5

"Literary Allusions in James's Prefaces," 1963.B100

"Literary Children of James and Clemens, The," 1961.B87

Milton, Dorothy, 1968.C10

"Mingled Vision: Point of View in the Novels of Henry James, 1871-1900, The," 1971.C5

"Minor Cultural Event, A," 1972.B80

Minter, Elsie Gray, 1964.C9

Miroiu, Mihai, 1970.B82

"Mirror of Allusion: The Ambassadors, The," 1961.B13

"Missing Word in Henry James's 'Four Meetings,' The," 1970.B48

"Miss Jessel and Lady Chatterley," 1960.B78

"'Miss Jessel': Mirror Image of the Governess," 1968.B89

Mitchell, Juliet, 1972.A6

Mitgang, Herbert, 1968.B74-75

Mix, Katherine Lyon, 1960.B65

"Mixed and Uniform Prose Styles in the Novel," 1960.B56 (rpt. 1967.B101)

Mizener, Arthur, 1964.B69; 1967.B73

Mlikotin, Anthony Matthew, 1961.C10; 1971.A4

"Modal Counterpoint in James's The Aspern Papers," 1968.B73

Modern American Criticism, 1963.B103

Modern Critical Spectrum, The, 1962.B110

Modern Fiction Studies, "Henry James Number," 1966.B67

Modern Novel: In Britain and the United States, The, 1964.B1

Modern Tradition: Backgrounds of Modern Literature, The, 1965.B22

Modern Writers, and Other Essays, 1969.B60

Modest Art: A Survey of the Short Story in English, The, 1968.B12

"Molds of Form: Comedy and Conscience in the Novels of Henry James, 1895-1901, The," 1961.C6

"Moment of The Portrait of a Lady, The," 1968.B36

Money (James's treatment of money), 1967.C11; 1968.B4; 1969.B4, B15, B34; 1973.A4

"Money as Myth and Reality in the World of Henry James," 1969.B4

"Money in the Novels of James, Wharton, and Dreiser," 1968.B4

"Monomyth in 'The Great Good Place,' The," 1963.B44

Monteiro, George, 1962.B73-75; 1963.B64-72; 1964.B70-71; 1965.A13; 1967.C10; 1969.B99-100; 1971.B85; 1972.B74; 1974.B46

Montgomery, Judith H., 1971.B86

Montgomery, Marion, 1960.B66; 1968.A1

Moody, A. D., 1961.B66

Mooney, Stephen L., 1961.B67

"Moonshine and Bloodshed: A Note on The American," 1962.B23 (rpt. 1972.B112)

Moore, Harry T., 1974.A4

Moore, John Rees, 1961.B76

Moore, Rayburn S., 1964.B72; 1974.B47

"Moral and Metaphorical Meanings of The Spoils of Poynton, The," 1960.B79

Moral and the Story, The, 1962.B34

"Moral Aspect of Henry James's 'International Situation,' The," 1968.B20

"Moral Awareness in The Spoils of Poynton," 1966.B46

"Moral Field: James, The," 1965.B129

Morality, 1960.B45, B70, B77, B79, B91, B92 (rpt. 1965.B8), B93-94, C3; 1961.B35, B52, B66; 1962.A4, B34; 1963.B94, B116, C2-3; 1964.B24, C1; 1965.A7, B47; 1966.B79 (rpt. 1968.A1), C1, C5; 1967.B85 (rpt. 1971.B67); 1969.B21, B48; 1971.B65; 1972.B17

"Morality in Henry James's Novels," 1963.B116

"Morality of Consciousness in Henry James, The," 1971.B65

"Moral or Historical Validity: Henry James, The Ambassadors," 1972.B36

"Moral Passion in The Portrait of a Lady and The Spoils of Poynton," 1966.B79

"Moral Perspective of The Ambassadors, The," 1969.B21

"Moral Values of the American Woman as Presented in Three Major American Authors," 1965.B91

Mordell, Albert, 1961.A3

"More About Gatsby's Guest List," 1972.B96

Morgan, Alice, 1970.B83

Morgan, H. Wayne, 1970.B33

Morris, R. A., 1973.B59

Morrison, Sister Kristin, 1961.B68

Morrison, Peggy Ann R., 1973.C15

Morse, Samuel French, 1970.B84

Moss, Leonard Jerome, 1960.B67

Mossman, Robert E., 1966.C7

"Mother in the Fiction of Henry James, The," 1962.C2

"Motive, Agency, and Act in James's The Aspern Papers," 1974.B63

Motoda, Shuichi, 1967.B74; 1968.B76; 1970.A3

Moynahan, Julian, 1972.B75

"Mr. Edmund Wilson and The Turn of the Screw," 1960.A6

"Mrs. Gaskell's 'The Old Nurse's Story': A Link Between Wuthering Heights and The Turn of the Screw," 1961.B2 (rpt. 1966.A5)

Mrs. Gaskell: The Basis for Reassessment, 1965.B128

"Mrs. Grose's Reading of The Turn of the Screw," 1974.B7

Mrs. Jack, 1965.B109

"Mr. Spilka's Reply," 1964.B94

"Mrs. Tristram and a 'Sense of Type,'" 1971.A7

"Mrs. Wharton and Mr. James," 1965.B25

"'Much Finer Complexity' of History in The American, The," 1972.B4

"Muddled Politics of Henry James's The Bostonians, The," 1972.B73

Mudrick, Marvin, 1962.B76

Mueller, Lavonne, 1968.B77

Mukherjee, Sujit, 1969.B101

Mukherji, Nirmal, 1963.B73; 1968.B78; 1969.B102

Mull, Donald Locke, 1967.C11; 1971.B87; 1973.A4

Mulqueen, James E., 1971.B88

Munford, Howard M., 1967.B75

Munzar, Jiří, 1971.B89

Murakami, Fujio, 1960.B68; 1961.B69; 1967.A6; 1974.B48

"Murderous Innocence: James's The Turn of the Screw," 1972.B27

Murdock, Kenneth B., 1964.A6

Murray, Donald M., 1963.B74; 1965.B79; 1967.A5; 1971.B90

"Museum World, The," 1963.A1

Mutarelli, Georgio, 1962.B77

"Mutual Perspective: James and Howells as Critics of Each Other's Fiction," 1967.B54

"My Dear Pinker: The Correspondence of Henry James with His Literary Agent," 1961.B18

Myers, Robert Manson, 1969.B103

"'Mystery' of Henry James's The Sacred Fount, The," 1962.B28

Myth and the Powerhouse, The, 1965.B86

"Mythic Approaches to The Turn of the Screw," 1970.A3

N

Nagano, Reiko, 1964.B73

Nagel, Paul C., 1971.B91

Naik, M. K., 1963.B75

Nakano, K., 1967.B76

Nakauchi, Masao, 1966.A8

Nakazato, Haruhiko, 1962.B78-79

Namekata, Akio, 1972.B80; 1967.A6; 1970.B85

"Names in James," 1966.B32

Otsu, Eiichiro, 1962.B85; 1966.A8

"'Our Doubt is Our Passion':
Ambiguity in Three of the Later
Novels of Henry James," 1961.C1

"Our Hawthorne," 1964.B98 (rpt.
1964.B79)

"'Our Lady of the Gulls': A Case
of Polite Revenge," 1971.B22

Owen, Elizabeth, 1963.B82;
1967.B80

Oxford Companion to English
Literature, The, 1967.B44

Ozick, Cynthia, 1963.B83

P

Page, Philip, 1974.B51, C13

"Pagoda Image in Henry James's
The Golden Bowl, The,"
1974.B37

Paik, Nak-Chung, 1964.B78

"Painter's Sponge and Varnish
Bottle, The," 1967.A5

"'Pandora' and Her President,"
1964.B35

Paniker, K. Ayyappa, 1973.B67

Parker, Hershel, 1965.B83

Parodies, 1960.B57; 1964.B39;
1967.B24; 1970.B51; 1971.B106;
1972.A2; 1974.B81

Parodies: An Anthology from
Chaucer to Beerbohm--and
After," 1960.B57

"Partial Analysis of 'The Bench
of Desolation,'" 1962.B64

"Parting of the Ways, The,"
1970.B118

Pastalosky, Rosa, 1971.B3

"Pastoralism as Culture and
Counter-Culture in English
Fiction, 1800-1928," 1972.B75

"Past Perfect Retrospection in
the Style of Henry James,"
1962.B113

Paterson, John, 1960.B70;
1964.A6; 1973.B63

Paths of American Thought,
1964.B87

Patnode, Darwin Nicholas,
1974.C14

Patrick, Michael D., 1972.B79

Patriotic Gore: Studies in the
Literature of the American
Civil War, 1962.B120

"Pattern in The Ambassadors,"
1964.A6

"Pattern of Limitations: The
Heroine's Novel of the Mind,
A," 1973.B47

"Pattern of Parallel and Double:
The Function of Myrtle in The
Great Gatsby, A," 1969.B24

"Patterns of Freedom in Henry
James's Later Novels," 1962.C4

"Patterns of Imagery in
Chapter XLII of Henry James's
The Portrait of a Lady,"
1969.B51

Patterson, Rebecca, 1960.B71

Paul, Sherman, 1965.B84

Pauly, Thomas Harry, 1971.B95

Payne, James Robert, 1974.B52

Pearce, Brian, 1969.B105;
1970.B89

Pearce, Howard D., 1974.B53

Pearce, Roy Harvey, 1962.B86;
1964.B79; 1969.B106

Pearson, Gabriel, 1972.A6

Pearson, Norman Holmes, 1968.B20

Pelican Guide to English Literature: The Modern Age, The,
1961.B35

Pendleton, James D., 1973.B64

Pendo, Mina, 1970.A8

"Perception in James's 'The Real
Thing,'" 1972.B106

"Percy Lubbock," 1967.B61

"Percy Lubbock: Disciple of
Henry James," 1968.C9

"Perfection of a Pattern: The
Structure of The Ambassadors,
The Wings of the Dove, and The
Golden Bowl," 1971.B88

"Performing Self, The," 1971.B97

Performing Self: Compositions
and Decompositions in the
Languages of Contemporary Life,
The, 1971.B98

Perloff, Marjorie, 1969.B107

Perlongo, Robert A., 1960.B72

Perosa, Sergio, 1966.B73

"Perpetuated Misprints," 1970.B89

Roselli, Daniel N., 1971.B106
Rosenbaum, Stanford Patrick,
 1961.C12; 1964.A6; 1966.A5,
 B82-84
Rosenberry, Edward H., 1961.B75
Rosenfield, Claire, 1963.B87
Ross, Maude Cardwell, 1965.B91
Ross, Morton L., 1966.B85
Rountree, Benjamin C., 1964.B82
Rourke, Constance, 1971.A7;
 1973.A6
Rovit, Earl, 1964.B83; 1965.B92
Rowe, John Carlos, 1972.C20;
 1973.B74
Roy, Claude, 1962.B96
Rubin, Louis D., Jr., 1961.B76;
 1963.B88; 1967.B86-87; 1969.A11
Ruggiero, Claudia Corradini,
 1973.B75
Ruhm, Herbert, 1961.B77;
 1962.B97; 1963.B89
Ruland, Richard, 1967.B88
Rupp, Richard H., 1970.B97
Russian Studies of American
 Literature: A Bibliography,
 1969.B86
Ryan, Marjorie, 1961.B78

S

Saalbach, R. P., 1971.B107
Sabiston, Elizabeth Jean,
 1969.B119; 1973.B76
Sachs, Viola, 1966.B86
"The Sacred Fount," (Tyler)
 1964.B99; (Edel) 1973.A6
"'The Sacred Fount': An Author
 in Search of His Characters,"
 1962.B57
"Sacred Fount and British
 Aestheticism: The Artist as
 Clown and Pornographer, The,"
 1971.B117
"Sacred Fount as a Comedy of the
 Limited Observer, The," 1963.B8
"Sacred Fount: James's Portrait
 of the Artist Manqué, The,"
 1960.B77
"Sacred Fount: Labyrinth or
 Parable?, The," 1960.B72

"Sacred Fount: 'The Actuality
 Pretentious and Vain' vs. 'The
 Case Rich and Edifying,' The,"
 1963.B112
"Sacred Fount: The Geometry in
 the Jungle, The," 1974.B24
"Sacred Fount: The Narrator and
 the Vampires, The," 1961.B71
"Sacred Fount: The Poetics of
 Nothing, The," 1972.B91
"Sacred Fount: The Scientific
 Method, The," 1972.B9
"'The Sacred Rage': The Time-
 Theme in The Ambassadors,"
 1961.B82
Saintsbury, George, 1971.A7
Saito, Hikaru, 1972.B84
Salisbury, Howard E., 1963.C3
Salomon, Roger B., 1964.B84;
 1968.B115; 1969.B120
"Salvation and Resurrection in
 James' 'The Beast in the
 Jungle,'" 1973.B42
Salzberg, Joel, 1972.B85-86
Samuel, Irene, 1965.B93
Samuels, Charles Thomas,
 1968.B85-86; 1971.A6
Sandeen, Ernest, 1967.A5
Sanders, Thomas E., 1967.B89
Sanford, Charles L., 1961.B79
Sanna, Vittoria, 1962.B98;
 1963.B90; 1964.B85
Sarmad, Nahid, 1974.C16
Sasaki, Miyoko, 1971.B108
"Satires of American Realism,
 1880-1900," 1962.B62
Saul, Frank Joseph, 1969.C10
Sayre, Robert F., 1962.B99;
 1964.B86
Scanlon, Lawrence E., 1963.B91
"Scapegoats and Martyrs of Henry
 James, The," 1974.B50
"Scene and Symbol: Changing Mode
 in the English Novel from
 George Eliot to Joyce,"
 1967.B28
Schechter, Harold, 1973.B77
Scherting, John, 1969.B121
Scheyer, Ernest, 1970.B98
Schelsinger, Arthur M., 1964.B87

"Shadow Within: The Conscious and Unconscious Use of the Double, The," 1963.B87

Shahane, V. A., 1961.B81

Shakespeare, William, 1965.B60 (rpt. 1969.A10); 1967.B69; 1972.B99, B109; 1973.B15

"Shakespeare and Henry James," 1967.B69

Shankovsky, Marilla Battilana, 1972.B88

Shaping Joy: Studies in Writer's Craft, A, 1971.B12

Sharma, O. P., 1969.B101

Sharp, Sister M. Corona, O.S.U., 1962.C8; 1963.A3; 1966.B88; 1967.A5; 1968.A1

Shaw, George Bernard, 1960.B23; 1963.A1; 1967.B103; 1971.B54; 1973.B38

Shaw, Sharon, 1974.B65

"Shaw the Reviewer and James's Guy Domville," 1971.B54

Sheldon, Pamela Jacobs, 1974.B66-67

Sheppard, E. A., 1974.A6

Shibuya, Yuzaburo, 1968.B87

Shine, Muriel Gruber, 1968.C12; 1969.A9

Shinn, Thelma J., 1973.B79

Shores of Light, The, 1963.A1

Short Fiction Criticism: A Checklist of Interpretation Since 1925 of Stories and Novelettes (American, British, Continental), 1800-1958, 1960.B87

"Short Note on a Long Subject: Henry James, A," 1967.B12 (rpt. 1971.B20)

Short Novels of Henry James, 1961.B61

Short stories, tales, and nouvelles,
Collections, 1961.B77, B85, B89, B97; 1962.B25; 1963.B2, B104; 1964.B28; 1965.B127; 1966.B28; 1968.B2; 1970.B31; 1973.B5
Criticism: 1960.A2; 1961.B93, B96-97, C14; 1962.B25 (rpt.

1963.A1); 1963.B24, B77, B89, B115, C1; 1964.A8, B9, B28; 1965.B58, B127; 1966.B3, B28, C2; 1967.B30, B96, C9; 1968.B12, B49, B70, B79, B90, C8; 1969.A5, B54; 1970.A7, B31, C2; 1971.B109, C15, C26; 1972.B102, C5, C15, C19; 1973.B5, C4, C20; 1974.A1, B41-42

"Short Story of Fantasy: Henry James, H. G. Wells, and E. M. Forster, The," 1966.B3

"Short Study of James's The Wings of the Dove: On Milly Theale, A," 1968.B87

"Shosetsu to Denki no Shud ai-sentaku to Imi," 1968.B57

Shriber, Michael, 1969.B123

Shucard, Alan R., 1973.B80

Shulman, Robert, 1968.B88

Shumsky, Allison, 1962.B100

Siegel, Eli, 1968.A9

Siegel, Paul N., 1968.B89

"'The Siege of London': Henry James and the Pièce Bien Faite," 1969.B57

"Significant Revision in The Wings of the Dove, A," 1972.B108

Silver, John, 1960.A6

Silverstein, Henry, 1962.B101

Simms, L. Moody, Jr., 1972.B88

Simon, Irène, 1962.B102

Simon, John Kenneth, 1966.B89

Simplified Approach to Henry James, A, 1964.A1

Singh, Brijraj, 1971.B112

"Sirens of Life and Art in Henry James," 1969.B84

"Sir Sidney Colvin in The Golden Bowl: Mr. Crichton Identi-fied," 1974.B83

Six American Novelists of the Nineteenth Century, 1968.B27

"Six Ways of Looking at Reality," 1960.B35

Sklare, Arnold B., 1960.B11

Sklepowich, Edward Anthony, 1972.C21

Skoumal, Aloys, 1971.B113

"Study in Theme and Technique in
the Autobiography of Henry
James, A," 1968.C7
Study in Yellow: The "Yellow
Book" and Its Contributors, A,
1960.B65
"Study of Classical Gesture:
Henry James and Madame de
Lafayette, A," 1966.B89
"Study of Henry James's 'Mdme.
de Mauves,' A," 1971.B63
Study of Literature: A Handbook
of Critical Essays and Terms,
The, 1960.B2
"Study of Point of View in
Selected Short Stories of Henry
James, A," 1963.C1
"Study of Point of View in Three
Novels by Henry James: The
Spoils of Poynton, The Wings of
the Dove, and The Golden Bowl,
A," 1965.C4
"Study of the Bildungsroman in
American Literature, A,"
1973.B37
"Study of the Concepts of Art,
Life and Morality in the
Criticism of Five Writers from
Pater to Yeats, A," 1971.B112
"Study of the Influence of the
Fairy Tale on the Fiction of
Henry James, A," 1974.C7
"Study of the Realistic Treatment
of Psychic Phenomena in Select-
ed Fiction of William Dean
Howells, Hamlin Garland, Henry
James, Frank Norris, and
Theodore Dreiser, A," 1972.B90
"Study of the Revisions of the
Tales of Henry James Included
in the New York Edition, A,"
1972.C19
"Study of the Style of Henry
James's Late Novels, A,"
1971.C14
Style, 1960.B12, B44, B47, B56
(rpt. 1967.B101), B57, B67,
B98 (rpt. 1964.A6; 1968.A11,
B115; 1969.A10); 1961.B15, B20;
1962.B35, B50, B52, B91-92,
B107, B111, B113; 1963.B13;

1964.B39, B103, C8; 1965.A2,
B14, C7; 1967.B71, B89, C5,
C9; 1968.B69; 1969.B46, B113;
1970.B61, B80, B93, B113, C10;
1971.B25, B50, B82, C3, C14,
C23, C26-27; 1972.A2, C2, C25;
1973.B81; 1974.A3, B87, B90,
C6
"Style and Meaning in American
Autobiography: William Dean
Howells, Henry James, Hamlin
Garland," 1974.B52
"Style and Point of View in the
Tales of Henry James," 1967.C9
"Style in Henry James," 1968.B69
"Subjective Adventure, The,"
1965.B107
"Subjective Adventure of Fleda
Vetch, The," 1964.B59 (rpt.
1968.A11)
"Subjective Pronoun in the Late
Style of Henry James, The,"
1971.B82
"Sublime Economy: Money as
Symbolic Center in Henry
James," 1967.C11
Subversive Vision: American
Romanticism in Literature, The,
1972.B47
Sullivan, Jeremiah J., 1973.B92
Sumner, Nan, 1971.B118
Sumner, Nathan, 1971.B118
"Survey of Early Reviews--
American, A," 1967.A5
"Survey of Early Reviews--
English, A" 1967.A5
Sutton, Horace, 1968.B75
Sutton, Walter, 1963.B103
Swan, Michael, 1963.B104
Swartz, D. L., 1967.B103
Swedenborg, Emanuel, 1960.B39;
1962.B59; 1967.B51; 1971.B127;
1972.B105
Sweetapple, R., 1970.B109
Swinden, Patrick, 1973.B93
Swinnerton, Frank, 1964.B96
"Switzerland in the Life and Work
of Henry James: The Clare
Benedict Collection of Letters
from Henry James," 1966.C3

"Two Novelists" [Meredith and James], 1972.B94

"Two Pairs of Gloves: Mark Twain and Henry James," 1960.B32

"Two Portraits of a Lady," 1960.B71

"Two Problems in The Portrait of a Lady," 1968.A1

"Two Sides of the Street, The," 1973.B26

"Two Sides of Washington Square, The," 1974.B29

"Two Taines of Henry James, The," 1971.B38

Two Worlds of American Art: The Private and the Popular, The, 1965.B115

Tyler, Gary R., 1966.B15

Tyler, Parker, 1963.B112; 1964.B99

"Tyranny of Conscience: Arnold, James, and Conrad's Lord Jim The," 1972.B32

"Tyranny of the Eye: The Observer as Aggressor in Henry James's Fictions, The," 1969.C2

Tytell, John, 1969.B138, C12; 1971.B124

U

Uchiyama, Tetsujiro, 1964.B100

Ueda, Tsutomu, 1962.B111

Ueno, Kazuko, 1974.B85

Ulanov, Barry, 1965.B115

"Una biografia di James," 1962.B76

"Unbiased Jamesian, The," 1961.B45

"Uncanny in the Supernatural Short Fiction of Poe, Hawthorne and James, The," 1968.B79

"Une lettre inédite de Henry James à Gustave Flaubert: Autour de Monckton Milnes, Lord Houghton," 1968.B18

"Un eseu despre Henry James: O aventură primejdiosă," 1973.B21

"'Unexpected light in shady places': Henry James and Life, 1883-1916," 1970.B51

"Unintentional Fallacy: Critics and The Golden Bowl," 1974.B26

"Universality in 'The Jolly Corner,'" 1962.B29 (rpt. 1970.A7)

Unknown Distance: From Consciousness to Conscience, Goethe to Camus, The, 1972.B32

"Un Monumento Biográfico a Henry James," 1973.B30

Unofficial Selves: Character in the Novel from Dickens to the Present Day, 1973.B93

"Unpardonable Sin in 'Washington Square,' The," 1973.B77

"Unpublished Henry James Letter, An," 1963.B72

"Unpublished Henry James on Whitman," 1969.B144

"Unpublished Review by Henry James, An," 1967.B59

"Un puritain hérésiarque," 1960.B62

"Unquiet Hearthside: A Study of the Parent-Child Relationship in the Fiction of Henry James, The," 1968.C10

"Un racconto italiano di Henry James: Daisy Miller," 1968.B5

Unrue, Darlene Harbour, 1972.C23

"Unweeded Garden: A View of The Aspern Papers," 1967.B43

"Uptown and Downtown in Henry James's America: Sexuality and the Business-Society," 1966.C6

Urgent West: The American Dream and Modern Man, The, 1969.B1

Uroff, M. D., 1972.B106

"Use of 'Everything' in The Wings of the Dove, The," 1972.B64

"Utopia of Henry James, The," 1962.B101

"Utopia: The Psychology of a Cultural Fantasy," 1970.B9

Volpe, Edmund L., 1961.B64;
1968.A1
Von Egmond, Peter, 1974.B86
Vorpahl, Ben M., 1971.B129

W

Wadden, Anthony T., 1971.C28
Wade, David, 1966.B101
Wagenknecht, Edward, 1970.B115
Wager, Willis, 1968.B105
Wagner, Linda Welshimer,
1965.B117
Walcutt, Charles Child,
1966.B102; 1968.B106
Waldock, J. A., 1960.A6
Waldron, Randall H., 1973.B103
Walker, Don D., 1960.B89;
1963.B114
Walker, Warren S., 1961.B93;
1963.B115; 1965.B118;
1967.B111
Wallace, Jack E., 1960.B90
Wallace, Ronald, 1972.B109, C24;
1973.B104-105
Wallace Stevens, 1970.B84
Walsh, William, 1964.B101
Walt, James, 1970.B116
Walters, Dorothy Jeanne,
1961.B94
Walters, Margaret, 1972.A6
Wanobu, Seiji, 1963.B116
Ward, Joseph A., 1960.B91-95;
1961.A6; 1963.B117; 1964.B102;
1965.B8, B119-21; 1967.A7;
1968.A11; 1969.B141
Warren, Austin, 1962.A4, B112;
1963.A1; 1966.B103; 1973.A6
"Washington Square," (Kronen-
berger) 1969.B81; (Lucas)
1972.A6
"Washington Square: A Psycho-
logical Perspective," 1970.A8
"Washington Square: o el
folletin bien hecho,"
1969.B31
[Washington Square] Romance and
Realism: An Introduction to
the Study of the Novel,
1961.B4
Wasiolek, Edward, 1960.B96-97

Watanabe, Hisayoshi, 1962.B113;
1964.B103; 1972.B110; 1974.B87
Watanabe, Toshiro, 1963.B118
"Watch and Chain of Henry James,
The," 1970.B24
"Watch and Ward: The Mixed
Beginning," 1970.C9
"Watch, Ward, the Jamesian
Themes," 1965.B24
Waterfall, Gaillard Fitzsimons,
1973.C19
Watkins, Floyd C., 1971.A7
Watson, George, 1964.B104;
1969.B142
Watt, Ian, 1960.B98; 1961.B65,
B95; 1964.A6; 1968.A11, B107,
B115; 1969.A10; 1973.B84
"Waymarsh's 'Sombre Glow' and
Der Fliegende Hollander,"
1973.B73
W. D. Howells and Art in His
Time, 1965.B59
"Weak Wings of Pride: An
Interpretation of James's
'The Bench of Desolation,'
The," 1965.B96
Weales, Gerald, 1962.B114
Weaver, Richard, 1968.B108
"Web as an Organic Metaphor in
The Marble Faun, Middlemarch:
A Study of Provincial Life,
and The Golden Bowl: The
Growth of Contextualism as an
Aesthetic Theory in the Nine-
teenth Century, The," 1971.B92
Webb, Howard, Jr., 1965.B64
Weber, Carl J., 1968.B109
"Week of the Angry Artist . . . ,"
1967.B40
Wegelin, Christof, 1962.A4,
B115; 1963.B119; 1964.A6;
1965.B8, B122; 1968.A1;
1969.B143; 1973.B106
Weilmann, Robert, 1962.B116
Weimer, David R., 1966.B104
Weiner, Rosemarie Bodenheimer,
1974.C19
Weinman, Geoffrey Stephen,
1968.C14
Weinstein, Arnold, 1974.B88

"Wounds of Judgment, The,"
1963.B12
Wright, Austin McGiffert,
1961.B96
Wright, Edgar, 1965.B128
Wright, Nathalia, 1965.B129
Wright, Walter F., 1962.A5;
1965.B8; 1968.A1, A11
Writer in the Room: Selected
Essays, The, 1968.B110
Writers of the Lost Generation,
The, 1969.B132
"Writer's Search for Reality,
The," 1970.B33
Wyatt, Bryant N., 1971.B132

Y

Yarina, Margaret Anne, 1973.C20
Year's Work in English Studies,
The, 1963.B122; 1964.B107;
1965.B125; 1966.B21; 1967.B19;
1968.B24; 1969.B61; 1970.B55;
1971.B51; 1972.B44; 1973.B35;
1974.B60
Yeazell, Ruth Bernard, 1972.C25;
1974.B90
Yellow Book, The, 1960.B65;
1964.B8
Yonezu, Nobushige, 1970.A3
Young, Mahonri Sharp, 1970.B122
Young, Thomas Beetham, 1974.B91
Young, Thomas Daniel, 1968.B115

"Young Henry James and the Les-
son of his Master Balzac,"
1961.B1
"Young Prophetess: Memories of
Spiritualism and Intimations
of Occult Consciousness in
Henry James's The Bostonians,
The," 1972.B56
Yu, Frederick Yeh-wei, 1972.B115

Z

Zabel, Morton Dauwen, 1960.B101;
1961.B97; 1968.B81
Zak, Michele Wender, 1974.B92
Zietlow, Edward R., 1966.B109;
1972.B112
Ziff, Larzer, 1963.B125;
1966.B110
Zimmerman, Everett, 1970.B123
Zola, Emile, 1960.B74; 1964.C9;
1966.B20; 1971.A5
Zolla, Elmire, 1966.B111
Zum Problem literarischer
Ökonomie: Henry James'
Erzahlungen Zwischen Markt
und Kunst, 1974.A1